THE BATTLE FOR ERETZ YISRAEL

THE BATTLE FOR ERETZ YISRAEL
Jews, G-d and Israel
1992-2011

Bernard J. Shapiro

iUniverse, Inc.
Bloomington

THE BATTLE FOR ERETZ YISRAEL
JEWS, G-D, AND ISRAEL, 1992-2011

Copyright © 2011 by Bernard J. Shapiro.

All rights reserved. No part of this book may be used or reproduced by any means, graphic, electronic, or mechanical, including photocopying, recording, taping or by any information storage retrieval system without the written permission of the publisher except in the case of brief quotations embodied in critical articles and reviews.

iUniverse books may be ordered through booksellers or by contacting:

iUniverse
1663 Liberty Drive
Bloomington, IN 47403
www.iuniverse.com
1-800-Authors (1-800-288-4677)

Because of the dynamic nature of the Internet, any web addresses or links contained in this book may have changed since publication and may no longer be valid. The views expressed in this work are solely those of the author and do not necessarily reflect the views of the publisher, and the publisher hereby disclaims any responsibility for them.

Any people depicted in stock imagery provided by Thinkstock are models, and such images are being used for illustrative purposes only.
Certain stock imagery © Thinkstock.

ISBN: 978-1-4620-0653-3 (sc)
ISBN: 978-1-4620-0654-0 (hc)
ISBN: 978-1-4620-0191-0 (ebk)

Library of Congress Control Number: 2011914236

Printed in the United States of America

iUniverse rev. date: 10/10/2011

Contents

PRAISE FOR THE AUTHOR.. xiii
PREFACE.. xxiii
ACKNOWLEDGMENTS... xxv
CHAPTER ONE: ABOUT THE FREEMAN CENTER.......................... 1
CHAPTER TWO: PARABLES 15
    The One Miracle (February 1994).. 16
    The Tale of The Mystic Buffalo – A Jewish Parable........................ 19
    Five Short Parables for Israel (January 2005).................................. 22
        Israel, Charlie Brown & Lucy 22
        Reboot Sharon, Save Israel and Ensure Security 22
        Making Peace with Wolves... 26
        Israel and the Camel Dung 27
        The Short Change Artist and Oslo... 29
    Sharon and the Cease-Fire – A Satire (June 2001) 31
    Arafat Sells his Nonviolence Rug to the Israelis
    Again (June 2001).. 33
    Some Thoughts(1952).. 34

CHAPTER THREE: ISRAELI HISTORY.. 35
    Jews, G-d, and Israel – My Zionist Passage (July 1992) 37
    Freeman Center Says Rush to Embrace 40
    O Land of Zion... 43
    Israel's Sacred Places—Why The Arab Thrust
    to Seize Control of Them (October 2006) 44
    Israel In The 21st Century—Three Alternate Futures Years
    2000-2010 (January 2000)... 48
    The Road Map and Israel's Survival Victory Or Defeat
    for Zionism—You Must Choose (June 2003) 57

CHAPTER FOUR: JEWISH HISTORY ... 95
The Temple Mount Faithful Fanatics or Jewish Patriots? (September 2000) ... 100
Chanukah and Jewish History Will We Be Maccabees or Victims? (December 1994) ... 103
A Letter That the Houston Chronicle Chose Not to Publish ... 105
Jerusalem as Israel's Capital ... 107
Chanukah and Jewish History ... 108
Redeeming the Temple Mount ... 111

CHAPTER FIVE: WORLD HISTORY ... 113
Harry W. Freeman's Favorite Quote (July 1992) ... 116
Shades of Munich (May 1998) ... 118
Notes from the Editor (April 1999) ... 120
Disorder in the World – Or Comparative Religion 101 ... 123

CHAPTER SIX: ARAB WARS OF EXTERMINATION AGAINST ISRAEL ... 127
Will There Ever Be True Peace Between Israel and the Arab States? (July 2002) ... 129
Arabs' Attitudes Toward Israel Has There Been Progress Since Oslo? (March 1995) ... 139
Israel's Virtual Surrender to Arafat—Some Observations (December 2000) ... 144
Is Peace Possible? (April 2001) ... 146

CHAPTER SEVEN: MILITARY AND STRATEGIC ISSUES: RESISTANCE TO APPEASEMENT ... 157
The Military Balance 1993 the Freeman Center Targets Jaffee ... 159
Will Israel Fall for the 'Mubarak Gambit' on the Golan? (September 1994) ... 164
Deterrence or Dhimmization Which Should Israel Choose? ... 167
Israel's Demographic and Security Challenge – Is Transfer the Only Rational Answer? ... 171
Oh L-Rd, How Shall I Make the Blind See? (November 1997) ... 177
Suicide Bombers and Israeli Government Responsibility (September 1997) ... 188
Notes on the Assassination of Terrorists (October 1997) ... 190

Withdrawal, Redeployment, Surrender or Just Plain Appeasement 195
The Primary Inherent Flaw in The Oslo Agreement That Will Lead to Military Conflict (October 1998) 196
"Peace In our Time?" Munich Re-Visited (November 1998) 198
Withdrawal from the Golan? A Dangerous Idea that Just Won't Go Away (July 1999) 201
Peace Talks with Syria Doomed to Failure (July 1999) 203
The Destruction of the State of Israel (October 1999) 205
The Golan Heights 211
Mark Langfan, Mortars and Katyushas (June 2001) 213
Separation, Security Fences & Buffer Zones the Primary Fallacy (March 2002) 220
The Art of the Fait Accompli – A New/Old Military Doctrine for Israel (October 2002) 223
Security Fences And Logical Fallacies (August 2003) 225
Israel-Syrian Resolution of Differences? (February 2004) 229
Sharon Threatens Gaza Pioneer Settlers with Civil War (July 2004) 232
Israel's Virtual Surrender 240
to Arafat & Terrorism Some Observations (September 2004) 240
Coping with Terrorism and Demography Israel's Virtual Surrender to Arafat & Terrorism (October 2004) 242
Seeing Through the Fog of War Orwell Meets Alice—Through the Mid-East Looking Glass (July 2006) 246
Israel's Failed Security Policy (July 2006) 252
The Nature of Peace and Peace Treaties (1993, 1994, 1995) (August 17, 2008) 257
Time to End Policy of Restraint By Bernard J. Shapiro (1998) 260
Fighting Terrorism and the Theater of the Absurd 264
Preemption or Destruction: which Should Israel Choose? 267

CHAPTER EIGHT: ISRAELI POLITICAL ISSUES 279
Communication and Public Policy Implications for Israel's Foreign Relations 280
The Peacemakers of Chelm 283
A Time for Peace, and A Time For War 285
Dayenu—It Would Have Been Enough 287
Ode to Sharon: A Demented Monster(September 2004) 291

The Silent Killers (January 2004) 292
Oslo Must Go – Will Netanyahu Do the Right Thing?
(July 1996).. 294
Oslo and Other Policy Conundrums (August 1996) 296
Bibi, Jonathan is Worried (November 1996) 302
Letter to Prime Minister Benjamin Netanyahu
(November 1996) 305
REboot Bibi, Save Israel and Ensure Security Wishful
Thinking (January 1997)... 308
Netanyahu, Our Prodigal Son – What Should the RIGHT
Do About Bibi's Plight? (May 1997)... 311
Further Redeployment in Yesha (Frd) Breaking News
of Great Importance an Editorial (December 1997) 314
Time to Stop the Surrender & The Appeasement of Terror 315
Referendum on Redeployment 317
Israel or Oslo: You Must Decide (October 1998)........................... 319
Freeman Center Analysis of Barak's New Wye Agreement
with Arafat (September 1999).. 322
The Freeman Center Publishes The Raviv Protocol
(December 1999) 324
Barak's Mental State—A Danger to Israel (August 2000) 333
Israeli Independence and American Foreign Policy
(May 2001) 335
Jewish Communities in Yesha (November 2002)......................... 339
Why Likud Voters Must Reject Surrender to Terrorism
(May, 2004) 350
Mccarthyism, Suppression of Free Speech Threatens
Israelis (July 2004) 356
Simple Rules for Creating A Giant Wave of Aliya to Israel 360
A Black Day For Israel (November 2004)...................................... 361
Sharon and Kahane Similarities and Differences
(April—May 2005) 367
I'm Mad As Hell Don't Ask Me to Be A Nice Jewish Boy
(June 2005) 369
Resistance: Moderation, Direct Action or Extremism
(August 2005).. 375

Victory Plan for Israel Updated November 3, 2005
(October-November 2005) 379
"If You Will It, It Need Not Be A Dream" . . . .
Theodore Herzl (1897) 383

CHAPTER NINE: U.S./ISRAEL RELATIONS 384
Perfidy Pollard & the Secret War Against the Jews
(August 1996) 386
Clinton and Israel the Double Standard at Work: Two Articles 389
Enough is Enough: Free Pollard Now! Time to End
the Abuse and Injustice (August 1997) 393
The Junkyard Dog Has His Jaws Clamped Hard
on Netanyahu's Leg(June 1998) 394
Americans Should Not Pay for the Rope to Hang Israel
(November 1999) 398
American Aid (December 1999) 400
American Foreign Policy and Israel A Maccabean
Perspective (July 2000) 401
Freeman Center Says: Disengage From American
Diplomacy with Arafat (July 2001) 405
Israel Acquiesces to Restrictions On Its Sovereignty
(August 2001) 406
Sharon and Bush Delude Israelis (May 2004) 410
Israeli Sovereignty and Foreign Policy
(October-November 2005) 415
Apocalypse Now the Planned Destruction of the
State of Israel (October-November 2005) 416
Advice to PM Netanayhu Before His Encounter
with Obama (May 2009) 422

CHAPTER TEN: ISLAM 427
Islamic Fundamentalism and Israel 428
The Terrorists are Free 434

CHAPTER ELEVEN: ARAB PROPAGANDA AND MEDIA BIAS 441
Arab Propagandists Join Forces With Anti-Semites (1963) 443
The Failure of the Jewish Media Is Suppression
of the Truth A Crime? 451
Verbal Defense A Necessity For Israel's Supporters
(May 1997) 453

To Letters to the Editor 455
Peace Now (Israeli Left) Exposed
How Americans for Peace Now (Apn)
Supports the Arabs (December 2002) 457
Arab Psychological/Propaganda Warfare Against Israel
How Israel
Can Defend Itself and Counterattack
|(October-November 2005) 459
Orwell Meets Alice—Linguistic DistortionS Through
the Mid-East Looking Glass (October-November 2005) 468
How Israel Can Improve Its Hasbara (Public Relations)
Why It Needs to (October-November 2005) 471

CHAPTER TWELVE: FREEMAN CENTER EDITORIALS AND PRAYERS 490

A Few Notes From Your Editor 491
The Maccabean Speaks An Interview with The Maccabean
(March 1997) On Syria, Lebanon, Plo & Other
Security Issues 494
Freeman Center Statement on Arab Violence
(September 30, 1996) 504
A Call to Action We Must Return to Zionism (June 1997) 508
Freeman Center Position on the Resumption of Talks
with the PA (July 1997) 512
An Important Note from the Freeman Center (August 1997) 514
My Rosh Hashana Prayer (5758) (September 1997) 515
Four Editorials By Bernard J. ShapirO 519
    Oslo: The Reality (March 1998) 519
    Simple Truths About Complicated Issues (April 1998) 522
    Observations & Condemnations (April 1998) 525
    My Message For Israel's 50th Anniversary (May 1998) 529
Editor's Notes for the New Year Elections (January 1999) 532
Is Peace Going to Break Out? The Harsh Reality
(June 1999) 533
Editorial Notes in the 21st Century The Freeman Center
Will Still Be Fighting For Eretz Yisrael (December 1999) 536
Freeman Center Peace Plan for Israel & Syria (January 2000) 538
Freeman Center Note on Polls (January 2000) 540
Why Not Give The Golan Heights to the Freeman
Center Instead of Assad? (April 2000) 542

Freeman Center Notes On Violence In Israel 544
Ten Reasons the Freeman Center Should Deal
With The Current Crisis Instead of Barak
(November 2000) 546
Reflection 2001 (January 2001) 547
Reflections and Reactions to Sharon's Victory (March 2001) 548
11 Things I Am Sick and Tired of (September 2001) 553
Straight Answers For Tough Questions (May 2003) 558
Notes on IsRaeli Policies (February 10, 2004) 562
Straight Answers for Tough Questions (June 2004) 566
To Israeli Consular Officials (March 2005) 571
The Freeman Center Urges Caution on the Israel Project
(October-November 2005) 576
Reflections of A Frustrated Zionist—Year End (2007)
(January 2008) 581
The Freeman Center Exposed—The Good and The Bad (?)
(January 2008) 590
Passover and Jewish Liberation (April 2008) 593
The Freeman Center Versus Aipac The Truth and The
Consequences (June 2008) 596
Let Freeman Center Take Over Israel Foreign
Ministry—War Crimes Charges Grow—Jerusalem Silent
(February 2009) 600
Notes to Bibi After His First Election—Still Important
(February 2009) 605
The Israel Quilt (April 2009) 615
My Prayer for Rosh Hashonah—5770 (September 11, 2009) 619
Freeman Center Disgusted At Bibi Groveling Before
Anti-Semites of Europe By Bernard J. Shapiro (2011) 635

CHAPTER THIRTEEN: CORRESPONDENCE WITH SHIMON PERES 637

CHAPTER FOURTEEN: CORRESPONDENCE WITH OTHER LEADERS 648

AUTHOR BIOGRAPHY 669

SUGGESTIONS FOR FURTHER READING 671

PRAISE FOR THE AUTHOR

Bernard J. Shapiro has been an advocate for Israel for more than 50 years. He understands that the antidote to ignorance is knowledge. The cure for mendacity is truth.

Richard H. Rolnick, M.D. (Houston)

Thanks for all you do for Israel and the Jewish People. G-d bless you . . .

Caroline Glick [Center For Security Policy and editor of The Jerusalem Post] lives in Israel

★

Keep up the great work that you are doing. I am honored by my association with you and **THE MACCABEAN** . . . Congratulations on your own very important work and your most moving/mobilizing effect on all us good guys . . . .

Louis Rene Beres, Ph.D., Professor of International Law and Political Science, **Purdue University**, Indiana (October 27, 1995)

★

In the long struggle to save Israel from itself, no American has been more important than Bernard Shapiro, Laboring tirelessly from his Freeman Center base in Houston, For tens of thousands of Americans and others who might have been barred from a candid, no-holds-barred view of Israel's place in the world, Bernard Shapiro's vital institution is always an authentic oasis of honesty and intelligence.

Bernard J. Shapiro

How sad it is that the past four prime ministers of Israel were not listening. How much better it would have been for Rabin, for Peres, for Netanyahu, and for Barak, to heed the informed warnings from Bernard J. Shapiro and the Freeman Center. Bless you for your remarkable service."

Amen!

★

Louis Rene Beres was educated at Princeton (Ph.D., 1971) and has often joined Bernard Shapiro in the battle against Israel's auto-destruction. He is Strategic and Military Affairs Analyst for **THE JEWISH PRESS.**

★

Bernard J. Shapiro's incisive, ironic style shatters the political doublespeak and leaves the reader with a clear picture of the situation. He courageously takes on Israel's government, a hostile media, and those who have lost faith in Jewish rights. Mr. Shapiro is a modern **Maccabean**, who will not rest until the peace process **"rests in peace."**

Herbert Zweibon (deceased may his name be blessed), (National Chairman, **Americans For A Safe Israel**, New York (January 30, 1995)

★

Your magazine is great and the Internet postings are extremely important. You are doing a great service for **Am Yisrael** . . . . Keep up the good work! With blessings from the city of the Patriarchs . . . .

David Wilder, Hebron (May 23, 1996)

★

You are most gracious. Thank you for your clear voice. If only there were those teachable with ears to hear . . . .

Christopher Barder, Editor **ISRAEL BULLETIN**, England (December 29, 1995)

*

I think it is great that you elicited a response from the Israeli Consul-General (Houston). The fact that he took the time to attack you means you must be doing something right (pun fully intended). Keep up the great work! . . . .

Michael Freund, **PEACE WATCH**, Israel (July 20, 1994)

*

Congratulations for the victory—good work! . . . . Sara Young, **WEBMASTER**, Israel (June 7, 1996)

*

I admire your ability to put all of your feelings into wonderful editorials. You speak for all of us. I respect your heart and just want to praise your direction and courage. It's from G-d. You sure speak for so many. G-d really has courageous voices everywhere. *Toda l'el*!!!! Shalom.

Carol L. Harmon, Maryland (6/ 6/96)

*

I would like to congratulate you for the excellent work which you have been doing for the cause of Israel and Jewish people. **The Maccabean** is "top notch" and so are your articles in the *Jewish Herald-Voice* . . . . Please keep up you excellent work. You have our full-hearted support.

Zvi Kalisky, MD, Houston (November 8, 1993)

*

Your excellent magazine provides very important and insightful information for Jews who are concerned about the situation here. That you are truly

Bernard J. Shapiro

committed to the survival of Israel and **Am Yisrael** is clearly evident from your own fine writings.

Shifra Hoffman, **Victims of Arab Terror**, Israel (Sept. 18, 1994)

★

Bernard, your "**Victory Plan For Israel**," is exactly what I have been calling for months. This is great! . . . .

Yehuda Poch, **JEWISH ACTION INITIATIVE**, Canada (June 6, 1994)

★

I read with horror the letter sent to you by the editors of the Houston-based ***Jewish Herald-Voice***.

Their attempt to equate condemnation of the Rabin government, with "Israel bashing" is outrageous.

Susan L. Rosenbluth, Editor, ***JEWISH VOICE AND OPINION***, New Jersey (December 22, 1993)

★

Like a growing number of Jews here and especially in Israel, I have become skeptical about the (peace) process and its possible results. Bernard Shapiro was the only columnist of whom I am aware who warned of the dangers from the moment the agreement was signed. He was doing the Jews a genuine, patriotic service . . . .

Steve E. Tabachnick, Ph.D. University of Oklahoma, (In a letter to ***Jewish Herald-Voice*** editors and publishers, Joe and Jeanne Samuels, December 3, 1993)

★

Your thought (re: **Tale of the Mystic Buffalo**) was brilliant and its execution perfect. Congratulations!

Ruth Brown, New York (February 24, 94)

★

On the whole your publication is excellent, essential information for those who are at all open to hear arguments . . . .

Elyakim Ha'etzni, Israel (January 29, 1995)

★

Thank you for your letter of June 6th and for the interesting scheme (my **Victory Plan For Israel**) that you have proposed . . . .

Ze'ev "Beny" Begin, Jerusalem (June 28, 1994)

★

Your publications and article are excellent . . . .

Rabbi Benzion Milecki, Australia (March 19, 1994)

★

The article on the transfer of the Arabs from Israel is brilliant! I do Hope that there is enough sanity for Israel to recognize the truth and practicality of your proposal. If it were implemented, it would not only save Jewish Lives but Arab lives as well. Isn't this important to recognize? No other solution matches it. With best wishes . . . .

David Basch, Connecticut (February 12, 1995)

Bernard J. Shapiro

★

Superb job (**Rabin & Kahane**), Bernard, *Chazak ve'ematz!*

Yehoshua Steinberg, Israel (November. 10, 1994)

★

So far, of all I've read and heard on the Hebron (massacre) story, you have said it best. Thank you.

Phil Chernofsky, Associate director of **OU/NCYSC Israel Center**, Jerusalem (February 28, 1994)

★

I have to tell you, even if I had to pay $100 for it, I wouldn't miss a single issue. Your publication brings me every month a collection of the most important articles regarding Israel and other matters of paramount interest to U.S. Jews. And there are summaries of other information and, of course, above all, your really excellent editorials . . . .

Gerardo Joffe, President, **FLAME** (January 27, 1995)

★

Yes, we will win—because you are on Israel's side (the real side) . . . .

Linda Truman, Clear Lake (1995)

★

You work under such extreme pressure, and you have so much devotion to Israel and the Jewish People that you need a constitution of tempered steel . . . .

Jacob Shapera, DMD, Connecticut (August 18, 1995)

★

We loved your *Dayanu* lyrics! Will use them at out next rally.

Beth Gilinsky, **Jewish Action Alliance**, New York (August 8, 1995)

★

Kol HaKavod, Bernard. You have it absolutely right! . . . .

Oregon, Sarah Mendelson (June 28, 1995)

★

You are doing a very important service to the Jewish people with your publication. You can expect more opposition in the future as the vicious hate campaign in this country spills over to the States as well. But the only weapon we have against falsehood is truth. We must shout out that truth even if no one wants to listen. Hopefully some will hear us . . . .

Gary Cooperberg, Hebron, (November 20, 1995).

★

I have enjoyed your publication immensely in the year I have received it, but for the depressing subject matter it is forced to deal with . . . . Continued success, and may our words somehow awaken all Jews to the dangers ahead . . . .

Rabbi Steven Pruzansky, New Jersey (December 20, 1995)

★

I read your editorial for this month's **Maccabean**—it is impressive. I am sure that people will take notice and sit up . . . .

Dr. Colin L. Leci, England (February 4, 1996)

Bernard J. Shapiro

★

Thank you for your existence on WWW!!! . . . .

Semyon (a new immigrant from Russia in Israel (2/13/96)

★

Shalom (in the good sense), I just wanted to write to say thank you for your articles and energy. I have to admit that the actions of our "leaders" and their words, and that of the media-do have a way of wearing us down and demoralizing us . . . . well, sometimes I wake up in the mornings and wonder if it's me that's nuts-So your articles are indeed refreshing and it's nice to know that there is still someone out there with the guts to say that there is indeed a difference between sanity and insanity, good and bad . . . . so keep up the good work and know that you efforts do have some effect.

Your friend, Joel Kronfeld, Department of Geophysics, **Tel Aviv University**, Israel (January 5, 1996)

★

Israel has been the foundation stone of your life. Many people weaken in their devotion to the Jewish State, but your loyalty as grown with the passage of time. G-d bless you.

Rabbi Jack Segal (Houston)

★

Your work for Israel during the last two decades defies description. The devotion and selfless struggle to educate the public about Israel deserves the highest honor.

Mark and Bill Langfan (Florida and New York)

✶

It has been an honor working with you for Israel this past 18 years. Your cooperation aided the success of our Christian Zionist outreach for Israel. We have always prayed that the Jewish community would defend Israel with the same passion that you do.

Dr. Frank and Alice Lanza (Houston)

PREFACE

When I wrote my first version of THE BATTLE FOR ERETZ YISRAEL in 1996, it ended with a victory for Israel. Unfortunately that victory was short lived. Benjamin Netanyahu had just defeated Shimon Peres in the elections following Yitzhak Rabin's assassination. We on the Right thought that Bibi would end the suicidal Oslo process. He didn't.

So the Battle goes on and it still has not ended now in 2011. Great changes have swept through the Middle East. Popular revolutions have swept Arab dictators from office, but they are being replaced by Moslem tyrannies even more hostile to Israel and the Jewish People.

Iran has come much closer to a capability to launch a nuclear war against Israel. Such a war with Israeli retaliation could lead an apocalypse none of us want to contemplate. I present a strong case for preemption for the reader.

Some of you will think my conclusions and suggestions are too harsh. Let me remind you of the very brutal conditions Jews have had to live with this last 2000 years. Israel is a ray of light in a dismal history and its citizens will never let it be extinguished, no matter the consequences.

ACKNOWLEDGMENTS

I would like to acknowledge the following individuals and organizations that have made my work and this book possible.

Harry W. Freeman (1888—1959), my beloved grandfather, for whom the Freeman Center is named. During my youth he constantly taught me and encouraged me to write. He taught me logic, analysis, and love of the Jewish people.

Joe Samuels, an old friend of my grandfather, offered me a column in his publication, the Jewish Herald-Voice (1990). This was not my first writing experience, but it was definitely the most important. The discipline of a weekly column gave me the skills to be a professional journalist. In 1995, I was fired from the paper for expressing Zionist views that upset the peace extremists of the Left in Houston.

The following authors and researchers have contributed greatly to the educational, intellectual, and ideological strength of the Freeman Center For Strategic Studies:

AUTHORS:

Herb Zwebon, Z"L and Helen Freedman of Americans for a Safe Israel gave me the ideological strength to keep up the fight.

Women in Green, Nadia and Ruth Matar, inspired me by their strength and unbridled patriotism in the battle for Eretz Yisrael.

Yoram Ettinger
Helen Freedman
Michael Freund
A. Ghosh Z"L

Bernard J. Shapiro

Elyakim Ha'etzni
Gerald Honigman
Gerrado Joffe
Rabbi Meir Kahane Z"L
Shmuel Katz Z"L
Dr. Irving Kett
Mark Langfan
William K. Langfan
Dr. Aaron Lerner
Ruth and Nadia Matar
Eugene Narrett, PhD
Dan Nimrod
Lt. Col. Shawn M. Pine Z"L
Dr. Steven E. Plaut
Joseph Puder
Gershon Salomon
Boris Shusteff
Herb Zweibon Z"L
David Wilder
Gail Winston
Emanuel A. Winston Z"L

I also want to acknowledge my webmasters, Abby Hazony, Leora Waldman and Shimshon Young of Excellence Internet Service, who have been with me for many years and helped me develop the Freeman Center website, and who were involved with many important aspects of the website, including the Maccabean Online, the Freemanlist, and the Freeman blog. I especially want to acknowledge Erin Cravey for her important technical support needed for the publication of this book.

The Freeman Center wishes to thank the following individuals and foundations for their financial support for our important educational activities in support of Israel's security and survival.

Platinum Supporters
Jack Berger
Fredman Family Charitable Trust III
William K. Langfan

Mark Langfan
Dr. Frank and Alice Lanza
Louis Lechenger Z"L
Drs. Richard H. and Ruth Rolnick
Morris Wilk
Gail Winston
Emanuel A. Winston Z"L
Herb Zweibon Z"L

Gold Supporters
Richard Booker
Gerardo Joffe
Dr. Irving Kett
Ari Levy
Dr. William Lipsky
Pastor Myrna Middleton
Leonard and Harriet Moskovit
Herbert L. Rechter
Emily and Albert Stein

Silver Supporters
Colette Berman
Helen Freedman
Susan and Steve Perin
David and Bethany Shapiro
Nathan Wolkovitz Z"L

CHAPTER ONE:
ABOUT THE FREEMAN CENTER

The Freeman Center for Strategic Studies aids Israel in her quest to survive in a hostile world. The Center was founded in Houston, Texas, in 1992 by Bernard J. Shapiro. Its activities include commissioning extensive research into the military and strategic issues related to the Arab-Israeli conflict and disseminating pertinent information to the Jewish community and worldwide. Its Board of Directors and Advisory Committee includes leading Pro-Israel activists from around the world.

Bernard J. Shapiro, a political analyst whose specialty is Israeli and Middle Eastern political and strategic issues, organized the **Freeman Center For Strategic Studies** in Houston, Texas in 1992.

The Freeman Center for Strategic Studies was named after Harry W. Freeman. Freeman was a Judaic scholar, fluent in six languages, and a brilliant attorney. He was a defender of the poor and the disadvantaged against the forces that kept them powerless.

Shapiro, who is executive director of **The Freeman Center**, made the following statement concerning its objectives:

"The primary purpose of the Freeman Center is to improve Israel's ability to survive in a hostile world. This will be accomplished through research into the military and strategic issues related to the Arab-Israeli conflict and Islamic terrorism and the dissemination of that information to the Jewish and non-Jewish community. Essential to Israel's survival, we feel, is the preservation of its present secure borders including Judea, Samaria, Gaza, and the Golan Heights. We will be strong allies of America in our common War against International Islamic terrorism. We will seek to improve Israel's image in this country as well as counteract Arab propaganda in the community and on college campuses. In pursuit of these goals we intend to maximize solidarity with Israel among both the Jewish and non-Jewish community and combat media bias. We will also work to strengthen Jewish communities in the Diaspora and help ensure their survival."

Those Who Fail To Learn From History Are Condemned To Repeat It

"In 1934, Harry W. Freeman, my grandfather, was already lecturing about the dangers of Hitler and Nazism. Nobody listened. The Holocaust was not prevented. Today Israel's enemies plan a second Holocaust against the Jews of Israel and the world. The governments and people of Europe not only acquiesce but actively aid in this genocidal plan through diplomatic and material support. The American State Department encourages this by actively striving to weaken Israel's strategic and military superiority. Their first stage is to use the so called "peace process" to weaken Israel and strip it of its strategic territories. They are being aided by the same hypocrites and accomplices in the West who failed to aid the Jews of Europe in their darkest hour.

Unfortunately, even left-wing Israelis have fallen victims to the seductive lure of peace and have begun a policy of appeasement similar to that tried with Hitler. The results will be no different.

"The Arab propaganda full of slanders and libels; the media bias against Israel replete with double standards and the rewriting of history are all working to the same end: making Israel appear illegitimate. Israel is the only country considered by many to be **guilty of original sin** by virtue of its very existence. This process has as its goal creating a world climate in which the **destruction** of Israel is acceptable. Many in the Jewish community are either apathetic or fail to recognize this threat.

"I founded the **Freeman Center For Strategic Studies** in order to create a powerful voice to arouse the Jewish community to the action necessary to frustrate the evil designs of the enemies of Israel. I need your help to accomplish this mission."

. . . . Bernard J. Shapiro

Future plans call for a building housing offices and meeting rooms. One special project is the creation of a **Museum of Jewish Warriors**—honoring Jewish fighters from Biblical times to the present. We feel that Jewish communities need to have a focus on Jewish heroism to complement the martyrdom of Holocaust Museums

CHAPTER ONE continued: INTRODUCTION

Israel and the Jewish people have been caught up in a whirlwind these last few years. In these last few weeks, it could have been called a roller coaster. From doom and gloom to elation, victory and hope for the future.

We saw an Israeli government abandon all the elements of national survival and security: strategic territory, water, national cohesion, intelligence capability, reverence for the Jewish character and Holy Places of the country. And we saw the Israeli people decisively say NO.

The late Prime Minister Yitzhak Rabin and his successor Shimon Peres were both caught up in a delusion of truly global proportions. They truly believed that by a grand act of self-emasculation, Israel could propel their Arab neighbors into making peace with them. That by denial of everything Jewish about their country, they could create a New Middle East where national identity didn't matter. Peres even desired acceptance into the Arab League.

During Israel's formative years, we in the Diaspora looked with pride as sabras (native Israelis) seemed to be overcoming the galut (ghetto) mentality of the exile. Here were proud Jews fighting for survival in a hostile neighborhood. Who would have guessed that the post-Zionists of the Israeli left would bring back the ghetto mentality in its most extreme form. Then came the Labor Party victory of 1992. A victory, I might add, derived from fraud, deception and treason. Once in power Rabin reneged on all his promises to the electorate: "no to a PLO state, no to negotiations with the PLO, no to surrender of the Golan". Surrender to Arab demands became a matter of high government policy.

With the help of anti-Jewish Arab Knesset members and the extreme leftist anti-Zionist Meretz party, Rabin and Peres began to systematically destroy Israel from within. Democratic norms of civil and human rights were thrown out and replaced with repression, torture and incarceration of their regimes political opponents. Terrorist murderer, Yassir Arafat was resurrected as Nobel Prize winner and national leader.

The very language we all use to talk and think was manipulated into Orwellian newspeak. A ridiculous concept, "land for peace," became the code word for the destruction of Israel. No nation in history had ever received peace from territorial sacrifice (ask the Czechs or for that matter Native Americans). This became the sacred cow of Middle East diplomacy and Rabin and Peres accepted it with the respect they should have given the Torah. The Oslo Agreement that would have led to the demise of Israel was called a "Peace Process." Those of us who opposed suicide were labeled "enemies of peace." Victims of Arab terrorism and hatred of Jews suddenly became "sacrifices for peace."

The world media joined in the manipulation of the truth with a vengeance. Those of us who loved Israel and supported its secure borders were called "right-wing extremists." The centrist Likud was labeled "hard-line, fascist, and racist." When Rabin was assassinated by a young law student, Likud leader Benjamin Netanyahu was labeled a murderer. No one paid much attention to the fact that he had been provoked and incited not by the Right but by Rabin's own secret service.

On May 29, 1996, the Israeli electorate swept the Labor/Meretz/Arab government into the dustbin of history. They elected Bibi Netanyahu and gave him a strong coalition of Zionist, religious, and pro-security parties. My hopes and prayers were with the new government.

Unfortunately, my expectations that we had won a permanent victory were false. Netanyahu failed to renounce Oslo and continued to accept the premise that it would bring peace. After he was defeated, new governments came in. Ariel Sharon, the head of the Likud Party, got elected in the 2004 election on a platform against the withdrawal from Gaza and on a strong pro-security platform. However, after taking office he had a total 180° turn in his political activities. He turned the Likud Party into the Kadima Party, which was made up of Left-wing, peace now oriented Israelis. Then he pursued a policy of appeasement with the Arabs, withdrew from Gaza, and expelled 10,000 Jews from their homes. This process of ethnic cleansing had very severe consequences for the whole country. Most of the people expelled are still refugees in Israel. Promises of compensation, resettlement, and new homes were never fulfilled by the government, and there developed a tremendous political schism between the Right and the Left in Israel.

This book documents the Battle for Eretz Yisrael as reflected in my writings and activities through the Freeman Center. It covers the years 1996 to 2009, from the sweet taste of victory to shattering betrayal. In order to give the reader the full impact of our struggle, I have included dozens of political cartoons, maps, mementos, flyers and poetry.

Of course, victories must be defended and extended. As Jews we have faced many defeats and many false hopes, yet we have survived 4000 years. We must understand that true PEACE will come with the Messiah and not necessarily from diplomacy. "And on that day the Lord will be One and his Name shall be One."

ISRAEL INDEPENDENCE AFTER 63 YEARS by Bernard J. Shapiro
Freeman Center For Strategic Studies
May 9, 2011

No one should fool themselves into thinking that giving the Arabs of Judea and Samaria Jordanian citizenship would solve anything in the long run. Jordan is not as friendly (population wise) as we are led to believe. Though the government is helpful and friendly, that could change in the blink of an eye. Should American troops leave Iraq and it falls to Iran, the consequences would be severe for Israel. With Syria, Lebanon, and Gaza under Iranian control, it could easily extend its reach to Jordan and the Judean-Samarian ridge overlooking Israel's vulnerable coast.

My Bottom Line (Conclusion)

Israel's central problem is psychological and no amount of beautiful rhetoric and wonderful proposals can change that.

When will the Nationalist Camp realize that we are "at war already" with the PLO/Hamas/Hezbollah supporting tyranny (the LEFT) that rules Israel? At what point will Israelis realize that the CIVIL WAR they fear, IS ALREADY TAKING PLACE AND THEY ARE LOSING? When will the true Zionists take over Israel and rid the country of the Arab and Jewish traitors.

After 2000 years of homelessness, we are privileged in this generation to see a new and productive Jewish State. Why do we let these evildoers threaten to take it from our hands?

Why don't members of the Nationalist Camp understand that FORCE is being used by only ONE side and that is the government. The monopoly on power must be broken or there is no hope.

Under the Nazis, the Jews of Warsaw numbered over 500,000. They were depleted with regular deportations aided by Judenrats (Jewish leaders). The Revolt in Warsaw began when the Jewish population was down to 50,000 (or 90% murdered). At what point is it OK to rebel?

Bernard J. Shapiro

Meekly letting a terrorist state emerge on the soil of Eretz Yisrael would be a rebellion against G-d, Torah and Jewish history. We should not allow it.

When is civil disobedience OK? When is civil war a better course than suicide? All throughout history there have been rebels and loyalists. History is usually written by the victors but truly there is seldom a universally accepted moral standard as to what is a proper rebellion and what is not. We can say with absolute certainty, however, that the Jewish return to Zion and our struggle today for Eretz Yisrael are more righteous than any other struggle for national liberation in the history of the world.

Conditions in Israel may have passed the period where civil disobedience would be effective. A massive outpouring of Israelis prepared to get arrested in civil disobedience would have stopped the Sharon's Expulsion of Jews Plan two years ago. Now, it appears that only civil disobedience and a willingness to fight for their homes will save the country. 600,000 Jews now are under threat of expulsion. 6 million are again under threat of extermination.

We expect the government to try to disarm Zionist patriots, to spy on them and to send agents provocateurs to discredit them. It is quite possible that the IDF will withdraw from Yesha and leaving the Jews with a difficult choice: being massacred or abandoning their homes. Their ability to defend themselves will have been thwarted by the government in collusion with the terrorists.

The Jews of YESHA must not be passive pawns in the political surrender of their homes. They must fight the Arabs, where necessary, to maintain their travel, water, and land rights. When the Israeli government retreats, leaving them behind PLO battle lines, they must be prepared to go on the offensive militarily to secure safe contiguous areas of Jewish control. The defeatist Israeli leaders, who have surrendered our Jewish rights to Eretz Yisrael, should be told that there are still proud Jews in YESHA who will give up neither their inheritance from Abraham nor their right of self-defense.

Exercising one's right to self-defense is a moral imperative. There is a lot of hypocritical talk coming from the government about the danger of Jew fighting Jew. These warnings are coming from the Left who delighted in shooting Zionist (Betar) teenagers swimming to shore after their forces sank the Altalena in 1948. These same hypocrites are putting the Jews of YESHA in life threatening peril. They care nothing about Jewish lives!

Should the Jews of YESHA be forced into military combat—most likely against Arabs, but, G-d forbid, perhaps also against Jews—they would be fully justified. They will be fighting for the security of Israel and the future destiny of the Jewish people. These brave Jews would be continuing the long tradition of Hebrew Warriors, including Joshua, David, the Maccabees and Bar Kochba, who fought against all odds to save their people and their country.

The glorious Hebrew Warriors who defeated five Arab armies in 1948, three in 1967, and two in 1973 must not surrender their Jewish homeland to evil terrorists, who delight in killing Jewish babies. The Brave Heroes of Zion must not limit themselves to passive civil disobedience. Freedom sometimes needs to be secured through the barrel of a gun.

If it is considered patriotic to die fighting Arabs for Israel's survival, then it is just as patriotic to fight against Jews who would lead Israel to destruction. While such internal Jewish fighting would be dreadful, it is a consequence of the government's disregard for the security and well being of its citizens. At this great time of trial and apocalyptic threat, the safeguarding of the future of the Jewish people's right to Eretz Yisrael must take precedence.

Israelis my age have fought and died in 6 wars and I understand their desire to be free of constant conflict. Unfortunately, there is no magic cure. I wish I could write more optimistic words. Sadly, beyond the neighboring states that Israel is negotiating with now lies another ring of unmitigated hostility led by Islamic fundamentalists in Iran.

As Jews we are all involved in this historic struggle to survive. It is not our fate or that of the Israelis that we should retire from this struggle. The only peace the Arabs are prepared to give us is the peace of the grave.

Bernard J. Shapiro

In blood and fire was Israel born and on a hot anvil was she forged. The brave young soldiers of Israel must take a quick glance back to the crematoria of Auschwitz and then go forth to face the enemy knowing that there is STILL no alternative (ein briera).

THE HOUSTON POST: JANUARY 25, 1934

Attorney Will Discuss Hitler

Harry Freeman Will Speak Friday at Temple Beth El.

Harry Freeman, well known Houston attorney, will deliver a lecture on the subject, "Hitlerism—A Threat to Civilization," at Temple Beth El, Crawford and Lamar, at 8 p. m. Friday. Mr. Freeman, who is a student of political and social history and frequent lecturer on these subjects before various organizations, stated, relative to the Friday evening subject:

"There is a growing tendency abroad to make of Hitler a great figure of a statesman-genius; to create a legendary greatness surrounding his accomplishments. That this is the result of efforts of organized Hitleristic propaganda in this land as well as in other countries is a fact known to some of us. Many, however, are innocent victims of this insidious propaganda."

Harry Freeman, Houston attorney, will speak on "Hitlerism" at Temple Beth El at 8 p. m. Friday.

THOSE WHO FAIL TO LEARN FROM HISTORY ARE CONDEMNED TO REPEAT IT

In 1934, Harry W. Freeman, my grandfather, was already lecturing about the dangers of Hitler and Nazism. Nobody listened. The Holocaust was not prevented. Today, in 1995 there are one billion Arab & Moslem people who plan a second Holocaust against the Jews of Israel. Their first stage is to use the so called "peace process" to weaken Israel and strip it of its strategic territories. They are being aided by the same hypocrites and accomplices in the West who failed to aid the Jews of Europe in their darkest hour. Unfortunately, even left-wing Israelis have fallen victims to the seductive lure of peace and have begun a policy of appeasement similar to that tried with Hitler. The results will be no different. The Arab propaganda full of slanders and libels; the media bias against Israel replete with double standards and the rewriting of history are all working to the same end: the delegitimation of Israel. Israel is the only country considered by many to be *GUILTY OF ORIGINAL SIN* by virtue of its very existence. This process of delegitimation has as its goal creating a world climate in which the **DESTRUCTION** of Israel is acceptable. Many in the Jewish community are either apathetic or fail to recognize this threat.

I founded the **FREEMAN CENTER FOR STRATEGIC STUDIES** in order to create a powerful voice to arouse the Jewish community to the action necessary to frustrate the evil designs of the enemies of Israel. I need your help to accomplish this mission. .... Bernard J. Shapiro

Freeman Center says rush to embrace PLO is foolish and ultimately dangerous

'... nothing more than an elaborate trap for Israel'

Asserting that the rush to embrace the Palestine Liberation Organization (PLO) is both foolish and ultimately dangerous, the Freeman Center For Strategic Studies has declared: "The pro-Israel community should react with extreme caution to the moves in Jerusalem to recognize the PLO."

Bernard J. Shapiro, director of the center, also said: "The proposed Gaza-Jericho plan worked out between Israeli Prime Minister Shimon Peres and representatives of the PLO, a terrorist organization, is nothing more than an elaborate trap for Israel. We should not forget that the PLO has violated and trampled on every agreement it has ever made during its nearly 30-year history. This includes agreements and solemn pledges made to the Arab governments of Egypt, Jordan, Syria and Lebanon, as well as the United States and the United Nations."

According to the Freeman Center, the PLO instituted a reign of terror, rape and murder locally as well as attacks on Israel in the two Arab countries where it gained a kind of "self-rule."

Shapiro continued: "Despite the media hype surrounding these developments, let me make something very clear: A leopard does not change its spots. You can say a *berachah* [blessing] over a ham sandwich, but that doesn't make it kosher. And a deal with the PLO is like a dance on quicksand – before you realize it, you have sunk into the muck and slime."

PEACE IN OUR TIME

Join my followers in the Peace March

Neville Chamberlain

AMERICANS FOR
  PEACE NOW
BINAH
BREIRA
NOAM CHOMSKY
CONAME
MICHAEL LERNER
  TIKKUN
MERETZ PARTY
  SHULAMIT ALONI
  YOSSI SARID
  BENI TEMKIN
  DEDI ZUCKER
NEW ISRAEL FUND
NEW JEWISH AGENDA
JEROME SEGAL
  JEWISH LOBBY
SHALOM AKSHAV
  PEACE NOW
MILTON VIORST

Harry W. Freeman, Early Texas Pioneer

By ROWENA FREEMAN GOLDFADEN and BERNARD SHAPIRO

"But what change in life upon arriving in America - Free America! Here I suddenly found myself unbridled, the air free, no stifling atmosphere - I could give free expression to the cravings of my soul! Life began to have a different meaning. What a blessing to have free assemblage, free speech, free press! Can an American who has always enjoyed these blessings appreciate what this means to one who was deprived of them until manhood?"

HARRY W. FREEMAN (1886-1959)

These exuberant words were uttered by Harry W. Freeman soon after arriving in Galveston from Russian controlled Poland at the turn of the century. He was born in wretched poverty in 1886. Left fatherless at the age of four, all of his youthful years were one long, bleak struggle against cold, deprivation, hunger, and persecution. He was finally forced to flee from his native land. This in brief is the inspiring story of Harry W. Freeman, who was for over forty years a successful lawyer in Houston, Texas.

In his native country, he began teaching Hebrew at the age of 12, and later studied to be a rabbi. From these studies he developed a life-long passion for Jewish history and Biblical scholarship. The Jewish ideal of social justice caused him to begin questioning the tyrannical and despotic rule of the Czars. He joined revolutionary movements and was subsequently forced to flee for his life. Disguised as a Russian peasant, he was smuggled across the border into Germany, where he boarded a ship at Bremen bound for Galveston and freedom. During 22 days in steerage, he used the time to master the English language.

It was in 1908 that Mr. Freeman arrived in the United States, making Houston his home. His hard work and fierce determination resulted in countless accomplishments. As a foundation, he used the education he had received in his native country and devoted himself to further studies. At the age of 22, he began working during the day and attending school at night. He later took a course in shorthand, then started work as a stenographer in the law office of Judge Henry J. Dannenbaum, a prominent Houston jurist. He remained with Judge Dannenbaum for three years, studying law in his spare time. Subsequently, he was employed by the United States Department of Justice in New York City, while continuing his law studies at night at New York University Law School for two years. He returned to Houston and was admitted to the bar in 1913.

His passion for social justice made him a fighter for women's rights long before the feminist movement began. Working with Judge Dannenbaum, he crusaded against White slavery, and was greatly responsible for its demise in Texas. Along with Judge Dannenbaum, he was a founding member of the Anti-Vice League of Houston. The goal of this organization was to combat commercialized vice through the publication of information and the enforcement of state and federal laws. He focused on the importance of education as a means of preventing the exploitation of women.

His belief in civil rights a half century before it was popular led him to defend an innocent Black man unjustly convicted in State Court of a major crime. Like all Texas Grand Juries at the time, the Grand Jury in this case excluded Blacks. On appeal to the United States Supreme Court, Mr. Freeman argued that the Grand Jury that indicted the defendant was illegally constituted by reason of such exclusion. The Supreme Court agreed and reversed the conviction. The result was a landmark decision in Constitutional law.

Mr. Freeman made an impact in other areas of law. For example, he authored a provision for a speedy and inexpensive remedy for obtaining possession of mortgaged real property following a foreclosure of a mortgage. This has become a basic provision included in most mortgages written in the State of Texas.

Among Mr. Freeman's many accomplishments was the establishment, with Louis A. Freed of the first chapter of the Zionist Organization of America in Houston. He was also the published author of numerous articles on Jewish history and Jewish issues. Mr. Freeman spoke five languages and was a brilliant Hebrew scholar.

In a resolution passed by the Houston Bar Association in memory of his sudden death, he was described as follows: "Largely self-educated, he was a man of indefatigable energy and wide cultural interests. He loved music, chess, literature and his fellow man. He practiced law with the determination that its goal should always be justice between men. He never compromised with truth. He was a student of the Talmud, and he lived the thought expressed in the Talmud that 'He who acquires more property acquires more problems, and he who acquires and practices more moral principles enjoys greater peace of mind.'"

Mr. Freeman was married for 44 years to Frieda Freeman, his childhood sweetheart. Together they had 2 daughters and a son and six grandchildren. He died in 1959 at the age of 73.

Publisher's note: As Julius Caesar allegedly said, "The good is oft interred with their bones" - such is the story with Harry Freeman. Not as yet listed in any of the books that deal with Texas' History of Jews, Harry Freeman still rates as one of the finest human beings ever to live in this state. The lives of those who knew him stand taller for this unique experience. The course of my own life ran smoother from having been touched by him.

— JOSEPH W. SAMUELS

THERE IS A CHOICE
You must decide or others will decide for you

Israel before Oslo

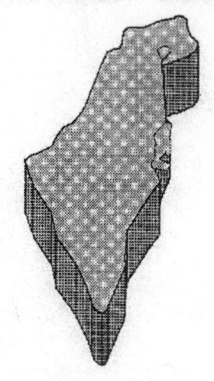

Israel after Oslo

PALESTINE

If you had to choose between water and thirst, what would you choose?

If you had to choose between secure borders that prevent war or indefensible borders that invite war and aggression, what would you choose?

If you had to choose between a rapidly growing population of Arab terrorists living in an area "safe" from intervention by the Israel Defense Forces.....and using that area to launch attacks on Jews by katyushas, suicide bombers and terrorism....or as an alternative placing that hostile population under tight military control, what would you choose?

If you had a choice of keeping Jewish Holy Places and Land under Jewish control or placing them under PLO control where they will be destroyed and desecrated, what would you choose?

DON'T LET HERZL'S DREAM DIE

>>>SUPPORT<<<

THE FREEMAN CENTER
P.O. Box 35661
Houston, Texas 77235-5661
Phone or Fax: 713-723-6016
E-mail: bernards@sbcglobal.net

CHAPTER TWO: PARABLES

Many things repeat themselves in the history of the world *("the more things change, the more they stay the same")* and especially for the Jewish People. I have found it very illustrative to relay many of my own parables to explain them in a simple form for the reader. Here are some of my best ones. Einstein once defined insanity as follows: "A man hits his head against a wall and it hurts and gives him a headache. He then does it repeatedly, hoping for a different result."

Since the advent of the current experiment in "peace making" (Oslo) successive Israeli governments keep hitting their heads against the wall of Arab hatred. No peace ever comes. Land for peace is really "Land for Dead Jews." The Leftists peace mongers say no sacrifice is too much for *"peace"* and the People of Israel keep hemorrhaging their blood and sovereignty in the Land G-d gave them for an inheritance for all time.

Bernard J. Shapiro

THE ONE MIRACLE

(February 1994)

I went to call on the L-rd in His house on the high hill, my head full of anxiety over five million Israeli Jews, having to grow up overnight. "If ever a people, Lord, needed a miracle!" The L-rd, He looked at me as a mountain might look at a molecule. "So you want a miracle," said the Lord. "My, my! You want a miracle." I suppose you mean that you want me to come sliding down a sunbeam and make five million egotists overnight into five million co-operative angels. "Brother," said the L-rd, in a voice that shook the windows," that isn't the sort of universe you're living in. And that isn't the sort of G-d I am."

The room was suddenly vast, with the stars set bright in the ceiling. "There is only one miracle," said the L-rd. "All else is cause and effect. All else is law." The thunder withdrew from the Voice, and the words came hushed and clear like the first stars in the twilight, each star a newborn glory. "There is only one miracle, and it is already accomplished. That miracle is the soul of the Jewish people.

The L-rd, He lifted His head and the Milky Way was His hair. "The Jewish soul is like the atom," He said. "Wonderfully like the atom. Consider the atom. So minute, no lens you can make can enlarge it to a point where your eye can see it, yet there's a whole solar system inside, whirling round a nucleus like the planets around the sun. So feeble in its unreleased state, yet actually the greatest force, save one, in creation. The greatest force in creation, save one."

The Lord strode through His house so the timbers whispered to each other, *"He's thinking of the soul tonight, of the Jewish soul, and the power asleep in the soul. He always shakes the house when He thinks of the power, the power asleep, asleep in the Jewish soul."*

"I have given you a soul," cried the L-rd, **"and you ask me to come down and do a magician's trick! The people who smashed the atom didn't beg Me to come with a thunderbolt and split the nucleus for**

them. They knew that there was power in the atom and they set to work to release it."

"There is power in the Jewish soul, when you break through and set it free, like the power of the atom. More powerful than the atom, it can control the atom, one of the few things in the world that can. I told you that the atom is the greatest force in the world, save one. That one is the Jewish soul."

"But," said the L-rd—and the stars in the sky seemed to stand still and listen—"The power must be released, as the atom-smashers released the power of the atom. They had to get past the electrons to get at the energy packed in the nucleus. And I have to get past a great deal of ego to release the power that is packed in the Jewish soul. I keep shooting My rays toward the nucleus, and the charged field keeps fending them off. But now and then one gets by, the nucleus is split, the power is released, and things begin to happen on a scale that makes men gasp and talk about miracles. The rebirth of Israel and the ingathering of the exiles is one such miracle. The spectacular victories of the Israeli army against overwhelming odds is another. But it isn't a miracle. It's just the soul of the Jew coming to its own. It's just the Jewish soul freed at last to be itself."

The L-rd, He looked at me and His eyes pierced like hot wires. "Perhaps there's something in you and numerous others that will have to be cracked open, if five million Israelis are going to grow up overnight. Something in you," said the L-rd, "something, perhaps, in you."

That was a joke, and I laughed. But the L-rd wasn't laughing. I hastened to reassure Him. "There's nothing the matter with me. It's the other fellow that's the trouble; all five million of them."

"I know all about the other five million Israelis," said the Lord, and I thought He seemed a little tired as He said it, *"but I don't at the moment seem able to see anyone but YOU."*

★

Bernard J. Shapiro

I adapted the parable above from an apocryphal tale I heard more than 40 years ago. The original author is unknown . . . . **Bernard J. Shapiro**

[Published in the Jewish Herald-Voice on February 10, 1994. Reissued in the Maccabean Online in May 1997 and June 2000.]

THE TALE OF THE MYSTIC BUFFALO

A Jewish Parable

My interest in the history of the Old West has led me many times to study the buffalo. No creature in America, except possibly the horse, has had as much influence on the course of history as this noble animal. Standing over 6 feet at the shoulder, it was indeed an impressive creature. To the Native Americans of the Great Plains, the buffalo was the source of all their needs. They harvested food and clothes from the buffalo and even used their hides to construct their homes. It was common for a warrior, who had gone many days without finding water, to save his life by killing a buffalo. The warrior would cut out its heart and drink the blood trapped in its chambers. The blood provided enough liquid and nutrition to continue his journey. The buffalo was so important to the Indians that it was worshipped in their rituals and ceremonies.

The buffalo were very brave and would fight vigorously against the wild animals that sought it as prey. But the buffalo had a great weakness: they could not understand man and the devastation that he brought. One could stand upwind from a large herd and shoot one at a time with a Sharp's 50 caliber or Hawken rifle. The herd would keep grazing, as if nothing happened. As the white man moved west it became clear that the best way to destroy the Indian was to destroy the buffalo. And so it was done. The vast herds that once covered the horizon for over 20 miles at a time were exterminated. The brave Native Americans were reduced to paupers dependent on government handouts of beef and grain.

Has it ever occurred to you that Jews and the Israelis are unfortunately like the buffalo? The non-Jews have been picking us off for thousands of years, yet we continue to act as if nothing has happened. Then came the Holocaust, and we were exterminated in large numbers like the buffalo, but in a more efficient manner. Israel was founded as a rebellion against the impotence and weakness of the buffalo-like Diaspora.

Israelis stopped being easy prey like the buffalo until recently. Then the Palestinians swooped down on the Israelis and started picking them off one by one. First they were cautious. Then when they saw that the Israelis would not react forcefully, they got bolder. The sight of Israeli soldiers, unable to react to 12-year-old Palestinian boys throwing stones, strengthened their resolve to throw the Jews out of Israel. Israelis interpreted the behavior of their military as moderate and compassionate, but the media thought it was brutal, and most important the Palestinians thought it was weakness. The poor buffalo (Israelis) were attacked everywhere—on the roads, in the cities, in the countryside. Hunting for Israelis became a great sport.

Then Labor came to power, with a famed military man, Yitzhak Rabin, at its helm. He would know what to do, said the Israeli people. He would solve this problem. Rabin's solution was simple: The Palestinians don't want us to live in some parts of Eretz Yisrael, so we will retreat. And so it was with the buffalo. First they were slaughtered in the Great Plains, and then in the deserts, the mountains and the forests. Soon there was no place to hide. And the Jews may retreat to the coast, leaving the hills of Judea and Samaria, but the hunters will come after them. There will be no peace but the peace of the grave.

And what about the heart of the Jewish people. The Palestinians are cutting it out. They have claimed Jewish history as their own. Jesus was proclaimed a Palestinian prophet. They claim descent from the Canannites, Jebusites, and Philistines as the rightful heirs to Israel. Jerusalem is really theirs and Yossi Beilin has a plan to give it to them. Hasan Tahboub, president of the PLO backed Supreme Muslim council, claims that Jews have no rights in the Cave of the Machpelah. That it is a Muslim site and Abraham was a Palestinian. Palestinians now talk about their "Diaspora" and about their "holocaust" at the hands of the Jews. Yes my friends, they are cutting the heart from the buffalo and drinking its lifeblood.

When will the buffalo return to its true self: the *Lion of Judah*?

[Published in ***THE JEWISH PRESS*** (NY)*,* February 25, 1994, *the **Jewish Herald-Voice***, April 21, 1994, and the March 1994 issue of ***The Caucus Current****.* Reissued in the Maccabean Online in May 1997, June 2000, June 2001, March 2004, and October-November 2005.]

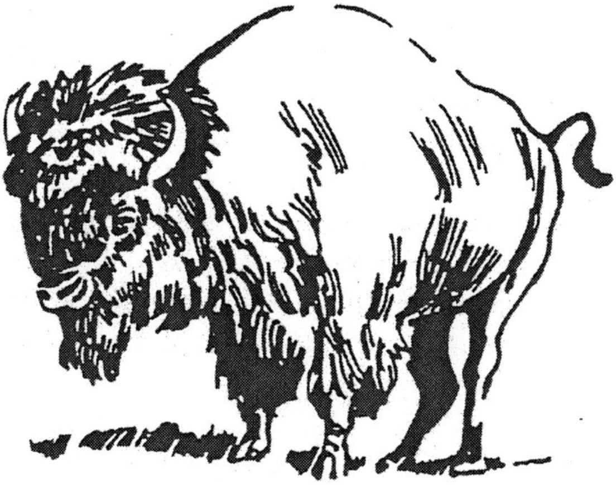

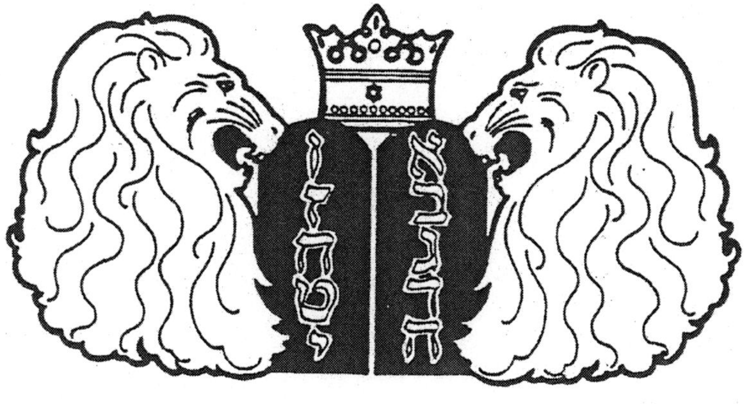

Bernard J. Shapiro

FIVE SHORT PARABLES FOR ISRAEL

(January 2005)

ISRAEL, CHARLIE BROWN & LUCY

As a kid, one of my favorite cartoons was Charlie Brown and his gang of offbeat characters. It is a little embarrassing to admit that my fondness for Charlie Brown extended way into my adulthood. There was something about him that seemed to correspond to my life. He was always trying to do good, but forces beyond his control kept intervening.

One of those forces was a nasty little girl named Lucy. She would promise Charlie to hold a football so he could kick it. Simple enough, except she never followed through on her promises. She would pull the football away and Charlie always landed on his back, stunned at the betrayal.

It may sound oversimplified to equate Israel with Charlie Brown, but I am going to do it. Israel has repeatedly tried to make a cease-fire and negotiate with the Palestinian Authority and Yasser Arafat. Of course, they always end up on their back with more suicide bombings, shootings, and sniper attacks.

And it continues today with Israeli PM Ariel Sharon and his faith in Mohammad Abbas to bring peace. Unfortunately, Israel will fall on its back but the injuries will be more than a backache—murder and mayhem most likely.

REBOOT SHARON, SAVE ISRAEL AND ENSURE SECURITY

Wishful Thinking

Let's face it; things have not gone well for Israel since Sharon was elected. While we all cheered his election and had very high expectations for his government, the reality has been shocking. Although he was elected by a national/ Zionist/religious coalition, Sharon seems to have undergone a radical transformation. With great skill he seems to have sacrificed his natural coalition on the right in order to curry favor with Bush and the Israeli left. The Labor-left leaders are having a rollicking good time watching Sharon trying to out-Peres Peres. Sharon seems to have mastered the "give the terrorist Arabs anything they want" trick that we all thought was peculiar to the previous government.

Conspiracy theorists are also hyperactive these days, with "explanations" for Sharon's bizarre conversion to the philosophies of the suicidal left. Here are some rumor categories for easy reference:

1. The American Connection: Bush and the State Department have exerted pressure of such magnitude that Sharon could not withstand it. The visible support from Bush was just a cover. In this theory, Arab money, the oil lobby and ex-government officials like James Baker are providing the incentive and intellectual cover for selling Israel out.

2. The Trilateral Connection: Men like David Rockefeller and Henry Kissinger, agents for the Trilateral Commission, "bought" Sharon in the 70's. Under this theory, the late Yitzhak Rabin was also bought so that they would have control of Israel regardless of which party was in power.

3. The Empty Shirt Theory: This theory holds that Sharon, despite his brilliant military record, is all "bulldozer". Once in office, it is revealed that he has no ideology and is a weak reed "blowing with the political wind."

4. The PLO A-Bomb Theory: About a year ago, the Freeman Center received confirmation that Iran had bought four nuclear devices from the Former Soviet Union (two from Russia, one from the Ukraine, and one from Kazakhstan). There is speculation that Arafat smuggled one into Israel via a tunnel from the Egyptian Sinai into PA Gaza. A Palestinian VIP, with permission to enter Israel without having to go through security, smuggled the bomb into the Tel Aviv area and buried it. Sharon was told by Arafat that if the Oslo process did not go forward to his satisfaction, Tel Aviv would be destroyed.

5. The Alien Abduction Theory: Many of our readers, who watched the **X-Files** on TV have written to me, convinced that Sharon was abducted by aliens. They insist that Sharon doesn't even exist and the image we see of him is projected telepathically by one of the **"aliens"** who abducted him.

For the record, I don't believe any of those theories. I have a simpler solution to the Sharon riddle. Sharon is like my computer; he needs to be rebooted periodically. For those not familiar with computers, let me explain. Every once in a while computers get confused and they freeze up. The screen stops working, the mouse has no effect, and generally you can't do anything. The solution is to turn the computer off and then turn it back on. This is called rebooting, and by some mysterious process everything begins to work properly. All the electrical connections suddenly know exactly what they are supposed to do.

Sharon's problem is that he knows what is best for Israel, but somehow has become frozen in a defective policy (**Oslo, the Roadmap, the Retreat**), and all his cognitive and operative controls are refusing to function. So we must reboot Sharon in order to save Israel and ensure security. Here's my plan:

Sharon needs to give up being Prime Minister for a period of six weeks. Three members of the cabinet, Uzi Landau, Michael Kliener, and Natan Sharansky, will share the duties of PM during this period of time. They will be trusted (by the rational public) with this responsibility because of their high integrity and proven devotion to Israel. Sharon will go to a quiet peaceful place—perhaps Safed—where he will be rebooted. Great Zionist thinkers, historians, philosophers and religious leaders will each spend one whole day with him discussing the major issues facing Israel's future. Elyakim Ha'etzni and Paul Eidelberg might spend Mondays with him and Shmuel Katz and Arie Stav on Tuesdays. David Wilder and Gary Cooperberg would come from Hebron on Wednesdays. Strategic analyst Lou Rene Beres and terrorist expert Yossef Bodansky, as well as Zionist leaders like Morton Klein and Herb Zweibon, would come from the US. Joe Gellert and Christopher Barder from England would come to visit Sharon on Thursdays. On Fridays, Sharon would be blessed by a visit from Ruth and Nadia Matar. Rabbis Eliezar Waldman and Zalman B. Melamed would conduct Shabbat Services and meet with Sharon every Shabbat. Dr. Aaron Lerner will spend Sundays with Sharon, going over all Oslo/Roadmap documentation.

If all goes according to my plan, Sharon will emerge from the six weeks retreat, rebooted and ready to be a **Maccabean** leader of Israel. He will have become a proud Jew, unafraid of the U.S. State Department, Mubarak, Arafat and the Israeli leftist fifth column. He will go forth with the blessing of Hashem, to blow the shofar loud and clear to all the world: *There is a new Israel. We will pursue our destiny with great vigor and without apology.*

★

Editor's Note: I modified this folk tale around 1994 and broadcast it during the early days of the Oslo appeasement process. It is now 2005 and we have Ariel Sharon as our Prime Minister. He is a man who historically knows how to do battle with the enemies of Israel. Has he lowered his guard, trying to be friends with everyone? Including the world that abandoned us many times to slaughter for over the last 2,000 years? . . . . Bernard J. Shapiro

A Folk Tale For Israelis

MAKING PEACE WITH WOLVES

How do you make peace with wolves? This question has faced man since he settled the land and domesticated animals for livestock. "G-d created the wolves too," man thought, "They too must have some kind of purpose, but why do they slaughter my sheep?" "I'll make peace with them" the man thought. "Surely they will understand what that means, for they are part of G-d's creatures."

So the man met with the wolves and promised them food and shelter if they would leave his sheep alone. The wolves, seeing desperation and weakness, agreed. They lived amongst the sheep, the man fed them and sheltered them, and they grew strong and multiplied. One day as the man went out to feed his flock and the wolves, he only found wolves, standing amongst the slain carcasses of his stock. "Why? Why have you killed my sheep?" the man screamed, "Haven't I fed you? Haven't I sheltered you? **WHY?**" The wolves looked at the man and smiled,

"Why, you ask, have we slain your sheep? Because **YOU LET US**, and after all we **ARE** still wolves!"

A government is like a shepherd; its **DUTY** is to the flock, **NOT** the wolves. This is a lesson Peres and his Labor government never learned. Peace is wonderful! Peace is what we all want for Israel (the world for that matter), but do we want the peace of a cemetery or the peace of a strong, secure nation? One of two things needs to happen; either the Israeli government needs to take off the rose colored glasses and see the wolves for what they are **OR the flock needs to get a new shepherd!**

Sharon, this applies to you.

ISRAEL AND THE CAMEL DUNG

A Jewish Parable

On his deathbed Neville Chamberlain, former British Prime Minister, said the following to his son:

"Everything would have worked out OKAY if Hitler had not lied to me."

*

The circumstances which led to this tale of **ISRAEL AND THE CAMEL DUNG** were first predicted by the wise men of Chelm sometime in the 18th century. At the time, these wise men were dismissed as fools. It took 200 years and the revival of the Jewish State for this prediction to come true.

Sometime in the early 1990's there was a wise King of Israel named Peres the Brilliant. The most serious threat to Israel came from an evil man named Yassir the Bloody. Now, Peres wondered how he could make peace with Yassir so that Israel would be loved throughout the Middle East. He and his favorite advisor, Beilin the Poodle, set out to make peace and change the Middle East forever.

First they sent emissaries to Yassir, and when they found that he was receptive, a meeting was scheduled. They couldn't meet in Israel, so they chose the next best place, Oslo. When they all entered the meeting room, everyone noticed a smell coming from a package held by Yassir. Peres didn't want to insult Yassir but was very curious and the odor was a bit overpowering. As was normal, Peres whispered to his Poodle to ask the delicate question. So Beilin asked Yassir and the rest is history.

You see, Yassir revealed that a gypsy had sold him a pot of camel's dung that had magical powers. Yassir agreed to sell it to Israel for a price. That price turned out to be the Oslo agreement. According to Yassir, who got it straight from the gypsy, Israel could use the power of the camel dung to wish for peace. Peres and his Poodle were very excited and concluded the Oslo deal with Yassir the Bloody. They then went back to Israel with the camel dung and said that they now had the power to create a peaceful New Middle East.

In the years that followed, peace never came to Israel. Israel had done everything right. They gave up land, water and Holy Sites to Yassir's bloody gang of Arabs. Periodically they checked with Arafat and complained that the camel dung wasn't working. The new King of Israel, Barak of the Wet Diaper, was told by Arafat that Israel must give him Jerusalem, the Golan, and the right of return of five million displaced Arabs. Since Barak was getting diaper rash and becoming very cranky, he decided that he must go along with Arafat to bring peace to Israel. Then their government was defeated.

Today a new king, Arik the Bulldozer, has arisen in Israel. With the encouragement of Peres the Brilliant, he has decided to make a deal with the new Palestinian Arab PM, Mohammad Abbas. Abbas explained that Arafat was wrong about camel dung and what Israel really needed for peace was goat dung. Convinced, Arik the Bulldozer accepted all of the Arab demands.

The rest is history. All those returning Arabs drove the Jews into the sea. No country would allow the Israelis to immigrate to their country. "Who needs Jews?" said the British. The Americans didn't have any room for Jews, since millions of illegal immigrants were coming without permission.

There in the great sea, sitting on a raft that was starting to sink, Peres the Brilliant, Beilin the Poodle, Barak of the Wet Diaper and Arik the Bulldozer were discussing the horrible disaster befalling Israel.

Peres summed up the situation in a very brilliant way: "Camel dung does not have magic powers and neither does goat dung. Everything would have worked out OKAY if Arafat and Abbas had not lied to us."

THE SHORT CHANGE ARTIST AND OSLO

Or Why One Shouldn't Make Redeployment Maps

During my 23 years as owner of House of Books in Houston, I learned many valuable lessons. One in particular seems to have an application to the current situation in Israel. Let me explain: In 1978, the store was victimized by a short change artist. One of my clerks was at the register when a well-dressed gentleman approached with a paperback book costing $2.95. He gave her a $20 bill and then began a back and forth exchange of money. In the end, the bookstore lost about $60.

I called the Houston Police Department and requested that an officer come to the store and brief my employees on how to prevent this crime from happening again. The officer came and told us a little story. It seems that Johnny Carson once asked a short change artist to come to his show and try to fool him while he was fully alert to what was going down. The criminal had no problem and his skill marveled the audience.

The Lesson: No matter how smart you are, a professional short change artist will win out. He is a pro. He does this day in and day out.

How To Stop The Short Change Artist: **You simply MUST NOT PLAY HIS GAME.** At the first hint of the scam, my employees were told to close the register and call security. They were specifically told NOT to try to outsmart or "keep up" with the short change artist.

How does this apply to Israel and the redeployment? Very simple. Think of Yassir Arafat and the US State Department as short change artists. They set up a scam called "Oslo" and the "peace process." They exchange promises for territory. They keep the territory but never keep their promises. Like I said, it is a scam. Along came the new Likud Prime Minister, Bibi Netanyahu, who believed that he was smart enough to control the **GAME**. Only he couldn't. No one can. He was up against pros who have been scamming nations for decades. The State Department has reneged on commitment after solemn commitment to the Jewish State. Still they continue, pledging friendship, while surgically inserting knives in our backs.

This high drama of Oslo, Roadmaps and Sharon's Retreat is just another manifestation of the attempt to control the **GAME**. There is only one way to win for Israel: Don't play!

We must tell Sharon and the world that the cash register of Eretz Yisrael is closed. The GAME is over. The scam is through.

SHARON AND THE CEASE-FIRE

A Satire

(June 2001)

The Freeman Center has calculated a number of important statistics which might be of interest to our readers. These raw figures relate to Sharon's cease-fire and Arafat's war. [All figures +/—4%]

1. Number of Jews that must be killed before Sharon ends cease-fire: 10,000

2. Number of Jews that must be maimed before Sharon ends cease-fire: 50,000

3. Number of times Israel will be condemned by the UN for allowing the Arabs to kill them: 1500

4. Number of times the US Secretary of State will ask for a cessation of violence on both sides: 10,000

5. Number of times the UN Secretary General Kofi Anan will blame Israel for excessive force: 8000

6. Number of times the Amnesty and the Red Cross blame Israeli for not dying faster so the conflict would be over sooner: 7000

7. Number of times construction of a Jewish home is considered the equivalent of mass murder in the media and diplomatic circles: 50,000

8. Number of times that Israel's left-wing news papers blame YESHA and religious Jews for Arab anti-Semitism: 25,000

9. Number of times Shimon Peres and Yossi Beilin will try to undermine Israeli government policy: 5000

Bernard J. Shapiro

10. How many members of the Israeli Left admit to having sexual fantasies about Arafat and his revolutionary chic: 500,000?

THE FREEMAN CENTER ASKS: WHEN WILL SHARON FULFILL HIS PROMISE TO BRING SECURITY TO HIS PEOPLE? IT IS PAST TIME TRYING TO PLEASE THE WORLD.

Notes and editorial from the June 2001 issue of THE MACCABEAN ONLINE

ARAFAT SELLS HIS NONVIOLENCE RUG TO THE ISRAELIS AGAIN

(June 2001)

What we are witnessing today is Arafat's attempt to sell the Israelis the promise of ending violence. He did it at Oslo, Gaza-Jericho, Oslo 2, Hebron, Wye, and Sharm. The world looked on and urged, indeed demanded that Israel pay a price to make the deal. This time it is "settlements." Last time it was land. Arafat continues to incite to murder and in fact is the true inheritor of the Nazi aim of exterminating the Jews, this time in Israel instead of Europe.

THE QUESTIONS:

ARE ISRAELIS SO LACKING IN HISTORICAL KNOWLEDGE THAT THEY DON'T UNDERSTAND THIS FACT?

Why is the Israeli Foreign Ministry praising The Mitchell Report, which is full of lies and distortions that impact very negatively on Israel?

Bernard J. Shapiro

SOME THOUGHTS

(1952)

He who knows not, **and knows not that he knows not**, is a **fool.**

Shun him

He who knows not, **and knows that he knows not**, is a **child.**

Teach him.

He who knows, **and knows not that he knows**, is **asleep.**

Awaken him.

He who knows, **and knows that he knows**, is **wise.**

Follow him.

CHAPTER THREE: ISRAELI HISTORY

The true history of Middle East Conflict Israel and the Arab/Muslim nations surrounding it has been greatly distorted in modern times. It is as if George Orwell book, *1984,* has become the media framework for discussing the conflict. More about this in my chapter on Arab Propaganda and Media Bias.

I have always felt that historians have mis-labeled the Middle East Conflict as an Arab-Israeli Conflict in earlier times and now as an Israeli-Palestinian Conflict. It is actually a 120 year war by the Arab and Muslims to exterminate the Jewish population in the same manner as the Nazis in Europe in the 1930's.

The Arabs were inspired by the modern anti-Semitism of Adolf Hitler and aided him during WWII. Their assistance was predicated on Hitler's promise to Hajj (Muhamed Effendi) Amin al Husseini, Grand Mufti of Jerusalem that after the war he would bring the Holocaust to Palestine. There was actually a plan on the drawing boards to set up two gas chambers and crematoria (one in Tel Aviv and one in Haifa) to dispose of the Jews. Attacks on the Jews of Palestine began in the 1880's as Jews began to return to their homeland from their involuntary exile in Europe. Many generations of Jews had remained in Israel since Roman times.

The historically in accurate view that the conflict began with the 1967 war and the occupation by Israel of Judea, Samaria and Gaza (YESHA) is simply false. One of the lessons of this book is that no matter how many times you deny the truth—*IT IS STILL THE TRUTH.*

Israel is a very small country, with few natural resources. In its 63 years of existence it developed an advanced hi-tech democratic capitalist economy despite constant warfare and terrorism.

JEWS, G-D, AND ISRAEL

My Zionist Passage

(July 1992)

In blood and fire was Israel born, and on a hot anvil was she forged. Her youth understood that life in the new Jewish homeland would require sacrifice. With stories of the stench of burning flesh from the ovens of Auschwitz embedded deep in their psyches, the young Israeli soldiers fight with the firm conviction that there is no alternative "ein brera." . . . . (from the author's private diary).

It was somewhat of a fluke that I became a Zionist. Having been raised in a congregation not known for its pro-Israel views, I could have lived my life without ever understanding the crucial link between Israel and the Jewish people. As it happened, I was in San Diego in 1959 and enrolled in a Jewish history course taught by a wonderful Reform rabbi. He required that we read two books: <u>The Course of Modern Jewish History</u> by Howard M. Sachar and <u>Exodus</u> by Leon Uris. While Sachar gave me the historical framework to understand the birth of Israel, it was Uris who made me feel involved. The San Diego Public Library provided me with many books on Israel and Jewish history and I eagerly read them all.

While I considered myself a Zionist by 1960 and made my first trip to Israel in that year, it would be seven years before fully understanding the connection between Israel and the Jewish people. Israel's victory in the Six Day War in 1967 was the background for the most meaningful experience of my life. I arrived in Israel a few days after the war ended and like many Jews, rushed to Jerusalem to see the Western Wall.

The Wall, the last remaining remnant of Solomon's Temple and sacred to Jews for over 2000 years, had been in Jordanian controlled Jerusalem since 1949. The Jordanians, acting with malice aforethought, had denied Jews access to their sacred holy place. I walked with hundreds of Jews, praying and singing through the Old City. The feeling of anticipation and exhilaration was contagious as we approached the Wall. As I stood a few feet away, I saw pious Jews pressing little scraps of paper into the cracks between the sacred stones. The pieces contained prayers, which legends hold go straight to G-d when placed in the holy Wall.

The people in front of me finished their prayers and suddenly I was pressed up close to the object of all our joy and hope. I had expected the stones to be rough and weathered after all this time, but they were smooth from 2,000 years of touching and kissing. The gentle caresses of Jews over the ages had worn soft finger grooves in the hard rock. As I placed my hands on this magnificent relic of our forefathers, I felt a surge of light and energy the likes of which I had never known. In what had to have been but the flash of a second, I felt at one with Jews from all periods of history. At the Passover Seder we are told to thank G-d for delivering us from Egypt as though we ourselves had been brought out of bondage. At that moment in Jerusalem, this Seder message was very real for me.

In an instant I saw the continuity of Jewish history and its unbreakable connection with *Eretz Yisrael* (Land of Israel). I understood how modern Israel is the beginning of the Third Temple Period and the spiritual heir to Joshua, Saul, David, Solomon, the Maccabees and Bar Kokhba. I frequently write about the security reasons for incorporating Judea, Samaria, and Gaza into the body of Israel. There is another side to this issue and that is the spiritual-religious side. The truth, which many find inconvenient, is that the Land of Israel was promised by G-d to Abraham and his seed in perpetuity. The Land of Israel is not speculative real estate to be bartered away for some high sounding false promises of peace. The hills and valleys of Judea and Samaria contain the collective memory of the Jewish people. It was here that the Israelites first entered the Holy Land. And it was here they fought the battles, built the towns, elected their kings and were preached to by their prophets and judges. And it was on this soil that they wrote the Holy Scriptures we call our Bible.

In my blinding flash of insight at the Wall, I also understood that Israel on its own soil was more powerful than the sum of its weapons and men. Jews, who had wandered the earth powerless for two millennia, attained great power when re-united with the soil of Israel. Anyone who has followed the Arab-Israeli conflict must be aware of the rising cost paid for Jewish blood. Before Israel was established, nations of the world took Jewish lives with impunity. Today, Arabs have discovered that the iron fist of Zahal (Israel Defense Forces) exacts a high price for even one Jewish life.

One thing is clear to me: the L-rd has blessed Israel by re-uniting Jerusalem and bringing Judea, Samaria, and Gaza back under its control. It would be a horrendous sin against G-d and common sense for Israel to renounce this inheritance to which it is entitled. Israel holds these lands as a sacred trust for the Jewish people in perpetuity.

It would not only be sinful, but also criminal, to abuse that trust by denying future generations of Jews their Holy Land—Land of their Fathers; the one tiny spot on Planet Earth given to them by G-d.

[This article was first published in the **Jewish Herald-Voice** on July 11, 1992. It was reissued in May 1997 and August 2000.]

Bernard J. Shapiro

Jewish Herald-Voice **(Houston) September 2, 1993, p. 6**

Freeman Center says rush to embrace

PLO is foolish and ultimately dangerous

" . . . nothing more than an elaborate trap for Israel"

Asserting that the rush to embrace the Palestinian Liberation Organization (PLO) is both foolish and ultimately dangerous, the Freeman Center for Strategic Studies has declared: "The pro-Israel community should react with extreme caution to the moves in Jerusalem to recognize the PLO."

Bernard J. Shapiro, director of the center, also said: "The proposed Gaza-Jericho plan worked out between Israeli Prime Minister Shimon Peres and representatives of the PLO, a terrorist organization, is nothing more than an elaborate trap for Israel. We should not forget that the PLO has violated and trampled on every agreement it has ever made during its nearly 30-year history. This includes agreements and solemn pledges made to the Arab governments of Egypt, Jordan, Syria and Lebanon, as well as the United States and the United Nations."

According to the Freeman Center, the PLO instituted a reign of terror, rape and murder locally as well as attacks on Israel in the two Arab countries where it gained a kind of "self rule."

Shapiro continued: "Despite the media hype surrounding these developments, let me make something very clear: A leopard does not change his spots. You can say a *berachah* (blessing) over a ham sandwich, but that doesn't make it kosher. And a deal with the PLO is like a dance on quicksand—before you realize it, you have sunk into the muck and slime."

*

Please note that this Press Release was issued on September 2, 1993, a full 11 days before Oslo was signed on the White House lawn (September

13, 1993). Everything it said has come horribly true. We at the Freeman Center properly analyzed the momentous events in the Middle East and we have been fighting the Oslo Appeasement Agreement ever since.

Please help us in our battle to save *Eretz Yisrael*.

Bernard J. Shapiro

AN IMPORTANT NOTE TO OUR READERS

March 1997

>The article below was written in 1993 with Rabin and Peres in mind. Unfortunately the new Likud government of Prime Minister Benjamin Netanyahu fulfills all the requirements of the residents of **Chelm**. How many times must we hear the word *"reciprocity"* and then watch it ignored. Must we talk about another unilateral withdrawal (Lebanon) and not see that the Arabs view our actions as weakness (which makes them demand more and become more aggressive). There is talk of building islands off the coast of Tel Aviv. They would be built at great cost. Do Israel's leaders **NOT SEE** the beautiful hills of Judea and Samaria that cry out for settlement? A huge breathing space for the crowded coast is being given to our enemies. Why? You say the Arabs are not happy with us living in **YESHA**. So what? They were never happy with Jews living anywhere in *Eretz Yisrael*.

It is a FOOL who bases his national goals on the hatred of his enemies. Has Israel become a *"ship of fools?"* And on this day, the Israeli government has released murderers of Jews. And they will kill more Jews. [See the **Arutz-7** report following my article.]

The Freeman Center has been fighting the **UTTER STUPIDITY** of Oslo since 1993. Our only weapon is the **TRUTH**. We have published in **THE MACCABEAN** over 5,000 pages of news, commentary and analysis by the best and brightest writers of our day. The **Freemanlist** has broadcast about 8,000 pages of great material across the Internet. Our website has been visited by over 6,500 people. Our fax broadcasts have sent thousands of pages to the Jewish leadership in this country. Despite all this, **CHELMITES** continue to function at the highest levels of the Israel government as well as the Jewish *"leadership"* in the Diaspora.

HaShem, *where have we failed?* . . . . **Bernard J. Shapiro, Editor**

O LAND OF ZION

Look to the east to a land far away but near
To a land where prophets roam and warriors do battle
Where the river Jordan flows in mystic splendor
Where hopes are born and dreams are realized
I look to a land of struggle, blood and tears
The Land is my people, the mother of the Jew
O Land of Zion, my heart longs for you.

✱

The soil of Zion is good beyond measure
It rewards those who care enough
To see its beauty and its grace
Past the sand and stones of neglect
The valleys blossom with the fruit of Eden
And the mountains are ablaze with color, they sparkle with the dew
O Land of Zion, my heart belongs to you.

✱

I wandered far and searched the earth for peace
But only in Zion was my heart at rest
And only in Jerusalem was my soul free at last
To seek the meaning of the universe and all its mysteries
To ponder the rebirth of my people and our destiny
Here in the hills and valleys of Israel, my understanding grew
O Land of Zion, my true love is with you.

✱

Written in Jerusalem in June of 1967 and first published in the Jewish Herald-Voice (Houston) on December 13, 1973.

[This poem was reissued in the Maccabean Online in May 1997, February-March 1999, and April 2004.]

Bernard J. Shapiro

ISRAEL'S SACRED PLACES—

Why The Arab Thrust To Seize Control of Them

(October 2006)

An editorial from the November 2001 issue of *THE MACCABEAN ONLINE*.

When the late Israeli Prime Minister, Yitzhak Rabin, and Foreign Minister Shimon Peres signed the Oslo Accords on the White House lawn (September 1993), they initiated a process whereby Israel would lose control of its Sacred Places and its Holy Land. Even before Oslo, Moshe Dayan had surrendered the most sacred of Jewish Holy Places, the Temple Mount, to the Arabs. There is much more involved here than politics as usual. I believe that there is something terrible dangerous about the removal of the Jews from their Sacred Places.

All over the world, from Stonehenge in England to the great temples of India, one finds Holy Places with great mystical power for the people who inhabit those lands. Some shrines of the East draw believers from across the globe. The power of these places cannot be explained scientifically. One only needs to step onto Mount Abu in India to feel the presence of great mystical forces. And then there is Banares, the Hindu's Holy City of Light casting a warm glow over the sacred Ganges River.

Islam arose in the 7th century on the foundation of a pagan (Meccan) religion that worshiped a large black stone, known as the Kaaba. Muhammad learned the rudiments of Judaism from the many Jews living in Arabia. He created the Islamic religion by re-writing the Jewish Holy Scriptures (calling it the Koran) and fusing it with the local pagan customs. One pagan concept became horribly significant as Islam spread both east and west across the world. The reverence for the Kaaba and the belief that Arab power derived from it became a brutal principle in the conquest of other peoples. As Islam was spread by the sword, the Sacred Places of conquered peoples were destroyed and occupied.

It became a standard practice to destroy an Indian, Persian, Zoroastrian, Buddhist, Jewish or Christian temple and build a mosque on its ruins. This was always interpreted by historians as a kind of one upmanship. A way to demonstrate the superiority of Islam and humiliate the defeated. Koenraad Elst in his recent book NEGATIONISM IN INDIA writes: "In all the lands it conquered, Islam has replaced indigenous places of worship with mosques. In Iran, there are no ancient Zoroastrians or Manichean shrines left. In Central Asia, there are no Buddhist temples left. Similarly, in India (except the far South where Islam penetrated rather late) there are practically no Hindu temples that have survived the Muslim period (over 10,000 destroyed).

But there are thousands of mosques built on the foundations of Hindu temples (for example, the Ayodhya temple)." In my opinion, this Islamic behavior was more than an exhibition of cruel superiority. It was based on the pagan belief that they would acquire the power of the defeated peoples by absorbing their Holy Places and making them theirs.

Let's see how these forces play out in the Arab war of extermination against the Jewish people (incorrectly called the Arab-Israeli Conflict). After Israel was conquered by the Arabs armies, the Temple Mount was used to build the Mosque of Omar (Dome of the Rock) and the Al Aska Mosque. While Jerusalem is not mentioned even once in the Koran, modern Arabs make great pretense by claiming it as one of their holy sites. This, of course is nonsense.

The Arab claim that each and every Jewish Holy Place is rightfully theirs has become quite common and accepted by the western media. First Jerusalem and the Temple Mount, then Hebron and the Cave of the Patriarchs, and on to the Tomb of Joseph (Nablus), Ramat Rachel and more.

The Western Wall, the last remaining remnant of Solomon's Temple and sacred to Jews for over 2000 years, had been in Jordanian controlled Jerusalem since 1949. The Jordanians, acting with malice aforethought, had denied Jews access to their sacred Holy Place. I visited the Wall for the first time in 1967.

Bernard J. Shapiro

When I placed my hands on this magnificent relic of our forefathers, I felt a surge of light and energy the likes of which I had never known. In what had to have been but the flash of a second, I felt at one with Jews from all periods of history. At the Passover seder we are told to thank G-d for delivering us from Egypt as though we ourselves had been brought out of bondage. At that moment in Jerusalem, this seder message was very real for me.

In an instant I saw the continuity of Jewish history and its unbreakable connection with Eretz Yisrael (Land of Israel). I understood how modern Israel is the beginning of the Third Temple Period and the spiritual heir to Joshua, Saul, David, Solomon, the Maccabees and Bar Kokhba. I frequently write about the security reasons for incorporating Judea, Samaria, and Gaza into the body of Israel. There is another side to this issue and that is the spiritual-religious side. The truth, which many find inconvenient, is that the Land of Israel was promised by G-d to Abraham and his seed in perpetuity.

The Land of Israel is not speculative real estate to be bartered away for some high sounding (false) promises of peace. The hills and valleys of Judea and Samaria contain the collective memory of the Jewish people. It was here that the Israelites first entered the Holy Land. And it was here they fought the battles, built the towns, elected their kings and were preached to by their prophets and judges. And it was on this soil that they wrote the Holy Scriptures we call our Bible.

In my blinding flash of insight at the Wall, I also understood that Israel on its own soil was more powerful than the sum of its weapons and men. Jews who had wandered the earth powerless for two millenniums attained great power when re-united with the soil of Israel.

What about the Arabs? They are destroying the Jewish people by taking over their Sacred Land. There is something very real and awe inspiring about the Jewish connection to Eretz Yisrael and the Arabs KNOW it and seek to destroy that mystical connection. With profound stupidity and avarice the political Left in Israel is cooperating with this evil project.

And worse, some religious Jews and members of the Right are also going along with the dismemberment of Israel. Some say it will save lives to appease the Arabs. Foolishness. The predatory Arabs already smell victory and each new concession makes their lust for Jewish blood grow.

Wouldn't the Arabs object to the removal of the Mosque of Omar (Dome of the rock) and the Al Aqsa mosque from the Temple Mount? Of course they would, but they have no legitimate rights in the area. "There is no reason the sovereign State of Israel, needs to allow this desecration Jewish Holy Places to continue." Today on the Mount, the Arabs are supreme. They are destroying all archaeological remnants of Jewish sites. They are storing weapons in their mosques to kill Jews.

One thing is clear to me: the L-rd has blessed Israel by re-uniting Jerusalem and bringing Judea, Samaria, and Gaza back under its control. **It would be a horrendous sin against G-d and common sense for Israel to renounce this inheritance to which it is entitled. Israel holds these lands as a sacred trust for the Jewish people in perpetuity.**

It would not only be sinful, but also criminal, to abuse that trust by denying future generations of Jews their Holy Land—Land of their Fathers; the one tiny spot on planet earth given to them by G-d.

An Editorial (Remember, the future is not fixed. We can change it for good or evil.)

ISRAEL IN THE 21ST CENTURY—

Three Alternate Futures

Years 2000-2010

(January 2000)

Not having the power of prophecy, this article is a projection of Israel's current trends into the future. One would not expect such a projection to be 100% accurate on every detail. It should however stay within fairly accurate parameters. You may want to save this paper to verify my projections.

Apart from my alternate realities, there is a fantasy shared by many Jews. That fantasy is of a Messianic Age where Arab and Jew will live in peace and prosper together. A fantasy of no more war, no more bloodshed, no more hatred. I did consider this as a fourth alternate reality, but rejected it on the basis of total lack of substantive evidence of its being possible.

It did however remind me of a story from the Moscow Zoo. During the 70's when the Soviet 'peace offensive' was at its height, there was an exhibit at the Moscow Zoo featuring a lion and a lamb living peacefully in the same cage. Tourists were amazed at this proof positive of possibility of peace. One reporter was not that convinced. After hours he showed up at the zoo and went talk to the zookeeper. Tell me the truth: "What is going on here?" The zookeeper was nonplused and answered quickly: "No big deal. We put a new lamb in the cage each morning."

ALTERNATE FUTURE #1—ISRAEL CEASES TO BE A JEWISH STATE

Israel continues its present course of sanctifying and making Oslo holy. Events follow as such:

1. 90% of Judea, Samaria and Gaza are given to Arafat.

2. A few Jewish areas remain but transit routes are controlled by hostile Arabs.

3. The Golan is given to Syria

4. There are promises of peace, access to water, early warning stations

5. Syria reneges on promises in line #4

6. Israel does nothing as it faces Syrian artillery overlooking the Galilee

7. Arafat is given Jerusalem including the Temple Mount but is not satisfied.

8. An intifada begins in the Galilee and the Negev as Arafat demands that those areas be annexed to Palestine.

9. The United Nations, the US State Department, the NY Times plus other morally deprived international bodies demand an immediate return to Palestine of these occupied territories.

10. Arafat, with European technical help manages to draw out the entire water supply in the Judean-Samarian mountain aquifer (from which Israel gets 30% of its water) for use by Palestinians.

11. Syria blocks the flow of water to Israel from the Jordan River sources on the Golan. These supplied Israel with 30% of its water.

12. Israel is forced to give up agriculture, watering lawns, washing cars, and even regular bathing. The odor of Oslo becomes overpowering.

13. Arafat demands that Israel accept the return of 7,000,000 refugees and the US State Department agrees that this will improve the climate for peace.

14. Even without Israel's agreement on refugees, hundreds of thousands pour into Palestine. This creates an uncontrollable pressure to expand territorially.

15. Many Arabs infiltrate into Israel and expand greatly the local Israeli Arab population.

16. Arabs began to demand that Israel cease being a Jewish country and just be a democracy.

17. The leftist/labor government of Israel is in coalition with the Arab parties so #16 is considered and passes the Knesset.

18. The early stages of removing the Jewish character of the state involve: taking the Magen David out of the Israeli flag, the word Jew out of Hatikvah, the national anthem, adding Moslem Holy Days, and especially re-writing all the history books to show the Jews as aggressors who stole Palestine and are prone to kill Arabs to use their blood to make matzoh.

19. Soon after becoming bi-national, Israel ceases to exist and the state merges with Palestine. The Jews become Dhimmis or second class citizens as in most Moslem countries.

ALTERNATE FUTURE #2—ISRAEL FIGHTS EXISTENTIAL WAR

1. The 'peace' process continues

2. Syria gets the Golan but guarantees that it will be demilitarized

3. Arafat gets 90% of Judea, Samaria and Gaza

4. Israeli Arabs in the Galilee and Negev areas demand to secede from Israel and become a part of Palestine

5. Israel refuses this demand and the Arabs start an intifada. It spreads to Palestine and attacks begin on Jews both on the roads and in their communities.

6. Israeli intelligence reveals that the Palestinian government is actively supporting, indeed started the anti-Jewish violence.

7. As the Jewish body count rises above the 500 mark, the Israeli government decides its patience has run out and retaliates heavily against Palestinian targets.

8. Egypt, Syria, Iraq, Iran, the US, the UN, and all Moslem and European nations demand that Israel stop its attacks on Palestinians.

9. The US State Department stops all aid to Israel until they cease their brutal attacks on innocent Arabs.

10. The UN passes its 2,345th resolution condemning Israel

11. As support for their position increases Arafat launches his first Katyusha rockets at Tel Aviv, Haifa and other sites on the coastal plain.

12. Israeli armed forces with air support invade Palestine to stop the attacks.

13. Israel's invasion triggers a much wider war.

14. Egypt, Syria, Iraq, and Iran launch missiles with anthrax and sarin gas warheads at major populated areas of Israel.

15. Egyptian, Iraqi, and Syrian paratroops land on the Samarian-Judean mountain ridge overlooking Israel. It had been given to Palestine for 'peace.'

16. It takes Syrian tanks 2-4 hours to cross the demilitarized Golan Heights and penetrate Israel.

17. It normally takes Israel 48-72 hours to achieve full mobilization. Unfortunately the Arabs have achieved the line of sight (from the mountains) ability to disrupt Israeli military communications. Also the Palestinians have totally disrupted the road system in Israel, making travel very difficult. Soldiers cannot reach their units, tank ammunition cannot reach the tanks, food and medical supplies cannot reach their destination.

18. Syrian troops close in on Haifa. Egyptian troops have crossed Sinai and are poised in Gaza to strike at Tel Aviv.

19. The desperate Israelis initiate the Sampson Option. This is a last ditch plan to destroy their enemies even at great losses to themselves.

20. Missile silos open in the most unreachable parts of the Negev and Galilee hills. Sleek Jericho 3 missile armed with nuclear warheads are launched deep into the heart of the Arab world. Three hours later the world learns that Cairo, Baghdad, Damascus, Tehran, Riyadh, Beirut, Mecca, Kabul, and Karachi no longer exist.

21. Small tactical nuclear weapons are used against the massed troops of Syria and Egypt.

22. With great difficulty, Israel survives, and sweeps the enemy from her land. Israel's death toll reaches 500,000 with many more wounded.

23. Half the country is uninhabitable due to anthrax and radiation poisoning. Cancer rates soar as a result of radiation in the atmosphere.

ALTERNATE FUTURE #3—ISRAEL GROWS STRONG AND PROSPERS

1. Opposition to the Golan give away grows. Even the security wing of what used to be the Labor Party has doubts about the wisdom of this move.

2. Before negotiations reach a conclusion, the Knesset brings down the Barak government. New elections are held.

3. Shas spiritual leader Rabbi Ovadiah finally understands the concept of saving Jewish lives (Pikuach Nephish) and realizes with great regret that Oslo and the Golan give away will cause the loss of many lives (and not the other way around).

4. A broad group of Israeli patriots forms a formidable alliance of religious Jews (Shas, NRP, and Agudat Yisrael), Russians (Yisrael B'Aliyah and

its leader Natan Sharansky and Knesset Golan lobby and its leader Yuli Edelstein and MK Avigdor Leiberman of Yisrael Beiteinu), and traditional Zionist parties like the Likud and its various breakaway factions.

5. Labor and Meretz form an alliance with the pro-PLO Arab parties, promising them an end to the Jewish nature of Israel. They propose that instead of a Jewish State there would be a democratic state with a lot of Jews in it.

6. Israel voters having a clear choice between leftist pro-Arabism and Zionism, choose the later.

7. For the first time since 1992 there is a truly Zionist government in Israel with a comfortable majority of 75 (out of 120) seats in the Knesset.

8. The new government begins immediately to correct the mistakes of the past.

9. Israel breaks off negotiations with Syria and issues a stern warning to them not to aid the Hezbollah in Lebanon. Syria is put on notice that any attack on Israeli forces in Lebanon will result in massive retaliation against Syrian interests. And further that Syrian interests will include both in Lebanon and in Syria itself.

10. Of course, after years of calling Israeli bluffs, the Syrians ignore the warning. Hezbollah attacks killing several Israeli soldiers.

11. Israel retaliates on a massive scale, destroying major economic infrastructure in both Lebanon and Syria. Under cover of the attack from the air, Israeli commandos land in Syria and destroy its stocks of anthrax bacteria, sarin gas, as well as its SCUD missile capacity. Syrian bases in Lebanon are mercilessly attacked and the weapons supply road from Damascus to southern Lebanon is taken out of operation completely.

12. Naturally the whole world condemns Israel and the Security Council is called into session. Israel in an act of beautiful irony sends a blind, deaf and dumb delegate to the UN.

13. The new Zionist government in Israel sends its troops into Palestinian Authority territory to arrest all know terrorists including Arafat himself. By a large percentage the Knesset votes that the Oslo agreement is null and void due to lack of Palestinian compliance to its terms.

14. The whole of Judea, Samaria, and Gaza are annexed and the Arab residents of the major cities are given autonomy (but not sovereignty) to run their affairs.

15. The difficult problem of ridding the country of its leftist/socialist/oligarchy is tackled head on.

16. Judges are all reviewed to determine if they guilty of using their leftist orientation to influence their decisions from the bench. The Israeli judiciary will be completely revamped with respectable and honest judges.

17. Once the judiciary is back to a normal democratic norm, an investigation is launched into the conspiracy to defame the religious/Zionist citizens of Israel.

18. The Raviv case and the whole investigation of the Rabin assassination are opened for judicial review.

19. The television stations run by the government will be completely reoriented toward Zionism and away from leftist pro-Arab programming.

20. The educational system will cease to be pro-Arab and will inculcate Jewish and Zionist values in the student body.

21. The private off the shore radio station (Arutz 7) will be permitted to operate from Israeli territory and also allowed to develop a private TV station.

22. The police and the GSS (Israel's Secret Service) will be programmed to support the national interests of Israel and not the wishes of Labor/Left/Peace Now supporters.

23. The economy will be allowed to develop freely with as little government interference as possible. The consumer and the environment will be protected. Most government corporations will be de-nationalized.

24. As taxes are slashed, a vigorous free enterprise system will develop; bring untold wealth to the country.

25. Building should be encouraged in all parts of the country (this includes YESHA).

26. Voting rights will be changed as follows: a. All Jews have the right to vote. b. Christians and Druze have the right to vote unless there is a history of security offenses. c. Moslems must perform 3 years of military or civilian service to Israel before obtaining the right to vote. They also must take a loyalty oath to the Jewish state and pass a security examination.

27. Nations posing a security threat to Israel will have that threat neutralized by the Israel Defense Forces. This includes Egypt, Libya, Iran, Iraq, Syria, Afghanistan, Pakistan et al.

28. Individual terrorists that pose a threat to Israel will be terminated with extreme prejudice.

29. Yes, the world will complain about all these actions and a competent information policy should be incorporated by the new government to counter these complaints. On a more philosophical basis Israel should heed international voices to exactly the degree they heeded the voices of the Jews during WWII. And Israel should protect the rights of Moslems to the exact degree that Moslems protect the rights of Jews.

30. The international community will try to boycott Israel. This effort will fail and is given up in a year or so. You see Jewish merchants worldwide continue to import and export to Israel using a variety of artificial fronts and entities. World commerce cannot be controlled as is evident with Iraq today.

31. Local Arab opposition and terrorism is simply crushed. No questions asked.

32. Aliya increases to Israel as a result of the crackdown on the Arab terrorists and because of the generally safe conditions in the country. No longer are there PA terrorist safe havens.

ISRAEL GROWS STRONG AND PROSPERS

THE JEWISH HOMELAND IS SAFE WELL INTO THE 21ST CENTURY

THE ROAD MAP AND ISRAEL'S SURVIVAL

VICTORY OR DEFEAT FOR ZIONISM—

YOU MUST CHOOSE

(June 2003)

It is clear to me that the present Likud government of Israeli Prime Minister Ariel Sharon is leading Israel to disaster. It is also clear that nothing external is compelling this self-destruction. The only thing that will save Israel is new elections. The only way to speed up elections and thus save Israel is by destabilizing the current government and causing it to fall. This would force new elections and stop the insane Oslo/Road Map process.

HISTORY

Over the last one hundred years, many governments have been destabilized by the action of a determined group of its citizens, not necessarily a majority. Two recent cases in this country are the Civil Rights Movement and the Anti-War in Viet-Nam Movement. There is no doubt that Lyndon Johnson chose not to run for a second term because of the anti-war movement. There is also no doubt the Afro-American population would not have been able to throw off the yoke of discrimination without non-violent protest. In Israel it is obvious that the intifada succeeded no doubt because of the Israeli government's reticence in crushing it.

It is this reticence by democratic regimes to crush popular uprisings that is the biggest weapon in the hands of groups wishing to destabilize their government. This principle does not work under autocratic governments such as Syria (Hama) and China (Tiananmen Square).

TECHNIQUES

1. Demonstrations—the larger the better. Demonstrations will not in and of themselves bring down a government. Good media coverage is essential to give the population a feeling that the tide of history is turning against the regime.

2. Civil disobedience—the key to success. There is one essential requirement for destabilizing a government and that is for a determined group of people to be willing to go to jail, be beaten by police, and suffer any consequence in the pursuit of their political aims. More will follow later on organizing civil disobedience.

3. The Wrench in the Machinery of Government

A. Physical—roads and bridges can be blocked by slow or stalled cars.

B. Electronic—computer networks, telecommunications can be adversely affected [10,000 people calling government offices at the same time can paralyze the system].

C. Psychological—photo's can be taken of police and military personnel who become involved in violent action against peaceful demonstrators. Available now are miniature video cameras that can be worn inconspicuously and send live feed to distant computers. At a time and place of your choosing, you can compromise those security officers involved in non-democratic violence against demonstrators. Their names and photos can be publicized.

4. Resistance

A. Open revolt against authority—Democracies are primarily based on voluntary compliance with the legal system. When that democracy ceases to govern in the best interests of its citizenry, with its security and survival, then it is lawful and justified to resist authority. This includes refusing to pay taxes, following illegal orders of the non-democratic army, traffic regulations etc.

B. Mass demonstrations, including the right of self-defense, are meant to intimidate the police and the government. The horrible vision of civil war will restrain the government. Knowing that the Zionist/Right will not physically resist, gives the government strength to pursue suicidal policies. The policy of not striking back at the Left (as experienced during the "season") begun in the pre-state days by Menachem Begin has had the effect of emasculating the Right in its relations with the Left.

STRATEGY

While it is preferable to wage a non-violent campaign, there are certain lessons one can learn from the Israel Defense Forces.

1. Most important: Do not give the enemy time to rest and re-group. The IDF always advances in one massive push to victory, never allowing the enemy a respite. The same must be true of the demonstrations against Sharon. It is a mistake to agree to a truce. A truce would give the government time to organize special police units including female police officers to handle demonstrators. The government has already learned that reservists do not like this heartrending undemocratic task.

2. Attack in many places at once, causing physical and psychological stress on the enemy. Demonstrators should not just take over hills in YESHA, but should take over government offices from Eilat to Metulla. Roads should be blocked all over the country. In Jerusalem, with its many government offices and a supportive religious population, you should be able to create and sustain chaos.

CONCLUSION

Half measures will not work. Either we are at war with this government or we are not. It was the IDF's failure to destroy the intifada that led to much of our trouble. Remember the principle of vaccinations: a tiny doze of the disease that allows the body to build its immune system. Half-measures allow Sharon to develop a resistance to the demonstrations. We must take the momentum and build continuously to the day of victory. **The decision is ours.**

A TIME FOR PEACE AND A TIME FOR WAR

We find all the expressions of horror at the recent Rabbi's ruling concerning a soldier's obligation to avoid abandoning army bases and settlements to terrorists, to be hypocritical, self-serving, and unfortunate. The Israeli government is in rebellion against everything that Israel, Zionism, and Judaism are all about. They are the ones causing the rift in the body politic and they will be totally responsible for any resulting violence.

When will the Nationalist Camp realize that we are "at war already" with a PLO supported government that rules Israel? At what point will Israelis realize that the **CIVIL WAR** they fear, IS **ALREADY TAKING PLACE AND THEY ARE LOSING?** Why don't members of the Nationalist Camp understand that FORCE is being used by only **ONE** side and that is the government? The monopoly on power must be broken or there is no hope.

Under the Nazis, the Jews of Warsaw numbered over 500,000. They were depleted with regular deportations aided by *Judenrats* (Jewish leaders). The Revolt in Warsaw began when the Jewish population was down to 50,000 (or 90% murdered). At what point is it OK to rebel? When is civil disobedience OK? When is civil war a better course than suicide? All throughout history there have been rebels and loyalists. History is usually written by the victors but truly there is seldom a universally accepted moral standard as to what a proper rebellion is and what is not. We can say with absolute certainty, however, that the Jewish return to Zion and our struggle today for *Eretz Yisrael* are more righteous than any other struggle for national liberation in the history of the world.

Conditions in Israel may have passed the period where civil disobedience would be effective. A massive outpouring of Israelis prepared to get arrested in civil disobedience would have stopped the Oslo Suicide Pact 10 years ago. With the Road Map the terrorists will be in charge. Jews will have a choice: being massacred or abandoning their homes. Their ability to defend themselves will have been thwarted by the government in collusion with the terrorists.

Following my five weeks of research in Israel, I spelled out (May-June 1994 issue of **THE MACCABEAN**) the nature of this inevitable conflict:

THE PRIMARY INHERENT FLAW IN THE OSLO AGREEMENT

THAT WILL LEAD TO MILITARY CONFLICT

1. The Palestinians expect and will demand that every Jew be removed from their areas of control including the whole of Judea, Samaria and Gaza and Jerusalem.

2. The Jews of YESHA not only plan to stay in their homes but will fight for them militarily. This obviously conflicts with #1.

I also stated (numbers updated to 2003): "The number of Jews in YESHA is about 250,000 (1994—144,000). Not counting women, children, and men over 50, leaves about 70,000 men capable of resisting a PLO armed force. These men are all IDF veterans and reservists with army issue Uzi's or M16's with at least two clips (30 rounds per clip) of ammunition per gun. During my visit I toured the whole area, and emphasized the need to get past the shock and make serious preparations for the coming battles. Among other things I recommended the following: (1) bring ammunition supplies up to a minimum of 300 rounds per gun (2) stockpile food, medicine and water supplies for 30 days in case the roads are impassable (3) Each community needs several trucks armored to withstand 60 caliber machine gun fire and small grenades (4) begin constructing bunkers and hardened firing positions.

All Jewish villages are on the hills with a commanding view of the area. The Arab villages control the roads creating a strategic situation similar to the pre-state fighting of 1947-48.

Nine years have passed and since that report and events are playing out exactly as I predicted. Arafat's PLO terrorists planned to take over Judea and Samaria under **Phase Two of the Oslo Plan**. The military struggle has begun in earnest. If anyone believes this to be unlikely, stay posted and we will see how the future plays out. The Jews of YESHA should not leave their physical well—being to the good graces of Arafat, Peres, Netanyahu, Barak, Mohammad Abbas or even Sharon. Certainly one should NOT trust the UN, EU, Russia, or the US State Department, who have their own interests

The Jews of YESHA must not be passive pawns in the political surrender of their homes. They must fight the Arabs, where necessary, to maintain their travel, water, and land rights. When the Israeli government retreats, leaving them behind PLO battle lines, they must be prepared to go on the offensive militarily to secure safe contiguous areas of Jewish control. The defeatist Israeli leaders, who have surrendered our Jewish rights to **Eretz Yisrael**, should be told that there are still proud Jews in YESHA who will give up neither their inheritance from Abraham nor their right of self-defense.

Exercising one's right to self-defense is a moral imperative. There is a lot of hypocritical talk coming from the government about the danger of Jew fighting Jew. These warnings came from the likes of Yitzhak Rabin who delighted in shooting Zionist (Betar) teenagers swimming to shore after his forces sank the *Altalena* in 1948. New more dangerous hypocrites are putting the Jews of YESHA and all of Israel in life threatening peril. They care nothing about Jewish lives!

Should the Jews of YESHA be forced into military combat—most likely against Arabs, but, G-d forbid, perhaps also against Jews—they would be fully justified. They will be fighting for the security of Israel and the future destiny of the Jewish people. These brave Jews would be continuing the long tradition of Hebrew Warriors, including Joshua, David, the Maccabees and Bar Kochba, who fought against all odds to save their people and their country.

The glorious Hebrew Warriors who defeated five Arab armies in 1948, three in 1967, and two in 1973 must not surrender their Jewish homeland to an evil terrorist regime, which delights in killing Jewish women, children, husbands, sons and daughters.

MAY THE ALMIGHTY WATCHMAN OF ISRAEL PROTECT HIS PEOPLE FROM THE DANGEROUS ROAD MAP TO ISRAEL'S DESTRUCTION. MAY HE LIBERATE HIS PEOPLE FROM NON-DEMOCRATIC LEADERS AND RESTORE ZIONIST RULE TO JERUSALEM.

[This article is updated from two editorials published in the September 1995 & August 1995 issues of **THE MACCABEAN**.]

★

***AND THE DECISION MUST BE FOR VICTORY,
ZIONISM AND THE JEWISH PEOPLE.***

★

***ALL IT TAKES FOR EVIL TO TRIUMPH
IS FOR GOOD MEN TO DO NOTHING.***

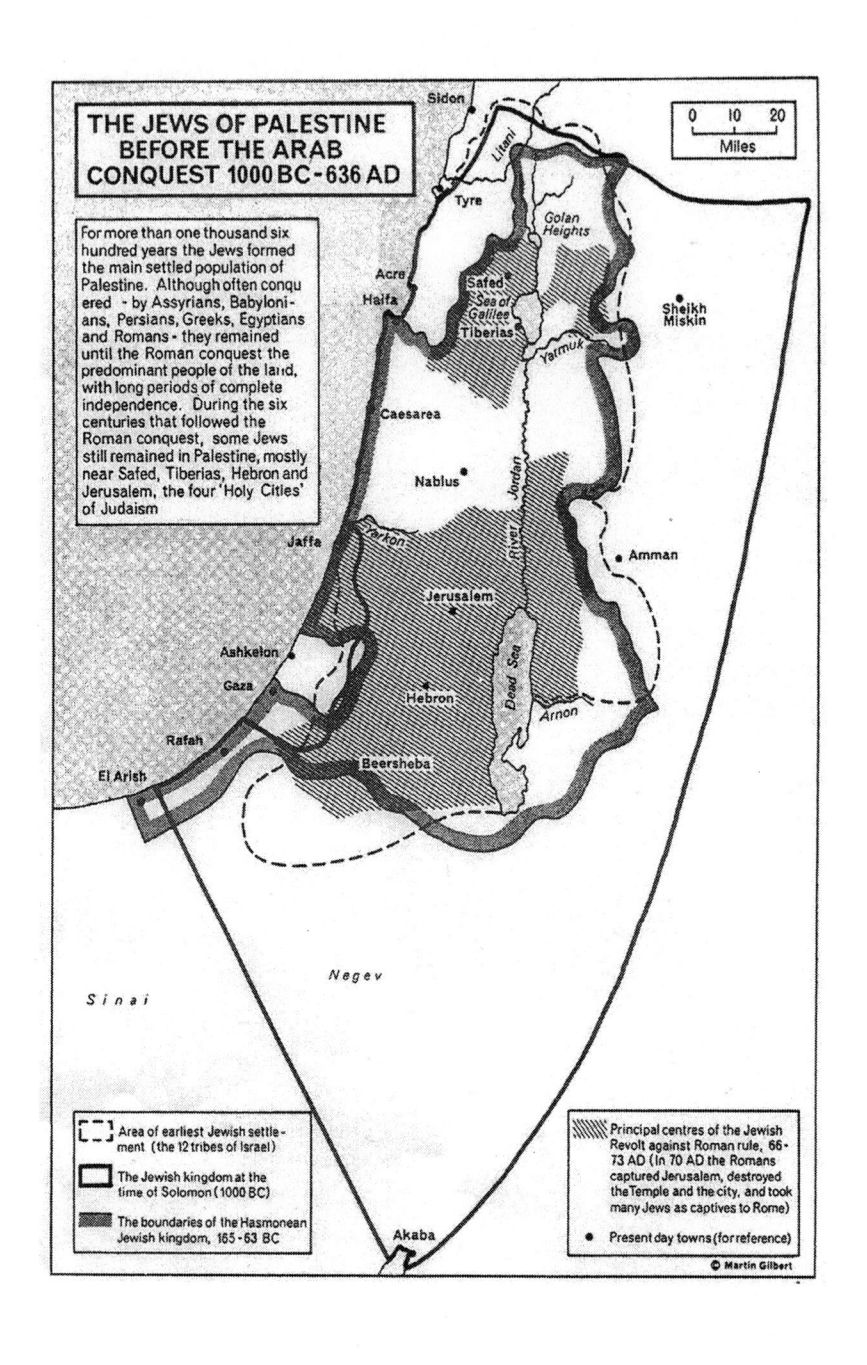

THE JEWS OF PALESTINE BEFORE THE ARAB CONQUEST 1000 BC - 636 AD

For more than one thousand six hundred years the Jews formed the main settled population of Palestine. Although often conquered - by Assyrians, Babylonians, Persians, Greeks, Egyptians and Romans - they remained until the Roman conquest the predominant people of the land, with long periods of complete independence. During the six centuries that followed the Roman conquest, some Jews still remained in Palestine, mostly near Safed, Tiberias, Hebron and Jerusalem, the four 'Holy Cities' of Judaism

```
[- - -]  Area of earliest Jewish settle-
         ment (the 12 tribes of Israel)

         The Jewish kingdom at the
         time of Solomon (1000 BC)

         The boundaries of the Hasmonean
         Jewish kingdom, 165 - 63 BC
```

Principal centres of the Jewish Revolt against Roman rule, 66-73 AD (In 70 AD the Romans captured Jerusalem, destroyed the Temple and the city, and took many Jews as captives to Rome)

• Present day towns (for reference)

© Martin Gilbert

BRITAIN AND THE ARABS 1917-1971

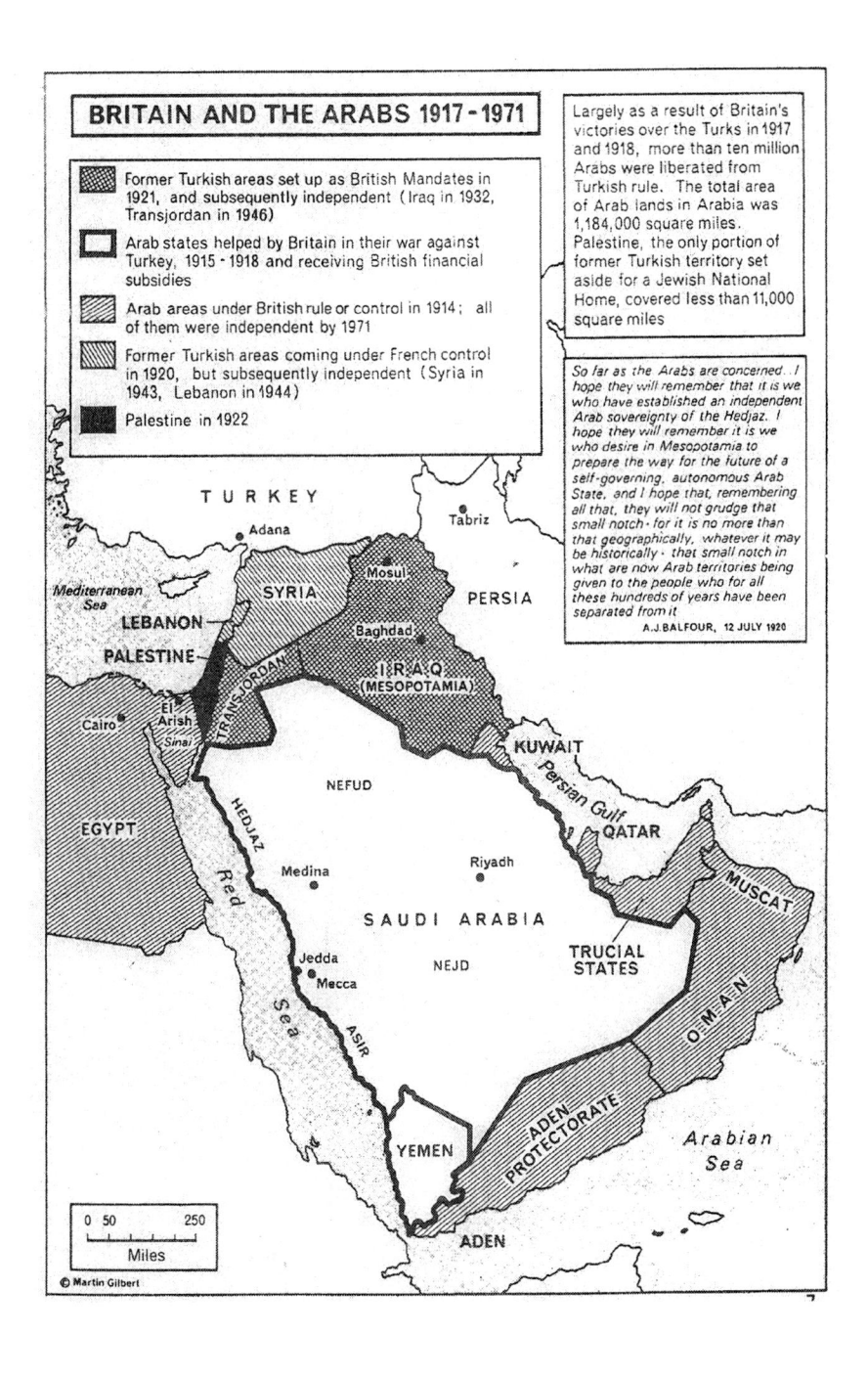

- Former Turkish areas set up as British Mandates in 1921, and subsequently independent (Iraq in 1932, Transjordan in 1946)
- Arab states helped by Britain in their war against Turkey, 1915-1918 and receiving British financial subsidies
- Arab areas under British rule or control in 1914; all of them were independent by 1971
- Former Turkish areas coming under French control in 1920, but subsequently independent (Syria in 1943, Lebanon in 1944)
- Palestine in 1922

Largely as a result of Britain's victories over the Turks in 1917 and 1918, more than ten million Arabs were liberated from Turkish rule. The total area of Arab lands in Arabia was 1,184,000 square miles. Palestine, the only portion of former Turkish territory set aside for a Jewish National Home, covered less than 11,000 square miles.

So far as the Arabs are concerned...I hope they will remember that it is we who have established an independent Arab sovereignty of the Hedjaz. I hope they will remember it is we who desire in Mesopotamia to prepare the way for the future of a self-governing, autonomous Arab State, and I hope that, remembering all that, they will not grudge that small notch - for it is no more than that geographically, whatever it may be historically - that small notch in what are now Arab territories being given to the people who for all these hundreds of years have been separated from it

A.J. BALFOUR, 12 JULY 1920

© Martin Gilbert

THE ZIONIST PLAN FOR PALESTINE FEBRUARY 1919

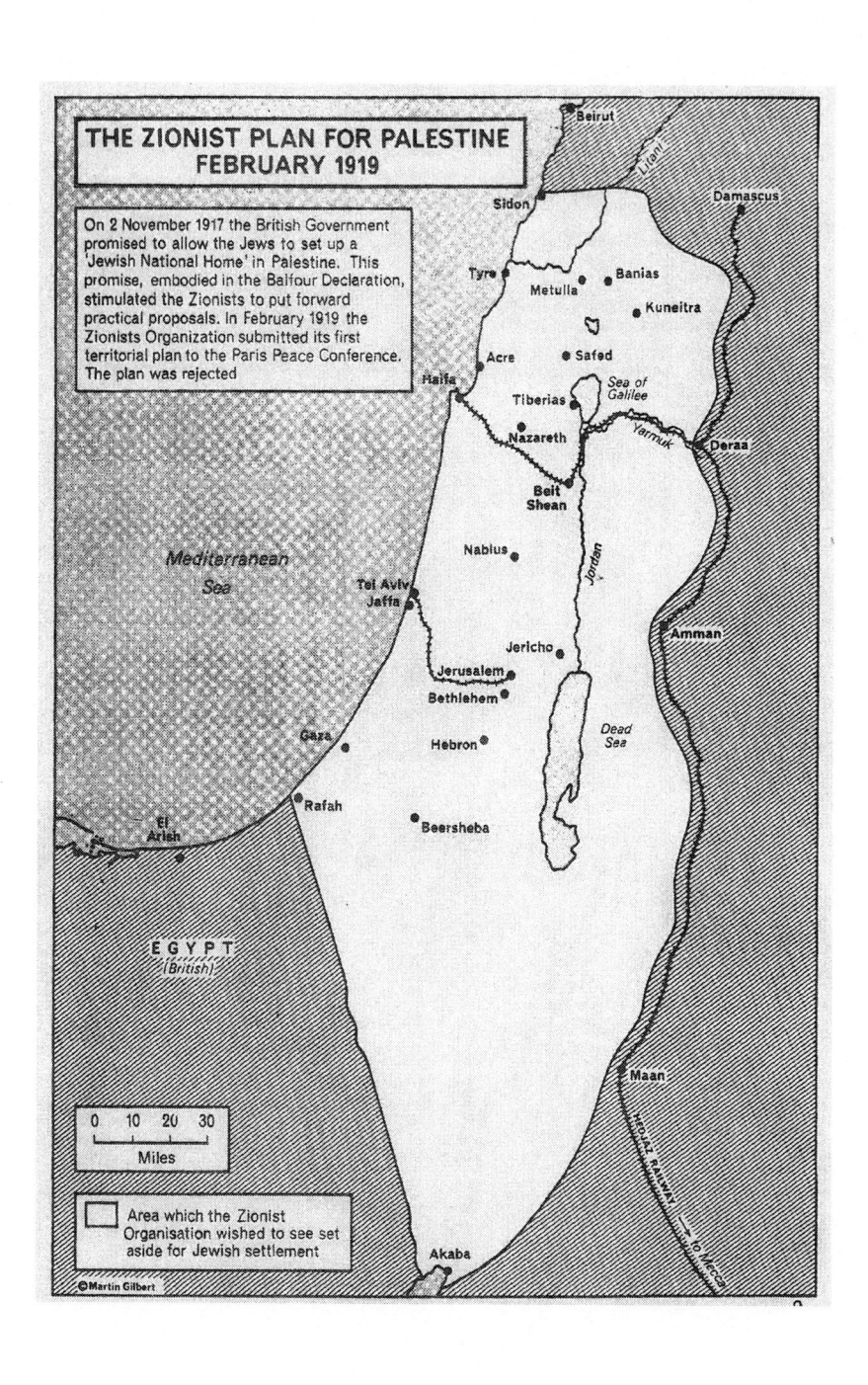

On 2 November 1917 the British Government promised to allow the Jews to set up a 'Jewish National Home' in Palestine. This promise, embodied in the Balfour Declaration, stimulated the Zionists to put forward practical proposals. In February 1919 the Zionists Organization submitted its first territorial plan to the Paris Peace Conference. The plan was rejected

□ Area which the Zionist Organisation wished to see set aside for Jewish settlement

© Martin Gilbert

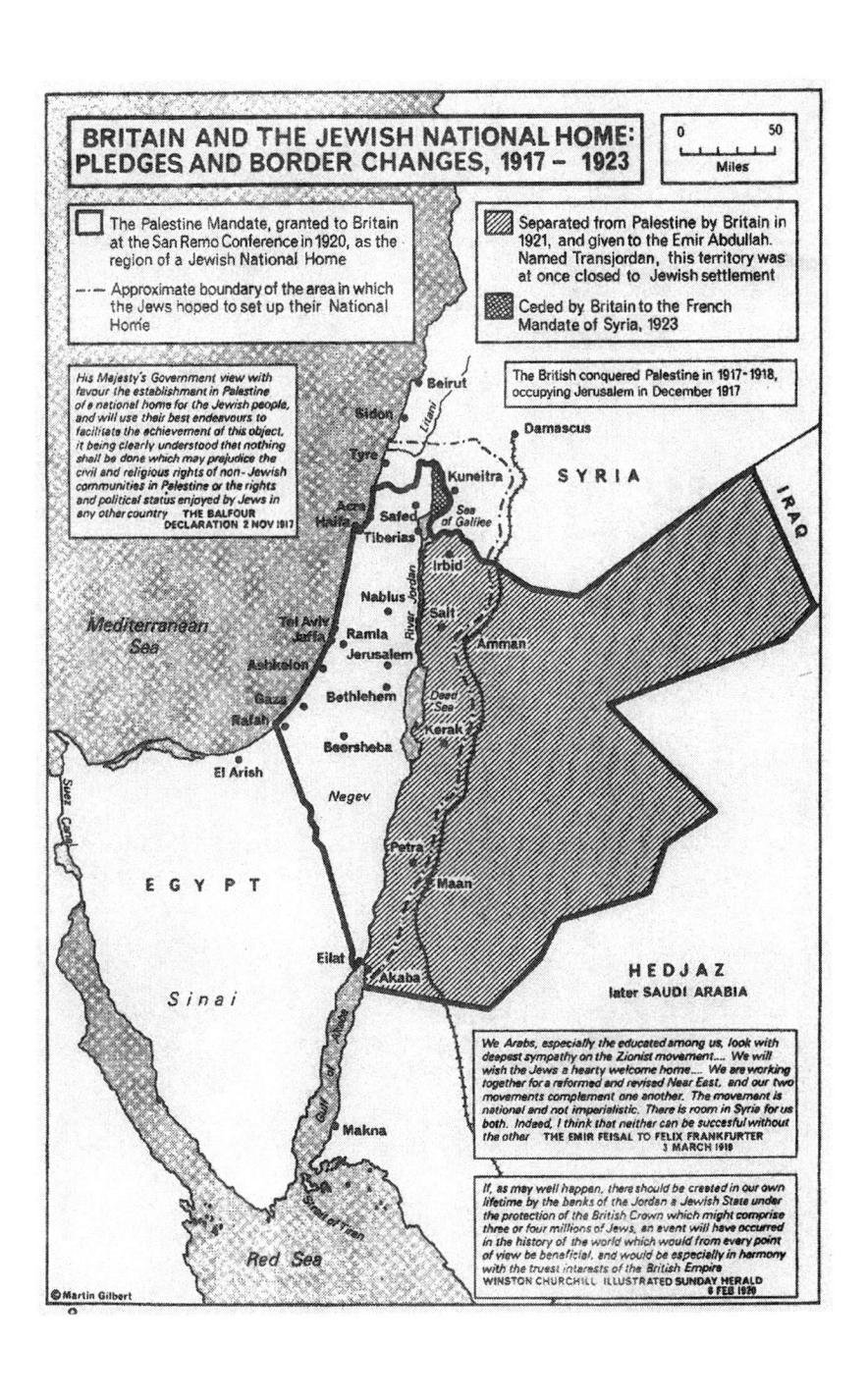

BRITAIN AND THE JEWISH NATIONAL HOME: PLEDGES AND BORDER CHANGES, 1917 – 1923

0 — 50 Miles

☐ The Palestine Mandate, granted to Britain at the San Remo Conference in 1920, as the region of a Jewish National Home

–·–·– Approximate boundary of the area in which the Jews hoped to set up their National Home

▨ Separated from Palestine by Britain in 1921, and given to the Emir Abdullah. Named Transjordan, this territory was at once closed to Jewish settlement

▩ Ceded by Britain to the French Mandate of Syria, 1923

His Majesty's Government view with favour the establishment in Palestine of a national home for the Jewish people, and will use their best endeavours to facilitate the achievement of this object, it being clearly understood that nothing shall be done which may prejudice the civil and religious rights of non-Jewish communities in Palestine or the rights and political status enjoyed by Jews in any other country **THE BALFOUR DECLARATION 2 NOV 1917**

The British conquered Palestine in 1917-1918, occupying Jerusalem in December 1917

Mediterranean Sea

Beirut
Sidon
Litani
Tyre
Kuneitra
Damascus
Acre
Haifa
Safed
Sea of Galilee
Tiberias
Irbid
Nablus
Salt
Tel Aviv
Jaffa
Ramla
River Jordan
Amman
Ashkelon
Jerusalem
Gaza
Bethlehem
Dead Sea
Rafah
Kerak
Beersheba
El Arish
Negev
Petra
Maan
Eilat
Akaba

SYRIA

IRAQ

EGYPT

Sinai

Suez Canal

Gulf of Aqaba

HEDJAZ later SAUDI ARABIA

Makna

Red Sea

Straits of Tiran

We Arabs, especially the educated among us, look with deepest sympathy on the Zionist movement.... We will wish the Jews a hearty welcome home.... We are working together for a reformed and revised Near East, and our two movements complement one another. The movement is national and not imperialistic. There is room in Syria for us both. Indeed, I think that neither can be successful without the other **THE EMIR FEISAL TO FELIX FRANKFURTER 3 MARCH 1919**

If, as may well happen, there should be created in our own lifetime by the banks of the Jordan a Jewish State under the protection of the British Crown which might comprise three or four millions of Jews, an event will have occurred in the history of the world which would from every point of view be beneficial, and would be especially in harmony with the truest interests of the British Empire **WINSTON CHURCHILL ILLUSTRATED SUNDAY HERALD 8 FEB 1920**

© Martin Gilbert

THE PEEL COMMISSION PARTITION PLAN, JULY 1937

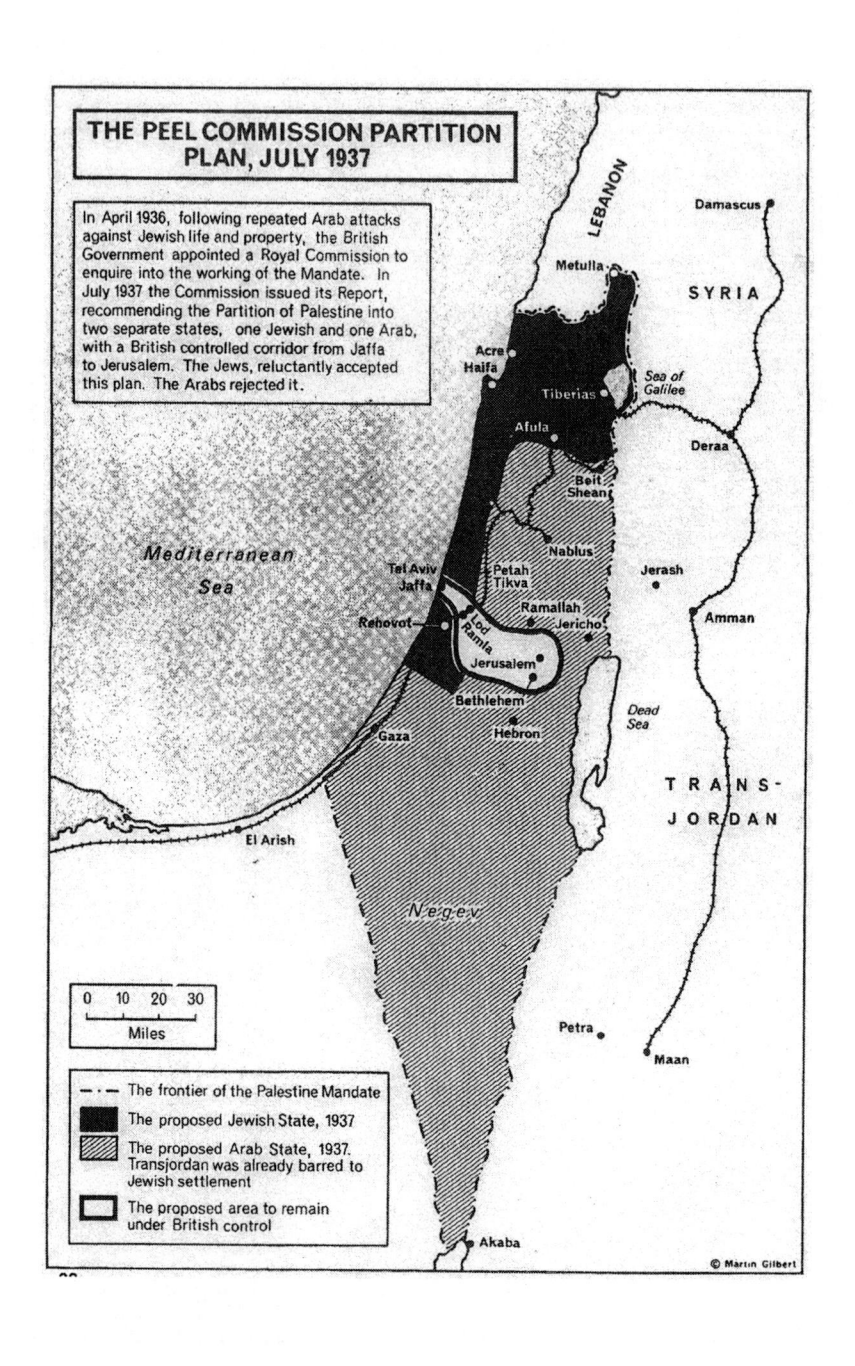

In April 1936, following repeated Arab attacks against Jewish life and property, the British Government appointed a Royal Commission to enquire into the working of the Mandate. In July 1937 the Commission issued its Report, recommending the Partition of Palestine into two separate states, one Jewish and one Arab, with a British controlled corridor from Jaffa to Jerusalem. The Jews, reluctantly accepted this plan. The Arabs rejected it.

0 10 20 30 Miles

- – · – The frontier of the Palestine Mandate
- ■ The proposed Jewish State, 1937
- ▨ The proposed Arab State, 1937. Transjordan was already barred to Jewish settlement
- ☐ The proposed area to remain under British control

© Martin Gilbert

THE UNITED NATIONS PARTITION PLAN, 1947

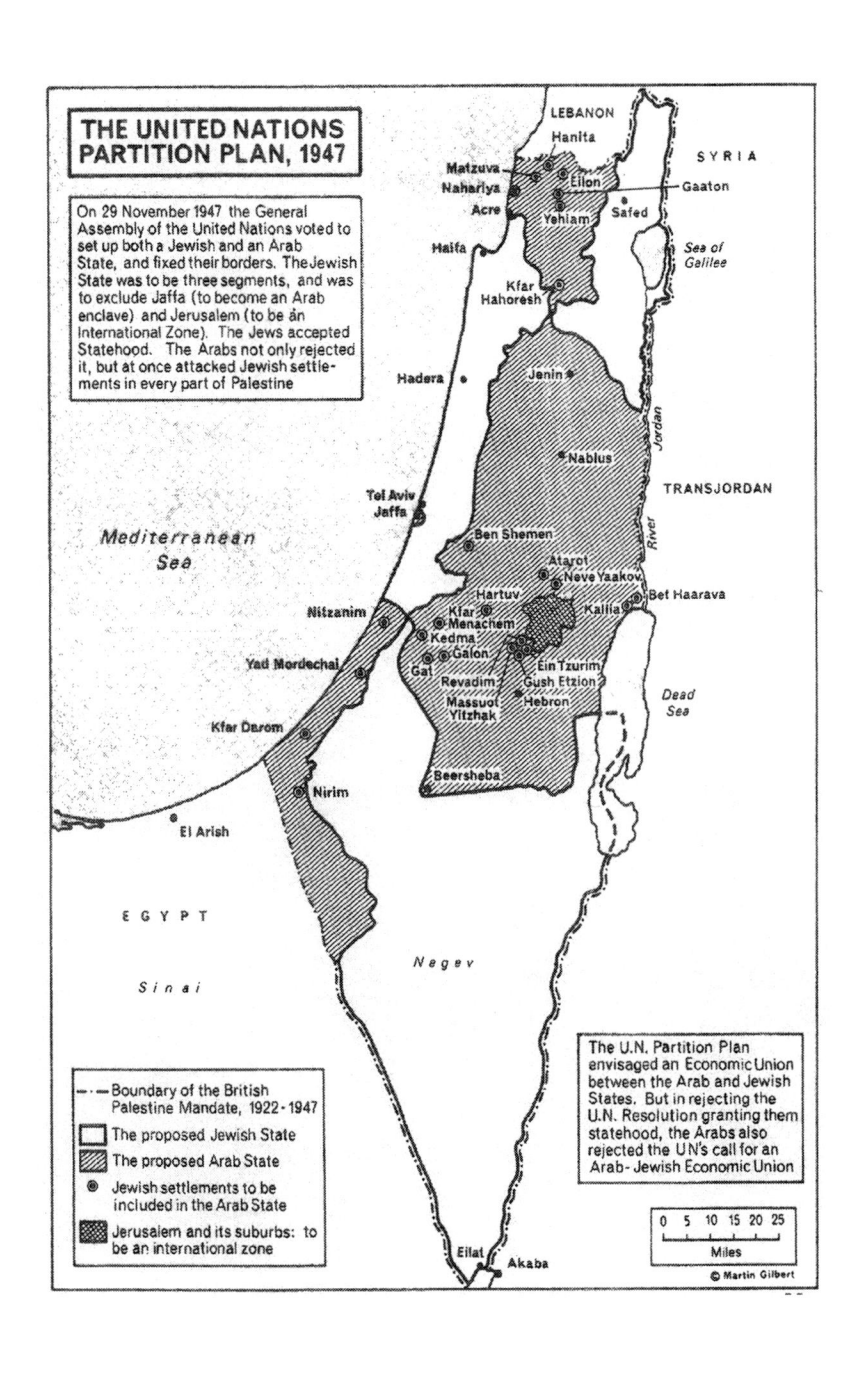

On 29 November 1947 the General Assembly of the United Nations voted to set up both a Jewish and an Arab State, and fixed their borders. The Jewish State was to be three segments, and was to exclude Jaffa (to become an Arab enclave) and Jerusalem (to be an International Zone). The Jews accepted Statehood. The Arabs not only rejected it, but at once attacked Jewish settlements in every part of Palestine

The U.N. Partition Plan envisaged an Economic Union between the Arab and Jewish States. But in rejecting the U.N. Resolution granting them statehood, the Arabs also rejected the UN's call for an Arab-Jewish Economic Union

- - - Boundary of the British Palestine Mandate, 1922-1947
▢ The proposed Jewish State
▨ The proposed Arab State
● Jewish settlements to be included in the Arab State
▨ Jerusalem and its suburbs: to be an international zone

0 5 10 15 20 25
Miles

© Martin Gilbert

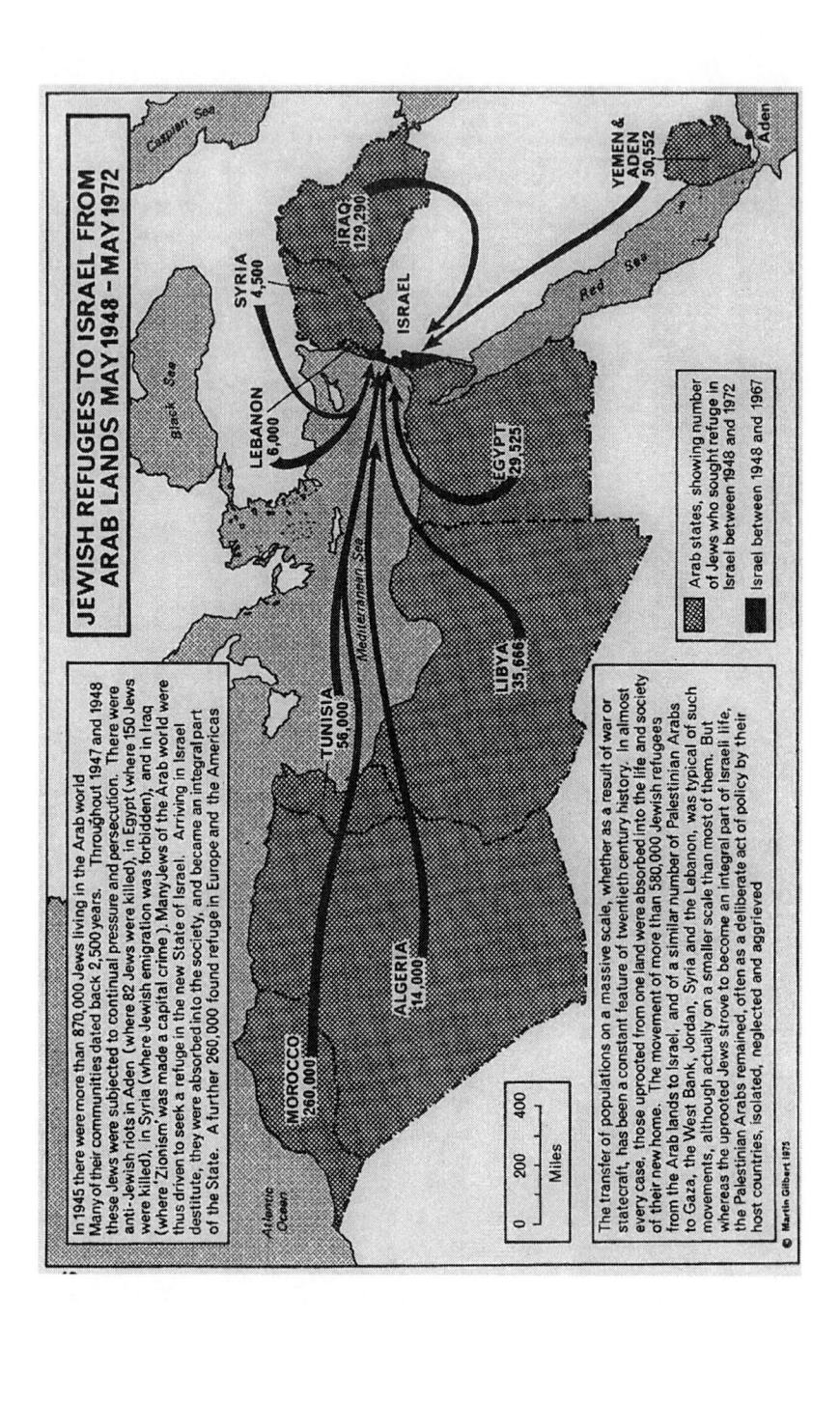

JEWISH REFUGEES TO ISRAEL FROM ARAB LANDS MAY 1948 – MAY 1972

In 1945 there were more than 870,000 Jews living in the Arab world. Many of their communities dated back 2,500 years. Throughout 1947 and 1948 these Jews were subjected to continual pressure and persecution. There were anti-Jewish riots in Aden (where 82 Jews were killed), in Egypt (where 150 Jews were killed), in Syria (where Jewish emigration was forbidden), and in Iraq (where 'Zionism' was made a capital crime). Many Jews of the Arab world were thus driven to seek a refuge in the new State of Israel. Arriving in Israel destitute, they were absorbed into the society, and became an integral part of the State. A further 260,000 found refuge in Europe and the Americas.

- MOROCCO 260,000
- ALGERIA 14,000
- TUNISIA 56,000
- LIBYA 35,666
- EGYPT 29,525
- LEBANON 6,000
- SYRIA 4,500
- IRAQ 129,290
- YEMEN & ADEN 50,552

Arab states, showing number of Jews who sought refuge in Israel between 1948 and 1972

Israel between 1948 and 1967

The transfer of populations on a massive scale, whether as a result of war or statecraft, has been a constant feature of twentieth century history. In almost every case, those uprooted from one land were absorbed into the life and society of their new home. The movement of more than 580,000 Jewish refugees from the Arab lands to Israel, and of a similar number of Palestinian Arabs to Gaza, the West Bank, Jordan, Syria and the Lebanon, was typical of such movements, although actually on a smaller scale than most of them. But whereas the uprooted Jews strove to become an integral part of Israeli life, the Palestinian Arabs remained, often as a deliberate act of policy by their host countries, isolated, neglected and aggrieved.

© Martin Gilbert 1975

THE SINAI CAMPAIGN OCTOBER – NOVEMBER 1956

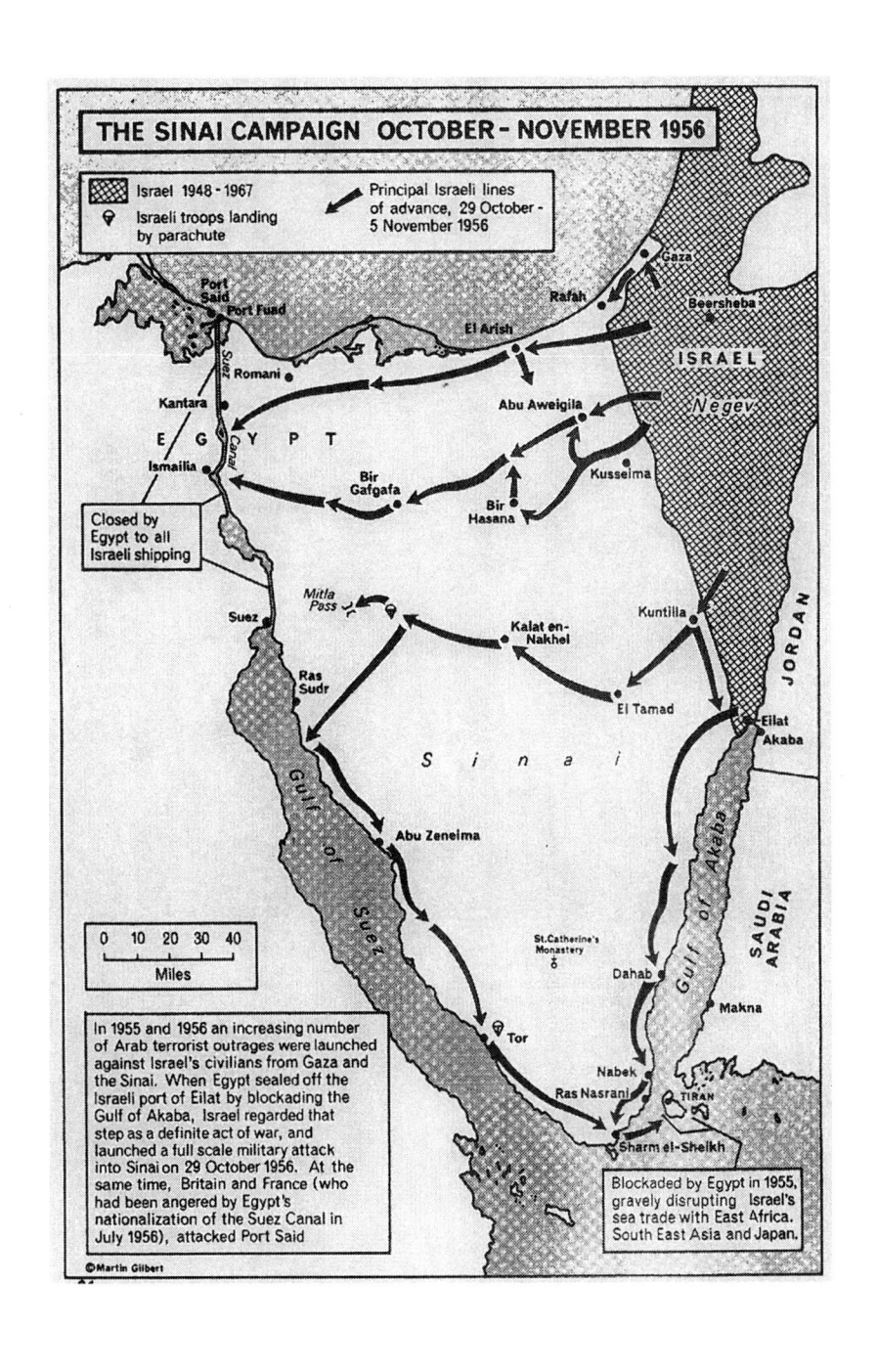

- Israel 1948 – 1967
- Israeli troops landing by parachute
- Principal Israeli lines of advance, 29 October – 5 November 1956

ISRAEL

Gaza • Beersheba • Rafah • El Arish • Abu Aweigila • Kusseima • Negev

EGYPT

Port Said • Port Fuad • Romani • Kantara • Ismailia • Bir Gafgafa • Bir Hasana

Suez Canal — Closed by Egypt to all Israeli shipping

Suez • Ras Sudr • Mitla Pass • Kalat en-Nakhel • Kuntilla • El Tamad • Eilat / Akaba

JORDAN

Sinai • Abu Zeneima • St. Catherine's Monastery • Dahab • Makna • Tor • Nabek • Ras Nasrani • TIRAN • Sharm el-Sheikh

Gulf of Suez • Gulf of Akaba • SAUDI ARABIA

0 10 20 30 40 Miles

In 1955 and 1956 an increasing number of Arab terrorist outrages were launched against Israel's civilians from Gaza and the Sinai. When Egypt sealed off the Israeli port of Eilat by blockading the Gulf of Akaba, Israel regarded that step as a definite act of war, and launched a full scale military attack into Sinai on 29 October 1956. At the same time, Britain and France (who had been angered by Egypt's nationalization of the Suez Canal in July 1956), attacked Port Said.

Blockaded by Egypt in 1955, gravely disrupting Israel's sea trade with East Africa, South East Asia and Japan.

© Martin Gilbert

THE FRONTIERS OF THE STATE OF ISRAEL 1949 - 1967

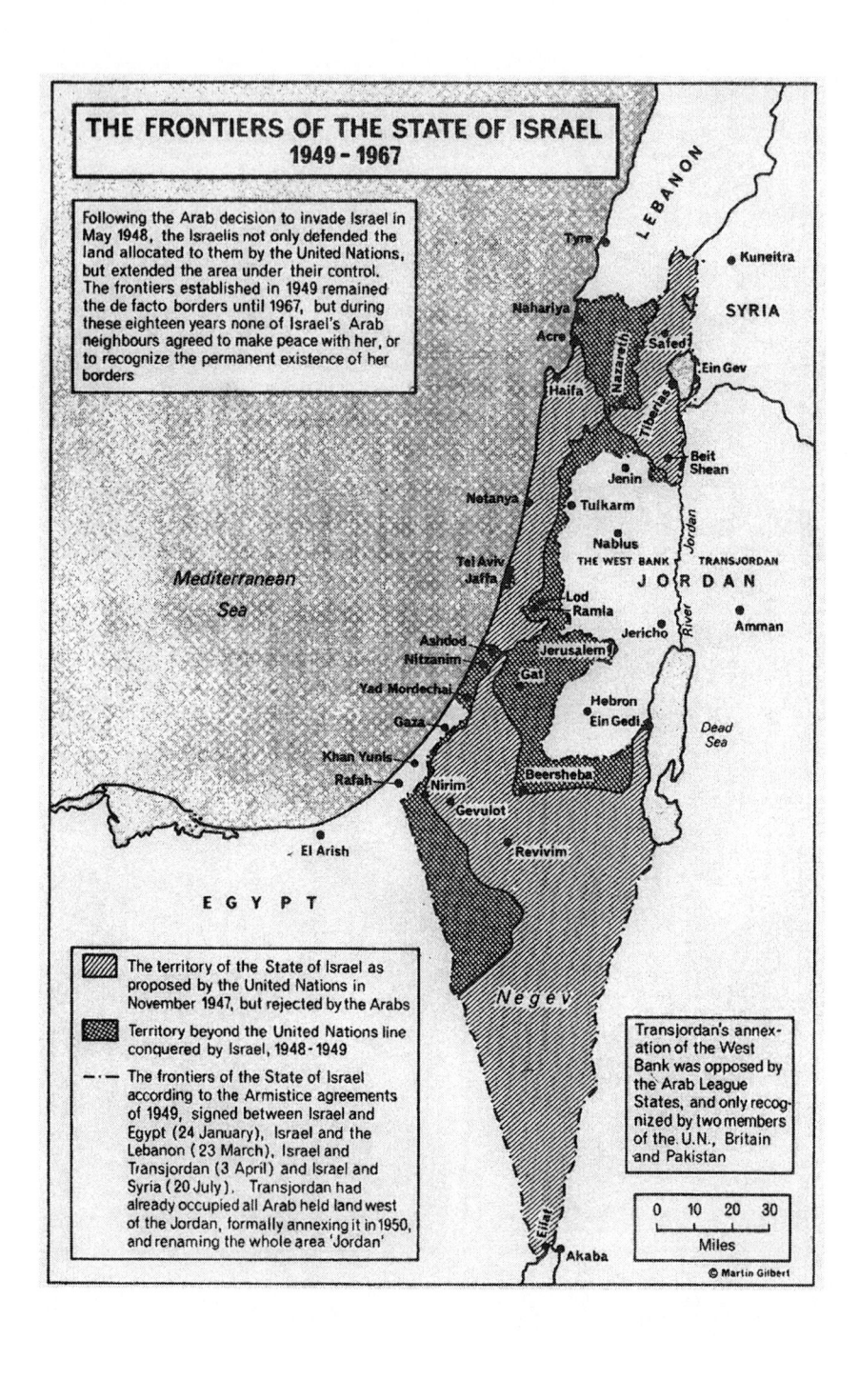

Following the Arab decision to invade Israel in May 1948, the Israelis not only defended the land allocated to them by the United Nations, but extended the area under their control. The frontiers established in 1949 remained the de facto borders until 1967, but during these eighteen years none of Israel's Arab neighbours agreed to make peace with her, or to recognize the permanent existence of her borders.

///// The territory of the State of Israel as proposed by the United Nations in November 1947, but rejected by the Arabs

▓▓▓ Territory beyond the United Nations line conquered by Israel, 1948-1949

—·— The frontiers of the State of Israel according to the Armistice agreements of 1949, signed between Israel and Egypt (24 January), Israel and the Lebanon (23 March), Israel and Transjordan (3 April) and Israel and Syria (20 July). Transjordan had already occupied all Arab held land west of the Jordan, formally annexing it in 1950, and renaming the whole area 'Jordan'

Transjordan's annexation of the West Bank was opposed by the Arab League States, and only recognized by two members of the U.N., Britain and Pakistan

0 10 20 30 Miles

© Martin Gilbert

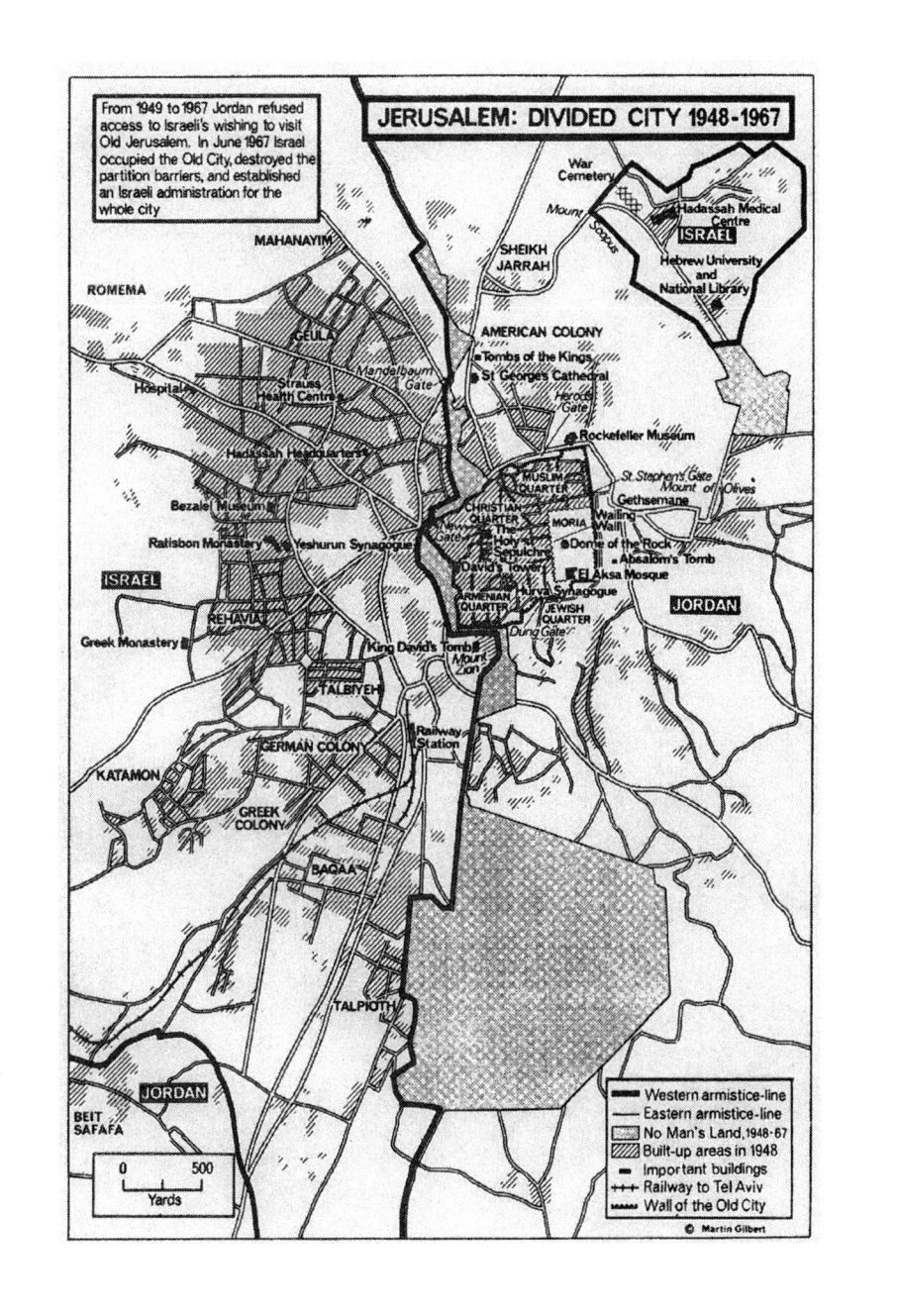

JERUSALEM: DIVIDED CITY 1948-1967

From 1949 to 1967 Jordan refused access to Israeli's wishing to visit Old Jerusalem. In June 1967 Israel occupied the Old City, destroyed the partition barriers, and established an Israeli administration for the whole city

ISRAEL
JORDAN

MAHANAYIM
ROMEMA
GEULA
SHEIKH JARRAH
War Cemetery
Mount Scopus
Hadassah Medical Centre
Hebrew University and National Library
Hospital
Strauss Health Centre
Mandelbaum Gate
AMERICAN COLONY
Tombs of the Kings
St Georges Cathedral
Herod's Gate
Hadassah Headquarters
Rockefeller Museum
Bezalel Museum
MUSLIM QUARTER
St. Stephen's Gate
Mount of Olives
Gethsemane
Ratisbon Monastery
Yeshurun Synagogue
CHRISTIAN QUARTER
Jaffa Gate
The Holy Sepulchre
MORIA Wailing Wall
Dome of the Rock
ISRAEL
David's Tower
ARMENIAN QUARTER
Hurva Synagogue
El Aksa Mosque
Absalom's Tomb
REHAVIA
JEWISH QUARTER
JORDAN
Greek Monastery
Dung Gate
King David's Tomb
Mount Zion
TALBIYEH
Railway Station
GERMAN COLONY
KATAMON
GREEK COLONY
BAQAA
TALPIOTH

JORDAN
BEIT SAFAFA

0   500
Yards

- ▬▬▬ Western armistice-line
- ── Eastern armistice-line
- ▦ No Man's Land, 1948-67
- ▨ Built-up areas in 1948
- ▬ Important buildings
- +++ Railway to Tel Aviv
- ⌇⌇⌇ Wall of the Old City

© Martin Gilbert

ISRAELI CONQUESTS 1967

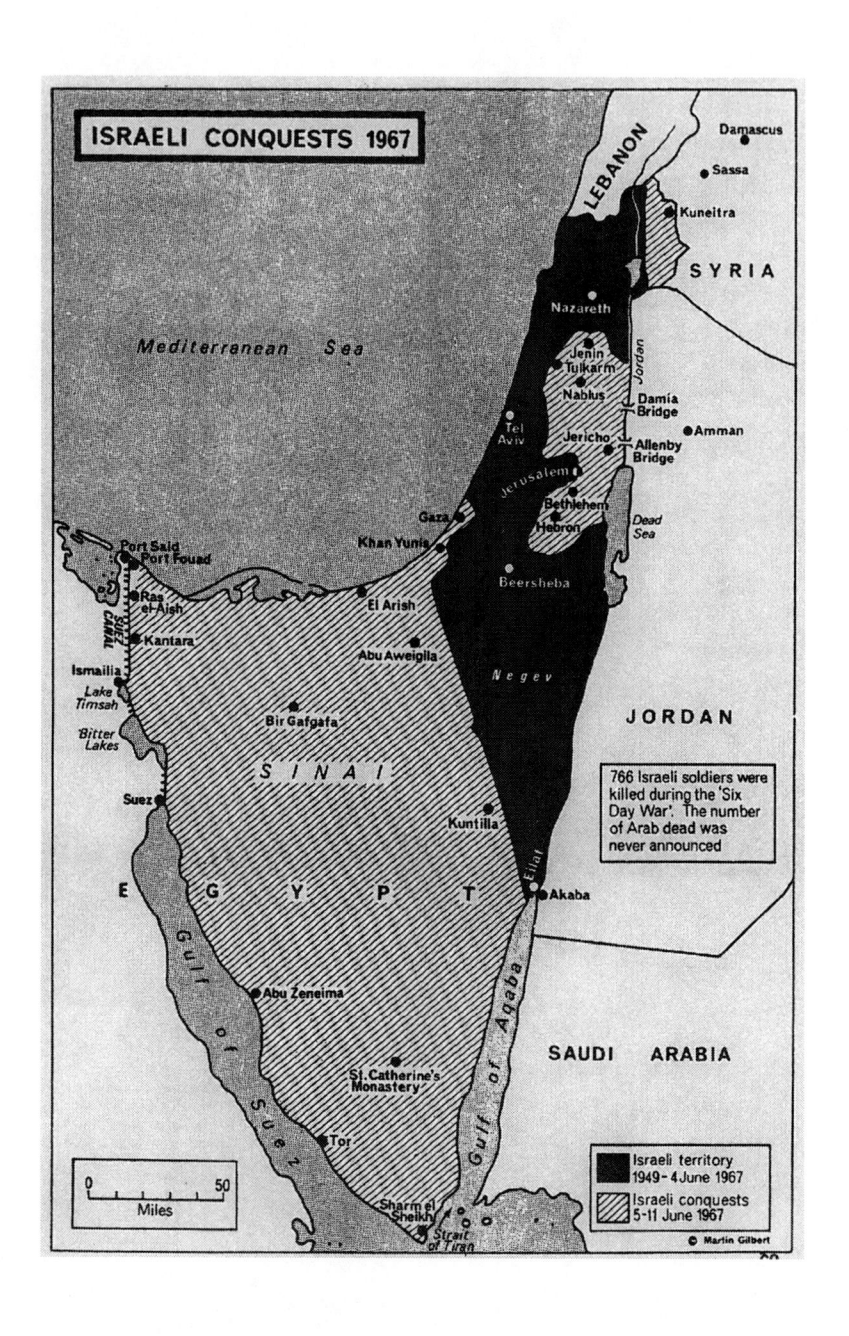

766 Israeli soldiers were killed during the 'Six Day War'. The number of Arab dead was never announced

■ Israeli territory 1949 – 4 June 1967
▨ Israeli conquests 5-11 June 1967

© Martin Gilbert

**THE HILLTOP LINE AT THE EASTERN BORDER OF
THE GOLAN HEIGHTS IS THE _ONLY_ DEFENSE LINE FOR
THE GOLAN AND THE GALILEE**

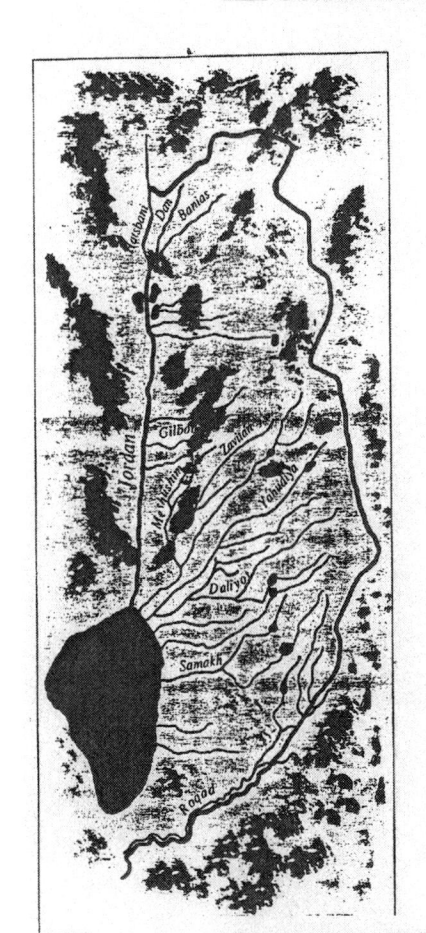

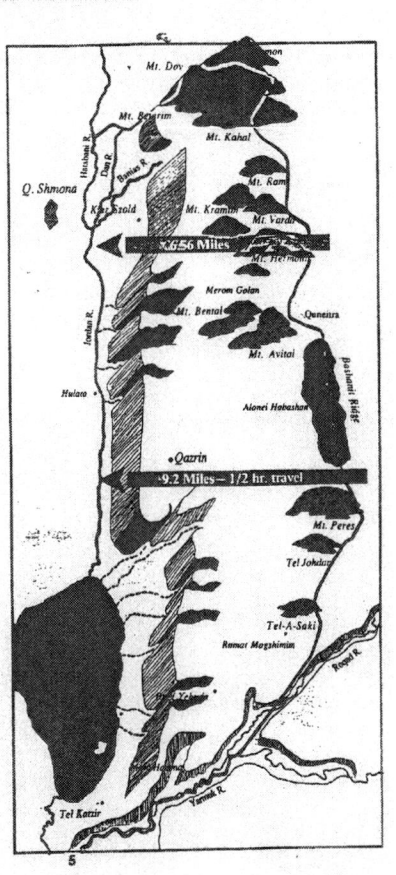

**THE KINNERET BASIN SUPPLIES 30%
(610 MILLION CU.M.) OF ISRAEL'S WATER CONSUMPTION
THE MOUNTAIN AQUIFER (JUDEA & SAMARIA)
SUPPLIES 38% (740 MILLION CU.M.)
OF ISRAEL'S WATER CONSUMPTION**

Rabin ~~is~~ *was* a Military Fraud

1. A medical expert (doctor) who fails to adequately disclose the risks of a medical operation (surgery) to his patient is a medical fraud.
2. A military expert (Rabin) who fails to adequately disclose the risks of a military operation (withdrawal) to his country (Israel) is a military fraud.
3. Therefore, Rabin ~~is~~ *was* a military fraud.

KATYUSHA ROCKET — RANGE OF KATYUSHA — 12.7 MI / 20.4 KM

The Katyusha Rocket "Multiple Rocket Launcher" BM-21 pictured above can be easily taken apart and smuggled into a "Demilitarized" Palestinian State. Individual Katyushas can be launched from a pipe with just a car battery. The rockets on this truck have a range of 12.7 miles (20.4 km). Katyushas can easily carry <u>chemical warheads</u>. One full salvo of rockets from the truck above would fire the explosive equivalent to 4 "Iraqi" type Scud missiles. No apartment in Tel Aviv will be safe.

Holds 70% of Jewish population and 80% of the Industrial Base

MILES 0 — 12.5
KILOMETERS 0 — 25

LEBANON, GOLAN HEIGHTS, Nahariyya, Akko, Haifa, Tiberias, Sea of Galilee, Nazareth, Israel, Hadera, Netanya, Herzliyya, WEST BANK Palestinian State, Tel-Aviv, Yafo, Ramla, JORDAN, Ashdod, Jerusalem, Jericho, Ashqelon, Gaza, Dead Sea, GAZA STRIP, Rafah, Mediterranean Sea, Beersheba, EGYPT

Map by Mark Langfan

"Demilitarized" Palestinian State =

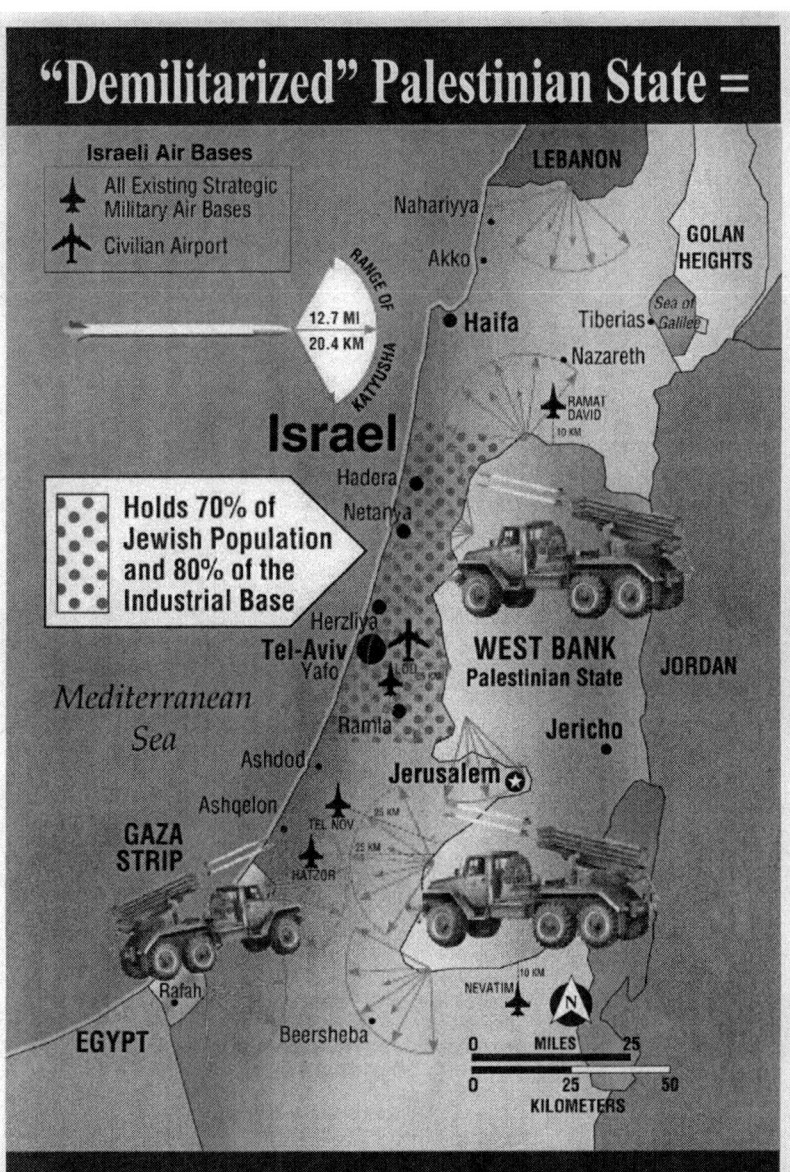

Israeli Air Bases
- All Existing Strategic Military Air Bases
- Civilian Airport

RANGE OF KATYUSHA: 12.7 MI / 20.4 KM

Holds 70% of Jewish Population and 80% of the Industrial Base

LEBANON
Nahariyya
Akko
Haifa
Tiberias
Sea of Galilee
Nazareth
GOLAN HEIGHTS
RAMAT DAVID 10 KM

Israel
Hadera
Netanya
Herzliya
Tel-Aviv
Yafo
LOD
Ramla

Mediterranean Sea

Ashdod
Ashqelon
TEL NOV 25 KM
HATZOR 25 KM

GAZA STRIP
Rafah
EGYPT
Beersheba

Jerusalem
WEST BANK
Palestinian State
Jericho
JORDAN

NEVATIM 10 KM

0 MILES 25
0 25 50 KILOMETERS

Katyushas carry chemical weapons too!

BERRY'S WORLD

"Well — quite frankly — in our case, the land-for-peace deal didn't work out too well."

Geronimo

White man say, "You want *peace now*, give us *land for peace*." So we give him our land. They still kill us.

White man speak with forked tongue. This PEACE NOW deal — — NO GOOD.

48

TIME
TRAITOR
OF THE YEAR
התעורר ישראל!
OSLO
הכוונות
מאחורי
הצהרת העקרונות

WAKE UP ISRAEL - JERUSALEM IS IN DANGER

FOR SALE
EXCLUSIVE COMMUNITY
JEWS FORBIDDEN TO LIVE HERE.
SALE OF THIS PROPERTY TO JEWS PUNISHABLE BY DEATH.
BY ORDER OF HIS MAJESTY KING HUSSEIN

WEST BANK
JUDEA & SAMARIA

ARAB APARTHEID

Sell-Out Theatre Presents

A Rabin-Arafat Production

GOOD-BYE ISRAEL
HELLO PALESTINE

The Greatest Story Ever Told!

Join in with the excitement as
Yitzchak & Yasser
dance together on the roof-tops.

Share the FUN, the ENJOYMENT,
the MASSACRES, the SONGS, the TEARS,
the LAUGHTER, and the SLAUGHTER.

A story of love, hate, betrayal and
eventual destruction, from the makers of:

- **Sink the Altalena!**
  (1948, Starring Y. Rabin)
- **Bomb the Buses**
  (Several runs, starring Y. Arafat
  with Y. Rabin and S. Peres in chief supporting roles)
- **Bloody Munich**
  (1972, Starring Y. Arafat)
- **Raid on Entebbe**
  (1976, produced and directed by Y. Arafat)
- **Mass Murder in Ma'alot**
  (1974, produced, presented, and directed by Y. Arafat)
- **Another One Bites the Dust**
  (an ongoing show, all about Israeli Soldiers out hitch-hiking,
  produced and directed by Y. Arafat, in collaboration with
  Rabin-Aloni Enterprises)
- **See No Evil, Hear No Evil**
  (1993, presented, and directed by Y. Arafat, Y. Rabin and S. Peres
  While terrorist attacks abound, Peres doesn't see them,
  Rabin ignores them, and Arafat hasn't
  a word of condemnation to make)

Appearing in Gaza-Jericho first
And soon all of Israel

OLEG © 94

September 15, 1993   *Rabin says that all is not what it seems clearly to be.*

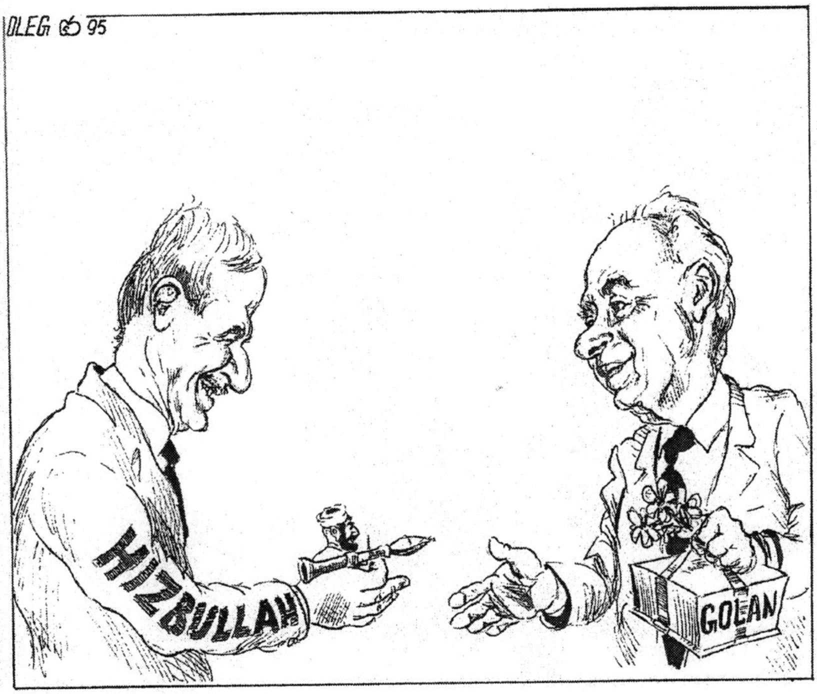
HIZBULLAH
GOLAN

1. I UNDERSTAND YOU NOW SUPPORT A PALESTINIAN STATE...

2. YES, WITH JERUSALEM ITS CAPITAL

OLEG © 96

3. WHY IS THAT?

4. BECAUSE OTHERWISE THE CAPITAL OF THE PALESTINIAN STATE WILL BE IN AMMAN!

November 30, 1993

Deputy Foreign Minister Yossi Beilin has become known as the only member of the government who tells the truth about its intentions.

TRANSFER
YOU RACIST AGITATOR! YOU DON'T BELONG IN THIS COUNTRY! GO BACK WHERE YOU CAME FROM!
I MEANT THE TRANSFER OF JEWS FROM THE TERRITORIES
WHY DIDN'T YOU SAY YOU WERE A PEACE-LOVING BELIEVER IN THE NEW MIDDLE EAST?!
MERETZ
OLEG © 94

IT'S PERFECTLY ALL RIGHT; THEY PROMISED THEY WILL ONLY HAVE 100,000 IN THERE
OLEG © 95

March 31, 1993

Israel's foreign minister Shimon Peres learning the characteristics of quicksand the hard way.

January 12, 1993 — *France announces support for sanctions against Israel.*

20
... אני שולל את
שמעון פרס תכלית השלילה
ורואה בעליית קרנו קלקלה מוסרית
ממארת ביותר.
אקרע קריעה על המדינה אם אראנו
יושב על כסאו של שר בישראל!
משה שרת - יומן אישי
כרך ה', עמ' 2301
שטר הגרלה מסי'
סדרה ב' № 710354
20
עשרים שקלים חדשים
ראיתי בחומרה רבה, וכפגם מוסרי
ממדרגה ראשונה, את האפשרות
שמפלגת העבודה תציע
לראשות הממשלה את שמעון פרס
שלא לבש את מדי צה"ל.
יצחק רבין "פנקס שירות" עמוד 418
זהירות!... לאיש זה אין כיסוי.
שמור שטר זה ודומיו להגרלות!
בהגרלת הביניים הראשונה זכתה ב-5000 ש"ח גב' דוכן מהרצליה
(מסי השטר הראשון שזכה - 290937)
הגרלת ביניים נוספת תערך ב-21.5.96.
הגרלה סופית ע"ס 10,000 ש"ח תערך ב-28.5.96.
תוצאות ההגרלות יפורסמו בטלמסר של זו ארצנו 03-63 88 486

November 1958

Well-intentioned voices at home and abroad repeatedly urge Israel's integration into the Middle Eastern scene.

INTEGRATION INTO WHAT?

November 1956.

The swift and victorious Sinai Campaign revives memories of ancient Jewish military glory.

WELL, WHAT DO YOU THINK OF IT?

CHAPTER FOUR: JEWISH HISTORY

Jewish history is a history of darkness and light. There were great periods in Jewish history when they were able to produce significant progress for the human race. They gave the world the belief in one G-d instead of a multitude of major and minor mythological gods. They gave the world its first true code of ethics in the Ten Commandments.

America was founded on much of the principles of the Holy Scriptures the Jews brought to the world. It was no accident that early pioneers in this country all took their names from the bible.

The Jews suffered degradation and persecution all over the world. On their own soil they grew in strength and for a while were able to protect themselves. Then with the Oslo suicide process, they began to lose that ability. In this collection of my articles, I will demonstrate to the reader how far into the darkness Israel has strayed in its futile pursuit of "peace."

Bernard J. Shapiro

THE VATICAN AND ISRAEL
Diplomatic Relations, Recognition & Reparations
by Bernard J. Shapiro (1992)

As most Jews are preparing to celebrate Israel's 44th year of independence, the Vatican is embroiled in a weighty discussion of whether to recognize the Jewish State. Most of us who have followed this issue over many years placed most of the blame for lack of relations on the Vatican's fear of offending the Arabs who have substantial Christian minorities in their countries.

During Israel's early years, the official Vatican excuse for not establishing relations was Israel's refusal to internationalize Jerusalem. That was a part of the 1947 United Nations Partition Plan that was rejected by the Arab states. The Jordanians who controlled the Christian Holy Places in Jerusalem during that time period also rejected internationalization. In modern times, the Vatican has recognized the impossibility of turning the clock back on Jerusalem, and now insists on a resolution of the Palestinian conflict before establishing relations.

Dr. Michael Kaniel, writing in the Jerusalem Post (April 25, 1992), analyzes the religious origins of the Vatican's anti-Israel policies. He shows how the real reason the Vatican has withheld formal recognition is because the Jewish State represents a vexing contradiction to Catholic theology. When Theodor Herzl met with Vatican Secretary of State Cardinal Merry del Val to request support of the Zionist movement on January 22, 1904, the cardinal said: "as long as the Jews deny the divinity of Christ . . . how can we agree to their regaining possession of the Holy Land? . . . They should first have to accept conversion." Three days later Pope Pius X told Herzl: "the Jews have not recognized our Lord; therefore we cannot recognize the Jewish people."

The persistence of the Jewish people goes against the Christian teaching that the Church is now the true Israel. Kaniel writes: "However, the foundations for modern anti-Semitism and the Church's antagonism to Jewish return to their ancestral homeland lies in the implacable contempt for Judaism and the Jewish people felt by all the Fathers of the Church, especially Justin, Augustine and Chrysostom. The Church Fathers taught that Jewish misfortune is Divine punishment for the rejection of Jesus, and that consequently Jews must be kept in degradation as living witnesses to the truth of Christianity—Justin Martry adding that the Land of Israel should be rendered a desert and Jews be forbidden to go to Jerusalem."

Because the Church held such anti-Semitic positions, a wide range of priests, monks, bishops, cardinals, and popes felt justified in almost any act that would injure the Jewish community of their region. Jews were forced to listen to conversion sermons. Blood libels were invented that claimed that Jews killed Christian children and used their blood to make matzo. Needless to say Jews were massacred every Passover to save the children. The masses were frequently encouraged to murder, rape and pillage the Jewish population. All in the name Christianity. The Church blamed the Jews for the Black Death in 1347-9 by claiming that they had poisoned the wells. This resulted in the massacres of Jews in 200 communities in Europe.

The Church forcibly converted many Jews and then had the Inquisitor hunt down, torture and burn to death those found to be still practicing Judaism. Jewish populations were expelled in dozens of countries at the whim of the Church (200,000 from Spain alone in 1492). All this was just the precursor to the Holocaust. Hitler told German Bishop Berning and Monsignor Steinman that he was merely going to do to the Jews "what the Church had done for 1500 years.

Israel and the Vatican are about to begin a dialogue that would mark the first concrete step forward on the long road to diplomatic relations. Israel radio last week said the Vatican was dispatching a delegation to Jerusalem in May to discuss ties. Both the Israel Foreign Ministry and the Holy See denied the story. Despite the denials, informed sources are pointing to numerous signals and the convergence of some important historical forces that will lead inevitably to such negotiations.

Some signs of the thaw in relations were seen recently when Avi Pazner, Israel's ambassador to Italy was warmly received by Pope John Paul II in the Vatican. Cardinal Joseph Ratzinger, the head of the Vatican's Congregation of Doctrine, came to Israel on what was described as a private Easter visit. Not only was he the most senior Vatican official to visit Israel since 1964, but he also initiated private discussions with Israeli officials concerning tax exemption for Vatican property in Jerusalem.

Historically, the Vatican is way out of step. The cold war is over and all the states of the former Soviet bloc including Eastern Europe have already established diplomatic relations with Israel. Both China and India and most of Black Africa have recently established (or in the case of Africa, reestablished) diplomatic relations with the Jewish State. With Arabs and Israelis actually engaged in peace negotiations, the rationalizations and excuses used by Vatican spokespersons in years past seem absurd today.

I would like the Israelis to take pause and not rush too eagerly into relations now that the long awaited talks with the Vatican are approaching. The Vatican needs relations with Israel badly now so that it can have a say concerning the Holy Places in Jerusalem. A topic likely to come up during Arab-Israeli peace talks.

The Jewish people have a long account to settle with the Church and we are within our rights to make a few demands before we grant them diplomatic recognition. The Vatican owes a debt of immense proportions to the Jewish people for its systematic plunder of its property during the last 1700 years. One of the reasons Jews were frequently expelled from European countries, was to allow confiscation of their property and wealth. The Church was not only the instigator of most expulsions but the prime beneficiary. All over Europe there are hundreds of former synagogues which have been stolen by the Church and converted to Christian religious buildings.

The Vatican library and hundreds of churches and monasteries throughout Europe are in possession of thousands of rare Hebrew manuscripts and books stolen from their rightful owners. Jewish ritual art and ceremonial objects of great value are in the hands of the Catholic church. At the very least, Israel must demand the return its manuscripts and Judaic objects. The ancient Jewish burying ground in the catacombs of Rome is still under Vatican control. This must stop.

Dagobert D. Runes in his book DESPOTISM A Pictorial History of Tyranny makes the observation that the Jewish population in ancient times was of such size e.g., in the year 70 C.E. Rome was 10% Jewish and Alexandria, Egypt had one million Jews) that through natural population growth could have reached 900 million by modern times. The one thing that interfered with that natural growth was the murder of Jews with the Church as the leading instigator.

I suggest that if it was legitimate to demand of Germany reparations after World War II, it is just a legitimate to demand reparations from the Vatican. Israel should offer the Vatican absolution for a penance of say: $100 billion plus the return of all Jewish property in their possession.

They may not accept such a proposal. They may be offended. But one thing is certain; they will know that we will not be victims anymore. They will know we have long memories. Someday they will have to deal with us.

★

Bernard J. Shapiro is the chairman of the Freeman Center For Strategic Studies www.freeman.org and editor of publications.

[This article was first published in the Jewish Herald-Voice (Houston) on May 14, 1992.]

Bernard J. Shapiro

Editor's Note: Arafat and the entire Moslem World are demanding full control and sovereignty over the Temple Mount. At the same time they are denying any Jewish connection to the Temple and the Israeli government of PM Ehud Barak is agreeing with them. I felt it necessary to revive this older article for the record.

A Timely Reissue **First Published on July 15, 1993 in the** *Jewish Herald-Voice***, Houston and reissued in the Maccabean Online in September 2000.**

THE TEMPLE MOUNT FAITHFUL

Fanatics or Jewish Patriots?

(September 2000)

I got a call a few weeks ago from a friend and supporter who lived in Clear Lake. She told me with much enthusiasm that Gershon Salomon, leader and founder of the Temple Mount and Land of Israel Faithful, would be in Houston for just one day. Did I want to meet him? I said yes immediately and began calling a few of my friends to join me for that meeting.

I was fairly ignorant about what the Temple Mount Faithful stood for. I knew they wanted to rebuild the Temple of Solomon or the Third Temple but not much else. When I started inviting people to the meeting, I discovered quite a lot of negative feeling toward them. Rabbi Moishe Traxler was very helpful in explaining to me the Lubavitch position regarding the rebuilding of the Temple. They very clearly prohibit any activity on the Temple Mount until the coming of the Messiah. The Israeli Consul General Meir Romem was quick to tell me about the horrible international consequences of attempting to rebuild the Temple. Romem also told me that he went to school with Salomon and that he was a charming person and Israeli war hero.

Others, including Rabbis of great note, told me the rebuilding of the Temple would require the introduction of animal sacrifices. My wife, a vegetarian and animal rights activist, was horrified by such a prospect.

Obviously, there was a lot to discuss with Salomon and I looked forward to our meeting.

In his private life, Salomon is an expert researcher and lecturer in Middle Eastern studies, specializing in the history of the national movement of the Kurdish people. He is an officer in the Israel Defense Forces and a 10th generation Jerusalemite. He is descended from Rabbi Avraham Solomon Zalman Zoref who settled in Jerusalem in 1811 and was one of the first Jewish pioneers dedicated to the redemption of the Holy Land. Rabbi Zoref was assassinated by Arabs who thought they could stop his Godly mission. Salomon has fought in all of Israel's wars. Badly wounded on the Golan, when a tank ran over his legs, he walks now with crutches.

It was in one of those battles, as he lay dying, that he felt God telling him that He was not through with him. Salomon understood that this was a divine call to consecrate himself to the Redemption of all of Israel including the Temple Mount. The Mount came back into Israeli hands as a result of the Six Day War liberation of Jerusalem. In an act of great stupidity, Israeli Defense Minister Moshe Dayan, a few days later, gave control of the Temple Mount to Moslem religious leaders. His reasoning was that this would prevent panic among the newly defeated Arab population. He also made great efforts to prevent Arabs from fleeing to Jordan. Today, as these same Arabs plot our demise, we realize how mistaken his policies were.

Gershon exploded all the myths about his group. Quoting Rambam, he explained that animal sacrifice is not necessary if the Temple is rebuilt. He talked about a process of **REDEMPTION.** First regain control of the Temple Mount. Second remove the Moslem buildings that desecrate our Holy Mount. Then the Temple (Beit Hamikdash) should be built. He was very clear on this: Building the Temple is preparatory process for Redemption. It is not an end in itself. Worship at the Temple would still await the Messiah. It is important, Salomon kept reiterating, that we **PREPARE** and **WORK** for Redemption. In other words, the Messiah will not come to Israel and reclaim the Temple Mount and rebuild the Temple. We must do those things **BEFORE** the Messiah comes, in order to **CAUSE** Him to come.

What about the Arabs? Wouldn't they object to the removal of the Mosque of Omar (Dome of the Rock) and the Al Aqsa mosque from the Temple Mount? Of course they would, but they have no legitimate rights in the area. From my Hindu friends I have learned how Moslem conquerors built mosques on Holy Places of other people in every part of the world. They did it to humiliate and degrade their subject nations. Salomon stated it bluntly, "There is no reason the sovereign State of Israel needs to allow this desecration of Jewish Holy Places to continue."

Today on the Mount, the Arabs are supreme. They are destroying all archaeological remnants of Jewish sites. They are storing weapons in their mosques to kill Jews. They have built a museum to Palestinian nationalism, including gut-wrenching pictures from the battles of Sabra and Shatila. Tourists from the world over are told Jews committed these killings (It was Christians).

Salomon was a gentle, inspiring and very religious person. His firm belief in the coming Redemption made the discussion of politics seem irrelevant. He is not a fanatic but a Jewish patriot of the highest rank. I am not competent to discuss Halacha with reference to the Mount. I do know that it is wrong for us to allow the Arab desecration of our people's most Holy Site. What about the consequences of our asserting our rights to the Temple Mount? The Moslems cannot hate us anymore, and the Christian world will be electrified with anticipation of the coming of the Messiah. In fact, Christians the world over will raise millions of dollars to help us rebuild the Temple. As in the days of Solomon, the nations of the world will send their best architects, artisans and materials to help build the Temple. Jews in the Diaspora will be inspired to "go up to Jerusalem" and join in the sacred process of Redemption. (*From my mouth to G-d's ear.*)

Before Israelis make fateful decisions about the Golan and YESHA, they should read the following lecture I gave back in 1993. **The realities today are much more obvious and considerably worse.**

CHANUKAH AND JEWISH HISTORY

Will We Be Maccabees Or Victims?

(December 1994)

The year is 70 C.B. and a young Roman legionnaire stands on a hill overlooking Jerusalem. While he watches it burn, he says to his comrades in Latin, *"**Judea Capta Est**"* (Judea is conquered). Yet like the legendary phoenix, rising from the ashes of its own destruction, Israel burst onto the world's stage 2,000 years later, with the lusty cry of an infant yearning to breathe free. Five Arab armies tried to destroy that new life before it could take hold. With blood and fire, including the sacrifice of one percent of its population (6,000 of its best young people), besieged Israel secured its independence.

Just nine short years earlier, European Jewry had faced its most devastating experience, the Holocaust. In the areas under Nazi occupation, the Jewish death rate was 90%. Despite revolts in dozens of camps, and heroic resistance with the partisans of free Europe, the Jews were unorganized, unarmed and ultimately became victims. During both the Holocaust and Israel's War of Independence, the world and its leaders were indifferent, if not hostile, to the fate of the Jews.

Jews in their own land, with their G-d, have great power, much more than the sum of arms and men. During Chanukah we should recall the legacy of the Maccabees. Remember how two "Hellenized Jews," Jason and Menelaus tried to destroy Judaism and force assimilation on the Jewish population. For generations, we have taught our children about the evil Antiochus and his attempt to suppress the Jews. In reality, there were traitors among our own people who led the way for Antiochus. Today in Israel, a similar situation has developed. Israeli Prime Minister Yitzhak Rabin and Foreign Minister Shimon Peres are leading a left-wing coalition that is blatantly hostile to everything Jewish. They are surrendering the heartland of Eretz Yisrael, promised in perpetuity to Abraham and his descendants by G-d. The educational system in Israel is being revamped to eliminate the study of Jewish sources, like the Bible. They are cultivating hatred of all things Jewish and especially religious Jews. Units of the Israel Defense Forces are being recruited from the non-religious population for the sole purpose of suppressing and possibly destroying the religious villages of **YESHA**.

Rabin and Peres, anxious to win favor with the Arabs, much like Jason and the Greeks, plan to give away Israel's strategic assets. Territory is not important if your new god is economics. While the Israeli government renounces anything Jewish, including Holy Sites, the Arabs seek strength and comfort in a revived Islam. Nothing portrays the difference between the Arabs and the Jews better than how each views his religion. Young Arab men, promised paradise, cry "ali Akbar" (**G-d** is Great), then sacrifice their lives to kill Jews in one great *jihad*. Jewish soldiers flee their posts, uncertain about their open-fire instructions, demoralized by a government which lies to them about the advent of peace.

Let us be Maccabees again. Let the IDF go into battle with the Maccabee cry, "All who are with **G-d**, follow me!" With the words: "Who is like unto Thee O **G-d** (the acronym of which spells out the word *Maccabee* in Hebrew) inscribed on their flags, the **G-d** inspired Jewish army swept the much larger enemy from the field in a great victory. It is this victory for which we celebrate Chanukah and not just the miracle of the oil burning eight days.

There is a simple but crucial lesson for us all in the above events. If we as Jews turn our backs on our religion and our G-d, we can expect disaster. The current government of Israel has brought down the wrath of G-d on the Israeli people for turning its back on our heritage. Like Judah Maccabee, angered by the treason of Jason and Menelaus, and outraged by Antiochus, we must revolt against Rabin and Peres. The nationalist opposition in Israel must unite behind one Zionist banner. They must fill the streets and jails with protesters. City after city must be shut down. This is war. All normal life must end until this evil Hellenistic regime is driven from power.

[This article was the cover editorial for the December 1994 issue of **THE MACCABEAN** and was published in *THE JEWISH PRESS* on December 9, 1994. It was revised and reissued in the Maccabean Online in January 1998, December 1998, December 2001, December 2002, December 2003, December 2004, and December 2006.]

A LETTER THAT THE HOUSTON CHRONICLE

CHOSE NOT TO PUBLISH

July 6, 1997
VIEWPOINTS EDITOR
HOUSTON CHRONICLE
Via Fax: 220-3575\

To The Viewpoints Editor:
Re: Your coverage of the Hebron violence (July 5th and many issues previously)

There are certain pertinent facts that are not being communicated to your readers. As a native Houstonian and also a Chronicle reader for over 40 years I feel it is my duty to bring this information to the public. Here is a short but important list:

1. Under the Hebron Agreement signed this year, with United States participation, Israel agreed to withdraw from over 80% of the city. The Palestinian Authority (PA) agreed to ensure security and stability. They also agreed, with US State Department coordinator Dennis Ross as witness, to maintain order among their population, fight terrorism, and prevent attacks on the Jewish community of Hebron and Israeli soldiers.

2. Violence doesn't **BREAK OUT** in Hebron by some *act of nature*. There has been violence for over three weeks precisely because Yassir Arafat and the PA believe it to be useful politically. When mobs of Arabs attack Israelis or attempt to break into the Jewish section of Hebron, Israeli troops find it necessary to defend both themselves and the Jewish Community. This is not violence breaking out (a morally neutral description) but, in truth, it is Arab aggression and Israeli defense. The two acts are not morally equivalent.

3. My third and final note is that there should never have been the need for Israeli troops to confront Arab attackers. The Hebron agreement clearly states that the PA's Hebron police force, of which there are over 1,000, are responsible for maintaining order among the Arab population. The fact that

they stand around and fail to prevent Arab mobs is clear proof that their political bosses have told them to do nothing. They clearly have the power and influence to prevent the violence in the first place.

Respectfully,

Bernard J. Shapiro, Executive Director

Freeman Center For Strategic Studies

Letter to *The Jerusalem Post* published on **Internet** on June 20, 1999

JERUSALEM AS ISRAEL'S CAPITAL

I am sick and tired of Israelis whining about the location of the American Embassy. Any normal country with one ounce of self-respect would have demanded that **ALL** embassies be located in its capital. Israel should announce that consulates and consulates-general would be welcome in Tel Aviv. **ONLY** Embassies would be permitted in Jerusalem. There would be temporary diplomatic difficulties, but in time, Israel's capital would be respected by the world community. Don't blame America; this is a problem of Israeli failure to exercise its proper right of sovereignty.

Bernard J. Shapiro

CHANUKAH AND JEWISH HISTORY

Will We Be Maccabees Or Victims?
(December 2006)

The year is 70 C.E. and a young Roman legionnaire stands on a hill overlooking Jerusalem. While he watches it burn, he says to his comrades in Latin, "Judea Capta Est" (Judea is conquered).Yet like the legendary phoenix, rising from the ashes of its own destruction, Israel burst onto the world's stage 2000 years later, with the cry of a lusty infant yearning to breathe free. Five Arab armies tried to destroy that new life before it could take hold. With blood and fire, including the sacrifice of one per cent of its population (6000 of its best young people), besieged Israel secured its independence.

Just nine short years earlier, European Jewry faced its most devastating experience, the Holocaust. In the areas under Nazi occupation, the Jewish death rate was 90%. Despite revolts in dozens of camps, and heroic resistance with the partisans of free Europe, the Jews were unorganized, unarmed and ultimately became victims. During both the Holocaust and Israel's War of Independence, the world and its leaders were indifferent, if not hostile, to the fate of the Jews.

Jews in their own land, with their G-d, have great power, much more than the sum of arms and men. During Chanukah we should recall the legacy of the Maccabees. Remember how two "Hellenized Jews," Jason and Menelaus tried to destroy Judaism and force assimilation on the Jewish population. For generations we have taught our children about the evil Antiochus and his attempt to suppress the Jews. In reality, there were traitors among our own people who led the way for Antiochus.

There arose in Israel, an almost similar situation when Israeli Foreign Minister Shimon Peres and Yossi Beilin led a leftwing coalition that was blatantly hostile to everything Jewish. They forced Israeli Prime Minister Yitzhak Rabin to go along with their nefarious schemes. They pushed through the Oslo Accords in the Knesset which surrendered the heartland of Eretz Yisrael, promised in perpetuity to Abraham and his descendants by G-d. The educational system in Israel was then revamped to eliminate the study of Jewish sources like the bible. They cultivated hatred of all things Jewish and especially religious Jews. Units of the Israel Defense Forces were recruited from the non-religious population for the sole purpose of suppressing and possibly destroying the religious villages of YESHA.

Peres, Yossi Beilin, Avraham Burg and other extreme leftists, anxious to win favor with the Arabs, much like Jason and the Greeks, planned to give away Israel's strategic assets. Territory is not important if your new god is economics. While the Israeli government renounced anything Jewish, including Holy Sites, the Arabs sought strength and comfort in a revived Islam. Nothing portrays the difference better between the Arabs and the Jews than how each views his religion. Young Arab men, promised paradise, cry "ali Akbar" (G-d is Great), then sacrifice their lives to kill Jews in one great jihad. Jewish soldiers filed to respond to the enemy, uncertain about their open-fire instructions, demoralized by a government, which lies to them about the advent of peace.

The Israeli people rose up in the 1996 election and threw out the party of appeasement that had abandoned Eretz Yisrael. Benjamin Natanyahu became Israeli Prime Minister and the National/Zionist/Religious groups breathed a collective sigh of relief. ONLY RELIEF DID NOT COME. For some reason known only to him, Netanyahu, Barak, PM Ariel Sharon, and now Olmert proceeded to implement the very same Oslo agreements the voters had rejected What should we do?

Let us be Maccabees again. Let us go into battle with the Maccabee cry, "All who are with G-d, follow me!" With the words: "Who is like untoThee O G-d (the acronym of which spells out the word Maccabee in Hebrew) inscribed on their flags, the G-d inspired Jewish army swept the much larger enemy from the field in a great victory. It is this victory for which we celebrate Chanukah and not just the miracle of the oil burning eight days.

There is a simple but crucial lesson for us all in the above events. If we as Jews turn our backs on our religion and our G-d, we can expect disaster.

The current government of Israel has brought down the wrath of G-d on the Israeli people for turning its back on our heritage. Like Judah Maccabee, angered by the treason of Jason and Menelaus, and outraged by Antiochus, we must revolt against Olmert as we did against Peres, Rabin and Sharon. The nationalist opposition in Israel must unite behind one Zionist banner. They must fill the streets and jails with protesters. City after city must be shut down.

Victory will not fall into our lap. It must be fought for and won. We must demonstrate that the strength of our will and the power of our belief cannot be defeated. Only then will victory come.

The Jews of Judea and Samaria and all of Israel must not be passive pawns in the political surrender of their homes. The defeatist Israeli leaders, who have surrendered our Jewish rights to Eretz Yisrael, should be told that there are still proud Jews in Judea, Samaria and Gaza who will give up neither their inheritance from Abraham, nor their right of self-defense.

The brave heroes of Zion must not limit themselves to passive civil disobedience, but must be on the offensive. My friends, it is may past time to mount an active civil disobedience campaign that will be celebrated by future generations as the Maccabees are today.

While such internal Jewish conflict would be dreadful, it is a consequence of the government's disregard for the security and well being of its citizens. At this great time of trial and apocalyptic threat, the safeguarding of the future of the Jewish people's right to Eretz Yisrael must take precedence.

REDEEMING THE TEMPLE MOUNT

by Bernard J. Shapiro

Back in 1993, I started inviting people to explain the significance of rebuilding the Temple Mount in Jewish history and its affect on the World. Rabbi Moishe Traxler was very helpful in explaining to me the Lubavitch position regarding the rebuilding of the Temple. They very clearly prohibit any activity on the Temple Mount until the coming of the Messiah. The Israeli Consul General (Houston) Meir Romem was quick to tell me about the horrible international consequences of attempting to rebuild the Temple.

Others, including Rabbis of great note, told me the rebuilding of the Temple would require the introduction of animal sacrifices. A friend, a vegetarian and animal rights activist, was horrified by such a prospect.

All the myths were refuted. Rambam explained that animal sacrifice is not necessary if the Temple is rebuilt. He talked about a process of REDEMPTION. First regain control of the Temple Mount. Second remove the Moslem buildings that desecrate our Holy Mount. Then the Temple (Beit Hamigdash) should be built. He was very clear on this: Building the Temple is preparatory process for Redemption. It is not an end in itself. Worship at the Temple would still await the Messiah. It is important, We must PREPARE and WORK for Redemption. In other words, the Messiah will not come to Israel and reclaim the Temple Mount and rebuild the Temple. We must do those things BEFORE the Messiah comes, in order to CAUSE him to come.

What about the Arabs? Wouldn't they object to the removal of the Mosque of Omar (Dome of the rock) and the Al Aqsa mosque from the Temple Mount? Of course they would, but they have no legitimate rights in the area. In fact, Jerusalem and the Temple Mount are not even mentioned in the Koran. From my Hindu friends I have learned how Moslem conquerors built mosques on Holy Places of other people in every part of the world. They did it to humiliate, degrade and acquire the spiritual power of their subject nations. There is no reason the sovereign State of Israel, needs to allow this desecration Jewish Holy Places to continue."

Bernard J. Shapiro

Today on the Mount, the Arabs are supreme. They are destroying all archaeological remnants of Jewish sites. They are storing weapons in their mosques to kill Jews. They have built a museum to Palestinian nationalism, including gut-wrenching pictures from the battles of Sabra and Shatila. Tourists from the world over are told Jews committed these killings (It was Christians).

I am not competent to discuss Halacha with reference to the Mount. I do know that it is wrong for us to allow the Arab desecration of our people's most Holy Site. What about the consequences of our asserting our rights to the Temple Mount? The Moslems cannot hate us anymore, and the Christian world will be electrified with anticipation of coming of the Messiah.

In fact, Christians the world over will raise millions of dollars to help us rebuild the Temple. As in the days of Solomon, the nations of the world will send their best architects, artisans and materials to help build the Temple. Jews in the Diaspora will be inspired to "go up to Jerusalem" and join in the sacred process of Redemption.

(From my mouth to G-d's ear).

CHAPTER FIVE: WORLD HISTORY

World history proves one thing conclusively. Mankind is but one step above the beasts of the jungle. Power is supreme and there is no such thing as International Law. All attempts to codify such law have ended in warfare and abuse of weaker nations at the hands of the stronger ones. For example, the United Nations today is a tool of anti-Semitic nations to abuse and restrict Israel's right of self defense.

Rather than cry and whine over this state of affairs, we must strengthen ourselves militarily and psychologically. Just say to the world, NO. We will take care of ourselves and you don't like it then write us a tough letter which we can then file in our circular file cabinet.

Some Jews in the face of all empirical evidence to the contrary believe peace is possible. In the book <u>Self Portrait Of A Hero: The Letters of Jonathan Netanyahu</u>

<u>(1963-1976),</u> **Jonathan Netanyahu,** the fallen hero of Entebbe and brother of Benjamin, said it best:

"I see with sorrow and great anger how a part of the people still clings to hopes of reaching a peaceful settlement with the Arabs. Common sense tells them, too, that the Arabs haven't abandoned their basic aim of destroying the State; but the self-delusion and self-deception that have always plagued the Jews are at work again. It's our great misfortune. They want to believe, so they believe. They want not to see, so they shut their eyes. They want not to learn from thousands of years of history, so they distort it. They want to bring about a sacrifice, and they do indeed. It would be comic, if it wasn't so tragic. What a saddening and irritating lot this Jewish people are!"

In our **Holy Scriptures** we read about the prophet Jeremiah. Jeremiah, who anguished over the fact that his people believed in false prophets of peace and didn't see the dangers facing Israel, cries out in despair, **"Peace, peace but there is no peace."**

Great issues of war and peace as related to Israel are being debated by Jews in Israel and America. There are strong opinions on both sides of the Atlantic as well as both sides of the major issues. Professor Paul Eidelberg of Bar-Ilan University reviews the historical facts:

"Between 1945 and 1978 the longest time without a war going on someplace was a mere 26 days. On an average day there are 12 wars being fought somewhere on earth. The consensus of scholars has been that the norm of international relations is not peace but war. As Eidelberg reports, "Indeed, the occurrence of 1,000 wars during the last 2,500 years indicates that *"peace" is little more than a preparation for war.* Which means that peace treaties are **WORTHLESS**, to say the least."

Eidelberg then quotes from a book by Lawrence Beilenson, entitled **THE TREATY TRAP**, saying, "After studying every peace treaty going back to early Roman times, Beilenson concludes that treaties are made to be broken. In fact, he shows that treaties for guaranteeing the territorial integrity of a nation are useless to the guaranteed nation and worse than useless insofar as they engender a false sense of security. *Such treaties can only benefit nations governed by rulers intending to violate them whenever expedient."*

Midge Dector on "peace"—"What I want to say is something that virtually the whole history of the 20th century teaches us and yet something we refuse to learn. And that is, when applied to the affairs of nations, peace is an evil word. Yes I said evil. And the idea of peace as we know it is an evil idea. From the peace of Versailles to "peace in our time" at Munich . . . each declaration of peace or expressions of longing for peace ended in slaughter. Not necessarily immediately and not necessarily directly, but slaughter all the same . . ."

"For there is no such thing as making peace. Nations who are friendly do not need to do so, and nations or people who are enemies cannot

do so. To cry peace, peace when there is no peace, the prophet Jeremiah taught us long ago, is not the expression of hope, not even superstition but a reckless toying with the minds and hearts of people whose very future depends on their capacity to rise every day to the harsh morning light of the truth."

Bernard J. Shapiro

HARRY W. FREEMAN'S FAVORITE QUOTE

(July 1992)

"If all mankind minus one were of one opinion and that one was of the opposite opinion, it would be just as wrong for the world to silence that one man as it would be for that man, if he had the power, to silence all mankind" . . . .

. . . . John Stuart Mill (ON LIBERTY).

I received two presents from Harry W. Freeman for Hanukkah in 1956: Mill's quote and a book, **GUIDES TO STRAIGHT THINKING** by Stuart Chase. They were among the most valuable presents I ever received . . . . Bernard J. Shapiro

ADDENDUM FROM FREEMAN CENTER:

THOSE WHO FAIL TO LEARN FROM HISTORY

ARE CONDEMNED TO REPEAT IT

In 1934, Harry W. Freeman, my grandfather, was already lecturing about the dangers of Hitler and Nazism. Nobody listened. The Holocaust was not prevented. Today (in 2009) there are 1,900,000,000 (1.9 billion) Arab & Moslem people who plan a second Holocaust against the Jews of Israel. Their first stage is to use the so called "peace process" to weaken Israel and strip it of its strategic territories. They are being aided by the same hypocrites and accomplices in the West who failed to aid the Jews of Europe in their darkest hour. <u>Unfortunately, even left-wing Israelis have fallen victims to the seductive lure of peace and have begun a policy of appeasement similar to that tried with Hitler. The results will be no different.</u>

The Arab propaganda full of slanders and libels; the media bias against Israel replete with double standards and the rewriting of history are all working to the same end: the de-legitimization of Israel. Israel is the only country considered by many to be **GUILTY OF ORIGINAL SIN** by virtue of its very existence. This process of de-legitimization has as its goal creating a world climate in which the **DESTRUCTION** of Israel is acceptable. Many in the Jewish community are either apathetic or fail to recognize this threat.

I founded the **FREEMAN CENTER FOR STRATEGIC STUDIES** (1992) in order to create a powerful voice to arouse the Jewish community to the action necessary to frustrate the evil designs of the enemies of Israel. I **need** your help to accomplish this mission. Many of you have taken the Freeman Center for granted. **It will not exist without financial aid from ALL OF YOU who understand** . . . . Bernard J. Shapiro

Bernard J. Shapiro

SHADES OF MUNICH

(May 1998)

Is there anyone out there who doesn't see the similarity between British actions today and those during the Munich Conference of 1938? It seems that another democratic country (Israel) is about to be sacrificed for Western interests. Those interests being dollars, oil and trade in weapons of mass destruction with the Arabs. How can Israelis be so stupid not to realize that when Israel is invited to dinner in London, they are the **MAIN COURSE**?

WHAT IF THE FREEMAN CENTER NEGOTIATED FOR ISRAEL IN LONDON?

Albright/Blair/Ross: It would be a great step for peace, if Israel would withdraw from 13.1% of its land.

Freeman Center: We would be happy to consider a withdrawal after the Palestinian Authority fulfills all its commitments agreed to in previous documents.

Albright/Blair/Ross: There will be violence if Israel doesn't withdraw from 13.1% of its land.

Freeman Center: We would be happy to consider a withdrawal after the Palestinian Authority fulfills all its commitments agreed to in previous documents.

Albright/Blair/Ross: America and Europe will be very upset with Israel if it doesn't withdraw from 13.1% of its land.

Freeman Center: We would be happy to consider a withdrawal after the Palestinian Authority fulfills all its commitments agreed to in previous documents.

Albright/Blair/Ross: The United Nations will pass resolutions against Israel if it doesn't withdraw from 13.1% of its land.

Freeman Center: We would be happy to consider a withdrawal after the Palestinian Authority fulfills all its commitments agreed to in previous documents.

Albright/Blair/Ross: It is time Israel made the hard decisions to withdraw from 13.1% of its land.

Freeman Center: We have made the hard decision to consider a withdrawal only after the Palestinian Authority fulfills all its commitments agreed to in previous documents.

Albright/Blair/Ross: This is totally unacceptable. President Clinton will be very upset with Israel

Freeman Center: We would be happy to consider a withdrawal after the Palestinian Authority fulfills all its commitments agreed to in previous documents.

Albright/Blair/Ross: [Exasperated, Albright asks one last question.] If Arafat did everything possible to comply with previous signed agreements, would you withdraw 13.1%?

Freeman Center: Are you crazy? *Eretz Yisrael* is our country. Though the Almighty has given us clear title in perpetuity, we have also won that title through our blood, sweat, and tears. No force on the face of the earth is strong enough to wrest it from our hands. Farewell, these negotiations are concluded.

Bernard J. Shapiro

NOTES FROM THE EDITOR

(April 1999)

SERBIA AND ISRAEL

There is no substantive difference between NATO bombing Serbia in support of a Moslem terrorist group (KLA) seeking secession and NATO bombing Israel in support of a Moslem terrorist group (PLO) seeking secession. ***Think about that fact.*** The media distortion of the nature of the Serbian conflict parallels the media distortion in the Arab-Israeli conflict. This is something the pro-Israel community needs to consider carefully. I have included in this issue five excellent articles on the Kosovo conflict. It is very important that you understand what is happening despite the overwhelmingly biased news media.

JERUSALEM

[Arutz Sheva News Service—March 15, 1999]

PALESTINIANS DEMAND WESTERN JERUSALEM, TOO

The Palestinians have demands not only on eastern Jerusalem, but on the western part as well. Palestinian Authority senior Abu Allah declared three days ago that the PA will insist on discussing western Jerusalem in the final-status negotiations. Arutz-7 correspondent Haggai Huber man reports that Abu Allah, who appeared before a gathering of the Fatah Youth movement, said he was speaking in the name of Yasser Arafat. Abu Allah also cited the recent European Union letter implying that Israel has no sovereignty over any part of Jerusalem.

Editor's Note: If you have confidence in the Israeli government defending Israeli interests in Jerusalem and elsewhere, here is a partial list of its broken promises:

1. No negotiations with the PLO (Rabin)

2. No PLO state (Rabin)

3. No withdrawal from the Golan (Rabin)

4. If Oslo doesn't work we will just end it (Rabin)

5. Orient House (PA Foreign Ministry) will be shut down (Netanyahu)

6. We will build Har Homa (Netanyahu)

7. We will demand extradition of PA murderers (Netanyahu)

8. We will demand PA reciprocity before continuing the Wye Accord (Netanyahu)

9. We will force the PA police and security forces out of Jerusalem (Netanyahu)

10. We will permit Jewish prayer on the **Temple Mount** (Netanyahu)

TO THE EUROPEAN UNION

In your rush to criticize Israeli sovereignty in Jerusalem, you seem to have forgotten the following:

Your ancestors lived in caves and had not yet mastered the art of language at the time King David made Jerusalem Israel's capital.

TIME FOR A NEW POLICY IN LEBANON

The Freeman Center believes that retaliation for Hizbullah attacks against the IDF and SLA in southern Lebanon, should be disproportionate. We believe that both Syrian and Lebanese infrastructure targets should be destroyed. We believe that the level of pain inflicted upon those that would kill Israelis should be so great as to inhibit such actions.

Israel has lost all deterrence in Lebanon (and also with the PA). That deterrence can only be regained by a policy of massive out of proportion retaliation for every attack on its forces. Israel must achieve a situation whereby its enemies will think twice or three times before authorizing an attack.

Civilians giving cover to the Hizbullah should be forced from the area. And this should be done without guilt or remorse. All agreements with international bodies concerning the activities of the IDF should be renounced. Full freedom of action must be reestablished.

We further believe that placing Israeli soldiers in a "no win" situation is terribly destructive of morale and jeopardizes the IDF's order of battle. The IDF was never intended to be a static defensive army. Rapid, unconventional aggressive responses to attacks are the natural order of things.

DISORDER IN THE WORLD

Or Comparative Religion 101

By Bernard J. Shapiro

It would be instructive for many of you to have taken the comparative religion course I took from Dagobert D. Runes at UC Berkeley in 1962. He later published his work in a book called DESPOTISM: A Pictorial History of Tyranny, published by Philosophical Library, 1963, Library of Congress Catalog Card No. 62-22269 (pre-dates the introduction of ISBN).

In the course he explained that Jews and Arabs were meant to fight, Christian's meant to turn the other cheek, and Hindus to be peaceful and loving. In reality religions may be interpreted differently by their followers. For example:

1. Arabs continue to be brutal, aggressive and seek world domination under their prophet Muhammad.

1. Following the defeat of Bar Kochba's revolt, many Jews were minorities in other lands. They began to turn the other cheek like Christians until the rise of Zionism. [Historical note: It took four years and one half of all the Roman Legions to defeat Bar Kochba, a minor Judean warrior, without full support of his own people, in a tiny desert land. The effort expended defeating Bar Kokba was one of the major factors causing the fall of the Roman Empire.]

2. Hindus stayed loving and peaceful until the arrival of the British, who taught them war. Moslems began to advance into the Indian sub-continent, raping, pillaging and murdering the innocent Hindus long before the arrival of the British. Many nationalist Hindus resent the British. But the British were interested in plunder and domination BUT NOT MURDER. The British, in fact saved India from total Islamic control. They did try forced conversion to Christianity but failed. Islam had a more effective method, tried by Catholics in Spain. Convert or die.

3. The Christians (no reflection intended toward GOOD Christians of today. Remember this is history and speaks in broad terms), while claiming to be peaceful, have been history's greatest mass murderers. They have greatly surpassed Islam in sheer numbers. For examples:

a. The Native Americans were virtually ethnically cleansed (read exterminated) from the North American continent.

b. Runes estimates that the Jewish population of Rome at the time of the empire's conversion to Christianity was 33%. Jews throughout the ancient world were a substantial portion of the world's population. He estimated under normal demographics the Jews would have numbered 1 billion people by the early 1960's. But Jews faced different demographic threats than other nations. In the name of Christ (primarily by Catholics), they were murdered, raped, forcibly converted, expelled, and looted.

Eventually the very efficient and techno minded Germanic Lutherans nearly exterminated the entire Jewish population. They did kill one third of the world's Jews as many claim, BUT 90% within their military grasp from France to Russia. Islam was in awe of German efficiency in killing Jews and beseeched Hitler to bring his 'solution to the Jewish problem' to the Middle East. Fortunately for my sake he did not win WWII but he lost (as did the Jewish people). Had he won I would not be alive to write this message to you.

That my friend is Comparative Religion 101, it should have taken you no more than 15 minutes to read and understand it. It took the Jewish people 3000 years. They apparently were very slow learners.

★

(February 2006)

The quotes below speak for themselves:

PLEASE COMPARE WINSTON CHURCHILL AND EHUD OLMERT IN CRISIS SITUATIONS

1) "We shall not flag nor fail. We shall go on to the end. We shall fight in France and on the seas and oceans; we shall fight with growing confidence and growing strength in the air. We shall defend our island whatever the cost may be; we shall fight on beaches, landing grounds, in fields, in streets and on the hills. We shall never surrender and even if, which I do not for the moment believe, this island or a large part of it were subjugated and starving, then our empire beyond the seas, armed and guarded by the British Fleet, will carry on the struggle until in God's good time the New World with all its power and might, sets forth to the liberation and rescue of the Old."

Winston Churchill
June 4, 1940 in a speech before the House of Commons

*

2) "We are tired of fighting, we are tired of being courageous, we are tired of winning, we are tired of defeating our enemies, we want that we will be able to live in an entirely different environment of relations with our enemies."

Ehud Olmert
June 9, 2005 in a speech to Israel Policy Forum in New York

This sort of attitude must be our RED LINE—we MUST NOT elect such a defeatist to be PM. Even this few weeks are already a disaster!

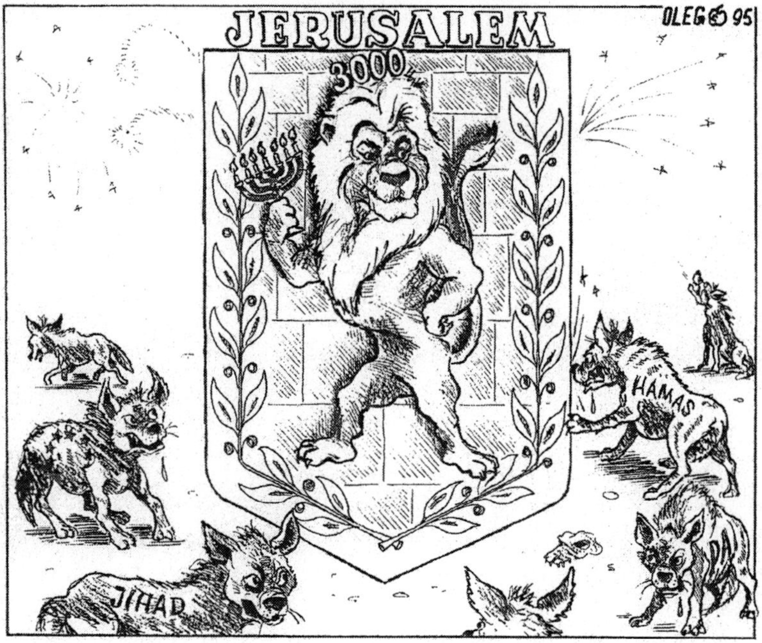
JERUSALEM
3000
OLEG 95
JIHAD
HAMAS

CHAPTER SIX: ARAB WARS OF EXTERMINATION AGAINST ISRAEL

Below is a list of the many wars that Israel has been forced to fight. This book is not a military history, but a political and strategical analysis of the struggle to save Israel. The reader should consult the bibliography for detailed books on the various wars.

ISRAEL HAS BEEN FORCED TO FIGHT A HUNDRED AND TWENTY YEAR WAR FOR SURVIVAL

1. Pre-state: Arab attacks on existing Jewish communities and Jewish resistance—1880's, 1921, 1929, 1936-9, 1947.

2. War of Independence (First Arab-Israeli War) 1948-9—Israel victorious but at the cost of 6000 killed.

3. Fedeyeen attacks—1949-56 & Israeli reprisals

4. Sinai Campaign—1956

5. Palestine Liberation Organization (PLO) formed and modern terrorist war begins against Israel—1964 (three years before so-called "occupied territories").

6. Six Day War—1967

7. War of Attrition at the Suez Canal—1969-70

8. Yom Kippur War—1973

9. International terrorism e.g. Entebbe—1976

10. Lebanese wars—1978 and Operation Peace For Galilee—1982

11. PLO/Hamas Intifada—1987-to present

12. Iraqi SCUD Attacks—1991

13. PLO/Labor/Meretz Peace Offensive—1992—War by

Appeasement and Deception

14. Israel War of Expulsion against the Jews of Gaza to please America and the Israeli Left—1995

15. Lebanese War—1996

16. Gaza—Operation Cast Lead—1996

17. Rocket, mortar attack from Gaza + continued terrorism to present day

Before Israelis make fateful decisions about the Golan and YESHA, they should read the following lecture I gave back in 1993. **The realities today are much more obvious and considerably worse.**

WILL THERE EVER BE TRUE PEACE

BETWEEN ISRAEL AND THE ARAB STATES?

(July 2002)

A Roman legionnaire stands on a hill overlooking Jerusalem. He watches the city burn and proclaims proudly, *"Judea capta est"*: Judea is destroyed. It will never rise again. Rome's rulers even decreed a change of name for Judea. Henceforth it would be named after the Philistines (or Palestine) and the Jewish connection would be obliterated forever.

Yet, like the legendary Phoenix rising from the ashes of its own destruction, the new nation of Israel burst onto the international scene in 1948, with the lusty cry of a newborn infant yearning to breathe free. Five Arab armies rushed to invade Israel and crush the life from the new Jewish State. With unbelievable bravery and heroism the new state survived. Six thousand of its young defenders gave their lives that Israel might live.

In blood and fire was Israel born, and on a hot anvil was she forged. Her youth understood that life in the new Jewish homeland would require sacrifice. With stories of burning flesh from the ovens of Auschwitz embedded deep in their psyches, the young Israeli soldiers fought with the firm conviction that there was **"no alternative"** (*ein brera*).

ISRAEL HAS BEEN FORCED TO FIGHT
A HUNDRED YEAR WAR FOR SURVIVAL

1. **Pre-state: Arab attacks** on existing Jewish communities and Jewish resistance—1921, 1929, 1936-9, and 1947.

2. **War of Independence** (First Arab-Israeli War) 1948-9—Israel victorious but at the cost of 6000 killed.

3. **Fedeyeen attacks**—1949-56 & Israeli reprisals

4. **Sinai Campaign**—1956

5. **Palestine Liberation Organization (PLO)** formed and modern terrorist war begins against Israel—1964 (three years before so-called "occupied territories").

6. **Six Day War**—1967

7. **War of Attrition** at the Suez Canal—1969-70

8. **Yom Kippur War**—1973

9. **International terrorism** e.g. Entebbe—1976

10. **Lebanese wars**—1978 and **Operation Peace For Galilee**—1982

11. **PLO/Hamas Intifada**—1987-to present

12. **Iraqi SCUD Attacks**—1991

13. **PLO/Labor/Meretz Peace Offensive**—1992—War by Appeasement and Deception

THIS ARAB / MOSLEM WAR AGAINST THE JEW IS NOT THE FIRST THAT THE JEWS HAVE FACED IN THEIR HISTORY

Our history unfortunately is filled with sad and traumatic episodes. In 1968, I bought a book entitled THE WAR AGAINST THE JEW by Dagobert Runes. This book documents the Christian persecution of the Jew throughout history. I mention this now, not to cast aspersions on modern day Christians, but to illustrate the nature and severity of the Jew's war for survival through the years. Runes writes: "No group or nation or alliance of nations in all known history has ever perpetuated on a hapless minority such sadistic atrocities over so long a time as the Christians have on the Jews. What the Germans did to six million Jews in the Second World War is only a continuation of long-established Christian bestiality toward the Jewish people, practiced by European Christians and especially the Catholic Church **EVERY DECADE OF EVERY CENTURY FOR THE LAST TWO THOUSAND YEARS."** Thankfully, most modern Christians have accepted the Jews and many are strong supporters of Israel.

As we struggle against the Arab and Moslem world, we find that a close connection exists between an old enemy, the Nazis, and our new enemy, the Arabs. Nazi anti-Semitic literature found wide acceptance in the Arab world before and after WWII. Haj Amin el-Husseini, the leader of the Palestine Arabs and Mufti of Jerusalem spent most of the War years in Berlin. He met with Hitler, Himmler and Eichmann and toured the gas chambers. He was so enthusiastic about the "final solution" that he lobbied Hitler personally to rid the Middle East of Jews after the war. Husseini suggested two death camps complete with gas chambers and crematoria: one near Haifa and the other near Tel Aviv, to carry out the "final solution" in Palestine. Husseini, also working for Hitler, organized the Bosnian Moslems into death squads which killed tens of thousands of Balkan Jews in the most brutal fashion possible, the details of which would sicken any audience.

IS PEACE POSSIBLE BETWEEN ISRAEL AND THE ARAB WORLD???

The answer is **YES**—But only after mind boggling changes in the Arab world. True peace can only be made after the Arab world undergoes democratization. Simply put, democracies rarely go to war with one another. All our major wars of the last two hundred years have been between dictators or between democracies defending themselves from dictators. When a ruler is elected by the people, he has a natural restraint preventing him from sending their sons and daughters into combat in an aggressive war. No such restraint exists anywhere in the Arab world.

The second major change required of the Arab/Moslem world is to create secular states not subservient to the rule of Islam. The problem for Israel with the rise of Islamic fundamentalism is the very hostile attitude that Islam has toward Jews and any non-Islamic person. Islam is all encompassing and guides behavior, law, religion and attitudes and relations with non-Moslems. Islam perceives the world as two separate parts:

1. The first is **Dar el-Islam**, or the World of Islam

2. All the rest is **Dar el-Harb**, or the world of the sword, or the world of war—that is those non-Muslim nations that have yet to be conquered.

The concept of **JIHAD**, or Holy War, has been understood by most of us, but there is another concept in the Koran with which few of us are familiar. But it is essential to understand this concept when relating to Moslems. That is the law of **HUDAIBIYA** which dates back to Muhammad and states clearly that "Muslims are permitted to lie and break agreements with non-Muslims." This applies to business, personal life and politics. Would a peace treaty be worth much if the other party is Moslem?

Islam divides the world between **Believers** and **Infidels**. Jews and Christians are relegated to the status of **Dhimmis**, or second class citizens. The Koran clearly calls on Moslems to degrade and humiliate both groups.

The Arab/Moslem world will have to develop a tradition of respect for women, minorities, and human rights in general before they will be ready for peace with Israel. It seems a bit odd that our State Department is pushing democracy and human rights from one end of the globe to the other—**WITH THE REMARKABLE EXCEPTION OF THE MIDDLE EAST**. Why are the Arabs insulated from pressure to democratize their societies?

It is obvious that no peace agreement would be worth anything with people believing in the above Islamic tenets, failing to practice democracy or show respect for minorities and human rights.

Israel's left-wing government headed by Yitzhak Rabin is engaged in a dangerous and ultimately fruitless effort to achieve peace with the Arabs through territorial concessions. A quick look at the map shows that the Arab world contains over 6 million square miles, compared to Israel's 10,840—or is roughly 547 times as great as Israel. Only a fool would believe that the way to peace in the Middle East is to give the Arabs more land. A look at history shows that the Arabs have tried to destroy Israel both before and after the 1967 war in which Israel acquired the land, giving it the secure borders it has now.

A quick reading of Arab statements on Israel reveals that their determination to destroy the Jewish state has not changed one iota. It was not by accident that the Palestine Liberation Organization was founded in 1964, three years before Israel controlled Judea, Samaria, and Gaza. Its National Covenant, its maps, its emblems, its stationery—all call for the liberation of Palestine from the Jordan to the Mediterranean.

The left-wing Jews in this country and in Israel, personified by the Peace Now movement and the Meretz Party, have given the Arabs a wonderful opportunity. Unable to conquer Israel by military means, they have succeeded in splitting Jewish ranks and spreading their propaganda about "peace in our time." The Arab victory plan is simply this: Seduce Israel into believing that peace is possible and get her to voluntarily give up her strategic territories in the Golan, Judea and Samaria. Once Israel's borders are narrow and vulnerable, terrorist raids and katyusha rockets will be used to terrorize the population.

Arab control of the Golan, and the mountains of Judea and Samaria, will allow them to cut off approximately 60% of Israel's water. Their positions on the high ground will allow them to eavesdrop and interfere with all Israeli telecommunications and radar. Large Arab standing armies can threaten to invade, causing Israel to mobilize its troops constantly—inflicting severe damage on its economy. Within years the Russian immigrants will stop coming to Israel because of the poor conditions. Native Israelis will become demoralized and begin emigrating in droves.

Finally, the Arabs will launch a surprise attack. Israel, lacking the buffer of the Golan and the mountains of Judea and Samaria, will be overrun. Most Jews will be killed, but some will escape thanks to American rescue ships. The US Congress will pass a resolution condemning the Arab attack and President Clinton will say Kadesh for Israel at a Washington synagogue. The UN will promptly condemn Israel for polluting the soil of Palestine with Jewish blood.

NOT A PRETTY PICTURE!—FORTUNATELY
THERE IS STILL TIME TO PREVENT IT FROM HAPPENING

Just like Hitler, who told the world of his ultimate aims in his book, <u>Mein Kampf</u>, the Arabs are not shy about telling us of their ultimate plans. The Islamic fundamentalists, like the Hamas movement or Islamic Jihad, want to destroy Israel in one stage. PLO has adopted a two-stage plan for Israel's destruction: first, get control of Judea and Samaria, and second, liberate the rest of Israel. Does this make the PLO "moderate"? Should we be negotiating our own demise with them?

Here is what the Palestinians say in their own words to their own people:

"I want to release a part of this Arab territory, and this cannot be done by war . . . Afterwards we would liberate the rest," Nabil Sha'at, Arafat's chief advisor in 1989.

Do you see his understanding of the need for a peace offensive with the aid of left-wing Jews and the US to force Israel's initial withdrawal?

Sha'at says later in 1989,

"If we achieve part of our territory, we will not relinquish our dream to establish one . . . state on all of Palestine."

PLO leader Abu Iyad says in 1988,

"The Palestinian state would be a skipboard from which we would be able to release Jaffa, Acre and all Palestine."

Later that same year Iyad says,

"The establishment of an independent Palestinian state on the West Bank and in the Gaza Strip does not contradict our ultimate strategic aim, which is the establishment of a democratic state in the whole territory of Palestine, but rather is a step in that direction."

The Battle for Eretz Yisrael

Yassir Arafat put it best when he said,

"The victory march will continue until the Palestinian flag flies in Jerusalem and in all of Palestine—from the Jordan River to the Mediterranean Sea and from Rosh Hanikra to Eilat."

Faisel Husseini, leader of the PLO and head of the negotiating team with Israel in Washington, is the nephew of Haj Amin Husseini the Mufti, mentioned earlier. Both he and Arafat consider the activities of the Mufti during WWII as heroic and in the best Arab tradition. And both claim all of Israel as their country—in their National Covenant, on their stationery, emblems and symbols.

DOES THAT SOUND LIKE "PEACE IN OUR TIME?"

Benjamin Netanyahu, in his new book <u>A PLACE AMONG THE NATIONS,</u> a wonderful book you all should read, writes about the peace of deterrence. That is: the peace resulting from Israeli strength both in its army and in strategic territory. He says, and I agree, that we must dig in our heels and remain steadfast, patiently waiting for our neighbors to accept and respect us on our present borders. Peace treaties reflect strategic realities. If Israel is weak, no treaty will protect it. He tells the sad story of how Czechoslovakia was forced to give up the strategic territory of the Sudetenland for "peace in our time" by Chamberlain at Munich in 1938. Netanyahu warns that the drive by the Labor Party to give up the Golan, Judea, Samaria and Gaza will have similar catastrophic results.

But, you ask, what are we to do with the Arabs who live in those areas, who are clearly unhappy with Israeli rule? I believe they should have control over their municipal affairs but not over the land of Judea, Samaria and Gaza. The Labor Party seems to be in a mad rush to give up Jewish claims to this part of Eretz Yisrael. Rabin's Labor Party should pay attention to the words of its founder and father of modern Israel, **David Ben Gurion,** who said, **"No Jew has the right to relinquish the right of the Jewish people over the whole Land of Israel. No Jewish body has such authority, not even the whole Jewish people have the authority to waive the right (to the Land of Israel) for future generations for all time."**

The Arabs who wish to live in peace with their Jewish neighbors are welcome. They can even manage their own civil and municipal affairs.

THOSE, HOWEVER, WHO WISH TO TAKE UP THEIR GUNS AND KNIVES TO KILL JEWS OR THROW ROCKS TO CRUSH JEWISH SKULLS, MUST BE DESTROYED OR DRIVEN FROM THE LAND OF ISRAEL. Rabbinical authorities have long recognized the ultimate religious priority of saving Jewish lives. For example, the Israeli army is permitted to operate fully on Shabbat because it is necessary to save Jewish lives.

Too many Jews are obsessed with what will satisfy the Arabs. I doubt if there is a single Palestinian or Moslem anywhere who worries about what is good for Israel or the Jewish People. We must remember the words of Hillel when he said, **"If I am not for myself, who will be for me? And if I am for myself alone, what am I?"** Hillel's message is clear: First, take care of yourself, your family and your people, and then try to help others.

Remember, it took the Christian world two thousand years to accept us as human beings, and this only after the mass murder of a third of our people. It may take the Arabs a while, maybe decades—but we have no choice but to be patient. The fact that we want peace badly does not mean that it is attainable. To strip Israel of strategic territory, like Czechoslovakia before WWII, in the pursuit of a phantom illusory peace will only lead to disaster.

Some Jews, in the face of all empirical evidence to the contrary, believe peace is possible. In the book <u>Self Portrait Of A Hero: The Letters of Jonathan Netanyahu (1963-1976)</u>, **Jonathan Netanyahu,** the fallen hero of Entebbe and brother of Benjamin, said it best:

"I see with sorrow and great anger how a part of the people still clings to hopes of reaching a peaceful settlement with the Arabs. Common sense tells them, too, that the Arabs haven't abandoned their basic aim of destroying the State; but the self-delusion and self-deception that have always plagued the Jews are at work again. It's our great misfortune. They want to believe, so they believe. They want not to see, so they shut their eyes. They want not to learn from thousands of years of history, so they distort it. They want to bring about a

sacrifice, and they do indeed. It would be comic, if it wasn't so tragic. What a saddening and irritating lot this Jewish people are!"

In our **Holy Scriptures** we read about the prophet Jeremiah. Jeremiah, who anguished over the fact that his people believed in false prophets of peace and didn't see the dangers facing Israel, cries out in despair, **"Peace, peace but there is no peace."**

I am sorry that I cannot offer you more encouraging words. What I present is:

A HARSH REALITY

We all want peace. We pray for peace in our Sabbath services every Friday night. After thousands of years, being **victims of persecution, expulsion, extermination, and discrimination,** it is natural that we yearn for peace with every ounce of our bodies and souls.

It is because our hunger for peace is so strong that we must be doubly cautious not to fall for a **pseudo-peace** that is really the wolf of war wrapped in sheep's clothing. Today none of us believe Chamberlain really negotiated **"peace in our time"** with Hitler. (Why do some Jews believe that Peres and Rabin really negotiated PEACE **with Arafat, one of today's Hitlers?)**

Israelis my age have fought and died in four wars and I understand their desire to be free of constant conflict. **Unfortunately, there is no magic cure.** I wish I could write more optimistic words. Sadly, beyond the neighboring states that Israel is negotiating with now lies another ring of **unmitigated hostility** led by Islamic fundamentalists in Iran.

As Jews we are all involved in this historic struggle to survive. It is not our fate or that of the Israelis that we should retire from this struggle. The only peace the Arabs are prepared to give us is the **peace of the grave.**

In blood and fire was Israel born and on a hot anvil was she forged. The brave young soldiers of Israel must take a quick glance back to the crematoria of Auschwitz and then go forth to face the enemy knowing that there is <u>STILL</u> **no alternative (*ein briera*).**

[This article was a lecture by Bernard J. Shapiro as part of the Torah Learning College, Congregation Beth Yeshurun, Houston, June 23, 1993. This article was published on August 16, 1993 in the *Jewish Herald-Voice*, in Houston, in the Maccabean Online, and in the Freemanlist (daily e-mail subscriber list). It was reissued in the Maccabean Online in May 1997, April 2000, July 2002, and October-November 2005.]

ARABS' ATTITUDES TOWARD ISRAEL

Has There Been Progress Since Oslo?

(March 1995)

A year and a half ago, I released a statement (*Jewish Herald-Voice*, September 2, 1993) on the Oslo "peace" process in which I said: " . . . the rush to embrace the Palestine Liberation Organization (PLO) is both foolish and ultimately dangerous . . . . it is a trap for Israel . . . the PLO has violated and trampled on every agreement it has ever made during its nearly 30-year history." I concluded: "Despite the media hype surrounding these developments, let me make something very clear: a leopard does not change its spots. You can say a *berachah* (blessing) over a ham sandwich, but that doesn't make it kosher. And a deal with the PLO is like a dance on quicksand—before you realize it, you have sunk into the muck and slime."

Events have proven that the statement above was accurate to an almost uncanny degree. Some have tried to paint a different picture of events in Israel. A massive documented report on PLO violations of the Oslo Agreement was compiled by Col. David Yahav, Assistant Chief Military Judge's advocate for International Law, and turned over to the Israeli government on December 13, 1994. This report shows deliberate and systematic violations of the Oslo Agreement by the PLO. As serious as the violations were, the Israeli reaction to it was equally serious. Israeli Foreign Minister Shimon Peres successfully suppressed the report and even denied its existence before the Foreign Affairs and Defense Committee of the Knesset. It was only in February of 1995 that MK Benie Begin leaked the full text of the document. While some of the facts contained in the report had appeared in local newspapers, it is the full text that is so damning. It demonstrates beyond any doubt the total disrespect in which the PLO held both the Oslo Agreement and their "partner in peace" the Israelis.

The real question is: Why have Israeli government leaders, including Peres, tried to suppress this report and prevent the Israeli public from acquiring this information? The answer, though disturbing, is quite simple: The reality of the post-Oslo period does not conform to the government's predictions and promises. If reality is not favorable to the "peace" process, then myth and fantasy must become paramount. The government has developed a universe of "smoke and mirrors" to hide the truth from the Israeli people. This fantasy universe has many components. Israeli leaders travel frequently to many countries, including Arabs countries previously forbidden to them. Photo ops appear in all the papers almost every day. Peres is with one world leader after another and in every place the "peace" process is praised. Government-controlled Israeli television is told not to cover opposition demonstrations; not to report attacks on Jews unless there is loss of life; not to interview or feature opposition spokespersons. The government has developed a whole vocabulary of **newspeak** (Orwellian term referring to words that mean the opposite or not what they seem). Jews killed in terrorist attacks are called "sacrifices for peace," as if their deaths serve some purpose. Opponents of the Oslo Agreement are labeled "enemies of peace," while terrorists are now labeled Islamic Fundamentalists, so that they will not be confused with the "good Palestinians."

There is a problem with the government campaign to obscure reality. It won't work. Reality has a way of imposing its will even on the most dedicated devotee of fantasy. The bombing near Netanya a few weeks ago in which 21 young soldiers were killed had a very sobering effect on most Israelis. And it was not just the murder and mayhem that made the Israelis change their attitude toward the "peace" process. The Palestinian reaction outraged many. The deaths of the Jewish soldiers brought out the true character of the Arab enemy. In Gaza there was a mass celebration in which condolences were shouted to the suicide bombers: ". . . Condolences to the heroes of the killing of 20 pigs and injuring of 60 monkeys." The family of one of the perpetrators issued a statement reading: "We take pride in the martyrdom of our son, who carried out a daring operation, thus becoming worthy of G-d's words."

One of the most enduring fantasies encouraged by the government is that the Arabs are changing their attitude toward Israel and the Jews. The official line is that we cannot expect full acceptance immediately, but that a process of reconciliation has begun and needs to be encouraged. Like the other myths of the "peace" process, this one falls in the face of reality. Following the terrorist attack at Beit Lid (near Netanya) the Palestine Center for Public Opinion surveyed Palestinians in the territories and discovered that 53% supported such attacks against Israelis (34% opposed, 13% no opinion).

PLO leader Yassir Arafat said the following on January 1, 1995 at a celebration of "Fatah Day": "We are all suicide-bombers, and I say to the martyrs and the suicide-bombers who already . . . Our sworn oath (to liberate Palestine) is still standing and it is still our obligation to continue the revolution." The Associated Press (January 23, 1995) reported the words of Sheik Abdullah Sham, spiritual leader of Islamic Jihad: "It is open war between us and the Israelis . . . The solution lies in the uprooting of the problem . . . the state of Israel . . . The Jihad (holy war) against the enemy will continue.

This rejection of Israel, despite its major concessions at Oslo, pervades the whole Arab world. Even in Jordan, where the "peace" is supposed to be more evident, we find the opposite. On February 13th, *El Quds* reported that the Jordanian Lawyers Association was enforcing a boycott of Israel, including *Palestinian* lawyers who had appeared before Israeli courts. On January 23rd the Chairman of the Israel Chamber of Commerce went to Amman hoping to meet his Jordanian counterpart. The Jordanian refused to meet him. Fahri Kawar, Secretary of the Union of Arab Writers, put it clearly: "Opposition to normalization with the enemy is a general national obligation which must be maintained in all fields." Muanes Elrazaz, head of the Association of Jordanian Writers, recently said: "The struggle is not just against Israel, rather the racist Zionist movement. This movement has tremendous international power . . . it controls most of the Western media." Nazia Abu Nidal: "The Zionist Jews who failed to establish normal ties with anyone in the course of two thousand years won't succeed in doing this with the Arabs . . . The Jewish Shylock will try to turn the Arabs into servants and workers for the Hebrew state and the chosen people." Dr. Hashem Rasib recently stated: "Those who favor normalization with the Zionist enemy . . . (forget that) The Zionists and Israel do not have a defined national culture. They represent the most racist and reactionary trends in the West which are the most inhuman and fascist. Our relations are one of struggle." Newspaperman Muhamed Harub: "I strongly oppose normalization, which is based on erasing the entire history of our continued struggle against Zionism."

Israel has had a "peace" agreement with Egypt for over 15 years, so if the process of reconciliation were to take place, it should have manifested itself there. Unfortunately, Egyptian hostility to Israel has been quite obvious to everyone except members of Israel's Foreign Ministry. In March 1994, Dr. Ahmed Zaree of Egypt's Al Azhar University completed a five-year study of university graduates and post-graduates, ages 30-35, who were in college when the Israeli-Egyptian peace treaty was signed. The study found that 92.8% regarded Israel as an expansionist, aggressive state headed by terrorists, fanatics and liars. Over 63% said that normalization of relations with Israel would constitute a major threat to national security.

In conclusion, it seems clear that there has been no change in the very negative Arab attitudes toward Israel. It is also clear that the Israeli government's attempt to hide this fact from the Israeli people will fail as myth runs headlong into reality. It is obvious that the very real and major concessions made by Israel to resolve its 100-year war with the Arabs have failed to accomplish that task. In fact, the concessions have whetted the appetite of the Arabs and their Jewish supporters for more serious concessions. At two One-Day Conferences held recently at Haifa University and at Tel Aviv University, Jewish leftists and Arab speakers appeared, calling for a "revolutionary" change in Jewish-Arab relations. Among the proposals raised were:

1. Abolishing Israel's Declaration of Independence.

2. Its replacement by a "New Accord" between Israel's Arabs and the State of Israel.

3. In this New Accord it will be stated that:

A. The Law of Return is Abolished.

B. All refugees from 1948 will be allowed to return from Lebanon and Syria to their original homes.

C. Return of all Arabs living within Israel who were forced out of their original villages to those homes (they mean Biram and Ikrit and others). All in all, this would involve 250,000 people.

D. Return of all lands in the Galilee that have been expropriated for public purposes to their Arab owners.

E. Abolishing the Israeli flag and its replacement by one without a Star of David.

F. Abolishing Hatikva as the national anthem, and its replacement by an anthem that does not threaten Arabs.

G. Abolishing the definition of Israel as a Jewish State and declaring it as a State of all its inhabitants.

H. Paying of reparations to Palestinian Arabs by the Jewish people (sort of like German reparations?) because of the theft of their property and their suffering throughout the 47 years of the existence of Israel. This because the State of Israel was created through an act of aggression by the Zionist Movement against Palestinians, one of whose aims was the expulsion of Arabs.

This is where the "so called peace" process is heading. *If you were on a train headed for Auschwitz and learned about what lay ahead—wouldn't you try to get off the train?* It is past time for Israelis to get off the Labor train.

[This article was published in the Jewish Herald-Voice on March 1, 1995 and the March 1995 issue of THE MACCABEAN. It was reissued in the Maccabean Online in May 1997.]

ISRAEL'S VIRTUAL SURRENDER

TO ARAFAT—

Some Observations

(December 2000)

1. It is apparent to many people that, despite his exalted military career, Prime Minister Ehud Barak is showing cowardice in the face of Palestinian attacks during the current war. While IDF soldiers and officers certainly are personally brave in the face of the enemy, Israel's political leadership is indecisive and non-aggressive. I ask you: When in Israel's military history did its forces not attack and occupy enemy positions from where live fire was coming? Only today is the IDF entangled with rules that prevent its ability to defeat the enemy decisively. The failure to engage the enemy with force and aggressiveness has led to a massive loss of deterrence on the part of Israel.

2. The repeated cease-fire talks with U.S. President Bill Clinton have made the Israelis look like a "banana republic" as well as fools for expecting Arafat's signature on an agreement to mean something tangible.

3. The level of lying on the part of the Palestinians about Arafat's war is an indicator of how unreasonable and "anti-peace" they really are.

4. It is clear to me that Barak is using Arafat's war for the purpose of causing the Jews of YESHA to evacuate their homes. This to save himself the difficulty of personally taking charge of the ethnic cleansing of Jews from the area. He has already given the green light to Arafat by his actions in not suppressing the war.

5. Barak's giveaways at Camp David should have brought down his government, yet he still rules. I am very disappointed at this. Where is the nationalist camp?

6. There is talk of international observers for YESHA. This would be a great victory of Arafat and justify his war against Israel. The Israeli response

should be a deafening no. From experience of 52 years, we all know that the UN, its bodies, and all International Forces are biased against Israel and in the pocket to the Arabs. The only purpose of such a plan would be to diminish Israel's rightful sovereignty in the area.

7. Barak's constant warnings and threats, for which he never acts, further reduce Israeli deterrence.

8. Allowing the news media to photograph teenagers throwing stones is bad for Israel's image. It is well know that these very same photographers avoid taking pictures of Palestinian gunfire. The print journalists avoid references to live fire from the Palestinian side. Many rioters wait for journalists to arrive before rioting. It is past time to remove journalists from the areas of clashes.

9. Oslo and Camp David must be terminated with extreme prejudice.

10. Israel must annex immediately areas B and C leaving the Palestinians with only A for now. Then the Palestinians must be told that those who engage in hostile activity against Israel will be expelled from the country. If hostility is widespread then the entire population should make a new home in Jordan.

IS PEACE POSSIBLE?

(April 2001)

Great issues of war and peace as related to Israel are being debated by Jews across America. Israelis are debating the same issues among themselves. There are strong opinions on both sides of the Atlantic as well as both sides of the major issues. What seems to be lacking in all these discussions is the proper historical context. Professor Paul Eidelberg of Bar-Ilan University reviews the historical facts.

Between 1945 and 1978 the longest time without a war going on someplace was a mere 26 days. On an *average* day there are 12 wars being fought somewhere on earth. The consensus of scholars has been that the norm of international relations is not peace but war. As Eidelberg reports, "Indeed, the occurrence of 1,000 wars during the last 2,500 years indicates that "*peace*" is little more than a preparation for war. Which means that *peace treaties* are WORTHLESS, to say the least."

Eidelberg then quotes from a book by Lawrence Beilenson, entitled THE TREATY TRAP, saying, "After studying every peace treaty going back to early Roman times, Beilenson concludes that treaties are made to be broken. In fact, he shows that treaties for guaranteeing the territorial integrity of a nation are useless to the guaranteed nation and worse than useless insofar as they engender a false sense of security. Such treaties can only benefit nations governed by rulers intending to violate them whenever expedient."

Midge Dector says this about "peace":

What I want to say is something that virtually the whole history of the 20th century teaches us and yet something we refuse to learn. And that is, when applied to the affairs of nations, peace is an evil word. Yes I said evil. And the idea of peace as we know it is an evil idea. From the peace of Versailles to "peace in our time" at Munich . . . each declaration of peace or expressions of longing for peace ended in slaughter. Not necessarily immediately and not necessarily directly, but slaughter all the same . . .

The Battle for Eretz Yisrael

For there is no such thing as making peace. Nations who are friendly do not need to do so, and nations or people who are hostiles cannot do so.

To cry peace, peace when there is no peace, the prophet Jeremiah taught us long ago, is not the expression of hope, not even superstition but a reckless toying with the minds and hearts of people whose very future depends on their capacity to rise every day to the harsh morning light of the truth.

On September 3, 1993, I wrote the following:

"The rush of events in the Middle East has been dizzying. The media hype, the talking heads, the worldwide expectations of peace in the Middle East is all quite staggering. Radio, TV, newspapers herald the coming of a new era of reconciliation between Israelis and Palestinians. The positive images are so abundant that any moment one might expect to see Isaiah on Nightline showing Ted Koppel video clips of lions lying down with lambs . . . . Despite the media hype surrounding Oslo, let me make something very clear: A leopard does not change its spots. And you can say a *berachaha* (Hebrew blessing) over a ham sandwich, but that doesn't make it kosher. And a deal with the PLO is like a dance on quicksand—before you realize it, you have sunk into the muck and slime."

On May 18, 1994, I wrote:

On May 17, 1994, in Johannesburg, Yassir Arafat called for a *"jihad* (holy war) until Jerusalem is restored to Moslem rule." He said this after undertaking many peaceful commitments since September, and after signing the Declaration of Principles in Washington and the Autonomy Agreement in Cairo. He also chose to draw a parallel between the Gaza-Jericho Agreement, which he signed with Israel, and the Hudaibiya Pact signed in 628 by the Prophet Muhammad with the leaders of the Quraysh tribe. Muhammad violated the agreement two years later and it has become a symbol for the Islamic principle that agreements and treaties with non-Moslems may be violated at will. There is a lesson for us all in this event.

On June 22, 1995, 'MA'ARIV' finally saw the truth:

Bernard J. Shapiro

"There is a growing impression that we are caught up in a mania (Oslo) to withdraw from all of the key positions that have ensured our existence up until now, without receiving anything appropriate in return."

IS PEACE POSSIBLE BETWEEN ISRAEL AND THE ARAB WORLD???

Only when the Arab/Moslem world is to create secular states not subservient to the rule of Islam. The problem for Israel with the rise of Islamic fundamentalism is the very hostile attitude that Islam has toward Jews and any non-Islamic person. Islam is all encompassing and guides behavior, law, religion and attitudes and relations with non-Moslems. Islam perceives the world as two separate parts:

1. The first is *Dar el-Islam* or the World of Islam.

2. All the rest is *Dar el-Harb* or the world of the sword or the world of war—that is those non-Muslim nations that have yet to be conquered.

The concept of *JIHAD* or Holy War has been understood by most of us but there is another concept in the Koran with which few of us are familiar. But it is essential to understand this concept when relating to Moslems. That is the law of *HUDAIBIYA* which dates back to Muhammad and states clearly that "Muslims are permitted to lie and break agreements with non-Muslims." This applies to business, personal life and politics. Would a peace treaty be worth much if the other party is Moslem?

Islam divides the world between Believers and Infidels. Jews and Christians are relegated to the status of *Dhimmis* or second class citizens. The Koran clearly calls on Moslems to degrade and humiliate both groups.

HITLER AND THE ARABS

(Abridged from an article by Jan Willem van der Hoeven which appears in this issue.)

"Hitler, Goebbels, Goering and the rest of the Nazis, inadequate to a man, were both pathological and pragmatic liars. They lied so convincingly and so hugely that most statesmen from other countries could not believe that what they were hearing was a lie . . . One of Hitler's biggest lies was constantly to assure the world of peaceful intentions while obviously planning war by building up massively strong armed forces." [John Laffin, 'Hitler warned us.']

Anis Mansour, editor of the Egyptian paper October and a Sadat confidant who accompanied the Egyptian leader to Jerusalem wrote: "The World is now aware of the fact that Hitler was right, and that the cremation ovens were the appropriate means of punishing [the Jews]."

Hitler's book, Mein Kampf, is still required reading in various Arab capitals and universities, and is widely distributed by others.

Samuel Katz writes in The Hollow Peace:

"The Arab attitude is pointedly and incisively expressed in modern Arabic literature, which is chock-full of unbridled hatred of Israel, of Zionism and of the Jewish people. The idea of the destruction of Israel is expressed in hundreds of books published on the subject of the 'dispute' itself, and anti-Israeli and anti-Zionist teaching has even been incorporated in school text-books, even, improbably enough, in arithmetic books."

The only reason that the Arabs have not yet done to the Israeli Jews what Hitler did to their forefathers in Europe is that they have thus far lacked the military means and weapons of mass destruction which were at Hitler's disposal, to do so.

That the Arabs have not done so to date has not been due to any reluctance on their part, but because, this time, there has been this difference: The Jews in Europe had no army to defend them. Thank G-d, the Jews in Israel have!

This deeply entrenched hatred of the Jews and love for Hitler and the Nazis surfaced during the time of one of the first Palestinian leaders, the Grand Mufti Haj Amin el Husseini, during the 1930's.

It is evident in what the Mufti said on Berlin radio while he was Hitler's guest in Germany. His words prove that there was total agreement between the Palestinian leader and this murderer of G-d's people:

"Kill the Jews—kill them with your hands, kill them with your teeth—this is well pleasing to Allah!"

<u>May Israel be wiser in relation to this death wish of her neighbors, than the Jews in Europe were. They belittled the writings and speeches of Hitler and the Nazis and were massacred as a result. May it not happen again!</u>

ARAFAT AS ENEMY

Dr. Aaron Lerner reports on March 15 that the Ramallah terror cell responsible for 8 murders and was prevented from blowing up a car bomb inside Jerusalem. The closure imposed on Ramallah that was the brunt of media criticism prevented them from achieving their objective. The group was coordinated by none other than Mahmoud Damra, the head of Force 17 in Ramallah.

Force 17 is not a Hamas force. It is not a group far beyond Arafat's sphere of influence. Force 17 is Arafat's own elite CIA trained presidential guard. The terrorist cell is also believed to be tied to Fatah leader Marwan Barghouti.

So much for the spin that Barghouti and other so-called "loose cannons" are responsible for terrorism. These terrorists aren't "loose cannons"—they are part of a terrorist force being coordinated by Arafat's most tightly controlled group.

This is where the left went wrong. They believed that you could make peace with your enemies by being nice, making concessions, and in every way appeasing their demands. Yet they immediately forgot that these people were just that: the enemy.

Dr. Lerner says the following": You can sit for hours and days in "dialog" with an enemy. You can share tons of humus and pitas and talk about your families etc. But that still does not mean that the person you are sitting with is any less an enemy.

In a way, it is the greatest insult one can give to the Palestinians to think that just because a Jew is willing to shake their hands and share a meal that this will change their goals. Their program to destroy Israel with a state of Palestine from the river to the sea.

The Israeli leftists were convinced that the post-dialogue terrorist leaders did not warrant the respect due an enemy devoted to our destruction. As a result, these Israeli leaders made no serious effort to address the security disaster that Oslo was creating.

Arafat is in fact the enemy and not a victim of loose cannons and therefore a new security policy must be introduced. The Palestinians are an enemy armed with anti-aircraft and anti-tank missiles, armored cars, mortar launchers, etc. It takes action to significantly neutralize that enemy force. To destroy their weapons store, their bunkers, their strategic positions.

Israel's leaders must talk today of destroying the terrorist infrastructure they must recognize that the most dangerous and powerful and significant "terrorist infrastructure" inside the Palestinian Autonomy is Yasser Arafat's own web of armed forces.

A HARSH REALITY

We all want peace. We pray for peace in our Sabbath services every Friday night. After thousands of years, being victims of persecution, expulsion, extermination, and discrimination, it is natural that we yearn for peace with every ounce of our bodies and souls.

It is because our hunger for peace is so strong that we must be doubly cautious not to fall for a pseudo-peace that is really the wolf of war wrapped in sheep's clothing. Today none of us believe Chamberlain really negotiated "peace in our time" with Hitler. Why do some Jews believe that Peres and Rabin really negotiated PEACE with Arafat, one of today's Hitlers?

Israelis my age have fought in four wars and I understand their desire to be free of constant conflict. Unfortunately there is no magic cure. I wish I could write more optimistic words. Beyond the neighboring states that Israel is negotiating with now lies another ring of unmitigated hostility led by Islamic fundamentalists like those in Iran.

As Jews we are all involved in this historic struggle to survive. It is not our fate or that of the Israelis that we should retire from this struggle. The only peace the Arabs are prepared to give us is the peace of the grave.

In blood and fire was Israel born and on a hot anvil was she forged. The brave young soldiers of Israel must take a quick glance back to the crematoria of Auschwitz and then go forth to face the enemy knowing that there is <u>still</u> no alternative (*ein briera*).

THE BOTTOM LINE

THE OSLO ACCORDS: A FAILURE—PEACE IMPOSSIBLE NOW

1. Giving world recognition to a terrorist organization as a representative of a legitimate national entity.

2. Terrorism—almost 600 killed thousands maimed and injured.

3. Armed Palestinian force in the heart of Judea, Samaria, and Gaza.

4. Incitement against Jews, Nazi like Anti-Semitism on PA TV, sermons, newspapers and in schools.

5. Arafat supports massive violence and terrorism against Jews and turns his back on promise of negotiations for peace.

6. Potential loss of strategic territory.

7. Loss of water resources.

8. Greatly divided Israel when unity was necessary to face the Arab threat.

9. And finally, the Arab/Muslim world rejects a Jewish state in their midst for deeply held cultural, religious and anti-Semitic reasons.

10. A victory for post-Zionism and a decline in Israeli patriotism.

March 1954

In considering complaints of the murder of Israel citizens, Colonel Hutchison, chairman of the Israel-Jordan Truce Commission, displays an outright pro-Arab bias.

I'VE NO IDEA WHO IT IS OR WHERE HE COULD BE...

Dry Bones

THE HAMAS WAR AGAINST THE JEWS IS A WAKE-UP CALL FOR US ALL. BOOM

AND LIKE ANY WAKE-UP CALL, THE FIRST REACTION IS TO ATTEMPT TO IGNORE IT AND GO BACK TO SLEEP

BUT WE KNOW THAT IF WE DON'T WAKE UP AND STOP IT NOW... IT'LL GO OFF AGAIN. BOOM

AND AGAIN BOOM AND AGAIN BOOM ...UNTIL WE DO!

KIRSCHEN
Cartoonists & Writers Syndicate

September 13, 1993

Different aspirations of our "peace" leaders.

CHAPTER SEVEN: MILITARY AND STRATEGIC ISSUES: RESISTANCE TO APPEASEMENT

The chapter covers basic concepts that are essential for defending Israel. It shows how much was learned in the past and much that is not applied at the present. The Israel Defense Forces (IDF) concept of rapid advance into enemy territory is still relevant. Unfortunately, this concept has been very modified by a false morality and desire show great restraint. Israel gets no international credit for its restraint and suffers increased losses among its own troops.

There is another factor of extreme importance. When Israel goes into battle and fails to fully destroy its enemy, the stage is set for another war a few years later. This causes repeated wars and many more casualties on both sides than a complete victory would have caused. By failing to annihilate the Arab terrorist enemy, Israel gives them the illusion that they can succeed the *next* time in their plans to exterminate the Jews of Israel.

In Israel's early military campaigns, the element of surprise, boldness and audacity were very evident. Now there seems to be a holding back to avoid international condemnation. For example, Iran's nuclear plants should have been attacked long ago. As time passes, the operation gets more difficult as Iran strengthens its defenses both underground and with missiles.

There are several principles that should guide the IDF. These come from several classical sources: Lao Tzu (The Art of War), Machiavelli (The Prince), Clauswitz (On War) and of course Jewish sources. Both Lao Tzo and Machiavelli believe in deception and guile as a tool of war. Clauswitz calls it "diplomacy." Whatever you call it, Israel has been losing this battle to the Arabs despite its spectacular military victories.

"He who is merciful when he should be cruel will in the end be cruel when he should be merciful." . . . **Midrash Samuel (Jewish rabbinic text from early Middle Ages)**

The quote above means that the IDF should not worry so much about civilian casualties when it fights the enemy. Did the Allies in WWII care about civilians when they burned Dresden or Hiroshima? Should the IDF attack with massive force, then victory would be quick and end result would less death and injury on both sides.

THE MILITARY BALANCE 1993

The Freeman Center Targets Jaffee

(Relates to the origin of the Freeman Center)

Last week, at a press conference, Joseph Alpher, director of the Jaffee Center For Strategic Studies, announced the publication of their new edition of "The Military Balance 1992-1993." The Jaffee Center is a part of Tel Aviv University and is highly respected in Labor and Meretz Party circles. The first "Military Balance" I read was the 1984 edition and I have kept up with the later editions.

I first met Alpher at an AIPAC meeting about two years ago, later learning that he was rumored to be a former Mossad agent. That meeting was quite stormy, as I disputed most of his analyses of Middle East politics, especially his statement that Syrian dictator Hafez Asad was ready for peace with Israel. Alpher rejected a proposal of mine to do a "Pro/Con" type commentary format in the Jewish Herald-Voice (Houston) and other papers. Although he turned me down, my meeting with him had positive results. It became clear to me that Alpher had access to massive amounts of information, yet could not prevent the politicization of his analysis and conclusions. I founded the Freeman Center For Strategic Studies primarily to provide the American Jewish Community with an alternative source of strategic information, free of political bias.

The new "**Military Balance 1992-1993**" continues this process of politicization. While I have not yet received it from Israel, the press releases alone are enough for great worry. This is the first time in more than a decade that the government of Israel has been in sync (politically) with the Jaffee Center. Israeli Prime Minister Yitzhak Rabin will no doubt use its findings to justify his drive for territorial retreat.

Following is a comparison between the Jaffee analysis of the Middle East and that of the Freeman Center:

Jaffee Center: Israel should open negotiations with the PLO.

Freeman Center: No to negotiations with the PLO. No to the concept that the PLO is moderate. The PLO seeks to destroy Israel in two stages. First, cause Israel to withdraw from its secure borders. Second, to use the new Palestinian foothold to complete the destruction of the Jewish State.

Jaffee: Israel should withdraw from the security zone in Lebanon because it is not big enough to stop Katyusha attacks anyway and its purpose was to stop infiltration. The security zone encourages attacks in the first place since it represents a foreign power on Lebanese soil. Syria and Lebanon can control the border area.

Freeman: The security zone was designed to contain the minimum of Lebanese territory for the maximum benefit in both the battles against infiltration and rocket attacks. With a range of 12 miles, the Katyusha could reach only one major Israeli population center, Kiryat Shmona. Just before the new round of fighting in Northern Israel, large Iranian cargo planes were observed off-loading at Damascus airport new high tech weapons for the Hezbollah. The weapons were put on Syrian military trucks and shipped to the Beeka valley in Lebanon and distributed to the Islamic fundamentalists (Party of God and Hezbollah). Included in the weapons were the Sagger anti-tank missiles, which took the lives of several Israeli soldiers, and a new improved Katyusha, capable of reaching targets 16 miles away with increased accuracy.

Eliminating the security zone would place virtually the whole Galilee within range of the new Katyusha, including such cities as Acre and Nahariya. Rabin had three choices in the current fighting: 1. Enlarge the security zone to cope with the new range of the new Katyusha, 2. Pummel Southern Lebanon into submission with massive artillery barrages, or 3. A search and destroy land operation. He chose the second option because the political consequences of occupying additional Lebanese territory far outweighed the benefits and a land operation would be too costly in Israeli lives. The Jaffee Center calls Rabin's shelling of southern Lebanon "excessive." The Freeman Center has always called for exacting the maximum penalty for the taking of Jewish lives. The Arabs must learn that there is a high price for the shedding of Jewish blood.

As for the Jaffee view that withdrawal from the security zone would take away the motive for Hezbollah attacks, the answer is simple. Why is there a security zone in the first place? Have the professionals at Jaffee forgotten what life was like in Northern Israel before the security zone? Can Syria and Lebanon keep peace on the Lebanese border? Of course they can. Don't forget that it was the supply of arms through Syria that started the current fighting. The Syrians get no credit in my book for ***temporarily stopping*** actions that cost Jewish lives. When it serves their purpose, the killing will begin again.

Jaffee: It is clear that a real advance in the peace process cannot be obtained without massive American involvement.

Freeman: While we appreciate the American interest in peace in the Middle East, we recognize two indisputable facts: 1. American geopolitical and economic interests and those of Israel are not identical though they converge in many areas 2. The traditional hostility to Israeli interests in the United States State Department remains a barrier to fair mediation between the Arabs and the Israelis by the US. At the Freeman Center we go beyond these factors and demand that any agreements be arrived at directly and independent of pressure from any party, including America. There is no nation in the world which would allow another to determine great issues of security and survival.

The very suggestion by the Jaffee Center of such American intervention belies an emasculated concept of Israeli sovereignty. One is reminded of the "court Jews" of medieval Europe groveling at the feet of their royal benefactors, seeking protection for their helpless Jewish kinsmen. When Herzl, the founder of modern Zionism, dreamed of the future Jewish State, it was a dream of proud Jews on an equal footing with all the nations of the world. When Jabotinzky founded the first modern Jewish army, which later became the Haganah, he did not anticipate that the future Jewish State would take orders from any nation. The nearly 20,000 Israelis who gave their lives defending the independence and security of their country would cry out from the grave if they knew of plans to turn Israel into a "banana republic" subservient to America. That sad result is inevitable if Israel accepts American intervention and security guarantees.

Jaffee: There is a limited amount of time to achieve peace, the so called "window of opportunity," and we should therefore move to the final arrangements and skip the interim agreement with the Palestinians.

Freeman: We conclude that there is no "window of opportunity" and that the concept enunciated by former President George Bush is a hoax similar to his "New World Order." There is a "window" but it is not for peace. Former Secretary of State James Baker promised his Arab allies in the Persian Gulf War that if they helped him against Iraq, HE (Baker) would help them force Israel to retreat to its 1967 borders. The so called "peace process" is an outgrowth of that promise by Baker. Peace was not a part of the promise—but a forced amputation of Israel's secure borders was to be labeled "peace." With regard to the negotiations with the Palestinians, the interim agreement is of extreme importance and cannot be "skipped." ***The very purpose of the interim time period is to test the good intentions of the Arabs.*** The very NATURE of the final arrangement depends on the EXPERIENCE of the interim arrangement.

Jaffee: Peace with the Arabs is possible now and if we don't make peace soon the Arabs will have nuclear weapons soon.

Freeman: Peace is possible with the Arabs, but only after mind-boggling changes in the Arab world. True peace can only be made after the Arab world undergoes democratization. Simply put, democracies rarely go to war with one another. All our major wars of the last two hundred years have been between dictators or between democracies defending themselves from dictators. When a ruler is elected by the people, he has a natural restraint preventing him from sending their sons and daughters into combat in an aggressive war. ***No such restraint exists anywhere in the Arab world.***

The second major change required of the Arab/Moslem world is to create secular states not subservient to the rule of Islam. The problem for Israel with the rise of Islamic fundamentalism is the very hostile attitude that Islam has toward Jews and any non-Islamic person. Islam is all encompassing and guides behavior, law, religion and attitudes and relations with non-Moslems. Islam perceives the world as two separate parts:

1. The first is **Dar el-Islam,** or the World of Islam

2. All the rest is **Dar el-Harb**, or the world of the sword, or the world of war—that is those non-Muslim nations that have yet to be conquered.

The concept of **JIHAD** or Holy War has been understood by most of us but there is another concept in the Koran with which few of us are familiar. But it is essential to understand this concept when relating to Moslems. That is the law of **HUDAIBIYA** which dates back to Muhammad and states clearly that "Muslims are permitted to lie and break agreements with non-Muslims." This applies to business, personal life and politics. ***Would a peace treaty be worth much if the other party is Moslem?***

Islam divides the world between **Believers** and **Infidels**. Jews and Christians are relegated to the status of **Dhimmis**, or second class citizens. The Koran clearly calls on Moslems to degrade and humiliate both groups. The Arab/Moslem world will have to develop a tradition of respect for women, minorities, and human rights in general before they will be ready for peace with Israel. It seems a bit odd that our State Department is pushing democracy and human rights from one end of the globe to the other—**WITH THE REMARKABLE EXCEPTION OF THE MIDDLE EAST**. Why are the Arabs insulated from pressure to democratize their societies?

It is obvious that no peace agreement would be worth anything with people believing in the above Islamic tenets, failing to practice democracy or show respect for minorities and human rights. It is also obvious that the Jaffee Center has a political agenda and uses its enormous resources and prestige to prove the validity of its political agenda. It would be far better if its research staff would examine the facts and then derive conclusions from those facts rather than vice versa.

[This article was published on August 16, 1993 in the *Jewish Herald-Voice*, in Houston.]

Bernard J. Shapiro

WILL ISRAEL FALL FOR THE 'MUBARAK GAMBIT' ON THE GOLAN?

(September 1994)

The word has gone forth from Jerusalem. Now there is no doubt, despite a multitude of denials. Israeli Prime Minister Yitzhak Rabin has already agreed to surrender the whole Golan Heights to Syrian dictator Hafez Assad. It took months of coaching, but finally Assad has learned to say the word "peace." Does he mean it? The United State's State Department has announced that once peace is made with Syria, then 18 other Arab countries will make peace with Israel. The pressure to accept a withdrawal will be immense. Golan residents are beginning massive resistance, including hunger strikes and demonstrations. Labor MK Avigdor Kahalani is organizing a faction in the Knesset to resist withdrawal from the Golan. He has tabled a bill to raise the vote necessary for approval of territorial change from a simple majority (61) to 70 Knesset members.

The time has come to clear the smoke and mirrors. There is a significant Israeli dilemma in the negotiating framework with Syria. I call this dilemma the **"Mubarak gambit."** After Egyptian dictator Anwar Sadat's death, his successor Hosni Mubarak discovered that Egypt could ignore its peace treaty obligations to Israel with impunity. Sadat had signed over 50 agreements and amendments to the Camp David Accords, which spelled out in great detail normalization of relations with Israel. These included trade, tourism, science, cultural and other attributes of peaceful relations. The late Menachem Begin, of blessed memory, fully believed that his sacrifice of Sinai, with its air bases and oil, was worth the inauguration of peaceful relations with the most important country in the Arab world.

With every passing year, it became clearer to Mubarak that the Israelis were too timid to protest Egyptian violations. It also became clear that America would continue to supply aid in the billions of dollars to Egypt, despite Egypt's obvious violations of their most solemn commitments to both President Jimmy Carter and Begin.

The Battle for Eretz Yisrael

From this experience Mubarak devised the *"Mubarak gambit,"* which sets out the principle **that an Arab country can promise Israel peace and full normalization as a negotiating tactic in order to force an Israeli withdrawal from territory. Then after the territory is recovered, the Arab country can ignore the normalization part of any agreement.**

It is such a painless gambit, one would have thought that all of Israel's neighbors would have rushed to use it. In the Arab world, however, symbolism is very important and it took many years before they were ready to use this tactic. Mubarak first convinced terrorist leader Yassir Arafat to try out the **"Mubarak gambit."** We all know what has happened, including the famous handshake on September 13, 1993. We also know that all of Arafat's promises to the Israelis, including revising the PLO Charter and stopping violence, have not been honored.

Now, after much tutoring, Assad has learned the principle. It has been with great difficulty that he even speaks about peace with Israel. While he is never very clear about his meaning of peace, one thing is clear: he has learned to use the *"Mubarak gambit."* We will be hearing a lot from him and State Department officials about how he has changed and now "really" wants peace. Don't believe it.

Most of you understand the strategic significance of the Golan Heights, so I will concentrate on the other side of the equation. If Syria wants Israel to exchange the Golan for peace, we must ask ourselves the following: (1) Is Syria capable of giving Israel peace? (2) Is peace really possible? (3) Does Syria deserve to get the Golan Heights? (4) Is the Golan really Israeli territory? (5) What are Syria's true intentions toward Israel?

Syrian dictator Hafez al-Assad, while very intelligent, is a sociopath with extreme paranoid delusions. His brutal record of killing everyone who disagrees with him or poses even the slightest political threat bears out this analysis. In my opinion, he is incapable of living up to any peace agreement with Israel. Whether peace is possible depends upon your relative propensity to believe in fairy tales. If you believe in the real possibility of achieving utopia or nirvana, and if you believe in the tooth fairy, then peace with Syria is not only possible but desirable.

Bernard J. Shapiro

Any review of Israel's relations with Syria would indicate that the Syrians do not deserve to get the Golan. This point is rarely mentioned but is important. The bloodthirsty behavior of the Syrians when they controlled the Golan (1948-67), makes me comfortable with depriving them of its return. When the Israeli Defense Forces conquered the Golan, we all vowed never to give it back. Nothing has changed.

Is the Golan really Israeli territory? The Golan was a part of the original League of Nations Mandate at the San Remo Conference in 1920 to Great Britain, for the purpose of establishing the Jewish National Home. In 1921, The British gave Eastern Palestine to Emir Abdullah, who named it Transjordan. Then in 1923, they gave the Golan to the French to become part of the French Mandate of Syria. In both cases, the intent of the League of Nations was violated and the area of the future Jewish state was diminished. Going back even further, one finds reference to the Golan as an Israelite territory in the Holy Scriptures (Deut. 4:43; Josh. 20:8; I Chron. 5:56). Israeli archaeologists have also found numerous ancient synagogues on the Golan.

My final question is: What is Syria's true intention? The answer can be found in a recent meeting of ten rejectionist Palestinian terrorists groups held in Damascus. They swore, with Assad's backing, to prevent peace with Israel and to work for its total destruction. Syria is also involved in an unholy alliance with Iran, whose aim is to make the Middle East *Judenrein* (Jew-free).

In conclusion, we find Syria *incapable* of making peace; that peace is *not possible* now anyway; that the Syrians *do not deserve* the Golan; that the Golan really *belongs to Israel*; and that war, not peace, is Syria's *true intention*. Assad may be whispering sweet nothings in Rabin's ear about peace, but we must tell Rabin not to be seduced.

[This article was published by The Jewish Press (NY) on September 23, 1994, the October 1994 issue of The Caucus Current, and the October 1994 issue of THE MACCABEAN. It was revised and published in the Maccabean Online in July 1999, January 2000, and February 2005, and reissued in the Maccabean Online in May 1997.]

DETERRENCE OR DHIMMIZATION

Which Should Israel Choose?

Back in 1965, in a small meeting room in Tel Aviv, former Defense Minister Moshe Dayan gave a pep talk to a group of RAFI (Rishimat Poalai Israel) volunteers, myself included. At that time, RAFI, a breakaway faction of the Mapai Party, included such notables as former Prime Minister David Ben Gurion and former Defense Minister Shimon Peres. Peres and Dayan had been considered the "hawks" of Mapai, and it was no accident that in the 1965 election they supported a strong defense and security policy.

Dayan was always interesting to listen to, but this talk was something special and we paid attention to every word. "The essence of Israel's security in this region (Middle East) is deterrence," he said. "When we formed the State in 1948-9, we were very weak. The Arab States had planes, tanks, heavy artillery and many more soldiers than us. We had very little heavy military equipment. In the period 1949-55, we absorbed almost a million immigrants. Tent cities sprung up all over the country. We were totally disorganized. Had the Arabs mounted another major invasion, we could have lost. We devised a solution to this problem. It was deterrence. Think about being lost in a forest and surrounded by hostile animals. If you light a torch, boldly approach them showing no fear—they will retreat. But, if you show fear—they will attack and you are lost. We used this principle to save Israel during those early years. Every time we were attacked, we retaliated tenfold. We showed daring and penetrated deep within their borders to attack our targets. We were fearless, brave, and even a bit bloodthirsty. You know the result. The Arabs were afraid and never attacked. Deterrence worked. By 1956, when we invaded Sinai, the Israel Defense Force was not just strong; it was invincible."

The story above was not told just for nostalgia. The lesson is extremely important for the survival of Israel today. Unfortunately, Israelis are daily witnessing the consequences of seven years of declining deterrence vis a vis its Arab population. In 1987, the intifada presented Israel with a new challenge. It was a new kind of war, but with the same aim of driving the Israelis out of their country. The Israelis fought the intifada with many handicaps, not the least of which were their own rules of conduct. Israeli soldiers failed to cope with attacks by teenage Arab boys. In the course of several years, the Arabs learned that the soldiers would not aggressively retaliate for their attacks. They became emboldened.

The Jews living in Judea, Samaria, and Gaza showed great fortitude, enduring thousands of attacks and still tripling their numbers. The serious security failure developed as Arabs became accustomed to attacking Jews and Israeli soldiers. By trying to remain humane in the face of massive attacks, Israel emboldened the Arabs to more and more attacks. Throwing concrete boulders, Molotov cocktails, and then using firearms at Israelis became the norm of behavior among the Arabs. The Israeli government allowed its citizens to be attacked solely because they were Jews. In no other country of the world would such a policy be tolerated. Just two weeks ago a reserve officer of the Israel Defense Forces made a wrong turn and ended up in the center of Ramallah, an Arab city. He was immediately attacked by a vicious mob of Arabs, murder in their eyes, who almost beat him to death. Deterrence had vanished.

While the Jews may not have been afraid like the man in the forest, the affect of multiple restrictions on the Israeli right of self-defense had the same result. That result was to increase the bloodlust of the Arab population and to multiply the Jewish casualties.

In 1991, the Persian Gulf War, with its SCUD attacks on Israel, further undermined Israeli deterrence. Having to depend on United States Forces instead of her own had a deleterious effect on Israeli self-confidence. It is notable that the Arab population of Judea and Samaria danced on their roofs and cried, "Gas the Jews" as the SCUD's headed for Tel Aviv. The self-assurance of the Israelis also declined immensely as a result of their cowering in sealed rooms during the missile attacks.

After the war, Shimon Peres and his associates began to search for a solution to the Arab-Israeli conflict that did not require deterrence. The answer, Peres thought, was to be found in the growing influence of the extreme left (Meretz Party) in Israeli's ruling Labor elite. For many years, the left in Israel and its supporters in America have promoted the doctrine of "Israeli guilt" for the continuing Arab-Israeli conflict. The leftists accepted the Arab propaganda version of Middle Eastern history and see their role as making amends for alleged "wrongs" committed against the Palestinian Arabs. When the Labor Party formed a coalition with Meretz, it was assumed that Meretz would be the junior partner. What we have witnessed is the virtual infusion of extreme left-wing philosophy into the body of Labor.

Peres took this "Israeli or Jewish guilt" and developed it into a "peace" policy based on rectifying "wrongs" committed against the Palestinian Arabs. The leftists saw the most serious "wrong" as being the occupation itself. Jewish rule over a minority of Arabs was considered so immoral, in and of itself, as to cause a destructive decline in Israeli democracy and public morality. The details of maintaining the occupation, like reserve duty in Gaza, were said to cause everything from violence in the home to reckless driving. Divorcing Israel from the territories was seen as a goal for Israel and not just a victory for the Arabs.

I describe the Peres "peace" policy as the "***dhimmization of Israel***." It was based on virtually giving the Arabs everything they wanted: a PLO state in most of the territories, control of land and water, return of refugees, and a shared status for Jerusalem. His belief was that by Israeli actions and concessions, he could terminate Arab hostility to Israel. Peres exhibited the fallacy of believing that anti-Semitism is caused by the "**bad behavior**" of Jews. He failed to understand that there are major forces of religion, history and psychology in the one billion strong Islamic world that cannot be manipulated by anything that Israel does. Would the Holocaust have been prevented if the Jews of Europe had been "nicer" to the Nazis? By shrinking Israel to a size that was non-threatening to the Arabs, Peres hoped to achieve for Israel the status of a ***dhimmis-nation*** in the Islamic world. ***Dhimmis*** status, you will recall, is the inferior third-class status afforded Jews in Arab countries throughout the centuries.

Israel, with its powerful military and independent citizens, had always been an affront to Moslems everywhere. Therefore, Jews should be made subservient, weak and dependent on the approval of their Moslem overlords. Peres understood that Israel in its present borders was too strong to be destroyed. He also understood that the Arabs were offended that they could not destroy Israel within its defensible borders. The Peres solution seems to involve making Israel weak, creating a PLO state, and generally groveling before Arab rulers. Such an emasculated ***dhimmis-like*** Israel, would now win the approval of the Islamic world. He would call it "peace." Some would call it appeasement. Some would cheer. Some would protest. Freeman Center members (and real Zionists) see the Peres/PLO plan as a nightmare and pray that Israel's leaders will come to their senses and return to a policy of deterrence, security and defense of Israeli interests.

[This article was published in the January 1995 issue of ***THE MACCABEAN***. It was reissued in the Maccabean Online in May 1997, and revised and reissued in the Maccabean Online in March 2000 and January 2006.]

ISRAEL'S DEMOGRAPHIC AND SECURITY CHALLENGE

Is Transfer the Only Rational Answer?

(June 1996)

[Editor's Note: This article was first published in the March 1995 issue of THE MACCABEAN. I am reissuing it because the issues it raises are of critical importance for Israel's future as a Jewish nation. The recent election proved how close we came to having Arabs decide the destiny of Israel.]

The Labor government of Israeli Prime Minister Yitzhak Rabin has brought his nation to a major turning point in its relations with its Arab neighbors. It is not the turning point Rabin or Israeli Foreign Minister Shimon Peres would have preferred. Rabin and Peres had a utopian plan to integrate Israel both politically and economically into a "New Middle East" that they would create. Their vision, especially that of Peres, pictured Arab-Jewish relations in a way that even Isaiah would be proud. The Olso agreement with PLO Chief Yassir Arafat was meant to resolve the outstanding conflicts with the Arabs and lead to a lasting peace. It was all a fantasy: a dream not based in reality. And it crashed into the solid wall of Arab/Moslem hatred of the Jews.

The Arabs, mind you, have been very clear as to what their goals were in the Arab-Israeli Conflict. Their plan was fully established and enunciated, and entailed the expulsion or murder of all the Jews of Eretz Yisrael and the establishment of an Islamic nation of Palestine between the river (Jordan) and the sea (Mediterranean). There are significant characteristics of Islamic culture that make peace impossible at the present time. Only after mind-boggling changes in the Arab world can TRUE peace be made. One such change is democratization. Simply put, democracies rarely go to war with one another. All our major wars of the last two hundred years have been between dictators or between democracies defending themselves from dictators. When a ruler is elected by the people, he has a natural restraint preventing him from sending their sons and daughters into combat in an aggressive war. No such restraint exists anywhere in the Arab world.

The second major change required of the Arab/Moslem world is to create secular states not subservient to the rule of Islam. The problem for Israel with the rise of Islamic fundamentalism is the very hostile attitude that Islam has toward Jews and any non-Islamic person. Islam is all-encompassing and guides behavior, law, religion and attitudes and relations with non-Moslems. Islam perceives the world as two separate parts:

1. The first is Dar el-Islam, or the World of Islam. 2. All the rest is Dar el-Harb, or the world of the sword, or the world of war—that is those non-Muslim nations that have yet to be conquered.

The concept of JIHAD or Holy War has been understood by most of us, but there is another concept in the Koran with which few of us are familiar. It is essential to understand this concept when relating to Moslems. That is the law of HUDAIBIYA which dates back to Muhammad and states clearly that "Muslims are permitted to lie and break agreements with non-Muslims." This applies to business, personal life and politics. Would a peace treaty be worth much if the other party is Moslem?

Islam divides the world between Believers and Infidels. Jews and Christians are relegated to the status of Dhimmis, or second class citizens. The Koran clearly calls on Moslems to degrade and humiliate both groups.

The Arab/Moslem world will have to develop a tradition of respect for women, minorities, and human rights in general before they will be ready for peace with Israel. It seems a bit odd that our State Department is pushing democracy and human rights from one end of the globe to the other—WITH THE REMARKABLE EXCEPTION OF THE MIDDLE EAST. Why are the Arabs insulated from pressure to democratize their societies?

It is obvious that a peace agreement with people believing in the above Islamic tenets, failing to practice democracy or show respect for minorities and human rights, would be worthless.

With a proper understanding of the above and full knowledge of the continuing Arab hatred of Israel and the Jewish people, we can discuss Israel's very serious demographic and security problems. In Judea,

Samaria, and Gaza there are about 1.8 million Arabs, while inside Israel's pre-1967 borders there are another 800,000. The Jewish population of Israel is about 4.5 million. The Oslo agreement commits Israel to negotiate the "right of return" of millions of Arabs who fled Israel in 1947-9 and 1967. With the high Arab birth rate and the influx of hundreds of thousands of returning Arabs, we could reasonably expect Israel to have an Arab majority by the year 2025. Let us agree on one thing: THIS IS NOT GOOD, and preventing it is a worthy Zionist activity.

Rabin and Peres both profess to wanting to maintain Israel as a Jewish country with a Jewish majority. Their solution was Oslo, with its separation of Judea, Samaria, and Gaza from pre-1967 Israel. Although they were quite willing to implement the transfer of Jews from the areas designated for the Palestinian Authority (PA), the idea of transferring Arabs was anathema. The problem with their solution lies in the fact that it leaves a rapidly growing population of 800,000 Arabs inside Israel and also permits their numbers being augmented by Arabs returning under the "right of return." The year and a half experience with the PA should convince anyone that the Oslo agreement leads inevitably to terrorism and irredentism. The PLO leaders show every indication of planning to liberate Jerusalem, Tel Aviv, Haifa and not just Gaza, Hebron and Knobbliest. The incident in Ramallah, where an Israeli soldier was almost beaten to death, shows accurately the bloodlust that permeates Palestinian society.

The answer to this demographic and security dilemma can be found as far back as the Torah. Rabbi Baruch Ben-Yosef explains to us that the source for the idea of transfer can be found in the story of Sarah telling Abraham in Genesis to expel Ishmael and his mother, Hagar the maid-servant. G-d tells Abraham to listen to Sarah. The sages reveal to us that Sarah was a greater prophet than Abraham, so he must listen to her. Why did she make such a cruel demand of Abraham, to expel his son?

Sarah saw that Ishmael felt that the land of Canaan belonged to him, as he was Abraham's eldest son. He was aware of the promise of G-d to Abraham. Sarah, realizing that her son Isaac's life would always be in danger because of Ishmael's claim to the land, wanted him expelled for good.

Thus TRANSFER was completed. We learn from this transfer the lesson for all others. We can never allow an (alien) nation to live in the land (of Israel) as he will always make a claim to the land. The concept of transfer is the only future for the State of Israel. Transfer provides the solution for survival. The real problem is not the actual transfer of the Arab enemy nation from the land. The real dilemma is confronting the false notions of morality and the confused perceptions of Judaism on the part of the Jews. Until this is corrected, it will be practically impossible to conduct any transfer, because of the Jews themselves, the ones who will benefit most from the transfer!

Rabbi Meir Kahane took up this theme in the 1970's & 80's and was ostracized by most Jewish communities and outlawed as a racist by the Knesset. Today there are several political parties in Israel that have come to accept the concept of transfer. A new political grouping, called Mishmeret Shalom, has transfer as its main policy aim to save Israel from a Jewish demographic collapse. After studying the Arab-Israeli Conflict for 35 years, I have come to the conclusion that transfer is neither racist nor impractical. That it would be challenging and difficult is correct.

Many liberal Jews believe that the very discussion of transfer is un-democratic and the practice totally immoral. Here is the Freeman Center Plan to transfer most of the Arabs from Eretz Yisrael:

1. Israel extends its full sovereignty to all of Eretz Yisrael from the Jordan to the Mediterranean Sea, from Golan to Eilat.

2. All Arabs living in Israel receive full civil rights but no political rights in the State of Israel. Civil rights include municipal affairs but no sovereignty on any part of Eretz Yisrael.

3. All Arabs unhappy with this arrangement will transferred to a destination of their choice or one of Israel's choosing.4. The IDF, police, and Jewish civilians are permitted to shoot to kill any Arab attacking them in any way including: stones, Molotov cocktails, knives, guns, etc.

5. All acts of terror are punished by either quick execution or expulsion from the country.

6. Arabs who choose to stay in the country are required to do three years national service, equivalent to the Jewish time of military service.

7. Money will be raised abroad and in Israel to finance the transfer of Arabs as a National goal. Economic incentives will be given to Arabs to leave Israel.

History shows us that the Arab population of Eretz Yisrael grew dramatically in proportion to the economic development of the country and the increase in opportunities for them. If the seven planks of the Freeman Center Plan are carried out then the demographic balance should soon begin to shift in favor of the Jewish population. The effects of this plan are clearly thus:

1. Termination of the Palestinians' plan to take over Israel as their country.

2. Depression on the part of the Arab population concerned about #1 and their emigration.

3. The tough treatment of terrorists will lead most to quit the country.

4. The transfer of Arabs unwilling to live in peace will further reduce the demographic gap.

5. National service will be abhorrent to the Arabs and they will leave the country.

6. Many Arabs would be glad to leave Israel given the proper economic incentives—especially now that there would be no hope for a Palestinian State.

There are those that will yell that this policy is not democratic. So what? Democracy is not Torah.

Even the Torah allows us to perform certain duties on the Sabbath in order to save lives. I contend that the Arab/Islamic world is at war with us and that the extraordinary measures that I have suggested should be implemented, despite the non-democratic character of some of them.

Once Israel has been made safe for all time as a Jewish country, we can cultivate the finer aspects of democracy, if we so choose.

[This article was revised and published in the Maccabean Online in April-May 2005 and October-November 2005. It was reissued in June 1996.]

OH L-RD, HOW SHALL I

MAKE THE BLIND SEE?

(November 1997)

OKAY, sometimes I do get frustrated. I spend all my time and energy bringing the truth about the harsh realities facing Israel and the Jewish people. Many good people, like the readers of **Israel National News** and *The Maccabean Online*, understand my feeling of despair at our total lack of influence in centers of power in Israel. We are searching for a new course of action that is more effective. Short of a miracle I don't know what to do. For the sake of history this editorial will review the relevant facts. It is my fond hope and prayer that someone in Prime Minister Ariel Sharon's office will read and understand our message:

THE HARSH REALITIES

We all want peace. We pray for peace in our Sabbath services every Friday night. After thousands of years, being **victims of persecution, expulsion, extermination, and discrimination,** it is natural that we yearn for peace with every ounce of our bodies and souls.

It is because our hunger for peace is so strong that we must be doubly cautious not to fall for a **pseudo-peace** that is really the wolf of war wrapped in sheep's clothing. Today none of us believe Chamberlain really negotiated **"peace in our time"** with Hitler. Why do some Jews believe that Peres and Rabin really negotiated *PEACE* with **Arafat, one of today's Hitlers?**

Israelis my age have fought in five wars and I understand their desire to be free of constant conflict. **Unfortunately, there is no magic cure.** I wish I could write more optimistic words. Beyond the neighboring states that Israel is negotiating with now lies another ring of **unmitigated hostility** led by Islamic fundamentalists like those in Iran.

As Jews we are all involved in this historic struggle to survive. It is not our fate or that of the Israelis that we should retire from this struggle.

Bernard J. Shapiro

The only peace the Arabs are prepared to give us is the **peace of the grave.**

In blood and fire was Israel born and on a hot anvil was she forged. The brave young soldiers of Israel must take a quick glance back to the crematoria of Auschwitz, and then go forth to face the enemy knowing that there is <u>still</u> **no alternative (*ein briera*).**

SELF-DELUSION

Just as bigots obscure reality about certain groups in an evil way, reality can be obscured by the seemingly well-meaning, who are deluded. This self-delusion, or self-deception, can sometimes have tragic consequences. Unfortunately, Jews throughout history have deluded themselves about their position in society. They pursue **utopian solutions** to complex political problems and disputes. Jews rejoiced as the enlightenment spread across Europe in the 18th and 19th centuries. Many were eager to give up their Jewishness and become German, French, Italian, and English. In the final analysis, those societies viewed them as Jews. Self-delusion came into collision with reality and left us with the stench of burning flesh from the ovens of Auschwitz. Many Russian Jews eagerly supported the communist idea of a worker's utopia with no nationalities and no religion. Reality taught them that their neighbors still considered them Jews.

The left-wing in Israel suffers from gross delusions about Arabs. In the face of all empirical evidence to the contrary, they believe peace is possible. In the book <u>Self Portrait Of A Hero: The Letters of Jonathan Netanyahu (1963-1976)</u>, Jonathan Netanyahu, the fallen hero of Entebbe and brother of Benjamin, said it best:

"I see with sorrow and great anger how a part of the people still clings to hopes of reaching a peaceful settlement with the Arabs. Common sense tells them, too, that the Arabs haven't abandoned their basic aim of destroying the State; but the self-delusion and self-deception that have always plagued the Jews are at work again. It's our great misfortune. They want to believe, so they believe. They want not to see, so they shut their eyes. They want not to learn from thousands of years of history, so they distort it. They want to bring about a

sacrifice, and they do indeed. It would be comic, if it wasn't so tragic. What a saddening and irritating lot this Jewish people are!"

I wish someone would explain to me why **ANY INTELLIGENT** Israeli could believe the nonsense (Oslo, Road Map, Geneva) its leaders are expounding. Professor Mark Steinberger (Department of Math and Statistics, State University of New York in Albany, New York) supplied the best answer I have ever heard:

"I would say that leftists must inhabit an alternate universe, except that we wind up having to pay the consequences for their detachment from reality. But while we do live in the same objective world, their vision of it seems to have nothing in common with ours. They do not comprehend reality as we see it, and when challenged with evidence that would seem to buttress our view, they seem either to dismiss it for theoretical reason or ignore it completely. One can list various dangers in the agreement, and give objective evidence that Palestinians have no desire for peace, but still want to drive our people into the sea. What is the reaction? They will tell you that self-determination and prosperity will change the Palestinians' outlook and behavior. On what do they base this? Not on evidence from Arab societies. Rather it is based on theory.

To me, this looks like an unwillingness to deal with reality, and it echoes the unwillingness of the Jewish community of the thirties to recognize the threat posed by the Nazis. Indeed, it seems we have learned nothing at all from our experience with Nazism. The Holocaust has become little more than a tale to frighten children: demons in a morality play. They have turned the Holocaust into an image divorced from real world happenings. Millions more Jews could die in Israel, but they refuse to even imagine the possibility. **They will not allow reality to interfere with their myths."**

Bernard J. Shapiro

IS PEACE POSSIBLE BETWEEN ISRAEL AND THE ARAB WORLD???

The answer is YES—But only after mind-boggling changes in the Arab world. True peace can only be made after the Arab world undergoes democratization. Simply put, democracies rarely go to war with one another. All our major wars of the last two hundred years have been between dictators or between democracies defending themselves from dictators. When a ruler is elected by the people, he has a natural restraint preventing him from sending their sons and daughters into combat in an aggressive war. No such restraint exists anywhere in the Arab world.

ISLAM AND JIHAD

The second major change required of the Arab/Moslem world is to create secular states not subservient to the rule of Islam. The problem for Israel, with the rise of Islamic fundamentalism, is the very hostile attitude that Islam has toward Jews and any non-Islamic person. Islam is all-encompassing and guides behavior, law, religion and attitudes and relations with non-Moslems. Islam perceives the world as two separate parts:

1. The first is **Dar el-Islam,** or the World of Islam

2. All the rest is **Dar el-Harb,** or the world of the sword, or the world of war—that is those non-Muslim nations that have yet to be conquered.

The concept of **JIHAD,** or Holy War, has been understood by most of us, but there is another concept in the Koran with which few of us are familiar. But it is essential to understand this concept when relating to Moslems. That is the law of **HUDAIBIYA**, which dates back to Muhammad and states clearly that "Muslims are permitted to lie and break agreements with non-Muslims." This applies to business, personal life and politics. Would a peace treaty be worth much if the other party is Moslem?

Islam divides the world between **Believers** and **Infidels**. Jews and Christians are relegated to the status of **Dhimmis**, or second class citizens. The Koran clearly calls on Moslems to degrade and humiliate both groups.

The Arab/Moslem world will have to develop a tradition of respect for women, minorities, and human rights in general before they will be ready for peace with Israel. It seems a bit odd that our State Department is pushing democracy and human rights from one end of the globe to the other—**WITH THE REMARKABLE EXCEPTION OF THE MIDDLE EAST**. Why are the Arabs insulated from pressure to democratize their societies?

It is obvious that no peace agreement would be worth anything with people believing in the above Islamic tenets, failing to practice democracy or show respect for minorities and human rights.

WAR AND PEACE

Great issues of war and peace as related to Israel are being debated by Jews in Israel and America. There are strong opinions on both sides of the Atlantic as well as both sides of the major issues. Professor Paul Eidelberg, of Bar-Ilan University, reviews the historical facts:

"Between 1945 and 1978 the longest time without a war going on someplace was a mere 26 days. On an average day there are 12 wars being fought somewhere on earth. The consensus of scholars has been that the norm of international relations is not peace but war." As Eidelberg reports, "Indeed, the occurrence of 1,000 wars during the last 2,500 years indicates that **'peace' is little more than a preparation for war.** Which means that peace treaties are **WORTHLESS**, to say the least."

Eidelberg then quotes from a book by Lawrence Beilenson, entitled **THE TREATY TRAP**, saying, "After studying every peace treaty going back to early Roman times, Beilenson concludes that treaties are made to be broken. In fact, he shows that treaties for guaranteeing the territorial integrity of a nation are useless to the guaranteed nation and worse than useless insofar as they engender a false sense of security. **Such treaties can only benefit nations governed by rulers intending to violate them** whenever expedient." [This also goes for the recent Oslo and Geneva treaties.]

NATURE OF PEACE

Midge Dector on "peace: "What I want to say is something that virtually the whole history of the 20th century teaches us and yet something we refuse to learn. And that is, when applied to the affairs of nations, peace is an evil word. Yes I said evil. And the idea of peace as we know it is an evil idea. From the peace of Versailles to 'peace in our time' at Munich . . . each declaration of peace or expressions of longing for peace ended in slaughter. Not necessarily immediately and not necessarily directly, but slaughter all the same . . ."

"For there is no such thing as making peace. Nations who are friendly do not need to do so, and nations or people who are hostile cannot do so. <u>To cry peace, peace when there is no peace, the prophet Jeremiah taught us long ago, is not the expression of hope, not even superstition, but a reckless toying with the minds and hearts of people whose very future depends on their capacity to rise every day to the harsh morning light of the truth.</u>"

THE COVENANT WITH ABRAHAM

The Land of Israel was given to Abraham for the Jewish People in perpetuity. David Ben Gurion, Israel's first Prime Minister and founder of the Labor Party, said the following about the Jewish People's connection to Israel:

"No Jew has the right to relinquish the right of the Jewish People over the whole Land of Israel. No Jewish body has such authority; not even the whole Jewish People have the authority to waive the right (to the Land of Israel) for future generations for all time."

A TIME FOR PEACE, AND
A TIME FOR WAR

We find all the expressions of horror at the recent Rabbi's ruling, concerning a soldier's obligation to avoid abandoning army bases and settlements to terrorists, to be hypocritical, self-serving, and unfortunate. The Israeli government is in rebellion against everything that Israel, Zionism, and Judaism are all about. They are the ones causing the rift in the body politic and they will be totally responsible for any resulting violence.

When will the National/Religious Camp realize that we are "at war already" with the left-wing tyranny that rules Israel (though seemingly not the ruling party)? At what point will Israelis realize that the **CIVIL WAR** they fear **IS ALREADY TAKING PLACE AND THEY ARE LOSING?** The monopoly on power must be broken or there is no hope.

History is usually written by the victors, but truly there are seldom universally accepted moral standards. We can say with absolute certainty, however, that the Jewish return to **Zion** and our struggle today for *Eretz Yisrael* are more righteous than any other struggle for national liberation in the history of the world.

Following my five weeks of research in Israel, I spelled out (May-June 1994 issue of **THE MACCABEAN**) the nature of this inevitable conflict:

THE PRIMARY INHERENT FLAW IN THE OSLO AGREEMENT
THAT WILL LEAD TO MILITARY CONFLICT

1. The Palestinians expect and will demand that every Jew be removed from their areas of control, including the whole of Judea, Samaria and Gaza.

2. The Jews of **YESHA** not only plan to stay in their homes but will fight for them militarily. **This obviously conflicts with #1.**

I also stated: "The number of Jews in **YESHA** is about 144,000 (now over 240,000). Not counting women, children, and men over 50, this leaves about 50,000 men capable of resisting a PLO armed force. These men are all IDF veterans and reservists with army issue UZIs or AR16s with at least two clips (30 rounds per clip) of ammunition per gun. All Jewish villages are on the hills, with a commanding view of the area. The Arab villages control the roads, creating a strategic situation similar to the pre-state fighting of 1947-48. During my visit I toured the whole area, and emphasized the need to get past the shock of the government's disregard for their interests and make serious preparations for the coming battles."

Among other things, I recommended the following: (1) bring ammunition supplies up to a minimum of 300+ rounds per gun (2) stockpile food, medicine and water supplies for 30 days in case the roads are impassable (3) all vehicles that have been equipped with shatterproof window to deflect rocks need to be re-equipped to become fully bullet-proof (4) Each community needs several trucks armored to withstand 60 caliber machine gun fire, small grenades and some protection from roadside bombs (5) begin constructing bunkers and hardened firing positions.

Nine years have passed since that report and events are playing out exactly as I predicted. The military struggle is about to begin in earnest. If anyone believes this to be unlikely, stay posted and we will see how the future plays out. The Jews of **YESHA** should not leave their physical well-being to the good graces of Arafat or Sharon.

The Jews of **YESHA** must not be passive pawns in the political surrender of their homes. They must fight the Arabs, where necessary, to maintain their travel, water, and land rights. When the Israeli government retreats, leaving them behind PLO battle lines, they must be prepared to go on the offensive militarily to secure safe contiguous areas of Jewish control. The defeatist Israeli leaders, who are willing to surrender our Jewish rights to **Eretz Yisrael**, should be told that there are still proud Jews in **YESHA** who will give up neither their inheritance from Abraham nor their right of self-defense.

Should the Jews of **YESHA** be forced into military combat, they would be fully justified. They will be fighting for the security of Israel and the future destiny of the Jewish people. These brave Jews would be continuing the long tradition of **Hebrew Warriors**, including Joshua, David, the

The Battle for Eretz Yisrael

Maccabees and Bar Kochba, who fought against all odds to save their people and their country.

The glorious **Hebrew Warriors** who defeated five Arab armies in 1948, three in 1967, and two in 1973 must not surrender their Jewish homeland to an evil terrorist, who delights in killing Jewish woman, children, even babies. The **Brave Heroes of Zion** must not limit themselves to passive civil disobedience. At this great time of trial and apocalyptic threat, the safeguarding of the future of the Jewish people's right to *Eretz Yisrael* must take precedence.

SERIOUS FLAWS IN THE OSLO, ROAD MAP AND GENEVA APPEASEMENTS

(1) The most fundamental flaw is the renunciation of **Jewish claims to Judea, Samaria, and Gaza**. The right of the Jewish people to the Land of Israel is God-given and cannot be renounced by a transitory Israeli government. The present government has no right to deprive future generations of Jews and Israelis of their legal patrimony.

(2) Yasir Arafat's PLO is **incapable of providing Israelis with the cessation of violence** they so dearly crave. The PA is, in fact, the primary source of terrorism and coordinates with Hamas and other Islamic fundamentalist factions that will continue to kill Jews.

(3) Without the presence of Israel's internal security force (Shin Bet) inside Judea, Samaria and Gaza, it will be **impossible to halt terrorism** or even keep it within present levels. The Israel Defense Forces maintain tremendous power, but are of little importance in day-to-day terrorism.

(4) Arafat's signature on any agreement and the PLO acceptance is of no consequence as **Arafat is a documented liar.** Muslims are permitted to lie to non-Muslims and break agreements with them under the Koranic law of **HUDAIBIYA**. Treaties and contracts with them are worthless.

(5) By virtue of these appeasements, the Israeli government has **validated Arab claims to the Land of Israel.** Decades of fighting Arab propaganda and distortions of history are trivialized and discounted.

(6) These appeasements put the status of **Jerusalem on the negotiating table**. Every previous government of Israel steadfastly stood by the principle of Jerusalem being non-negotiable.

(7) All of **Israel's military and civilian communications could be easily monitored** from the hills of Judea and Samaria.

(8) While Israeli radar and military installations are limited by these current appeasements, the future is less certain. Eventually **the Arab population will force the Israelis out.**

(9) Whether they admit it publicly or not, Israeli leaders know that this is the **first step to a Palestinian state.**

(10) The **"Palestinian right of return" has been acknowledged** for the first time by the Israelis and could result in a flood of Arabs to Judea and Samaria.

(11) The inevitable increase in Arab population will result in **tremendous pressure on Israel's water supply.** As Arab wells are dug in the Judean and Samarian hills, the natural mountain aquifer that supplies much of Tel Aviv and the coastal plain with water will be seriously depleted. Such depletion will cause the salt water of the Mediterranean Sea to penetrate Israel's coastal strip, thus destroying all water supplies. This process can be witnessed in California, where sea water has already penetrated five miles into the coast.

(12) Some **70% of Israel's population and industry** is concentrated in a small strip of coast and greater Tel Aviv. That population will be **immediately threatened by Katyusha or Quassam rockets.** Fired singly from the hills of Judea and Samaria, and set with timers, they will be virtually impossible to stop. The Israeli government plan to coordinate with the Palestinian police is akin to working with the fox to guard the henhouse. The Palestinian police are being recruited from among the terrorists, who delight especially in murder and mutilation of bodies. Will they arrest and turn over a terrorist who kills Israelis and then escapes to Gaza?

(13) Judea and Samaria have geographical features that are extremely significant for Israeli security. Most important is the Judean-Samarian mountain ridge running north and south and parallel to the Jordan River. From the Jordan to the top of the ridge, the elevation is very sharp and fast, causing a channeling of enemy forces into five passes easily controlled by much smaller Israeli forces on the mountain top. On the other hand, the slope from the top down on the western slope to the coast makes it possible for enemy troops to attack Israeli cities on the coastal plain, with the IDF being unable to anticipate the route of attack, channel it and destroy it.

From the top of the mountain ridge Israeli radar is able to see as far as Iraq, providing an early warning of hostile military activity. In other words, the Judean-Samarian Mountains are not just a barrier but also a radar point. The surrender of such a strategic asset, with great topographical significance for defending Israel from attack from the East, would be the height of foolishness.

(14) The **Jewish residents of Judea, Samaria, and Gaza** will no doubt be **victims of ethnic cleansing**. The Arabs will insist on a Jew-free country like Jordan, Saudi Arabia, and Kuwait. The government has already begun **confiscating the weapons of Jews**, which could cause them to become vulnerable to massacre like the Bosnians.

(15) The air and seaports planned for Gaza will facilitate the entry of weapons and terrorists, threatening the security of Israel.

(16) The proposed "safe passages" for the PA will facilitate the movement of terrorists and weapons from Gaza to Judea and Samaria.

Is there any need to say more? Please copy and distribute this information as widely as possible. Please urge Prime Minister Ariel Sharon to read it and respond correctly and urgently to the dangers presented.

Bernard J. Shapiro

SUICIDE BOMBERS AND

ISRAELI GOVERNMENT RESPONSIBILITY

(September 1997)

The Freeman Center sends condolences to the families of the victims of today's triple suicide bombing on Ben Yehuda Street in Jerusalem. At the same time, we must accuse the Israeli government of dereliction of duty and perhaps also negligence for continuing the **Oslo Suicide Process**. The Israeli government of Prime Minister Benjamin Netanyahu has at its disposal a powerful military and has good intelligence that a group of people plan to murder its citizens. When that government fails to act, then it is negligent. This is what continues to happen in Israel.

How many times have we heard demands from the Netanyahu government that "Arafat must fight terrorism?"

How many times has this government published lists of Palestinian Authority non-compliance with the terms of the Oslo Accords?

How many warnings have been issued to Arafat?

The Freeman Center has repeatedly broadcast the truth through many public forums. That truth is a simple concept: **The fox cannot guard the chickens. The wolf will not cohabit with the sheep and not make a meal of them.** Arafat is doing his job quite well. He is killing Jews, which is his claim to fame. The job of protecting Israelis and fighting terrorism rightfully belongs to the Israel Defense Forces **ALONE**. To believe that this job could be subcontracted out to world renowned Jew killers was always a delusion.

The Oslo Accords were always the **Kevorkian Plan—*Land for Suicide***, with the U.S. President and State Department assisting. At least half of the population of Israel and a much greater proportion of American Jews have accepted this voluntarily, some with enthusiasm. That, of course, makes the Kevorkian comparison even more accurate.

I have just one question for all of those supporters of Israeli suicide: How many dead Jews will it take for you to see the **HARSH REALITY**? How many body parts strewn across Israeli streets will it take for you to **RE-EVALUATE** the wisdom of making a pact with the **DEVIL**? Remember, as Faust pointed out: *When you deal with the devil, you lose your soul.*

Netanyahu was elected on a platform opposed to Oslo, terrorism, and lack of reciprocity. I say to him now: DO IT. I say it loud and I will say it often. I pray he hears the message and acts accordingly.

Bernard J. Shapiro

NOTES ON THE ASSASSINATION OF TERRORISTS

(October 1997)

1. The Israeli government has the right and duty to eliminate individuals actively engaged in either the planning or execution of terrorist acts against Israelis and Jews.

2. Terrorism knows no national boundaries and therefore counter-terrorism must recognize no borders.

3. The left-wing (Labor & Meretz) leaders and media in Israel are demonstrating their total disregard for Israeli security by launching an orgasm of criticism of Israeli Prime Minister Benjamin Netanyahu over this issue. We saw this happen during the Lebanese war. The suicidal Oslo agreements they made with Arafat greatly undermined Israeli security and, in fact, led to more terrorism. For them to attack Bibi now is totally irresponsible. Have they forgotten the hit teams of Labor leaders like Golda Meir and Yitzhak Rabin?

4. Bibi has shown unfortunate weakness in the face of pressure from Jordan, Canada and the US. I will say more about this later.

5. I have one plea to all Israelis: Join ranks and fight terrorism together. When a bomb goes off in Jerusalem, the terrorist does not check first to see if the victims voted Labor or Likud . . .

∗

JERUSALEM APARTMENTS OF MOSKOWITZ

I am very disappointed with the decision of the Israeli Government to force the eviction of the Jewish families in Jerusalem. The "so-called compromise" is an insult to Jewish sovereignty in Israel's own capital.

There is a clear implication that the Israeli government ousted the Jews from their residence in Jerusalem under the legal precedent of "clear and present danger to the peace and security." Does anyone know of any plans by these residents to commit terrorist acts or to attack the Arabs living in the vicinity with stones, Molotov cocktails, or bullets? If they had such plans then they would represent a "danger."

On the other hand, I believe that if the Arabs were planning disruptions of public safety and order, **then it is the Arabs who should be ousted**. Let us be moral, legal and in all ways just. To blame the potential victim for the crime of the criminal does not satisfy the Biblical injunction to deal justly with your fellow man. Bibi: take note.

JEWISH RIGHTS

The Freeman Center supports the *RIGHT* of Jews to live anywhere in *Eretz Yisrael* and condemns government and opposition spokesmen who claim such acts will result in violence. It is the Israeli government's job to protect the peace and tranquility of its citizens. If any Arab should perpetrate violence, incite to violence or in any way violate the law they should arrested and prosecuted for such crimes of violence. We realize that the Arabs do not like Jews living in Jerusalem as neighbors. We suggest they find somewhere else to live. Perhaps Jordan or Saudi Arabia, where there are no Jews, since they have long since been banned, expelled or murdered.

SUICIDE BOMBERS AND ISRAELI GOVERNMENT RESPONSIBILITY

The Freeman Center sends condolences to the families of the victims of today's triple suicide bombing on Ben Yehuda Street in Jerusalem. At the same time, we must accuse the Israeli government of dereliction of duty and perhaps also negligent homicide for continuing the **Oslo Suicide Process**. The Israeli government of Prime Minister Benjamin Netanyahu has at its disposal a powerful military and has good intelligence that a group of people plan to murder its citizens. When that government fails to act, then it is negligent. This is what continues to happen in Israel.

How many times have we heard demands from the Netanyahu government that "Arafat must fight terrorism?"

How many times has this government published lists of Palestinian Authority non-compliance with the terms of the Oslo Accords?

How many warnings have been issued to Arafat?

The Freeman Center has repeatedly broadcast the truth through many public forums. That truth is a simple concept: **The fox cannot guard the chickens. The wolf will not cohabit with the sheep and not make a meal of them.** Arafat is doing his job quite well. He is killing Jews, which is his claim to fame. The job of protecting Israelis and fighting terrorism rightfully belongs to the Israel Defense Forces **ALONE**. To believe that this job could be subcontracted out to world renowned Jew killers was always a delusion.

The Oslo Accords were always the **Kevorkian Plan**, with the U.S. President and State Department assisting Israel to commit suicide. At least half of the population of Israel and a much greater proportion of American Jews have accepted this plan voluntarily, some with enthusiasm. That, of course, makes the Kevorkian comparison even more accurate.

I have just one question for all of those supporters of Israeli suicide: How many dead Jews will it take for you to see the **HARSH REALITY**? How many body parts strewn across Israeli streets will it take for you to **RE—EVALUATE** the wisdom of making a pact with the **DEVIL**? Remember, as Faust pointed out: *When you deal with the devil, you lose your soul.*

Netanyahu was elected on a platform opposed to Oslo, terrorism, and lack of reciprocity. I say to him now: **DO IT.** I say it loud and I will say it often. I pray he hears the message and acts accordingly.

MY WASHINGTON TRIP

I am pleased to report that I found tremendous understanding for our position in the Congress. Because of the huge backlog of mail (E and postal) on my desk, I will have to write a more detailed report next week.

Let me just say that there has been a watershed change in Congress toward Israel and Oslo, the latter being recognized as **DEAD** by key leaders. Since May of 1995, we have been sending **THE MACCABEAN** to key members of the House and Senate who deal with foreign policy and security.

Although we did not get much feedback during those years since 1995, I found out in Washington, during my recent visit, that it was being read. And, most importantly—over time, slowly but surely, it has been an important tool for change and education. We are not the only one involved. **AFSI** has been vigorous in its efforts, as have other organizations like **ZOA**, **Jewish Action Alliance**, **CAMERA** & **YESHA**, **AMCHAI** and **Women in Green**. For all of you who have been frustrated, let me say:

"Things are changing—our work has not been vain."

I LEFT WASHINGTON REINVIGORATED AND REDEDICATED TO, AND ESPECIALLY MORE OPTIMISTIC ABOUT, OUR BATTLE FOR THE SECURITY AND SURVIVAL OF ISRAEL.

Of course, **NOW** we must bring the Israeli government and Bibi to the realization that he will have the support of the Congress, should he take the difficult steps necessary to ensure the survival and well-being of Israel. (And, of course, that he should no longer use the excuse of American pressure for continuing the Kevorkian Process of Oslo.)

MY MESSAGE TO BIBI AT THE NEW YEAR

THE CONGRESS WILL SUPPORT ANY ACTION OF YOUR GOVERNMENT NECESSARY FOR THE SECURITY AND SURVIVAL OF ISRAEL.

I realize that there will be pressure (maybe great pressure) from the State Department and the President in relation to Oslo. If you will stand firm and **clearly** enunciate a policy that will provide security and survival for Israel, the American people and their representatives in Congress **WILL SUPPORT YOU**. You are facing primarily psychological pressure. You must be able to stand eyeball to eyeball and say **NO** when necessary to a great power.

SHANA TOVA

With Love Of Israel And Faith In HaShem

Bernard J. Shapiro, Editor

WITHDRAWAL, REDEPLOYMENT, SURRENDER

OR JUST PLAIN APPEASEMENT

The new American plan for Israeli redeployment is inimical to Israel's interest and destructive of Israeli security and survival. **It is neither supported by the American people as represented by the US Congress nor by a majority of Israel's citizens.** I believe that it will give a boost to the process, started in Oslo, that will lead eventually to the destruction of Israel and the mass murder of its Jewish population. That is, unless the Israeli government takes immediate action to disassociate itself from this "suicide" plan. **Why Netanyahu, whom we supported, would accept such an irrational plan is beyond comprehension.**

The **Freeman Center** has done its best to educate both the Israeli and international community as to the *HARSH REALITIES* in the Middle East. Since we began operation in July of 1993, we have broadcast by fax and email, printed in **THE MACCABEAN**, or placed on our web site, a total far in excess of 20,000 pages of commentary and strategic analysis outlining the dangers Israel is facing due to Oslo. **No one of you can use the (Holocaust) excuse that "you didn't know."**

Bernard J. Shapiro

THE PRIMARY INHERENT FLAW

IN THE OSLO AGREEMENT THAT

WILL LEAD TO MILITARY CONFLICT

(October 1998)

1. The Palestinians expect and will demand that every Jew be removed from their areas of control including the whole of Judea, Samaria and Gaza. **This obviously conflicts with #2.**

2. The Jews of **YESHA** not only plan to stay in their homes but will fight for them militarily. The number of Jews in **YESHA** is about 170,000. Not counting women, children, and men over 50 leaves about 40,000 men capable of resisting a PLO armed force. These men are almost all IDF veterans and reservists with army issue UZI's or M-16 with about two clips (30 rounds per clip) of ammunition. All Jewish villages are on the hills with a commanding view of the area. The Arab villages control the roads creating a strategic situation similar to the pre-state fighting of 1947-48. The Jews in **YESHA** are in some shock and can't believe that their government is really doing this to them. There a great need to get past the shock and make serious preparations for the coming battles.

3. FREEMAN CENTER RECOMMENDATIONS:

(1) Increase dramatically the number of weapons in the hands of **YESHA** residents.

(2) bring ammunition supplies up to a minimum of 300 rounds per gun

(3) stockpile food, medicine and water supplies for 30 days in case the roads are impassable

(4) all vehicles that have been equipped with shatterproof windows to deflect rocks need to be re-equipped to become fully bullet-proof

The Battle for Eretz Yisrael

(5) Each community needs several trucks armored to withstand 50 caliber machine gun fire and small grenades

(6) Each **YESHA** community needs to begin constructing bunkers and hardened firing positions.

(7) Artillery and mortars need to be acquired that are capable of hitting nearby Arab villages participating in the siege of **YESHA** communities.

MORE QUESTIONS THAN ANSWERS:

1. When war breaks out between the Palestinians and **YESHA**, will the IDF intervene on the side of the Palestinians? or the Jews?

2. Will the IDF try to evict Jews from their homes in **YESHA**?

3. When war breaks out between the Palestinians and **YESHA** will the IDF prevent other Arab countries like Egypt, Jordan, Syria, and Iraq from intervening on the side of the Palestinians?

4. Will hostility to the Israeli government's policies affect donations to Federations Appeals, JNF and Israel Bonds?

5. Will American Jews support the forcible eviction of Jews from their homes in Israel to make the area *Judenrein* for the Palestinian?

6. Is there a **moral** *difference* between the transfer of Arabs from Judea, Samaria and Gaza and the transfer of Jews from the same area?

[Author Note: Part of this call for preparedness was printed following my trip to Israel in 1994. I studied in detail the security conditions in Israel and **YESHA**. Unfortunately little has been done to improve the situation.]

"PEACE IN OUR TIME?"

Munich Re-visited

(November 1998)

WRITTEN BEFORE THE WYE PLANTATION NEGOTIATIONS

At the Wye Plantation in Maryland we are witnessing a replay of **Munich 1938.** The players are different but the outcome will be the same. Clinton and Albright are taking the role of British Foreign Minister, Neville Chamberlain. Yassir Arafat assumes the role of fellow Jew-murderer, Adolf Hitler. And Israel has the dubious task of being a good Czechoslovakia. A "piece of paper" may emerge and the White House will declare: *"Peace in our Time."* Of course Clinton has already committed itself to the Palestinian goal of a State (which Arafat claims is from the "river to the sea.") He and Hillary see the elevation to statehood of Palestinian terrorists, who have murdered not only Israelis but also Americans, as the highest form of international morality.

Those of you who care about Israel, please join with me in a prayer for the **FAILURE** of this **EVIL AND ILL CONCEIVED** appeasement conference . . .

AFTER THE WYE AGGREEMENT

Never mind that all of Arafat's "concessions" had already been made at **Oslo in 1993,** the **Oslo-Jericho, Oslo-Jericho II,** and **Hebron Accords.** Why shouldn't he sell the same rug to the Israelis for the fifth time? While he agreed to fight terrorism, change the PLO Covenant, stop Nazi-like incitement against Israelis and Jews, extradite terrorists, and destroy terrorists bases, we all know he will not live up to any of it. After all **HE IS THE TERRORIST AND INCITER.** Can one convince the wolf **NOT** to dine on sheep. Never mind that every American guarantee to Israel at Hebron, signed by U.S. Secretary of State, Warren Christopher, was breached. Never mind that every promise made by Prime Minister Netanyahu in his election campaign of 1996 has been violated.

Rafael Eitan of **Tsomet** had this to say of the Wye Agreement: **"There is no way this agreement cannot be a disaster. The 13% withdrawal is wrong on its own and when you add this to the fact that our delegation had apparently caved in and failed to get anything at all from the other side, one wonders why they went out there at all. It was possible to capitulate with less humiliation at home. This is not how an independent state negotiates. This is how a vassal state handles its affairs."**

The important thing to remember is that this is one more domino falling. One more step in the eventual destruction of Israel and its replacement with a new terrorist State of Palestine. In the February 1997 issue of **THE MACCABEAN** we published a report of **The Task Force on Terrorism and Unconventional Warfare of the U.S Congress** entitled: **APPROACHING THE NEW CYCLE OF ARAB-ISRAELI FIGHTING** by Yossef Bodansky and Vaughn S. Forrest. This intelligence paper outlined how Arafat signed an agreement (on behalf of Palestine) with Syria, Iraq, Egypt and Iran for a combined effort to destroy Israel. The strategy was simple: The Palestinians would disrupt life in Israel through forest fires, intifada, katyusha rockets, road blocks, sniper attacks, and assaults on isolated Jewish communities. Then, while Israel's ability to mobilize its reserve forces was paralyzed by the disorder, there would be a simultaneous attack by Arab nations. That attack would be preceded by a massive missile bombardment on Israeli population centers. Commando units of the various Arab armies would land by helicopters in areas Israel has turned over to Arafat. They would be equipped with the latest anti-air missiles and a wide variety of artillery capable of making life unbearable along Israel's densely populated coastal area from Tel Aviv to Haifa . . .

I don't need to go on much further. We all know about the grim days at the beginning of the **Yom Kippur War**. A war nearly lost because of a conceptual failure (that the Arabs would never dare attack). My dear friend, what we are witnessing today is a horrendous conceptual failure: That Oslo can bring peace. The evidence has already come in and we have reported it: *Oslo has failed*; in fact, it never had a chance of success.

Israelis have fought in five wars and I understand their desire to be free of constant conflict. **Unfortunately there is no magic cure.** I wish I could write more optimistic words. Beyond the neighboring states that Israel is negotiating with now lies another ring of **unmitigated hostility** led by Islamic fundamentalists like those in Iran. Jews have always lived in a jungle some call the world. As in most jungles, only the strong survive. The moment an animal stops fighting for survival he becomes the main course for another hungry jungle beast. The attempt to integrate into the Middle East jungle was always naive though well meaning.

As Jews we are all involved in this historic struggle to survive. It is not our fate or that of the Israelis that we should retire from this struggle. The only peace the Arabs are prepared to give us is the **peace of the grave.**

In blood and fire was Israel born and on a hot anvil was she forged. The brave young soldiers of Israel must take a quick glance back to the crematoria of Auschwitz and then go forth to face the enemy knowing that there is **still no alternative (*ein briera*).**

[An earlier version of this article was published by *The Jewish Press* (NY) on September 23, 1994, the October 1994 issue of *The Caucus Current*, and the October 1994 issue of **THE MACCABEAN**]

WITHDRAWAL FROM THE GOLAN?

A Dangerous Idea That Just Won't Go Away

(July 1999)

Last week United States Secretary of State Warren Christopher toured the Middle East trying to get the peace talks started. Everyone seemed eager to get the talks going again, except the Palestinians who want to use the deportee issue to force concessions from the Americans and Israelis. No party seemed more anxious for the talks to resume than the Syrians, who sincerely believe that a return of the Golan Heights is within sight.

Labor Party Prime Minister Yitzhak Rabin is primarily responsible for this sudden Syrian interest in negotiation with Israel. He has launched "trial balloons" about an Israeli withdrawal from the Golan. He has given the Israeli public mixed signals saying that Israel would never "come down from the Golan," and then saying there would be "withdrawal on the Golan" but not "withdrawal from the Golan." Rabin has further confused the public by saying that Jews living on the Golan would not be affected, since the withdrawal he envisions involves just the Israel Defense Forces. His negotiators have told the Syrians that the" extent of the withdrawal" would be determined by the "extent of the peace" offered by Syria.

Likud party leader Benjamin Netanyahu reported on February 24, 1994 in an interview with David Landau (JTA) in Jerusalem that Israel and the US were discussing a three-stage plan for a total Israeli withdrawal from the Golan. All of this may be confusing to you, and it should. All such talk and negotiation about withdrawal from the Golan is dangerous, misleading, and ultimately harmful to Israel's interest.

In conclusion we find Syria incapable of making peace; that peace is not possible now anyway; that Syria offers Israel nothing; that the

Syrians do not deserve the Golan; that the Golan really belongs to Israel; and that war, not peace, is Syria's true intentions. Assad may whisper sweet nothings in Rabin's ear about peace, but I trust that Rabin will not be seduced.

Written sometime in 1994, **true today!**

PEACE TALKS WITH SYRIA

DOOMED TO FAILURE

(July 1999)

We should not be upset at this development. We must understand the **"Alice in Wonderland"** world we inhabit. When the Israel Defense Forces were slugging it out with the terrorist forces of Hezbollah in Southern Lebanon, United States President Bill Clinton praised Syrian dictator Hafez al-Assad for showing restraint in the face of Israeli attacks. This, despite the fact the Syria was responsible for whole escalation of violence in the area.

Surely Clinton and his State Department aids know that Syria controls the territory from which the Hezbollah attack Israel. Surely they know that weapons and money for Hezbollah operations pass through Syrian controlled territory in Lebanon. And surely they know that Syria is using the violence in Lebanon to pressure Israel to make ill-advised concessions on the Golan Heights.

This ability of US and sometimes Israeli officials to modify the truth in discussions and plans for the Middle East is the central reason the Peace Talks are doomed to failure and they should be. Close observers of the Middle East were shocked when Syria was exonerated for its role in the Pan Am 103 bombing.

When Syria massacred 600 Christian soldiers (POW's with their hands tied) in Lebanon during the Persian Gulf Conflict, the media and the US State Department failed to even protest. In fact, Syria was praised and rewarded ($3 billion) for its support of Desert Storm, though its soldiers were instructed not to fire a single shot at the Arab enemy. The Israeli negotiators have consistently failed to tell the Israeli public the truth about Syrian policy.

Assad mumbles to a western journalist **(Editor's Note: In 1999 it is Patrick Seale, British author and biographer of Assad)** that he might possibly, maybe, could, almost accept a Jewish entity someplace on the planet earth. The media and some Israeli officials proclaim loudly, *"ASSAD READY FOR TRUE LASTING MESSIANIC PEACE WITH ISRAEL."*

US Secretary of State Warren Christopher is traveling through the Middle East telling the regions leaders not to miss this opportunity for peace. It just isn't so. When real peace comes to the Middle East, we will not hear phrases like "risks for peace" or "territories for a promise of, maybe, could be peace if it snows in Houston in July". When real peace comes we will see the *"Mosiach coming into the Jerusalem on a white ass."*

THE DESTRUCTION

OF THE STATE OF ISRAEL

(October 1999)

There have been two major stages in modern Israel's development: Construction—the building of the State and Destruction—the tearing down of the state. What follows is a brief description of these significant stages.

A Roman legionnaire stands on a hill overlooking Jerusalem. He watches the city burn and proclaims proudly, *"Judea capta est"* Judea is destroyed. It will never rise again. Rome's rulers even decreed a change of name for Judea. Henceforth it would be named after the Philistines (or Palestine) and the Jewish connection would be obliterated forever.

Yet, like the legendary Phoenix, rising from the ashes of its own destruction, the new nation of Israel burst onto the international scene in 1948, with the lusty cry of a newborn infant, yearning to breathe free. Five Arab armies rushed to invade Israel and crush the life from the new Jewish State. With unbelievable bravery and heroism the new state survived. Six thousand of its young defenders gave their lives that Israel might live.

In blood and fire was Israel born, and on a hot anvil was she forged. Her youth understood that life in the new Jewish homeland would require sacrifice. With stories of burning flesh from the ovens of Auschwitz embedded deep in their psyches, the young Israeli soldiers fought with the firm conviction that there was **"no alternative"** (*ein brera*).

The history of the modern State of Israel can be divided into two stages. The first began with Theodore Herzl's convening of the First Zionist Congress in Basle, Switzerland in 1897. Herzl proclaimed prophetically that there would be Jewish State in 50 years: *"If you will it, it need not be a dream."* In the half century that followed, with blood sweat and tears, a modern Jewish State was born.

Israel prospered as millions of new immigrants returned to their homeland. Displaced persons from Europe, survivors of the Holocaust, were reborn as proud citizens of a proud Zionist State. Jews from Arab lands, expelled from their homes of over a thousand years were welcomed in an Israel yet to be built. Jews from Russia, Ethiopia, Europe and the Americas joined the exotic mixture that makes up the Jewish State's vibrant character.

In 1967 Israel fought and won an impossible war of survival and with the help of HaShem. Jerusalem, Judea, Samaria, and Gaza were returned to their rightful owner. The covenant with Abraham had been fulfilled.

"And it came to pass, that when the sun went down, and there was thick darkness, behold a smoking furnace, and a flaming torch that passed between these places. That day the L-RD made a covenant with Abraham saying: *"UNTO THY SEED HAVE I GIVEN THIS LAND."* . . . . **Genesis 15:17-18**

Some Israelis and many liberal/left intellectuals from the West were disconcerted by Israel's great victory. They loved the Jews as victims and could not appreciate them as victors. As Golda Meir use to say: A lot world leaders would love to say the nicest eulogies should Israel be destroyed. She preferred Israel to survive as do I. This period following the **Six Day War** was the beginning of the second stage that I call the deconstruction of Israel. This period marked the rise of the post-Zionists and historical revisionists. There was, indeed, also a surge of Zionist messianic fervor following the Six Day War. Unfortunately the Left managed to persevere and infiltrate the universities, schools, media, judiciary, and military of Israel. Over a 25 year period they were able to destroy most Zionist principles and destroy the nation's patriotism.

In rapid succession, a series of events turned the deconstruction from a gradual drift to a sickening free fall. Those events in brief:

1. 1987—Intifada & Loss of Deterrence

The Israeli government lacked the will to put down the revolt decisively. The Israeli Defense Forces were defeated by 12 year old Arab boys. It is important to note that the world media used this conflict to slander Israel and create a myth of David (Arab) versus Goliath (Israel).

Back in 1965, in a small meeting room in Tel Aviv, former Defense Minister Moshe Dayan gave a pep talk to a group of RAFI (Rishimat Poalai Israel) volunteers, myself included. At that time, RAFI, a breakaway faction of the Mapai Party, included such notables as former Prime Minister David Ben Gurion and former Defense Minister Shimon Peres. Peres and Dayan had been considered the "hawks" of Mapai and it was no accident that in the 1965 election they supported a strong defense and security policy.

Dayan was always interesting to listen to, but this talk was something special and we paid attention to every word. "The essence of Israel's security in this region (Middle East) is deterrence," he said. "When we formed the State in 1948-9, we were very weak. The Arab States had planes, tanks, heavy artillery and many more soldiers than us. We had very little heavy military equipment. In the period 1949-55, we absorbed almost a million immigrants. Tent cities sprung up all over the country. We were totally disorganized. Had the Arabs mounted another major invasion, we could have lost. We devised a solution to this problem. It was deterrence. Think about being lost in a forest and surrounded by hostile animals. If you light a torch, boldly approach them showing no fear—they will retreat. But, if you show fear—they will attack and you are lost. We used this principle to save Israel during those early years. Every time we were attacked, we retaliated tenfold. We showed daring and penetrated deep within their borders to attack our targets. We were fearless, brave, and even a bit bloodthirsty. You know the result. The Arabs were afraid and never attacked. Deterrence worked. By 1956 when we invaded Sinai, the Israel Defense Force was not just strong, it was invincible."

The story above was not told just for nostalgia. The lesson is extremely important for the survival of Israel today. Unfortunately Israelis are daily witnessing the consequences of seven years of declining deterrence vis a vis its Arab population. In 1987, the intifada presented Israel with a new challenge. It was a new kind of war, but with the same aim of driving the Israelis out of their country. The Israelis fought the intifada with many handicaps, not the least of which were their own rules of conduct. Israeli soldiers failed to cope with attacks by teenage Arab boys. In the course of several years, the Arabs learned that the soldiers would not aggressively retaliate for their attacks. They became emboldened.

THE LESSON: What seemed like moderation and civilized behavior to Israelis was seen as brutality by the West and <u>weakness</u> by the Arabs. The failure to learn this lesson still continues.

2. 1990-91—Persian Gulf War & Loss of Deterrence

The failure to retaliate against Iraq for its SCUD attacks greatly weakened Israel's policy of deterrence. All the world saw Israelis cowering in their sealed rooms. The Arabs loved the sight and it emboldened the Palestinian Arabs. More serious damage was done to the Israelis psyche. From a proud macho national image, was born a new vulnerable, dependent (on America), ghetto mentality. The Israeli public was "tired of fighting" and felt they could not cope with the new threats to their survival. The looked for a new peaceful solution.

3. 1993—Oslo Accords: The movement toward destruction speeds up

The Israelis had always yearned for peace. Shimon Peres, Yossi Beilin and others secretly negotiated the Oslo Accords, which created a Palestinian State. Israelis were told that this was a "peace" agreement, but they soon found out that it would lead to more death and destruction. Eventually they would learn of its fatal consequences in strategic territory, water and the surrender of its Holy Places. Oslo set in motion the following negative forces:

Creation of a new political entity which claimed Israeli territory, water and history as its own

Cast in doubt Jewish rights to Israel

Put Israel's capitol, Jerusalem, up for negotiation

Placed Arab refugee return and compensation up for negotiation

Created terrorist safe havens in all PA territory

Created terrorist passageways across Israeli territory

Israel became a collaborator and promoter of Palestinian terrorism and gave a lesson to future terrorists that if they just kill enough people over a long period of time they could become successful.

Israel is giving up the strategic territory that protects it and has allowed a hostile army to develop in its very heartland.

There is much more, but you get the picture.

Here are the benefits that Israel received as a result of its participation in Oslo:

0 (zero)

Israel did not get peace, cooperation, good neighbors, an end to anti-Semitic incitement, security, etc . . . .

. . . . they got nothing!!

THE BOTTOM LINE

The process that is going on now is nothing less than the destruction of the State of Israel. Everything that is happening strengthens the Arab claim to *Eretz Yisrael*. Nothing helps Israel.

The truth, which many find inconvenient, is that the **Land of Israel** was promised by **G-d** to Abraham and his seed in perpetuity. **The Land of Israel** is not speculative real estate to be bartered away for some high sounding false promise of peace. The hills and valleys of Judea and Samaria contain the collective memory of the Jewish people. It was here that the Israelites first entered the **Holy Land**. And it was here they fought the battles, built the towns, elected their kings and were preached to by their prophets and judges. And it was on this soil that they wrote the **Holy Scriptures** we call our Bible.

The Israeli governments of Rabin, Peres, Netanyahu, and Barak are transitory. They hold office for a few years and then pass into history. <u>G-d's covenant with Abraham is eternal</u>. Israel holds these lands as a sacred trust for the Jewish people for all time. It would not only be sinful, but also criminal, to abuse that trust by denying future generations of Jews their Holy Land—Land of their fathers; the one tiny spot on planet earth given to them by God.

THE GOLAN HEIGHTS

Going . . . Going . . . Going . . . Gone . . . Gone . . . Gone . . .

(January 2000)

The Meretz/Labor government of Prime Minister Ehud Barak works vigorously to rid Israel of the burden of the Golan Heights. You may be sure that they are likely to succeed unless a powerful countervailing force can be created to oppose them. In exchange for a piece of paper signed by Syrian dictator Hafez Assad, Barak is willing to relinquish the following:

> 35-40% of Israelis scarce water resources. Former Agriculture Minister Ya'acov Tzur said that water sources on the Golan Heights were of "vital importance" to the future of the State. "The water coming from the Golan to the Lake Kinneret catchment area is between 200 million and 300 million cubic meters [per year]," he said. "This is a critical, vital and even fateful matter in terms of the future of the State. I have to say that I'm not aware of any replacement for this water." [The Jerusalem Post December 27]

> The electronic surveillance/intelligence outpost on Mount Hermon. No amount of techno-wizardry can replace fixed mountaintop installations with line of sight radar and electronic surveillance. All talk about third-party intelligence, AWACS, or even balloons is absurd. Israel has the best possible intelligence now. Why destroy it and then search for an inferior crutch to replace a healthy system.

> Forward Israel Defense Force positions within artillery range of Damascus. It is this military position that keeps the Syrians from starting a war. Once the IDF is removed by a pseudo "peace" the probability of WAR increases.

> Defensive positions along a ridge line of mountains on the Golan that allow a small force to hold off a large invasion force while the necessary mobilization takes place.

The right of some 18,000 Israelis to stay in their homes and businesses. This represents acceptance of the idea of ethnic cleansing as a legitimate tool of government.

<u>The Golan is legitimate territory of the State of Israel annexed by the Knesset n 1981.</u> Not only does Israel have a legal claim as a victim of aggression from Syria, but historically the Golan was always considered a part of the Land of Israel, even in Biblical times. The Golan was a part of the original League of Nations Mandate for Palestine and at the San Remo Conference in 1920 it was given to Great Britain, for the purpose of establishing the Jewish National Home. In 1921, The British gave Eastern Palestine to Emir Abdullah, who named it Transjordan. Then in 1923, they gave the Golan to the French to become part of the French Mandate of Syria. In both cases, the intent of the League of Nations was violated and the area of the future Jewish state was diminished. Going back even farther, one finds reference to the Golan as an Israelite territory in the Holy Scriptures (Deut. 4:43; Josh. 20:8; I Chron. 5:56). Israeli archaeologists have also found numerous ancient synagogues on the Golan.

And finally in the words of the late Yitzhak Rabin: "<u>Whosoever gives up the Golan Heights, abandons the security of the State of Israel.</u>"

There are some Israelis who believe that a peace agreement with Assad would bring about a Messianic Age in the Middle East. They also believed that a deal with PLO terrorist Yasir Arafat would bring "peace." and of course, they believe in the tooth fairy. The rising stack of dead Jews would seem to disprove the proposition that lions are indeed lying down with lambs.

Israelis need not behave like lemmings. Why the rush to suicide?

GAMLA SHALL NOT FALL AGAIN

MARK LANGFAN, MORTARS AND KATYUSHAS

(June 2001)

Back in September of 1992 a young New York attorney, Mark Langfan, published a landmark article in JINSA's magazine, Security Affairs. It was entitled, DEMILITARIZATION RISKS, and boldly pointed out the dangers of allowing the creation of a Palestinian State or Authority in Judea, Samaria and Gaza. As you will learn from this article it has become frighteningly prophetic. In the light of very recent news from Israel, please read the following excerpts from Langfan's original article:

A "demilitarized autonomous zone" has been proposed as a solution for a gradual lessening of Israeli administration of the territories of Judea, Samaria and the Gaza Strip. At some point in the ongoing Middle East peace talks, the exact legal meaning of the term "demilitarized autonomous zone" will have to be agreed upon by Israel, the surrounding Arab states, the Palestinians and, if necessary, outside peace keeping guarantors. (Ed. note: Prime Minister of Israel, Yitzhak Rabin, has announced that negotiations on Palestinian autonomy in the territories will proceed rapidly.) <u>One problem facing Israeli negotiations will be a structure to prevent determined individuals from smuggling impermissible weapons into the "demilitarized zone."</u>

In this regard, the Israeli negotiating team must grapple with the reality that, no matter what settlement is reached, there will continue to exist well-funded, organized and violent Palestinian nationalistic and Islamic extremist elements which will attempt to smuggle weapons into the "demilitarized zone" which they will use to kill Israelis.

In evaluating how strong a security net is required to prevent smuggling, the Israeli negotiating team must evaluate the relative dangers of small and easily transported weapons. A standard terrorist weapon, for purposes of such a discussion, is the Soviet-designed Katyusha artillery rocket. For over 20 years, the Katyusha has been used extensively by terrorists in Lebanon to bombard northern Israel.

While Katyusha rockets are usually fired in barrages of dozens at a time, they can also be fired singly. If launched into the very densely populated Tel Aviv-Netanya corridor, they would surely kill and spread unimaginable terror. Israel's coastal corridor contains 70 percent of Israel's population and 80 percent of her industrial base. The technological simplicity and ease of transportability of many weapon systems with sufficient range to cause havoc and death in Israel make smuggling of weapons into the West Bank a grave concern for Israeli negotiators.

Internal security measures are another issue to be addressed. The greatest protection Israel now has against terrorist attacks and weapons smuggling is the maintenance of an intense surveillance regime in the territories. If internal jurisdiction was transferred to an independent Palestinian entity, Israel would lose this crucial ability. Unlike the barren deserts and hills of the Egyptian and Jordanian border regions, the West Bank has hundreds of cities, towns and villages. Therefore, terrorists operating from the West Bank could easily find safe refuge within the surrounding population.

In addition, what right of action will Israel have if a Katyusha or other weapon is fired into Israel from the "demilitarized autonomous zone?" If such reprisal is restrained in expectation of justice being served by the authorities of the "autonomous zone," what is the Israeli recourse when nothing happens? There will exist plausible deniability in the failure of the "autonomous zone" authorities to capture terrorist. Unlike in state-to-state relations, there is the likelihood that no one person or group of persons will have the authority or means to halt attacks on Israelis.

*

PA SMUGGLES WEAPONS INCLUDING KATYUSHAS

Dr. Aaron Lerner reports on May 7, 2001 that a Palestinian weapons boat seized yesterday represent major a change in the threat against Israel. This evening the Commander of the Israeli Navy Yedidya Yaari told a press conference televised live from Haifa Port that a weapons boat had been seized by the Israeli Navy. The operation was handled by professional Lebanese smugglers who took the boat ("Santorini") from North Lebanon and were supposed to leave the weapons in barrels off the Gaza Coast for pick upon behalf of the Palestinian Authority. The weapons were believed to have been sent by Ahmed Jibril.

The weapons captured were displayed at the press conference as was the boat. The boat had been monitored over the weekend. Yaari noted that on board the ship a wide variety of weapons were discovered, among them surface to air missiles, RPG launchers, mortars, mines, weapons, and many kinds of ammunition.

List of Weapons:

20 RPG-7 launchers
9 Sights for RPG-7
100 PG-7 rockets
50 OG-7 rockets
150 Propellant for RPG-7
120 Anti-tank grenades RKG
4 SA-7 Strella anti-aircraft missiles
2 60mm mortar
98 60mm mortar bombs
50 107mm Katyusha rockets including fuses
62 TMA-5 mines
8 TMA-3 mines
24 Various hand grenades
30 Hungarian Kalashnikov assault rifles with 13,000 rounds of 7.62mm rounds for ammunition
116 Magazines for Kalashnikovs

Dr. Aaron Lerner reports further that the SA7 Strella anti-aircraft missiles have a range allowing them to shoot down Israel aircraft over Israeli airspace from inside the Palestinian Autonomy. Channel Two Television military correspondent Roni Daniel noted that the anti-tank weapons found on the boat would have been able to pierce the armo being used by Israel in the conflict with the Palestinians. He also pointed out that the Katyusha range would bring much of the Sharon Plain (greater Tel Aviv area) within striking distance from within the Palestinian Autonomy.

Ha'aretz (IMRA) reports that Minister of Defense Ben Eliezer said today that "very soon you will be stunned to hear things that will make it clear just how large the extent o smuggling has become. It is possible that we will soon see the Palestinians move from the stage of mortar shelling to new and more dangerous stages.

Danny Rubinstein (Ha'aretz 8 May 2001) says that the weapons were meant for many fighters. (IMRA) Israel Radio reported this morning that the spokesman for the PHLP-GC in Gaza said the weapons were meant for general distribution to security forces in Gaza and not the PHLP-GC) Based on information gathered during questioning, the source of the weapons and other military materials found on a ship headed for Gaza is the Popular Front for the Liberation of Palestine-General Command (PFLP-GC) headed by Ahmed Jibril.

This relatively small organization, whose activities are nearly all abroad, including in Syria and Lebanon, has nearly no presence in the West Bank and Gaza. It is therefore difficult to suggest that such a large quantity of weapons was meant only for the members of Jibril's organization in Gaza. The Katyusha rockets and the Strella SA-7 anti-aircraft missiles, the explosives and other materials, were meant to reach bigger groups in Gaza, with the operational capability to distribute them to trained persons who are capable of using them.

In other words, if these weapons were not directly meant for the Palestinian Authority, they would surely have reached organizations linked with the PA. These comprise the various "resistance committees," and other gangs of Fatah members (the Tanzim), the Hamas and the Islamic Jihad, who operate in cahoots with the Palestinian security services and who initiate the majority of the shooting incidents.

Ahmed Jibril, 70, is a Palestinian born near Abasiya (Yehud). A former Syrian officer, he once headed one of the leftist organizations against Arafat and fought on the side of renegades from Fatah and Syrian troops against the PLO during the latter part of the war in Lebanon in 1982. During the last decade, Jibril has forged links with Iran and Islamic radicals.

During the previous Intifada, in early 1988, Jibril lent his assistance by setting up a radio station, Al Quds, in Syrian territory on the Golan Heights, which broadcast to the territories. In recent years, several operations were initiated by Jibril's operatives in southern Lebanon, but all failed.

Ha'aretz (May 8, 2001) correspondents Amnon Barzilai and David Ratner and Aluf Benn quote Navy Commander-in-Chief Yedidia Ya'ari that there was no guarantee that similar shipments had not successfully reached the PA in the past. There would undoubtedly be similar smuggling attempts in the future, he said. Israel Radio senior diplomatic correspondent Yoni Ben Menachem reported today that Prime Minister Ariel Sharon told a foreign press briefing today that the arms smugglers caught over the weekend smuggling anti-aircraft missiles, Katyushas and other weapons to Gaza successfully delivered THREE shipments to Gaza in the past.

"The arms that were captured change the balance of forces between us and the Palestinians, particularly the 107mm Katyushas, which have a range of 8.5 kilometers," Ya'ari told reporters during a press conference at the naval base in Haifa. "Even more worrying are the Strella personal anti-aircraft missiles, which are capable of hitting aircraft inside Israeli territory."

Prime Minister Ariel Sharon informed the U.S. administration of the captured ship yesterday, terming it "an extremely grave violation of all the agreements that [PA Chairman Yasser] Arafat signed with Israel." This was "not a minor violation, but an attempt [by the Palestinians] to equip themselves with serious weaponry that could injure Israeli citizens," he said. The message was relayed to U.S. National Security Advisor Condoleeza Rice at a meeting with Finance Minister Silvan Shalom, who is now in Washington; Shalom asked Rice to pass it on to President George W. Bush.

Israel Radio also reported that a senior defense source said he believes the Palestinians have mortars and mortar launchers in the West Bank. <u>The correspondent relaying the story noted that the much ridiculed warnings</u>

<u>by Sharon and others that Oslo would ultimately lead to the cities of Israel being threatened by shelling are now becoming reality.</u>

Arutz Sheva reports in its broadcast on May 8 that Defense Minister Binyamin Ben-Eliezer said "The extent of these weapons makes a mockery of all our security-coordination meetings with the Palestinians," said. "We talk about peace and returning to the negotiating table, while they are preparing for war." He was referring to the discovery on Sunday of a vessel laden with heavy weapons headed for the Gaza coast from Lebanon. The shipment contained four anti-aircraft Strella missiles, 120 anti-tank missile launchers, rocket-propelled grenades, and mortar shells. In addition, there were Kalachnikov submachine guns with 13,000 7.62 mm bullets, Katyusha rockets with a range of 8.5 kilometers—as opposed to the 1.5-kilometer range of the mortars used by the PA until now—as well as dozens of RPG launchers, mortar bombs, mines, and more. The shipment was sent by terrorist leader Ahmed Jibril's Popular Front for the Liberation of Palestine. Israeli officials invited international diplomats to see the wide array of weapons saved from reaching their destination in the PA. The Oslo and Wye Agreements forbid the PA from holding weapons such as Katyushas, rockets, and mortar launchers, and it is bound to hand them over to U.S. officials for destruction.

Voice of Israel reporter Yoni Ben-Menachem said today, "A government minister reminded me that in 1994, after the 'Gaza and Jericho first' agreement, then-Likud MK Ariel Sharon told the Knesset that it will only be a matter of time before the PA fires Katyushas from Gaza onto Ashkelon; later, then-Labor party Minister Chaim Ramon mocked Sharon and said, 'Where are the Katyushas that you promised us?' Now it looks like we will soon see them . . ."

Israeli defense leaders said today that the Palestinians already have weapons of the type that were seized Sunday. Smuggling of weapons to the PA has been taking place for years, chiefly via underground tunnels from Egypt to Rafiach and in Arafat's plane. Other Palestinian VIPs, whose cars went unchecked through Israeli checkpoints, also smuggled in various weapons. A security source told Arutz-7 today, "Almost every time a VIP car returned from Jordan, we saw that it was heavily weighted down—but we were not allowed to check it."

THE BOTTOM LINE

As Langfan predicted the Palestinian Authority would smuggle weapons, including Katyushas in to the areas under its control to attack Israel. The rapid rise in the use of mortars by the PA terrorists points to a testing of Israeli resolve. The relative difficulty of the IDF to stop the mortar attacks has been noted by the enemy. As has the ability to terrorize and kill with a weapon fired from a distance. The Left who mocked Langfan's warnings and those of the Nationalists Camp will live to see their delusions crumble as the bloodbath accelerates.

*

Mark Langfan is a New York-based attorney who has written on Middle Eastern affairs and security issues confronting Israel. He has created a three-dimensional topographical model of Israel to explain the implications of strategic height and depth for Israel's security. This model has been endorsed by the Spokesman's Office of the Israel Defense Forces and is used by JINSA. Langfan is also the Freeman Center Military Analyst.

SEPARATION, SECURITY FENCES

& BUFFER ZONES

The Primary Fallacy

(March 2002)

The idea of separation has much appeal to an Israeli population feeling threatened daily by hostile Arabs. The Israeli government recently advanced an elaborate plan to construct hi-tech fences and new military checkpoints between Israel and the Palestinian West Bank in an effort to reduce the risk of militant violence. Israeli security officials brought the plan before the Knesset a day after Islamic extremists opened fire on an Israeli bus near the West Bank town of Hebron, killing two Jewish settlers and wounding five. The separation plan involves building extensive fences, other barriers and restricting Palestinian access into Israel through eight to ten crossings points. The border would be heavily patrolled by Israeli soldiers and police. Cost estimates range from $300 million to $500 million. An economic report on the draft plan said the cost would be too high and separation would lead to political and economic instability in the PLO areas, perhaps intensifying the danger of attacks from opponents of the Israeli-PLO peace process. Analysts such as Dore Gold, Emanuel Winston and Ze'ev Schiff have discussed many of the reasons why it simply won't work.

For another reason why it is the wrong approach to security, it is worth repeating a story I wrote, which appeared in an article entitled, **DETERRENCE OR DHIMMIZATION (THE MACCABEAN**, January 1995): Back in 1965, in a small meeting room in Tel Aviv, former Defense Minister Moshe Dayan gave a pep talk to a group of RAFI (Rishimat Poalai Israel) volunteers, myself included. At that time, RAFI, a breakaway faction of the Mapai Party, included such notables as former Prime Minister David Ben Gurion and former Defense Minister Shimon Peres. Peres and Dayan had been considered the "hawks" of Mapai and it was no accident that in the 1965 election they supported a strong defense and security policy.

The Battle for Eretz Yisrael

Dayan was always interesting to listen to, but this talk was something special and we paid attention to every word. "The essence of Israel's security in this region (Middle East) is deterrence," he said. "When we formed the State in 1948-9, we were very weak. The Arab States had planes, tanks, heavy artillery and many more soldiers than us. We had very little heavy military equipment. In the period 1949-55, we absorbed almost a million immigrants. Tent cities sprung up all over the country. We were totally disorganized. Had the Arabs mounted another major invasion, we could have lost. We devised a solution to this problem. It was deterrence. Think about being lost in a forest and surrounded by hostile animals. If you light a torch, boldly approach them showing no fear—they will retreat. But, if you show fear—they will attack and you are lost. We used this principle to save Israel during those early years. Every time we were attacked, we retaliated tenfold. We showed daring and penetrated deep within their borders to attack our targets. We were fearless, brave, and even a bit bloodthirsty. You know the result. The Arabs were afraid and never attacked. Deterrence worked. By 1956 when we invaded Sinai, the Israel Defense Force was not just strong, it was invincible."

The story above was not told just for nostalgia. The lesson is extremely important for the survival of Israel today. Unfortunately Israelis are daily witnessing the consequences of seven years of declining deterrence vis a vis its Arab population. In 1987, the intifada presented Israel with a new challenge. It was a new kind of war, but with the same aim of driving the Israelis out of their country. The Israelis fought the intifada with many handicaps, not the least of which were their own rules of conduct. Israeli soldiers failed to cope with attacks by teenage Arab boys. In the course of several years, the Arabs learned that the soldiers would not aggressively retaliate for their attacks. They became emboldened. The Jews living in Judea, Samaria, and Gaza showed great fortitude, enduring thousands of attacks and still tripling their numbers. The serious security failure developed as Arabs became accustomed to attacking Jews and Israeli soldiers. By trying to remain humane in the face of massive attacks, Israel emboldened the Arabs to more and more attacks. Throwing concrete boulders, Molotov cocktails, and then using firearms at Israelis became the norm of behavior among the Arabs. The Israeli government allowed its citizens to be attacked solely because they were Jews. In no other country of the world would such a policy be tolerated.

During the Persian Gulf War Israel allowed Iraq to fire Scud missiles into its major cities without retaliating. This was a major blow to Israeli deterrence in the Middle East. Then finally, the Oslo Appeasement Agreement of 1993 which resurrected a terrorist gang to the role of competitor for Eretz Yisrael.

Several weeks ago a reserve officer of the Israel Defense Forces made a wrong turn and ended up in the center of Ramallah, an Arab city. He was immediately attacked by a vicious mob of Arabs, murder in their eyes, who almost beat him to death. Deterrence had vanished.

While the Jews may not have been afraid like the man in the forest, the affect of multiple restrictions on the Israeli right of self defense had the same result. That result was to increase the bloodlust of the Arab population and to multiply the Jewish casualties. For Israelis to seek security behind a security fence is a total reversal of the traditional policy of deterrence. From the days of Orde Wingate during the Arab riots of 1936-9, Israeli military strategists have always emphasized the doctrine of striking the enemy deep within his territory. Retaliation, deep penetration raids were the hallmark of the IDF. To return to a siege mentality hiding behind electrified ghetto walls would be the beginning of the end of Israeli independence. No barrier whether the Bar Lev Line or the Maginot Line can resist a determined enemy willing to risk money and lives to breach it.

In conclusion, I believe that the only way for Israel and her beleaguered citizens to achieve security, both personal and national, is by reasserting those traditional methods of combat that will re-establish deterrence in the minds of the Arab enemy.

[This article was published in the *Jewish Herald-Voice* (Houston) on April 5, 1995 and in the April 1995 issue of **THE MACCABEAN**.]

THE ART OF THE FAIT ACCOMPLI

A New/Old Military Doctrine For Israel

(October 2002)

Israel in recent years has seemed to have forgotten many lessons of the past. I call those "lessons" the art of the *fait accompli*. Today we have the sorry example of:

1. Israel taking military action
2. Not completing the action
3. Pausing in the middle of the action allowing public opinion and US and world pressure to interfere with an ongoing action
4. Retreat from the action allowing the appearance of weakness in the face of pressure

In the past Israel's Defense Forces performed many heroic acts that cat can only be described as *fait accomplis* or "creating facts on the ground." Some outstanding examples:

1. Orde Wingates' night squads
2. Illegal immigration of Holocaust survivors into Israel
3. Retaliatory raids into Arab countries in response to attacks on Israel
4. The Sinai Campaign 1956
5. The Six Day War 1967
6. The rescue of Jews at Entebbe
7. The assassination of the PLO Munich murderers
8. The bombing of Iraq's nuclear reactor at Osirak
9. The Peace for Galilee war in Lebanon

Of course there are many more examples, but the common denominator among them is that the world and the US disapproved of them all. And if they were not carried out Israel's eterrence and security would have been greatly diminished.

One of my great disappointments in the last two years is the restraint exercised by the IDF. The effect of this restraint is to allow the Arabs to constantly adapt to Israel's strategy. They have a very high learning curve. In order to stamp out terrorism it is necessary to excise the whole institutions

Bernard J. Shapiro

that support it. Just like a cancer that must be cut out completely to prevent it from metastasizing, the terrorists must be destroyed completely.

I am not a military expert, yet my observations seem like common sense and I hope Israel will begin again to follow them.

SECURITY FENCES AND LOGICAL FALLACIES

(August 2003)

[Author's Note: Israeli Prime Minister Ariel Sharon has followed former PM Ehud Barak, who in turn followed the lead of former PM's Yitzhak Rabin and Shimon Peres in suggesting a separation wall between Israel and the Arabs. It is not a new idea and as far back as 1995, I explained why it won't work. Here is an update of that article.]

The idea of separation has much appeal to an Israeli population feeling threatened daily by hostile Arabs, who since September 2000 have waged a murderous terror campaign against them. The Israeli government has already begun construction of a security fence consisting of a concrete wall and hi-tech devices between Israel and the Arabs in Judea and Samaria. The goal is to reduce the risk of terrorist violence, especially homicide bombing. Some 200 kilometers of the security fence have already been built. In addition to barriers, Arab access into Israel is restricted to ten or more crossings points. The border would be heavily patrolled by Israeli soldiers and border police. Cost estimates range from $1-2 billion.

For many reasons this is the wrong approach to security. It is worth repeating a story I wrote, which appeared in an article entitled, **DETERRENCE OR DHIMMIZATION (*THE MACCABEAN*,** January 1995): Back in 1965, in a small meeting room in Tel Aviv, former Defense Minister Moshe Dayan gave a pep talk to a group of RAFI (Rishimat Poalai Israel) volunteers, myself included. At that time, RAFI, a breakaway faction of the Mapai Party, included such notables as former Prime Minister David Ben Gurion and former Defense Minister Shimon Peres. Peres and Dayan had been considered the "hawks" of Mapai and it was no accident that in the 1965 election they supported a strong defense and security policy.

Dayan was always interesting to listen to, but this talk was something special and we paid attention to every word. "The essence of Israel's security in this region (Middle East) is deterrence," he said. "When we formed the State in 1948-9, we were very weak. The Arab States had planes, tanks, heavy artillery and many more soldiers than us. We had very little heavy military equipment. In the period 1949-55, we absorbed

Bernard J. Shapiro

almost a million immigrants. Tent cities sprung up all over the country. We were totally disorganized. Had the Arabs mounted another major invasion, we could have lost. We devised a solution to this problem. It was **deterrence**. Think about being lost in a forest and surrounded by hostile animals. If you light a torch, boldly approach them showing no fear—they will retreat. But, if you show fear—they will attack and you are lost. We used this principle to save Israel during those early years. Every time we were attacked, we retaliated tenfold. We showed daring and penetrated deep within their borders to attack our targets. We were fearless, brave, and even a bit bloodthirsty. You know the result. The Arabs were afraid and never mounted a coordinated military campaign against us. **Deterrence worked**. By 1956 when we invaded Sinai, the Israel Defense Force was not just strong, it was invincible."

The story above was not told just for nostalgia. The lesson is extremely important for the survival of Israel today. Unfortunately Israelis are daily witnessing the consequences of sixteen years of declining deterrence vis a vis its Arab population. In 1987, the intifada presented Israel with a new challenge. It was a new kind of war, but with the same aim of driving the Israelis out of their country. The Israelis fought the intifada with many handicaps, *not the least of which were their own rules of conduct*. Israeli soldiers failed to cope with attacks by teenage Arab boys. In the course of several years, the Arabs learned that the soldiers would not aggressively retaliate for their attacks. They became emboldened. The Jews living in Judea, Samaria, and Gaza showed great fortitude, enduring thousands of attacks and still tripling their numbers. The serious security failure developed as Arabs became accustomed to attacking Jews and Israeli soldiers. By trying to remain humane in the face of massive attacks, Israel allowed and emboldened the Arabs to more and more attacks. These attacks grew more and more deadly including homicide bombers in the large cities of Israel like Tel Aviv, Jerusalem, Haifa, and Netanya. Throwing concrete boulders, Molotov cocktails, and then using firearms at Israelis became the norm of behavior among the Arabs. Progressing rapidly to mines and bombs—human and other. The Israeli government allowed its citizens to be attacked solely because they were Jews. *In no other country of the world would such a policy be tolerated*.

During the Persian Gulf War Israel allowed Iraq to fire 39 Scud missiles into its major cities without retaliating. This was a major blow to Israeli deterrence in the Middle East. The Oslo Appeasement Agreement of 1993 resurrected a terrorist gang and brought it into the heart of Israel. It then pursued a policy of terror and propaganda to become a fraudulent competitor for the rights to **Eretz Yisrael**. Of course their goal was never "peace" or a two state solution, but to replace Israel with Palestine "from the river to the sea."

A couple of years ago two reserve officers of the Israel Defense Forces made a wrong turn and ended up in the center of Ramallah, an Arab city. They sought safety in a PA police station. The PA turned them over to a vicious mob of Arabs, murder in their eyes, who beat them to death. Their bodies were mutilated and the Arabs cheered at the bloody hands of the murderers. **Deterrence had vanished**.

While the Jews may not have been afraid like the man in the forest, the affect of multiple restrictions on the Israeli right of self defense had the same result. That result was to increase the bloodlust of the Arab population and to multiply the Jewish casualties. For Israelis to seek security behind a security fence is a total reversal of the traditional policy of deterrence. From the days of Orde Wingate during the Arab riots of 1936-9, Israeli military strategists have always emphasized the doctrine of striking the enemy deep within his territory. Retaliation, deep penetration raids were the hallmark of the IDF. To return to a siege mentality hiding behind electrified ghetto walls would be the beginning of the end of Israeli independence. No barrier whether the Great wall of China, the Bar Lev Line or the Maginot Line can resist a determined enemy willing to risk money and lives to breach it.

Today, there is a great deal of political opposition to the security fence from the US State Department, President George W. Bush and the Arabs (who oppose anything that might aid Israeli security). My opposition is based on two factors: (1) It is a fallacious security concept and (2) It might be used as way to divide and abandon parts of the Jewish Homeland.

A security fence means nothing in the face of a determined enemy with rockets and mortars. Israel has an enemy willing to sacrifice its youth as human bombs to breach the fence. A fence can easily be dug under with the sophisticated equipment presently being used in Gaza to smuggle weapons.

The so called Road Map is a continuation of Israel's retreat from a policy of deterrence, expression of its sovereign right to military self defense and preemption.

In conclusion, I believe that the only way for Israel and her beleaguered citizens to achieve security, both personal and national, is by reasserting those traditional methods of combat that will re-establish deterrence in the minds of the Arab enemy.

[Parts of this article were published in the Jewish Herald-Voice (Houston) on April 5, 1995 and in the April 1995 issue of THE MACCABEAN.]

ISRAEL-SYRIAN RESOLUTION OF DIFFERENCES?

(February 2004)

There were many factual and analytic errors in a recent article by Alon Ben-Meir on Israel-Syrian peace possibilities. The article appeared in the Jewish Herald-Voice (Houston) on January 22, 2004.

Here are a few points by Ben-Meir and my counterpoints (facts):

Ben-Meir statement: Most issues were resolved in negotiations between Israel and Syria in 2000.

FACT: The issues were not resolved and Syria rejected the very generous offers of Israeli PM Ehud Barak. There was **NO** deal and the government of Israel changed. It is absurd to suggest that the new Israeli government should honor offers by an opposition party defeated overwhelmingly by the Israeli electorate that brought the Likud to power.

Meir: Geopolitical changes since the defeat of Iraq make Syrian-Israeli peace more likely.

FACT: It is true that the geopolitical situation in the Middle East has changed, but this has greatly weakened the despotic, anti-Israel, terrorist supporting government of Syria. In fact, the authoritative London—based Jane's Intelligence Digest reports today that the US is seriously considering confronting Syria militarily with the aim of "regime change." Increasing pressure on Syria can be found in the recent Syrian Accountability Act signed by US President George Bush last December. Syria would certainly welcome peace talks with Israel as a way to relieve the pressure to changes its policies, including its brutal occupation of Lebanon. It should not be forgotten that American troops in Iraq are facing Syrian facilitated terrorists and weapons.

Meir: Israel would benefit from a peace of reconciliation with Syria.

FACT: The Israel border with Syria has been the most peaceful in the last 37 years. A retreat from the strategic mountains of the Golan would certainly result in renewed aggression by Syria. It would also stimulate more attacks on Israel from every hostile Arab force. The view of Israel "running" from Lebanon was a direct cause of Arafat's decision to start the Oslo war of September 2000. The reader should remember the Munich Appeasement Agreement with Hitler in 1938. Appeasement and concessions to dictators makes them hungry for more and **DOES NOT** lead to peace.

BRIEF COMMENTARY:

Moshe Arens, who served three times as Israel's Defense Minister, wrote in a recent article (Haaretz, January 20, 2004), that Syrian crime should not pay. He recounts their many crimes:

1. Two invasions of Israel, 1948 & 1973
2. Brutal shelling of peaceful Israelis 1948-67
3. Vicious torture of Israelis falling into their hands
4. And finally support for multiple terrorists organizations including Hisbullah

Arens says that to reward them by a retreat from the Golan would encourage future aggression by making it a win-win option: for example: lose territory and then get it back through negotiations.

I want to express the opinion that the time has come to clear the smoke and mirrors. There is a significant Israeli dilemma in the negotiating framework with Syria. I call this dilemma: the *"Mubarak gambit."* After Egyptian dictator Anwar Sadat's death, his successor Hosni Mubarak discovered that Egypt could ignore its peace treaty obligations to Israel with impunity. Sadat had signed over 50 agreements and amendments to the Camp David Accords, which spelled out in great detail normalization of relations with Israel. These included trade, tourism, science, cultural and other attributes of peaceful relations. The late Menachem Begin, of blessed memory, fully believed that his sacrifice of Sinai, with its air bases and oil, was worth the inauguration of peaceful relations with the most important country in the Arab world.

From this experience Mubarak devised the *"Mubarak gambit,"* which sets out the principle **that an Arab country can promise Israel peace and**

full normalization as a negotiating tactic in order to force an Israeli withdrawal from territory. Then after the territory is recovered, the Arab country can ignore the normalization part of any agreement.

Mubarak first convinced terrorist leader, Yassir Arafat, to try out the **"Mubarak gambit."** We all know what has happened, including the famous handshake on September 13, 1993. We also know that all of Arafat's promises to the Israelis, including revising the PLO Charter and stopping violence, have not been honored.

In my opinion, whether peace is possible depends upon your relative propensity to believe in fairy tales. If you believe in the real possibility of achieving utopia or nirvana; and if you believe in the tooth fairy, then peace with Syria is not only possible but desirable.

Bernard J. Shapiro

SHARON THREATENS GAZA PIONEER SETTLERS WITH CIVIL WAR

(July 2004)

By Emanuel A. Winston, *a Middle East analyst & commentator* and member of the Board of Directors of the Freeman Center For Strategic Studies and one of its research associates. and Bernard J. Shapiro, *Executive Director of the Freeman Center For Strategic Studies and Editor of its monthly Internet magazine,* **The Maccabean Online** *and its daily email broadcast,* **The Freemanlist.**

As predicted, Gaza has become the launching pad for rockets as they were launched against the town of Sderot, killing four year old Afik Zahavi and a 49 year old Russian grandfather immigrant who were walking to kindergarten. Sderot has endured over 70 Kassam rocket attacks in the past three years, but until Monday June 28th no one had died. On Tuesday after the funeral, another six rockets hit Sderot. While Prime Minister Sharon was visiting Sderot at 4 PM he said *"Kassam rocket will not return to Sderot again, when we're through with our current IDF actions."* Two minutes later 3 Kassam rockets were fired and fell very close to the PM with his mouth open in dismay. The Shabak and secret service ran him out of there like a bat out of hell. Too bad Sharon's bodyguards couldn't have protected and saved the life of Afiki Zahavi, the 4 year old and the grandfather who were murdered yesterday.

Sharon said he will withdraw regardless and added the personal threat that those who resist his orders of evacuation should realize *"There is a price to pay!"* That threat has several meanings.

One: He will confiscate all properties and not pay their owners anything and give them to the Arab Muslim incoming refugees kicked out by their current Arab hosts from all Arab nations.

Two: He will use the threat often employed by Yitzhak Rabin to order the secret police to create false grounds for political arrests and harass all those who dare to defy his will. (Regrettably, the once admired Secret Services have been political contaminated and used by Prime Ministers, both Left and Right, to enforce their own political agenda.)

Three: *"He will build detention camps for settlers in case of mass resistance. The Army and Police are training special forces to carry out the evacuation".* (1) These are purposely selected thugs without conscience.

As President George W. Bush attempts to bring democracy to Iraq and the Middle East, Sharon (with the encouragement of Bush and the U.S. Arabist State Department) are erasing democracy from Israel—knowingly starting a Civil War in Israel.

Israel has seen her Prime Ministers make terrible decisions while ignoring any advice from Cabinet Ministers, Members of Knesset (Parliament) and the will of the people by their votes. Whenever necessary, they utilize the Israeli Supreme Court to give a thin covering of legality to their politics—as in the recent decisions to realign the Security Fence to protect the Arab Muslims and leave the Jews at greater risk.

These would-be dictators truly believe that, whatever comes into their minds and leaves by way of their mouths is always an infallible decision and not to be questioned. Those who have known Sharon as close friends understand that Sharon always believes his own thoughts and ideas are infallibly correct and not ever to be questioned. Those who question or oppose are quickly pushed far away as punishment for speaking their minds.

I remind the reader that all through the Oslo debacle, since 1993, October, each time there was a massive suicide bombing—continually demonstrating that there was no peace—Rabin and Peres claimed that this would not stop their "Peace Process" which, of course, was non-existent. Now Sharon echoes the Leftist mantra that, he too will disengage from the hostile Arab Muslims as a lesson in "peace making" and whoever is opposed to losing their homes, farms, synagogues, businesses, schools—or being threatened by moving hostile Arab Muslims with sophisticated weapons closer to their borders within a shrunken Israel is wrong and doesn't want peace.

From the scrambled connections in Sharon's mind, augmented by Bush and the State Department, he has issued a proclamation of abandonment of the Land, Gaza and Gush Katif (with the rest of Judea and Samaria soon to follow, then half of Jerusalem and probably the Golan Heights as pushed by the U.S. State Department). Paralleling this insanity is a push by French President Jacques Chirac and Shimon Peres to resurrect Yassir Arafat yet again. (More on this in another article.)

Do the Pioneering Settlers who were urged to turn barren desert into productive farm land by all the past Israeli governments now have to listen to a self-proclaimed Herod/Sharon of 2004/5 to leave because he alone says so?

NO, THEY DO NOT, nor must anyone else follow docilely while this befuddled old man plays with the lives of thousands. By thousands, I mean not only the 8000 Jewish men, women and children of Gaza/Gush Katif but ALL the cities and towns in the South, including Beersheva and even the centers of Tel Aviv and Jerusalem who will be placed in harm's way.

The rockets and missiles which were at first crude and inaccurate are gaining sophistication in terms of accuracy, distance and explosive power. Once Gaza/Gush Katif is *'Judenrein'* (free of Jews), including IDF patrols, checkpoints and forays to keep the Terrorists off balance, Islamic Terrorists from all over will consolidate. They will be provided with high quality missiles from Iran, Syria, North Korea and China—among others.

Gaza will very soon become the greatest terrorist enclave in the world with the ability to project Terror across most of Israel and the region. The so-called 'foreign fighters' (*'Mujahadin'*) who came from all the Arab/Muslim countries to fight Americans in Iraq will flow into Gaza with no restrictions.

Once consolidated, the level of sophisticated attacks on Israel proper with far better missiles, explosives and rockets *'et al'*, most coming through Egypt, will make Sharon crawl into his 'hidey-hole' as did Saddam Hussein. Sharon's farm near Sderot will be in easy firing range of the Gaza International Muslim Terrorists.

The laws being used by Sharon are not holy writ conferring upon government the right to put the Jewish nation or any segment of her people at deadly

The Battle for Eretz Yisrael

risk because a self-anointed dictatorial Prime Minister thought it was a good idea—or (for his spot in the history books?).

Think of the history of the Jewish people from Biblical times through today where we can clearly see the disasters caused by ego-driven decisions made by Kings or Prime Ministers who 'knew' that only they were right.

Assimilationist Jews have always been with us. Jews who loved the Land and accepted their birthright always fought them throughout the centuries. There are hundreds of examples of such battles between good and evil, between Jew and Jew. Some examples:

JEW FIGHTING JEWS

1. The prophet Samuel railed against King Saul and established the principle that Kings of Israel were not absolute monarchs (or dictators). They were subject to the will of G-d and the people of Israel. They could not violate Torah principles and not receive punishment. Often the whole people of Israel were punished. Today, Sharon is acting like an absolute dictator in violation of Judaic traditions and may certainly bring down the wraith of G-d on Israel and the Jewish people as well as himself.

2. During Chanukah we should recall the legacy of the Maccabees. Remember how two "Hellenized Jews," Jason and Menelaus tried to destroy Judaism and force assimilation on the Jewish population? Today we call them Leftists, Peace Now, assimilationist, post-Zionist Jews. For generations we have taught our children about the evil Antiochus and his attempt to suppress the Jews. In reality, there were traitors among our own people who led the way for Antiochus.

Let us be Maccabees again! Let us go into battle with the Maccabee cry, *"All who are with G-d, follow me!"* With the words: *"Who is like unto Thee O G-d"* (the acronym of which spells out the word: *"Maccabee"* in Hebrew) inscribed on their flags, the G-d inspired Jewish army swept the much larger enemy from the field in a great victory. It is this victory (and the freedom for Jews in Jerusalem and Eretz Yisrael) for which we celebrate Chanukah and not just the miracle of the oil burning eight days.

Bernard J. Shapiro

There is a simple but crucial lesson for us all in the above events. If we as Jews turn our backs on our religion and our G-d, we can expect disaster. The current government of Israel has brought down the wrath of G-d on the Israeli people for turning its back on our heritage. Like Judah Maccabee, angered by the treason of Jason and Menelaus, and outraged by Antiochus, we must revolt against Sharon. The nationalist opposition in Israel must unite behind one Zionist banner. They must fill the streets and jails with protesters. City after city must be shut down.

We must respond to the Civil War which he has mounted against his own people, with the strongest Civil Disobedience we can muster. Victory will not fall into our lap. It must be fought for and won. We must demonstrate that the strength of our will and the power of our belief cannot be defeated. Only then will victory come.

3. During WWII the Nazis forced the Jews in their control into ghettos. In order to control the huge numbers of Jews, it was necessary to establish a *'Judenrat'* made up of Jewish leaders. As the Holocaust unfolded, the *'Judenrats'* were told to select Jews for "re-settlement" (extermination). In order to maintain their status and privileges, of course they complied. They basically led the Jews, like sheep, to their slaughter.

Some Jews, like those in Warsaw, wanted to rebel against the Nazis. The Jewish leadership forbade it and refused to cooperate in self defense measures. In fact, they betrayed many brave Jews who were organizing the resistance.

After The Warsaw ghetto's original population of 500,000 had been reduced to barely 50,000, the revolt began. Many lives could have been saved had the revolt begun much sooner with the cooperation of the Jewish leadership. Today in Israel, Sharon and his followers and supporters on the Left are acting like the *'Judenrats'*, taking orders from Bush, the UN, the EU and even Mubarak of Egypt. The result will be another disaster upon the people of Israel.

The Pioneering Settlers followed the recommendations of all prior governments which were both *'de facto'* and *'de jure'*—law intended for them to settle the Land. Having done so, with their own sweat and money, it is not up to an old fool who will soon be gone to proclaim dictatorial rule under a thin veneer of so-called democracy to abandon the Land. The Jewish Nation has specifically urged, under law and common practice, that the Pioneering Settlers to go forth to the furthest borders to create a safety net against the numerous Arab Muslim invaders and Terrorists. This they have done for more than three generations and the contract to the nation has been fulfilled.

The Inner City dwellers benefitted from this line of protection as well as the agricultural produce and manufactured goods the Settlers created. But, they have forgotten what the Pioneers have done for them. This is especially true for those called assimilated Leftists who wish to open the flood-gates to Arab Muslims in massive numbers.

I use the term: "Arab Muslims" advisedly because wherever there were Arab Christians before Yassir Arafat was brought back in with his Palestinian Authority from Tunis, the Arab Muslims have repressed the Christians who have emigrated out. For example, Bethlehem was 80% Christian before Arafat took control, now there is only a minor percentage of Christian Arabs in Bethlehem.

We all recall the Biblical statement: *"Now comes a new ruler who knew not Joseph"*. Which means that the Pioneers have done their best for Israel but, now it's time to forget them and send them away on the off chance it will appease a non-people who have called themselves Palestinians since 1967. The new Pharaohs forgot that Joseph saved the Land and her people from seven years of famine and decided to enslave them. Sharon, too, as the new dictator wishes, demands obedience or, as he threatens, he will get even.

We are all familiar with George Santayana's homily: *"Those who forget history are doomed to repeat it."* We are indeed repeating it as Israel's enemies close in with the assistance of assimilated Jewish rulers.

We Jews have indeed been at war with each other for centuries. There were always the assimilated pacifists who sought to appease the Greeks (Hellenists) or those who invited in the Romans like King Herod in order to preserve their own rule.

Today, we have the Peresites and Sharon, who seeks to solidify his power by appeasing the Bush Dynasty and the Arabist State Department all making promises to an old fool who does not understand that few of those promises will be kept.

As Herod was hated, so too will Sharon be hated. As Sharon surrounds himself with thicker layers of security, knowing the same people who once loved him are beginning to hate him. Herod was hated as a tyrant who, according to an Israeli archeologist I have spoken to, had a certain egomaniacal mind-set about his legacy after death. He wanted the women in his funeral entourage to weep in a heart-broken parade. He left instructions that husbands of the women in court were to be slain so their wives' weeping would be quite real. He also funded guards at the entrance to his tomb for 60 years, lest the people in their hatred invade his tomb and scatter his bones in the desert or into a cesspool.

One can understand why Sharon no longer visits the towns of YESHA (Yehuda, Shomron and Gaza), given his tyrannical ways and the hatred he has engendered. But, Sharon has nothing to fear from the Pioneers of YESHA—other than perhaps being ridiculed as their failed hero. As for the thugs being trained to attack the settlers with force, that is another story.

Know this: Sharon has initiated and engineered a War Against the Jews of Gaza/Gush Katif and everywhere else. He cannot claim he is an innocent victim of a war he brought against the peaceful Pioneers of Gaza and YESHA.

Sharon is initiating Civil War but, wishes it to appear as if the Pioneering Settlers are the provocateurs.

The eminent psychologist Carl Jung recognized this syndrome of a false attack. The aggressor would first blame his intended victim that it was him/them who intended to attack. So, whatever the aggressor did to his victim was seem to be acceptable and the victim's fault. Therefore, Sharon has demonized the Pioneering Settlers of Gaza/Gush Katif and made them human sacrifices to appease the Arab Muslims, their International Terrorist Organizations and their Arab and/or Muslim countries as well as the Bush

Dynasty and cronies, led by the Arabist U.S. State Department. Jung had it right!

✱

1. "Army Bracing for Worst as Settlers Threaten to Resist Withdrawal Plan" by Leslie Susser JTA Daily Briefing, June 29, 2004 [from Crisis-in-Israel@yahoogroups.com*]*

Bernard J. Shapiro

ISRAEL'S VIRTUAL SURRENDER

TO ARAFAT & TERRORISM

Some Observations

(September 2004)

1. It is apparent to many people that, despite his exalted military career, Prime Minister Ariel Sharon is showing cowardice in the face of Palestinian attacks during the current war. While IDF soldiers and officers certainly are personally brave in the face of the enemy, Israel's political leadership is indecisive and non-aggressive. I ask you: When in Israel's military history did its forces not attack and occupy enemy positions from where live fire was coming? Only today is the IDF entangled with rules that prevent its ability to defeat the enemy decisively. The failure to engage the enemy with force and aggressiveness has led to a massive loss of deterrence on the part of Israel.

2. The repeated cease-fire talks and restraint demanded by the Americans have made the Israelis look like a "banana republic" as well as fools for expecting Arafat's signature on an agreement to mean something tangible.

3. The level of lying on the part of the Palestinians about Arafat's war is an indicator of how unreasonable and "anti-peace" they really are. Of course, they are truthful about their ultimate goal of destroying Israel and committing genocide against its Jewish population.

4. It is clear to me that Sharon is using Arafat's war for the purpose of causing the Jews of YESHA to evacuate their homes. This was meant to save himself the difficulty of personally taking charge of the ethnic cleansing of Jews from the area. Unfortunately today, he leading the forces demanding the ethnic cleansing of Jews from *Eretz Yisrael*. Sharon has already given the green light to Arafat, Hamas and Islamic Jihad, by his actions in not suppressing the war and destroying Israel's enemies.

5. Sharon's giveaway of Gaza and the Shomron and his plans to make all of YESHA *Judenrein* should have brought down his government, yet he still rules. I am very disappointed at this. Where is the nationalist camp?

6. There is talk of international observers for YESHA. This would be a great victory of Arafat and justify his war against Israel. The Israeli response should be a deafening no. From experience of 56 years, we all know that the UN, its bodies, and all International Forces are biased against Israel and in the pocket to the Arabs. The only purpose of such a plan would be to diminish Israel's rightful sovereignty in the area.

7. Sharon's constant warnings and threats, for which he never acts, further reduce Israeli deterrence.

8. Allowing the news media to photograph teenagers throwing stones is bad for Israel's image. It is well know that these very same photographers avoid taking pictures of Palestinian gunfire. The print journalists avoid references to live fire from the Palestinian side. Many rioters wait for journalists to arrive before rioting. Others actually collaborate with journalists to start riots strictly for the anti-Israel propaganda it inevitably brings the Arab cause. It is past time to remove journalists from the areas of clashes.

9. Oslo, Camp David, Road Map, Geneva, and the Disengagement (Retreat—Appeasement to terror) must be terminated with extreme prejudice.

10. Israel must annex immediately all of YESHA. Then the Palestinians must be told that those who engage in hostile activity against Israel will be expelled from the country. If hostility is widespread then the entire population should make **a new home in Jordan.**

Bernard J. Shapiro

COPING WITH TERRORISM AND DEMOGRAPHY

Israel's Virtual Surrender to Arafat & Terrorism

(October 2004)

[Author Note: This article is an update and revision of my September editorial.]

It is apparent to many people that, despite his exalted military career, Prime Minister Ariel Sharon is showing cowardice in the face of Palestinian attacks during the current war. While IDF soldiers and officers certainly are personally brave in the face of the enemy, Israel's political leadership is indecisive and non-aggressive. I ask you: When in Israel's military history did its forces not attack and occupy enemy positions from where live fire was coming? Only today is the IDF entangled with rules that prevent its ability to defeat the enemy decisively. The failure to engage the enemy with force and aggressiveness has led to a massive loss of deterrence on the part of Israel.

Sharon's plan to retreat from Gaza and parts of Samaria and expel its Jewish citizens can only be a stimulus for greatly increased terrorism. As the Arabs see the Jews respond to violence with surrender of their Holy Land, they will draw the appropriate conclusions: More terror will bring more retreat and expulsion of Jews. Their voracious appetite for Jewish blood will grow geometrically. In their evil visions they will believe that it is possible to progress from Gaza to Judea and Samaria and then to all of Israel in one massacre after another. Finally they will see the destruction of Israel as within the realm of possibility.

The repeated cease-fire talks and restraint demanded by the Americans have made the Israelis look like a "banana republic" as well as fools for expecting Arafat's signature on an agreement to mean something tangible. The failure to pursue **VICTORY** by the IDF allows the Arabs to regroup, learn from their experience and prepare for the next round of fighting. They have a high learning curve. If the Security Fence stops suicide bombers, then they will fire rockets over it, tunnel under it or have Israeli Arabs inside the fence carry out the attacks. Like a surgeon who must totally excise a cancer or it will metastasize and destroy whole body, the IDF must eliminate completely terrorism and those who support it.

There is talk of international observers for **YESHA**. This would be a great victory of Arafat and justify his war against Israel. The Israeli response should be a deafening no. From experience of 56 years, we all know that the UN, its bodies, and all International Forces are biased against Israel and in the pocket to the Arabs. The only purpose of such a plan would be to diminish Israel's rightful sovereignty in the area.

Sharon's issues constant warnings and threats, for which he never acts, further reducing Israeli deterrence. If Israel wants to rid itself of terrorism, it must first get rid of its AG, pro-Arab Supreme Court, and pro-Arab anti-Zionist media. Then it must release from all restraint the IDF to totally destroy the PA and other terrorist groups. And finally it must expel all the disloyal and terrorists supporting residents of Israel. It is not brain surgery. This does not require going beyond the international standard for survival of a nation state.

Oslo, Camp David, Road Map, Geneva, and the Disengagement (Retreat—Appeasement to terror) must be terminated with extreme prejudice. Israel must annex immediately all of YESHA. Then the Palestinians must be told that those who engage in hostile activity against Israel will be expelled from the country. If hostility is widespread then the entire population should make a new home in Jordan.

The level of lying and manipulation of the media by the Palestinians about Arafat's war is an indicator of how unreasonable and "anti-peace" they really are. **Of course, they are truthful about their ultimate goal of destroying Israel and committing genocide against its Jewish population.** Allowing the news media to photograph teenagers throwing stones is bad for Israel's image. It is well know that these very same photographers avoid taking pictures of Palestinian gunfire. The print journalists avoid references to live fire from the Palestinian side. Many rioters wait for journalists to arrive before rioting. Others actually collaborate with journalists to start riots strictly for the anti-Israel propaganda it inevitably brings the Arab cause. It is past time to remove journalists from the areas of clashes.

It is clear to me that Sharon is using Arafat's war for the purpose of causing the Jews of **YESHA** to evacuate their homes. This was meant to save himself the difficulty of personally taking charge of the ethnic cleansing of Jews from the area. Unfortunately today, he leading the forces demanding the ethnic cleansing of Jews from Eretz Yisrael. Sharon has already given the green light to Arafat, Hamas and Islamic Jihad by his failure to suppress and destroy them.

Sharon's giveaway of Gaza and the Shomron and his plans to make all of YESHA *Judenrein* should have brought down his government, yet he still rules. I am very disappointed at this. Where is the nationalist/religious camp?

One way to defeat terrorism is to create a giant wave of new immigrants to Israel. This will demonstrate to the Arabs that Israel is growing and strengthening. They will see facts on the ground that makes it increasingly impossible to destroy Israel and create a Palestinian state in its place.

Here are some of the methods needed to create that wave of aliya:

Terrorism must be crushed and all existential threats to the State of Israel must be preemptively destroyed. Why move to a country unable to protect its Jewish population? Then Israel should annex all state lands within the borders of Israel (post 1967). Annex all property stolen from the Jewish People during the last 2000 years, including Church and Waqf property (exceptions, of course for Holy Places. The term Holy Places does not include fraudulent claims of Muslims to Jewish or Christian Holy Places.). Then remove all illegal Arab buildings and farms.

All those in Israel must do military or community service for 3 years (including Arabs). The right to vote and be a citizen will depend on such service plus a loyalty oath to the Jewish State. Anyone with aspirations to create a Palestinian State should be removed from Israeli citizenship roles.

Israel must reaffirm that it is a Jewish State and **NOT** a democratic (one man one vote) state of all its citizens. The loyal citizens of Israel whether Jewish, Christian, Druze, Beduin or Arab will have equal rights. Prof. Paul

Eidelberg's constitution with constituency elections is the best course to preserve Israel as a Jewish democracy and should be adopted.

Judea & Samaria should be opened up for massive building, thus creating giant suburbs close to the heavily populated Israeli coastline. A system of toll roads, and light rail will connect these suburbs to the coast from Ashdod to Nahariya. This will solve the overpopulation along Israel's coast and create a better quality of living for all Israelis.

Israel must learn to deal harshly with anyone who raises up a rock to crush Jewish skulls, or a knife, gun or bomb to kill Jews. Without regard to international criticism, they should be killed or expelled from *Eretz Yisrael*.

Most troubling to me is the current campaign by the Israeli government to stifle legitimate criticism of its retreat/surrender policies. I strongly believe that this will impact negatively on aliya to Israel. Many potential new immigrants (especially those from Western countries) regard free speech, free assembly and the right to protest government policies as essential to a democratic society. They view the current drift in Israel toward McCarthyism and suppression of free speech (with the treat of imprisonment) as extremely distasteful.

Israel **NEEDS** as many Jewish immigrants as possible and we must make the country more acceptable from the standpoint of security, economics, and freedom from coercion.

A final thought: It took Jews 2000 years to regain *Eretz Yisrael*. We should most emphatically not allow the world who wished us dead to influence our decisions on how we should LIVE.

Bernard J. Shapiro

SEEING THROUGH THE FOG OF WAR

Orwell Meets Alice—Through The Mid-East Looking Glass

(July 2006)

Israel is at war and you need to know how to separate fantasy from reality. Understanding the meaning of words in such a situation is very difficult for even the best linguist or psychologist. We must go back and remember the classic book by George Orwell, 1984, in which a totalitarian government manipulates the meaning of words to confuse its citizens about reality. He called this new language "newspeak". While Orwell's book was an attempt to satirize the Soviet communist regime, its meaning extends much more broadly.

A QUICK DECODER

1. Remember that Arabs lie and the figures given for civilian casualties are greatly exaggerated. Since most Hizbollah and Hamas terrorists wear civilian clothes and mix with the local population, it is very easy to distort the true toll on civilians.

2. Damage to Lebanese infrastructure is also greatly exaggerated. Photographers and reporters in Lebanon MUST repeat the Arab terrorist propaganda line or be tortured or executed. No such threat hangs over reporters in Israel. When the media reports from both sides, you can get a very distorted picture. We tend to think that the veracity of the two sides is equal.

3. It is a hoax that there is **NO MILITARY** solution to Hezbollah, Hamas, Iran and genocidal terrorism. Those that come to kill Jews must be destroyed. There is no other choice. No "Mr. Nice Guy". The most moral position for Israel is to protect its own citizens and soldiers.

4. It is a hoax that the UN can do anything good for Israel. That also goes for Europe, Egypt and Saudi Arabia. The usefulness of international forces

separating Arab terrorists from Israeli defenders is nil, nada, zero. In fact, it is a negative, inhibiting Israel's defensive measures.

All diplomacy is also a hoax. Only the power of the IDF allows Israel to survive. Right and justice are nice, but in the final analysis, a nation's ability to survive depends on raw military power. Treaties, cease fires and negotiations are useless.

5. It is a hoax that public opinion is of great significance to Israel's survival. A strong aggressive public relations campaign is quite important, but is NO substitute for unflinching resolve to protect Israel's security and guarantee its survival.

Golda Meir once said: "I would rather have a thousand angry editorials directed at Israel, than one beautiful eulogy."

I would have to use the words of Harry Truman to express my contempt for the world that has murdered, raped, pillaged, expelled, forcibly converted and finally exterminated us. As Truman once said: "They ain't worth a bucket of warm spit."

6. Another hoax is that Israel depends on American aid and must be willing to sacrifice its security to the interest of its ally. The reality is that Israel and America have a very useful symbiotic relationship. The many ways in which the U.S. benefits from the relationship hardly need enumeration—intelligence, technology, counterterrorism techniques and much more. America gets its money's worth and more. **BUT THIS IS NEVER MENTIONED IN POLITE CIRCLES.**

For that matter, much or most of the monetary foreign aid to Israel is spent in the U.S. and goes into the American economy. It is Israeli leaders, for their own political purposes, who fail to utilize Israeli power to alter its asymmetric relationship to America.

7. Another hoax of the Left and the Islamists, for the past 13 years, is that when Israel defends itself it hurts its cause. That is, it should try to "win the hearts and minds" of the enemy, and "harming civilians" is counterproductive. Of course, we know that Hamas and Hezbollah

barbarically and illegally operate freely within civilian neighborhoods in S. Lebanon and the PA.

A very wise Rabbi Schiff gives the analogy:

"If you and I were neighbors, and I allowed a family to move into my house in my living room and shoot rockets at your house from my yard, and to store their rockets in my basement, and the police do nothing about it for years, and have 'Peace Now' on my lawn telling you not to harm me standing in my kitchen—what would you do?"

Orwell Meets Alice—Through The Mid-East Looking Glass

We have been treated to the modern equivalent of Orwellian newspeak, not to mention a harrowing trip through Alice's looking glass. One could not help but notice the extent to which the Arabs were being portrayed as pure and innocent. A casual observer would certainly think that all violence in the Middle East was a product of bloodthirsty Jewish settlers roaming the Judean-Samarian hills looking for Arab prey.

The PLO/PA leadership, its hands dripping with Jewish and Arab blood, demanded protection from the vicious Jewish residents of Judea, Samaria and Gaza (YESHA). It refused to return to negotiations until its demands were met. The gullible international media took this whole charade seriously. The United Nations began debating a resolution to give protection to the poor vulnerable Palestinians. The PLO demanded that all Jewish communities of YESHA be ethnically cleansed of those rotten murderous Jews. At the very least they needed to be disarmed, to make them easier targets for Arab terrorists.

The high and the mighty beseeched Arafat to return to the talks with Israel. The late Israeli Prime Minister Yitzhak Rabin, obviously anxious to please his PLO friends, began a crackdown on Kach and Kahane Chai and other so-called Israeli extremists. Consider this "logic": Rabin determined that Baruch Goldstein acted alone in his reprisal act. He then decided to outlaw the organizations associated with him. Guilt by association is what made McCarthy big in the 50's. It was wrong then and it is wrong now.

The Battle for Eretz Yisrael

Reality Check: Now Kach and Kahane Chai have been labeled as terrorist organizations, although they never have committed a single act of terror as a body. The PLO, which is guilty of thousands of murders of Arabs and Jews, continuing still, is labeled a "partner for peace" and will be given arms to kill some more (as "policemen").

Reality Check: Are Arabs in danger from armed Israelis in YESHA? Some research reveals the following figures since the famous handshake on September 13, 1993:

Israelis killed by Arabs = over 1600, plus 10,000 injured and maimed for life

Arabs killed by Arabs = over 500

Arab attacks on Israeli targets = 25,000+

Private Israeli attacks on Arabs = 1 (Goldstein killed 29)

(Of course MANY terrorists were killed in their **FAILED** attempts to murder Jews. This point is NOT relevant to this discussion).

It is clear that except for the attack by Goldstein, the Arabs have not been threatened by Jews and certainly need no special protection. If you travel to YESHA you will notice that every Jewish village needs a security fence, while every Arab village is open. Doesn't this tell you who is threatened and who isn't? All the talk about disarming the Jews is a cover for the Arab desire to murder them. And if you desire murder, wouldn't it be nice to disarm your victim first?

The media has begun to adopt another tactic which we should protest. In the New York Times, The Los Angeles Times, The Washington Post, The Houston Chronicle, CNN and most of the other media, opponents of the suicidal Oslo, Roadmap and Jewish Expulsion Plan are being referred to as rightwing extreme, Arab-hating and anti-peace groups. Do you ever remember the PLO, PA, Hezbollah or Hamas ever being referred to as Jew-hating groups, although their covenants and speeches are filled with hatred of Jews? Arafat and then Abbas often referred to Jews as "filthy, sons of monkeys and pigs", but are still rarely referred to in the media as Jew-haters.

Reality Check: To the best of my knowledge there is a distinct difference between Jewish feelings about Arabs and Arab feelings about Jews. Arabs are taught from the earliest grades to despise Jews, and their clerics preach hatred (Itbach El Yahoud—slaughter the Jews) in many of their services. Jews, on the other hand do not preach hatred, but those who are not brain dead recognize, after 120 years of being attacked, that Arabs mean them harm. The media is totally obfuscating the truth about the conflict by the use of such clichéd phrases as "Arab-hating Jews" or "cycle of violence."

Another problem with media coverage of the Israel-PLO/PA so-called "peace negotiations", is the way their opponents are described. Arabs opposed to the deal because they want to kill or expel all Jews from "Palestine" immediately, are equated with Jews and Israelis who want Israel to survive in secure borders. Opponents of national suicide are called "anti-peace", as opposed to supporters of such suicide being "pro-peace".

Reality Check: Most opponents of the deal with Arafat/Abbas oppose it because it is suicidal for many strategic, historical and objective reasons. None of us are anti-peace. We just recognize that the path chosen by the Rabin/ Peres/Barak/Olmert governments will lead not to the hoped for and advertised peace, but to Israel's destruction.

In another bizarre twist of logic the Los Angeles Times reports that Israel's leading peace group, Shalom Achshav (Peace Now), had urged Sharon to remove 500,000 Jewish inhabitants of YESHA (including Jerusalem) to avert widespread bloodshed under Palestinian self-government, and to forcibly evict all Jews within five years. They said that their continued presence, "fostering violence and bloodshed, endangers peace prospects."

Reality Check: The facts demonstrate that it is the Palestinians and not the Jews that are the cause of 99.9% of the violence. Why not remove the Palestinians? What Peace Now is really admitting is that there is **NO PEACE** nor any prospect of **PEACE**.

The liberal Jewish establishment and most of the media were appalled when Rabbi Meir Kahane first began talking about transferring the Arabs from Eretz Yisrael. Most are still appalled at this idea. A new idea has come into fashion, though, among these same righteous Jews: transferring the Jews from YESHA (heartland of Eretz Yisrael). Former Secretary of State James Baker once said it would be a good idea to use the $10 Billion in US loan guarantees to buy out and transfer the Jews from YESHA. US President Bill Clinton seemed to like the idea and so did Rabin's coalition partner Meretz.

Reality Check: There is no moral difference between transferring either Jews or Arabs from YESHA. What Kahane said years ago about the inability of Jews and Arabs to live together is being validated today by the same people who condemned him.

The 120-year war of extermination launched by the Arabs against the Jews of Israel has had many twists and turns. Sadly, it seems headed for Alice's looking glass and the world of 1984, where black is white, war is peace and good is evil.

ISRAEL'S FAILED SECURITY POLICY

(July 2006)

Israel has, without a doubt, the best military in world. The Israel Defense Forces are quite capable of achieving any objective the Israeli government puts before it. The soldiers of the IDF are brave, patriotic and exceptionally well trained and equipped. Unfortunately Israel's political leadership is confused, inept and lacking in Zionist motivation.

Israel has been unable to stop the **War of Extermination** against it, because it lacks the political will to do what is necessary. The current campaign to secure the release of Cpl. Gilad Shalit, the captured IDF soldier, illustrates this fact. The Israeli government has given the military very limited objectives, primarily the release of the soldier. Proper strategic planning would use the sad situation of Shalit's capture to achieve a number of far reaching and important objectives.

Already Olmert has done several things that prevent the accomplishment of these aims. He has stopped the offensive in Gaza to allow time for negotiations to release Shalit. He has allowed Israel's enemy, Egypt, to intervene, and given the terrorists time to re-group and make demands. Yesterday, Defense Minister Peretz even authorized the shipment of 600 truckloads of supplies to relieve the siege.

The Israeli objectives should be:

1. The release of the soldier.
2. Elimination of the terrorist leadership in the PA.
3. Item #2 means successfully destroying the newly elected Hamas government.
4. Immediate annexation of all territory in Judea and Samaria that has strategic and religious value (which means all).
5. Withdraw citizenship and voting rights from Israeli Arabs who support terrorism against the State of Israel.
6. Create municipal councils but not sovereignty for Arab cities in the newly annexed areas.

7. Encourage Arab emigration by strict enforcement of taxes, building permits, national service requirements, and by providing funds to aid in emigration.
8. Dramatically increase Jewish immigration to Israel by reducing taxes and regulations on business. Immigration will soar once the lands of Judea and Samaria are opened up for massive Jewish settlement.
9. The Zionist/Jewish character of Israel must be affirmed and the cost of Jewish blood must rise dramatically as the government develops a zero tolerance for terrorism.

All of the above objectives are achievable. It is my hope that the Olmert government will be replaced soon with a new Zionist government committed to the objectives I have listed. A failure of the present government to achieve the first three objectives would only hasten its being massively repudiated by the public.

There are a few other things that make my blood boil. Here is a list and the explanations.

12 THINGS I AM SICK AND TIRED OF:

1. I am sick and tired of the slowly escalating actions of the IDF to fight terrorism.

The slow escalation allows PA terrorism to become immune to Israel's strategy. It allows them to smuggle more guns, missiles, mortars and anti-aircraft missiles into PA territory. This is much the same as with bacterial infections. If the antibiotic is not strong enough to eliminate it, then the disease will return in a much more virulent form. I would suggest that the IDF launch a massive offensive against the terrorists until victory.

2. I am sick and tired of the Israeli government's fear of collateral damage to the enemy.

The Arabs have no such qualms. In fact they target civilians in bestial suicide bombings. PA weapons factories, weapons storage depots and bomb making facilities should be blasted off the face of earth even if it causes civilian casualties. Remember that *"he who is merciful to the cruel, will end up being cruel to the merciful."*

3. I am sick and tired of Israeli PM Olmert's policy of restraint.

The adjustment to accepting the killing of Jews is an abomination. A Jew here or there murdered daily, pretty soon adds up to a lot of dead and maimed Jews. I remember when the Al Aksa terror on Israel began in September 2000, the IDF general staff opened a file called "Operation Thorns", a plan for the retaking of the PA areas. They estimated Israeli dead at 300. Since then there have been almost 1500 Jews killed, which is five times the estimated combat deaths (plus 10,000 wounded, many maimed for life), with no apparent consequences to the terrorists' ability to inflict casualties on Israel. There is one extremely important variable. The PA has used the last six years to build bunkers, firing positions, smuggle in heavy weapons and missiles, create an underground arms industry and organize an army of 80,000. The defeat of PA now would certainly be more costly. And it will grow with time. There is a very short window of time to defeat the PA terrorists with minimal losses. Many political analysts and military experts agree that Israel must take decisive action NOW.

4. I am sick and tired of the US State Department urging Israel to show "restraint."

Despite the fact that the CIA knows exactly WHO (PA) is attacking WHOM (Israel) the State Department continues call for a stop to the "cycle of violence." Whenever Israel is attacked viciously, there is rush to tell Israel "to turn the other cheek".

5. I am sick and tired of Shimon Peres trying to arrange another appeasement for the PA.

He claims to be seeking a cease fire and a return to negotiations. Let me be honest with you. I don't want negotiations with either Hamas or Abbas, I want to crush them and their terrorist gangs.

6. I am sick and tired of the continued UN presence within the borders of Israel.

It's time to remove them and assert Israel's sovereignty. Israel should work to have the world withdraw its recognition of Arab refugee camps and refugees. It should condemn the hypocritical treatment of the Arab countries in exploiting these people for political purposes. Israel should declare in a strong voice that there are NO refugees. That status is not permanent and obviously should not apply to people living in the same place for 58 years.

7. I am sick and tired of the international boycott of Jerusalem as Israel's capital.

Israel should unilaterally announce to the nations of the world that all embassies MUST be in Jerusalem. (Consulates may be in Tel Aviv or any other place they want). Israel will no longer permit its eternal capital to be disrespected.

8. I am sick and tired that under both Labor and Likud governments, Arutz Sheva, Israel National Radio, has not been fully legalized.

Whatever happened to freedom of speech? Arutz Sheva should not only be allowed to establish facilities on land but also a television channel. I am also sick and tired of government television being controlled and dominated by the extreme left that does not represent the Israeli public. A lot of the time they represent the Arabs and not Israelis.

9. I am sick and tired of Israel's trying to be \'Mister Nice Guy\' to a hypocritical world.

Europeans are increasingly comparing Israel to the Nazis. Over half of all the resolutions of the UN since its founding have been directed against Israel. At the conference on how to condemn Israel in Durban, South Africa, UN head Kofi Anan condemned Israel for existing. In fact, at a recent meeting at the UN, there was a map of "Palestine", which included all of Israel. The Arab world openly plots the destruction of Israel. I am sick and tired of the vilification of "settlers".

10. I am sick and tired of Israel tolerating Moslem restrictions and desecrations on the Temple Mount.

The excuse that it would cause violence to exercise our rights there is absurd. Israel has the capability to enforce security. Virtually everything Israel wants do in the Land of Israel displeases the Arabs, who want us to leave. Jews should be allowed to pray on the Temple Mount and the destruction of Jewish antiquities by the Moslem waqf needs to be stopped immediately.

11. I am sick and tired of PA demonstrations of the fierceness of their terrorists and how they will destroy Israel.

Why not knock off a bunch of them during their demonstrations? Maybe they would be more circumspect.

12. And most important, the IDF and police should never be used for political purposes. Their purpose is to protect Israelis and not to expel them from their homes or persecute them.

I believe that we will defeat our current adversaries. We will succeed and survive from three sources of our strength: Love of **Tanach** (Torah), Love of **Eretz Israel** (Land of Israel, and Love of **Am Yisrael** (People of Israel).

. . . . In blood and fire was Israel born, and on a hot anvil was she forged. Her youth understood that life in the new Jewish homeland would require sacrifice. With stories of the stench of burning flesh from the ovens of Auschwitz embedded deep in their psyches, the young Israeli soldiers fight with the firm conviction that there is still no alternative, **"ein breira."**

To that I would like add something the American soldiers used to say during the heaviest fighting in Viet Nam. This is dedicated (slightly revised) to the brave IDF soldiers who face the enemy every day: **Yea, though I walk through the Valley of Death, I will fear no evil because the Almighty fights with me for the Restoration of Zion and for love of HIS people, Israel.**

. . . . And for the Jews of YESHA, I believe that He will *NOT* allow Olmert to expel them from the heartland of *ERETZ YISRAEL*.

THE NATURE OF PEACE AND PEACE TREATIES

(1993, 1994, 1995)

(August 17, 2008)

DEDICATED TO THE MEMORY OF GEORGIAN INDEPENDENCE

MAY ISRAEL LEARN THE LESSONS OF HISTORY SO AS NOT TO REPEAT THE MISTAKES OF THE PAST.

Great issues of war and peace as related to Israel are being debated by Jews across America. Israelis are debating the same issues among themselves. There are strong opinions on both sides of the Atlantic as well as both sides of the major issues. What seems to be lacking in all these discussions is the proper historical context. Professor Paul Eidelberg of Bar-Ilan University, reviews the historical facts.

Between 1945 and 1978 the longest time without a war going on someplace was a mere 26 days. On an average day there are 12 wars being fought somewhere on earth. The consensus of scholars has been that the norm of international relations is not peace but war. As Eidelberg reports, "Indeed, the occurrence of 1,000 wars during the last 2,500 years indicates that "peace" is little more than a preparation for war. Which means that peace treaties are **WORTHLESS**, to say the least."

Eidelberg then quotes from a book by Lawrence Beilenson, entitled **THE TREATY TRAP**, saying, "After studying every peace treaty going back to early Roman times, Beilenson concludes that treaties are made to be broken. **In fact, he shows that treaties for guaranteeing the territorial integrity of a nation are useless to the guaranteed nation, and worse than useless insofar as they engender a false sense of security. Such treaties can only benefit nations governed by rulers intending to violate them whenever expedient."**

Midge Dector says this about "peace"

What I want to say is something that virtually the whole history of the 20th century teaches us and yet something we refuse to learn. *And that is, when applied to the affairs of nations, peace is an evil word. Yes I said evil. And the idea of peace as we know it is an evil idea. From the peace of Versailles to "peace in our time" at Munich . . . each declaration of peace or expressions of longing for peace ended in slaughter. Not necessarily immediately and not necessarily directly, but slaughter all the same . . .*

For there is no such thing as making peace. Nations who are friendly do not need to do so, and nations or people who are hostile cannot do so.

To cry peace, peace when there is no peace, the prophet Jeremiah taught us long ago, is not the expression of hope, not even superstition but a reckless toying with the minds and hearts of people whose very future depends on their capacity to rise every day to the harsh morning light of the truth.

On September 3, 1993, I wrote the following:

"The rush of events in the Middle East has been dizzying. The media hype, the talking heads, the worldwide expectations of peace in the Middle East are all quite staggering. Radio, TV, newspapers herald the coming of a new era of reconciliation between Israelis and Palestinians. The positive images are so abundant that any moment one might expect to see Isaiah on Nightline showing Ted Koppel video clips of lions lying down with lambs. Though studying the same history as many of those cheering recent developments, I see nothing to be happy about.

Once again I find myself marching to a different drummer. It has happened before, with my support for the civil rights movement (early 60's) and then the anti-war in Viet Nam struggle. Despite the media hype surrounding these developments, let me make something very clear: A leopard does not change its spots. And you can say a berachaha (Hebrew blessing) over a ham sandwich, but that doesn't make it kosher. And a deal with the PLO is like a dance on quicksand—before you realize it, you have sunk into the muck and slime."

On May 18, 1994, I wrote:

On May 17, 1994, in Johannesburg, Yassir Arafat called for a "jihad (holy war) until Jerusalem is restored to Moslem rule." He said this after undertaking many peaceful commitments since September, and after signing the Declaration of Principles in Washington and the Autonomy Agreement in Cairo. He also chose to draw a parallel between the Gaza-Jericho Agreement, which he signed with Israel, and the Hudaibiya Pact signed in 628 by the Prophet Muhammad with the leaders of the Quraysh tribe. Muhammad violated the agreement two years later and it has become a symbol for the Islamic principle that agreements and treaties with non-Moslems may be violated at will. There is a lesson for us all in this event.

On June 22, 1995, \'MA\'ARIV\' finally saw the truth:

Ma'ariv comments on Meretz's role in the current Government, and says that "the Labor Party is implementing Meretz's ideology. The saying about the tail wagging the dog is being realized every time Rabin carries out what Peres—under the influence of Beilin, who thinks like Sarid—advises him."

The editors note that "Meretz has yet to prove one thing: that the way in which it is leading the Government is good for the State of Israel," and add that *"there is a growing impression that we are caught up in a mania to withdraw from all of the key positions that have ensured our existence up until now, without receiving anything appropriate in return."* The paper says that "a little anxiety about the future would not hurt Meretz's leaders, instead of the satisfied smile like a cat that has just swallowed a canary.

TIME TO END POLICY OF RESTRAINT

By Bernard J. Shapiro (1998)

"He who is merciful when he should be cruel will in the end be cruel when he should be merciful." . . . Midrash Samuel (Jewish rabbinic text from early Middle Ages)

"Yehi that I walk though the Valley of Death, I will fear no evil, because I am the meanest son of a bitch in the Valley" . . . . Viet Nam soldiers after watching their friends get blown up by the enemy.

"And the Almighty is with me and my cause is JUST." (circa 1968 and adapted by the Freeman Center for IDF)

From the very early days of the *Haganah* and continuing with the emerging Israel Defense Forces (IDF), there was a policy of self-restraint or *havlagah*. This policy mandated that defenders could only return fire, hold their positions, and never to engage in counter-terror. This policy was based on the false premise that the Arab masses did not support the war against the *Yishuv* (the Jewish population before independence) and then the State of Israel and would be brought into the conflict if Israeli forces were too aggressive. There were some good and practical reasons for **restraint** in the early days. There was legitimate fear that the British would cut off immigration if the Jews were to go on the offensive against the Arabs. *Havlagah* was essentially a *Haganah* (Labor/Socialist) policy and many supporters of Jabotinsky's Revisionist Zionist movement broke off from them to form fighting units (*Irgun Zvai Leumi* and **Stern**) unrestrained by that policy.

The modern IDF was dominated by Labor and quickly adopted the policy of restraint and the concept of *"purity of arms"* as its official doctrine. The later reinforced the former by adding that a soldier should never have to obey an illegal order to commit some atrocity. The enemy, including prisoners of war, should be treated with dignity and civilian populations should be spared as much harm as possible, *even if this causes greater Israeli casualties.* There was some flexibility in this strict moral code. A young officer named Yitzhak Rabin (1948) was sent to fire on Jewish teenagers swimming to flee the sinking **Altalena** (he killed 16 of them). Many retaliatory raids were launched against terrorist targets in neighboring countries, killing numerous civilians as collateral damage.

This policy of restraint may have been practical during the pre-state days and even during the early years of Israeli independence. These periods were characterized by weakness and relative dependence on foreign goodwill. Following the **Six Day War** in 1967, the need for *havlagah* decreased and the damage it caused began to become more evident. Israel became the preeminent power in the Middle East, yet failed to grasp the strategic opportunities that came with such dominance. Here are some of the historical highlights of the failed policy of restraint:

1. Following the **Six Day War** (1967) and the capture of Jerusalem, Moshe Dayan turned over control of Judaism's most sacred place, the **Temple Mount**, to Moslem authorities. He did it to appease their sensibilities to the Israeli capture of the city. Jewish rights were ignored to please the defeated Arabs, who had plotted our destruction. Dayan also prevented a mass exodus of Arabs from **YESHA**, which ultimately led to the problems we face today.

2. During the **War of Attrition** with Egypt (1969-70), the Israeli forces adopted primarily a defensive posture. They built a system of bunkers (**The Bar Lev Line**) along the Suez Canal. Israeli soldiers were heavily pounded daily by Egyptian artillery. Finally they began to use aircraft to strike targets deep into Egypt. The policy of restraint kept them from striking anything but military and minor economic targets. Israeli soldiers died because the government was inhibited from causing Egypt **'real'** pain.

3. The Yom Kippur War of 1973 is a classic example of restraint run amok. Israeli military intelligence did not fail to recognize the approaching danger as has been the common account. In fact, Israel's leaders made the political decision not to utilize the great power of the IDF to crush the Egyptian and Syrian armies that they **KNEW** were planning to attack. Thousands of Israeli soldiers died needlessly.

4. The Camp David Accord (1978) with Egypt was another example of the failure to exert Israeli power. The oil fields of Sinai would have given

Israel economic independence from America. The cost of redeployment from Sinai placed Israel in almost permanent debt to American diplomacy (often pro-Arab). Did Israel achieve anything worthwhile at Camp David? I think not and believe history will bear me out. Egypt has become one of the most ant-Semitic and hostile Arab countries in the world. As a result of Camp David, the Egyptian army now threatens Israel, having been equipped with the most modern American weapons.

5. During the **War in Lebanon** (1982), the IDF reached Beirut and then failed to complete the destruction of the PLO. Our enemies were allowed to escape and prepare to fight another day. Why didn't the Israeli Navy sink the ships loaded with PLO troops (including Arafat) as they fled Beirut? **RESTRAINT!**

6. In 1987 the *intifada* began and the Israeli forces showed great restraint and thus were incapable of crushing it. Of course, Israel received no credit in the Western media for such restraint. The failure to defeat this uprising began a process of demoralization among the Israeli population.

7. The Persian Gulf War (1991) and the SCUD attacks on Israel led to further demoralization. The failure to adequately respond to Iraq's aggression and the humiliating sealed rooms, led to a rapid decline in Israeli morale and desire to defend itself. More and more Israelis began to feel impotent, weak and fatigued with the continuous battle for survival. The Oslo Accords were the logical outcome of this depression and feeling that they could not sustain the struggle.

8. The Oslo Accords (1993) were the ultimate failure of the policy of restraint. Israel actually was very powerful. The IDF was unequaled in the Middle East. Yet despite this power, its leaders were ready to grant equal status to a band of murderers and ultimately create a state of "Palestine" which would challenge its right to the **Land** and its **capital of Jerusalem.**

9. Israeli forces in Lebanon (today) are restricted in their ability to fight the Hizbollah and other terrorists. They must be given a free hand to 'punish' all those who facilitate attacks on them including Syria, Lebanon, and Iran. No more agreements that tie Israeli hands.

The damage caused by *havlagah* (restraint) has been immense and it far past time to reverse that policy. Israel must massively and disproportionately retaliate for terrorist attack. The murderers of Jews must be plucked from their safe havens in Palestinian Authority areas. Oslo must be declared null and void due to Arafat's non-compliance with its terms. No more giving him *"one more chance."* <u>The test is over. HE FAILED! He and his cronies should be arrested and tried for murder</u>.

MAY THE LION OF JUDAH RISE ON THIS ROSH HASHANA AND RECLAIM THE SOUL OF ISRAEL AND WITH A MIGHT HAND VANQUISH HER ENEMIES . . . .

FIGHTING TERRORISM AND THE THEATER OF THE ABSURD

By Bernard J. Shapiro
March 11, 1996

On Wednesday, March 13, 1996, we will witness a grand farce on an international stage. President Bill Clinton has assembled a group of some 31 nations to hold an "Anti-Terrorist Conference" on the shores of Sharm a-Sheikh, which lies on the coast of Egyptian Sinai. While no one can argue with fighting terrorism, the real purpose of the meeting is to shore up both the sagging political fortunes of Israeli Prime Minister Shimon Peres and Clinton's meager foreign policy credentials.

Terrorism is not fought with political theater, but with constant vigilance, good intelligence, and steadfast political will. The Israeli government has facilitated the present state of rampant terrorism in its country through negligence and ill considered "peace" moves. Some of the more important actions by the Israeli government which have impacted negatively on its citizens are the following:

1. Abandonment of its intelligence network of Arab agents in Judea, Samaria, and Gaza. These Arabs were the "eyes and ears" of Shin Bet (Israelis internal security agency). Working with them over 90% of terrorist actions were prevented. When the Oslo Agreement was signed, Israel made a political decision to cooperate with the Palestinian Authority security apparatus. Intelligence information was exchanged which compromised the identities of Israeli informers. The Palestinians systematically tortured and murdered over 1200 Arabs believed to be "collaborators" with Israel. While retaliation against these individuals was specifically forbidden in the Oslo Agreement, both Israel and the United States chose to ignore this brutal fact.

2. The creation of territory under the control of the Palestinian Authority had the immediate effect of also creating safe havens from which terrorist could operate. The assembly of high-tech suicide bombs became practical with a secure home base in which to train operatives and store explosive material. PLO Chief Yasir Arafat has protected the terrorist infrastructure

of both Hamas and Islamic Jihad and allowed them to increase in strength and effectiveness.

3. The release of over 11,000 terrorist prisoners as a part of political arrangements made the concept of "punishment for a crime" obsolete. This had a significant influence in creating a climate for future terrorist actions.

4. The failure of the Palestinian Authority to extradite known terrorists had the affect of guarantying safety to anyone committing murder inside Israel and escaping the few miles into PA territory. While extradition of terrorists is guaranteed in the Oslo Agreement, it has never been carried out. Israel has chosen to ignore this violation and has lobbied the US Congress to ignore it also. After every terrorist outrage, Arafat has had a few people arrested with much fanfare, only to release them quietly a few days later.

5. The greatest political error by the Israelis has been the false assumption that Arafat would fight Hamas. It is no coincidence that Arafat attended the funeral of "the engineer," credited with inventing the car-bomb. At the funeral he praised the master bomber as a martyr to the Palestinian cause and urged his audience to emulate him. He called for jihad, a holy war to destroy the Jews and create a Palestinian state from the "river (Jordan) to the sea (Mediterranean) with Jerusalem as its capital." Hamas's Sheikh Mahmoud Zahar on the relationship between Hamas and the PLO: "Like the wings of a bird, they must work together."

Clinton has invited Arafat to the summit and is trying to get Syria's Hafez Asad to come also. What is the purpose of inviting terrorists to an anti-terrorist summit? It reminds one of hiring the fox to guard the hen house. Nothing can be accomplished at this conference except photo-ops and political games. Fighting terrorism requires a lot of hard work, away from the spotlight. It requires good intelligence acquired through building the confidence of informers that they will not be compromised. It also requires intelligence of another sort. The kind that can distinguish between friend and foe.

On September 3, 1993, the Jewish Herald-Voice published my press release from the Freeman Center: "The rush of events in the Middle East

Bernard J. Shapiro

has been dizzying. The media hype, the talking heads, the worldwide expectations of peace in the Middle East are all quite staggering. Radio, TV, newspapers herald the coming of a new era of reconciliation between Israelis and Palestinians. The positive images are so abundant that any moment one might expect to see Isaiah on Nightline showing Ted Koppel video clips of lions lying down with lambs. Though studying the same history as many of those cheering recent developments, I see nothing to be happy about. Once again I find myself marching to a different drummer. It has happened before, with my support for the civil rights movement (early 60's) and then the anti-war in Viet Nam struggle." Despite the media hype surrounding these developments, let me make something very clear: A leopard does not change its spots. And you can say a berachaha (Hebrew blessing) over a ham sandwich, but that doesn't make it kosher. And a deal with the PLO is like a dance on quicksand—before you realize it, you have sunk into the muck and slime."

What I wrote then has proven to be true. I am saddened by this. I would have preferred to be wrong. The 220 Israelis who have died and the 900 horribly maimed by terrorists' bombs would then be alive and well.

Preemption or Destruction: Which Should Israel Choose?

Israel has been swept with Arab violence and terrorism since the late 19th century. Israeli Prime Ministers have tried but failed to stem the tide. Ariel Sharon, well known for his tough tactics in quelling terrorism in Gaza in the 70's, has also failed.

Back in 1965, in a small meeting room in Tel Aviv, former Defense Minister Moshe Dayan gave a pep talk to a group of RAFI (Rishimat Poalai Israel) volunteers, myself included. At that time, RAFI, a breakaway faction of the Mapai Party, included such notables as former Prime Minister David Ben Gurion and former Defense Minister Shimon Peres. Peres and Dayan had been considered the "hawks" of Mapai and it was no accident that in the 1965 election they supported a strong defense and security policy.

Dayan was always interesting to listen to, but this talk was something special and we paid attention to every word. "The essence of Israel's security in this region (Middle East) is deterrence," he said. "When we formed the State in 1948-9, we were very weak. The Arab States had planes, tanks, heavy artillery and many more soldiers than us.

We had very little heavy military equipment. In the period 1949-55, we absorbed almost a million immigrants. Tent cities sprung up all over the country. We were totally disorganized. Had the Arabs mounted another major invasion, we could have lost. We devised a solution to this problem. It was deterrence. Think about being lost in a forest and surrounded by hostile animals. If you light a torch, boldly approach them showing no fear—they will retreat. But, if you show fear—they will attack and you are lost. We used this principle to save Israel during those early years. Every time we were attacked, we retaliated tenfold. We showed daring and penetrated deep within their borders to attack our targets. We were fearless, brave, and even a bit bloodthirsty. You know the result. The Arabs were afraid and never attacked. Deterrence worked. By 1956 when we invaded Sinai, the Israel Defense Force was not just strong, it was invincible."

The story above was not told just for nostalgia. The lesson is extremely important for the survival of Israel today. Unfortunately Israelis are daily witnessing the consequences of seven years of declining deterrence vis a vis its Arab population. In 1987, the intifada presented Israel with a new challenge. It was a new kind of war, but with the same aim of driving the Israelis out of their country. The Israelis fought the intifada with many handicaps, not the least of which were their own rules of conduct. Israeli soldiers failed to cope with attacks by teenage Arab boys. In the course of several years, the Arabs learned that the soldiers would not aggressively retaliate for their attacks. They became emboldened.

The Jews living in Judea, Samaria, and Gaza showed great fortitude, enduring thousands of attacks and still tripling their numbers. The serious security failure developed as Arabs became accustomed to attacking Jews and Israeli soldiers. By trying to remain humane in the face of massive attacks, Israel emboldened the Arabs to more and more attacks. Throwing concrete boulders, Molotov cocktails, and then using firearms at Israelis became the norm of behavior among the Arabs. The Israeli government allowed its citizens to be attacked solely because they were Jews. In no other country of the world would such a policy be tolerated. Just two weeks ago a reserve officer of the Israel Defense Forces made a wrong turn and ended up in the center of Ramallah, an Arab city. He was immediately attacked by a vicious mob of Arabs, murder in their eyes, who almost beat him to death. Deterrence had vanished.

While the Jews may not have been afraid like the man in the forest, the affect of multiple restrictions on the Israeli right of self defense had the same result. That result was to increase the bloodlust of the Arab population and to multiply the Jewish casualties.

In 1991, the Persian Gulf War, with its SCUD attacks on Israel, further undermined Israeli deterrence. Having to depend on United States Forces instead of her own had a deleterious effect on Israeli self-confidence. It is notable that the Arab population of Judea and Samaria danced on their on their roofs and cried, "Gas the Jews" as the SCUD's headed for Tel Aviv. The self-assurance of the Israelis also declined immensely as a result of their cowering in sealed rooms during the missile attacks.

After the Gulf War, Shimon Peres and his associates began to search for a solution to the Arab-Israeli conflict that did not require deterrence. The answer, Peres thought, was to be found in the growing influence of the extreme left (Meretz Party) in Israeli's ruling Labor elite. For many years, the left in Israel and its supporters in America have promoted the doctrine of "Israeli guilt" for the continuing Arab-Israeli conflict.

The leftists accepted the Arab propaganda version of Middle Eastern history and see their role as making amends for alleged "wrongs" committed against the Palestinian Arabs. When the Labor Party formed a coalition with Meretz, it was assumed that Meretz would be the junior partner. What we have witnessed is the virtual infusion of extreme left-wing philosophy into the body of Labor.

Peres took this "Israeli or Jewish guilt" and developed it into a "peace" policy based on rectifying "wrongs" committed against the Palestinian Arabs. The leftists saw the most serious "wrong" as being the occupation itself. Jewish rule over a minority of Arabs was considered so immoral, in and of itself, as to cause a destructive decline in Israeli democracy and public morality. The details of maintaining the occupation, like reserve duty in Gaza, were said to cause everything from violence in the home to reckless driving.

Divorcing Israel from the territories was seen as a goal for Israel and not just a victory for the Arabs.

I describe the Peres "peace" policy as the "dhimmization of Israel." It was based on virtually giving the Arabs everything they wanted: a PLO state in most of the territories, control of land and water, return of refugees, and a shared status for Jerusalem. His belief was that by Israeli actions and concessions, he could terminate Arab hostility to Israel. Peres exhibited the fallacy of believing that anti-Semitism is caused by the "bad behavior" of Jews. He failed to understand that there are major forces of religion, history and psychology in the one billion strong Islamic world that cannot be manipulated by anything that Israel does.

Would the Holocaust have been prevented if the Jews of Europe had been "nicer" to the Nazis? By shrinking Israel to a size that was non-threatening to the Arabs, Peres hoped to achieve for Israel the status of a dhimmis-nation in the Islamic world. Dhimmis status, you will recall, is the inferior third-class status afforded Jews in Arab countries throughout the centuries.

Now Prime Minister Barak was willing to give the Golan Heights to Syria despite the full knowledge that this would weaken Israel and make it more vulnerable to attack. The concurrent loss of one third of Israel's water resources would further weaken Israel. What is hard for rational Jews and Israelis to understand is that weakening Israel is precisely the purpose of the 'peace process.'

Israel, with its powerful military and independent citizens, had always been an affront to Moslems everywhere.

Therefore, Jews should be made subservient, weak and dependent on the approval of their Moslem overlords. Peres understood that Israel in its present borders was too strong to be destroyed. He also understood that the Arabs were offended that they could not destroy Israel within its defensible borders. The Peres solution seems to involve making Israel weak, creating a PLO state, and even groveling before Arab rulers. Such an emasculated dhimmis-like Israel, would now win the approval of the Islamic world. He would call it "peace." Some would call it appeasement. Some would cheer. Some would protest. Freeman Center members (and real Zionists) see the Peres/Barak/PLO/Syria plan as a nightmare and pray that Israel's leaders will come to their senses and return to a policy of deterrence, security and defense of Israeli interests.

The Bottom Line

Israel must preempt the threats described in the article below and NOT ACCEPT A FIRST STRIKE AS INEVITABLE. Survival depends on it. Ein Brera.

★

Bernard J. Shapiro is executive director of the Freeman Center For Strategic Studies www.freeman.org *and editor of its monthly Internet magazine,* The Maccabean Online, the Freemanlist, and the Freeman Blog.

★

Israel Braces For The Iranian Rain Of Fire

militarystrategy.com

November 5, 2010: The head of Israeli military intelligence warned his political superiors that the next major war Israel encountered would likely result in much higher Israeli casualties, especially to civilians. There is also growing concern about Russia selling advanced anti-aircraft systems to Syria, which could pass them on to Iran.

All this could be traced back to preparations Iran has been making for over a decade. Using their oil wealth, and weapons smuggling network, Iran has armed Syria, Hezbollah (the Shia militia in southern Lebanon) and Hamas (the Palestinian terrorist group that runs Gaza) with over 50,000 rockets, plus numerous other weapons. Most of the rockets are short range (about 10 kilometers), but several thousand have a much longer reach, and can hit targets throughout Israel.

The Iranian master plan is for Hezbollah, Hamas, Syria and Iran to simultaneously fire as many missiles and rockets into Israel as they can. Even if there are no ground forces to follow up such an attack, the casualties (civilian and military) in Israel would be seen as a great Islamic victory, and would demoralize the Israelis. While Israeli defensive moves could do great damage to Syria, Lebanon and Gaza, Iran considers it a reasonable plan. Hezbollah, Syria and Hamas are not so sure, but Iran already has all the rockets and missiles in place.

Israeli military planners have seen this coming. Over the last three years, Israel has been revising its civil defense plans, and how to deal with the growing arsenal of rockets and ballistic missiles aimed at it. The latest change is the announcement that the military is dispersing its stocks of supplies, equipment and spare parts to a larger number of (better protected) locations.

The basic defense plan assumes a future war with Syria, and gives the local officials an idea of what to expect. Currently, the Israelis estimate that there would be as many as 3,300 Israeli casualties (including up to 200 dead) if Syria tried to use its long range missiles against Israel. If the Syrians used chemical warheads, Israeli casualties could be as high as 16,000. Over 200,000 Israelis would be left homeless, and it's believed about a 100,000 would seek to leave the country.

Israel now assumes that Iran would also fire some of its ballistic missiles as well, armed with conventional warheads. But the big danger is Syria, which is a client state of Iran. Syria has underground storage and launch facilities for its arsenal of over a thousand SCUD missiles. Armed with half ton high explosive and cluster bomb warheads, the missiles have ranges of 500-700 kilometers. Syria also has some 90 older Russian Frog-7 missiles (70 kilometer range, half ton warhead) and 210 more modern Russian SS-21 missiles (120 kilometer range, half ton warhead) operating with mobile launchers.

There are also 60 mobile SCUD launchers. The Syrians have a large network of camouflaged launching sites for the mobile launchers. Iran and North Korea have helped Syria build underground SCUD manufacturing and maintenance facilities. The Syrian missiles are meant to hit Israeli airfields, missile launching sites and nuclear weapons sites, as well as population centers. Syria hopes to do enough damage with a missile strike to cripple Israeli combat capability.

Israel has long been aware of the Syrian capabilities and any war with Syria would probably result in some interesting attacks on the Syrian missile network. The SCUD is a liquid fuel missile and takes half an hour or more to fuel and ready for launch. So underground facilities are a major defensive measure against an alert and astute opponent like Israel.

But Syria has been adding a lot of solid fuel ballistic missiles to its inventory, and recently transferred some of these to Hezbollah, in Lebanon. Hezbollah and Syria would likely coordinate an attack on Israel. Hamas, in Gaza, is a semi-client of Iran, and might be persuaded to join in as well.

No unclassified government planning documents have discussed what Israel would do in response to such an attack, but in the past, Israel has threatened to use nukes against anyone who fired chemical weapons at Israel (which does not have any chemical weapons). But current plans appear to try and keep it non-nuclear for as long as possible.

GOD, ONE-AND-ONLY:
WILL I HAVE TROUBLE GETTING
THRU PLO/HAMAS SECURITY?
MOSES
alvarez '94

August 5, 1992

Israeli soldiers often feel they need a lawyer by their side, to ensure they don't open fire before their lives are <u>really</u> endangered.

August 16, 1993   *Christopher assures Rabin about the returning Hamas deportees.*

I DON'T UNDERSTAND WHY YOU WORRY SO MUCH ABOUT SECURITY...
OLEG © 95

Dry Bones

Panel 1: BEHOLD! THE EMPEROR HAS PUT ON MAGICAL NEW GARMENTS OF PEACE!

Panel 2: BUT A BOY CRIED OUT... THE "EMPEROR" IS NAKED! SHHH! GASP

Panel 3: WHICH MADE THE PARADE MASTER VERY ANGRY!! SEIZE THAT RIGHT WING FANATIC! HIS BELIEF IS TOO WEAK TO SEE THE EMPEROR'S NEW CLOTHES!

Panel 4: AND SO THE EMPEROR KNEW THAT HE WOULD NEVER HAVE TO CHANGE HIS CLOTHES, OR HIS WAYS, OR HIS OBJECTIVES!

CHAPTER EIGHT: ISRAELI POLITICAL ISSUES

Israel has a complicated political system of proportional representation. With 120 members of a unicameral legislature called the Knesset. The, unfortunately leads to a fragmented body with 10-12 political parties represented. The balance for many years was dominated by the Socialist Zionist Left but today the Zionist Religious Right is predominate.

Unfortunately many segments of the ruling elite still represent the Left while the electorate has shifted to the Right. Examples are the Supreme Court, the media, the police, the Shin Bet (Secret Service), many judges, most academics and the Border Police.

The Left has become a force for appeasement and surrender in Israel and has aligned itself with the traitorous anti-Israel Arabs. The high birth rate of the religious community will eventually solve this problem (hopefully not to late).

Bernard J. Shapiro

COMMUNICATION AND PUBLIC POLICY

IMPLICATIONS FOR ISRAEL'S FOREIGN RELATIONS

[Editor's Note: This article was originally published on February 4, 1993. I feel that its message is critical to the success of the new Netanyahu government.]

Virtually every news commentator compares Israel's temporary removal of 400 terrorists to Lebanon with the heinous crimes of Iraqi dictator Saddam Hussein. The United Nations is being asked not to have a double standard for Iraq and Israel. In fact, the Palestine Liberation Organization, having been recognized as the world's highest moral arbiter, has been asked by the United Nation's Secretary General Boutros-Ghali to draft a resolution condemning Israel and calling for sanctions. Something is obviously wrong with this picture. It is time for Israelis and their supporters to recognize that Israel has a public relations problem.

The actions Israel took to defend its security were quite moderate by Middle East standards. Its ability to explain what and why it took such action was inadequate. Along with most of the pro-Israel community, I'm a frequent critic of Israeli information policies. I had a pleasant lunch last week with an Israeli official and we discussed this very issue. As a result of our conversation, I am convinced that the Israeli government is doing everything in its power to communicate its message to the media, political leaders, and general public. It's just not working.

What is needed is a whole new approach to Israeli public relations. Let's call it: THE MARKETING OF ISRAEL, and look at the problem from an advertizing perspective. About nine months ago, I discussed with an executive of a major advertising company the possibility of producing television spots supporting Israel's positions on various political issues. I became discouraged upon learning that the major stations do not permit "advocacy" commercials. And then Yitzhak Rabin was elected in Israel's national elections and there was a major turn for the better in Israel's image.

I think it is time to take a second look at my concept but expand it to include radio, magazines, cable television (cable will accept this type of commercial) and newspapers. The ads should range from the very soft evocative travel type to some hard hitting but subtle political messages. Pretend that Israel is a corporation with a vast market in the United States. Receipts from that market top $6 Billion Dollars (including US economic and military aid, UJA, Israel Bonds, JNF, plus all the other campaigns from Yeshivas to the Technion). What would you spend to protect a market of that magnitude? One half of one percent would equal $30 million. You can run for president with thirty million dollars. In a wild fantasy, let's say we have that much money. And let's say we hire a talented creative ad man to develop a multi-faceted, multi-media, and multi-year campaign to win the hearts and minds of the American people.

This should not be an impossible task. Israel is a good product, lots of virtues, few vices. (Can you imagine convincing the American people to love Saddam?) We could do nothing, but the consequences are not so good. Public opinion polls are beginning to show the Arabs winning more and more sympathy. Yes, Arabs who keep their women in bondage; Palestinians who disembowel pregnant teachers in front of their classes; Syrians who peddle narcotics to American inner city youth and commit mass murder if provoked; Saudis who threaten to behead a man for practicing Christianity; all of these and more are almost as popular as Israel. The Arabs are good at smearing the good name of Israel. Just listen to Hanan Ashrawi some time. No matter what the question, she manages to fit in a lie about Israel in her answer. Israel has already lost the college campus, half of the Afro-Americans, a good portion of the Protestants except for the Baptists and the Evangelicals and some in the Jewish community.

The Israel government needs to realize that we are living in a new world where telecommunications brings us closer than ever before to each other. In the fifties when Israel was criticized, Ben Gurion used to say, "It's not what the world thinks, but what the Jews do that is important." It is a different world now and for every Israeli policy, the public relations aspect must be examined. I am definitely not calling on Israel to submit to public opinion but instead to organize and mold it for their benefit. I don't want Israel immobilized by fear of bad public relations. I want Israel to plan, with the help of experts, a strategy to counteract the negative effects of any public policy move. Would Rabin send his soldiers into battle without a detailed plan and strategy to win? The time has come for Israel to develop a strategy to win the public relations battle. The Jewish community in this country is more than willing to lend its money and advertizing talent to aid in this task. Let's do it! (Are you listening Bibi?)

[This article was reissued in the Maccabean Online in June 1996 and October-November 2005.]

THE PEACEMAKERS OF CHELM

As a child, my grandfather used to entertain me with delightful tales about the foolish Jews of Chelm. Chelm was said to be a tiny **shtetal** (Jewish village) in the Russian Pale of Settlement during czarist times. Its inhabitants were known primarily for their foolishness.

In most of these tales one finds that a resident of Chelm becomes fixed upon an idea which is totally a variance to objective reality. An example: One day a visitor from Chelm took refuge for the night at the home of a famed Rabbi. He told the Rabbi's housekeeper to wake him early and to lay out his clothes so he could dress and depart the next morning without disturbing the Reb. After waking, he dressed in the dark and mistakenly put on the Rabbi's clothes, complete with long black coat and black hat. Upon arriving back in Chelm, he saw his reflection in the large mirror in the entryway to his home. Full of anger and scorn, he yelled, "That stupid housekeeper! He woke the Rabbi instead of me!"

Chelm has been on my mind lately as I view the current move to give Israel's sacred patrimony to the Arabs. I raised this issue through one of my computer networks, saying, "I wish someone would explain to me why **ANY INTELLIGENT** Israeli could believe the nonsense (PLO/Israel deal) its leaders are expounding." A wonderful response came from Professor Mark Steinberger (Department of Math and Statistics, State University of New York in Albany, New York). He writes: "This has also been bothering me lately. I would say that leftists must inhabit an alternate universe, except that we wind up having to pay the consequences for their detachment from reality.

But, while we do live in the same objective world, their vision of it seems to have nothing in common with ours. They do not comprehend reality as we see it, and when challenged with evidence that would seem to buttress our view, they seem either to dismiss it for theoretical reason or ignore it completely.

One can list various dangers in the agreement, and give objective evidence that Palestinians have no desire for peace, but still want to drive our people into the sea. What is the reaction? They will tell you that self-determination and prosperity will change the Palestinians' outlook and behavior. On what do they base this? Not on evidence from Arab societies. Rather, it is based on theory.

Indeed, one can point to the fact that warfare, macho-one upmanship, racist hegemonism and Islamic fanaticism are endemic to Arab cultures, including the more prosperous ones such as Egypt and Lebanon. The leftist response is either to ignore the point or to counter with accusations of insensitivity and Eurocentrism.

To me, this looks like an unwillingness to deal with reality, and it echoes the unwillingness of the Jewish community of the Thirties to recognize the threat posed by the Nazis.

Indeed, it seems we have learned nothing at all from our experience with Nazism. The Holocaust has become little more than a tale to frighten children: demons in a morality play. They have turned the Holocaust into an image divorced from real world happenings. Millions more Jews could die in Israel, but they refuse to even imagine the possibility.

THEY WILL NOT ALLOW REALITY TO INTERFERE WITH THEIR MYTHS."

The stories from Chelm have amused Jews for many generations. Many of us, however, are not amused that the peacemakers of Israel seem to be operating in the best tradition of the colorful inhabitants of Chelm.

[Published in the Jewish Herald-Voice on December 23, 1993 and reissued in the Maccabean Online in March 1997.]

A TIME FOR PEACE,

AND A TIME FOR WAR

By Bernard J. Shapiro

We find all the expressions of horror at recent statements concerning a soldier's obligation to avoid abandoning army bases and settlements to terrorists, to be hypocritical, self-serving, and unfortunate. The Israeli government of Ehud Barak is in rebellion against everything that Israel, Zionism, and Judaism are all about. They are the ones causing the rift in the body politic and they will be totally responsible for any resulting violence.

When will the Nationalist Camp realize that we are "at war already" with the PLO supported tyranny that rules Israel? At what point will Israelis realize that the CIVIL WAR they fear, IS ALREADY TAKING PLACE AND THEY ARE LOSING? Why don't members of the Nationalist Camp understand that FORCE is being used by only ONE side and that is the government. The monopoly on power must be broken or there is no hope.

Under the Nazis, the Jews of Warsaw numbered over 500,000. They were depleted with regular deportations aided by *Judenrats* (Jewish leaders). The Revolt in Warsaw began when the Jewish population was down to 50,000 (or 90% murdered). At what point is it OK to rebel? When is civil disobedience OK? When is civil war a better course than suicide? All throughout history there have been rebels and loyalists. History is usually written by the victors but truly there is seldom a universally accepted moral standard as to what is a proper rebellion and what is not. We can say with absolute certainty, however, that the Jewish return to Zion and our struggle today for *Eretz Yisrael* are more righteous than any other struggle for national liberation in the history of the world.

A massive outpouring of Israelis prepared to get arrested in civil disobedience would have stopped the Oslo Suicide Pact years ago. The government plan to withdraw the IDF from settlements in YESHA is nothing more than a than a way to make them insecure in the face of Arab attacks. The ultimate aim being to cause them to evacuate their homes and save the government the trouble of ethnic cleansing them for Arafat. Jews will have a choice: being massacred or abandoning their homes. Their ability to defend themselves will have been thwarted by the government in collusion with the terrorists.

Following my five weeks of research in Israel, I spelled out (May-June 1994 issue of THE MACCABEAN) the nature of this inevitable conflict:

Author's Note: Dayenu was originally written for Rabin and Peres. It applies to Olmert, Barak, Livni, and Sharon as well.

Dear Friends:

Like most of you, I am frustrated, angry and depressed over the actions of the Israeli government. We must, however, get over the depression and then use our anger to spur ourselves to greater action on behalf of Israel. *EIN BRERA*. In that spirit I offer the following chant or song to sing at demonstrations (slightly abridged from the popular song sung at Passover). Please distribute as widely as possible:

With Love of Israel, Bernard J. Shapiro [August 7, 1995]

TO THE ISRAELI GOVERNMENT OF RABIN AND PERES

DAYENU—IT WOULD HAVE BEEN ENOUGH

If you had collaborated with enemy to get elected to office,

Dayenu—It would have been enough to rebel against your rule

If you had collaborated with the enemy and not given away our **Sacred Land** and **Holy Places**,

Dayenu—It would have been enough to rebel against your rule

If you had collaborated with the enemy; given away our **Sacred Land** and **Holy Places**; and not divided the **People of Israel** setting brother against brother,

Dayenu—It would have been enough to rebel against your rule

Bernard J. Shapiro

If you had collaborated with the enemy; given away our **Sacred Land** and **Holy Places**; divided the **People of Israel**; and not beaten and abused women and children,

Dayenu—It would have been enough to rebel against your rule

If you had collaborated with the enemy; given away our **Sacred Land** and **Holy Places**; divided the **People of Israel**; beaten and abused women and children; and not suppressed our freedom of speech,

Dayenu—It would have been enough to rebel against your rule

If you had collaborated with the enemy; given away our **Sacred Land** and **Holy Places**; divided the **People of Israel**; beaten women and children; suppressed our freedom of speech and not endangered our water supply,

Dayenu—It would have been enough to rebel against your rule

If you had collaborated with the enemy; given away our **Sacred Land and Holy Places**; divided the **People of Israel**; beaten women and children; suppressed our freedom of speech; endangered our water supply and not released terrorist murderers into our midst,

Dayenu—It would have been enough to rebel against your rule

If you had collaborated with the enemy; given away our **Sacred Land** and **Holy Places**; divided the **People of Israel**; beaten women and children; suppressed our freedom of speech; endangered our water supply; released terrorist murderers into our midst and not surrendered our strategic mountains that protect us from attack,

Dayenu—It would have been enough to rebel against your rule

If you had collaborated with the enemy; given away our **Sacred Land** and **Holy Places**; divided the **People of Israel**; beaten women and children; suppressed our freedom of speech; endangered our water supply; released terrorist murderers into our midst; surrendered our strategic mountains; and not created a Palestinian State dedicated to the destruction of Israel,

Dayenu—It would have been enough to rebel against your rule

If you had collaborated with the enemy; given away our **Sacred Land and Holy Places**; divided the **People of Israel**; beaten women and children; suppressed our freedom of speech; endangered our water supply; released terrorist murderers into our midst; surrendered our strategic mountains; created a Palestinian State and not broken **G-d's Covenant with Abraham**,

Dayenu—It would have been enough to rebel against your rule

If you had collaborated with the enemy; given away our **Sacred Land** and **Holy Places**; divided the **People of Israel**; beaten women and children; suppressed our freedom of speech; endangered our water supply; released terrorist murderers into our midst; surrendered our strategic mountains; created a Palestinian State; broken **G-d's Covenant with Abraham** and not defamed religious Jews and their **TORAH**,

Dayenu—It October 27, 2009would have been enough to rebel against your rule

If you had collaborated with the enemy; given away our **Sacred Land** and **Holy Places**; divided the **People of Israel**; beaten women and children; suppressed our freedom of speech; endangered our water supply; released terrorist murderers into our midst; surrendered our strategic mountains; created a Palestinian State; broken **G-d's Covenant with Abraham**; defamed religious Jews and their **TORAH** and not jeopardized Jewish rule in **Jerusalem**,

Dayenu—It would have been enough to rebel against your rule

TO THE ISRAELI GOVERNMENT OF RABIN AND PERES:

You have done all of these things. You have collaborated with the enemy; given away our **Sacred Land** and **Holy Places**; divided the **People of Israel**; beaten women and children; suppressed our freedom of speech; endangered our water supply; released terrorist murders into our midst: surrendered our strategic mountains; created a Palestinian State; broken **G-D's Covenant with Abraham**; defamed religious Jews and their **TORAH** and even jeopardized Jewish rule in **Jerusalem.**

DAYENU! WE HAVE HAD ENOUGH OF YOUR RULE! BY YOUR ACTIONS YOU HAVE FORFEITED ANY CLAIM TO LEGITIMACY. DAYENU!

"FOR ZION'S SAKE I WILL NOT HOLD MY PEACE,

AND FOR JERUSALEM'S SAKE I WILL NOT REST"

ODE TO SHARON: A DEMENTED MONSTER

(September 2004)

Oh Land of my Fathers, lovely land of freedom,
Where has thou gone?
To a *New Middle East* of retreat and appeasement, across a sea of fog.
Deep into the fantasy world of Beilin & Peres goes Sharon.
Oh love of my fathers, hope of my people,
What has become of your promise of Zion?
Why do you wander drunk and sick?
What has become of thee?

★

I see no more a land of freedom, love and justice.
I see no more the hope and prayer of the Jew.
I see a monster, a demented monster.
Tell me oh beast, oh mighty beast of prey,
How many dirty deals did you make with our enemies today?
How many Jewish villages did you put in harms way?
How many Jewish homes and families will you bulldoze?
How many Jewish prayers for *Eretz Yisrael* did you wreck and bury?
And tell me, how many children will die at the
Hands of the murderers you appease and have set free today?
Tell me the truth, oh beast, oh mighty beast of prey.

★

Oh demented monster, why did you come?
When will you go?
You'll go when the settlers are all gone.
You'll go when religious Jews are no longer in your way.
You'll go when all Zionists have forsaken Zion.
You will go when Israel is *Judenrein*.
You'll go when *They* are all dead.
Oh beast, oh mighty beast of prey.
It is *We*, the people of Israel, who are *They*.

Bernard J. Shapiro

[Author's Note: This poem was originally written for Beilin, Peres, Sarid, and Burg, but it also applies to Barack, Sharon, Livni, and Olmert.]

THE SILENT KILLERS

(January 2004)

When did the blood begin to flow?
The left-wing Jews watch in silence.
When did they start the killing?
The left-wing Jews do not make a sound.
Why do they make so many die?
The left-wing Jews are happy and do not want trouble.
When every Israeli is dead there, where will the Arabs go to kill more Jews?
The left-wing Jews are sleeping and do not see the blood.
How will they get rid of the bodies so no one will know?
**We need to censor the news; shut down Arutz Sheva,
Deceive the people for the good of Israel.**

✲

It's all right for the settlers to die.
Rabin said they are not real Israelis. "They can spin like propellers"
Let the Arabs burn those damn right-wing villages.
Mofaz said that it costs too much to protect them.
You'd better stop protesting and calling Beilin and Peres traitors.
You damn settlers are dirty Jewish rats.
Go ahead, crack their skulls, show them who is boss.
We don't need these people,
Let them go back where they came from.
Imprison the settler, beat up the demonstrator, it's for the good of Israel.
If you don't like what we are doing,
Leave and let the Arabs kill whom we want.
Murder, mutilate, maul, decimate, the Arabs will solve our problem.
Blast, burn, bomb, torture, kill, kill, kill,
Our Arab friends will solve the problem.
The left-wing Jews demand silence.

★

The left-wing Jews want you to shut up, be quiet, go away.

The left-wing Jews don't see any blood on their hands.

The left-wing Jews just can't be bothered with such matters.

The left-wing Jews don't want to listen to the cries of the dead.

The left-wing Jews believe in Beilin, Peres, Sarid and Burg.

They are killers, silent killers.

Bernard J. Shapiro

Oslo Must Go

Will Netanyahu Do The Right Thing?

(July 1996)

There is a fallacy in thinking that Israel can pursue the "piece process" in a new Likud-like manner. As most of us know, this "Oslo process" does not lead to peace, but to the destruction of Israel and its replacement with "Palestine." Perhaps this point is so obvious that I should not be devoting this issue to it. However, Israel's new Prime Minister, Benjamin Netanyahu, and many of his advisors continue to express the view that "international agreements" must be honored, including the Oslo Accords. It is true that Israel's new government has announced its intention to conduct the negotiations differently from Labor. And Netanyahu has made a point of demanding PLO compliance with their commitments under Oslo. He has also wisely stated that the security interests of Israel will be protected.

The problem with Netanyahu's plan is two-fold:

(1) The Oslo Accords are not really sanctioned by international law, as you will discover in this issue; and

(2) Israeli security can never be protected under the Oslo Accords, despite the best of intentions. Many in the new government believe that the key is demanding strict compliance on the part of the PLO. This is also an illusion, since a perfectly compliant PLO would still pose a serious threat to Israeli survival by virtue of its negative impact on Israeli security, water supplies, and national morale.

Many Israelis believe that to renounce Oslo would result in adverse international repercussions. While there is some truth in this fear, it need not be paramount. There are good and bad ways to carry out government policy. The Oslo Accords represent a clear and present danger to Israel and, therefore, must be renounced in the least damaging way. I would recommend the following course of action:

1. David Bar-Illan, Netanyahu's new communication director, should prepare and then launch a public relations campaign designed to re-educate the American public and their political leaders to the hidden truth about Oslo (i.e. PLO non-compliance, security threats, denial of legitimate Jewish rights, etc.)

2. The implementation of Oslo should be frozen until complete PLO compliance.

3. Slowly at first (then more rapidly later), Israel should begin to strengthen and build up the Jewish communities in YESHA, including Hebron. Territorial blocks, military bases, and the roads connecting them to each other and the rest of Israel should be annexed officially and taken off the negotiation table. Eventually all public domain land should be added to this territory.

4. Jerusalem should be immediately cleared of PLO police and officials. Massive building of Jewish apartments and government buildings should encircle the city. The boundaries of Jerusalem should be extended to Maale Adumim. For the time being, the Temple Mount should come under joint Jewish/Moslem control, with times for prayer divided in an equitable fashion. [Jewish prayer guaranteed on the Mount according to halakhah.]

The Palestinian Arabs would soon abandon their dream of creating a new state of Palestine on the ashes of the Jewish state. The international community would soon accept Israel's right to protect its own interests. Israel would be gradually burying Oslo without actually doing it blatantly. Netanyahu must realize that Israel can't be a little bit pregnant. We must either accept Oslo (and Palestine) or reject it.

As for meeting with Arafat, Bibi must remember this bit of folk wisdom: When you sup with the devil, be sure to use a long spoon.

Bernard J. Shapiro

Oslo and Other Policy Conundrums

(August 1996)

Nothing has bothered me more than Israeli Prime Minister Benjamin Netanyahu's constant reaffirmation of the Oslo Agreement and his stated intention to honor its provisions. As we have reported in this publication, in many learned articles, the Oslo Accord will result in the destruction of the Jewish state. Why then does the new Israeli government continue to promise compliance? I have no doubt about Bibi's dedication to Israel, Zionism, and the Jewish people. Being puzzled and confused by this seemingly inappropriate policy, I recently questioned a friend close to the Likud. "Why is Bibi doing this?" I asked anxiously.

"We must live up to Oslo—it is a signed agreement," said my friend.

I am surprised at your answer. Your response on Oslo sounds like the fairy tale refrains: "Land for Peace" or "The New Middle East". There is NO historical basis for nations living up to "signed agreements" one minute beyond the point at which they serve their national interests. For example:

1. Egypt's agreements with Israel at Camp David

2. Dozens of treaties by the US with Native Americans

3. The Armistice Agreements with Egypt, Syria, Lebanon, and Jordan in 1949.

4. The Munich "Peace in Our Time" of 1938.

5. The North Korean Treaty in 1953.

6. The US agreement (1957) to protect Israeli shipping to Eilat

7. The US—North Vietnam Treaty protecting independence of South Vietnam.

8. And finally, over 100 agreements signed by Arafat with other Arab countries.

I could go on, but you get the picture.

The proper historical context relating to treaties and signed agreements was provided by Professor Paul Eidelberg of Bar-Ilan University:

"Between 1945 and 1978 the longest time without a war going on someplace was a mere 26 days. On an average day there are 12 wars being fought somewhere on Earth. The consensus of scholars has been that the norm of international relations is not peace, but war." As Eidelberg reports, "Indeed, the occurrence of 1,000 wars during the last 2,500 years indicates that "peace" is little more than a preparation for war. Which means that peace treaties are WORTHLESS, to say the least."

Eidelberg then quotes from a book by Lawrence Beilenson, entitled THE TREATY TRAP, saying, "After studying every peace treaty going back to early Roman times, Beilenson concludes that treaties are made to be broken. In fact, he shows that treaties for guaranteeing the territorial integrity of a nation are useless to the guaranteed nation, and worse than useless insofar as they engender a false sense of security. Such treaties can only benefit nations governed by rulers intending to violate them whenever expedient."

THE BOTTOM LINE: If Bibi wants to follow Oslo for Public Relations reasons, that is one thing. I hope he doesn't fall into the trap of believing (what he says) that "signed agreements" have some intrinsic value like "TORAH." There is a very real danger that the constant repetition of statements that he will "live up to signed agreements" will tend to create a dynamic of its own.

My friend replied: "Once an elected PM of Israel signed Oslo 2r, Oslo became a valid agreement that Israel has to honor. I am not saying that it is a GOOD agreement; it is terrible, but valid. Regarding the legality of an agreement signed with terrorists—If the world had protested Oslo, that would be one thing. But the world and Israel did not protest at the time—You cannot go back after signing and say 'It is invalid. Arafat is a terrorist. It is too late . . .' The whole purpose of agreements is for nations to honor them, even when in the short term it is not in their interest to do so. My point is that when nations sign agreements they are expected to honor them for better or for worse. Obviously, Oslo is not a good agreement—but it is already fact. The trick is to make it work as best as possible . . ."

I replied: "You have never answered my central point that 'nations historically do not comply with agreements that are no longer in their national interests.'"

1. For discussion's sake, let's say Oslo is "legal"

2. You and Bibi both agree that it is a BAD agreement for Israel

3. Therefore, why should Israel comply, when other nations would not think twice about renouncing a bad agreement?

Some have argued that Israel must act on the basis of a HIGHER moral or legal standard. While Jews generally like to think of themselves as superior, in practice this creates a DOUBLE STANDARD. During the intifada we saw how quickly the application of a double standard to Israeli behavior becomes anti-Semitism and a focal point for anti-Israel media coverage. I believe that Israel has the same right as other nations to violate treaties and agreements that cease to be in their national interest.

Zvi, an Israeli friend of mine, had this to add to our dialogue on Oslo: "Oslo should be portrayed both in Israel and here as an illegitimate agreement, which was conceived by illegal actions of the former government, which has led to tremendous bloodshed and which, in the long run, endangers Israel's security. It shouldn't bind the present government, or at least they should not state it repeatedly, because by doing so they will tie their hands and they will never be able to get out of it . . ."

THE BEST POLICY: Gradually move away from the Oslo Agreements, mention them less and less, and blame Arafat for their collapse. By all means stop investing in them any undeserved legitimacy.

POLLARD

The Freeman Center and its members are outraged by the continued imprisonment and abuse of Jonathan Pollard, who has sacrificed a great part of his life in defense of Israel. That he was put in such a terrible dilemma of having to spy on his country in order to save Jewish lives is a tragedy. His actions did not happen in a vacuum, as you will read in my article, PERFIDY, reprinted in this issue. We call on the Israeli government to do everything it can to free Pollard. We agree that Pollard violated the law and should accept punishment. On the other hand, based on the prison sentences of other persons convicted of spying for our allies, his sentence was quite excessive. Pollard never meant to harm American security, and in fact, didn't. In other words, ENOUGH IS ENOUGH. It is time for Israel to demand an end to this shameful affair.

TERRORISM

The Freeman Center expresses its outrage and condemnation at the recent incidents of terrorism directed at Americans and Israelis. Terrorism is not an act of nature . . . it can be controlled and prevented. Unfortunately, the US has not taken the steps necessary to combat it on an international scale. This would involve more than cosmetic sanctions against the terrorist nations of Iran, Syria, Iraq, Libya, and Sudan.

In a recent report to the Task Force on Terrorism and Unconventional Warfare, of the US Congress, on terrorism, Yossef Bodansky, the Freeman Center's World Terrorism Analyst, had the following to say:

"The bomb that killed, wounded or blinded hundreds of US servicemen in Saudi Arabia was the work of several months, involving many groups with ties to radical states, above all Iran." He told the Congressmen on the task force: "We must keep our eye on the big picture. We are dealing with a long-term state sponsored grand strategy, with a huge and extremely sophisticated and costly operation. It is not just costly in cash, but in a high-quality personnel training system that is geared to bring about, to implement this long-term strategy. The main issue is not running after perpetrators of one action or another—not that we should not do that and bring them to justice one way or another. But we should deal with the sponsoring state, and we should make sure they do not do that. We should preempt and prevent."

Mr. Bodansky said the bombing is part of an unfolding process designed to force the United States out of the Persian Gulf and install an Iranian-backed regime in Saudi Arabia. Furthermore, the terrorist network stretching across the Muslim world is ready to strike in America. The infrastructure is in place. Tehran will give the signal, though how and when can only be guessed. He named a multimillionaire Saudi Arabian, Usama Bin Ladin, now in Afghanistan, as chief organizer of the terrorist network.

ISRAEL'S CONSULAR CORP

During the last four years, many in the Israeli consular corp in America have distinguished themselves as purveyors of misinformation and as proponents of censorship, blacklisting and interference in the American Jewish community. Many are still in place in Israeli consulates all across the US. They are working to sabotage the new policies of the Netanyahu government and are continuing a policy blacklisting the American Jews who opposed the suicidal policies of the previous government. THIS MUST STOP! As difficult as this may seem, those guilty members of the foreign service must be removed from American consulates by dismissal or re-location to some distant post where they can do no more harm.

THE TEMPLE MOUNT

Netanyahu has spoken and written very clearly about the rights of Jews to pray on the Temple Mount. Yet a few days ago, on Tisha b'Av, Israeli police forcibly prevented Jews from exercising the basic human right to pray at their Holiest Place. The reason was to prevent a riot by Moslems. In my view, the proper function of Israeli police is to prevent violence, not to appease it. We support the Jewish right to pray at any place in Israel and we will be watching the new Israeli government's commitment to protecting the religious rights of all faiths, including Jews.

The Mount returned to Israeli hands as a result of the Six Day War liberation of Jerusalem. In an act of great stupidity, Israeli Defense Minister Moshe Dayan gave control of the Temple Mount to Moslem religious leaders a few days later. His reasoning was that this would prevent panic among the newly defeated Arab population. He also made great efforts to prevent Arabs from fleeing to Jordan. Today, as these same Arabs plot our demise, we realize how mistaken his policies were.

I learned from history how Moslem conquerors built mosques on top of the Holy Places of other peoples in every part of the world. They did it to humiliate and degrade their subject nations. There is no reason the sovereign State of Israel needs to allow this desecration of Jewish Holy Places to continue. Today on the Mount, the Arabs are supreme. They are destroying all archaeological remnants of Jewish sites. They are storing weapons in their mosques to kill Jews. They have built a museum to Palestinian nationalism, including gut-wrenching pictures from the battles of Sabra and Shatila. Tourists from the world over are told Jews committed these killings (It was Christians).

While I am not competent to discuss Halacha with reference to the Mount, I do know that it is wrong for us to allow the Arab desecration of our people's most Holy Site. I also believe that Jews have the right to pray at all of their Holy Sites, including the Temple Mount. What about the consequences of our asserting our rights to the Temple Mount? Can the Moslem world hate us anymore?

ADMINISTRATIVE DETENTION

It is past time to free the Jews being held under administrative detention orders carried over from the previous Israeli government. They were being held because of their political beliefs. Such orders, while an abuse of judicial power when used against Jews, are necessary in dealing with Arab terrorism. Also, the deportation of Jews from Israel because of their political beliefs is outrageous and a violation of all Jewish principles. There should be no need to debate this issue, as the correct course for Bibi is obvious.

Shapiro's Rule #1: We must know the truth about our enemies and never drop our guard.

Bibi, Jonathan Is Worried

(November 1996)

Long before I had ever heard of Benjamin Netanyahu (Bibi), I had read about his older brother Jonathan, Hero of Entebbe. In 1980, I read a book of Jonathan's letters entitled: SELF-PORTRAIT OF A HERO, The Letters Of Jonathan Netanyahu [1963-1976]. A lot of reviewers at the time spoke about the beautiful prose, the passion and the great potential of this hero cut down in his youth. While I saw all those things, it was Jonathan's deep love of Israel and his fervent patriotism that attracted me most. There was something else that one could sense on every page. That was his deep understanding of Jewish history and the role of Israel in it. One of my favorite passages, which I have quoted often, could have been written today in the context of the Oslo Accords. Here is that excerpt:

"I see with sorrow and great anger how a part of the people still clings to hopes of reaching a peaceful settlement with the Arabs. Common sense tells them, too, that the Arabs haven't abandoned their basic aim of destroying the State; but the self-delusion and self-deception that have always plagued the Jews are at work again. It's our great misfortune. They want to believe, so they believe. They want not to see, so they shut their eyes. They want not to learn from thousands of years of history, so they distort it. They want to bring about a sacrifice, and they do indeed. It would be comic, if it wasn't so tragic. What a saddening and irritating lot this Jewish people is!"

I am sure that Bibi, growing up in the shadow of his fallen brother, must have felt an overpowering need to succeed. There must have been a need to learn more, achieve more, and to rise to the top of his chosen field. The struggle was partly to "make his brother proud," and partly to prove to himself that he was made of the "right stuff." That is, the stuff with which HEROES are made.

The Battle for Eretz Yisrael

And Bibi did it all: military excellence, diplomacy at the highest level, and finally political success in his brilliant campaign for Prime Minister. He has proven his worth to everyone, including himself. Now, poised at center stage during the most critical time of Israel's history, Bibi seems to have lost his inner direction. Often he speaks with a voice that would make Jonathan cheer, and then his actions leave much to be desired. For example, on October 24, 1996, the Prime Minister's office sent me a list of the ten most egregious PLO violations (printed in this issue) of the Oslo Accords. It was quite devastating: this account demonstrating the PLO's total disregard for its peace obligations.

This impressive list could be used as a part of a major Israeli public relations (hasbara) campaign to justify terminating its obligations to implement Oslo, including the abandonment of Hebron. Unfortunately, Bibi will NOT do this. He should have given the list to PLO terrorist chief, Yasser Arafat, with the admonition that all implementation of Oslo would cease until complete compliance. He didn't. Bibi has spoken often of the need for reciprocity, while continuing to negotiate without it.

I want to tell a little story to explain what I believe is happening to Bibi. My grandfather, Harry W. Freeman, settled in Texas at the turn of the century. He was already fighting injustice to women and Afro-Americans by 1912, liquidating white slavery in Galveston by 1930 and speaking about the dangers of Hitler and Nazism in 1933. Growing up in Texas, I used to love the rodeo which came to Houston once a year. One of my favorite contests was the wild bronco bull ride. Cowboys would mount these ferocious creatures and hold on tight until they were thrown. It all lasted little more than 12 seconds. It was much later that I learned that a leather strap was tied tight behind the bull's testicles to make him buck more ferociously. Even the biggest, strongest and most experienced Texans were able to ride the bull for only a few seconds.

This brings me back to Bibi, who is trying to ride the "Oslo bull." The Palestinian Arabs are filled with rage and hatred of Jews, with all the ferocity of the bull angered by the leather strap . . . Much of their rage comes straight from Nazi anti-Semitism, brought to the Middle East by their former mufti, Haj Amin el-Husseini. The Palestinian Arabs, filled with both Nazi and Islamic hatred of Jews, make the Oslo bull impossible to ride. Their aspirations for a state that REPLACES Israel is evident to anyone who takes the time to listen to what they are saying. As much as Bibi would like to master the Oslo process and protect Israeli interests, it is impossible. It is a bull he can never ride. This is a harsh reality. There is a history lesson that Jonathan understood well: Enemies must be defeated and destroyed. The idea that one makes peace with your enemies is just a hoax of the Left.

The Americans did not make peace with the Native Americans; they destroyed them . . . The same is the case with Hitler's Germany and the Emperor's Japan. Midge Dector had this to say about peace:

"For there is no such thing as making peace. Nations who are friendly do not need to do so, and nations or people who are hostile cannot do so. To cry peace, peace when there is no peace, the prophet Jeremiah taught us long ago, is not the expression of hope, not even superstition, but a reckless toying with the minds and hearts of people whose very future depends on their capacity to rise every day to the harsh morning light of the truth."

Bibi must recognize the essential truth that both his brother and Dector have expressed so eloquently. He must read his own list of PLO violations. And then he must get off the Oslo bull and lead his people, Israel, to victory. Jews the world over are praying that he will fulfill his great destiny as a leader of Israel. They pray that he will pursue with all his vigor the Zionist goals of settling the Land, protecting the Holy Places, and ingathering the Jewish exiles. They pray that he will strengthen the military and infuse it with the high morale of days past. In my heart I know that Jonathan is watching over Bibi with love and affection. And Bibi, in my heart I fear that he is as worried as me.

FREEMAN CENTER FOR STRATEGIC STUDIES

P.O. Box 35661-5661 Houston, Texas 77235-5709

Phone or Fax: 713-723-6016 * E-mail: bernards@sbcglobal.net

November 15, 1996

The Honorable Benjamin Netanyahu
Prime Minister of Israel
Prime Minister's Office
Jerusalem, **ISRAEL**

Dear Mr. Prime Minister:

As lifelong supporters and friends of Israel, we urge you to reconsider the redeployment from Hebron as well as the implementation of the Oslo Agreement.

When you spoke before both houses of the United States Congress, you stated that you would demand reciprocity on the part of the Palestinians before proceeding with the implementation of Oslo. As your memo of October 24, 1996 entitled **"LIST OF MAJOR PLO VIOLATIONS"** clearly enunciates, there has been no PLO compliance. This failure of the PLO clearly gives you ample recourse. Many legal scholars, such as Professor Louis Rene Beres (International Law, Department of Political Science, Purdue University), have proven that Oslo has no standing in international law. I quote from his article: **TERMINATING OSLO I AND II: AN OBLIGATION UNDER INTERNATIONAL LAW:** *An informed brief for permissible abrogation by the State of Israel*:

"It is generally believed that the **Oslo Accords** between Israel and the PLO are fully binding under international law. Exactly the opposite is true. Because these non-treaty agreements run counter to absolutely incontrovertible legal expectations, Israel is now obligated to terminate the agreement./ . . . . / . . . . / . . . The Oslo Agreements do not constitute treaties because they link a state with a nonstate party. In and of itself, this incontestable fact, drawn from the **Vienna Convention on the Law of Treaties**, certainly does not call for termination. But because the nonstate party in this case happens to be a terrorist organization whose leaders must be punished for egregious crimes, any agreement with this party that offers rewards rather than punishment is entirely null and void. Indeed, in view of the peremptory expectation known in law as ***Nullum crimen sine poena***, "No crime without a punishment," the state party in such an agreement—in this case the State of Israel—violates international law by honoring the agreement."

There is, therefore, no legal or moral reason for you to implement an agreement that is so destructive to the interests of the State of Israel.

It is true that you have also proclaimed Oslo to be a devastatingly bad agreement for Israel. Unfortunately, you have been misinformed as to your obligations to implement what you agree is a bad agreement. As Prime Minister, your obligation is to the **People of Israel** and not to a terrible agreement between a previous government and a known terrorist. We would also like to remind you of the brilliant words of Karl Von Clausewitz, who said (Von Krigge 1833): *"War is not merely a political act, but also a political instrument, a continuation of political relations, a carrying out of the same by other means."* Any analyst who has studied carefully the behavior of the Palestinian Authority since the Oslo signing in 1993 would conclude the following: **The Palestinians are using the Peace Process as another means to achieve the victory over Israel which they were unable to achieve in direct confrontation or war.** This is exactly what Clausewitz understood so well in the 19th century and many Israelis fail to understand today.

The Left will never support you and the National/Religious Camp will never forgive you for betraying your campaign promises. Should you follow the foolish course of your predecessors, you will certainly fail to protect the security and well-being of Israel. And thus, history will record you as the man who brought about the fall of the **Third Temple**.

We emphatically urge you to marshal the strength of character that runs in your heroic family, and say **NO** to those who would dismember *Eretz Yisrael*. And then you should not only save Hebron, but begin a major building program that would bring 50,000 Jews to live in the Hebron-Kiryat Arba metropolitan area.

With Love of Israel and Faith in Hashem.

Respectfully Yours,

Bernard J. Shapiro

Bernard J. Shapiro, Executive Director

Freeman Center For Strategic Studies

Bernard J. Shapiro

REBOOT BIBI, SAVE ISRAEL AND ENSURE SECURITY

Wishful Thinking

(January 1997)

Let's face it. Things have not gone well for Israel since Bibi was elected. While we all cheered his election and had very high expectations for his government, the reality has been shocking. Although he was elected by a national/Zionist/religious coalition, Bibi seems to have undergone a radical transformation. With great skill, he seems to have sacrificed his natural coalition on the right in order to curry favor with Arafat and the Israeli left. The Labor and Meretz leaders are having a rollicking good time watching Bibi trying to out-Peres Peres. Bibi seems to have mastered the "give Arafat anything he wants" trick that we all thought was peculiar to the previous government.

Conspiracy theorists are also hyperactive these days with "explanations" for Bibi's bizarre conversion to the philosophies of the suicidal left. Here are some rumor categories for easy reference:

1. The American Connection: Clinton and the State Department have exerted pressure of such magnitude that Bibi could not withstand it. In this theory, Arab money, the oil lobby and ex-government officials like James Baker are providing the incentive and intellectual cover for selling Israel out.

2. The Trilateral Connection: Men like David Rockefeller and Henry Kissinger, agents for the Trilateral Commission, "bought" Bibi in the 70's. Under this theory, the late Yitzhak Rabin was also bought so that they would have control of Israel regardless of which party was in power.

3. The Empty Shirt Theory: This theory holds that Bibi is all spit-and-polish with no substance. His political philosophy was written by Yoram Hazony in order to get elected. Once in office, it is revealed that he has no ideology and is a weak reed "blowing with the political wind."

4. The PLO A-Bomb Theory: About a year ago, the Freeman Center received confirmation that Iran had bought four nuclear devices from the Former Soviet Union (two from Russia, one from the Ukraine, and one from Kazakhstan). There is speculation that Arafat smuggled one into Israel via a tunnel from the Egyptian Sinai into PA Gaza. A Palestinian VIP, with permission to enter Israel without having to go through security, smuggled the bomb into the Tel Aviv area and buried it. Bibi was told by Arafat that if the Oslo process did not go forward to his satisfaction, Tel Aviv would be destroyed.

5. The Alien Abduction Theory: Many of our readers who watch the X-Files on TV have written to me, convinced that Bibi was abducted by aliens. They insist that Bibi doesn't even exist and the image we see of him is projected telepathically by one of the "aliens" who abducted him.

For the record, I don't believe any of those theories. I have a simpler solution to the Bibi riddle. Bibi is like my computer; he needs to be rebooted periodically. For those not familiar with computers, let me explain. Every once in a while computers get confused and they freeze up. The screen stops working, the mouse has no effect and generally you can't do anything. The solution is to turn the computer off and then turn it back on. This is called rebooting, and by some mysterious process everything begins to work properly. All the electrical connections suddenly know exactly what they are supposed to do.

Bibi's problem is that he is basically a good Right thinking politician who somehow has become frozen in a defective policy (Oslo), and all his cognitive and operative controls are refusing to function. So we must reboot Bibi in order to save Israel and ensure security. Here's my plan:

Bibi needs to give up being Prime Minister for a period of six weeks. Three members of the cabinet, Uzi Landau, Ariel Sharon, and Raful Eitan, will share the duties of PM during this period of time. They will be trusted (by the rational public) with this responsibility because of their high integrity and proven devotion to Israel. Bibi will go to a quiet, peaceful place—perhaps Safed, where he will be rebooted. Great Zionist thinkers, historians, philosophers and religious leaders will each spend one whole day with him discussing the major issues facing Israel's future. Elyakim Ha'etzni and Yohanan Ramati might spend Mondays with him, and Shmuel Katz and Arie Stav on Tuesdays. David Wilder and Gary Cooperberg would come from Hebron on Wednesdays. Zionist leaders like Morton Klein and Herb Zweibon from the US; Dan Nimrod from Canada; and Conrad Morris, Joe Gellert and Christopher Barder from England would come to visit Bibi on Thursdays. On Fridays, Bibi would be blessed by a visit from Ruth and Nadia Matar. Rabbis Eliezar Waldman and Zalman B. Melamed would conduct Shabbat Services and meet with Bibi every Shabbat. Dr. Aaron Lerner will spend Sundays with Bibi going over all Oslo documentation.

If all goes according to my plan, Bibi will emerge from the six weeks retreat, rebooted and ready to be a Maccabean leader of Israel. He will have become a proud Jew, unafraid of the U.S. State Department, Mubarak, Arafat and the Israeli leftist fifth column. He will go forth with the blessing of Hashem, to blow the shofar loud and clear to all the world:

There is a new Israel. We will pursue our destiny with great vigor and without apology.

NETANYAHU, OUR PRODIGAL SON

What Should The RIGHT Do About Bibi's Plight

(May 1997)

Israeli Prime Minister Benjamin (Bibi) Netanyahu is in trouble. While he will not be charged with a crime, there is no question that his political standing has fallen. How he came to be embroiled in the most damaging scandal of his political career is also well known. I would like to discuss the proper response of the National Camp to unfolding events.

Bibi has been like the prodigal son who takes the family inheritance and squanders it foolishly. He was elected on a Zionist platform by one of the largest Jewish majorities in Israeli history (over 11%). His election was a clear signal from the voters of concern about the direction of the Oslo Process. Yet like the prodigal son, he took the political power given him by the electorate, and began to use it to complete the self-destructive process begun by the previous Labor/Meretz/PLO government.

Bibi's current troubles stem from his desire to secure a majority in the Knesset for the abandonment of Hebron. He desperately needed the votes of Shas, an ultra-Orthodox political party with a long history of fraud and scandal. While I am not a religious scholar, it has occurred to me that Bibi may be feeling the **Wrath of HaShem** for his share in undermining the Jewish claim to Hebron, burial place of the Patriarchs. We know from the **TANACH** that **HaShem** loved and cared deeply for Abraham, Isaac and Jacob. Perhaps **He** is showing **His** displeasure at Bibi's actions.

With all that said, I must confess the following: Bibi is **OUR** prodigal son. We must guide him back to the **Right** path. Now there is no substitute. The Left has unsheathed their long knives and has begun to lust for blood. The viciousness of the Israeli media and the politically corrupted police and judiciary must be stopped. They seek to overturn the voter's democratic choice by innuendo, slander and damaging leaks. The charges against Bibi are at their very worst a form of political "backroom" bargaining. Such behavior has been common to every Israeli government since 1948. In fact, it was David Ben Gurion, Israel's first premier, who initiated the policy of "paying off" the ultra-Orthodox to join his coalition.

Do we value the concept of "equal protection under the law" and judicial impartiality? The Left is guilty of far greater crimes against the State than Bibi. How many of you remember Alex Goldfarb, who was given a new Mitsubishi to bolt the Tsomet Party and give Peres and Rabin a majority for the Oslo Accord? Was the late Yitzhak Rabin ever charged with the cold-blooded murder of 17 Jewish teenagers in 1948 during the Altalena incident? The Israeli police never investigated whether Shimon Peres, Yossi Beilin and others violated Israel law by:

(1) collaborating with the enemy

(2) damaging Israeli security by aiding known terrorists

(3) perpetrating the self-destructive hoax of Oslo against the will of the Israeli people

(4) plotting with enemies of Israel to turn over strategic territory to them which would facilitate their destruction of the Jewish State.

The Left is also guilty of compromising the quality of the IDF by promoting fellow leftist officers instead of the most qualified. The leftist police have pursued an agenda of punishing Jews who defend themselves against Arab attack. And then the government releases Arab murderers to kill more Jews. The Israeli television channels are so biased that it is easier for Yasser Arafat to get an interview than the Prime Minister. Leftist educators have recently launched a campaign to strip everything Jewish or Zionist from Israel's schools. Speakers who have unconventional views are prevented from speaking on college campuses. Freedom of speech is only for the Left. I could go on. **The Leftist rot in Israel runs very deep.**

The bottom line is this: Israeli society has many problems. Bibi is certainly not the worst problem. We must support him during this current crisis. It could work to our favor. With the National Unity government removed from the table, Bibi is more dependent than ever on his Nationalist coalition. The Left is literally salivating for his fall. Bibi and his traditional allies must reunite and proceed with the management of Israeli affairs in a more activist Zionist fashion. That means **ACTUAL** building permits in **YESHA** (in a simplified process) instead of mere *TALK ABOUT PERMITS*.

The new revitalized coalition must consider doing the following:

1. **ACTUALLY DEMANDING RECIPROCITY** from Arafat instead of just *TALKING* about it.

2. Demanding that all provisions of Oslo be complied with. This includes everything from the PLO Covenant, extradition of terrorists, disarming and destruction of Hamas and Islamic Jihad infrastructure, reducing the size of the PLO army to stated terms, turning in of all prohibited weapons (anti-tank, anti-air, grenades, bombs, etc.), and an end to incitement against Israel and Jews, etc. etc.

3. All of above to be done within 60 days or Oslo is terminated. **PERIOD**.

4. The Leftists must be weeded out of government media, the police, Consular Corp and the judiciary.

5. **Moledet** should be brought into the government even if this means that the Third Way, (no bargain for the Nationalists) decides to leave.

This is only a beginning. First we need to salvage this government and then make it **RIGHT**.

Bernard J. Shapiro

FURTHER REDEPLOYMENT IN YESHA (FRD)

Breaking News Of Great Importance

An Editorial (December 1997)

Editor's Note: The Freeman Center helped to rally the Zionist forces against a planned surrender of Israeli land to Yassir Arafat and his terrorist PA. I believe that we have scored a partial victory. The reader should be aware of government uses of *"trial balloons."* Things looked very bleak, indeed, on November 28, yet by the 30th the situation had improved greatly. No one can evaluate with certainty the effect of the massive protests, demonstrations and letter/fax campaigns launched by the **Right**. See below.

An Editorial & An Appeal (Freeman Center Broadcast—November 28, 1997)

TIME TO STOP THE SURRENDER &

THE APPEASEMENT OF TERROR

TIME TO RECLAIM ZIONISM AND DEFEND ISRAEL FROM DESTRUCTION

Israeli Prime Minister Benjamin Netanyahu is about to cross a **RED LINE** that will result in the creation of a Palestinian **TERRORIST** State, leading to the eventual destruction of Israel. I speak of his plan for a further surrender of Israeli land to a murderous band of terrorists. The fall of the **Third Temple** will not occur in one day, one month or even a year. There will be a slow but steady grinding down of Israeli morale and faith in their country.

All the things we know about the 'Palestinians' confirm this view. Israel's agriculture will turn brown as the new entity competes for limited water. Terrorism will increase. There will be increased strategic vulnerability. Israeli military deterrence will continue its steady decline. Millions of Arabs will demand the **"right of return"** and return to Israel. While all Israeli parties oppose such a return, we know they **LIE** and in the end will continue the appeasement process. They will declare: **"One last step to *peace*. Do not forsake *peace* because of this ONE LAST CONCESSION."** And Jerusalem will go the same way. *One last thing for peace*. And so it was with Chamberlain and Hitler. *There is never an end to blackmail.*

Israeli Arabs will demand the right to link up with "Palestine." Diaspora Jews will stop coming on aliya for fear of their future and many more Israelis will move to NY and LA. Arab voters will be a deciding factor in the Knesset and they will demand that Israel cease to be a Jewish State. Finally, Jews will lose control and all that will remain of Israel will be one more corrupt terrorist Arab country.

When the government tells you that they will demand reciprocity before they redeploy, tell them they **LIE**. From 1993 until today no Israeli government has stopped Oslo because of lack of reciprocity.

Bernard J. Shapiro

If you love Israel, you must do everything in your power to call a halt to this redeployment **(to hell)**. Write, fax, phone Cabinet Ministers and tell them to save Israel . . . . **VOTE NO ON THE REDEPLOYMENT AND SURRENDER TO APPEASEMENT AND TERRORISM** . . . . **Bernard J. Shapiro, Editor**

REFERENDUM ON REDEPLOYMENT

To the Voter:

Please read the description of the effects of redeployment and then vote for or against. Your informed consent is very important to us. Following a redeployment you should expect the following:

1. The areas from which Israel redeploys will become safe havens for terrorists, who will murder your children, wife and other loved ones.

2. The PA will continue to refuse to extradite terrorist murderers

3. PA schools will continue to teach hatred of Jews and Israelis

4. About 30% of Israel's water supply will be damaged or made unavailable

5. Many Jewish communities will be slowly strangled by PA activities including interfering with electric or water supply. The roads leading to those communities will become deathtraps with PA sponsored terrorists attacking vehicles with gunfire, Molotov cocktails and boulders.

6. Katyusha rockets smuggled by tunnel into PA territory from Egypt will begin raining on Tel Aviv and other Israeli cities.

7. The PA will continue to refuse to amend its Covenant calling for the destruction of Israel.

8. The PA will promise to live up to its commitments if Israel turns over Jerusalem to Palestinian Arab control for its capital.

9. The Israeli government will buy the rug for the **SIXTH** time.

10. This process will continue with each PA demand: right of return for refugees; Israeli Arabs to join "Palestine" along with their territory in the Galilee and Negev; that Jews should either convert to Islam or go back where they came from.

Bernard J. Shapiro

To the Voter:

Now that you have the facts, please vote:

(A) For Redeployment—

(B) Against Redeployment—

ISRAEL OR OSLO: YOU MUST DECIDE

(October 1998)

As talks in Washington seem to be reaching a conclusion, I wish to remind our readers of what the Freeman Center position on such talks is. There is no possible successful negotiation with Arafat. There are many security based reasons for this position and we have discussed those extensively in the past.

Now we feel it necessary to state our position in the area beyond security and into the spiritual realm. Should Arafat become as peaceful as a choir boy or as honest as a boy scout for a period of 1000 years, we would still not give him even one grain of sand of *Eretz Yisrael*.

We further believe that any Israeli government, whether Likud or Labor, are custodians of the **Land of Israel**, to be held in perpetuity as an inheritance for the Jewish people. We agree with **DAVID BEN GURION**, founding father and first Prime Minister of Israel, who said this about territorial concessions:

"No Jew has the right to relinquish the right of the Jewish people over the whole Land of Israel. No Jewish body has such authority, not even the whole Jewish people has the authority to waive the right (to the Land of Israel) for future generations for all time." (Zionist Congress, Zurich, 1937)

It is the height of arrogance, indeed it is a rebellion against the **Almighty**, that the Israeli government negotiates the abandonment of *Eretz Yisrael*. The consequences will be more dreadful than can be imagined. Some important Jewish voices that agree with the Freeman Center:

A MACCABEAN RESPONSE

Below is the letter from the Jewish leader Simon, the only survivor of the five Maccabee brothers to the Seleucid king Antiochus, whom they had just defeated. Antiochus demanded the return of the 'occupied territories'—that is territories the Maccabees liberated during their recent war.

Simon writes: "We have neither taken foreign land nor seized foreign property, but only the inheritance of our fathers, which at one time had been unjustly taken by our enemies. Now that we have the opportunity, we are firmly holding the inheritance of our fathers."

Benjamin Netanyahu, leader of the **Likud Party** (and *BEFORE* becoming Prime Minister of Israel) in his book A PLACE AMONG THE NATIONS writes the following when told that **Judea** and **Samaria** are foreign "occupied" lands:

"This land, where every swing of a spade unearths remnants of the Jewish past and where every village carries the barely altered Hebrew names of old; this land, in which the Jews became a nation and over which they shed more tears than have been shed by any other people in history; this land, the loss of which resulted in an exile of the Jews such as has been suffered by no other people and the spilling of a sea of blood such as has been spilled by no other nation; this land, which never ceased to live as a distant but tangible home in the minds of Jewish children from Toledo in medieval Spain to the Warsaw ghetto in our own century; this land, for which the Jews fought with unsurpassed courage and tenacity in ancient as in modern times—this is the "foreign land" that world leaders now demand be barred to Jews and that Israel (should) unilaterally forsake. The answer to such absurd demands must be a resounding NO!"

THE END GAME

You have seen many articles in **THE MACCABEAN** which describe in excruciating detail the apocalyptic security dangers that Oslo brings to Israel. I must report that there is only a brief window left to save Israel. We are definitely in the **END GAME.** The time may be less than eight months. Our actions will have a profound effect on Jewish history for all time. Israelis never rose en masse to protest Oslo and after the assassination of Rabin the fear of leftist persecution had a chilling effect on mass demonstrations.

VICTORY PLAN

If Israel is to be saved then two things must happen: (1) the Land for Israel Knesset members must increase their numbers and seriously threaten Netanyahu's rule and (2) large and credible numbers of Israelis must take to the streets and demand an end to the Oslo Suicide Process. These two groups (1 + 2) will re-enforce each other and with good *hasbara* (information) it is possible to achieve victory for Israel. The Freeman Center will be there with *hasbara*, but a change of government policy must be won in Israel.

Bernard J. Shapiro

FREEMAN CENTER ANALYSIS OF BARAK'S

NEW WYE AGREEMENT WITH ARAFAT

(September 1999)

As an agreement nears completion, we have been asked by numerous sources to explain in a simple manner the true nature of the new Wye Agreement negotiated by Israeli Prime Minister Ehud Barak. Broken into its essential ingredients this is what has been agreed to:

Palestinian Tactical/Political/Strategic Benefits

1. Increased land area for terrorist safe havens

2. Increased ease of access from terrorist safe havens to potential Jews to murder

3. Vastly increased vulnerability of Jewish communities to terrorist attack

4. Freedom from prison of a large number of veteran well-trained terrorists, who will be able to train a whole new generation of murderers of Jews [To protect Israeli's Barak is demanding that they sign a paper saying that they will not kill any more Jews. This Israeli form of mental masturbation could also be used to empty the overcrowded prisons in America]

5. A safe passage for terrorists to move from Gaza to Judea and Samaria

6. A port for Palestinian terrorists to bring in heavy military weapons for the future wars with Israel

7. An opportunity to sow discord among the Israelis

8. International recognition/aid/ and thanks from Europe and America for agreeing to accept these benefits

American Tactical/Political/Strategic Benefits

1. Increased influence in the Arab world for a few minutes

2. The State Department, which never supported the establishment of Israel in 1948, will finally get to *"stick it to those pesky Jews."*

European Tactical/Political/Strategic Benefits

1. They will get to *"stick it to those pesky Jews"* for the second time this century

Israeli Tactical/Political/Strategic Benefits

1. Post-Zionist Israelis will finally succeed in destroying their evil state

2. Shimon Peres will be able to push his grand idea of a very large boat to carry the Israelis on the seas. Land, as he says, is passé . . . . no longer necessary . . .

3. As Israel self-destructs, suicide-prone individuals will be considered **"prophetic"** and great leaders.

Such a deal . . . . ***Oy Veh*** . . . .

Bernard J. Shapiro

THE FREEMAN CENTER PUBLISHES

THE RAVIV PROTOCOL

(December 1999)

1. Freeman Center military experts have examined the **Raviv Protocol** and find nothing in it that impacts negatively on Israeli security. *We find exactly the opposite*. We feel that Israel's democracy would be in grave danger if politicians and the GSS are allowed to cover-up and suppress all evidence of unethical and anti-democratic behavior. Below is today's *Jerusalem Post* story on the suppression of this document. The Israeli Supreme Court justices saw fit to use a "security" excuse to ban what is obviously a matter of political censorship. This would seem to indicate that the plot to withhold the truth about the Rabin assassination has reached the highest levels of the Israeli judiciary.

Below you will find an English translation of the actual **Raviv Protocol** and that is followed by information on its significance.

At the Freeman Center we believe that democracy is served best by an informed electorate. Only a vigorous, free and uncensored press can provide a nation with an informed electorate capable of making wise decisions about its leadership.

VERY IMPORTANT
RAVIV DOCUMENT
AN Unofficial Translation of the Document

Document dated June 16, 1996 File 403

Summary of a Meeting on the Swearing-In Ceremony of the Eyal Organization Meeting Date: May 2, 1996

In attendance: 1. Attorney-General Ben-Yair 2. Noam Solberg—Senior Assistant to the Attorney-General 3. Edna Arbel—State Attorney 4. Talia Sasson—Head of the anti-incitement unit of the State Attorney's office. 5. N. Ben-Or—Head of the Criminal Division in the State

Attorney's Office 6. Leora Chavilio, Senior Assistant in the Jerusalem District Attorney's office. 7. Chezi Kallo—direct GSS handler of Avishai Raviv 8. G. Ben Ami—GSS official 9. Eli Barak—Head of the Jewish Division of the GSS after Carmi Gillon, and during the Ya'akov Perry era, head of Perry's office. 10. Ledor, Jerusalem District Attorney

Synopsis of deliberations on evidence 133/95 The swearing-in ceremony of the Eyal Organization, a document from 29.3.96 from Leora Chavilio; the summary report of the Eyal swearing-in ceremony; document from 5.2.96 from Y. Rodman

Attorney-General: We have all seen the videotape. Anyone who was there, on location, could have understood that this was not an authentic ceremony. Even the Shamgar Commission explicitly noted this in its report.

L. Chavilio: I didn't notice that the inauthentic sections were intentionally edited out of the video. I see a problem with issuing an indictment against the reporter.

A-G: Perhaps some disciplinary action can be taken against him?

C. Kallo: We are talking here about the handling of a problematic agent. The loss-benefit evaluation looks like this: He served as our agent for 8-9 years. Within this time period, he generally worked well, except for the last year. He transmitted to us thousands of pieces of information . . . During the last year, he lost control, and we were able to nip the problem in the bud. He underwent an initial investigation, and admitted [to his actions]. We continued to employ him. As for the story of the videotape [of the staged Eyal swearing-in ceremony]—from our perspective, this is a most serious episode. Our officials deliberated on the matter, and decided that he was out of control and that it was impossible to permit him to continue operating . . .

But we established new rules of operation . . . and that he would undergo psychological examinations. It was made quite clear to him that we wouldn't continue along the same path, and that he would not receive immunity for crimes he committed. In hindsight now, if we had gone ahead and broken off our ties with him—maybe he would have given us the murderer [of Yitzchak Rabin].

A court case against him would essentially be a case against the General Security Services (GSS). We would have to reveal all of our rules operation, something that would cause serious operational damage. We have to remember that our opponents pose some serious threats today. During a trial, everything would come out into the open.

I don't remember any trial against a GSS agent that was conducted behind closed doors. Great damage could be caused—revelation of operational strategies, etc.

N. Ben-Or: The attorney who represented Avishai Raviv will have a strong ideological bias, and it is possible that he would join forces with extremist elements, and that together, they would reveal secrets.

T. Sasson: They would do everything they could to reveal secrets.

G. Ben-Ami: As far as his criminal intentions are concerned: Did he intend to commit a crime? They suspected that Raviv was a GSS collaborator and he had to prove himself [to right-wing activists] He had to remove all their suspicions that he was an agent. Dorit Beinish gave approval for his activities next to Bar-Ilan University, to incriminate someone else who would then be caught. He had to protect himself. Any Defense Attorney will call Raviv to the witness stand.

E. Barak: Raviv was part of a violent group—the fact is that they suspected him of being a GSS collaborator. He had to, at all times, prove that he was as "active" as them . . .

Ledor: We have to close the file "due to lack of public interest." An indictment [against Raviv] could seriously harm the GSS. We have to accept the GSS opinion on this. We close a lot of files in this manner, due to a "lack of public interest." The harm is clear—the trial would look crooked. Holding it "behind closed doors" just won't help.

Ben-Or: I am bothered by the criminal aspect of this—I am not sure that it won't end in a finding of "not guilty." Then we will be in a strange situation. This person was working in a problematic situation. His involvement in Eyal was illegal. They didn't allow him to bring television cameras. A police agent who is commissioned to 'buy' drugs is not allowed to smoke them himself, etc. When you're in the trenches, though, it's difficult, and sometimes [an agent] will "give himself permission" to break a law. Maybe he will argue the defense of "necessity," maybe the justification that he had to "earn the trust of those around him." I don't want to make a decision about his criminal culpability.

A-G: We see this as a serious matter. I don't dismiss the damage to the organization [the GSS]. Even the revelation of his code name caused great damage. But the additional damage is relatively insignificant, and we can make an effort to minimize it. It is possible to conduct proceedings behind closed doors. The case itself is very serious and there is a real public interest in filing criminal charges. This episode shocked television viewers and caused enormous damage, a virtual public storm! I just don't see how we can avoid beginning [criminal] proceedings.

Ben Ami: Another factor [that must be considered]: The GSS ability to hire agents, and the organization's handling of already existing agents. Our sources demand that the Service ensure that they will not be revealed. It will be hard [if Raviv goes to trial] to handle present agents and hire new ones.

A-G: Sec.(b)(1); The whole trial will take place behind closed doors. The Shamgar Commission was also held behind closed doors. It is possible.

Sasson: Let's assume that there is evidence. The television clip made an impression on me. We see from Chezi Kallo's words what kind of damage [such a trial] would cause to the GSS. I must work with the assumption that there would be such damage. We have to weigh the benefits [of bringing him to trial] against the losses. It has to be evaluated in cold [objective] terms.

E. Arbel: From the perspective of the Attorney-General and the State Attorney's office: It is impossible to evaluate the evidence when we know that what is available there does not give an accurate portrait of what went on. The man was an agent. We don't know what the true picture was at the time. We can't know the clear details of the situation until he gets up on the witness stand, and maybe he will say that he was operating according to the directions of the GSS. It is impossible to say whether there is or is not evidence against him. The file [swearing-in] was staged. The lines were not clearly demarcated for Avishai Raviv. What would have happened if he would have prevented the murder? With all the difficulties that this [decision] entails, I am not sure that we can accomplish our goal. With a heavy heart, I suggest we close the file [against him].

A-G: Section 4(a)—I don't see a problem with the evidence. I don't see any problems in terms of his criminal intent. It is impossible to close the case without public exposure.

Ledor: Some time ago, we put together a format that we could use for a situation in which we announce that a file is being closed.

Arbel: It is simpler to defend the closing of a file due to a lack of evidence; it is possible that he [Raviv] wanted to convince them that he was "one of them." I see a problem with this. And if there is a problem with the evidence, it is easier to explain things [to the public]. I don't have to wait and come to the Court for it to say all this. My desire is to issue an indictment, but the risk is so big. We can in fact explain this to the Supreme Court; it's possible to defend [such an approach].

E. Barak: In actual fact, during the entire time that Raviv served as an agent for us, there were many "incidents." He could very well testify about the [numerous] cases in which we gave him directions. The entire story of his service will be revealed, and there will be legal difficulties. Even after the [Eyal] television broadcast, they continued to employ him.

Sasson: A "lack of evidence" and a "lack of public interest" together constitute good reasons [for closing the file]

A-G: I don't want to be involved in closing the file. I won't get into explaining. In any case, we have to send a letter to the Israel Broadcast Authority in which we express our bad feelings at the video clip [the swearing in ceremony of Eyal]. We have to write something against [TV reporter] Eitan Oren. I can't be involved in this. Were I to be the only one to decide, I would issue an indictment. But, as I said, I don't want to be involved in this. I would like to request that the issue be transferred over to the State Attorney's office, that the State Attorney's office make a decision on this, and issue a statement to the plaintiffs

THE SIGNIFICANCE OF THIS DOCUMENT

November 2, 1999

RAVIV DOCUMENT CENSORED ON-AIR

A "secret document" of a meeting of General Security Service and State Prosecution officials reveals that the two bodies made a "pact to hide "facts about GSS agent provocateur Avishai Raviv, according to MK MichaelEitan. It also shows that GSS agents, only a few months after the assassination, felt that "if we had cut off our connections with Raviv, maybe he would have turned the murderer over to us." Television talk show host Nissim Mishal, whose guest MK Eitan was about to reveal the contents of the document on air last night, suddenly received instructions from Attorney-General Elyakim Rubenstein that the document's disclosure would "endanger public security," and was forbidden. Arutz7 has learned that the document may be seen on the internet at <http://208.150.6.139/>

Both Mishal and Eitan reacted with surprise to the order, saying there was nothing secret about the document. Eitan said, "When you try to fight the GSS and the State Prosecution, they are just too strong—they control things in this country that not even the Prime Minister, or the government, or the Knesset, controls, and they ignore the public—they claim 'public security,' when it's really only their own internal issues." Eitan claims that Rubenstein is attempting to prevent the revelation of a pact between the GSS and the Prosecution to hide the fact that Raviv did not act on his own.

The document also quotes a GSS agent as telling the Attorney-General and the others at the meeting that a previous State Prosecutor had approved activity by Raviv at Bar Ilan University that would incriminate "someone else." The document shows that both the Prosecution and the GSS representatives were seeking ways to close the investigation against Raviv, while Attorney-General Rubenstein was against closing it.

Arutz-7's Haggai Segal notes that Rubenstein's action was fairly unprecedented. Segal said that when two GSS agents were imprisoned in Amman after the bungled assassination attempt of a Hamas leader, the head of the Mossad begged the press not to publicize the news in order not to hurt chances for a quick release—but Rubenstein did not intervene to order or ask the media to be silent.

2. MK EITAN ON THE DOCUMENT

MK Michael Eitan reacted with bitterness to the order blocking the publication of the document. He told Arutz-7 today, "Instead of answering my grave complaints about the fact that the Shabak and the State Prosecution made a pact and submitted false information to the government ministers, and concealed information from the government and the public—they accuse me of leaking classified information, so that I'll have to answer their charges, instead of them answering clearly my charges. For example, I claimed that when the head of the GSS came before the special security cabinet forum—which I convened when I was a government minister—to discuss indicting Raviv, the GSS head told us clearly that the GSS decided that it should not investigate him, and that the police found that Raviv knew nothing and was not involved in the assassination. But I tell you that this is totally misleading and false—the Shabak DID interrogate him, and the whole story was meant to mislead the ministers . . . They simply want to ensure that the story of Avishai Raviv not be made public . . . This document contains nothing that will harm state security . . . Do you have any doubt that Attorney-General Elyakim Rubenstein would trouble himself to call television stations and newspapers and threaten them if he thought that the document would not embarrass the Prosecution?!"

"The large picture," concluded Eitan, "is that this document shows that my long-time basic assumption is correct, that there is a pact between the GSS and the Prosecution to go above the levels responsible for them, and even above the law. They run things as if they are above every suspicion, and no one can ask or raise any doubts about them . . . How could it be that the newspapers are not rising up against threats by the Atty.-Gen. not to publish a document that has no bearing on state security! [The Prosecution] doesn't want it published because it will show how the two bodies work together to fool the government and the public, and they don't want it publicized because it's THEM. Civil rights of people have been trampled—trampled! And instead of punishing those who were guilty, and instead of leading the campaign to look out for civil rights, the Prosecution cooperated with them, became a rubber stamp, and became their partner."

MK Benny Elon said that the document shows how anxious the relevant bodies were to ensure that Avishai Raviv would not be tried, in order that he not take the witness stand: "They searched for excuses not to hold the trial, such as 'no public interest' and 'insufficient evidence,' and Rubenstein tried to disassociate himself from these ideas, and said that he doesn't want to be involved in closing the file."

TO OUR READERS ON THE RAVIV COVERUP

On November 3, 1999 our Freeman Center Broadcast published the Raviv Document. At the time it had been suppressed (censored) by the Israeli Justice Department with the consent of the Israeli Supreme Court on the grounds of "national security." We assured you that security was not an issue. Yesterday, the Israeli Supreme Court reversed its position and agreed with the Freeman Center that the document had been suppressed for purely political ends. **Please read the details below** . . . . **Bernard J. Shapiro, Editor**

Subj: Important—

Date: 11/11/1999 12:49:43 PM Central Standard Time

To: BSaphir@aol.com

Dear Mr. Shapiro,

You might want to send out an announcement to your email list to the effect that today, The Israeli Supreme Court struck down Attorney-General

Elyakim Rubenstein's gag order on the secret Avishai Raviv document! Judges Matza and Dorner harshly reprimanded the Attorney-General for claiming that "national security" prevented the publication of the document. For a full report on the issue, readers can check Arutz-7 news at our website.

ARUTZ-7 NEWS—FRIDAY, NOVEMBER 12, 1999

CALLS FOR INVESTIGATIONS FOLLOW PUBLICATION OF DOCUMENT

Calls continue to be heard for an official committee of inquiry into the workings of the General Security Service and/or the State Prosecution, following the publication yesterday of the heretofore-secret Raviv-Beinish document. Housing Minister Rabbi Yitzchak Levy (NRP) demands that the GSS be investigated for continuing to employ Avishai Raviv despite his activities. MK Tzvi Hendel called upon Prime Minister Barak yesterday to establish a public commission to look into the State Prosecution's role in approving Avishai Raviv's incitement against the right-wing with the purpose of "delegitimizing it and causing it to be reviled by the public."

In addition, popular calls for the resignation of Justice Dorit Beinish from the Supreme Court have been heard. Atty.-Gen. Elyakim Rubenstein, who was sharply criticized yesterday by the Supreme Court for his attempt to prevent the document's publication, issued a defense of Beinish, in light of the document's damaging impression about her. The no-longer secret protocol quotes a GSS agent as saying that because Raviv had to remove suspicions that he was a GSS agent, "Beinish approved activities by Raviv . . . and that he would cause someone else to be incriminated, who would be caught." Rubenstein explained last night that what actually happened was that Beinish had agreed to an urgent GSS request for Raviv to take an action that would incriminate one of the agency's operatives—with that operative's consent. It was noted, however, that the document says "another person," and not "another operative," and that it nowhere implies that this was done with his consent.

BARAK'S MENTAL STATE—

A DANGER TO ISRAEL

(August 2000)

The great under-reported story in the Jewish and national media including the **Jewish Herald-Voice** (Houston) is the continued deterioration of Israel Prime Minister's Ehud Barak's mental state.

In the past months Barak has done the following:

1. Began the process of ethnic cleansing (a war crime under the Geneva Conventions) for Jews from 96% of Judea and Samaria and Gaza.

2. He has offered to give up sovereignty on the Temple Mount and half of Jerusalem to terrorist anti-Semites. Arafat demands also the Old City plus the Western Wall and Barak will give him what he wants as the record proves.

3. Just this week, Barak agreed to give Arafat control of $3 Billion of oil and gas off the coast of Gaza

4. He has agreed to give up the Golan Heights with it strategic mountains and 35% of Israel's water supply, already at drought conditions.

5. He has agreed give Arafat control of the strategic Jordan Valley and the Judean-Samarian mountain ridge that protects Israel from invasion from the east (Syria, Iraq, Iran).

6. He has agreed to turn over the following Jewish Holy places to Arafat's gang of Jew murderers: Tomb of Rachel, Tomb of Jacob, Cave of the Macpala (Tomb of the Patriarchs).

7. Barak has cease governing the country, does not consult with anyone that does not agree with him.

There is an obvious psychiatric diagnosis for such behavior: the grandiose phase of mania. People in such mental state take wild gambles with money and behavior. They believe themselves above the law, super intelligent and capable of doing anything. Eventually they crash and burn having lost their fortunes and their health.

BARAK IS GAMBLING AWAY THE HERITAGE, LAND AND SECURITY OF ISRAEL. HE MUST BE STOPPED IN A DEMOCRATIC PROCESS IMMEDIATELY .... Bernard

An Editorial for the May 2001 issue of THE MACCABEAN ONLINE

ISRAELI INDEPENDENCE AND

AMERICAN FOREIGN POLICY

(May 2001)

The American people when properly polled come out consistently in support of Israel. There are at least 50 million Evangelical Christians who are friends and dedicated supporters of Israel. Many of America's presidents have bucked the US State Department to help Israel with arms and money. The US Congress and Senate have consistently been friends of Israel. Martin Luther King, Jr. expressed his love of Israel many times. My own grandfather, for whom the Freeman Center was named, expressed his love of America upon his arrival on our shores:

"But what a change in life upon arriving in America—Free America. Here I suddenly found myself unbridled, the air free, no stifling, atmosphere—I could give free expression to the cravings of my soul! Life began to have a different meaning. What a blessing to have free assemblage, free speech free press! Can an American who has always enjoyed these blessings appreciate what it means to one who was deprived of them until manhood?"

Unfortunately there are institutions in America that don't love Israel as much as most of us do. Israel's relations with America go back even before statehood in 1948. During the critical years of WWII, the Zionist community of both America and Israel appealed to President Franklin Roosevelt to take action to stop the Holocaust. They were rebuffed at every turn. It was apparent that neither America nor any of its allies were very interested in saving Jewish lives. England was the most persuasive when arguing that the Jews saved would want to go to Palestine. This would anger the Arabs and should be avoided at all cost. It is true that European Jewry would have been a vast reservoir of new citizens for the emerging State of Israel. Their sheer numbers would have eliminated the Arab demographic problem in the new State. American policy came down solidly on the side of dead Jews as opposed to live Jews.

Bernard J. Shapiro

When Israel declared its independence in 1948, we were all pleased that the American president, Harry S. Truman, made America the first nation in the world to recognize the Jewish State. Yet even here there was a dark side to American Foreign Policy. The State Department had argued in vain against the recognition of Israel. When they didn't succeed at that they successfully placed an embargo of arms to Middle Eastern States. Seemingly neutral it only affected Israel since the British and French were arming the Arabs. So we have the spectacle of American recognition of Israel's independence while at the same time refusing the arms it needed to survive, to defend their lives.

Following Israel's Sinai Campaign in 1956, Eisenhower and Dulles forced Israel to withdraw with little political gain. Two "benefits" appeared to be: a UN Force in Sinai to guarantee free passage for Israel in the Gulf of Eilat; and an American promise to guarantee such free passage. In 1967 the UN Force disappeared as did the American promise, which the State Department claimed they could not verify.

In the period since 1967, the US State Department has devoted an excessive amount of time developing and promoting plans to force Israeli withdrawal to the 'suicide' borders of pre-1967. With amazing regularity, the State Department has failed to be honest about violations of the agreements it has negotiated between the Arabs and Israelis. The US has been blind to Arab violations from the failure to see missile movements in Egypt (1970-76) to the failure to see Palestinian violations of the Oslo and Wye Agreements. This US blindness has always been one way. The Israelis are subjected to constant misinterpretations of agreements. For example, never having agreed to a freeze in Jewish building, US spy satellites are active daily counting houses in YESHA. And then publicly rebuking Israel for a normal activity of a sovereign country.

In order to pressure Israel, stories appear on a regular basis claiming that Israel is transferring American technology to third parties. In every case they are proven false, but the constant repetition is meant to weaken Israel diplomatically. The State Department has orchestrated a media campaign to damage Israel's reputation in general and Israeli Prime Ministers in particular. A few examples:

1. Sharon is the "hardline" PM of Israel while other world leaders are Statesman. Arafat is a 'leader'

2. Ethnic cleansing is bad in Kosovo but the ethnic cleansing of Jews from YESHA is good

3. All disputed land in YESHA 'belongs' to Arabs even when Israel has clear title

4. All foreign capitals are recognized 'except Jerusalem'

5. Israeli soldiers defending themselves from attack have been treated by the media as the 'bad guy'

6. Rock throwers who can crush you skull have been treated as 'demonstrators or protesters' by the media

7. Jewish villages are 'settlements' and 'illegitimate' while Arab villages are all considered legitimate

The list could on but now we must say something that should have been said a few years ago. All the mediators like Dennis Ross and all the shuttles of the Secretary of State to help secure a peace between terrorists and Israel following Oslo are fruitless. They serve only one function and that is to strip Israel of its strategic and water resources for the benefit of Arab plans to destroy her in stages. America benefits by a presumed gratitude (which will not exist) from the Arab states and Arafat.

It is very important for Israel to disengage from its close embrace with American diplomacy. It should be obvious to all that American and Israeli interests differ markedly in relation to the negotiations with the Palestinians. America has by its own admission ceased to be either pro-Israel or a neutral mediator (the Americans claim to be 'even-handed'). American policy in the final analysis will leave Israel with indefensible borders and an irredentist Palestinian neighbor yearning for all the land "from the river to the sea." Then, of course, they will also want Jordan.

Bernard J. Shapiro

Moshe Arens has confirmed recently that Israel's strong ties to American military aid have stifled the growth of Israel's domestic production and R & D. It has also prevented the export of Israel's military equipment to other countries making domestic production very costly. This is due to the fact that products need a large market to justify development costs.

Much more can be gained for Israel by negotiating directly with the Arabs. This used to be Israeli policy. In reality, Arafat has ceased negotiating with Israel and now is negotiating only with Washington. It may be necessary to give up American aid dollars and possibly weapons to break out of the current US embrace. It will certainly be difficult, but in the end, there will exist a truly free and sovereign Israel. Now Israel is somewhere between a friend and a banana republic, beholden to the whims of America.

This is my message for Independence Day. The alternative is to learn nothing from history: placing Israel's destiny in America's hands as was done during WWII. America won the war, but 90% of Europe's Jews were already dead. I would prefer Israel to survive.

JEWISH COMMUNITIES IN YESHA

(November 2002)

I plan to discuss the Right of the Jewish People to Eretz Yisrael including Judea, Samaria and Gaza—Yesha for short. I also will discuss the strategic importance of Yesha and how the Jewish communities there contribute to Israel's security, prevent the establishment of a Palestinian terrorist state next door and fulfill Biblical commandments.

GENESIS 15:17-18:

And it came to pass, That day the L-RD made a covenant with Abraham saying:

"UNTO THY SEED HAVE I GIVEN THIS LAND IN PERPETUITY."

*

DAVID BEN GURION, founding father and first Prime Minister of Israel, had this to say about territorial concessions:

"No Jew has the right to relinquish the right of the Jewish people over the whole Land of Israel. No Jewish body has such authority, not even the whole Jewish people have the authority to waive the right (to the Land of Israel) for future generations for all time."[Zionist Conference, Basle, Switzerland, 1937]

THE JEWISH RIGHT TO ERETZ YISRAEL was expressed in a letter from the Jewish leader Simon, the only survivor of the five Maccabee brothers to king Antiochus, whom they had just defeated. Antiochus demanded the return of the 'occupied territories'—that is territories the Maccabees liberated during their recent war.

Simon writes: "We have neither taken foreign land nor seized foreign property, but only the inheritance of our fathers, which at one time had been unjustly taken by our enemies. Now that we have the opportunity, we are firmly holding the inheritance of our fathers."

★

Israeli Prime Minister Benjamin Netanyahu in his book **A PLACE AMONG THE NATIONS** writes the following when told that Judea and Samaria are foreign "occupied" lands:

"This land, where every swing of a spade unearths remnants of the Jewish past and where every village carries the barely altered Hebrew names of old; this land, in which the Jews became a nation and over which they shed more tears than have been shed by any other people in history; this land, the loss of which resulted in an exile of the Jews such as has been suffered by no other people and the spilling of a sea of blood such as has been spilled by no other nation; this land, which never ceased to live as a distant but tangible home in the minds of Jewish children from Toledo in medieval Spain to the Warsaw ghetto in our own century; this land, for which the Jews fought with unsurpassed courage and tenacity in ancient as in modern times—this is the "foreign land" that world leaders now demand be barred to Jews and that Israel (should) unilaterally forsake."

The answer to such absurd demands must be a resounding NO!

★

The modern Jewish return to **Eretz Yisrael** began in 1882. Between 1882 and 1914 there were dozens of Jewish "settlements" (I prefer the term Jewish communities both then and now). Some of the more important ones were Tel Aviv, Hadera, and Rischon Letzion,Hayelet Hashacher, Rosh Pina, Metula, Kfar Saba and Petah Tikva. Between 1921 and 1925 Jews settled throughout the Jezereel Valley. In fact, the return of Jews to Eretz Yisrael was the raison etre of the Zionist Movement and a commandment to Jews everywhere to return to Zion. This process continues today 120 years after it began.

★

Unfortunately, Jews throughout history have deluded themselves about their position in society. They pursue utopian solutions (like Oslo) to complex political problems and disputes. Jews rejoiced as the enlightenment spread across Europe in the 18th and 19th centuries. Many were eager to give up their Jewishness and become German, French, Italian, and English. In the final analysis those societies viewed them as Jews. Self-delusion came into collision with reality and left us with the stench of burning flesh in the ovens of Auschwitz. Many Russian Jews eagerly supported the communist idea of a worker's utopia with no nationalities and no religion. Reality taught them that their neighbors still considered them Jews.

The left-wing in Israel believes in a common humanity of shared values with the Arabs. In the face of all empirical evidence to the contrary they believe peace is possible. In the book <u>Self Portrait Of A Hero: The Letters of Jonathan Netanyahu (1963-1976)</u>, Jonathan Netanyahu, the fallen hero of Entebbe and brother of Benjamin, said it best: "I see with sorrow and great anger how a part of the people still clings to hopes of reaching a peaceful settlement with the Arabs. Common sense tells them, too, that the Arabs haven't abandoned their basic aim of destroying the State; but the self-delusion and self-deception that have always plagued the Jews are at work again. It's our great misfortune. They want to believe, so they believe. They want not to see, so they shut their eyes. They want not to learn from thousands of years of history, so they distort it. They want to bring about a sacrifice, and they do indeed. It would be comic, if it wasn't so tragic. What a saddening and irritating lot this Jewish people are!"

★

In 1967 I traveled to Israel a few days after the Western Wall fell into Israeli hands. As I placed my hands on this magnificent relic of our forefathers, I felt a surge of light and energy the likes of which I had never known. In what had to have been but the flash of a second, I felt at one with Jews from all periods of history. At the Passover Seder we are told to thank G-d for delivering us from Egypt as though we ourselves had been brought out of bondage. At that moment in Jerusalem, this Seder message was very real for me.

In an instant I saw the continuity of Jewish history and its unbreakable connection with **Eretz Yisrael** (**Land of Israel**). I understood how modern Israel is the beginning of the Third Temple Period and the spiritual heir to Joshua, Saul, David, Solomon, the Maccabees and Bar Kokhba. I frequently write about the security reasons for incorporating Judea, Samaria, and Gaza into the body of Israel. There is another side to this issue and that is the spiritual-religious side. The truth, which many find inconvenient, is that the **Land of Israel** was promised by **G-d to Abraham** and his seed in perpetuity. The **Land of Israel** is not speculative real estate to be bartered away for some high sounding (but false) promises of peace. The hills and valleys of **Judea and Samaria** contain the collective memory of the Jewish people. It was here that the Israelites first entered the **Holy Land**. And it was here they fought the battles, built the towns, elected their kings and were preached to by their prophets and judges. And it was on this soil that they wrote the **Holy Scriptures** we call our Bible.

In my blinding flash of insight at the Wall, I also understood that Israel on its own soil was more powerful than the sum of its weapons and men. Jews who had wandered the earth powerless for two millenniums attained great power when re-united with the soil of Israel. Anyone who has followed the Arab-Israeli conflict must be aware of the rising cost paid for Jewish blood. Before Israel was established, nations of the world took Jewish lives with impunity. Today, Arabs have discovered that the iron fist of Zahal (Israel Defense Forces) exacts a high price for even one Jewish life. Unfortunately, following the signing of the Oslo Agreements, Jewish blood has become cheaper.

One thing is clear to me: the **L-rd** has blessed Israel by re-uniting Jerusalem and bringing Judea, Samaria, and Gaza back under its control. It would be a horrendous sin against **G-d** and common sense for Israel to renounce this inheritance to which it is entitled. Israel holds these lands as a sacred trust for the Jewish people in perpetuity.

It would not only be sinful, but also criminal, to abuse that trust by denying future generations of Jews their Holy Land—Land of their Fathers; the one tiny spot on planet earth given to them by G-d.

A LETTER FROM SHILOH, by Yisrael Medad

"The faith of these "settlers" who should properly be termed "revenants," people who have returned to a place after a long absence", their commitment and their determination, are intangibles that some Diaspora Jews still find difficult to grasp. To some Diaspora Jews, especially those who have traditionally championed a more liberal or leftwing approach to Zionism, the Oslo process is still strong after nine years of abject failure. For them, it seems, my community is an impediment to fulfillment of the Oslo vision of two states, one Jewish, the other devoid of Jewish communities.

To those who still champion the Oslo process, peace requires that Jews be banned from the heart of the Jewish people's historic homeland, Judea and Samaria, as they were for 19 years after Israel's 1948 War of Independence. To them, the quarter-million Jews who reside there are always "the settlers." Their communities constitute "human rights violations," they are an "illegal occupation" and must be dismantled for their vision of peace to be fulfilled.

My home in Shiloh was never occupied, to use a phrase too liberally applied, by Arabs, though there are Arab villages nearby. Calling Shiloh a "settlement" implies something foreign, intrusive and temporary, something that is purposefully and maliciously imposed. To us, however, "settling" is the most natural thing for a Jew to do: to reside where his forefathers dwelled, where his kings ruled and his prophets spoke.

No, we are not violators of justice and international law. If there is any substance to the charges of ethnic cleansing and human rights violations so frequently tossed about, it relates to what the Arab leadership and its supporters have done and continue to do. We have done our best to avoid hindering Arabs as they continue to live here and in Israel, and have founded our communities almost exclusively on unused and unpopulated hilltops. Arab terrorists and their supporters justify killing our children and women just because we live here."

The letter ends.

*

As I stand before you tonight, I must emphatically declare that the ethnic cleansing of Jews from Judea, Samaria, and Gaza is NO different from ethnic cleansing anywhere in the world.

The Arabs who wish to live in peace with their Jewish neighbors are welcome. They can even manage their own civil and municipal affairs.

THOSE, HOWEVER, WHO WISH TO TAKE UP THEIR BOMBS, GUNS AND KNIVES TO KILL JEWS OR THROW ROCKS TO CRUSH JEWISH SKULLS, MUST BE DESTROYED. Rabbinical authorities have long recognized the ultimate religious priority of saving Jewish lives. For example, the Israeli army is permitted to operate fully on Shabbat because it is necessary to save Jewish lives.

*

Too many Jews are obsessed with what will satisfy the Arabs. I doubt if there is a single Palestinian or Moslem anywhere that worries about what is good for Israel or the Jewish People. We must remember the words of Hillel when he said, "If I am not for myself, who will be for me? And if I am for myself alone, what am I?" Hillel's message is clear: First take care of yourself, your family and your people and then try to help others.

*

Remember it took the Christian world two thousand years to accept us as human beings, and this only after the mass murder of a third of our people.

It may take the Arabs a while, maybe decades or even hundreds of years—but we have no choice but to be patient. The fact that we want peace badly does not mean that it is attainable. To strip Israel of strategic territory like Czechoslovakia before WWII in the pursuit of a phantom illusory peace will only lead to disaster.

*

In our Holy Scriptures we read about the prophet Jeremiah. Jeremiah, who anguished over the fact that his people believed in false prophets of peace and didn't see the dangers facing Israel, cries out in despair, "Peace, peace but there is no peace."

Midge Decter writes "For there is no such thing as making peace. Nations who are friendly do not need to do so, and nations or people who are hostile cannot do so. To cry peace, peace when there is no peace, the prophet Jeremiah taught us long ago, is not the expression of hope, not even superstition but a reckless toying with the minds and hearts of people whose very future depends on their capacity to rise every day to the harsh morning light of the truth."

★

The glorious **Hebrew Warriors** who defeated five Arab armies in 1948, three in 1967, and two in 1973 must not surrender their Jewish homeland to an evil terrorist, who delights in killing Jewish babies. The **Brave Heroes of Zion** must not limit themselves to fruitless negotiations. At this great time of trial and apocalyptic threat, the safeguarding of the future of the Jewish people's right to *Eretz Yisrael* must take precedence.

SERIOUS FLAWS IN THE OSLO AGREEMENT AND SERIOUS REASONS TO MAINTAIN JEWISH SETTLEMENT AND CONTROL IN JUDEA, SAMARIA AND GAZA

(1) The most fundamental flaw is the renunciation of **Jewish claims to Judea, Samaria, and Gaza**. The right of the Jewish people to the Land of Israel is God-given and cannot be renounced by a transitory Israeli government. The present government has no right to deprive future generations of Jews and Israelis of their legal patrimony.

(2) Yasir Arafat's PLO is **incapable of providing Israelis with the cessation of violence** they so dearly crave. There are ten rejectionist PLO factions plus Hamas and other Islamic fundamentalist factions, including Arafat's own terrorist gangs that will continue to kill Jews.

(3) Without the presence of Israel's internal security force (Shin Bet) inside Judea, Samaria and Gaza, it will be **impossible to halt terrorism** or even keep it within present levels. The Israel Defense Forces maintain tremendous power but are of little importance in day-to-day terrorism, unless they are able to project their power into Yesha as Sharon has done.

(4) Arafat's signature on the agreement and the PLO acceptance is of no consequence as **Arafat is a documented liar.** Muslims are permitted to lie to non-Muslims and break agreements with them under the Koranic law of *HUDAIBIYA*. Treaties and contracts with them are worthless.

(5) By virtue of this agreement, the Israeli government has **validated Arab claims to the Land of Israel**. Decades of fighting Arab propaganda and distortions of history are trivialized and discounted.

(6.) This agreement puts the status of **Jerusalem on the negotiating table** as a final status issue. Every previous government of Israel steadfastly stood by the principle of Jerusalem being non-negotiable.

(7) All of **Israel's military and civilian communications could be easily monitored** from the hills of Judea and Samaria. The quick mobilization of the IDF could be rendered impossible by Palestinian attacks.

(8) Israel would lose control of the Judean-Samarian mountain ridge which protects it from attack from the east. The steep slope from the Jordan River to the crest of the ridge is difficult to traverse and can be blocked by a relatively small force of the IDF Should a Palestine State arise **the Arab population will force the Israelis out.**

(9) Whether they admit it publicly or not, Israeli leaders know that this is the **first step to a Palestinian state.**

(10) The **"Palestinian right of return" has been acknowledged** for the first time by the Israelis and could result in a flood of Arabs to Judea and Samaria.

(11) The inevitable increase in Arab population will result in **tremendous pressure on Israel's water supply.** As Arab wells are dug in the Judean and Samarian hills, the natural mountain aquifer that supplies much of Tel Aviv and the coastal plain with water will be serious depleted. Such depletion will cause the salt water of the Mediterranean Sea to penetrate Israel's coastal strip, thus destroying all water supplies. This process can be witnessed in California, where sea water has already penetrated five miles into the coast.

(12) Some **70% of Israel's population and industry** is concentrated in a small strip of coast and greater Tel Aviv. That population will be **immediately threatened by mortars and Kyushu rockets.** Fired singly from the hills of Judea and Samaria, and set with timers they will be virtually impossible to stop. The Israeli government plan to coordinate with the Palestinian police is akin to working with the fox to guard the henhouse. The Palestinian police are being recruited from among the terrorists who delight especially in murder and mutilation of Jewish bodies. Will they arrest and turn over a terrorist who kills Israelis and then escapes to Gaza?

(13) The **Jewish residents of Judea, Samaria, and Gaza** will no doubt be **victims of ethnic cleansing.** The Arabs will insist on a Jew-free country like Jordan, Saudi Arabia, and Kuwait.

(14) The air and seaports planned for Gaza will facilitate the entry of weapons and terrorists, threatening the security of Israel. The air space above Israel including Ben Groin Airport would easily be threatened. A Palestinian State could NOT be demilitarized. Look at the PA today.

(15) The proposed "safe passages" for the PA will facilitate the movement of terrorists and weapons from Gaza to Judea and Samaria.

(16) HITLER AND THE ARABS

"Hitler, Goebbels and Goering were pathological and pragmatic liars. Arafat also lied at Oslo as he fully intended to carry out his staged plan of 1974. Under this plan he would accept any part of Palestine until he could conquer the remainder. The Nazis lied so convincingly and so hugely that most statesmen from other countries could not believe that what they were hearing was a lie . . . One of Hitler's biggest lies was constantly to assure the world of peaceful intentions while obviously planning war. Arafat has done the same.

The only reason that the Arabs have not yet done to the Israeli Jews what Hitler did to their forefathers in Europe is that they have thus far lacked the military means and weapons of mass destruction which were at Hitler's disposal, to do so.

That the Arabs have not done so to date has not been due to any reluctance on their part, but because, this time, there has been this difference: The Jews in Europe had no army to defend them. **Thank G-d, the Jews in Israel have!**

May Israel be wiser in relation to this death wish of her neighbors, than the Jews in Europe were. They belittled the writings and speeches of Hitler and the Nazis and were massacred as a result. May it not happen again with Arafat!

I am sorry that I cannot offer you more encouraging words. What I present is:

A HARSH REALITY

We all want peace. We pray for peace in our Sabbath services every Friday night. After thousands of years, being **victims of persecution, expulsion, extermination, and discrimination,** it is natural that we yearn for peace with every ounce of our bodies and souls.

It is because our hunger for peace is so strong that we must be doubly cautious not to fall for a **pseudo-peace** that is really the wolf of war wrapped in sheep's clothing. Today none of us believe Chamberlain really negotiated **"peace in our time"** with Hitler. Why do some Jews believe that Peres and Rabin really negotiated *PEACE* **with Arafat, one of today's Hitlers?**

Israelis my age have fought in four wars and I understand their desire to be free of constant conflict. **Unfortunately there is no magic cure.** I wish I could write more optimistic words. Beyond the neighboring states that Israel is negotiating with now lies another ring of **unmitigated hostility** led by Islamic fundamentalists like those in Iran.

As Jews we are all involved in this historic struggle to survive. It is not our fate or that of the Israelis that we should retire from this struggle. The only peace the Arabs are prepared to give us is the **peace of the grave.**

In blood and fire was Israel born and on a hot anvil was she forged. The brave young soldiers of Israel must take a quick glance back to the crematoria of Auschwitz and then go forth to face the enemy knowing that there is <u>still</u> **no alternative (*ein briera*)**.

Bernard J. Shapiro

WHY LIKUD VOTERS MUST REJECT SURRENDER TO TERRORISM

(May, 2004)

There are many reasons Likud voters should reject PM Ariel Sharon's plan to surrender Gaza to terrorist Arabs and expel its peaceful productive Jewish residents. I have broken these reasons into three categories: moral, strategic and security. Also I will discuss the fact that U.S. President George Bush's commitments to Sharon have no practical value and are of little more than "smoke and mirrors" to cover up a flawed plan. Then I will review the guarantees Israel has given Bush to achieve these delusions. When you look at the whole picture, I believe you will agree that all Likud members should vote a resounding **NO** against this surrender to terrorism plan.

MORAL

1. The expulsion of Jews from Gaza is no different from the expulsion of Jews from any country. This includes the expulsions from Israel by the Romans, Assyrians and Babylonians. In Europe Spain, England, Germany, France, Poland and Russia drove Jews from their homes of many centuries. That Jews should be expelled from *Eretz Yisrael* by a Jewish government makes it all the more morally reprehensible.

2. Gaza is clearly a part of the **Holy Land** given by G-d to Abraham for the **Jewish People** in perpetuity. Sharon has no right to take it upon himself to divest all of us of our inheritance.

3. Sharon claims that the removal of Jews from Gaza would strengthen Israel's ability to protect other Jews. This goes against all Torah principles which state that it is wrong to sacrifice one Jew to save another.

4. One of the greatest moral flaws is the attempt to stifle debate on this crucial decision for the future of Israel. Sharon has refused to debate the issue. The media presents only one side, that of retreat. Israeli politicians are blackmailed into thinking that to go against Sharon's surrender the United States would be upset (which it would not).

5. Surrender to terrorism will embolden it and increase the killing worldwide and not just in Israel.

STRATEGIC

Gaza has always been strategically important. Throughout history it has been the route of invasion from North Africa into Israel and beyond. Egypt has used Gaza to attack Israel during warfare and with terrorism since before the State of Israel was declared. Jutting like a finger into the heart of Israel it sits only 40 miles from Tel Aviv. Rockets and missiles from Gaza, after retreat, will certainly hit Israeli population centers. Already the strategic port of Ashdod has been struck and most areas in the Negev will become front line communities.

Worse still from a strategic standpoint will be the absence of good intelligence on the ground in Gaza. This will make impossible the targeted assassinations terrorist leaders. It will also create a safe haven for the terrorists to do research and development on advanced weapon systems like missiles capable of carrying biological or chemical warheads.

SECURITY

Israelis are being promised security by leaving Gaza. Unfortunately this will not be the case for a number of reasons:

1. Arabs will still enter Israel to work and a certain number will be homicide bombers.

2. The Gaza fence will not be a perfect barrier to infiltration of terrorists into Israel. With the increased motivation resulting from Israeli retreat, they will seek new innovative ways to cross the barrier. For example, their success in building tunnels into Gaza will be re-directed to tunneling into the Negev from Sinai or directly under the fence.

3. Israelis should expect the terrorists to place greater emphasis on involving Israeli Arabs in acts and support of terrorism. There will be no let up in the terrorist pressure despite assurance that leaving Gaza will have beneficial effects.

PRESIDENTIAL DECLARATIONS—*Are They Binding?*

Yoram Ettinger recently published a list of American commitments from history that have proven how worthless those promises were "when push came to shove." We should certainly not rely on American promises in our decision to vacate strategic territory and compromise or moral values and security interests. Here is his list of infamy:

> **FACT**: According to the US Constitution, no presidential declaration/promise is binding without a Congressional legislation or ratification.
>
> **FACT**: President Bush's statements (Apr. 7, 2004) on the "1967 Lines" and the "Claim of Return" are not binding. He did not oppose the "claim of return", did not recognize Israel's sovereignty over major settlement blocks in Judea & Samaria, and did not support Israel's sovereignty beyond the "1967 Lines." Presidents Johnson and Reagan stated (September 10, 1968 and September 1, 1982) that Israel should **not** be expected to withdraw to the "1967 Lines", but it has not prevented their successors—and did not prevent them—to expect such a withdrawal.
>
> **FACT**: President Clinton committed (in 2000) $800MN to Israel, to induce a withdrawal from So. Lebanon. Israel withdrew, Palestinian terrorism escalated, but the committed assistance has not been extended.
>
> **FACT**: Saudi F-15s are stationed at Tabuq, south of Eilat, threatening Israel, in defiance of President Reagan's 1981 commitment to Congress and to Israel.
>
> **FACT**: President Bush promised (in 1991) to direct 30% of US bombing to Western Iraq, in order to destroy the Scud missile launchers, dissuading Israel from a preemptive offensive against Iraq. However, only 3% of the bombing were directed at W. Iraq, the launchers were not destroyed, but Israel was hit in its Soft Belly.

FACT: President Nixon committed (in 1970) the US to oppose the deployment of missiles, by Egypt, toward Sinai. Missiles were deployed, Israeli complaints were ignored by the US, and the 1973 War erupted taxing Israel with 2,800 fatalities (more than 100,000 in US terms).

FACT: President Eisenhower issued (in 1957) Executive commitments to Israel, in return for a full withdrawal from Sinai. In 1967, Egypt violated the agreement with the US and Israel, the Egypt-Syria-Jordan axis tightened around Israel, President Johnson did not implement the 1957 commitments, which paved the road to the Six Days War.

FACT: Presidential candidate Bush made a commitment (in 2000) to relocate the US embassy to Jerusalem. In 2004, the embassy is still located in Tel Aviv.

Presidential Commitments—The Limits

FACT: According to the US Constitution, international treaties and commitments assumed by the president must be ratified by 2/3 of the Senate, in order to be constitutionally binding.

FACT: According to the US Constitution, the Power of the Purse is on Capitol Hill. No presidential financial commitment stands, unless legislated by Congress (which is constrained by rigid budget caps).

FACT: According to the US Constitution, the president and/or Congress can rescind any international commitment by issuing an Executive Order and/or by a congressional vote.

FACT: A President may bypass Congress by Executive Agreements and Executive Orders, which could be rescinded by the president, by his successors and by Congress.

FACT: US international commitments (including NATO) are characterized by ambiguity, lack of specificity and by the absence of automaticity of implementation, in order to preserve the interests of the US (rather than the interest of other countries).

THE BOTTOM LINE:

The contention that presidential declarations/promises are carved in stone reflects misunderstanding of the US democracy, a dangerous delusion and ignorance of precedents, which have taxed Israel severely.

In return for an ambiguous, non-specific presidential declaration—devoid of an automatic trigger—Israel is expected to carry out a specific, certain and tangible retreat, which would constitute—according to Israel's Chairman of the Joint Chiefs of Staff (Dec. 3, 2003)—a tail wind to Palestinian terrorism.

ISRAEL'S COMMITMENTS TO BUSH

Israel made many commitments to Bush which greatly limit Israel's sovereignty and its ability to act in its national interests. Some of them are listed below:

1. No settlement growth beyond the limits placed on Israel by the Americans. US Ambassador Kurtzer, who has a pro-Arab bias, will determine those limits.

2. Removal of unauthorized outposts. The list of such outposts will be presented to Ambassador Kurtzer within 30 days.

3. Palestinian revenues should be dispersed. This matter is pending in various courts of law in Israel, awaiting judicial decisions.

4. The Israeli government remains committed to the two-state solution—Israel and Palestine living side by side in peace and security—as the key to peace in the Middle East.

5. The Israeli government remains committed to the road map as the only route to achieving the two-state solution.

6. The Government of Israel supports the United States' efforts to reform the Palestinian security services to meet their road map obligations to fight terror. Israel also supports the American efforts, working with the international community, to promote the reform process, build institutions, and improve the economy of the Palestinian Authority and to enhance the welfare of its people, in the hope that a new Palestinian leadership will prove able to fulfill its obligations under the road map. The Israeli Government will take all reasonable actions requested by these parties to facilitate these efforts. **[This is the most ridiculous of commitments. Can you train terrorists to fight terrorism?]**

THE BOTTOM LINE

I hope the Likud voters will review carefully the material presented here. I believe there is an overwhelming case for voting no on the surrender referendum for moral, strategic and security reasons. And also, the commitments of Bush and Sharon do nothing to change the realities on the ground and we should be wary of falling for "nice words" that mask the real issues. The future of Israel is in your hands now, please do the responsible thing.

Bernard J. Shapiro

MCCARTHYISM, SUPPRESSION OF

FREE SPEECH THREATENS ISRAELIS

(July 2004)

I want to make something perfectly clear to all my readers. No one should even think about harming Israeli PM Ariel Sharon personally. He is a hero of Israel. For reasons none of us really know he has made political and security decisions that are terribly wrong. He may have good intentions. He may be becoming senile and as some doctors suggest, the victim of mini-strokes that have affected his behavior.

On the other hand, we must fight his self-destructive policies with all the might at our disposal. The fate of Israel is in our hands and not that of only Sharons. Mass movements can effect great political change. Most of the public is apathetic. A strong movement with good leadership is capable of producing major improvements in the national situation.

In Israel, the major mass movement has been leftist oriented. This does not have to last forever as evidenced in the most recent election when the Right (as opposed to the wrong) won over 70% of the vote. Unfortunately, Sharon made a 180% turn to the left against the will of those who elected him.

The response of the Right must become massive. Resistance to the ethnic cleansing of Jews must be powerful. I participated in the mass movement for civil rights in America and was a part of the March on Washington in 1963. Standing with 200,000 people and listening to Dr. Martin Luther King's "I Have A Dream" speech stirred my soul.

The Jews of Russia and America who fought the Communists to liberate the Jewish People were not afraid. They suffered great hardships, but in the end they were free and their battle was instrumental in the Fall of Communism in the Soviet Union.

WHERE ARE THE LEADERS OF ISRAEL?

This brings me to a most important part of my article. The GSS (General Security Service), under orders from Sharon, is targeting opponents of his national suicide plan. The Nationalist Camp should expect "dirty tricks" and agents provocateurs, who will attempt to discredit them with the Israeli public. They did it after Oslo and increased the intensity after the assassination of Yitzhak Rabin. [See my article below from December 1995.]

With the help of the leftist elite in the media and politics, McCarthysim and suppression of free speech will threaten Israelis. Normal democratic debate on life and death government policies will be called extremism. The specialist in Orwellian (1984 Newspeak) linguistic manipulation will be hard at work convincing Israelis that black is white, war is peace. Don't let them intimidate you or your friends.

You must bravely speak the truth. Fear no one as the G-d of Israel walks with you. Like the brave Jews of Russia and the Afro-Americans in the US, you must march proudly to defend Eretz Yisrael, Zionism, and the Jewish People. No earthly power can stop you. Ein Breira.

★

Bernard J. Shapiro

McCarthyism in Israel Must be Stopped
[December 1995]

The leftist coalition ruling Israel has cynically used the tragic assassination of Israeli Prime Minister Yitzhak Rabin to launch a vicious campaign of slander against the pro-security and religious majority in their country. The hate and divisions in Israel were created by Labor from the earliest days of the State and have been perpetuated by the left-wing ever since. Nothing, however, equals the present outpouring of hate for the opposition. Government ministers are openly equating the democratic opposition to the suicidal policies of the government with the cold-blooded irrational murder of Rabin. They seek to intimidate the opposition in order to carry out their misguided policies without protest. There have been calls to restrict the normal democratic practices of freedom of speech, press, assembly and protest. There is again talk of silencing the pro-security radio station, Arutz 7.

I say to the leaders of Israel: If you are looking for a villain in this tragedy, take a hard look in the mirror. You reap what you sow.

The following comment comes from Gary Cooperberg, the press officer for the city of Kiryat Araba: "I do not rejoice at Rabin's death. I mourn the fact that his policies drove a decent Jew to commit such a desperate act. One can call a process of self destruction "peace". But the self deception cannot go on indefinitely. If you keep heating a pressure cooker it will eventually explode. Only when the leaders of the Jewish state come to grips with reality and govern with regard to the will of those whom they presume to govern will there be hope for us to avoid the further catastrophe of civil strife." There is a massive smear campaign being waged against the pro-security camp in Israel and America. I believe quite strongly that history will view our efforts as heroic and in the best Jewish/Zionist tradition. Hatzofeh, in a recent editorial writes: "We are alarmed at the unceasing incitement against the national and religious public," and regret that "only a few left-wing personalities are speaking out against this." The paper warns against McCarthyism, and declares that "persecution and incitement together, are a dangerous phenomenon that is liable to steer us into an abyss if it is not stopped or halted immediately." Conclusion: Someone needs to explain to our critics that people are responsible for their own actions. Writers, poets, actors, singers, film makers, TV producers and publishers are always being told by self-appointed moralists that THEY are responsible for the crimes of some disturbed individual.

It just isn't so! If criticism of the government caused murder, then there would not be a single free democracy anywhere in the world.

I understand the pressure you must feel from the massive smear campaign being waged against the pro-security camp in Israel and America. I believe quite strongly that history will view our efforts as heroic and in the best Jewish/Zionist tradition. Even if all mankind opposed my work for Israel, I would continue until my last breath. I persevere not for myself; not for this generation; but so that all future generations of Jews shall possess Eretz Yisrael, in perpetuity, according to the Covenant of G-d with Abraham. The international and Jewish media has also adopted the BIG LIE of opposition complicity in this tragic assassination. At the Freeman Center, we take the truth seriously, and will continue to give you the facts no matter how harsh the reality.

For the sake of Zion we demand an end to McCarthyism in Israel!

[This article was the cover editorial for December 1995 issue of The Maccabean.]

SIMPLE RULES FOR CREATING

A GIANT WAVE OF ALIYA TO ISRAEL

By Bernard J. Shapiro

(Revised from original editorial of August 2004)

1. Crush terrorism and pre-empt all existential threats to the State of Israel. **Why move to a country unable to protect its Jewish population?**
2. Annex all state lands within the borders of Israel (post 1967). Annex all property stolen from the Jewish People during the last 2000 years, including Church and Waqf property (exceptions, of course for **Holy Places**. The term Holy Places does not include *fraudulent* claims of Muslims to Jewish or Christian Holy Places.). Remove all illegal Arab buildings and farms.
3. Require all voting citizens of Israel to do military or community service for 3 years (including Arabs). The right to vote and be a citizen will depend such service + a loyalty oath to the Jewish State.
4. Re-affirm that Israel is a Jewish State and **NOT** a democratic (one man one vote) state of all its citizens. The loyal citizens of Israel whether Jewish, Christian, Druze, Bedouin or Arab will have equal rights.
5. Adopt Prof. Paul Eidelberg's constitution with constituency elections.
6. Open up Judea & Samaria for massive building, thus creating giant suburbs close to the heavily populated Israeli coastline. A system of toll roads, and light rail will connect these suburbs to the coast from Ashdod to Nahariya. This will solve the overpopulation along Israel's coast and create a better quality of living for all Israelis.
7. Anyone in Israel who raises up a rock to crush Jewish skulls, or a knife, gun or bomb to kill Jews should be expelled from *Eretz Yisrael*. Those not loyal to the State of Israel as a Jewish State and wish to replace it with an Arab/Muslim country **should lose all citizenship rights and be encouraged to leave.** If they incite hatred and anti-Jewish feelings, they should be expelled.
A final thought: It took Jews 2000 years to regain *Eretz Yisrael*. We should most emphatically not allow the world who wished us dead to influence our decisions on how we should **LIVE**.

A BLACK DAY FOR ISRAEL

(November 2004)

Yesterday was a BLACK DAY FOR ISRAEL. The consequences of the Knesset vote on the expulsion of Jews will be horrendous and is not fully understood.

The Jews have faced expulsions many times throughout their history—the largest from Spain in 1492. Today we witness the first time Jews have been expelled by a Jewish government from their own nation.

The immediate consequence of this vile act by the Sharon government is the total fracture of the national consensus. It is a rupture of the historical roots of Israel in Zionism. The ruling Likud Party will be split and there is a possibility that the anti-Zionist left will emerge as the most significant influence on Israeli politics after being defeated in the last election by a landslide.

Democratic principles are being undermined and critics of Sharon's policies are being threatened with imprisonment.

What can we expect in the future following the surrender to terrorism. For one, Gaza will become a haven and training base for terrorists from all over the world. New weapons will be introduced in large number including rockets capable of reaching Israel's major cities. Just like the days before the Six Day War, terrorists will infiltrate into Israel from Gaza bringing death and destruction in their wake.

The most significant damage will be to Israeli morale. While the Arabs will feel elated at this victory over Israel, Jews will become depressed and their feelings of national pride will be greatly diminished. Many Jews will seek to avoid joining the IDF and its elite units. Many more will immigrate to other countries, disgusted with Israeli anti-Jewish policies.

The goal of improving Israel's demographic balance by leaving Gaza will fail as fewer Jews will immigrate to Israel as the security situation deteriorates. As increasing numbers of Jews emigrate and the Arab birthrate continues to grow Israel will find itself in the same difficult position. There are other answers to the problem like transfer, but the leftist government will refuse to even discuss it.

HOW CAN WE SAVE ISRAEL AND PREVENT EXPULSION OF JEWS

[**Writer's Note:** This editorial is conceptually based on the history of both the American Revolution and Martin Luther King Jr's struggle to emancipate the black population of the United States. Of course it is modern and on the struggle for Israel, but the voices of George Washington, Patrick Henry and Dr. King ring loudly in my heart and soul.]

It is clear to all of us that the present Likud government of Israeli Prime Minister Ariel Sharon is leading Israel to disaster. It is also clear that nothing external is compelling this self-destruction. The only thing that will save Israel is new elections.

THAT COULD BE TOO LATE! ISRAEL WILL BE LOST!

The only way to speed up elections and thus save Israel is by destabilizing the current government and causing it to fall. This would force new elections and stop the insane Oslo/Road Map process.

HISTORY

Over the last one hundred years, many governments have been destabilized by the action of a determined group of its citizens, not necessarily a majority. Two recent cases in this country are the Civil Rights Movement and the Anti-War in Viet-Nam Movement. There is no doubt that Lyndon Johnson chose not to run for a second term because of the anti-war movement. There is also no doubt the Afro-American population would not have been able to throw off the yoke of discrimination without non-violent protest. In Israel it is obvious that the intifada succeeded no doubt because of the Israeli government's reticence in crushing it.

It is this reticence by democratic regimes to crush popular uprisings that is the biggest weapon in the hands of groups wishing to destabilize their government. This principle does not work under autocratic governments as witness Syria (Hama) and China (Tiananmen Square).

TECHNIQUES

1. Demonstrations—the larger the better. Demonstrations will not in and of themselves bring down a government. Good media coverage is essential to give the population a feeling that the tide of history is turning against the regime.

2. Civil disobedience—the key to success. There is one essential requirement for destabilizing a government and that is for a determined group of people to be willing to go to jail, be beaten by police, and possibly be killed in the pursuit of their political aims. More will follow later on organizing civil disobedience.

3. The Wrench In The Machinery Of Government

A Physical—roads and bridges can be blocked by slow or stalled cars.

B. Electronic—computer networks, telecommunications can be adversely affected [10,000 people calling government offices at the same time can paralyze the system].

C. Psychological—photos can be taken of police and military personnel who become involved in violent action against peaceful demonstrators. Available now are miniature video cameras that can be worn inconspicuously and send live feed to distant computers. At a time and place of your choosing their names can be revealed—you can compromise those security officers involved in non-democratic violence against demonstrators. Their names and photos can be publicized, leading to fear and a sense of insecurity.

4. Violence—ONLY TO DEFEND ONE'S LIFE

A. Armed resistance to non-democratic police and military actions is not the best course of action since the military, police and security services will always be stronger and better equipped.

B. Open revolt against authority—<u>Democracies are primarily based on voluntary compliance with the legal system. When that democracy ceases to govern in the best interests of its citizenry, with its security and survival, then it is lawful and justified to resist authority.</u> This includes refusing to pay taxes, following illegal orders of the non-democratic army, traffic regulations etc.

C. Mass demonstrations, including the right of self-defense, are meant to intimidate the police and the government. The horrible vision of civil war will restrain the government. Knowing that the Zionist/Right will not physically resist, gives the government strength to pursue suicidal policies. <u>The policy of not striking back at the Left (as experienced during the "season") begun in the pre-state days by Menachem Begin has had the effect of emasculating the Right in its relations with the Left.</u>

STRATEGY

While it is preferable to wage a non-violent campaign, there are certain lessons one can learn from the Israel Defense Forces.

1. Most important: Do not give the enemy time to rest and re-group. The IDF always advances in one massive push to victory, never allowing the enemy a respite. The same must be true of the demonstrations against Sharon. It is a mistake to agree to a truce. This time will be used to organize special police units including female police officers to handle demonstrators. The government has already learned that reservists do not like this heartrending undemocratic task.

2. Attack in many places at once, causing physical and psychological stress on the enemy. Demonstrators should not just take over hills in YESHA, but should take over government offices from Eilat to Metulla. Roads should be blocked all over the country. In Jerusalem, with its many government offices and a supportive religious population, you should be able to <u>create and sustain chaos</u>.

CONCLUSION

Half measures will not work. Either we want to bring down this government or we don't. You cannot be both meat and milk. It was the IDF's failure to destroy the intifada that led to much of our trouble. Remember the principle of vaccinations: a tiny doze of the disease that allows the body to build its immune system. Half-measures allow Sharon to develop a resistance to the demonstrations. We must take the momentum and build continuously to the day of victory. **The decision is ours.**

A TIME FOR PEACE, AND A TIME FOR WAR

We find all the expressions of horror at the recent Rabbi's ruling concerning a soldier's obligation to avoid abandoning army bases and settlements to terrorists, to be hypocritical, self-serving, and unfortunate. The Israeli government is in rebellion against everything that Israel, Zionism, and Judaism are all about. They are the ones causing the rift in the body politic and they will be totally responsible for any resulting violence.

When will the Nationalist Camp realize that we are "at war already" with a PLO supported government that rules Israel? At what point will Israelis realize that the **CIVIL WAR** they fear, **IS ALREADY TAKING PLACE AND THEY ARE LOSING?** Why don't members of the Nationalist Camp understand that **FORCE** is being used by only **ONE** side and that is the government. The monopoly on power must be broken or there is no hope.

Under the Nazis, the Jews of Warsaw numbered over 500,000. They were depleted with regular deportations aided by Judenrats (Jewish leaders). The Revolt in Warsaw began when the Jewish population was down to 50,000 (or 90% murdered). At what point is it OK to rebel? When is civil disobedience OK? When is civil war a better course than **suicide**? All throughout history there have been rebels and loyalists. History is usually written by the victors but truly there is seldom a universally accepted moral standard as to what a proper rebellion is and what is not. We can say with absolute certainty, however, that the Jewish return to **Zion** and our struggle today for *Eretz Yisrael* are more righteous than any other struggle for national liberation in the history of the world.

Bernard J. Shapiro

The Jews of **YESHA** must not be passive pawns in the political surrender of their homes. They must fight the Arabs, where necessary, to maintain their travel, water, and land rights. When the Israeli government retreats, leaving them behind PLO battle lines, they must be prepared to go on the offensive militarily to secure safe contiguous areas of Jewish control. The defeatist Israeli leaders, who have surrendered our Jewish rights to *Eretz Yisrael*, should be told that there are still proud Jews in **YESHA** who will give up neither their inheritance from Abraham nor their right of self-defense.

Exercising one's right to self-defense is a moral imperative. There is a lot of hypocritical talk coming from the government about the danger of Jew fighting Jew. These warnings came from the likes of Yitzhak Rabin who delighted in shooting Zionist (Betar) teenagers swimming to shore after his forces sank the *Altalena* in 1948. New more dangerous hypocrites are putting the Jews of **YESHA** and all of Israel in life threatening peril. They care nothing about Jewish lives!

The glorious **Hebrew Warriors** who defeated five Arab armies in 1948, three in 1967, and two in 1973 must not surrender their Jewish homeland to an evil terrorist, who delights in killing Jewish women, children, husbands, sons and daughters. **The Brave Heroes of Zion** must not limit themselves to passive civil disobedience but must on the offensive.

While such internal Jewish fighting would be **DREADFUL**, it is a consequence of the government's disregard for the security and well being of its citizens. At this great time of trial and apocalyptic threat, the safeguarding of the future of the Jewish people's right to *Eretz Yisrael* must take precedence.

AND THE DECISION MUST BE FOR VICTORY, ZIONISM AND THE JEWISH PEOPLE.

ALL IT TAKES FOR EVIL TO TRIUMPH IS FOR GOOD MEN TO DO NOTHING.

SHARON AND KAHANE

Similarities And Differences

(April—May 2005)

Israeli Prime Minister Ariel Sharon has spoken to his nation many times following the devastating terrorist attacks, bombing and ariel bombardment with missiles and mortars. One would have hoped that Israel's leader would have taken the opportunity to inspire his people and bring them together during this difficult time. One would have hoped for a speech worthy of Churchill, rallying the nation to the task of fighting terrorism. Instead we were treated to a rambling, incoherent speech full of defeatism, political venom, and attempts to blame everyone, except himself for the tragedy. Very disturbing was his attempt to blame the Jews of YESHA for the security breach that made possible the bombings in Tel Aviv and Jerusalem. It was not a rational speech. Perhaps the stories of his senility are true.

One element of his pitiful diatribe needs special attention. Sharon repeatedly stressed the necessity of separating Arabs from Jews. Over and over he talks about not wanting Jews and Arabs to mix; of building walls of separation between them. Does Sharon not realize that this was the exact policy of the late Rabbi Meir Kahane (May his murder be avenged.)? There is, of course, one big difference between Sharon and Kahane. Kahane was a Jewish leader who cared about *Eretz Yisrael* and wanted it for the Jewish people. Sharon is the father of the Palestinian State and cares nothing for Judaism or the Land of Israel. Where Kahane would "transfer" Arabs from Israel to make the land safe for Jews, Sharon wants to "transfer" Jews from Israel to curry favor with his terrorist partners and Jew-killers in the Palestinian Authority. Sharon wants to make Palestine completely Jew-free which is also the goal of the Palestine Liberation Organization.

Kahane was made an outlaw by the political establishment for views, which in comparison to Sharon's, appear rational, Zionist, and patriotic. How does Sharon plan to keep Jews and Arabs separate in Jerusalem and still keep the city unified under Israeli sovereignty? Perhaps these speeches by Sharon and Ehuh Olmert are "trial balloons" to test the idea of dividing Jerusalem. What about the 300,000 Arabs of the Galilee? By Sharon's logic we must give this territory to the emerging nation of Palestine. What about the Negev? Haifa? Jaffa? Jews and Arabs live mixed all over Israel. What we can demand is that those who are not prepared to live in peace with their Jewish neighbors, be transferred to someplace across the border.

The decision as to who should be transferred should be based on what promotes Israel's security and what furthers the Zionist and Torah goal of settling the Land. Decisions about Israel's future and its borders should not be made by a left-wing secularist who cares nothing about either Zionism or Judaism.

We must say NO to Sharon. And we must say it so loud that the earth will tremble under his feet and the heavens will hear our prayers.

I'M MAD AS HELL

DON'T ASK ME TO BE A NICE JEWISH BOY

(June 2005)

I was mad as hell at the Oslo sell out of Israel—and I am still mad as hell. I will tell you why. After 2000 years of statelessness, we Jews finally achieved a rebirth of our independence in our ancient homeland, Israel. After 57 years of struggle, sacrifice, blood and tears, Israel had defensible borders and the most powerful army in the Middle East. So what does Israeli Prime Minister Ariel Sharon do? He follows in the footsteps of Former PM Yitzhak Rabin and Shimon Peres, getting advice from Yossi Beilin.

HE PLANS TO SURRENDERS ISRAEL'S HEARTLAND, GIVEN IN PERPETUITY

TO THE JEWISH PEOPLE, TO ITS MOST IMPLACABLE ENEMY.

HE NEGOTIATES AS IF ISRAEL LOST ALL ITS WARS

The present Israeli government is leading its war-weary population, not to PEACE but to ANNIHILATION.

Sharon, Peres and Olmert would like you to believe that peace, economic prosperity, and utopia await the people of Israel once the \'withdrawal\' (retreat) from YESHA is implemented. Their first step is the deportation of Jews from Gaza And the Shomron. Then it will be easy to progress to the total ethnic cleansing of Jews from Judaea and then from parts of Jerusalem.

Appeasement has never brought peace and it won't now. Here is the more likely scenario:

1. Terrorists will raid at will from Gaza and elsewhere in the new "Palestinian state." Morters, rockets and missiles will begin to rain down on Israeli communities.

2. After surrendering its strategic heartland, Israel will begin to be struck by katyushas (and even smaller mortors and missiles will be able to reach Tel Aviv and other population centers on Israel's coast randomly across the central coastal plain. In every case Arafat (or who ever controls the Arab population after he dies) will disclaim responsibility and the international community will show no sympathy for Israel's plight. Indeed, Israel will be condemned by the world when it attempts cross border retaliatory raids.

3. Hundreds of thousands of Arabs will pour into "Palestine" through the border checkpoints. They will create a large hostile population on Israel's borders who will rejoice in MORE terrorism to gain the REST of Israel.

4. Thousands of wells will be drilled on the Judean and Samarian hills by these Arabs, depriving Israel of 30% of its water supply.

5. The intifada (Oslo War), which started in 2000, will start again in earnest to drive the Jews from what is left of Israel. Israelis will continue to murdered, bombed, shot, knifed and stoned. Their bodies will be mutilated. Jewish blood will be very cheap again as in the time of the Nazis. In the meantime, the Palestinian military will get arms from the Arab countries and the West financed by United States, Europe and wealthy Arab countries. It will be Bosnia all over again, with only a matter of time before the last Jew is killed or expelled from Eretz Yisrael. The Arab old promise to "drive the Jews into the Sea" could be a sad reality.

6. A new intifada will be started among the Israeli Arabs. Why shouldn't they join the new Palestine with their fellow Arabs?

7. Having been so weakened by the above events, Israel agrees to withdraw from "Arab" areas of the 1949 borders.

8. The "so called" demilitarized Judean-Samarian hills protecting Israel's coastal concentration of population and industry around Tel Aviv, are occupied by Iranian, Jordanian, and Syrian troops. It takes 20 minutes to re-militarize this area.

9. Egypt, Syria, and Jordan sensing Israeli blood, join the Arab coalition for an all-out attack.

10. Israel is destroyed but does get a favorable obituary in the New York Times. The United Nations, however, condemns the deceased Jewish state for polluting the sacred land of Palestine with "filthy Zionist pig blood."

That sounds quite extreme and people keep telling me to tone down my rhetoric. "Don't be so strident", they tell me. It's good advice and maybe I would be more convincing if I didn't show so much passion in my writing. I'll do my best, but aren't you MAD also? Can any Jew, who understands history, not be anguished by the present course of events? This is a serious issue of life and death for our fellow Jews. And it is a deadly serious issue of survival for Israel. That's why I\m mad as hell. So don't ask me to be a nice Jewish boy . . . .

. . . . And while I am talking about why I am mad as hell, here are a few more things I am sick and tired of.

11 THINGS I AM SICK AND TIRED OF

There are a few things more that make my blood boil. Here is a list and the explanations:

1. I am sick and tired of the slowly escalating actions of the IDF to fight terrorism.

The slow escalation allows PA terrorism to become immune to Israel's strategy. It allows them to smuggle more guns, missiles, mortars, anti-aircraft missiles into PA territory. This is much the same as bacterial infections. If the antibiotic is not strong enough to eliminate it, then the disease will return in a much more virulent form. I would suggest that the IDF launch a massive offensive against the terrorists until victory.

2. I am sick and tired of the Israeli government's fear of collateral damage to the enemy.

The Arabs have no such qualms. In fact they target civilians in bestial suicide bombs. PA weapons factories, weapons storage depots and bomb making facilities should be blasted off the face of earth even if it causes civilian casualties. Remember that "he who is merciful to the cruel, will end up being cruel to the merciful."

3. I am sick and tired of Israeli PM Sharon's policy of restraint.

The adjustment to accepting the killing of Jews has become is an abomination. A Jew here or there murdered daily, pretty soon adds up to a lot dead and maimed Jews. I remember when the Al Aska terror on Israel began last September, The IDF general staff plans to re-opened a file called "Operation Thorns" which could re-take the PA areas. They estimated Israeli dead at 300.

Since then there have been almost 1000 Jews killed which is more than three times the estimated combat deaths with no apparent consequence to Arafat's ability to inflict casualties on Israel. There is one extremely important variable. The PA has used the last three years to build bunkers, firing positions, smuggle in heavy weapons and missiles, create an underground arms industry and organize an army of 80,000. The defeat of PA now would certainly be more costly. And it will grow with time. There is a very short window of time to defeat the PA terrorists with minimal losses. Many political analysts and military experts agree that Israel must take decisive action now.

4. I am sick and tired of the US State Department urging Israel to show "restraint."

Despite the fact that the CIA knows exactly WHO (PA) is attacking WHOM (Israel) the State Department continues call for a stop to the "cycle of violence." Whenever Israel is attacked viciously, there is rush to tell Israel "to turn the other cheek".

5. I am sick and tired of Shimon Peres trying to arrange another appeasement for the PA.

He claims to be seeking a cease fire and a return to negotiations. Let me be honest with you. I don't want negotiations with Abbas, I want to crush him and his terrorist gang.

6. I am sick and tired of the continued UN presence within the borders of Israel.

It's time to remove them and assert Israel's sovereignty. Israel should work to have the world withdraw its recognition of Arab refugee camps and refugees. It should condemn the hypocritical treatment of the Arab countries for exploiting these people for political purposes. Israel should declare in a strong voice that there are NO refugees. That status is not permanent and obviously should not apply to people living in the same place for 56 years.

7. I am sick and tired of the international boycott of Jerusalem as Israel's capital.

Israel should unilaterally announce to the nations of the world that all embassies MUST be in Jerusalem. Consulates may be in Tel Aviv or any place they want. Israel will no longer permit its eternal capital to be disrespected.

8. I am sick and tired that under both Labor and Likud governments, Arutz Sheva, Israel National Radio has not been fully legalized.

Whatever happened to freedom of speech? Arutz Sheva should not only be allowed establish facilities on land but also a television channel. I am also sick and tired of government television being controlled by the extreme left that doesn't represent the Israeli public. A lot of the time they represent the Arabs and not Israel's.

9. I am sick and tired of Israel's trying to be Mister Nice Guy to a hypocritical world.

Europeans are increasingly comparing Israel to the Nazis. Over half of all the resolutions of the UN since its founding have directed against Israel. At the recent conference on how to condemn Israel in Durban, South Africa, UN head Kofi Anan condemned Israel for existing. The Arab world openly plots the destruction of Israel.

10. I am sick and tired of Israel tolerating Moslem restrictions and desecrations on the Temple Mount.

The excuse that it would cause violence to exercise our rights there is absurd. Israel has the capability to enforce security. Virtually everything Israel wants do in the Land of Israel displeases the Arabs, who want us to leave. Jews should be allowed to pray on the Temple Mount and the destruction of Jewish antiquities by the Moslem waqf needs to be stopped immediately.

11. I am sick and tired of PA demonstrations of the fierceness of their terrorists and how they will destroy Israel.

Why not knock off a bunch of them during their demonstrations. Maybe they will be more circumspect.

12. And most important, the IDF and police should never be used for political purposes. Their purpose is to protect Israeli's and not expel them from their homes or persecute them.

I believe that we will defeat our current adversaries. We will succeed and survive from three sources of our strength: Love of Tanach (Torah), Love of Eretz Israel (Land of Israel, and Love of Am Yisrael (People of Israel) . . . . In blood and fire was Israel born, and on a hot anvil was she forged. Her youth understood that life in the new Jewish homeland would require sacrifice. With stories of the stench of burning flesh from the ovens of Auschwitz embedded deep in their psyches, the young Israeli soldiers fight with the firm conviction that there is still no alternative "ein brera."

To that I would like add something the American soldiers used to say during the heaviest fighting in Viet Nam. This is dedicated (slightly revised) to the brave IDF soldiers who face the enemy every day: Yeah though I walk through the Valley of Death, I will fear no evil because the Almighty fights with me for the Restoration of Zion and for love of HIS people, Israel.

. . . . And for the Jews of Gaza and the rest of YESHA, I believe that He will NOT allow JEWS TO EXPEL JEWS FROM ERETZ YISRAEL.

RESISTANCE: MODERATION, DIRECT ACTION OR EXTREMISM

(August 2005)

The struggle to save Gaza and North Shomron does not seem to have succeeded so far. I believe that one of the reasons is the failure of Yesha officials and NGO activists to unite in a serious pro-active effort. This is not to disparage the many wonderful rallies and demonstrations. The great marches south toward Gaza were very impressive. But, they did not stop the Sharon "bulldozer." Everyone concerned with Israel's security and survival must re-evaluate his course of action in these final desperate days before the expulsion of Jews.

1. First of all we must admit that moderation and restraint simply do not work in the current situation. The government simply ignores or represses these acts with massive use of police and military forces. We have also seen that extremism also is a failed policy. Whenever the government can blame its democratic opponents with extreme acts (even if they did NOT commit them), the public support for our goals diminishes. Obviously actions that would be deemed extreme are not beneficial to our cause.

That leaves us with only one policy direction and that is direct action. By direct action, I mean a very pro-active plan to stop the deportation. This means more than one giant rally or march. It means measures to totally shut down the country. I have written about the techniques before. Unfortunately all the measures suggested in my earlier editorials have not been utilized, so I am going to repeat them now.

The only way to speed up elections and thus save Israel is by destabilizing the current government and causing it to fall. This would force new elections and stop the insane Oslo/Road Map/retreat process.

History

Over the last one hundred years, many governments have been destabilized by the action of a determined group of its citizens, not necessarily a majority. Two recent cases in this country are the Civil Rights Movement and the

Anti-Vietnam War Movement. There is no doubt that Lyndon Johnson chose not to run for a second term because of the anti-war movement. There is also no doubt the African-American population would not have been able to throw off the yoke of discrimination without non-violent protest. In Israel, it is obvious that the Intifada succeeded because of the Israeli government's reticence in crushing it.

It is this reticence by democratic regimes to crush popular uprisings that is the biggest weapon in the hands of groups wishing to destabilize their government. This principle does not work under autocratic governments, as witness Syria (Hama) and China (Tiananmen Square).

Techniques

1. Demonstrations—The larger, the better. Demonstrations will not in and of themselves bring down a government. Good media coverage is essential to give the population a feeling that the tide of history is turning against the regime.

2. Civil disobedience—The key to success. There is one essential requirement for destabilizing a government and that is for a determined group of people to be willing to go to jail, be beaten by police and possibly be killed in the pursuit of their political aims. More will follow later on organizing civil disobedience.

3. The Wrench in the Machinery of Government

A. Physical—Roads and bridges can be blocked by slow or stalled cars

B. Electronic—Computer networks, telecommunications can be adversely affected [10,000 people calling government offices at the same time can paralyze the system].

C. Psychological—Photos can be taken of police and military personnel who become involved in violent action against peaceful demonstrators. Available now are miniature video cameras that can be worn inconspicuously and send live feed to distant computers. At a time and place of your choosing, their names can be revealed; those security officers involved in non-democratic violence against demonstrators can be compromised. Their names and photos can be publicized, leading to fear and a sense of insecurity.

4. Violence—Only to defend one's life.

A. Armed resistance to non-democratic police and military actions is not the best course of action, since the military, police and security services will always be stronger and better equipped.

B. Open revolt against authority. Democracies are primarily based on voluntary compliance with the legal system. When that democracy ceases to govern in the best interests of its citizenry, for its security and survival, then it is lawful and justified to resist authority. This includes refusing to pay taxes, violating illegal orders of the non-democratic army, etc.

C. Mass demonstrations, including the right of self-defense, are meant to intimidate the police and the government. The horrible vision of civil war will restrain the government. Knowing that the Zionist Right will not physically resist gives the government strength to pursue suicidal policies. The policy of not striking back at the Left (as experienced during the "Season") begun in the pre-state days by Menachem Begin has had the effect of emasculating the Right in its relations with the Left.

Strategy

While it is preferable to wage a non-violent campaign, there are certain lessons one can learn from the Israel Defense Forces.

1. Most important: do not give the enemy time to rest and re-group. The IDF always advances in one massive push to victory, never allowing the enemy a respite. The same must be true of the demonstrations against Sharon. It is a mistake to agree to a truce. The time will be used to organize special police units, including female police officers, to handle demonstrators. The government has already learned that reservists do not like this heartrending, undemocratic task.

2. Attack in many places at once, causing physical and psychological stress on the enemy. Demonstrators should not just take over hills in Judea, Samaria and Gaza, but should take over government offices from Eilat to Metulla. Roads should be blocked all over the country. In Jerusalem, with its many government offices and a supportive religious population, it should be possible to create and sustain chaos.

Conclusion

Half measures will not work. Either we want to bring down this government or we don't. You cannot be both meat and milk. It was the IDF's failure to destroy the Intifada that led to much of our trouble. Remember the principle of vaccinations: a tiny dose of the disease allows the body to build its immune system. Half-measures allow Sharon to develop a resistance to the demonstrations. We must take the momentum and build continuously to the day of victory. The decision is ours. In these final days, the battle of the forces of light must defeat the forces of darkness. Nothing short of a total effort will work. We must not let up until victory is assured.

May G-d bless the Holy Warriors of Zion and bring them VICTORY!

VICTORY PLAN FOR ISRAEL

Updated November 3, 2005

(October-November 2005)

Thank for your letter of June 6th and the interesting scheme (my Victory plan for Israel) that you have proposed . . . . Ze'ev "Beny" Begin, Jerusalem (June 28, 1994)

PROBLEM:

How to rally the right-wing Nationalist forces and bring down the Sharon/Labor/Meretz government.

SOLUTION:

1. Formation of a United Front, consisting of the following elements: Likud, Tsomet, Moledet, NRP, Lubavitch, YESHA Council, This Is Our Land, Gush Emunim, Women For Israel's Tomorrow, Temple Mount Faithful, Victims of Arab Terror, plus any other compatible group.

2. The United Front to call itself The Maccabee Party and would be run by a council of all constituent bodies. Members would agree not to fight with each other or threaten to withdraw until the Peres/Sharon/Meretz post Zionist government has fallen and new elections are scheduled. Hopefully they would also stay together through a new election and victory bringing the Nationalist camp to power.

3. Members of the United Front to call themselves, Maccabees or Maccabeans.

[Please ignore the fact that my Internet magazine is called THE MACCABEAN. I chose that name for the same reason that the United Front should choose it: Immediate name recognition with a heroic period in Jewish history—a period of WARRIORS and NOT appeasers and collaborators with our enemies!]

4. The Maccabees should begin political activity immediately with a series of marches not demonstrations. Marches and parades should grow rapidly in size and should display POSITIVE rather than NEGATIVE signs and slogans. Examples: (1) The Maccabees Will Save Israel (2) The Maccabees Mean Victory (3) The Maccabees Will Drive The Pagans From Jerusalem (4) Only the Maccabees Can Save Jerusalem (5) The Maccabees Will Make Jewish History (6) You can think of many more, this was just a sample.

5. In the parades and marches, the Maccabees adopt the colors of blue and white like the Israeli flag. Also a liberal amount of orange to show that we remember the crime committed against the Jews of Gush Katif. Everyone dresses in white tops and blue bottoms with perhaps an orange band around the upper arm or head.

6. Israeli flags are used everywhere including cars, buildings, and massive displays of flags during parades.

7. A Maccabee symbol similar to the one on my letter, blue on white arm band is worn by all Maccabees all the time until a new government is installed. As the arm bands proliferate throughout Israel, everyone including government officials and foreign correspondents will be able to gauge the growing strength of the Maccabee Party.

MACCABEE PARTY PLATFORM:

[Illustration of party platform—not written in stone—subject to discussion. But beware of spending too much energy on platform details. Keep your eyes on the prize: the fall of Sharon/Peres and the saving of Israel from dismemberment.]

1. All of Eretz Yisrael is the rightful possession of the Jewish people.

2. Israeli sovereignty extended to all of Eretz Yisrael.

3. Jerusalem is the united captal of Israel and all foreign embassies must be in Jerusalem. Countries not wishing to have an embassy in Jerusalem are welcome to have consulates in other Israeli cities.

4. The Arabs, who wish to live in peace with their Jewish neighbors, are welcome and should have full civil rights including self-rule in their villages and towns.

5. Item #4 does not imply or give any political sovereignty to the Arab population.

6. Those Arabs that desire to do harm to their Jewish neighbors or who claim sovereignty over any part of Eretz Yisrael should be re-settled among other Arab countries.

7. Arabs resisting item #6 should be forcibly removed from Eretz Yisrael.

8. Economic and political incentives for the Arabs to emigrate other countries.

9. Israel's economy should become a fully open free enterprise economy. Government regulations, taxes, and bureaucracy that have inhibited economic growth for 45 years should be removed immediately. All government enterprises should be privatized as soon as practical.

10. In all matters Israeli foreign policy should be conducted in a manner that reflects the dignity and sovereignty of the Jewish state. There should be an end to the bowing and scraping reminiscent of ghetto Jews, complete with the acceptance of insults from friend and foe alike.

11. A new constituency based constitution similar to the one I proposed as the Rafi Party platform in 1965 and Prof. Paul Eidelberg is proposing now.

12. Plus whatever you wish . . . .

WHAT WILL MAKE THIS PLAN WORK:

1. It is positive and exciting and will restore momentum to the Right-wing.

2. The Right is in an almost clinical depression. This plan will cause a dramatic mood shift by focusing on the future and victory.

3. Since I am proposing this plan, and I have no political following in Israel, then each member of the Nationalist/Religious camp is free to agree to a plan that is not proposed by a political contender.

4. Marches, parades. flags, and symbols make good TV news. Good visual images.

5. The use of Blue and White and massive displays of flags will associate the Israeli flag with the Maccabee Party. Every flag displayed will promote the Maccabee Party.

6. Many members of the Likud Party would leave a sinking ship if there was an alternative. If they see the public rallying to the Maccabee Party and they see that you are in the ascendancy and Maccabee Party offers them a role as a faction in the party then maybe 7-10 Labor MK's will join.

7. If #6 works then there will be new elections.

8. The Maccabee Party must maintain unity and compete in the elections with great professionalism. Then:

9. VICTORY FOR ISRAEL

*

"IF YOU WILL IT, IT NEED NOT BE A DREAM"

... Theodore Herzl (1897)

It is as simple as that. If you put your heart and soul into this campaign, you can win. By force of WILL, you can create The Maccabee Party, and save Israel from disaster.

Will you do it???

DISCUSS>>>DEBATE>>>TAKE ACTION>>>VICTORY
[This plan was published as the cover editorial in the September 1995 issue of THE MACCABEAN. Originally written on June 6, 1994]

CHAPTER NINE: U.S./ISRAEL RELATIONS

Paul Eidelberg recently wrote that Israel aids American in many ways through vast improvements in medicine, economics, agriculture, physics and especially with military and intelligence activities. Israel constantly relays to the U.S. lessons of battle and counter-terrorism, which reduce American losses in Iraq and Afghanistan, prevent attacks on U.S. soil, upgrade American weapons, and contribute to the U.S. economy. Innovative Israeli technologies boost U.S. industries.

The vice-president of the company that produces the F16 fighter jets told Yoram Ettinger that Israel is responsible for 600 improvements in the plane's systems, modifications estimated to be worth billions of dollars, which spared dozens of research and development years.

Without Israel, the U.S. would have to deploy tens of thousands of American troops in the eastern Mediterranean Basin, at a cost of billions of dollars a year. In 1981, Israel bombed the Iraqi nuclear reactor, thus providing the U.S. with the option of engaging in conventional wars with Iraq in 1991 and 2003, thereby preventing a possible nuclear war and its horrendous consequences.

In 2005, Israel provided America with the world's most extensive experience in homeland defense and warfare against suicide bombers and car bombs. American soldiers train in IDF facilities and Israeli-made drones fly above the Sunni Triangle in Iraq, as well as in Afghanistan, providing U.S. Marines with vital intelligence that saved many American lives.

But I have not mentioned Israel's greatest gift to America's well-being and prosperity, a gift of incalculable value, exceeding by far all that Israel receives from the U.S. For Israel provides America with 25,000 high tech workers, 324 scientists, 902 doctors who studied medicine in Israel, 1,800 Israeli professors and lecturers, 171 high ranking military officers, and thousands of other professional people whose contribution to the American economy is priceless.

With all of the above, one would expect America to be very friendly to Israel. They don't know all of these facts, but are in fact very friendly. The American Government headed by Barak Hussein Obama is extremely hostile. The State Department has been hostile to the Israel and the Jewish People for generations. The horrible truth is that long before the Holocaust, the US State Department worked diligently to prevent Jews from escaping Europe to the relative safety of America or Palestine.

What all of the above tells me and I express in my writings, is that Israel must "take care of itself." It must not depend on any force other than its military, its intelligence, the righteousness and its G-d.

Bernard J. Shapiro

PERFIDY

Pollard & The Secret War Against The Jews

(August 1996)

Last week I received a large parcel with Jonathan Pollard's return address, complete with his prisoner number 09185-016. Inside I found about 500 photo-copied documents, including virtually every op-ed written about his case, plus copies of hundreds of letters written to President Bill Clinton on his behalf by important personalities, Jewish organizations, Senators, Congressmen, and lawyers. The sheer volume and diversity of the material was quite overwhelming. I had long been a supporter in the "justice for Pollard battle." In short, I didn't need convincing. There was no cover letter with the material and I wondered about Pollard's motive for sending it to me.

I started looking through the material, anxiously searching for a clue as to why it was sent. First skimming rapidly and then reading intently, slowly the missing pieces began to appear in the puzzle. The answer is closely tied to a new book by John Loftus and Mark Aarons entitled, THE SECRET WAR AGAINST THE JEWS: How Western Espionage Betrayed the Jewish People (St. Martins Press, 1994). Pollard had included among the papers several book reviews of this monumental book (658 pages) which exposes many of the dark secrets of the CIA, British Intelligence (M16), and our own State Department. Here are just a few samples of the startling revelations:

1. In order to entice Sadat to sign a treaty with Israel at Camp David, the CIA provided Egypt with satellite photos, intercepts, the location of Israel's nuclear force, and virtually every Israeli military secret. Carter had no knowledge that his Camp David Accords were supplemented by intelligence given to Egypt that betrayed Israel.

2. To evade the laws requiring proper authorization for wire taps, the CIA and M16 would bug each other's targets and regularly exchange information. A favorite target of the CIA was politically active American

supporters of Israel. Files were even kept on every Jewish child attending summer camp in Israel.

3. In order to spy on Arab terrorists, M16 infiltrated many organizations and even took a leading role in planning and training terrorists for attacks on Israel. Although they had advance notice of a planned attack on a Pan Am or El Al plane in Rome in 1973, they "forgot" to mention it to the Mossad, with whom they were supposed to share intelligence.

4. The CIA set up a special "Jew room" in 1945-6 devoted to spying on Israel and Jewish Americans. No Jew was allowed to work there. The US Navy banned Jews from serving in their surveillance ships.

5. In 1967 Israel notified America of its planned attack. The Americans promptly tried to warn Egypt and Syria. As the battles progressed the Americans did everything possible to spy on Israel and provide that information to Israel's enemies. The USS Liberty, a CIA surveillance ship, sailed close to the southern Israeli shore and close to northern Sinai, and began monitoring the battles there. The gathered information was sent to a British listening post in Cyprus, complete with precise electronic maps of the holes in Israeli lines. It was then relayed to the Egyptian, Syrian, and Jordanian military. Fortunately, the short duration of the war prevented the Arabs from utilizing the intelligence. The fact of American perfidy remains.

Pollard's misfortune was to land right in the middle of this dark and dirty game of betraying Israel. As a naval intelligence officer, he began to notice a large flow of extremely important intelligence from the Middle East which was not being shared with Israel as agreed to in numerous American-Israeli agreements. During his trial, Defense Secretary Casper Weinberger told the judges that Pollard's spying had greatly damaged American security. Aldrige Ames had yet to be uncovered but had already left a trail of dead US agents in Europe. Weinberger knew that Pollard could not have been responsible for compromising American agents, but took advantage of this information to successfully get Pollard a life sentence despite an earlier plea bargain. Later, when Pollard was up for parole last year, the CIA leaked the story that Pollard was continuing to be a danger to American security. President Bill Clinton ignored a massive amount of high level appeals to commute Pollard's sentence, despite the fact that he had promised during the election campaign to be lenient.

Why is it so important to certain government agencies like State and the CIA to keep Pollard locked up? The answer is clearly a desire to protect those agencies from too much scrutiny concerning their anti-Israel bias and actions. Most of the American people and their elected representatives are quite friendly to Israel. The Jewish community has always considered America a friend and ally. I believe that a tremendous revulsion would sweep this country if the truth about America's treachery toward Israel gained wide exposure. Pollard was in the "belly of the beast" and knows the awful truth. Can you imagine Pollard on Nightline telling Ted Koppel how the US has been giving Israel's military secrets to her enemies or how the State Department plotted to deprive Israel of the fruits of its military victories?

I believe that pro-Israel activists need to begin demanding that all the branches of the US government live up to the friendship for Israel expressed by the electorate.

[This article was published in the *Jewish Herald-Voice* (Houston, Texas) on March 22, 1995 and in the April 1995 issue of *THE MACCABEAN*.]

CLINTON AND ISRAEL

The Double Standard At Work: Two Articles

Article One

By Bernard J. Shapiro (January 1997)

On December 16th, President Clinton attacked Israel verbally, accusing the Netanyahu government of causing a major threat to peace and possibly bringing about the end of the world as we know it. Also, former Secretary of State James (F**K the Jews) Baker and seven other former national security employees attacked Israel. Let me get this straight: Arafat and the Arab world commit murder and incitement to murder, stockpile missiles armed with poison gas and lethal anthrax biological weapons, riot, commit the drive-by murder of a woman and her 12-year-old child, fail to amend their charter calling for the destruction of Israel, import heavy weapons in preparation for war with Israel, burn Israeli flags, violate every provision of the Oslo Accords, refuse to extradite terrorist murderers, become safe havens for terrorists, abuse the human rights of their own people, including murder and torture, and more **ad nauseam.**

Netanyahu authorizes tax incentives for Israelis living under harsh conditions and perhaps the building of a few houses on Jewish-owned land within the boundaries of sovereign Israel.

AND IT IS ISRAEL THAT IS VIOLATING THE PEACE OF THE WORLD!!!!!!!!!!!!!

Give me a break! Clinton is either stupid, anti-Israel, anti-Semitic, a puppet of the oil companies, being blackmailed by the Arabs who have pictures of him **in a compromising position** or he is just misguided. One thing I am sure of: As a Rhodes scholar, Clinton is not stupid.

When will the Israeli government take the **KICK ME** sign off their back and stop taking such abuse (even from their "allies")? Maybe I am naive, but shouldn't Israel be full of **MACCABEES**?

Bernard J. Shapiro

Article Two

Freeman Center member George Theiss sent this letter to President Clinton via AOL:

[12-19-96].

Dear Mr. President:

President Clinton, you and several former Secretaries of State and National Security Advisors (Brzezinski, Baker & Company) openly condemned Israel for expanding existing settlements. But why did neither you, nor they, publically condemn the murder of an Israeli woman and her 12 year old son by Palestinian terrorists? Why did neither you nor they condemn the violation of every line of the Oslo Accords by Yassir Arafat?

Examples of Palestinian violations are numerous, but here are just a few examples:

Failure to hand over Palestinian terrorists to Israeli authorities.

Failure to amend the PLO Charter calling for the destruction of Israel.

Open calls for Jihad (Holy War) by Arafat (in Arabic, not in English) against Israel.

Palestinian Police shooting Israeli soldiers, unprovoked, on a "tunnel pretext".

Desecration of Jewish Holy Places, such as Joseph's tomb in Shechem (Nablus).

Why were you, Brzezinski, Baker and Company also silent about the Muslim States arming themselves with weapons of mass destruction? Why not condemn their open threats to wipe out Israel? Why be silent about their desire to commit genocide?

Why not condemn brutal dictatorships in Syria, Iran, Iraq, Egypt, Libya, Sudan and Saudi Arabia? Are they not a threat to peace, according to you, Brzezinski, Baker and Company?

Why are Arab and Iranian missiles (purchased from North Korea and China) armed with Chemical, Biological (and possibly Nuclear) warheads not a problem to you champions of the peace process?

Baker and Bush, who started this lopsided peace process, both once called Texas their home. Neither would have ever dreamed of returning Texas to Mexico. After all, America won Texas fair and square in the Mexican War. And all's fair in love & war.

So why the double standard for Israel? Israel won its ancient homeland in the Golan, the West Bank, and the Gaza Strip fair and square in the Six Day War of 1967—after centuries of illegal Muslim occupation of their God-given Jewish land.

Baker & Bush might argue that Israel should surrender these lands, because there are many Arabs living there. But there are many Mexicans living in Texas. Is that a reason to give back Texas to Mexico?

Baker and Bush might argue that Israel should surrender these lands, because the Arabs were there first. But the Mexicans were in Texas before the Americans came. Is that a reason to surrender Texas to Mexico?

Don't you, Brzezinski, Baker & Company know that the ultimate goal in the Muslim mind is the destruction of Israel? Don't you know, from their own statements, that the PLO & Hamas don't want peace, they want the genocide of the Jews?

Didn't the CIA, nor your State Dept. Arabists, tell you what the Palestinians say in Arabic? They say "First we kill the Saturday people, then we kill the Sunday people. Kill the Jews, wherever you find them."

But with Arab oil wealth propping up weak American banks, what are New World Order buffs like you to do, Mr. President? With Islamic terror spreading to America, what are Trilateral Commission strategists like Brzezinski & Baker to say?

Is it your answer to apply double standards and speak double talk? Keep Texas, but pressure Israel to surrender the strategic Golan Heights and West Bank? Call Israeli settlements a grave threat to peace, but remain silent about Muslim Jihad?

Have you never heard President Clinton, how you, Brzezinski, Baker & Company will one day have to stand before Almighty God to give account of yourselves? How will you justify your support of Muslim dictators in their Jihad of genocide against Israel?

I thank God for brave men like Jesse Helms and Ben Gilman, who will still stand up for Israel, the only country in the Middle East that genuinely wants peace. And I respect men like Kissinger and Schultz, who refused to sign the letter to Netanyahu.

Sincerely,

George Theiss

USMC Vietnam Veteran

ENOUGH IS ENOUGH: FREE POLLARD NOW!

TIME TO END THE ABUSE AND INJUSTICE

(August 1997)

At this time I am not going to review the whole Pollard case. I would just like to clarify a few issues and raise a few questions. About twice a month I receive an envelope from Jonathan Pollard (prisoner #09185-016) direct from his cell at a federal prison in North Carolina. In it are copies of all the letters and articles written about his case in the last few weeks. I have been getting these letters for about five years and my file now contains more than 1,000 documents.

What has become obvious to me as I study the case is that there are significant changes in the reason for keeping Pollard in prison. In the beginning, there was rage on the part of then Defense Secretary Casper Weinberger. His plan to keep vital security information from Israel had been thwarted by a loyal American Jew who could not stomach another Holocaust. Then Pollard was kept in prison to prevent him from telling the American people the truth about his actions and about the torture he suffered at the hands of his cruel jailers.

Today, there is a new obstacle to Pollard's release. I believe that there are people in the State Department and the White House who are literally holding Pollard hostage to force concessions from Israel during the final status talks with Arafat. Arafat is reported to have told Clinton, during one of their private conversations, that Pollard should not be released until the Israelis agree to a Palestinian state with Jerusalem as its capital.

Pollard was guilty of violating U.S. law, for which he has spent *more* time in jail than anyone else guilty of a similar crime. His human rights were brutally violated and he was tortured in a psychiatric facility for nine months (against U.S. law). He has now become a political prisoner and hostage. **Enough is enough; the Freeman Center respectfully pleads:**

FREE POLLARD NOW!

Bernard J. Shapiro

BRIEF NOTES FROM THE EDITOR

THE JUNKYARD DOG HAS HIS JAWS CLAMPED HARD ON NETANYAHU'S LEG

(June 1998)

[The **New York Times** (May 11, 1998) reported today from Jerusalem that the administration has given Netanyahu a two-week extension to reconsider his stance. "We are sticking by the points we laid out," an unidentified U.S. official close to the negotiations was quoted as saying. "We agreed to a reprieve to make it absolutely clear we're doing everything we can." After her own difficult talks with Netanyahu in London last week, Albright appeared to rule out abandoning U.S. attempts to mediate between the two Mideast leaders.]

EDITOR'S NOTE: It is obvious that the jaws of a **junkyard dog** (Clinton/Albright) are clamped tight around Netanyahu's leg. The US will not take **NO** for an answer from Israel. While ignoring Arafat's PA violations of Oslo, this American administration has decided to **BREAK** Netanyahu and **FORCE** him into action inimical to the security interests of his country.

How to extricate himself and his country from the jaws of this vicious beast is a challenge. My suggestion is to call for a total break in negotiation on a redeployment for at least 6 months. During that period Israel would test the PA willingness to comply with Oslo. For example, during those six months the PA must:

1. Amend its covenant

2. Cease all incitement against Israel and Jews from its media and educational system

3. Extradite all terrorist murderers to Israel for prosecution

4. Cease cooperation with terrorist organizations including Fatah, Hamas and Islamic Jihad

5. Totally destroy all infrastructures of terrorist organizations like Fatah, Hamas, and Islamic Jihad

6. Reduce its armed forces to the numbers of men and weaponry permitted in the Oslo agreement

7. Prosecute vigorously all criminals who steal from Israel and seek refuge in PA territory.

Should the PA not demonstrate six months of compliance with the above requirements, Netanyahu should officially announce that the Oslo Accords have been abrogated and terminated by Yasser Arafat and the PA. Israel now feels no more obligation to discuss, negotiate are in any way deal with this now defunct agreement. Netanyahu should extend Israeli law to all areas of Yesha not under the security control of the PA and announce that it might take control of other areas if they become a threat to Israeli security.

Yes, there would be repercussions on the international scene. These problems will disappear in time. The alternative is for **ISRAEL TO DISAPPEAR IN TIME.**

[This plan is based on the principle of Israel's current recognition of Oslo and working within its legal framework. Please don't be confused: The Freeman Center does **NOT** recognize Oslo, either legally or morally.]

THE TEMPLE MOUNT

I believe that buildings of any kind constructed on **Holy Jewish Sites**, for the express purpose of humiliating the Jewish people, should be removed promptly. [**Editor's Note:** I am not calling for their destruction—just moving them to a non-Jewish site. Please see article in this issue entitled: **Palestinian Officials Disparage Jewish Sites**.] The decision should not be delayed on the political consideration of appeasing the very same people who chose to desecrate a Jewish site.

I have discussed the issue of re-building the **Temple** with Gershon Solomon, head of the **Temple Mount Faithful**. He tells me that his purpose is to prepare for the re-building while not actually finishing the job. Removal of the pagan sites that desecrate the **Jewish Temple Mount** is just one thing that must be done to prepare for the day of building the **Third Temple**. Perhaps the actual re-building will need to wait for the *Moshiach* and perhaps the **Temple** will come down from heaven. I am not able to judge those things. I do believe strongly that the actual building will need to wait for the *Moshiach*.

I believe that **HaShem** weeps at the sight of the desecration of the **Temple Mount**. I also believe that as Jews we should work toward the coming of the *Moshiach*. One step would be to cleanse the **Temple Mount** and make it ready for the **Third Temple**. That the Arabs would be unhappy, is a given. That I care about **HaShem** more than Arabs, is also a given. If you want to call me names like extremist/fanatic, so be it. My destiny lies with **G-d**, not with the petty insults of men.

MY RESPONSE TO A LEFTIST WHO DISPUTED MY RIGHT TO SPEAK OUT ON ISRAEL

To Alon: For your information:

1. I am empowered as an American citizen to care about American foreign policy and especially about the morality and effectiveness of giving our tax dollars to terrorist murderers and anti-Semites like Arafat and Mubarak.

2. I am empowered as a Jew to care about the health, security and fate of Jews anywhere on earth. I fought for Soviet Jews in the 70's and & 80's. Was this none of my business? I have fought Arab propaganda on the college campuses my whole adult life. Was this none of my business? I am an avid student of Jewish history and it is a dark and bleak history of persecution, murder, dispossession, torture and forced conversion. I can't do anything about the past but learn from its lessons. I was born during the Holocaust and could do nothing then. But today, when I see danger to Jews anywhere, I will raise my voice with a might roar. I will not rest until I have done my best to alert the Jews of Israel and elsewhere to the imminent dangers they face. If I am wrong, then **HaShem** will judge me, not you Alon.

3. You are obviously a case of the pot calling the kettle black. I remember how actively the Left/Labor tried to undermine Shamir in America every time he visited here. I remember especially the distorted ads promoted by Project Nishama to deceive the American people. I remember the left allying itself with the enemies of Israel in the Middle East and at the State Department in the joint project of dismembering Israel.

4. You say you don't want to be rational. *YOU HAVE SUCCEEDED.*

THE DOOMSDAY CLOCK IS TICKING . . . .

When Labor leaders Shimon Peres and Yitzhak Rabin scammed the Israeli public into believing that Oslo would bring peace, a **DOOMSDAY CLOCK** started ticking. Time for the Jewish state was running out. The election of Benjamin Netanyahu caused the **CLOCK** to pause. A few months later when he proved that he would continue the process of self-destruction started by Labor, the **CLOCK** started to tick again.

Today, America's top **CLOCK** repairman, Dennis Ross, is in Israel. His goal is to oil the mechanism of the **CLOCK** and make it go faster.

As we celebrate Israel's 50th anniversary, let us remember the **DOOMSDAY CLOCK**. How many years and Independence Days does Israel have left before the **CLOCK** runs out. What are you doing to save Israel? Are you spouting platitudes about peace or are you telling the truth the Jewish community?

If you are not part of the solution, then you are a part of the problem. If you want to help, join the Freeman Center or go on aliya and make your voice heard in Israel.

Remember the CLOCK is ticking . . . .

. . . . Bernard J. Shapiro, Editor

AMERICANS SHOULD NOT PAY

FOR THE ROPE TO HANG ISRAEL

(November 1999)

Today's (October 26th) **Jerusalem Post** has an opinion piece which attacks all opponents of the Wye Aid Package as wild and crazy right-wing extremists bent on doing great harm to Israel's security. It mentions by name two of Israel's most intelligent advocates, Yossi Ben-Aharon and Yoram Ettinger. Let me make something perfectly clear, Ettinger and Ben-Aharon know exactly what they are doing and saying. Israel, unfortunately, has become like an alcoholic drug crazed relative. It is our love for Israel that makes good Zionists like Ettinger want to intervene to save her. The addiction to Oslo and the American aid deemed necessary to make it work must be stopped. The Israelis must learn that they can't continue to behave in a self destructive manner and then expect American dollars to rush in and save them from disaster. To continue aid to Israel under these circumstances make us an **ENABLER** to Israel's dysfunctional policies. As I have said before, Americans should NOT pay for the rope so Israel can hang herself . . . .

BARAK JOINS RANKS OF HISTORY'S ETHNIC CLEANSERS OF JEWS

The Freeman Center strongly condemns Israeli Prime Minister' Ehud Barak's plans to ethnically cleanse Jews from **YESHA**. Bernard J. Shapiro, Freeman Center director, noted that throughout history there have been evil men who have sought to eradicate the presence of Jews in their territories. Assyrians, Babylonians, Greeks, Romans, Arabs, Persians, Catholics, Germans, Egyptians, Syrians, Jordanians, Iraqis, and Palestinian Arabs all tried but failed to destroy the Jews.

Now a new **Chamberlain-like** ruler, Barak, has joined the ranks of ethnic cleansers. Though democratically elected in Israel, he rules without Zionism, Judaism or morality. He should be reminded of the fate all those before him who have tried to destroy the Jewish people and remove them from their **Holy Land**. Whether Barak intends to destroy the Jewish people or not can be argued but his actions will certainly lead to that unfortunate end.

I do not believe that my words are incitement. Rather the whole Oslo appeasement process is an incitement against the Jewish people and their right to **Eretz Yisrael** . . . . Bernard J. Shapiro, Editor

[**Editor's Note:** Barak just released 151 more veteran terrorists being help in Israeli prisons. These are the men who murdered and maimed not only Jews but also Arabs and Americans. They will no doubt be of service to Arafat as trainers of a new generation of terrorists. Imagine, if you are able, how the victims of these men must feel as they are released as heroes to the cheers of their fellow Arabs.]

THE HARSH REALITY

The soothsayer told Caesar to *"beware the Ides of March,"* but he was too wrapped up in his own glory to imagine the possibility of his own demise. The best military/political/strategic analysts of the Freeman Center have estimated Israel's life expectancy to be 30 months. In order to prevent the inevitable destruction of the Jewish state, policy changes must be made within the next 12 months. This is today's *Harsh Reality*. Averting your eyes and refusing to hear the truth will not prevent this from happening.

AMERICAN AID

(December 1999)

The aid earmarked for implementation of the Wye Surrender Agreement was passed in the House this morning. Apparently the Israeli leadership has sold out the Jewish People's birthright in Judea and Samaria for $1.3 billion and plans to sell the Golan for $20 billion. There may already be secret negotiations to sell the rest of Israel to a conglomerate of Arabs, Europeans and Americans. Perhaps $100 billion will be the price for the illegal sale of the Jewish State. The Freeman Center will continue to inform our readers that Eretz Yisrael belongs to Am Yisrael (the People of Israel) in perpetuity. The disposal of that Land by Rabin, Peres, Netanyahu, and Barak constitutes the sale of stolen property and someday proper judicial charges will be brought against them.

DEFINITION OF PEACE CRIMINAL

A peace criminal is a person or organization that uses the eternal seductive lure of peace to aid the enemies of Israel, who wish to destroy or replace her and expel or exterminate its Jewish population. Peace Now is the preeminent example of a peace criminal organization. In the near future we will present a full discussion of the peace criminal, their organizations, and propose legislation to end their depredations on Israel and the Jewish people.

An Editorial **from the May 1999 issue of THE MACCABEAN**

AMERICAN FOREIGN POLICY AND ISRAEL

A Maccabean Perspective

(July 2000)

This article is quite critical of American Foreign Policy; therefore, I would like to say a few positive things up front.

The American people when properly polled come out consistently in support of Israel. There are at least 50 million Evangelical Christians who are friends and dedicated supporters of Israel. Many of America's presidents have bucked the US State Department to help Israel with arms and money. The US Congress and Senate have consistently been friends of Israel. Martin Luther King, Jr. expressed his love of Israel many times. My own grandfather, for whom the Freeman Center was named, expressed his love of America upon his arrival on our shores:

"But what a change in life upon arriving in America—Free America. Here I suddenly found myself unbridled, the air free, no stifling, atmosphere—I could give free expression to the cravings of my soul! Life began to have a different meaning. What a blessing to have free assemblage, free speech free press! Can an American who has always enjoyed these blessings appreciate what it means to one who was deprived of them until manhood?"

Unfortunately there are institutions in America that don't love Israel as much as most of us do. Israel's relations with America go back even before statehood in 1948. During the critical years of WWII, the Zionist community of both America and Israel appealed to President Franklin Roosevelt to take action to stop the Holocaust. They were rebuffed at every turn. It was apparent that neither America nor any of its allies were very interested in saving Jewish lives. England was the most persuasive when arguing that the Jews saved would want to go to Palestine. This would anger the Arabs and should be avoided at all cost. It is true that European Jewry would have been a vast reservoir of new citizens for the emerging State of

Israel. Their sheer numbers would have eliminated the Arab demographic problem in the new State. American policy came down solidly on the side of dead Jews as opposed to live Jews.

When Israel declared its independence in 1948, we were all pleased that the American president, Harry S. Truman, made America the first nation in the world to recognize the Jewish State. Yet even here there was a dark side to American Foreign Policy. The State Department had argued in vain against the recognition of Israel. When they didn't succeed at that they successfully placed an embargo of arms to Middle Eastern States. Seemingly neutral it only affected Israel since the British and French were arming the Arabs. So we have the spectacle of American recognition of Israel's independence while at the same time refusing the arms it needed to survive, to defend their lives.

Following Israel's Sinai Campaign in 1956, Eisenhower and Dulles forced Israel to withdraw with little political gain. Two "benefits" appeared to be: a UN Force in Sinai to guarantee free passage for Israel in the Gulf of Eilat; and an American promise to guarantee such free passage. In 1967 the UN Force disappeared as did the American promise, which the State Department claimed they could not verify.

In the period since 1967, the US State Department has devoted an excessive amount of time developing and promoting plans to force Israeli withdrawal to the 'suicide' borders of pre-1967. With amazing regularity, the State Department has failed to be honest about violations of the agreements it has negotiated between the Arabs and Israelis. The US has been blind to Arab violations from the failure to see missile movements in Egypt (1970-76) to the failure to see Palestinian violations of the Oslo and Wye Agreements. This US blindness has always been one way. The Israelis are subjected to constant misinterpretations of agreements. For example, never having agreed to a freeze in Jewish building, US spy satellites are active daily counting houses in YESHA. And then publicly rebuking Israel for a normal activity of a sovereign country.

In order to pressure Israel, stories appear on a regular basis claiming that Israel is transferring American technology to third parties. In every case they are proven false, but the constant repetition is meant to weaken Israel diplomatically. The State Department has orchestrated a media campaign to damage Israel's reputation in general and Prime Minister Benjamin Netanyahu in particular. A few examples:

1. Netanyahu is the "hardline" PM of Israel while other world leaders are Statesman. Arafat is a 'leader'

2. Ethnic cleansing is bad in Kosovo but the ethnic cleansing of Jews from YESHA is good

3. All disputed land in YESHA 'belongs' to Arabs even when Israel has clear title

4. All foreign capitals are recognized 'except Jerusalem'

5. Israeli soldiers defending themselves from attack have been treated by the media as the 'bad guy'

6. Rock throwers who can crush you skull have been treated as 'demonstrators or protesters' by the media

7. Jewish villages are 'settlements' and 'illegitimate' while Arab villages are all considered legitimate

The list could on but now we must say something that should have been said years ago. It is very important for Israel to disengage from its close embrace with American diplomacy. It should be obvious to all that American and Israeli interests differ markedly in relation to the negotiations with the Palestinians. America has by its own admission ceased to be either pro-Israel or a neutral mediator (the Americans claim to be 'even-handed'). American policy in the final analysis will leave Israel with indefensible borders and an irredentist Palestinian neighbor yearning for all the land "from the river to the sea." Then, of course, they will also want Jordan.

Much more can be gained for Israel by negotiating directly with the Arabs. This used to be Israeli policy. In reality, Arafat has ceased negotiating with Israel and now is negotiating only with Washington. It may be necessary to give up American aid dollars and possibly weapons to break out of the current US embrace. It will certainly be difficult, but in the end, there will exist a truly free and sovereign Israel. The alternative is to learn nothing from history: placing Israel's destiny in America's hands as was done during WWII. America won the war, but 90% of Europe's Jews were already dead. I would prefer Israel to survive.

FREEMAN CENTER SAYS:

DISENGAGE FROM AMERICAN DIPLOMACY WITH ARAFAT

(July 2001)

One of the tactics of American diplomacy is to make "suggestions" and get Israeli reactions. After Israel says no, they make the suggestion again, and again and again and again and again and again until Israel agrees. There is implied pressure but no blatant pressure. It is a form of psychological warfare.

There is another trick to American diplomacy. It is getting Israel to agree to a small concession (sort of the camel's nose under the tent or the thin edge of the wedge) and then beginning a process of expanding it. Since Arafat never makes any concessions, the Americans keep asking Israel to split the remaining difference.

Israel has no red lines so is a perfect candidate for manipulation. Serious security needs are bartered away. Israel's right of self defense is off the table to be replaced with intricate discussions on when to start a cooling off period and political negotiations. Sharon says he will not negotiate under fire and terrorism which continues until today. The Americans and the terrorists say they want negotiations with the continued killings. Why discuss negotiations at all when Arafat sold the rug of nonviolence many times before at Oslo, Gaza-Jericho, Oslo 2, Wye, Hebron, Sharm, Taba etc. He is a pathological liar and murderer so why even discuss negotiations with him.

Sharon says everyday that Israel has the right of self-defense but then does nothing. He is like the kid at school who says to the bully: If you hit me one more time I will really get you. He gets hit and then repeats his threat. Will he ever act?

Essentially we have an Orwellian situation where the parties say black is white, war is peace, terrorism is a cease fire.

Bernard J. Shapiro

ISRAEL ACQUIESCES TO RESTRICTIONS

ON ITS SOVEREIGNTY

(August 2001)

For over 50 years Israel has fought for survival in a very hostile neighborhood. After winning 6 major wars, Israel still finds its sovereignty questioned by its Arab neighbors and the international community. Some six or more international or UN peacekeepers have been given the task of patrolling Israel's borders as well as cities like Hebron and Jerusalem. A new observer forces is being demanded by the Palestinian Authority today.

As early as Israel's victory in its War of Independence, it was saddled with numerous United Nations entities and troops. It very borders were considered "temporary" and a "right to return" was granted to a hostile Arab population.

Faced with continuous terrorist (fadeyeen) raids from Egypt, Israel joined France and England in the Sinai Campaign (1956). After winning a great victory, Israel was forced to withdraw by US President Dwight Eisenhower and Secretary of State John Foster Dulles. They received promises of free passage through the straits of Eilat and a UN protection force in Sinai. Both of which evaporated in 1967.

Israel's spectacular victory in the Six Day War gave it some breathing space from foreign intervention. Even the UN which had piled up a huge record of one sided anti-Israel resolutions, passed a fairly balanced one. Israel was not required to return to its old borders but to new secure ones following peace agreements.

Unfortunately Israel had only a brief period of feeling secure. A certain concept (mechdal) set in the military and the public that the Arabs would never launch an attack on Israel. Though there are differences among historians, most agree that Israeli intelligence knew some 72 hours before Egypt and Syria launched their surprise attack on Yom Kippur 1973. Israel's political leadership including Golda Meir and Moshe Dayan consulted

Washington and were told not to launch a first strike. We all know what disaster resulted. What many don't know is that Israel's desperate need for resupply was used by Washington to force Israel to submit to concessions in the post-war negotiations. On both the Syrian and Egyptian fronts Israel was force to withdraw from badly won territory with no gain.

In the Peace for Galilee War of 1982, Israeli forces trapped PLO Yassir Arafat and his terrorist gangs in West Beirut. Northern Israel and Southern Lebanon were freed from his terror. The US and international community demanded that he be allowed to escape the encirclement and sail to Tunis free of consequences for the damage he had wrought in Lebanon and Israel. The media totally distorted Israel's military operation and left a black eye that has yet to recover.

The Intifada of 1987 came and Israel was unable to defeat teenage Arab boys who threw stones at Israeli soldiers and civilians. Every time the army tried to control the situation it got very strong media and international condemnation. The result was a feeling of helplessness that ultimate led to Oslo. The view that there was no military solution to Israel's relations with the Arabs became common on the Left.

The Persian Gulf War of 1991 was the most critical. Israeli acquiescence to restrictions on its sovereignty in recent history. Israel was always proud of its military tradition of fighting its own battles and not being dependant on foreign forces. When the US forced Israelis to cower in sealed rooms and not fight back against the Iraqi SCUD missile attacks, it had a major negative effect on Israeli morale and its deterrence level in the Middle East. The post-war period found Israelis weakened and led the Labor Party to begin negotiations on the disastrous OSLO APPEASEMENT. Labor leaders Shimon Peres and Yossi Beilin thought that by creating a Palestinian State in Judea, Samaria and Gaza they would bring an end to the historical conflict between Jew and Arab. They had another goal which was to limit Jewish sovereignty and increase Labor's election chances by pleasing Israeli Arabs.

Once Oslo began in earnest, Israel began to face affront after affront to its sovereignty. A Palestinian army began to develop and constant anti-Jewish incitement began to be a regular PA feature in its schools, mosques, TV, and newspapers. Every provision of the Oslo Agreement was violated by the PA and the Israeli government meekly ignored them. Terrorism began almost immediately after the signing of Oslo. Buses started blowing up and Arab attacks intensifies. Unfortunately many Israelis were so deluded by the vision of "peace" that they failed to see the harsh reality in front of them.

The PA got bolder and bolder in its insults to Israel. From its pollution of Israeli water supplies to its harassment of Jews visiting the Temple Mount. The Moslem Waqf began to destroy Jewish antiquities on the Mount and no Israeli authority stepped in to stop it. In almost every instance the Israelis backed down from insisting on their rights. To the Israelis this may have seemed moderation but to the Arabs it was weakness.

At Camp David (2000) Israeli Prime Minister Ehud Barak, PA leader Yasir Arafat, and US President Bill Clinton met to hammer out a final status "peace agreement" between Israel and the Palestinians. Barak made an offer to Arafat that would have been disastrous for Israeli security and Arafat REFUSED. Why? Simply put, Arafat was not prepared to make peace with Israel of any size. For him Palestine must rise on the ashes of a destroyed Israel with all the land from the "river to the sea."

Following the breakdown of the talks, Arafat launched the terrorist Rosh Hashona War, attacking Jews all over the country. Israel's responses were moderate at first but gradually increasing in deadliness. As Israel counter-attacked in both military and economic terms, a chorus of criticism arose. The Europeans, the UN, the Americans all demanded that Israel stop defending itself. International observers were demanded by the Europeans and the Palestinians. The US wanted CIA or State Department observers. The Israelis, knowing full well the futility of biased observers opposed the idea. Judging from past experience, I would predict that Israel will give in on this point.

The Temple Mount is now totally off-limits to Jews although the right of Jews to pray there has been affirmed by the Supreme Court. The police chief has prevented them from exercising their rights under the threat of Arab violence. Can you imagine the US (in the 60's) refusing to send in troops to protect the right of black students to attend public schools in the South, DESPITE the threat of White violence.

The erosion of Israeli patriotism began with the post-Zionist movement founded in academia in the 70's and 80's. This movement taught that the Zionist movement was not based on the legitimate national cravings of the Jewish people. It was described as the brutal exploitation of another people, the Arabs.

Once a portion of the Jewish people believed in this ruinous philosophy, it was possible to justify any compromise with the Arabs, even at the expense of the Jewish State.

Israel's founding father, David Ben-Gurion, and Zionist leaders, Theodore Herzl and Ze'ev Jabotinsky are probably restless in their graves over current events.

Bernard J. Shapiro

SHARON AND BUSH DELUDE ISRAELIS

(May 2004)

We are now witness to the second greatest hoax perpetuated on the Israeli people in the last 11 years. The first, of course, was the great Oslo peace hoax of Shimon Peres, Yitzhak Rabin and Yossi Beilin in 1993. Israelis should have learned from that bitter and bloody experience. While some had the foresight to recognize the fatal flaws in the Oslo process, others were quite blind. The blind were not necessarily evil, but craved "peace" so much that they were willing to take dangerous gambles with the lives of their neighbors. Unfortunately, leading the blind were truly evil men who cared not about **Eretz Yisrael** and the **Almighty's** promise to Abraham.

As the Oslo process fell apart, the stack of Jewish dead and maimed bodies began to grow at an alarming rate. Diplomats with little understanding of the dynamics of the Middle East, began to come up with plans to "save" Oslo. Their names—Mitchell, Tenet, Wye, Camp David, Taba, The Roadmap—have sunk into the dustbin of history. All of them failed because they never properly analyzed the true situation in the Middle East. They never understood the simple fact that **NO** plan could ever work. They didn't fully grasp and internalize the fact that the Arab goal of destroying Israel and the Israeli goal to live and not be destroyed were irreconcilable.

There is a certain psychopathology in Middle East diplomacy. I see a sort of obsessive/compulsive behavior on the part of all the so-called peacemakers. They keep banging their heads against the hard rock of reality and get a headache. And then they do it again, thinking they will get a different result. This ailment which used to be predominant only in Israeli leftist circles has now afflicted Israeli PM Ariel Sharon. Despite his vast service to the Israeli nation, he too has become subject to this psychiatric disorder.

Sharon believes that his retreat from Gaza will somehow change the harsh realities he has faced all his life. Nothing could be further from the truth.

Sharon went to Washington to seek approval from US President George Bush for his plan to retreat from Gaza and surrender to terrorism. His motivation, of course, was to enhance his chances of winning the Likud referendum on the plan to be held on May 2nd.

FREEMAN CENTER ANALYSIS OF BUSH COMMITMENTS TO SHARON

Bush: I welcome your disengagement (retreat) plan. I hope it will lead to two states living sided by side in peace and security.

Sharon: Thank you for your support.

Shapiro: There is no evidence of an Arab desire to live in peace with Israel. Your vision, Mr. President, is not based on the harsh realities of the Middle East.

Bush: The right to self defense and need to fight terrorism are equally matters of international agreement. The two-state vision and the roadmap are designed to implement it and command nearly universal support.

Sharon: Thank you for your vision of peace.

Shapiro: Mr. President, you have said nothing that will be of benefit to Israel in its fight against terrorism. While you acknowledge the right of self defense, every organ of the international community denies it to Israel. Even Your State Department has never accepted Israel's right to defend itself, other than empty phrases short on specifics and long on restrictions. There is no roadmap to peace, since there can be **NO** peace between the victim and his murderer.

Bush: There will be no security for Israelis or Palestinians until they and all states in the region and beyond join together to fight terrorism and dismantle terrorist organizations. I want to reiterate the US commitment to Israel's security within secure defensible borders. We will aid the PA security forces (terrorists) to enable them to fight terrorism and dismantle terrorist organizations (themselves).

Sharon: Thanks you Mr. President. Without your agreement I believe Israel would have no right of self defense and certainly no right to fight terrorism.

Shapiro: Mr. President, thanks for nothing. Israel's right to self defense is inherent in all sovereign states and it will continue to fight terrorism, with or without your permission. May I remind you that it is the Arabs, including the PA, that are responsible for terrorism in this region. To continue the failed path of many before you and expect them to fight terrorism is foolish and dangerous. Would you ask the fox to guard the hen house or the wolf to shepherd the lambs?

Bush: We will ask Egypt to help with security in Gaza after Israel withdraws.

Sharon: Thank you Mr. President.

Shapiro: Mr. President, Egypt has done nothing to further peace in the region and has facilitated the building of tunnels from the Sinai into Gaza to smuggle weapons to the terrorists. How are we to believe that will help with security?

Bush: The Arab refugees will be permitted to settle in the Palestinian state and should not be settled in Israel.

Sharon: Thank you Mr. President. If it weren't for your strong stand on this issue we would be forced to accept millions of refugees (most of them fake) into Israel, which would cease to be a Jewish State. You have really saved us.

Shapiro: Thanks a lot Mr. President, for nothing. Israel never planned to allow millions of hostile Arabs to enter its borders. So what have you done for us? Anyway, by my calculation, there are **NO** Arab refugees. It is not a status you can inherit for generations. Look up in your Webster's dictionary and you will find that the definition of a refugee is someone who has been displaced due to war or other catastrophe. Very few of the so-called Arab refugees fit that category, and they are equal (though less in number) to the Jews displaced from Arab countries.

Bush: Israel will not have to return to the 1949 Armistice lines.

Sharon: Thanks Mr. President.

Shapiro: Those lines were never borders due to Arab insistence, thinking they would be able to destroy Israel in the future. They didn't. They kept losing. There are now no official borders and while there is some territory disputed, it is Israel's right to annex, settle or retreat from it. Sorry Arabs, you should not really have a say in this decision.

Bush: The Palestinians must fight terror and dismantle terrorist organizations.

Sharon: Of course, that is what I have been saying.

Shapiro: By my calculation this is the 122nd time the PA has been asked to or promised to fight terrorism. Will anyone ever "get it?' The Arabs **ARE** the terrorists. Asking them to fight terrorism is like asking them to stop being Arabs. It won't happen. Forget this losing proposition. Continuing is that psychopathology of obsessive/compulsive disorder I spoke about earlier.

So in reality, Sharon got nothing substantive from Bush during his trip to Washington. The media spin and the Arab protest are all a part of the delusion Sharon wishes to perpetuate on Likud voters. **JUST SAY NO!**

DECEPTION, DELUSION AND IGNORANCE

*Israel will **NOT** be destroyed by the acts of deception, delusion, and ignorance demonstrated at the White House today. There is a **Higher Authority** than either **Sharon or Bush**. His promise to Abraham WILL NOT be broken. The pagans of Arabia will NOT be victorious. But each and everyone of us must actively fight for **Eretz Yisrael**. Those members of the Likud must vote against retreat and defeat. Those abroad, with relatives in Israel, must let them know that Israel was promised in perpetuity to the*

Jewish People, including those abroad, and **CAN NOT** be divested by any temporal government. Those that seek to abandon Israel must not succeed. Our efforts must be tireless and our faith mighty if we are to win this battle.

ISRAELI SOVEREIGNTY AND FOREIGN POLICY

(October-November 2005)

Once you pay tribute to a foreign power, the demands keep coming. My whole life I have called for Israeli independence in all things related to security and national sovereignty. We have wept as Israel became a banana republic instead of refusing to bow before any nation. We have demonstrated that due to its technological prowess, Israel needs to grovel before no nation. We have demonstrated that Israel's contribution to American security is so great that it would NOT be pushed around, if it stood its ground. As we enter the New Year, we pray that Israeli leaders will learn the lessons of history and restore pride and self esteem to their people . . . .

Bernard J. Shapiro

APOCALYPSE NOW

The Planned Destruction Of The State Of Israel

(October-November 2005)

There have been two major stages in modern Israel's development: Construction—the building of the State and Destruction—the tearing down of the state. What follows is a brief description of these significant stages.

A Roman legionnaire stands on a hill overlooking Jerusalem. He watches the city burn and proclaims proudly, "Judea capta est" Judea is destroyed. It will never rise again. Rome's rulers even decreed a change of name for Judea. Henceforth it would be named after the Philistines (or Palestine) and the Jewish connection would be obliterated forever.

Yet, like the legendary Phoenix, rising from the ashes of its own destruction, the new nation of Israel burst onto the international scene in 1948, with the lusty cry of a newborn infant, yearning to breathe free. Five Arab armies rushed to invade Israel and crush the life from the new Jewish State. With unbelievable bravery and heroism the new state survived. Six thousand of its young defenders gave their lives that Israel might live.

In blood and fire was Israel born, and on a hot anvil was she forged. Her youth understood that life in the new Jewish homeland would require sacrifice. With stories of burning flesh from the ovens of Auschwitz embedded deep in their psyches, the young Israeli soldiers fought with the firm conviction that there was "no alternative" (ein brera) . . . . (from the author's private diary)

The history of the modern State of Israel can be divided into two stages. The first began with Theodore Herzl's convening of the First Zionist Congress in Basle, Switzerland in 1897. Herzl proclaimed prophetically that there would be Jewish State in 50 years: "If you will it, it need not be a dream." In the half century that followed, with blood sweat and tears, a modern Jewish State was born.

Israel prospered as millions of new immigrants returned to their homeland. Displaced persons from Europe, survivors of the Holocaust, were reborn as proud citizens of a proud Zionist State. Jews from Arab lands, expelled from their homes of over a thousand years were welcomed in an Israel yet to be built. Jews from Russia, Ethiopia, Europe and the Americas joined the exotic mixture that makes up the Jewish State's vibrant character.

In 1967 Israel fought and won an impossible war of survival and with the help of HaShem. Jerusalem, Judea, Samaria, and Gaza were returned to their rightful owner. The covenant with Abraham had been fulfilled.

"And it came to pass, that when the sun went down, and there was thick darkness, behold a smoking furnace, and a flaming torch that passed between these places. That day the L-RD made a covenant with Abraham saying: "UNTO THY SEED HAVE I GIVEN THIS LAND. . . . . Genesis 15:17-18

Some Israelis, and many liberal/left intellectuals from the West were disconcerted by Israel's great victory. They loved the Jews as victims and could not appreciate them as victors. As Golda Meir use to say: A lot world leaders would love to say the nicest eulogies should Israel be destroyed. She preferred Israel to survive as do I. This period following the Six Day War was the beginning of the second stage that I call the deconstruction of Israel. This period marked the rise of the post-Zionists and historical revisionists. There was, indeed, also a surge of Zionist messianic fervor following the Six Day War. Unfortunately the Left managed to persevere and infiltrate the universities, schools, media, judiciary, and military of Israel. Over a 25 year period they were able to destroy most Zionist principles and destroy the nation's patriotism.

In rapid succession, a series of events turned the deconstruction from a gradual drift to a sickening free fall. Those events in brief:

1. 1987—Intifada & Loss of Deterrence

The Israeli government lacked the will to put down the revolt decisively. The Israeli Defense Forces were defeated by 12 year old Arab boys. It is important to note that the world media used this conflict to slander Israel and create a myth of David (Arab) versus Goliath (Israel).

Back in 1965, in a small meeting room in Tel Aviv, former Defense Minister Moshe Dayan gave a pep talk to a group of RAFI (Rishimat Poalai Israel) volunteers, myself included. At that time, RAFI, a breakaway faction of the Mapai Party, included such notables as former Prime Minister David Ben Gurion and former Defense Minister Shimon Peres. Peres and Dayan had been considered the "hawks" of Mapai and it was no accident that in the 1965 election they supported a strong defense and security policy.

Dayan was always interesting to listen to, but this talk was something special and we paid attention to every word. "The essence of Israel's security in this region (Middle East) is deterrence," he said. "When we formed the State in 1948-9, we were very weak. The Arab States had planes, tanks, heavy artillery and many more soldiers than us. We had very little heavy military equipment. In the period 1949-55, we absorbed almost a million immigrants. Tent cities sprung up all over the country. We were totally disorganized. Had the Arabs mounted another major invasion, we could have lost. We devised a solution to this problem. It was deterrence. Think about being lost in a forest and surrounded by hostile animals. If you light a torch, boldly approach them showing no fear—they will retreat. But, if you show fear—they will attack and you are lost. We used this principle to save Israel during those early years. Every time we were attacked, we retaliated tenfold. We showed daring and penetrated deep within their borders to attack our targets. We were fearless, brave, and even a bit bloodthirsty. You know the result. The Arabs were afraid and never attacked. Deterrence worked. By 1956 when we invaded Sinai, the Israel Defense Force was not just strong, it was invincible."

The story above was not told just for nostalgia. The lesson is extremely important for the survival of Israel today. Unfortunately Israelis are daily witnessing the consequences of seven years of declining deterrence vis a vis its Arab population. In 1987, the intifada presented Israel with a new challenge. It was a new kind of war, but with the same aim of driving the Israelis out of their country. The Israelis fought the intifada with many handicaps, not the least of which were their own rules of conduct. Israeli soldiers failed to cope with attacks by teenage Arab boys. In the course of several years, the Arabs learned that the soldiers would not aggressively retaliate for their attacks. They became emboldened.

THE LESSON: What seemed like moderation and civilized behavior to Israelis was seen as brutality by the West and weakness by the Arabs. The failure to learn this lesson still continues.

2. 1990-91—Persian Gulf War & Loss of Deterrence

The failure to retaliate against Iraq for its SCUD attacks greatly weakened Israel's policy of deterrence. All the world saw Israelis cowering in their sealed rooms. The Arabs loved the sight and it emboldened the Palestinian Arabs. More serious damage was done to the Israelis psyche. From a proud macho national image, was born a new vulnerable, dependent (on America), ghetto mentality. The Israeli public was "tired of fighting" and felt they could not cope with the new threats to their survival. The looked for a new peaceful solution.

3. 1993—Oslo Accords: The movement toward destruction speeds up

The Israelis had always yearned for peace. Shimon Peres, Yossi Beilin and others secretly negotiated the Oslo Accords, which created a Palestinian State. Israelis were told that this was a "peace" agreement, but they soon found out that it would lead to more death and destruction. Eventually they would learn of its fatal consequences in strategic territory, water and the surrender of its Holy Places. Oslo set in motion the following negative forces:

*Creation of a new political entity which claimed Israeli territory, water and history as its own

*Cast in doubt Jewish rights to Israel

*Put Israel's capitol, Jerusalem, up for negotiation

Placed Arab refugee return and compensation up for negotiation

*Created terrorist safe havens in all PA territory

*Created terrorist passageways across Israeli territory

*Israel became a collaborator and promoter of Palestinian terrorism and gave a lesson to future terrorists that if they just kill enough people over a long period of time they could become successful.

*Israel is giving up the strategic territory that protects it and has allowed a hostile army to develop in its very heartland.

*There is much more, but you get the picture.

Here are the benefits that Israel received as a result of its participation in Oslo: 0 (zero)

Israel did not get peace, cooperation, good neighbors, an end to anti-Semitic incitement, security, etc . . . .

 . . . . Israelis got nothing!!

THE BOTTOM LINE

The process that is going on now is nothing less than the destruction of the State of Israel. Everything that is happening strengthens the Arab claim to Eretz Yisrael. Nothing helps Israel.

The truth, which many find inconvenient, is that the Land of Israel was promised by G-d to Abraham and his seed in perpetuity. The Land of Israel is not speculative real estate to be bartered away for some high sounding false promise of peace. The hills and valleys of Judea and Samaria contain the collective memory of the Jewish people. It was here that the Israelites first entered the Holy Land. And it was here they fought the battles, built the towns, elected their kings and were preached to by their prophets and judges. And it was on this soil that they wrote the Holy Scriptures we call our Bible.

The Israeli governments of Rabin, Peres, Netanyahu, Barak and Sharon are transitory. They hold office for a few years and then pass into history. G-d's covenant with Abraham is eternal. Israel holds these lands as a sacred trust for the Jewish people for all time. It would not only be sinful, but also criminal, to abuse that trust by denying future generations of Jews their Holy Land—Land of their fathers; the one tiny spot on planet earth given to them by God.

Bernard J. Shapiro

ADVICE TO PM NETANAYHU

BEFORE HIS ENCOUNTER WITH OBAMA

(May 2009)

Like most of us, who are concerned with the survival and security of Israel, I am concerned. There are so many forces bent on our destruction that a true Zionist hardly knows where to turn, much less what to do. I have been thinking about it for many many, months, even years. Below are the simple thoughts of a frustrated Zionist.

TO NETANYHU—WHEN YOU MEET OBAMA

1. Tell him that he is now president of a great country that Israelis have always loved. He should do his best not to destroy it by turning it into a third-world Socialist non-democratic nation.

2. Please remind him that Israel is a sovereign Jewish nation and will not take orders from either him, the UN, EU, NATO, or the Arab dictators. Let him understand that when his people (white, black and Muslim) were still barbarians the Jewish People had already built a great civilization based on Justice and Monotheism.

3. Explain to him that there can be no peace treaty with Muslims, because they do not keep treaties. Israel is too smart to sign another piece of paper for a fake peace. For 16 years, Israeli leaders have pissed away territory, security and deterrence for NOTHING. We have had enough.

4. There have been a long line of officials in the US State Department and CIA, who have worked hard to damage Israel's ability to survive in its very hostile neighborhood. Time after time, they pull Israel back from total victory over its enemies. Those days are gone forever.

5. We are sick and tired of your Justice system targeting good Jews like Jonathan Pollard for exceptional anti-Semitic treatment. I say to you with full authority and intent that we will capture and try every CIA agent in Israel unless Pollard is released within 10 days. Enough is enough.

6. The United States often threatens to cut off military supplies to Israel, should we not do what you order us to do. No longer. On the other hand, we plan to eliminate you from our intelligence network and military supply line. That is unless you are willing to transform our relationship to one of equal partnership and not the asymmetry of a banana republic.

7. On the topic of a PA terrorist state. It is not going to happen. In fact, the hostile terrorists that live within our borders will be encouraged peacefully, but forcefully to find another place to live. They cannot be citizens in a country they hate and wish to destroy.

8. The American military training of terrorists will stop, whether you want it to or not. American aid to terrorists, whether in Gaza or YESHA is finished. Get used to it.

9. Iran's nuclear program will be destroyed whether you like it or not, sooner rather than later. You might not want us to fly over Iraq, we will. Just try to stop us. In every air combat test in America between Israel and American pilots, you lost 99% of the time. It you want to sacrifice your wonderful pilots, just send them against us. NATO forces acted tough against little Serbia a few years ago and then acted like cowards when Georgia's independence was at stake.

This is not a warning, it is a promise: Should NATO ever go to war against us, we will destroy their forces in a short time and then bomb all the capitals of Europe and the Middle East.

10. Please let him know that the enemies of Israel will be destroyed. American is not Israel's most important ally. Israel is America's greatest ally. Israel's most important ally is the Almighty, Who neither slumbers nor sleeps and will smite the enemies of Israel with a mighty Hand.

11. Nearly fifty years ago, I came to understand that Israel was the "canary in the coal mine." I refer to the world. If Israel cannot survive in the tiny land (Eretz Yisrael) that G-d gave to the Jews in perpetuity, then the world will not exist.

12. And finally, Bibi should inform Obama, that Jews are entitled to settle the whole Land of Israel. This is not negotiable and is a gift from G-d and not man. The hills and valleys of Judea and Samaria must be populated with hundreds of new Jewish communities. This will relieve the population pressure on the Tel Aviv—Haifa coast. The Jews expelled from Gaza must be encouraged to return and reclaim that historically Jewish territory. Will the world or the Arabs like it. Of course not. I don't care. They don't want us to live in any place on Earth.

We will no longer ask permission to breathe. Zionism will be renewed and re-invigorated as a powerful act of self-liberation.

The rebuilding and strengthening of Israel becomes the primary mission of those who project Jewish survival far into the 21st century and beyond. The liberation of Jerusalem in 1967 was another step in the redemption of our people. Yet, in our time, governments have arisen in Israel, that would barter our national heritage for false promises of "peace in our time."

The truth, which many find inconvenient, is that the Land of Israel was promised by G-d to Abraham and his seed in perpetuity. The Land of Israel is *NOT* speculative real estate to be bartered away for some seductive (false) promises of peace.

One thing is clear to me: the Lord has blessed Israel by re-uniting Jerusalem and bringing Judea, Samaria, and Gaza back under its control. It would be a horrendous sin against G-d and common sense for Israel to renounce this inheritance to which it is entitled. Israel holds these lands as a sacred trust for the Jewish people in perpetuity. It would not only be sinful, but also criminal, to abuse that trust by denying future generations of Jews their Holy Land—Land of their Fathers; the one tiny spot on planet earth given to them by G-d.

The hills and valleys of Judea and Samaria contain the collective memory of the Jewish People. It was here that the Israelites first entered the Holy Land. And it was here they fought the battles, built the towns, elected their kings and were preached to by their prophets and judges. And it was on this soil that they received the Holy Scriptures we call our Bible.

December 7, 1993

The American restauranteur is eager to serve the main dish.

July 1957

America's fair and impartial policy toward the Middle East . . .

REAR VIEW and FRONT VIEW

CHAPTER TEN: ISLAM

Islam is a twisted and barbaric interpretation of the Jewish religion and its offspring, Christianity. Long before the world was conscious of the dangers of Islamic fundamentalism, I wrote several articles on the subjects and the Freeman Center did serious work on the subject.

Far from being a religion of peace, as some political and media commentators would have you believe, Israel is religion of war. Everywhere the followers of Muhammad have gone, they have brought death and destruction in their wake. From its earliest days, Islam was spread by the sword, not by the virtue of its ideas. A conquered people had a simple choice: conversion or death.

Jews and Christians were considered infidels and were subservient to Moslems and subject to special rules and restrictions.

Bernard J. Shapiro

Islamic Fundamentalism and Israel

Part I: Early Relations Between Jews and Islam

Muhammad was born in Mecca around 570 C.E. and began having visions telling him that he was the Messenger of God when he was twenty-five years old. Jewish traders and merchants lived throughout the Arabian peninsula and he had the opportunity to discuss with them in great detail their religion. Muhammad saw himself as the prophet of a new monotheistic religion, Islam. He felt that as the most recent prophet, his revelations took precedence over those of Moses and Jesus. In fact, he was quite critical of Christians for claiming that Jesus was the son of God, considering that a violation of the principle of monotheism.

Muhammad had a difficult time converting the Arabs of his home town, Mecca, to his new religion. He was abused there and actually became an outlaw and was literally forced to flee. In the year 622 Medina had a thriving Jewish population, and it was here Muhammad sought refuge. He knew that the Jews believed in monotheism (in fact he learned it from them) and he felt that they would be fertile ground for his new religion. He found out, much to his displeasure, what the Christians of Europe already knew: the Jews were a stubborn lot and simply would not change their religion.

Muhammad felt betrayed by the Jews who rejected his new faith and proceeded to fill the Qur'an with anti-Jewish passages. (The early Christians did much the same thing, turning some of their gospels into anti-Jewish diatribes.) This, in a nutshell, is the origin of the Islamic antipathy to the Jewish people. The Qur'an often uses the word dhilla (humiliation or abasement) to indicate the status God has assigned to those who reject Muhammad, and in which they should be kept until they accept him. In the Qur'an (II,61) we read thus in a chapter on the Children of Israel, "They were consigned to humiliation and wretchedness: they brought the wrath of God upon themselves, and this because they used to deny God's signs and kill His Prophets unjustly and because they disobeyed and were transgressors."

During over 1,300 years under Islamic rule, Jews were tolerated along with Christians as people who had revealed religions and prophets of God. Since they did not accept Muhammad as the final authoritative true prophet of God they were assigned to the inferior status of Dhimmis. In Moslem society there were three classes of the population that were inferior and had no rights: slaves, women, and non-believers. The Jews as Dhimmis were much better off than slaves or women, but they were inferior to every Moslem male in the country. For example, in Iran in the nineteenth century the law read "A Jew must never overtake a Muslim on a public street. He is forbidden to talk loudly to a Muslim. A Jewish creditor of a Muslim must claim his debt in a quavering and respectful manner. If a Muslim insults a Jew, the latter must drop his head and remain silent."

Christians were preferred to Jews in Moslem society because they had not opposed the Prophet actively as the Jews were claimed to have done. Christians, though ugly, were seen as less ugly than Jews, whose ugliness is accentuated by inbreeding. Al-Jahiz, a fourteenth century Arab commentator noted:

> "The reason that the Christians are less hideous—though they certainly are ugly—is that the Israelite marries only another Israelite, and all of their deformity is brought back among them and confined with them . . . . they therefore have not been distinguished either for their intelligence, their physique, or their cleverness. As the reader certainly knows, the same is the case with horses, camels, asses when they are inbred."

The laws in Islamic countries used to debase and humiliate Jews were many and varied. In brief: Jews had to live in separate parts of town since they were considered unclean; they had no right to trade in stuff goods; if they entered a Moslem street they were to be stoned; they were not allowed to go out in the rain since the rain would wash dirt off of them that could sully the feet of Moslems; if a Jew was recognized on the street he must be insulted and beaten unmercifully; if a Jew entered a shop he was forbidden to inspect the goods and must pay whatever price the merchant asked; ad nauseam.

The reason for my historical outline of Jewish-Islamic relations is to set the stage for an analysis of what has become today a vicious conflict. The rise of Islamic fundamentalism in the Middle East brings the Arab-Israeli conflict to a new primal stage. It is important for Jews to understand reality when it comes to issues of Israel's security. Issues of war and peace must be discussed in a framework of knowledge and understanding. Too many people in the Western world fail to understand the meaning of Arab and Islamic history. Even worse, they fail to understand the Islamic mind set and its deeply held beliefs. Israel is headed toward a cataclysmic confrontation with the Islamic world.

Part II: The Conflict Today

In part one, we learned how hatred and discrimination against Jews originated in the Islamic world. In part two we will see the conflict between Israel and the Islamic world in its modern day incarnation. When we speak of Islamic fundamentalism, we are talking about a state where political rule and religious authority are vested in the same entity. That entity is the supreme religious personality or Ayatollah as in Iran. Mohammed established the tradition of unified political and religious rule. After his death a series of Caliphs (e.g., Abu Bakr, Omar, Osman and Ali) ruled the Arabs as both religious and secular leader. The Qur'an was the source of all legislation and Islam was supreme in all aspects of life.

Today there are only three Islamic fundamentalist nations: Iran, Sudan, and Pakistan. The influence of the fundamentalists is much stronger than these few countries seem to show. Islamic movements are very strong in Algeria, where they recently won a democratic election. A military coup prevented them from coming to power, but their strength was demonstrated recently by their ability to assassinate the president of that country. The fundamentalists are gaining strength in Jordan, Libya, Tunisia, and Egypt. The conservative Arab monarchies of Saudi Arabia, Kuwait, and Oman are very vulnerable to the message of Islamic fundamentalism. The five republics of the former Soviet Union in central Asia have predominately Moslem populations and already have been penetrated by Iranian emissaries hoping to spread their brand of Islamic fundamentalism.

The problem for Israel is very simple, but also devastating in its impact on the possibility of peace with its neighbors. The fundamentalists have added the dimension of religion to the nationalist struggle between the Arabs and Israel. While there was no shortage of hatred for Israel and the fact that the Arabs were Moslems was always a factor before, now we have a xenophobic religious jihad (holy war). Recently, a group of Moslem clerics gathered in Jerusalem and issued a religious opinion, or fatwa, which bars any negotiated agreement with Israel. It also states that temporary agreements may be reached like taking over Judea and Samaria, if it is in the Arabs' interests, but permanent peace is forbidden and the battle to liberate all of the occupied Moslems lands (i.e. Israel) must continue. Let there be no misunderstanding. The message of Islamic fundamentalism to Israel and the Jewish people is: no compromise—war until total victory over the infidels (Jews).

In pursuit of that aim, Iran hosted an International Conference to Support the Islamic Revolution of Palestine on October 19-22, 1991. The conference was held a few days before the Madrid Peace Conference and was mostly ignored by the press, which focused on Madrid. It was attended by over 400 delegates from 60 Moslem countries, including Egypt, which is supposed to be at peace with Israel. A veritable who's who of the terrorist world, including Ahmed Jibril (Pan Am 103), attended. The conference hall had a 100 foot banner across the front proclaiming: "ISRAEL MUST BE DESTROYED."

Even today, Islamic forces are engaged in warfare against Israel. The battles across the Lebanese border are primarily with the Hizballah and Islamic Jihad, both supported and run by Iran. Inside Israel, especially in the Gaza Strip, the fundamentalists are organized under the name Hamas and are responsible for most of the stabbings and other attacks on Israeli civilians. Members of Hamas are responsible for many brutal murders of their rivals in the Palestinian community and so called "collaborators" with Israel.

The Algerian model is quite instructive of how the fundamentalists operate. They are perfectly willing to compete in democratic elections, but once in power all aspects of democracy would disappear. In much the same way as Adolf Hitler came to power in Germany in 1933 following elections, the Islamic militants would exploit the desire for democracy in many Arab countries. Once in power they would make the Qur'an the principle source of legislation with all the dire consequences for women and minorities. The fate of non-Moslem minorities would be similar to that meted out to black Christians and Animists of Southern Sudan: expulsion, forced starvation, and mass murder.

Israel faces an apocalyptic threat from the Islamic fundamentalist nations as they rush to acquire nuclear weapons. In Iran alone, some 25 Russian nuclear scientists have joined hundreds of Iranians, Pakistanis, Algerians, and Libyans in a "Manhattan" type project to develop nuclear weapons. There are un-confirmed reports that Iran already possesses four Soviet nuclear warheads illicitly bought from the Moslem Republic of Kazakhstan. It is widely known that Pakistan is well on the way to a nuclear bomb. Syria, Libya, Algeria, and Iraq could have nuclear weapons by the year 2000. It is important to remember that 75% of Israel's population and industrial base is concentrated along the narrow coastal strip from Tel Aviv to Haifa. Two to four nuclear bombs the size of the one dropped on Hiroshima (equivalent to 10,000 tons of TNT) targeted on this area would practically annihilate the Jewish state.

Israel's answer to this threat was spelled out a few weeks ago by OC Air Force Maj.-Gen. Herzl Budinger when he said, "Israel must create the greatest disruption, whether military or political, in order to prevent the introduction of nuclear weaponry in the region." (Translation: preemptive military action if political action fails.)

The Islamic threat is serious and no one should minimize its true nature. During WWII the chief Islamic leader among the Palestinians was Haj Amin al-Husseni, the Grand Mufti of Jerusalem. He traveled to Berlin to lend his support to Hitler. After viewing the death camps he petitioned Hitler and I quote, "You should accord to Palestine and to the other Arab countries the right to solve the problem of Jewish elements in Palestine and other Arab countries in accordance with ./..../... the same method that the question is now being settled in the Axis countries." At that time the extermination of Jews was in full swing, so there can be little doubt about what the Mufti meant by solving the Jewish problem. Because of the victory of the Labor Party in Israel's recent elections, there seems to be an unrealistic, almost euphoric, feeling that peace is just around the corner. In the Book of Esther we find the story of Purim. You may remember that Queen Esther succeeded in foiling Haman's evil plan to kill the Jews of Persia. It is significant that Haman was hanged and the Jews were saved and not that King Ahashuerus negotiated peace between Haman and the Jews. The simple lesson is that there is no way to make peace with someone as evil as Haman who wants to destroy you. This might sound pessimistic, but a study of Jewish history would lead one to believe that only the pessimists were realistic. Consider this: The German Jews who were pessimists fled Germany in the 30's; the optimists went to Auschwitz in the 40's!

[This article appeared in the Jewish Herald-Voice on June 25, 1992, and was reissued in the Maccabean Online in October 1996 and August 2002.]

Bernard J. Shapiro

Arutz Sheva News (February 12, 1997)

THE TERRORISTS ARE FREE

Thirty women terrorists were released from prison early this morning, including four murderesses (two who killed Jews) and six who were imprisoned on criminal charges. The release was enabled after the Supreme Court rejected a second petition by the Terror Victims Association at approximately 9 PM last night. One of the freed terrorists—Rola Abu Dahu, who murdered Yigal Shachaf—said this morning that she would continue to "wage a violent struggle against the Israeli occupation." She said that the areas of occupation include also Jaffa and Acre. She also said that she was not asked to sign a declaration that she would not engage in terror activities as a pre-condition for her release. An excerpt of an interview with her on Army Radio follows:

Army Radio (Q): Why were you sentenced to 25 years imprisonment?

Abu Dahu (A): I was a member of a group which belongs to the PLO, and I fought against the occupation.

Q: You were an accomplice to the murder of Yigal Shachaf, right?

A: That's what they say.

Q: What do you say?

A: I say that I fought against the occupation. It doesn't matter what I did; the principle is that I fought against the occupation.

Q: Before your release, did you have to sign that you will refrain from fighting against the occupation?

A: I didn't make any such promise; I was just released from jail.

Q: How will you fight now?

A: I am just out of jail, so I don't know exactly. But I will continue.

Q: Will you do everything, including the type of activity which brought you to jail?

A: I will (long pause) fight with my nation to bring freedom to my land.

Q. When you speak of occupation, are you referring only to the lands which Israel conquered in 1967 or to the whole of the Land of Israel?

A. You know that most of the land is not in our hands.

Q. What is missing, all of Jerusalem?

A. Yes, Jerusalem is missing, along with many other places.

Q. What else, Jaffa?

A. For example.

Q. Acre also?

A. For example.

In response to Abu Dahu's threats, MK Chanan Porat (National Religious Party) said today that he demands that the State Attorney's Office produce the declarations signed by the freed terrorists prior to their release. He said that he suspects that the State Attorney's Office was not telling the truth when it said that the terrorists were required to sign such documents, and that he would pursue the matter until it is clarified.

The common denominator: ARAB ANTI-SEMITISM

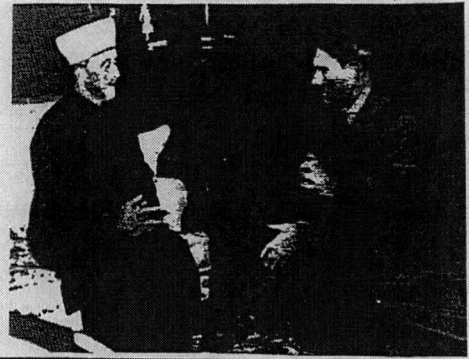

an′ti–Sem′i·tism (an′ti-sĕm′ĭ-tĭz·m; -sĕ′ mĭ-tĭz′m), n. Opposition to, hatred of, or agitation against, Jews. **an′ti–Sem′ite** (-sĕm′ īt; -sē′ -mīt), n. **—an′ti–Semit′ic** (-sĕ-mĭt′ĭk), adj. *(Webster's Dictionary)*

Partners in hate: Mufti Haj Amin Al-Husseini (the undisputed leader of Palestinian Arabs), and Adolf Hitler, Berlin, November 21, 1941. The Mufti lobbied Hitler to bring the gas chambers to Palestine to "solve the Jewish problem there."

NOTE TO READER

In this issue of **THE MACCABEAN**, we enclose a sample of some of the most venomous, outrageous and virulent anti-Semitic caricatures ever published. These cartoons come from a study of Arab anti-Semitic caricatures being published (August 1995) in a Hebrew version by *NATIV*, together with Zamora Bitan Publishers. An English version will appear in the next few months. This anti-Semitic profanity is not coming, this time, from Germany, although there is no doubt the Nazi magazine, "*De Sturmer*" would have been proud to publish them. What is most disturbing, these cartoons are being published daily in government controlled newspapers by our so called 'peace' partners, Egypt, Jordan, Syria and the Palestinian Authority. In view of the enormous risk imposed by the Israeli government upon the Jewish people in the name of "peace," it has become urgent to unveil to the world the harsh reality behind the smiles, the handshakes and Nobel Prize awarding ceremonies and to display the true and ugly face of Arab anti-Semitism. Arie Stav, editor of *NATIV*, has taken it upon himself to attempt this difficult but crucial task.

"Tishrin", Syria, March 1995

The Jewish devil holds the menorah against the background of the Jewish Bible. "Tishrin" is the official Syrian newspaper.

Taken from "*El-Am*", Lebanon, December 1993
As you can plainly see from the cartoon, the peace negotiations are only a smokescreen for the real intentions of the Arabs. With one hand the Arab is squeezing the face of the Jewish monster, and the other hand is cutting the Israeli flag.

This cartoon was published in the Jordanian paper *Al-Dustur* on June 4, 1990. The American administration is shown tipping the United Nations vote against the Arabs in favor of Israel.

The Zionist devil is composed of settlers and the army.

March 1, 1993   *Islamic militants bomb the World Trade Center in New York.*

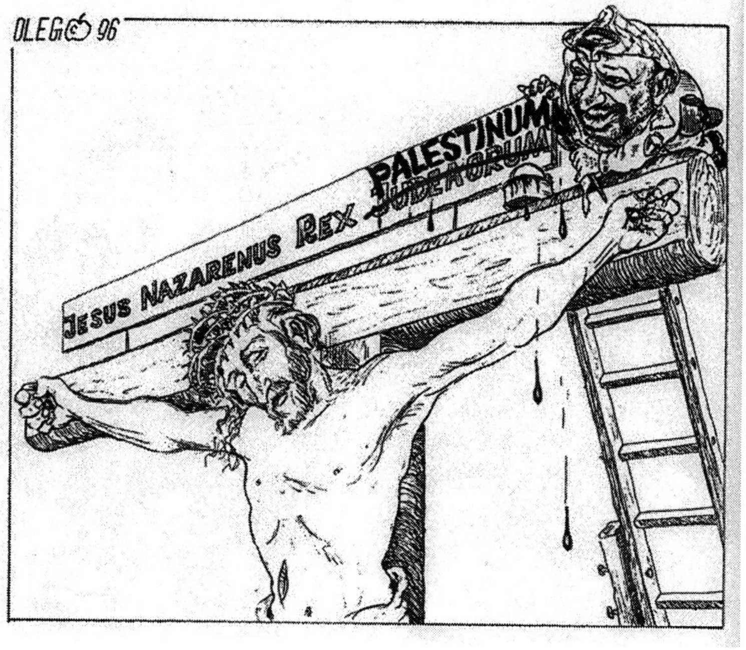
JESUS NAZARENUS REX
PALESTINUM

CHAPTER ELEVEN: ARAB PROPAGANDA AND MEDIA BIAS

The history of the Middle East conflicts have been distorted through an ant-Semitic and anti-Israel lens. Many commentators claim that they are not anti-Semitic but only against unjust Israeli policies. They claim that they protest mistreatment of Israel's Arab population. In truth, Arabs in Israel have far more civil rights and protections than in any Arab country in the world.

While Israel is accused of being an "apartheid" state, it is the Arab states that are truly racist. All races and religions are free in Israel but not in Arab countries. A simple trip to Israel reveals Jews and other minorities of all colors and faiths. Only the Arab minority has developed a "victim mentality." There are about 10 members of the Arab community in Israel's Knesset, elected in Democratic elections. In no Arab country are Arabs free to elect their representatives.

Unfortunately, many in this minority have moved from opposition to Israeli government policies to active treason and terrorism. The right of peace protest has been abused and become a method of violence against the peaceful Jewish population of Israel. While the Media portrays this violence by Arabs as peaceful, it most certainly is not.

Rocks, molotov cocktails, knives and bullets are certainly violent. When Jews defend themselves, they are accused of aggression.

I am a firm believer in equal rights and equal justice for all people in Israel. However, those who raise their hands to kill Jews and conspire with terrorists to destroy the Jewish State, should be driven from the Land.

Bernard J. Shapiro

It is important to note that the Arab countries, especially Saudi Arabia, Syria, and Iran are still the world's largest publisher of "hard core" anti-Semitic literature like the PROTOCOLS OF THE ELDERS OF ZION. Syria's Defense Minister recently wrote a book to prove that accusations of "blood libel" against the Jews were true. That is that ***"Jews kill Christians, especially children, to use their blood in the preparation of rnatza during Passover."*** I have added a few author notes to update some of the text.

ARAB PROPAGANDISTS JOIN FORCES

WITH ANTI-SEMITES

(1963)

"It is time that Americans realize that these teeming masses of Zionists who infest their cities and sit astride the arteries of their commerce are, in every sense of the word, aliens."

The above quotation, in passion and paranoiac ring could have come from the pen of anyone of our local hatemongers, whose rhetoric we have come to know well over the past half century. Yet, these words are neither the work of a professional rabble-rouser, nor of a right-wing extremist; rather they come from a presumably scholarly work written by Musa Khuri, an Arab college professor.

This points up two rather disturbing realities: That Arab propaganda has broadened in area of attack w Jewish populations Out-side of Israel; it has, in effect, joined forces with local anti-Semites. Secondly, this propaganda apparatus, sanctioned, as it is, by duly recognized governments which together form an influential political power bloc, has lent these local anti-Semitic efforts the aura of respectability.

Arab propaganda constitutes a formidable threat to the Jewish people. This essay will focus upon the Arab propaganda effort in this country first by examining its history, institutions arid aspirations, and secondly, by analyzing the techniques and themes that it uses to achieve its goals. Finally, we will attempt to measure the effectiveness of this endeavor.

Ironically, the initial inspiration for this effort was stimulated by the success of the Zionist movement in this area. For while the Arabs used political obstructionism and violence to oppose the creation of a Jewish State, the Zionists built up a propaganda apparatus that succeeded in convincing the majority of Americans of the efficacy and rightness of a Jewish State in Palestine. The Zionist diplomatic victory in securing the UN partition of Palestine1 convinced the Arabs of the necessity of attracting favorable public opinion.

Bernard J. Shapiro

Arab propaganda first entered the country in an organized fashion after World War Ir, when several of the newly liberated Middle Eastern nations formed the Arab League, binding themselves together politically for the first time in modern history.

A year later, the member states of the League established the first Arab office of Information in Washington, D.C The Institute of Arab-American Affairs, founded in the same year, supposedly to promote Arab-American cultural exchange and friendship, was revealed to be concerned primarily with heading off American support of a Jewish State. While national rivalries between the Arab gates prevented anything like a coordinated propaganda campaign, the cumulative amount of propaganda increased as each state embarked upon its own campaign.

After the creation of the State of Israel, the Arab League Information Offices began to take on a more professional look. This re-organization was achieved during the years 1948-1955, due, primarily. to the efforts of Abdul Rahman Azzam Pasha, then Secretary General of the Arab League. He came to America in 1950 to stir up support for a unified propaganda effort In January, 1955, the *new* Arab Information Center was opened in New York with a budget of $400,000. It set out to do the job prescribed by Azzam Pasha; and was headed by the former Egyptian Ambassador to the US., Kamil Rahim What do the Arabs hope to gain by this great effort and expense? Bluntly speaking: **to bring about conditions that would facilitate the destruction of the State of Israel** they concentrate most of their propaganda in the United States, because they feel that *this* country **was** the greatest single influence that contributed to the creation of Israel and that *it still is* the major force standing in the way of **Israel's destruction**.

The Arabs, therefore, aim to neutralize the impact of America on the Middle East and, if possible, to draw her over to their side. This requires that the propaganda apparatus achieve the following effects: To drive a wedge between Israel and the American Jewish community; to alienate the Jew from the rest of America, and destroy his political and economic strength; and to convince the American people, and through them the American government, that it must adopt a pro-Arab, anti-Israel foreign policy.

Let us briefly examine these three conditions and understand why their achievement is absolutely necessary before an Arab policy of eliminating Israel can hope to succeed. The Arabs have always looked at the Jews of America as allies of Israel, and it is against this alliance that the bulk of the Arab propaganda is directed. During the past fifteen years, the Jews of America have given invaluable material and political support to the State of Israel. American Jewish aid has helped make possible the absorption of over 1,000,000 immigrants in Israel, and has given impetus to her economy. The Arabs, therefore, believe that they must destroy this relationship as a precondition to destroying the state. Recognizing that such a campaign might not succeed, the Arabs have devised other means of limiting the effectiveness=B7 of the American Jew. If Israel cannot be made alien to the American Jew, then the Jew can be made alien to his non-Jewish neighbor. Isolate the Jew, and you isolate Israel; destroy Jewish prestige in America, and you destroy Israel's; weaken Jewish economic and political strength and you weaken Israel's potential to survive.

And finally, they believe that a long-range program to win wide-spread support of their policies from the American people is essential. If they can do this they will be able to prevail upon the American government to take a pro-Arab. anti-Israel position in its foreign policy. These ideas and projected goals are certainly plausible and, to a great degree, necessary, if Israel is to be destroyed with impunity.

To achieve these goals, the Arab Information Center has published voluminous material and has distributed it extensively. School and public libraries regularly receive large amounts of unsolicited propaganda; civic, church and political clubs are treated to a host of polished Arab speakers who are able to lecture on a wide variety of subjects but always manage to direct the discussion to the Arab-Israeli conflict; hundreds of anti-Israel letters are kept flowing to large and small papers across the country.

The themes and techniques exploited in the letters, books, pamphlets and speeches follow a pattern. Virtually all Arab propaganda is based on the following postulates:

The establishment of Israel represents a great "imperialistic" injustice to the Arabs.

The Arabs of Palestine were expelled from their homes by "alien" invaders who seized their country.

Muhanimad T. Mehdi spells this out explicitly in his recent pamphlet <u>The Question of Palestine</u>:

"The question of Palestine is basically a problem of intrusion of a group of foreigners, largely Europeans, into the Arab land of Palestine, against the will of the Arab people, but with British and later American and Western support."

A wide variety of proposals, arguments, themes and accusations based on these postulates appear periodically in Arab propaganda. In all of their efforts the distinction between Zionist and Jew is blurred, although the Arabs frequently claim to have no quarrel with the Jews, but only with the Zionists. We will deal with this lack of precise distinction, when we discuss the use of anti-Semitic themes in its propaganda.

Here, then, are some examples of recurrent themes:

An 'international" Zionist (often Zionist-Jewish or Zionist-Jewish-Communist depending on the audience) conspiracy was able to take aver Palestine because:

(a) *It controls the mass media in this county.*

(b) *It controls the wealth of this country.*

(c) *It controls both political parties*

Arabs never wished a close relationship with Communist countries, but were forced to do so because of the creation of Israel, and the Western role in bringing it about.

Israel is guilty of stealing land and property that belongs to Arabs; of military aggression; of creating tension to help it pleas for aid.

The UJA. is not a chanty; therefore contributions should not be tax-exempt.

Highly Organized, well financed "minority groups" pressure the American government to adopt programs that are supposedly in their respective private interest, but are, in fact, detrimental to the United States.

The Zionists (Jews) are, in reality, loyal to Israel, and, therefore, aliens to America.

Communism is not only legal, but popular in Israel, which constitutes a Communist menace in the Middle East.

Israel benefits from anti-Semitism in the sense that it uses it as an excuse to increase immigration and ask for more aid

Israel preaches peace, but is guilty of aggression; it desires territorial expansion.

There would be peace if Israel accepted U.N. Resolutions

American prestige in the Middle East is damaged, end Arab-American friendship is inhibited by American supporters of Zionism.

Desecration Christian and Moslem holy places.

Charges of atrocity.

Israel persecutes the Arab minority

The Jews have been worse than even the Nazis in their relations to the Arabs.

While this list could certainly be extended, it does include the most frequently-used arguments of Arab propaganda. Direct collusion, involving payoffs and exchanges of material, has been uncovered and published by the Anti-Defamation League in its recent book on the exploitation of anti-Semitism for political purposes, Cross-Currents. The book gives an account of how Gerald L. K. Smith received large gifts from Arab sources for publishing stories on the *"Palestine question"* in his publication. **The Cross and the Flag**; and how Frank Briton supports himself by rewriting Arab material for American audiences. and selling his own works. such as **"Behind' Communism."** *"Atom Treason"* and *"Hollywood Treason"* to Arab publishers for distribution in the Middle East.

Publishers of other right-wing extremist magazines like Conde McGinley (**Common Sense**) Gerald Winrod (**Defender**) and the American Mercury, have used their vehicles for the vilest kind of Arab Propaganda. And the publications of the American Council for Judaism, **Jewish Newsletter** and **Issues** have aimed at alienating Jewish readers from the state of Israel. [**Author's Note**: Today the primary American Jewish groups fulfilling this propaganda function for the Arabs are: **New Israel Fund**, **Americans for Peace Now**, **New Jewish Agenda**, and Michael Lerner's *TIKKUN*. In Israel there are several political groups which support the Arab propaganda position. They include the **Meretz Party**, **Shalom Akshav**, and the left-wing of the **Israel Labor Party**.]

Joe Alex Morris Jr. in an article that appeared in the **New York Herald Tribune**, reveals that American bigots not only distribute Arab propaganda' but also supply Anti-Semitic material to the Arabs. He writes:

"Spreaders of racial and religious bigotry in the United States are among the prime suppliers of propaganda to the Arabs in their political and propagandistic war against Israel"

The Arab states utilize anti-Semitic material in their propaganda because it seems to be the most effective way of alienating and intimidating the American Jew. This goal can best be realized by utilizing the reservoir of prejudice in this country. It is really quite simple: If the policies and ideas of a Gerald L. K. Smith become widely accepted, then Congress will be forced to pass anti-Jewish legislation and adopt an anti-Zionist foreign policy. Smith in his book, <u>Christian Nationalism Vs. Jew-Communist Internationalism</u> alternates the term "Jew-Communist" with "Jew-Zionist" in various chapters. Thus. Smith's readers are prone to accept the Arab conception of the Zionist conspiracy: that took over Palestine and plans to take over other Arab nations and, finally, the world.

Here is how the Arabs take this and-Semitic theme and exploit it for their purposes: Haj Amin el-Husseini, former Mufti of Jerusalem, Grand Mufti of Palestine, Hitler's Middle Eastern propaganda specialist during the war and head of the Arab Republic of Palestine" in exile, declared, recently, in Baghdad:

"The Palestine tragedy is unequaled in history. The Zionist imperialistic plot against Palestine was most inhumane and base. World Judaism plans to take over most of the Arab countries to fulfill its so-called historical dream of a homeland between the Nile and Euphrates. The Imperialist Jewish plot is not aimed at Palestine only ... —"

It seems clear from what has been said that an unholy alliance exists between native bigots and Arab propagandists in their aim of destroying the Jewish position in America. The third goal of Arab propaganda is to secure grass-roots support from the American people. It hopes to achieve this in a number of ways:

Exploitation of organizations "devoted" to explaining Arab cultures to America; "service" organizations, such as The American Friends of the Middle East (financed by the large oil companies) which purport to be aimed, solely, at promoting Arab-American friendship; through student exchange and similar pro-grams; personal indoctrination of individuals by carefully selected Arab students (over 5,000 in this country). The effectiveness of this ubiquitous propaganda machine seems to be increasing as the skill and experience of its director improves. Today the Arabs are not easily caught in compromising positions with native hate-mongers as they were in previous years. The tone of the propaganda has become less vile, subtler, psychologically oriented. [**Author's Note:** The most important improvement in Arab propaganda is its ability to utilize Jewish and left-wing groups for its anti-Israel campaign.]

And yet, the factor which impedes its progress the most is the overall decline of bigotry in this country. The ADL has discovered that where reservoirs of prejudice exist, they are reinforced by the introduction of

Arab propaganda. It can only be hoped that with the improvement in the educative process, communication and means of world travel, that there will be a decline in prejudice, and a concomitant decline in the effectiveness of Arab propaganda.

THE FAILURE OF THE JEWISH MEDIA

Is Suppression Of The Truth A Crime?

By Bernard J. Shapiro (April 1996)

Likud MK Benny Begin: "There is a voluntary suppression of the 'bad' news relating to the Oslo Project in the world's press".

At the International Press Institute (IPI) World Congress currently being held in Jerusalem, MK Benny Begin (Likud) charged that editors and journalists were not interested in news which reflected badly on the so-called "peace process". He said that it was most difficult to penetrate the press with stories on violations of the spirit and letter of the Oslo Accords. One newspaper editor told a reporter that the news was inflammatory and asked if the reporter wanted peace.

Begin spoke before editors and media executives from 85 countries and asked in summation: "when will a free press allow the people to know the truth". [From a special Shomron News Service (SNS) Report on March 28, 1996]

Begin's remarks were directed to members of the world press, but we all are aware that an even worse situation exists with regard to the Jewish press. Attempts to publish the full facts and logical consequences of the Oslo Agreement in Jewish newspapers has been almost totally prevented. Editors of most Jewish weeklies have maintained a uniform commitment to ignorance. What their readers don't know, want hurt them. Why ruffle the feathers of their local Israeli consulate?

The Jewish Telegraphic Agency (JTA), which provides a large number of Jewish papers with their news, has been dominated by a Peace Now/ Labor philosophy for years. It would be unthinkable for them to provide an honest assessment of the Oslo Process. After all they are committed to "peace."

My own personal experience with the Jewish Herald-Voice is illustrative of the problem faced at most Jewish papers. After writing a column on

Bernard J. Shapiro

Israel for three years, I was dismissed following an expose (June 7, 1995) entitled "THE JERUSALEM COVERUP."

My article revealed the ongoing discussions by the Israeli government to divide Jerusalem. At the time, the Israeli government was denying the existence of such talks. Today, this information is common knowledge. The editors insisted that their dismissal of me was not censorship but merely related to my use of strong language. By the way, in an examination of the previous six months of my columns, they were unable to locate any such "strong language." What really bothered them was my continued criticism of both the Oslo Agreement and the Israeli government.

Since I had developed my own publication, THE MACCABEAN, I let the matter of my column drop. However I did decide to test their sincerity concerning censorship. Over the last 18 months, I supplied the Jewish Herald-Voice with about 200 excellent articles by fax and e-mail. Articles not by myself, but by well known military and political commentators of national scope as well opposition Israeli leaders. All of the articles had one thing in common, they disputed intelligently the validity of the Oslo Process and the Israeli government's commitment to it. NONE WERE PUBLISHED.

My personal experience has been duplicated in the editorial offices of Jewish papers across America. What we are witnessing is a massive (though not necessarily conspiratorial) cover up of the truth about the dangers inherent in the Oslo Process. This coverup, designed to keep the Jewish community in ignorance, reminds one of the darkest days of the Holocaust. Then, as now, Jewish leaders and editors saw fit to hide the truth from the Jewish community.

Is the suppression of the truth where Jewish lives are at stake—a crime?

VERBAL DEFENSE

A Necessity For Israel's Supporters

(May 1997)

Israel is being defeated linguistically every day in the pages of newspapers, in the news broadcasts, even in the speeches of political leaders and State Department officials. Even many Jews fall into the trap of using the accepted anti-Israel language. We must start using the correct language to describe events in Israel. That goes for the Israeli government spokesman as well as private pro-Israel groups like ours.

Samples:

1. **CNN/ABC/NBC/CBS/NPR/NY TIMES Headline**:

Israeli kills two Arabs in West Bank.

Militant Jewish settler kills two Arabs in West Bank.

Linguistically Accurate Headline:

Terrorists attack Jewish civilian and are killed in firefight.

Innocent Jew attacked by Arab mob. Jew survives due to courageous action.

★

2. **CNN etc**:

Israelis cause terrorist bombing by grabbing Arab East Jerusalem.

Israelis provoke violence by building on Arab land in Arab East Jerusalem.

Should Be:

Arab terrorist murderers were sent by Arafat to kill Jews & bombed a Tel Aviv cafe.

✷

3. **CNN etc:**

Arafat says Bibi at fault for breaking down of peace talks.

Should Be:

Arafat, a documented liar and terrorist murderer, tried to blame Israel for the breakdown in peace talks.

✷

We need to be linguistically aggressive and accurate all the time. Call a spade a spade. No more Mr. Nice Guy to the Arabs who lie and slander us at every opportunity.

(March 2001)

To our readers:

TIME magazine this week (issue of February 26, 2001) has a five page article (Waiting For History) praising Yassir Arafat. It includes a full color full page portrait. It is slick Arab propaganda. It is filled with inaccurate history and should be countered by the pro-Israel community.

The Freeman Center recommends that as many of you as possible write to *TIME*. Below is my letter:

TIME MAGAZINE LETTERS VIA FAX: 1-212-522-8949
Time & Life Building
Rockefeller Center
New York, NY 10020
February 21, 2001

TO LETTERS TO THE EDITOR

Re: Your unbridled praise of Yasser Arafat (Time, February 26, 2001).

Contrary to your author's commentary, Arafat has brought misery, poverty, human rights abuses and a ruthless dictatorship to his people. He runs a klepocracy where aid funds end up in his or his cronies pockets with the Palestinian people seeing none of it.

Despite your praise he has a history of murder and terrorism that continue even today. The *intifadeh* is no more than a *pogram* designed to kill or murder Jews. The daily incitement against Israelis and Jews can only be described as worthy of the Nazis. It is broadcast on TV, taught in the schools, and preached in sermons. American and Israeli intelligence are aware that roughly 80% of all terror attacks and shooting at Israelis is authorized by the Palestinian Authority under Arafat.

Since the Oslo Agreement was signed, Arafat has failed to live up to a single item of his obligations. His promise to end the violence is a mockery as he perpetuates more violence. He and Israeli Prime Minister Yitzhak Rabin promised to negotiate differences. "No more war, no more bloodshed," they said. Arafat refuses to negotiate, but only demands. If he doesn't get his way, he returns to violence.

The article fails to adequately tell the story of Arafat's bloody history from the civil war in Lebanon (100,000 killed), the attempted takeover of Jordan, and finally terrorism against Israelis and Americans.

The ultimate failure of the article is to ignore how much the Palestinian people could have gained by this time with better leadership. Everything from economic development, a state, human rights, and improved standard of living.

Bernard J. Shapiro, Executive Director
Freeman Center For Strategic Studies

PEACE NOW (ISRAELI LEFT) EXPOSED

HOW AMERICANS FOR PEACE NOW (APN)

SUPPORTS THE ARABS

(December 2002)

The following chart demonstrates clearly how closely the positions of APN parallel those of Arab/PLO positions. (Written and published originally in 1993.)

Position or Policy	Peace Now	Arab PLO	Freeman Center Shapiro/ AFSI
1. Israel should return to 1967 borders	*YES*	*YES*	*NO*
2. Status of Jerusalem should be negotiated with Palestinians	*YES*	*YES*	*NO*
3. Jews have the right to settle in Judea, Samaria, and Gaza	*NO*	*NO*	*YES*
4. Jewish settlements in Judea, Samaria, & Gaza are illegal	*YES*	*YES*	*NO*
5. Supported linking the loan guarantees to a freeze in settlement	*YES*	*YES*	*NO*
6. Favors American pressure to force an Israeli withdrawal to '67 borders	*YES*	*YES*	*NO*

7. When an Arab mob attacks Israeli soldiers and some Arabs are killed, this situation is described as:	*HUMAN RIGHTS VIOLATION*	*HUMAN RIGHTS VIOLATION*	*SELF-DEFENSE*
8. Israeli control of Judea, Samaria, and Gaza is the cause of the Arab-Israeli Conflict	*YES*	*YES*	*NO*
9. Slander Israel in the Media and International Conferences	*YES*	*YES*	*NO*
10. Wish to strip Israel of the strategic mountain ranges in Judea, Samaria, & Golan making it vulnerable to attack	*YES*	*YES*	*NO*

IF IT LOOKS LIKE A DUCK, WALKS LIKE A DUCK, QUACKS LIKE A DUCK, AND BEHAVES LIKE A DUCK,

THEN ONE CAN ASSUME THAT IT IS A DUCK

OR AT LEAST PRO-DUCK.

ARAB PSYCHOLOGICAL/PROPAGANDA

WARFARE AGAINST ISRAEL

How Israel Can Defend Itself And Counterattack

[(October-November 2005)

The Arabs have always been adept at psychological/propaganda warfare due to their culture of lies and verbal skills. Students of Islamic practices have long recognized that in Arab society it is the norm to prevaricate and deceive. An Arab who tells the truth about serious events affecting ideology, history, and "disputed" matters is considered foolish and naive. How this sociological pattern manifests itself in the Arab War of Extermination Against Israel is the subject of this article.

History is very illuminating on the changes and evolution of Arab psychological warfare against Israel. In the beginning (1888-1939) the Arabs in general, and the Arabs of British Mandate Palestine tended to operate on the basis of religious fanaticism and anti-Jewish incitement. Arab leaders like Haj Amin el-Husseini, the British appointed Mufti of Jerusalem, began to organize squads of terrorists (the called *fedayeen*) to attack Jews as early as the 1920's. The massacre of the Jews of Hebron in 1929 preceded the establishment of Israel by almost 20 years.

In these early years the motivation was to sow fear in the hearts of Jews and prevent their integration into the country. It was also meant to scare away potential new Jewish immigrants. A very important other motivation for the Arabs was to convince the British that the influx of Jews into Palestine was the cause of instability and war and ***thus should be stopped***. This policy succeeded dramatically in 1939 when the British White Paper, limiting Jewish immigration into Palestine, was issued. The White Paper trapped millions of European Jews seeking refuge from the Nazis by closing the doors of the Jewish Homeland.

During World War II, the Arab goal shifted as Haj Amin el-Husseini became a regular guest of Adolf Hitler in Berlin. There he watched as Hitler's plans to exterminate all of European Jewry emerged. Greatly please with the

Holocaust, he lobbied Hitler to bring the gas chambers and crematoria to Palestine after the war. He drew up plans to set up extermination centers near Tel Aviv and Haifa.

Of course we know that the Nazis lost the war and these plans never came to such an evil fruition.

After the war, the Palestinian Arabs continue a war of terrorism against the Jewish community of Palestine. Again, they hoped that the British would abandon their promises to allow the development of a Jewish National Home. Frustrated with the fighting between Jews and Arabs and the growing Jewish resistance their rule, the British turned the entire issue over to the United Nations. This resulted in the Partition Resolution passed on November 29, 1947, which divided Palestine into two states (one Jewish and one Arab).

The Arab States declared war on the new Jewish State and Israel was reborn (1948) in blood and fire. Arab psychological warfare shifted gears in the following years (1948-67) and the cry was to "throw the Jews into the sea." This cry was repeated often by Palestinian Arab leader Ahmed Shuqeiri, both in the media and in the halls of the United Nations. Israel was seen as a potential victim of Arab aggression until the Six Day War when it suddenly became Goliath to the Arab David.

The Arabs understood after the wars of 1967 and 1973 (Yom Kippur War) that Israel could not be defeated by military means. They were forced to come up with a new psychological/propaganda plan. This new strategy ceased calling for the extermination of the Jews and the destruction of Israel.

The most important improvement in Arab propaganda is its ability to utilize Jewish and left-wing groups for its anti-Israel campaign. Extreme left-wing political parties like Meretz and Labor joined pro-Arab organizations like Peace Now, Betzelem, Peace Forum and Tikkun to form a broad coalition of Jews willing and anxious to be political pawns in the hands of those that sought Israel's destruction. Since 1967 that propaganda has changed to emphasize **"Palestinian self determination"**, Palestinian **"rights"** and to enlist the support of **"human rights"** and leftist groups.

The Battle for Eretz Yisrael

It is important to note that the Arab countries, especially Saudi Arabia, Syria, and Iran are still the world's largest publisher of "hard core" anti-Semitic literature like the PROTOCOLS OF THE ELDERS OF ZION. Syria's Defense Minister recently wrote a book to prove that accusations of "blood libel" against the Jews were true. That is that *"Jews kill Christians, especially children, to use their blood in the preparation of rnatza during Passover."*

Arab propaganda is based on deception and misdirection through the following demands and claims:

DEMANDS

1. Self determination for "palestinians" in a new State of Palestine
2. Return of the "occupied" territories
3. Return of the Arab refugees
4. Return of all property of Arabs who lost it as a result of their failed attempt to exterminate the Jewish population of Palestine

CLAIMS

1. The State of Israel dispossessed the "palestinians" and stole their country
2. The Jews/Israelis were racists
3. The Jews/Israelis were worse than the Nazis
4. The Jews/Israelis were guilty of genocide against the "palestinians"
5. Jews had no historical connection to Eretz Yisrael (Israel)
6. The "palestinians" were the indigenous people of Palestine
7. Terrorism by "palestinians" is justified as resistance to "occupation"

ARAB MANTRA

"It is time that Americans and Europeans realize that these teeming masses of Zionists who infest their cities and sit astride the arteries of their commerce are, in every sense of the word, aliens."

The above quotation, in passion and paranoiac ring could have come from the pen of anyone of our local or international hatemongers, whose rhetoric we have come to know well over the past half century. Yet, these words are neither the work of a professional rabble-rouser, nor of a right-wing extremist; rather they come from a presumably scholarly work written by Musa Khuri, an Arab college professor.

This points up two rather disturbing realities: That Arab propaganda and it psychological warfare against Israel has broadened into an attack Jewish populations outside of Israel. It has, in effect, joined forces with anti-Semites, both from the extreme right and the extreme left to delegitimize Israel and the Jewish people and facilitate their destruction. Secondly, this Arab, European and Jewish left wing propaganda apparatus, sanctioned, as it is, by duly recognized governments which together form an influential political power bloc, has lent these local anti-Semitic efforts the aura of respectability.

What do the Arabs hope to gain by this great effort and expense? Bluntly speaking: **to bring about conditions that would facilitate the destruction of the State of Israel** they concentrate most of their propaganda in the United States, Europe, the United Nations and Islamic nations. A lot of emphasis in recent years has been on the United States, because they feel that *this* country *was* the greatest single influence that contributed to the creation of Israel and that *it still is* the major force standing in the way of **Israel's destruction**.

The Arabs, therefore, aim to neutralize the impact of America on the Middle East and, if possible, to draw her over to their side. This requires that the propaganda apparatus achieve the following effects: To drive a wedge between Israel and the American Jewish community; to alienate the Jew from the rest of America, and destroy his political and economic strength; and to convince the American people, and through them the American government, that it must adopt a pro-Arab, anti-Israel foreign policy.

To achieve these goals, Islamic organizations like the Arab Anti-Defamation League, the Council of Arab Affairs have published voluminous materials and have distributed them extensively. School and public libraries regularly receive large amounts of unsolicited propaganda; civic, church and political clubs are treated to a host of polished Arab speakers who are able to lecture on a wide variety of subjects but always manage to direct the discussion to the Arab-Israeli conflict; hundreds of anti-Israel letters are kept flowing to large and small papers across the country. Of even more importance, almost every major American university has an Islamic Studies Center financed and funded by Arab money. The centers are teaching a false biased anti-Israel history of the Middle East to a whole new generation of students, including uninformed Jewish students.

The themes and techniques exploited in the letters, books, pamphlets and speeches follow a pattern. Virtually all Arab propaganda is based on the following postulates:

* The establishment of Israel represents a great "imperialistic" injustice to the Arabs.

* The Arabs of Palestine were expelled from their homes by "alien" invaders who seized their country.

Muhanimad T. Mehdi spells this out explicitly in his pamphlet <u>The Question of Palestine</u>:

"The question of Palestine is basically a problem of intrusion of a group of foreigners, largely Europeans, into the Arab land of Palestine, against the will of the Arab people, but with British and later American and Western support."

A wide variety of proposals, arguments, themes and accusations based on these postulates appear periodically in Arab propaganda. In all of their efforts the distinction between Zionist and Jew is blurred, although the Arabs frequently claim to have no quarrel with the Jews, but only with the Zionists. We deal with this lack of precise distinction, when we discuss the use of anti-Semitic themes in its propaganda. Here, then, are some examples of recurrent themes:

An 'international" Zionist (often Zionist-Jewish or Zionist-Jewish-Communist depending on the audience) conspiracy was able to take aver Palestine because:

(a) It controls the mass media in this county.

(b) *It controls the wealth of this country.*

(c) *It controls both political parties*

1. Israel is guilty of stealing land and property that belongs to Arabs; of military aggression; of creating tension to help its pleas for aid.
2. The UJA is not a charity; therefore contributions should not be tax-exempt.
3. Highly Organized, well financed "minority groups" pressure the American government to adopt programs that are supposedly in their respective private interest, but are, in fact, detrimental to the United States.
4. The Zionists (Jews) are, in reality, loyal to Israel, and, therefore, disloyal to America.
5. Israel benefits from anti-Semitism in the sense that it uses it as an excuse to increase immigration and ask for more aid.
6. Israel preaches peace, but is guilty of aggression since it desires territorial expansion.
7. There would be peace if Israel accepted U.N. Resolutions.
8. **American prestige in the Middle East is damaged, end Arab-American friendship is inhibited by American supporters of Zionism**.
9. Israel desecrates Christian and Moslem holy places.
10. Israel commits atrocities.
11. Israel persecutes the Arab minority.
12. The Jews have been worse than even the Nazis in their relations to the Arabs.

Here is how the Arabs take this and-Semitic theme and exploit it for their purposes: Haj Amin el-Husseini, former Mufti of Jerusalem, Grand Mufti of Palestine, Hitler's Middle Eastern propaganda specialist during the war and head of the Arab Republic of Palestine" in exile in Baghdad said:

"The Palestine tragedy is unequaled in history. The Zionist imperialistic plot against Palestine was most inhumane and base. World Judaism plans to take over most of the Arab countries to fulfill its so-called historical dream of a homeland between the Nile and Euphrates. The Imperialist Jewish plot is not aimed at Palestine only . . . ."

COUNTERATTACK

The Palestine Liberation Organization, which has been recognized as the world's highest moral arbiter recently asked the United Nation's Secretary General Kofi Anan to draft a resolution condemning Israel and calling for sanctions. Something is obviously wrong with this picture. It is time for Israelis and their supporters to recognize that Israel has a public relations problem.

The actions Israel takes to defend its security are quite moderate by Middle East standards. Its ability to explain what and why it took such action is inadequate. Along with most of the pro-Israel community, I'm a frequent critic of Israeli information policies.

What is needed is a whole new approach to Israeli public relations. Let's call it: **THE MARKETING OF ISRAEL**, and look at the problem from an advertizing perspective. About eight years ago, I discussed with an executive of a major advertising company the possibility of producing television spots supporting Israel's positions on various political issues. I became discouraged upon learning that the major stations do not permit "advocacy" commercials.

I think it is time to take a second look at my concept but expand it to include radio, magazines, cable television (cable will accept this type of commercial) and newspapers. The ads should range from the very soft evocative travel type to some hard hitting but subtle political messages. Pretend that Israel is a corporation with a vast market in the United States. Receipts from that market top $6 Billion Dollars (including US economic and military aid, UJA, Israel Bonds, JNF, plus all the other campaigns from Yeshivas to the Technion). What would you spend to protect a market of that magnitude? One percent would equal $60 million. You can run for president with sixty million dollars. In a wild fantasy, let's say we have that much money. And let's say we hire a talented creative ad man to develop a multi-faceted, multi-media, and multi-year campaign to win the hearts and minds of the American people (and later the Europeans).

This should not be an impossible task. Israel is a good product, lots of virtues, few vices. (Can you imagine convincing the American people to love Saddam or Osama bin Ladin?) We could do nothing, but the consequences are not so good. Public opinion polls are beginning to show the Arabs winning more and more sympathy despite terrorism. Today the movement of university students and their professors, blacks, and the leadership of the Democrat Party toward support of Arab anti-Israel goals is truly frightening. Yes, Arabs who keep their women in bondage; Palestinians who disembowel pregnant teachers in front of their classes; Syrians who peddle narcotics to American inner city youth and commit mass murder if provoked; Saudis who threaten to behead a man for practicing Christianity; all of these and more are almost as popular as Israel. The Arabs are good at smearing the good name of Israel. Just listen to Hanan Ashrawi some time. No matter what the question, she manages to fit in a lie about Israel in her answer. Israel has already lost the college campus, half of the Afro-Americans, a good portion of the Protestants except for the Baptists and the Evangelicals and some in the Jewish community.

A FINAL NOTE

Israel must stop being inhibited from its national Zionist mission because of Arab psychological intimidation. The Israelis must know that they are **NOT** racist despite accusations of racism from racist Arabs and their left wing fellow travelers. In their military/strategic policy, Israel must act in its own best interests and that of its citizens and **NOT** at the command of any other nation. The security and survival of Israel and the Jewish community has the highest priority in Jewish law and **MUST** be observed. And I mean by that, the Israel Defense Forces must be given complete freedom to destroy the enemy. Israel's political establishment **MUST NOT** negotiate with an enemy seeking its destruction in the false hope of preventing the final battle between the forces ***of good and evil (light and darkness)***.

THE BOTTOM LINE

The Israel government needs to realize that we are living in a new world where telecommunications brings us closer than ever before to each other. In the fifties when Israel was criticized, Ben Gurion used to say, "It's not what the world thinks, but what the Jews do that is important." It is a different world now and for every Israeli policy, the public relations aspect must be examined. I am definitely not calling on Israel to submit to public opinion but instead to organize and mold it for their benefit. I don't want Israel immobilized by fear of bad public relations. I want Israel to plan, with the help of experts, a strategy to counteract the negative effects of any public policy move. Would Sharon send his soldiers into battle without a detailed plan and strategy to win? The time has come for Israel to develop a strategy the win the public relations battle. The Jewish community in this country is more than willing to lend its money and advertizing talent to aid in this task. Let's do it! (Are you listening Sharon?)

Bernard J. Shapiro

ORWELL MEETS ALICE—LINGUISTIC DISTORTIONS

Through The Mid-East Looking Glass

(October-November 2005)

Since the unfortunate reprisal against Arabs in Hebron ten years ago, there has been a dramatic decline in the accuracy of the media. We have been treated to the modern equivalent of Orwellian newspeak, not to mention a harrowing trip through Alice's looking glass. One could not help but notice how pure and innocent the Arabs were being portrayed. A casual observer would certainly think that all violence in Middle East was a product of bloodthirsty Jewish settlers roaming the Judean hills looking for Arab prey.

The PLO leadership, its hands dripping with Jewish and Arab blood, demanded protection from the vicious Jewish residents of Judea, Samaria, and Gaza (YESHA). It refused to return to the negotiations until its demands were met. The gullible international media took this whole charade seriously. The United Nations began debating a resolution to give protection to the poor vulnerable Palestinians. The PLO demanded that all Jewish communities of YESHA be ethnically cleansed of those rotten murderous Jews. At the very least they should be disarmed. The high and the mighty beseeched Arafat to return to the talks with Israel. Israeli Prime Minister Yitzhak Rabin, obviously anxious to please his PLO friends, began a crackdown on Kach and Kahane Chai and other so-called Israeli extremists. Consider this: Rabin determined that Baruch Goldstein acted alone in his reprisal act. He then decides to outlaw the organizations associated with him. Guilt by association is what made McCarthy big in the 50's. It was wrong then and it is wrong now. Reality Check: Now Kach and Kahane Chai have been labeled as terrorist organizations although they never have committed a single act of terror as a body. The PLO, which is guilty of thousands of murders of Arabs and Jews, continuing still, is labeled a "partner for peace" and will be given arms to kill some more (as policemen).Reality Check: Are Arabs in danger from armed Israelis in YESHA? Some research reveals the following figures since the famous handshake on September 13, 1993: Israelis killed by Arabs = 1400+Arabs killed by Arabs = 200+Arab attacks on Israeli targets = 15,000+Israeli

The Battle for Eretz Yisrael

attacks on Arabs = 1(Goldstein killed 29) It is clear that except for the attack by Goldstein, the Arabs have not been threatened by Jews and certainly need no special protection. If you travel to YESHA you will notice that every Jewish village needs a security fence, while every Arab village is open. Doesn't this tell you who is threatened and who isn't? All the talk about disarming the Jews is a cover for the Arab desire to murder them. And if you desire murder, wouldn't it be nice to disarm your victim first? The media has begun to adopt another tactic which we should protest. In the New York Times, The Los Angeles Times, The Washington Post, The Houston Chronicle, CNN and most of the other media opponents of the suicidal Oslo, Roadmap, Jewish Expulsion Plan are being referred to as right wing extreme Arab-hating and anti-peace groups. Do you ever remember the PLO or Hamas ever being referred to as Jew-hating groups, although their covenants and speeches are filled with hatred of Jews? Arafat, who has been quoted on many occasions as referring to Jews as, "filthy, sons of monkeys and pigs," is never referred to in the media as a Jew-hater. Reality Check: To the best of my knowledge there is a distinct difference between Jewish feelings about Arabs and Arab feelings about Jews. Arabs are taught from the earliest grades to despise Jews and their clerics preach hatred (Itbach El Yahoud—slaughter the Jews) in every service. Jews, on the other hand do not preach hatred, but those that are not brain dead recognize, after 100 years of being attacked, that Arabs mean them harm. The media is totally obfuscating the truth about the conflict by the use of such terms as Arab-hating Jews. Another problem with media coverage of the Israel-PLO deal is the way its opponents are described. Arabs opposed to the deal because they want to kill or expel all Jews from "Palestine" immediately are equated with Jews and Israelis who want Israel to survive in secure borders. Opponents of the deal are called anti-peace as opposed to supporters being pro-peace. Reality Check: Most opponents of the deal with Arafat oppose it because it is suicidal for many strategic, historical and objective reasons. None of us are anti-peace. We just recognize that the path chosen by the Rabin/ Peres government will lead not to the hoped for and advertised peace, but to Israel's destruction. In another bizarre twist of logic the Los Angeles Times reports that Israel's leading peace group, Shalom Achshav (Peace Now), has urged Sharon to remove 500,000 Jewish inhabitants of YESHA(including Jerusalem) to avert widespread bloodshed under Palestinian self-government, and to forcibly evict all Jews within five years. They said that their continued presence, "fostering violence and bloodshed endanger peace prospects."Reality Check: The facts demonstrate that it is the Palestinians and not the Jews that are the cause of 99.9% of the violence. Why not remove the Palestinians? What Peace Now is really admitting is that there is NO PEACE or any prospect of PEACE. The liberal Jewish establishment and most of the media were appalled when Rabbi Meir Kahane first began talking about transferring the Arabs from Eretz Yisrael. Most are still appalled at this idea. A new idea has come into fashion, though, among these same righteous Jews: transferring the Jews from YESHA (heartland of Eretz Yisrael). Former Secretary of State James Baker recently said it would be a good idea to use the $10 Billion in US loan guarantees to buy out and transfer the Jews from YESHA. US President Bill Clinton seemed to like the idea and so did Rabin's coalition partner Meretz. Reality Check: There is no moral difference between transferring either Jews or Arabs from YESHA. What Kahane said years ago about the inability of Jews and Arabs to live together is being validated today by the same people who condemned him. The 100-year war of extermination launched against the Jews of Israel by the Arabs has had many twists and turns. Sadly it seems headed for Alice's looking glass and the world of 1984, where black is white, war is peace and good is evil. FREEMAN CENTER's FAVORITE QUOTE:"In Germany they first came for the Communists and I didn't speak up because I wasn't a Communist. Then they came for the Jews, and I didn't speak up because I wasn't a Jew. Then they came for the trade unionists and I didn't speak up because I wasn't a trade unionist. Then they came for the Catholics, and I didn't speak up because I was a Protestant. Then they came for me—and by that time no one was left to speak up."—Pastor Martin Niemoller (A Righteous Gentile)

HOW ISRAEL CAN IMPROVE ITS HASBARA (PUBLIC RELATIONS)

Why It Needs To

(October-November 2005)

Virtually every news commentator compares Israel's temporary removal back in 1996 of 400 terrorists to Lebanon with the heinous crimes of Iraqi dictator Saddam Hussein. The United Nations was being asked not to have a double standard for Iraq and Israel. In fact, the Palestine Liberation Organization, having been recognized as the world's highest moral arbiter, has been asked by the then United Nation's Secretary General Boutros-Ghali to draft a resolution condemning Israel and calling for sanctions. Something is obviously wrong with this picture. It is time for Israelis and their supporters to recognize that Israel has a public relations problem.

The actions Israel took to defend its security were quite moderate by Middle East standards. Its ability to explain what and why it took such action was inadequate. Along with most of the pro-Israel community, I\'m a frequent critic of Israeli information policies. I had a pleasant lunch last week with an Israeli official and we discussed this very issue. As a result of our conversation, I am not convinced that the Israeli government is doing everything in its power to communicate its message to the media, political leaders, and general public. It's just not working.

What is needed is a whole new approach to Israeli public relations. Let's call it: THE MARKETING OF ISRAEL, and look at the problem from an advertizing perspective. About nine months ago, I discussed with an executive of a major advertising company the possibility of producing television spots supporting Israel's positions on various political issues. I became discouraged upon learning that the major stations do not permit "advocacy" commercials. Fortunately, this has changed.

I think it is time to take a second look at my concept but expand it to include radio, magazines, cable television (cable will accept this type of commercial) and newspapers. The ads should range from the very soft evocative travel type to some hard hitting but subtle political messages.

Pretend that Israel is a corporation with a vast market in the United States. Receipts from that market top $9 Billion Dollars (including US economic and military aid, UJA, Israel Bonds, JNF, Hadassah plus all the other campaigns from Yeshivas to the Technion). What would you spend to protect a market of that magnitude? Two percent would equal $180 million. You can run for president with that kind of money. In a wild fantasy, let's say we have that much money. And let's say we hire a talented creative ad man to develop a multi-faceted, multi-media, and multi-year campaign to win the hearts and minds of the American people.

This should not be an impossible task. Israel is a good product, lots of virtues, few vices. Can you imagine convincing the American people to love Osama Bin Ladin? We could do nothing, but the consequences are not so good. Public opinion polls are beginning to show the Arabs winning more and more sympathy. Yes, Arabs who keep their women in bondage and cut off their clitorises to deny them sexual pleasure; Palestinians who disembowel pregnant teachers in front of their classes; Syrians who peddle narcotics to American inner city youth and commit mass murder if provoked; Saudis who threaten to behead a man for practicing Christianity; all of these and more are almost as popular as Israel. The terrorists Arabs delight in the mass murder of Israel and Jewish civilians. They're especially blowing arms and legs off women and children.

The Arabs are good at smearing the good name of Israel. Just listen to Hanan Ashrawi some time. No matter what the question, she manages to fit in a lie about Israel in her answer. Israel has already lost the college campus, half of the Afro-Americans, a good portion of the Protestants except for the some Baptists and the Evangelicals and some in the Jewish community. Unfortunately many American Jews are ignorant or apathetic about the fate of Israel.

The Israel government needs to realize that we are living in a new world where telecommunications brings us closer than ever before to each other. In the fifties when Israel was criticized, Ben Gurion used to say, "It's not what the world thinks, but what the Jews do that is important." It is a different world now and for every Israeli policy, the public relations aspect must be examined. I am definitely not calling on Israel to submit to public opinion but instead to organize and mold it for their benefit. I don't want

Israel immobilized by fear of bad public relations. I want Israel to plan, with the help of experts, a strategy to counteract the negative effects of any public policy move. Would Sharon send his soldiers into battle without a detailed plan and strategy to win. The time has come for Israel to develop a strategy the win the public relations battle. The Jewish community in this country is more than willing to lend its money and advertising talent to aid in this task. Let's do it!

HASBARA AND REALITY

THE JERUSALEM POST reported several years ago on plans at the Israeli Foreign Ministry to abolish its "hasbara" or information efforts. It reported, "The decision to abolish hasbara is in keeping with the then Foreign Minister Shimon Peres\' view that \'if you have good policy, you do not need hasbara. And if you have bad policy, hasbara will not help.\'" Those of us who have been in the trenches, fighting Arab propaganda for years, were stunned by this policy change. Most of all, we were stunned by this apparently incorrect perception of reality.

The propaganda battlefield, from which the Foreign Ministry seems eager to withdraw, is a surreal Kafkaesque landscape filled with the evil utterances of that unholy alliance of Arabs and anti-Semites. Their propaganda targets the Jewish community in America as well as Israel for a one simple reason: Anything that weakens the Jewish community and reduces their status in America ultimately limits the ability of Jews to aid Israel politically and financially. George Orwell would be quite at home with the "newspeak" of the "politically correct" bigots. Language, history, and religion become a twisted mass of bizarre concepts such as Zionism = racism.

CAMERA (Committee for Accuracy in Middle East Reporting in America) regularly reports on the most glaring examples of media bias to its members. Over the past few months, we have been shocked to discover that Encyclopedia Britannica has joined in the distortion of Israeli history to conform to what's "politically correct." In its description of the Six Day War of 1967 there is no mention of the Egyptian removal of UN troops, the closing of the Straits of Tiran (an act of War by international law), the movement of 100,000 troops into Sinai or the huge mobs in Cairo whipped to a frenzy by Gamal Abdul Nasser with cries of "DEATH TO THE JEWS" The Britannica account of the \'67 war reads, "The Arab-Israeli War of 1967 devastated the Arab nations. In six days in June, Israel not only dispatched the combined forces of Egypt, Syria and Jordan, but also overran vast tracts of Arab territory . . . which formally had been parts of mandated Palestine." For the average reader of the supposedly authoritative Britannica, Israel launched an aggressive war to seize land and devastated innocent Arabs. PRECISELY THE VERSION OF HISTORY THE ARABS WANT!

A quick scan of recent CAMERA literature reveals that the New York Times\' correspondents for Israel, have a decidedly ant-Israel viewpoint. Harper's Magazine has published 22 viciously anti-Israel articles in the last five years. Public Broadcasting Service (PBS) shows one biased report after another on the Middle East. National Public Radio (NPR) has become a hotbed of the most anti-Israel and anti-Semitic programs in the nation. And it is taxpayer supported! The American Library Association (ALA) has begun taking official anti-Israel positions and its 18,000 members are urged to carry books on the Middle East supporting the Arab version of history. The ALA's annual meeting several years included a panel discussion entitled, "Israeli Censorship: There and Here." Israel has a free press (though 90 % leftist) and censors only for security reasons. On the other hand the Arab world is the most censored and restricted in the world, with death penalties for authors who go against the law of Islam. Why is the ALA discussing Israel and no other country? The answer: attacking Israel is politically correct.

What we are witnessing is the success of Arab propaganda in America. The following excerpt from ARAB PROPAGANDISTS JOIN FORCES WITH ANTI-SEMITES (my first published article in 1965 and still true today) should warn us of the consequence of abandoning the information field to the Arabs. "What do the Arabs hope to gain by this great effort and expense? Bluntly speaking—to bring about conditions that would facilitate the destruction of the State of Israel. They concentrate most of their propaganda in the United States, because they feel that this country was the greatest single influence that contributed to the creation of Israel and that it still is the major force standing in the way of Israel's destruction."

It is my hope that the Israel Foreign Ministry will heed this warning and reassess their policy on hasbara before any more damage is done to the reputation of Israel and the Jewish community in this country.

ARAB PROPAGANDA AND ITS GOALS

"It is time that Americans realize that these teeming masses of Zionists who infest their cities and sit astride the arteries of their commerce are, in every sense of the word, aliens."

The above quotation, in passion and paranoiac ring could have come from the pen of anyone of our local hate mongers, whose rhetoric we have come to know well over the past half century. Yet, these words are neither the work of a professional rabble-rouser, nor of a right-wing extremist; rather they come from a presumably scholarly work written by an Arab college professor.

This points up two rather disturbing realities: That Arab propaganda has broadened its area of attack against Jewish populations out-side of Israel; it has, in effect, joined forces with local anti-Semites. Secondly, this propaganda apparatus, sanctioned, as it is, by duly recognized governments which together form an influential political power bloc, has lent these local anti-Semitic efforts the aura of respectability.

The Arabs, therefore, aim to neutralize the impact of America on the Middle East and, if possible, to draw her over to their side. This requires that the propaganda apparatus achieve the following effects: To drive a wedge between Israel and the American Jewish community; to alienate the Jew from the rest of America, and destroy his political and economic strength; and to convince the American people, and through them the American government, that it must adopt a pro-Arab, anti-Israel foreign policy.

Arab propaganda constitutes a formidable threat to the Jewish People and Israel. It must be counter-balanced by a strong and vigorous defense of Israel and the Jewish People. Recent efforts, like that of the Israel Project will fail as will the Israeli Foreign ministry effort. The reason for that failure is their attempt to disavow Zionist ideology and pursue a delusional "peace" with those who wish to destroy us.

Bernard J. Shapiro

What do the Arabs hope to gain by their propaganda against Israel Bluntly speaking they plan to bring about the conditions that would facilitate the destruction of the Jewish State.

The Arabs, there for aim to neutralize the impact the impact of America on the Middle East. In many ways they have turned the United States into their ally in the process of dismemberment of Israel. Let us briefly examine these three conditions and understand why their achievement is absolutely necessary before an Arab policy of eliminating Israel can hope to succeed. The Arabs have always looked at the Jews of America as allies of Israel, and it is against this alliance that the bulk of the Arab propaganda is directed. During the past fifteen years, the Jews of America have given invaluable material and political support to the State of Israel. American Jewish aid has helped make possible the absorption of over 1,000,000 immigrants in Israel, and has given impetus to her economy. The Arabs, therefore, believe that they must destroy this relationship as a precondition to destroying the state. Recognizing that such a campaign might not succeed, the Arabs have devised other means of limiting the effectiveness of the American Jew. If Israel cannot be made alien to the American Jew, then the Jew can be made alien to his non-Jewish neighbor. Isolate the Jew, and you isolate Israel; destroy Jewish prestige in America, and you destroy Israel's; weaken Jewish economic and political strength and you weaken Israel's potential to survive.

And finally, they believe that a long-range program to win wide-spread support of their policies from the American people is essential. If they can do this they will be able to prevail upon the American government to take a pro-Arab. anti-Israel position in its foreign policy. These ideas and projected goals are certainly plausible and, to a great degree, necessary, if Israel is to be destroyed with impunity.

To achieve these goals, the Arab Information Centers and the funding of Islamic studies at most major American Universities has turned a whole generation of scholars and students against Israel. School and public libraries regularly receive large amounts of unsolicited propaganda; civic, church and political clubs are treated to a host of polished Arab speakers who are able to lecture on a wide variety of subjects but always manage to direct the discussion to the Arab-Israeli conflict; hundreds of anti-Israel letters are kept flowing to large and small papers across the country.

The themes and techniques exploited in the letters, books, pamphlets and speeches follow a pattern. Virtually all Arab propaganda is based on the following postulates:

The establishment of Israel represents a great "imperialistic" injustice to the Arabs.

The Arabs of Palestine were expelled from their homes by "alien" invaders who seized their country.

Muhanimad T. Mehdi spells this out explicitly in his pamphlet The Question of Palestine:

"The question of Palestine is basically a problem of intrusion of a group of foreigners, largely Europeans, into the Arab land of Palestine, against the will of the Arab people, but with British and later American and Western support."

A wide variety of proposals, arguments, themes and accusations based on these postulates appear periodically in Arab propaganda. In all of their efforts the distinction between Zionist and Jew is blurred, although the Arabs frequently claim to have no quarrel with the Jews, but only with the Zionists. We will deal with this lack of precise distinction, when we discuss the use of anti-Semitic themes in its propaganda.

Here, then, are some examples of recurrent themes:

An \"international" Zionist (often Zionist-Jewish or Zionist-Jewish-Communist depending on the audience) conspiracy was able to take aver Palestine because:

(a) It controls the mass media in this county.

(b) It controls the wealth of this country.

(c) It controls both political parties

Israel is guilty of stealing land and property that belongs to Arabs; of military aggression; of creating tension to help it pleas for aid.

The UJA. is not a chanty; therefore contributions should not be tax-exempt.

Highly Organized, well financed "minority groups" pressure the American government to adopt programs that are supposedly in their respective private interest, but are, in fact, detrimental to the United States.

The Zionists (Jews) are, in reality, loyal to Israel, and, therefore, aliens to America.

Israel benefits from anti-Semitism in the sense that it uses it as an excuse to increase immigration and ask for more aid

Israel preaches peace, but is guilty of aggression; it desires territorial expansion.

There would be peace if Israel accepted U.N. Resolutions

American prestige in the Middle East is damaged, end Arab-American friendship is inhibited by American supporters of Zionism.

Desecration Christian and Moslem holy places.

Charges of atrocity.

Israel persecutes the Arab minority

The Jews have been worse than even the Nazis in their relations to the Arabs.

MEDIA BIAS AND THE ARAB ISRAELI CONFLICT

WORD	MEDIA DISTORTION	TRUTH
1. Palestinian	dispossessed natives	Recent arrivals land purchased
2. PLO	Palestinian repesentatives	Terrorist group
3. Hamas	Moslem religious group	Terrorist group
4. battle	Israel kills Arabs	Arabs who attacked Israelis were killed
5. Judea, Samaria and Gaza	Arab or Palestinian occupied territory	Israeli land by intern'l law
6. Arab rioter	demonstrator, protestor	Murderer and attempted murderer
7. peace negotiation	"territories for peace"	Ceding territory makes makes Israel more vulnerable and increases likelihood of war
8. Jerusalem	occupied Arab Jerusalem	Jerusalem has always been Jewish
9. human rights	Israel violates Arab rights	Israelis don't lie down and die without a fight
10. Zionism	racisim	The Jewish People's liberation movement- nationalist struggle

MEDIA METHODS OF DISTORTION

1. Double standard
2. Excessive focus on Israel
3. Anti-semitism
4. Unfair comparisons to Nazis
5. Code words
6. Twisted logic
7. Lack of context
8. Use of false history

ARAB PROPAGANDA & COMBATING IT

IT IS REAL COMBAT
FOR THE HEARTS AND MINDS OF AMERICANS

1. False peace offers--support from Jewish left
2. Arab-Israeli Conflict narrowed and changed to Palestinian-Israeli Conflict
3. Arab refugees kept until they became Palestinian national movement
4. Re-writing history to make propaganda
5. Portraying themselves as victims instead of aggressors--appeals for sympathy
6. Use of anti-semitism--blood libel--conspiracy theory
7. Wild charges--lies, the bigger the better
8. Distortion of human rights
9. Murder and threats to intimidate journalists
10. Comparing Israelis/Jews to Nazis

IMPORTANT NOTES ON HASBARA

PART ONE: THE HASBARA ADS

1. Repetition is the key to success of this campaign. Just like advertising in general, your message must be presented at least 20 times to be cognitively assimilated by the target audience.

2. A pattern of repetition and presentation might be the following. (This is just a suggestion): Publish ads in this order: 1,2, 3, 1, 2, 3, 4, 5, 6, 4,5, 6, 1,2, 3, 4, 5, 6, >>Go through the whole sequence of 10 ads with this pattern. And then repeat on a continuous basis until your goal is reached

3. No more than a week should pass between ads. Better twice a week.

4. All major media should be utilized

PART TWO: PRESS RELEASES

1. The ads above are for correcting historical myths. There is also a major role for daily press releases.

2. The Arabs have launched a massive press release campaign that result is lies and slander against Israel **EVERY DAY**. Israel must fight back.

3. The first step is to eliminate the Israel' reluctance to criticize harshly the PA, Oslo, US, Europe, Arab states.

4. The gloves must come off. Daily (or twice daily) press releases should offer a continuous stream of criticism for the parties damaging Israeli interests.

5. Remember: *the squeaking wheel gets the grease*. Arafat screams at the drop of a hat, often based on lies, and his words are picked up by every major media in the world.

6. **He who speaks first gets attention.** Your staff must prepared to be first on a 24 hour basis in the press release battle.

[**Editorial Note:** It is time to stop calling for progress in the 'peace process' (Oslo). We all know it will never work, Arafat will never fulfill his obligations and incitement against Israel by the PA will never stop. No more time is needed to **PROVE** this. It makes the Israeli government look foolish to keep proclaiming loyalty to an agreement that **CAN NOT** work and is a great danger to Israeli security and survival.]

December 22, 1992

The expulsion of Islamic militants brought on an orgy of media sympathy.

Court of last resort...

...ARMED KIBBUTZNIKS GUN DOWN OUR "FREEDOM FIGHTERS" BEFORE WE CAN GET TO THE CHILDREN'S HOUSE...

...CIVIL GUARDS IN NAHARIYA STOP US BEFORE WE CAN GET TO THE SCHOOL...

ISRAELI JETS BOMB AND STRAFE OUR HEADQUARTERS IN SOUTHERN LEBANON...

WE'VE GOT ONLY ONE CARD LEFT TO PLAY IF WE WANT TO CONTINUE KILLING ISRAELI KIDS!

A DIRECT APPEAL TO WORLD PUBLIC OPINION?

EXACTLY!

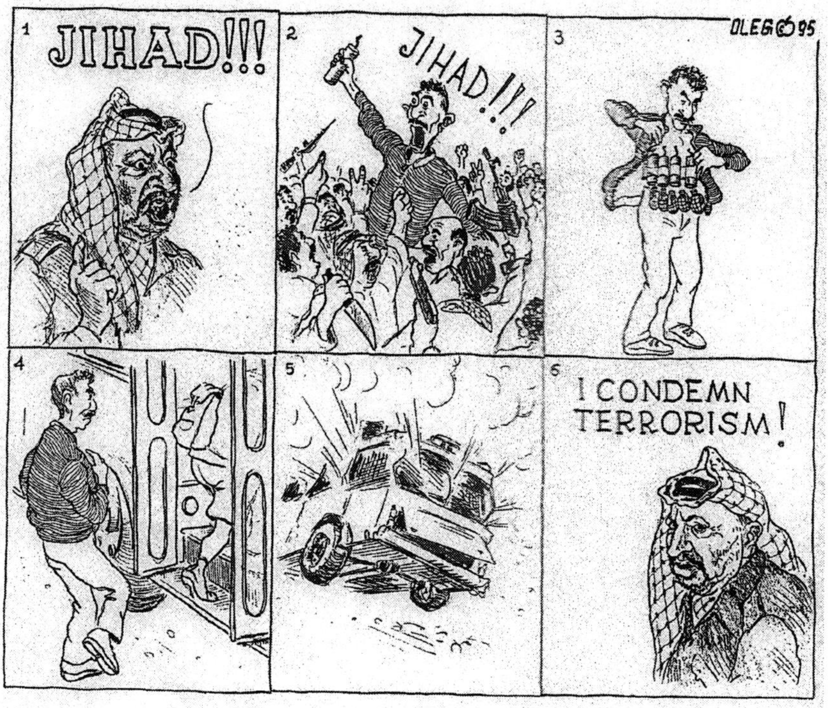
1
JIHAD!!!
2
JIHAD!!!
OLEG©95
3
4
5
6
I CONDEMN TERRORISM!

ARAB PROPAGANDISTS JOIN FORCES WITH ANTI-SEMITES

By BERNARD J. SHAPIRO

"It is time that Americans realize that these teeming masses of Zionists who infest their cities and sit astride the arteries of their commerce are, in every sense of the word, aliens."

The above quotation, in its passion and paranoid ring could have come from the pen of anyone of our local hatemongers, whose rhetoric we have come to know well over the past half century. Yet, these words are neither the work of a professional rabble-rouser, nor of a right-wing extremist; rather they come from a presumably scholarly work written by Musa Khuri, an Arab college professor.

This points up two rather disturbing realities: That Arab propaganda has broadened its area of attack to Jewish populations outside of Israel; it has, in effect, joined forces with local anti-Semites. Secondly, this propaganda apparatus, sanctioned, as it is, by duly recognized governments which together form an influential political power bloc, has lent these local anti-Semitic efforts the aura of respectability.

Bernard J. Shapiro is a former member of SZO and is now studying in Israel.

Arab propaganda constitutes a formidable threat to the Jewish people. This essay will focus upon the Arab propaganda effort in this country first by examining its history, institutions and aspirations, and secondly, by analyzing the techniques and themes that it uses to achieve its goals. Finally, we will attempt to measure the effectiveness of this endeavor.

Ironically, the initial inspiration for this effort was stimulated by the success of the Zionist movement in this area. For while the Arabs used political obstructionism and violence to oppose the creation of a Jewish State, the Zionists built up a propaganda apparatus that succeeded in convincing the majority of Americans of the efficacy and rightness of a Jewish State in Palestine. The Zionist diplomatic victory in securing U.N. partition of Palestine, convinced the Arabs of the necessity of attracting favorable public opinion.

Arab propaganda first entered the country in an organized fashion after World War II, when several of the newly liberated Middle Eastern nations formed the Arab League, binding themselves together politically for the first time in modern history.

A year later, the member states of the League established the first Arab office of Information in Washington, D.C. The Institute of Arab-American Affairs, founded in the same year, supposedly to promote Arab-American cultural exchange and friendship, was revealed to be concerned primarily with heading off American support of a Jewish State.

While national rivalries between the Arab states prevented anything like a coordinated propaganda campaign, the cumulative amount of propaganda increased as each state embarked upon its own campaign.

After the creation of the State of Israel, the Arab League Information Offices began to take on a more professional look. This re-organization was achieved during the years 1948-1955, due, primarily, to the efforts of Abdul Rahman Azzam Pasha, then Secretary General of the Arab League. He came to America in 1950 to stir up support for a unified propaganda effort. In January, 1955, the new Arab Information Center was opened in New York with a budget of $400,000. It set out to do the job prescribed by Azzam Pasha; and was headed by the former Egyptian Ambassador to the U.S., Kamil Rahim.

What do the Arabs hope to gain by this great effort and expense? Bluntly speaking—to bring about *conditions that would facilitate the destruction of the State of Israel.* They concentrate most of their propaganda in the United States, because they feel that this country *was* the greatest single influence that contributed to the creation of Israel and that it still *is* the major force standing in the way of Israel's destruction.

The Arabs, therefore, aim to neutralize the impact of America on the Middle East and, if possible, to draw her over to their side. This requires that the propaganda apparatus achieve the following effects: To drive a wedge between Israel and the American Jewish community; to alienate the Jew from the rest of America, and destroy his political and economic strength; and to convince the American people, and through them the American government, that it must adopt a pro-Arab, anti-Israel foreign policy.

Let us briefly examine these three conditions and understand why their achievement is absolutely necessary before an Arab policy of eliminating Israel can hope to succeed. The Arabs have always looked at the Jews of America as allies of Israel, and it it against this alliance that the bulk of the Arab propaganda is directed. During the past fifteen years, the Jews of America have given invaluable material and political support to the State of Israel. American Jewish aid has helped make possible the absorption of over 1,000,000 immigrants in Israel, and has given impetus to her economy. The Arabs, therefore, believe that they must destroy this relationship as a precondition to destroying the state.

Recognizing that such a campaign might not succeed, the Arabs have devised other means of limiting the effectiveness of the American Jew. If Israel can not be made alien to the American Jew, then the Jew can be made alien to his non-Jewish neighbor. Isolate the Jew, and you isolate Israel; destroy Jewish prestige in America, and you destroy Israel's; weaken Jewish economic and political strength and you weaken Israel's potential to survive.

And finally, they believe that a long-range program to win widespread support of their policies from the American people is essential. If they can do this they will be able to prevail upon the American government to take a pro-Arab, anti-Israel position in its foreign policy.

These ideas and projected goals are certainly plausible and, to a great degree, necessary, if Israel is to be destroyed with impunity.

To achieve these goals, the Arab Information Centers have published voluminous material and have distributed it extensively. School and public libraries regularly receive large amounts of unsolicited propaganda; civic, church and political clubs are treated to a host of polished Arab speakers who are able to lecture on a wide variety of subjects but always manage to direct the discussion to the Arab-Israeli conflict; hundreds of anti-Israel letters are kept flowing to large and small papers across the country.

The themes and techniques exploited in the letters, books, pamphlets and speeches follow a pattern. Virtually all Arab propaganda is based on the following postulates:

The establishment of Israel represents a great "imperialistic" injustice to the Arabs.

The Arabs of Palestine were expelled from their homes by "alien" invaders who seized their country.

Muhammad T. Mehdi spells this out explicitly in his recent pamphlet *The Question of Palestine:*

"*The question of Palestine is basically a problem of intrusion of a group of foreigners, largely Europeans, into the Arab land of Palestine, against the will of the Arab people, but with British and later American and Western support.*"

A wide variety of proposals, arguments, themes and accusations based on these postulates appear periodically in Arab propaganda. In all of their efforts the distinction between Zionist and Jew is blurred, although the Arabs frequently claim to have no quarrel with the Jews, but only with the Zionists. We will deal with this lack of precise distinction, when we discuss the use of anti-Semitic themes in its propaganda.

Here, then, are some examples of recurrent themes:

— *An "international" Zionist (often Zionist-Jewish or Zionist-Jewish-Communist depending on the audience) conspiracy was able to take over Palestine because:*

a. *It controls the mass media in this country.*

b. *It controls the wealth of this country.*

c. *It controls both political parties.*

— *Arabs never wished close relationship with Communist countries, but were forced to do so because of the creation of Israel, and the Western role in bringing it about.*

— *Israel is guilty of stealing land and property that belongs to Arabs; of military agression; of creating tension to help its pleas for aid.*

— *The U.J.A. is not a charity; therefore contributions should not be tax-exempt.*

- *Highly organized, well financed "minority groups" pressure the American government to adopt programs that are supposedly in their respective private interest, but are, in fact, detrimental to the United States.*
- *The Zionists (Jews) are, in reality, loyal to Israel, and, therefore, aliens to America.*
- *Communism is not only legal, but popular in Israel. This constitutes a Communist menace in the Middle East.*
- *Israel benefits from anti-Semitism—in the sense that it uses it as an excuse to increase immigration and ask for more aid.*
- *Israel preaches peace, but is guilty of agression; it desires territorial expansion.*
- *There would be peace if Israel accepted U.N. Resolutions.*
- *American prestige in the Middle East is damaged, and Arab-American friendship is inhibited by American supporters of Zionism.*
- *Desecration of Christian and Moslem holy places.*
- *Charges of atrocity.*
- *Israel persecutes the Arab minority.*
- *The Jews have been worse than even the Nazis in their relations to the Arabs.*

While this list could certainly be extended, it does include the most frequently-used arguments of Arab propaganda.

Direct collusion, involving payoffs and exchanges of material, has been uncovered and published by the Anti-Defamation League in its recent book on the exploitation of Anti-Semitism for political purposes, *Cross-Currents*. The book gives a fascinating account of how Gerald L. K. Smith receives large gifts from Arab sources for publishing stories on the "Palestine question" in his publication, *The Cross and the Flag*; and how Frank Briton supports himself by rewriting Arab material for American audiences, and "selling" his own works, such as "Behind Communism," "Atom Treason" and "Hollywood Treason" to Arab publishers for distribution in the Middle East.

Publishers of other right-wing extremist magazines like Conde McGinley *(Common Sense)*, Gerald Winrod *(Defender)* and the *American Mercury* have used their vehicles for the vilest kind of Arab Propaganda. And the publications of the American Council for Judaism—*Jewish Newsletter* and *Issues*—have, in recent years, aimed at alienating Jewish readers from the State of Israel.

Joe Alex Morris Jr., in an article that appeared in the New York Herald Tribune, reveals that American bigots not only distribute Arab propaganda, but also supply Anti-Semitic material to the Arabs. He writes:

"*Spreaders of racial and religious bigotry in the United States are among the prime suppliers of propaganda to the Arabs in their political and propagandistic war against Israel.*"

The Arab states utilize anti-Semitic material in their propaganda because it seems to be the most effective way of alienating—and intimidating—the American Jew. This goal can best be realized by utilizing the reservoir of prejudice in this country. It is really quite simple: If the policies and ideas of a Gerald L. K. Smith become widely accepted, then Congress will be forced to pass anti-Jewish legislation and adopt an anti-Zionist foreign policy. Smith in his book, *Christian Nationalism Vs. Jew-Communist Internationalism* alternates the term "Jew-Communist" with "Jew-Zionist" in various chapters.

Thus, Smith's readers are prone to accept the Arab conception of the Zionist conspiracy—that took over Palestine and plans to take over other Arab nations and, finally, the world.

Here is how the Arabs take this anti-Semitic theme and exploit it for their purposes: Haj Amin el-Husseini, former Mufti of Jerusalem, Grand Mufti of Palestine, Hitler's Middle Eastern propaganda specialist during the war and head of the "Arab Republic of Palestine" in exile, declared, recently, in Baghdad:

> "The Palestine tragedy is unequalled in history. The Zionist-Imperialistic plot against Palestine was most inhumane and base. World Judaism plans to take over most of the Arab countries to fulfill its so-called historical dream of a homeland between the Nile and Ephrates. The Imperialistic-Jewish plot is not aimed at Palestine only..."

It seems clear from what has been said that an unholy alliance exists between native bigots and Arab propagandists in their aim of destroying the Jewish position in America.

The third goal of Arab propaganda is to secure grass-roots support from the American people. It hopes to achieve this in a number of ways: Exploitation of organizations "devoted" to explaining Arab cultures to Americans; "service" organizations, such as The American Friends of the Middle East (financed by the large oil companies) which purport to be aimed, solely, at promoting Arab-American friendship; through student exchange and similar programs; personal indoctrination of individuals by carefully selected Arab students (over 5,000 in this country).

The effectiveness of this ubiquitous propaganda machine seems to be increasing as the skill and experience of its director improves. Today the Arabs are not as easily caught in compromising positions with native hate-mongers as they were in previous years. The tone of the propaganda has become less vile, subtler, psychologically oriented. And yet, the factor which impedes its progress the most is the overall decline of bigotry in this country. The A.D.L. has discovered that where reservoirs of prejudice exist, they are re-enforced by the introduction of Arab propaganda. It can only be hoped that with the improvements in the educative process, communication and means of world travel, that there will be a decline in prejudice, and a concomitant decline in the effectiveness of Arab propaganda.

EDITOR'S NOTE:

While this article was written in 1965, it still accurately reflects the history and main principles of Arab propaganda. Since 1967 that propaganda has changed to emphasize "Palestinian self determination", Palestinian "rights" and to enlist the suport of "human rights" and leftist groups.

It is improtant to note that the Arab countries, especially Saudi Arabia, Syria, and Iran are still the the world's largest publisher's of "hard core" anti-Semitic literature like the PROTOCOLS OF THE ELDERS OF ZION. Syria's Defense Minister recently wrote a book to prove that accusations of "blood libel" against the Jews were true. That is that "Jews kill Christians, especially children, to use their blood in the preparation of matza during Passover."

CHAPTER TWELVE: FREEMAN CENTER EDITORIALS AND PRAYERS

Sometimes I just felt like speaking out on specific issues in the news and once a year at Rosh Hashona (Jewish New Year) I have issues note and prayers for the reader. I hope they will be meaningful to you as well.

A FEW NOTES FROM YOUR EDITOR

The Freeman Center has a vital role to play in the future battles to preserve Eretz Yisrael. With your help we will fight the distorted media, inform the Jewish community and defend Israel in the public arena.

Are all of you as disgusted as me at the way Netanyahu's victory was trashed by the electronic and print media? I have coined a new term for such commentary. I call it linguistic terrorism. Instead of suicide bombs, they put the word hard line in front of Bibi's name. Dedication to Jewish Jerusalem is hard line. Demanding security for Israel is pursuing the policies of fear. Netanyahu will be judged on how he fulfills the Oslo Accord. Was Arafat ever so judged? Is he fulfilling his commitments? Of course not!

James Baker says that Bibi will be judged on how he manages the American-Israel relationship. We know what he means. Why doesn't he just say instead: " . . . how well he licks the Secretary of State's boots?"

To all of the columnists, journalists, diplomats and government bureaucrats, please listen carefully:

Israel is a sovereign Jewish country. Jerusalem is its capital. Its new Zionist/Religious/Pro-Security government will be much less tolerant of your interference in its internal affairs. And for your information, internal means from the Jordan River to the Mediterranean Sea. Jews can and will live anywhere in Eretz Yisrael. No one will pay attention to your complaints about "settlements." We are going to call them Jewish communities. I realize that many of you live in neighborhoods that exclude Jews. There will be no such neighborhoods in Israel.

And to our good American friends: It is time you understood that Israel is the best security bargain you could possibly have. Your aid is certainly appreciated, but this is not a one-way street. Israel's contribution to American security is immense, though unpublicized for fear of offending Arab sensibilities. So please save us from having to ignore any threats of cutting off foreign aid if Israel doesn't toe the line like a banana republic. And it is time to free Jonathan Pollard, exactly like Israel has freed dozens of CIA operatives caught in Israel. He has suffered enough.

Bernard J. Shapiro

The Netanyahu Connection:

In 1980, during my years as owner of House of Books (Houston's only Jewish bookstore) a handsome young medical student asked to order a new book of letters by Jonathan Netanyahu, fallen hero of Entebbe. When I produced a copy, entitled: *SELF-PORTRAIT OF A HERO The Letters of Jonathan Netanyahu* (1963-1976), he was quite surprised and identified himself as a cousin of Jonathan's studying at the Texas Medical Center. For the next several months, he returned to the store often, ordering dozens of copies to send to friends and relatives. His name was Gil, and now I realize how much he looked like Bibi. Also, I have quoted some of the brilliant passages from Jonathan's letters in several of my articles.

When Benjamin Netanyahu's book, *A PLACE AMONG THE NATIONS*, was released in 1993, I eagerly read it. I found the book exceptional in its understanding of Jewish history and in its treatment of Israel's unique destiny. I published a glowing review in the Jewish Herald-Voice as well as giving many book reviews in the community. When the Freeman Center was founded, Bibi's book was the first ordered for our book list. At our founding fundraiser, a copy was given to every contributor. Since then we have sold hundreds of copies. I was so impressed that I wrote Netanyahu and asked him to be "Honorary President" of the Freeman Center. He declined due to other commitments.

After the disaster of Oslo became apparent, Ben Ronn, a cousin of Bibi's and a successful Houston businessman, asked me to help him form a bi-partisan group called JEWS CONCERNED FOR ISRAEL'S FUTURE. The group never took off, but Ben joined the Freeman Center and helped to strengthen our organization.

Some Suggested Do's & Don'ts For Netanyahu's New Government:

Do restore pride and dignity to Israel's foreign policy.
Do restore deterrence to the Israel Defense Forces.
Do crush any resumption of the intifada.
Do arrest all members of the Palestine National Council guilty of crimes of violence.
Do restore Zionism and Jewish pride to Israel's school system.

Do rid the media of leftist jerks and create a vigorous information system with an aim to reform and not propagandize.

Do demand freedom for Jonathan Pollard.

Do live up to your campaign promise to free the economy, reduce taxes, and sell off all government industries not connected to security.

Do put Natan Sharansky in charge of immigration and absorption.

Do take politics out of the Israel Defense Forces and the Security Forces, even if this means removing leftist officers of high rank.

Do respect the civil and human rights of Israel's Arab inhabitants but . . . .

Don't give them the political right to change Israel from a Jewish State to a state with a lot of Jews.

Don't go to Egypt to talk to Mubarak. Let him come to you.

Do support the efforts of Dr. Paul Eidelberg in his quest to create an Israeli constitution that protects the Jewish character of Israel.

Don't jump every time the American State Department acts upset with your actions.

Do annex all of YESHA and re-affirm the Golan Annexation.

Do pass a law requiring a two-thirds majority of the Knesset and consent of the Prime Minister to alter above annexations.

Do vigorously settle Jews in Jerusalem and extend its municipal boundaries to Maale Adumim.

Do carry out the plan to add 500,000 Jews to YESHA.

Do, as a first step, open all completed apartments for purchase and occupation.

And finally, do restore Jewish rights to the Temple Mount, including the right to prayer.

Bernard J. Shapiro

THE MACCABEAN SPEAKS

An Interview With The Maccabean (March 1997)

On Syria, Lebanon, PLO & Other Security Issues

SYRIA

Reporter: Israel is facing many serious security problems with Syria, Lebanon, Iran and the PLO. Tell us how you would negotiate with Syria, for example.

Maccabean: The first thing I would do is stop talking about the Golan as primarily a security issue. I would repeat often that it is Israeli territory with a long Jewish history, which also happens to be vital for Israeli security and water supplies.

Reporter: The Syrians are demanding that you agree to withdraw from the Golan before peace talks can begin.

Maccabean: It is true that this is a Syrian demand. I would present the following Israeli demands:

1. Syria must relinquish all claims of sovereignty on the Golan as compensation for the pain, suffering and loss of life they caused Israel during their occupation of it.

2. Since peace agreements with non-democratic countries are useless, we would insist on full democratization in Syria before beginning negotiations. This would naturally include full civil and human rights for its citizens, including minorities.

3. We would certainly insist on Syria breaking ties with terrorist organizations like Hizbullah and terrorist states like Iran, Libya, Iraq, and the Sudan.

4. Syria would have to withdraw its occupation troops from Lebanon and allow a true representative government to develop there.

5. And finally, we would demand that Syria stop producing and selling drugs and counterfeit money on the world markets.

Reporter: Those are very tough demands. How can you ever make peace with Syria if those are your pre-conditions?

Maccabean: These are the pre-conditions that make peace with Syria possible. Anything less is foolishness.

LEBANON

Reporter: Lebanon is intimately connected to the question of Syria. How would you resolve the seemingly endless Israeli losses in that troubled country?

Maccabean: The biggest problem for Israel in Lebanon is its self-inflicted restriction on the use of military power. Israel is like a giant, fighting pygmies and then deciding to tie one hand behind its back and wearing a blindfold on one eye and perhaps even hobbling one leg. There is one essential principle of military success and that is to use overwhelming force at a speed that keeps the enemy off balance and vulnerable. The defensive limited war being fought by the IDF in Lebanon is a recipe for failure. It plays into the hands of the enemy by fighting the type of war they are best prepared to face. The United Nations and United States connections serve only to limit Israel's freedom of action.

Reporter: How would you fight this war in Lebanon?

Maccabean: The first thing I would do is reverse the political losses Israel suffered since Operation Accountability and the Grapes of Wrath.

1. This would be done by a continuous massive artillery and aerial bombardment on all areas associated with the Hizbullah. Ignore all international repercussions, vigorously proclaiming the right of self-defense. All monitoring organizations should be ignored and renounced.

2. Syrian bases in Lebanon that have supplied the terrorists should be destroyed.

3. Israeli troops should clear the area up to the Litani of all hostile forces.

4. While not extending the security zone permanently, Israel should announce that the whole of southern Lebanon from the Litani to the Israeli border is an area of operations and a free fire zone. Israel should further declare that no normal life will take place until the Hizbullah are disarmed and expelled.

5. Syrian economic interests in Lebanon will be destroyed, including the drug producing areas of the Bekka Valley.

6. It should be made clear that *new* rules apply to Lebanon. Rather, all parties should know that there are **NO RULES** that limit Israeli action there. Lebanon is a jungle. Let Israeli soldiers march into that jungle exclaiming: *"Yea though I walk through the Valley of the Shadow of Death, I will fear no evil, because the L-rd is with me and anyway I am the meanest SOB in the valley."*

Reporter: It sounds like you are against the traditional policy of "restraint" in the IDF.

Maccabean: That policy may have been important in the past, but today we face a barbarian enemy who sees our restraint as weakness, making him more aggressive. He must be disabused of that notion.

PLO

Reporter: What do you think of Netanyahu's handling of the Palestinian negotiations properly?

Maccabean: Let me make one thing perfectly clear: Oslo is a death sentence for Israel. To ask if Bibi is handling the negotiations with the Palestinians properly is to engage in an oxymoronic fantasy. There are no "good" negotiations with Arafat. The PLO makes no secret of its intention to replace Israel from *"the river to the sea."* To negotiate is to play their game. And it is a **zero-sum game**: what they gain for Palestine is subtracted from Israel.

Reporter: But aren't you ignoring the political reality on the ground? Can you really turn the Oslo clock back?

Maccabean: History is full of territorial and political reversals. Just look at Europe during the last 150 years. For Israel to survive, Oslo must go. This will mean a war with the Palestinians and maybe some Arab countries. It is the price of survival. Freedom is won with the blood of patriots but must be preserved with the blood of our children. It is an illusion to believe that we can survive in this hostile region without fighting cruel wars. Appeasement only makes those inevitable wars more difficult to win. Even in Biblical times, the Israelites faced constant conflict.

Reporter: What about the reactions, indeed the outrage, from America and Europe?

Maccabean: We will have to accept some economic discomfort and political isolation. But this is the price of freedom of action to preserve our country. Our consular officials will need to earn their pay explaining our positions to the world. Looked at logically it should not be that hard. After all, the previous Labor government made an agreement with a mass murderer, who planned to destroy us, and now we have come to our senses. There is a large reservoir of good will for Israel in America. Millions of Christians and Jews are fundamentally on our side. Properly guided they can ease the damage from our new policy.

JERUSALEM

Reporter: Jerusalem has been in the news lately with regards to new Jewish housing at Har Homa. The Americans have expressed dissatisfaction with not only housing but new roads around the city. What do you think?

Maccabean: First let the Israeli government complain to the US about the highways near Washington and housing projects there, etc. Let the Americans realize how ridiculous this sounds. The Israeli government needs to rid itself of the idea that America should either be consulted or give its approval for any Israeli action. Enough is enough! American diplomats like Dennis Ross and Martin Indyk should be politely informed that their help in making decisions is no longer desired. My plan for Jerusalem:

1. Rapid building in all sectors of the city to increase not only the numbers of Jews but the prosperity of the city.

2. Close all PLO offices in the city (as opposed to just saying that you are going to do that).

3. Remove the Moslem Waqf from control of the Temple Mount and encourage Jewish worship there in areas not forbidden by the Torah. Remove all evidence of Palestinian control on the Temple Mount.

4. Complete all roads necessary to connect Jerusalem to all areas of the country.

5. Annex Bethlehem and all territory as far east as Maale Adumin to a greater Jerusalem.

6. Evict all PA police and security personnel from Jerusalem.

7. Take over all educational institutions and introduce positive pro-Israel, Zionist courses in the curricula of all schools, including Arab ones.

UNCONVENTIONAL WEAPONS

Reporter: Before we close, let me ask you about the growing threat of chemical, biological and nuclear weapons from Syria, Iran, and Iraq. How would you deal with this threat?

Maccabean: Preemption, preemption, and preemption. Anything else is a foolhardy gamble with Israeli lives.

TERRORISM

Reporter: Has terrorism become an existential threat to Israel, and how should we deal with it?

Maccabean: Contrary to what many experts believe, terrorism has, in fact, become an existential threat to Israeli survival. This is for two important reasons. First, it exposes Israel's rapidly declining level of deterrence vis-a-vis the Arabs. This leads to an increased frequency and seriousness of attacks. Secondly, the repeated assaults on the Israeli people have a deleterious effect on the health of the nation. This process is much like a living organism that is attacked repeatedly by infection, suffers a failure of its immune system and dies. The Chinese call it the *"death of a thousand cuts."* No single terrorist attack will bring down the State of Israel, but repeated attacks weaken morale and the will to fight. Oslo is the perfect example of the policies of a nation that has lost the will to fight, to survive.

Reporter: How did this terrorist threat develop?

Maccabean: Terrorism derives among other things from the decline in Israeli deterrence. Unfortunately, Israelis are daily witnessing the consequences of ten years of declining deterrence vis-a-vis its Arab population. In 1987, the intifada presented Israel with a new challenge. It was a new kind of war, but with the same aim of driving the Israelis out of their country. The Israelis fought the intifada with many handicaps, not the least of which were their own rules of conduct. Israeli soldiers failed to cope with attacks by teenage Arab boys. Over the course of several years, the Arabs learned that the soldiers would not aggressively retaliate for their attacks. They became emboldened.

The Jews living in Judea, Samaria, and Gaza showed great fortitude, enduring thousands of attacks and still tripling their numbers. The serious security failure developed as Arabs became accustomed to attacking Jews and Israeli soldiers. By trying to remain humane in the face of massive attacks, Israel emboldened the Arabs to more and more attacks. Throwing concrete boulders, Molotov cocktails, and then using firearms at Israelis became the norm of behavior among the Arabs. The Israeli government allowed its citizens to be attacked solely because they were Jews. In no other country of the world would such a policy be tolerated.

In 1991, the Persian Gulf War, with its SCUD attacks on Israel, further undermined Israeli deterrence. Having to depend on United States Forces instead of her own had a deleterious effect on Israeli self-confidence. It is notable that the Arab population of Judea and Samaria danced on their on their roofs and cried, *"**Gas the Jews**"* as the **SCUD**s headed for Tel Aviv.

The self-assurance of the Israelis also declined immensely as a result of their cowering in sealed rooms during the missile attacks.

Israel, with its powerful military and independent citizens, had always been an affront to Moslems everywhere. Therefore, Jews should be made subservient, weak and dependent on the approval of their Moslem overlords. Peres understood that Israel in its present borders was too strong to be destroyed. He also understood that the Arabs were offended that they could not destroy Israel within its defensible borders. The Peres solution seems to involve making Israel weak, creating a PLO state, and generally groveling before Arab rulers. Such an emasculated ***dhimmis-like*** Israel, would now win the approval of the Islamic world. Labor, the US and Europe would call it "peace." Some would call it appeasement. Some would cheer. Some would protest. Freeman Center members (and real Zionists) see the Peres/PLO (and now Netanyahu) plan as a nightmare and pray that Israel's leaders will come to their senses and return to a policy of deterrence, security and defense of Israeli interests.

Reporter: But how would you stop terrorism?

Maccabean: Terrorism is not an act of nature like an earthquake. It can be fought and controlled if there is the political will to do so. The key is the political will to fight a tough and dirty battle. Netanyahu doesn't have that will today, but Israeli leaders in the past have shown us how it can be done.

Terrorist groups like Hamas or Islamic Jihad operate within a community of supporters who supply them with weapons, safe houses, intelligence, and new recruits for their units. The first step in counteracting a terrorist movement is to infiltrate its organizational structure. For this you need members of the community willing to help you for money, protection or even conviction. Israel's General Security Services (GSS) successfully infiltrated the major terrorist organizations in the past. This has always been the quintessential prerequisite to successful military operations against those terrorists.

When Israel signed the Oslo agreement with the PLO in September of 1993, it agreed to share intelligence with them and to cooperate with them in the preservation of security for both Jews and Arabs. In the course of that intelligence sharing, Israel revealed to the PLO the names of Arabs in Judea, Samaria, and Gaza who had aided them in their battle against terrorism. The PLO then directed its police and security forces to murder all of these Arabs as "**collaborators with the enemy**." Thus, the eyes and ears of Israeli intelligence were destroyed.

The Oslo deal signed by the PLO also called for the extradition of Arabs guilty of crimes in Israel, to be returned to Israel for trial. The PLO was to crack down on all terrorist groups within the area of its jurisdiction (Gaza and Jericho). The Oslo script was not followed. PLO controlled areas became "safe havens" for terrorist groups to organize and plan their murderous operations. The Israeli Defense Forces (IDF) was effectively banned from those areas and Hamas members could stroll the streets of Gaza unmolested with their machine guns. The PLO police refused to perform any police function in relation to terrorists, devoting themselves to civil problems like robbery and rape.

It is now three and a half years since Oslo, and the terrorist groups have grown and prospered in the friendly atmosphere created by the Rabin/Peres/Netanyahu government's pursuit of "peace." It is true that a dedicated suicide bomber is extremely difficult to stop. This is the very reason that a proper security approach requires destroying the environment in which suicide bombers are nurtured.

There are no magic solutions, but here is what needs to be done to restore security to the Israeli population:

1. The Oslo PLO/Israel deal must be cancelled.

2. The IDF will have to destroy all terrorist bases in the PA areas. Heavy artillery and air strikes should be used to devastate and paralyze the population. An escape route into Sinai should be opened for refugees.

3. A new network of Israeli agents will have to be built up. (This takes time.)

4. All Hamas social institutions should be destroyed.

5. The use of explosive sniffing dogs should be authorized.

6. The borders of Gaza should be closed, with no Arab workers crossing into Israel. This should be permanent. It should cause great economic hardship in Gaza and eventually lead to the emigration of Arabs from there.

7. Issue the following new security rule: Soldiers and Jewish civilians are allowed to shoot to kill anyone attacking them (including attacks with any object larger than a grain of sand). No qualifications, no prosecutions.

8. All terrorists guilty of murder or attempt to murder should be executed, with their bodies cremated to prevent their graves from becoming sites of veneration. Executions should be performed quickly to prevent international outcry and terrorist attempts to free the condemned.

9. All Arab prisoners that were released early should be rearrested and jailed or given the choice of leaving Israel for good.

These are tough actions, but they will work. There is no way to fight terrorism with "kid gloves." If you are not willing to get "down and dirty" with them, they will win. The terrorist has no guilt like some Jews. His motivation is clear, and in the case of the suicide bomber, he believes paradise awaits him.

Reporter: And finally, how would you rate the new Likud Prime Minister Benjamin Netanyahu?

Maccabean: He has been more than a great disappointment to the security-minded Israeli voter. The majority voted for him in an effort to rid Israel of the disaster of Oslo inflicted by the previous Labor government. Many from the Religious/Zionist sector of the population voted for him with the fond hope of restoring Jewish pride and Jewish values to the country. Both of these groups have been traumatized by Bibi's reversal of positions on everything important to them, from Hebron to Jerusalem. It is as if Bibi was a "**Manchurian Candidate**," secretly programmed for a different (leftist) agenda following election. His actions have revealed a contempt for the voters who put him in office. But worse still, those actions reveal that his security concepts are similar to the self-destructive Labor/Meretz/Arab alliance that brought us the catastrophe of Oslo. Just as Labor was brought down by the National Camp, Bibi will have to be replaced by someone true to the principles of Zionism, security, Judaism, and **Eretz Yisrael.**

We should all pray that **HaShem** will deliver us from the false leaders that afflict us.

Reporter: Thank you for taking the time for this important interview.

Bernard J. Shapiro

Freeman Center Statement on Arab Violence

(September 30, 1996)

The Freeman Center views the Arab violence against the Jewish community of Israel and its Holy Places as nothing less than a 20th century pogrom. Only this time there is a difference: The Jewish community has the Iron Fist of Zahal (the Israel Defense Forces) to protect them from the murderous mob. We offer our heartfelt condolences to the soldiers and civilians who have died in this violence perpetuated and incited by Arafat and the PLO.

The Freeman Center makes the following observations and recommendations:

1. This violence was orchestrated to diminish the Israeli claim to Jerusalem. Therefore, the Israeli government must move quickly to reinforce is sovereignty in the whole Jerusalem area. This means:

    A. The expulsion of the PLO police units from the city
    B. The removal of all PLO offices and officials from the city including its Wakf officials
    C. Annexing the area to the east of Jerusalem as far as Maale Adumim to its municipal borders
    D. Massive Jewish housing in the eastern portion of the city
    E. The prosecution of Islamic clerics guilty of incitement to violence against Jews
    F. Assertion of the Jewish right to pray on the Temple Mount

2. The Freeman Center calls for the foundation of 14 new Jewish communities in YESHA to be named after the Israeli soldiers who bravely gave their lives defending Jews in the recent violence.

3. The Freeman Center believes that it was a mistake for Netanyahu to agree to a summit in Washington next week. Such a meeting will have the following negative effects:

A. It creates a tremendous opportunity for pressure on Israel to make concessions to Arafat.

B. It creates the appearance of moral equivalence between Arafat and Netanyahu. That has the effect of equating the Jews who were attacked and defended themselves with the mobs that attacked them. Murderer and victim should never be equated.

C. Natanyahu cannot expect anything like a fair hearing in Washington. Lies will be equated with truth. Israel's sovereignty in Jerusalem will be disputed along with Israel's right to take even minimal actions in its capital.

4. The Freeman Center believes, however, that Netanyahu is tremendously talented and is the best Prime Minister Israel ever had when it comes to dealing with the Americans. In light of the above, we recommend the following:

A. Netanyahu should come to the summit with a list of DEMANDS and not come to Washington as a defendant in the dock. Offense is the best defense. Some possible demands:

a. Arafat must publicly condemn violence.
b. Arafat must apologize for the behavior of his police force and his fellow Arabs.
c. Arafat must turn over to Israel for prosecution all of his police who opened fire on Israelis.
d. Arafat must comply with all provisions of the Oslo Accord, including extradition of the 20-odd terrorist murderers he is currently harboring in PA territory despite Israel's legal extradition requests.

B. Netanyahu must vigorously defend Israeli actions in Jerusalem and use the opportunity to educate the American public on the Jewish history of Jerusalem. He should also explain that Jerusalem is not a Holy Islamic city and not even mentioned in the Koran. He should explain that the Islamic sites were put on the Temple Mount for the express purpose of defaming the Jewish people and defiling their Holy Place. At the time, the Moslem world was militarily supreme in Jerusalem and the Jews could do nothing. Today Israel is supreme and need not grovel before a terrorist like Arafat.

5. The Freeman Center believes that the massive media distortion in this country can be traced to latent anti-Semitism. The distortions were very blatant and include the following outrageous actions:

A. All major networks and CNN produced maps of the Temple Mount showing in error the site of the Dome of Rock over 300 meters closer to the excavated tunnel than reality. This was done to reinforce the Arab claim that somehow the tunnel affected their Holy sites.

B. All major newspaper & TV reports described the tunnel as close or under the Arab sites. This is totally false, as the tunnel runs on the outside of the Temple Mount.

C. All major media kept repeating the Arab lies about the tunnel without any objective report. For example: When reporting an Arab lie like, "The tunnel damages the foundations of the Dome of Rock," the reporter never bothers to add that this is blatantly false.

D. All major media failed to point out that Jerusalem is a Jewish city and Israel has full sovereignty. They falsely claimed that the Oslo Accord requires Israel to forgo any action in Jerusalem. There is nothing in the Oslo Accord that limits Israeli rule. There is an agreement to negotiate the final status of the city, but nothing that requires Jerusalem to be frozen in time.

6. The Freeman Center believes that the Oslo Agreement is an albatross around the neck of Israel. The sooner it is removed the better. We do not believe that there is a "peace process." We do not believe that any action on the part of Netanyahu will damage the "peace process" since it doesn't exist.

The Freeman Center stands by my press release of September 3, 1993:

"The rush of events in the Middle East has been dizzying. The media hype, the talking heads, and the worldwide expectations of peace in the Middle East are all quite staggering. Radio, TV, and newspapers herald the coming of a new era of reconciliation between Israelis and Palestinians. The positive images are so abundant that any moment one might expect to see Isaiah on Nightline showing Ted Koppel video clips of lions lying down with lambs. Though studying the same history as many of those cheering recent developments, I see nothing to be happy about. Once again I find myself marching to a different drummer. It has happened before, with my support for the civil rights movement (early 60's) and then the anti-war in Vietnam struggle. Despite the media hype surrounding these developments, let me make something very clear: A leopard does not change its spots. And you can say a berachaha (Hebrew blessing) over a ham sandwich, but that doesn't make it kosher. And a deal with the PLO is like a dance on quicksand—before you realize it, you have sunk into the muck and slime."

You may have noticed that I devoted little space to defending Israel's actions in relation to the tunnel. The reason is that the tunnel is irrelevant to the violence caused by the vicious Arab hatred of Jews. Some have said that we should try not to offend the Arabs. Please note that being an independent Jew in the land of Israel also greatly offends the Arabs. Zionism represents a great turning point in Jewish history, when Jews decided never again to ask permission TO LIVE IN ERETZ YISRAEL. HaShem in His Wisdom gave this Land to the Jewish people in perpetuity. That is all the permission Netanyahu needs to exercise Israeli rule in its ancient capital: Jerusalem.

Respectfully submitted With Love of Israel.

Bernard J. Shapiro

A CALL TO ACTION

We Must Return To Zionism

(June 1997)

In 1897 in Basle, Switzerland, Theodore Herzl founded the World Zionist Organization. There were great accomplishments in the last 100 years. Much has happened to the Jewish people, who found themselves on a roller coaster with many traumatic ups and downs. The Holocaust was the lowest point and the establishment of Israel was a high point. There was the great victory of 1967 and the trauma of 1973. Zionism flourished, Israel prospered, and Judea, Samaria and Gaza were settled. The Ethiopian return to Zion brought tears to our eyes with pride. The great Russian migration to Israel literally changed the country forever.

And then a cataclysmic and horrific event took place. A small clique of charlatans, with anti-Zionist delusions, took over the Israeli government in 1992. They deceived the Israeli voters by placing ("Mr. Security") Yitzhak Rabin at the head of their ticket. They promised security and then proceeded to dismantle the Jewish State. 100 years of Zionism are being undone in a few years. The new Likud government of Prime Minister Benjamin Netanyahu does not seem to have the political will to undo the damage of Oslo.

In the past few years, it seems that the main effort of Israeli governments was the creation of a Palestinian state. The word peace was perverted and distorted, coming to mean surrender and appeasement.

It is time for real Zionists to take charge of Israel's future. Zionists who will populate the lands of YESHA. And do it without apology or timidity. The leaders of Israel must pursue security policies without regard to the opinions of those who did nothing to help us during the Holocaust. The People of Israel must understand that they have caused a revolution in Jewish history. We have moved from weakness to the power of self-determination.

WE MUST NOT GO BACK TO THE OLD VULNERABLE DAYS. SURVIVAL INTO THE 21ST CENTURY REQUIRES SELF-SUFFICIENT POWER AND ACTIONS.

SOME THOUGHTS ON THE FAILURE

TO IMPLEMENT REAL ZIONISM

It is obvious that the Palestinians will continue to violate their Oslo commitments. Their behavior is in keeping with their character. It is normal for them to kill Jews, break agreements, lie to the media and even abuse their own people. Like the wolf and the sheep, it is just nature that one will devour the other. The Palestinians are working very seriously to create a state from the river to the sea, with Jerusalem as their capital. We are not surprised.

What bothers us greatly is the impotence (indeed inactions) of the Israeli government in protecting the vital interests of the Israeli people. Instead of lists of PLO violations, *DO SOMETHING!* **DEMAND COMPLIANCE**. In the old days, terrorists were destroyed in Gaza and Beirut by the long arm of **ZAHAL** (Israel Defense Forces). How is it that they can now find refuge in Nablus and Jericho?

We say to Netanyahu, "Arafat and Mubarak are laughing at you. At the Freeman Center we are crying. We had worked for a stronger leadership. A leadership that would mobilize Israel to face the ominous challenges of the 21st Century."

TALKING ABOUT HAR HOMA

The Freeman Center urges the Israeli government **NOT** to talk about Har Homa. Instead, talk about the PA endorsement of terrorism and their lack of compliance with existing agreements. Bibi should talk to Mubarak only in Jerusalem and only after Azam is released from Egyptian imprisonment. And then Mubarak could be asked to help rid Egypt's newspapers of anti-Semitic articles and cartoons and to allow its citizens to visit and trade with Israel. Har Homa is nobody's business but the Israeli people and any Arab, American, or European that brings it up should be shown the door.

Bernard J. Shapiro

OSLO HAS CAUSED STRATEGIC DAMAGE TO ISRAEL'S SECURITY

The problem is the ability of the Palestinians to disrupt the IDF's mobilization schedule. Of course, the IDF can crush them in a head to head battle. But some 50,000 well-armed terrorists (with anti-tank and anti-air missiles, Katyushas etc.) could slow Israel down, while missile barrages from Syria, Iraq, and Iran containing VX nerve gas would contribute to the general breakdown of Israel's ability to fight. Israel would still win, but at great cost. Do you remember the **SCUD** attacks and how much it disrupted life in Israel? Syria alone has 1,000 missiles loaded with VX nerve gas and anthrax bacteria. We are talking chaos. Of course Israel can nuke these countries, but there is a great imbalance in this psychological deterrence factor. America and Russia operated on the principle of **MAD** (Mutually Assured Destruction) for 50 years. This will not work for Israel because its Arab enemies see victory in **DESTROYING** Israel in a **JIHAD**. Arabs killed would go to paradise while the Jews would be sent straight to hell.

It is this imbalance in attitudes toward human life that makes the situation so unstable. The Freeman Center believes firmly in the principles of "**preemption, preemption and preemption**." No nation hostile to Israel should be allowed to possess non-conventional weapons. Regardless of public opinion, they need to be taken out.

ISRAEL'S SOVEREIGNTY IN YESHA

Sovereignty is quite often a unilateral act. America's sovereignty in Texas and California was never recognized by Mexico and certainly was a unilateral act based on superior military power. Israel's sovereignty in *Eretz Yisrael* has considerably more international sanction (League of Nations Mandate etc.) than America ever had. That the international climate has shifted (to anti-Semitism) doesn't alter the issue. Of course, with the granting of *Eretz Yisrael* to the Jews by **HaShem** there are certainly moral rights.

In the final analysis, *Zionism was the Jewish people's act of unilateral sovereignty over what was morally and rightfully theirs BUT denied by mankind.*

ISRAELI POWER

I wouldn't quibble over details; I would exercise our right and utilize our power for the good of the Jewish people. A lot of people misjudge the power of a united Jewish people in pursuit of justice for Israel. (**Pray that we would unite!**) We are not that weak, only intimidated by the big powers and the Arabs. *Israeli strength has always been greater than the sum of arms and men.* The Maccabees defeated numbers much greater than theirs. Bar Kochba held off the Roman Empire for many years before succumbing to the force of **ONE HALF** of Rome's Legions. I know they lost in the end, but many historians say that the huge losses of Rome in this battle with Bar Kochba and his men so weakened them that it led to Rome's decline. It is important to note that the Romans are **NO MORE** and we Jews control Israel and Jerusalem.

THE DOUBLE STANDARD

Some well-meaning Jews believe that Israel should behave at a higher standard of morality than its Arab neighbors. They urge Jews to refrain from retaliating for Arab attacks. **While I have never supported murder for murder's sake, killing the enemies that come to slay us is fully in keeping with Jewish law.** Was it wrong for the fighters of the Warsaw Ghetto to kill Nazis? For the IDF to raid terrorist bases? For Netanyahu to travel to Beirut to kill PLO terrorists? To kill the enemies of Israel, before they commit murder, is certainly a *mitzvah*. And I am not talking about unjustified murder. I am talking about real enemies, including those who throw Molotov cocktails and other lethal objects. The double standard is really a form of anti-Semitism. A complete discussion of this subject can be found in chapter 10 (**Why Jews Must Behave Better Than Everybody Else**) of Professor Ed Alexander's new book, **THE JEWISH WARS** (no relation to the book by Josephus about Masada).

Bernard J. Shapiro

FREEMAN CENTER POSITION ON

THE RESUMPTION OF TALKS WITH THE PA

(July 1997)

It appears that there is a lot of pressure on Israel for the resumption of talks with the Palestinian Authority. America, the UN and the Europeans are quite anxious that talks should resume. They fear that failure to renew talks would doom the Oslo Accords. Prime Minister Benjamin Netanyahu also says that he wants the talks to start. The Israeli Labor Party and its allies, Meretz and the terrorist PLO, are very upset that talks about Israel's complete surrender are not being held. Almost all parties have been drawing an inaccurate conclusion as to the reasons for the break in talks. Some have suggested that Israeli building in Har Homa and in YESHA is related to the impasse. The truth needs to be told.

In the light of this immense, almost universal, interest in restarting talks, the Freeman Center has developed a plan. I must warn you ahead of time that our plan is based on two things: What is good for Israel's security and what would facilitate peace (as opposed to the "peace process").

THE FREEMAN CENTER POSITION

THE PALESTINIANS MUST DO THE FOLLOWING:
1. Extradite to Israel the terrorist murderers in their areas.
2. They must cease all acts of terrorism and cooperation with other terrorist organizations.
3. They must move quickly to destroy and disarm all terrorist organizations in their territory, e.g. Hamas & Islamic Jihad.
4. Repeal the Palestinian Covenant and write a new one than encourages democracy, human rights and recognition of Israel in its present borders.
5. Stop the pollution of Israeli water as well as the improper handling of sewage.
6. Comply with all of their obligations under the Oslo agreements.
7. They must cease the murder of Israeli citizens as well as their own.
8. They must cease the torture of their own people.

9. They must limit the number of police and their arms to that specified in the Oslo Accords.
10. They must cease the anti-Jewish incitement on their radios, TVs, newspapers, and in mosques.
11. They must cease their anti-Jewish incitement in their educational institutions.
12. They must stop the stealing and profiteering from donor aid money and use it to help their people, as it was intended.

THE ISRAELIS MUST DO THE FOLLOWING:
1. Build and settle Har Homa on an accelerated basis.
2. Expand all Jewish villages in YESHA to include all of the public lands.
3. Build new Jewish communities on strategic land and especially on land that gives contiguity to other Jewish areas.
4. Destroy all illegal Arab buildings, especially those near bypass roads and in Jerusalem.
5. Evict all Arabs who have occupied public lands illegally.
6. Grant to Israeli soldiers and civilians the right of self-defense, including lethal fire at anyone attacking them.

We feel that this plan would go a long way toward creating a just and lasting State of Israel in a piece of the Middle East.

Bernard J. Shapiro

AN IMPORTANT NOTE FROM

THE FREEMAN CENTER

(August 1997)

Many Israelis and American Jews seem to have a cognitive disorder that prevents them from critically analyzing the serious threats to their existence. At the Freeman Center we have tried to present the facts in many different formats: print, e-mail, the World Wide Web, fax and public speakers. We have used the best political, military and strategic analysts and the sheer volume of our output has surpassed 10,000 pages since 1993. Yet Oslo's true believers in the **Kevorkian Plan—*Land for Suicide*** still seem firmly in control. I ask each of you to do your best to wake up the leaders of Israel before it is too late. Support for the Freeman Center is one of the ways to help in this "wake up" process. For many Israelis, the truth will only be realized as their throats are slit. In a pool of their own blood they will utter incredulous words: *"You mean you really didn't want to make peace?"*

It takes money to carry out our many pro-Israel activities. The monthly cost of printing, postage, phone, fax, computer upgrades and repair, web maintenance, online and web fees and many other expenses keep growing. Subscription rates and dues have not increased since 1993. The number of free copies we send to political and media leaders has grown to over 100 copies a month (includes the State and Defense Departments, the Senate and House Committees on Foreign Relations). We also send copies to selected Zionist/Nationalist leaders in Israel.

THE BOTTOM LINE: Without financial help from you, we will not be able to continue to fill the information gap (the truth about the Arab-Israeli conflict) in the media. Please take the time to write us a check.

I promise that it's a *mitzvah and you will feel good about doing it* . . .

. . . . *Bernard J. Shapiro, Executive Director*

MY ROSH HASHANA PRAYER (5758)

(September 1997)

As I survey the fragile planet we call home, my mind makes note of the chaos, blood, and tears. The cries of a million lost souls shatter the night in a million corners of the Earth. The sensitive and compassionate among them try to feed the hungry, heal the sick, and clothe the naked. One by one their energies dissipate. They try to hold back the tide with a teaspoon and then see the impossibility of the task. The Jewish people are but a cosmic speck in this universe. To many Jews who feel deeply about their own people, that speck becomes the whole world. Other Jews are irrevocably tied to non-Jewish pursuits.

May we as a people open our eyes and begin to see the world as it really is. Without becoming depressed and morose, we must realize that there are powerful forces in the world that wish us ill. May we mobilize our strength to fight our enemies until they are defeated. May we not succumb to false prophets of peace. We all want peace. We pray for peace in our Sabbath services every Friday night. After thousands of years, being victims of persecution, expulsion, extermination, and discrimination, it is natural that we yearn for peace with every ounce of our bodies and souls. It is because our hunger for peace is so strong that we must be doubly cautious not to fall for a pseudo-peace. Today none of us believe Chamberlain really negotiated **"peace in our time"** with Hitler. Why do some Jews believe that Peres and Rabin really negotiated **"peace"** with Arafat, one of today's Hitlers? The Jewish people must learn the value of unity in the face of so many enemies who wish them ill.

I pray that Israelis who have fought in countless wars will understand that there is no magic cure, though they crave to be free of constant conflict. As Jews we are all involved in this historic struggle to survive. It is not our fate or that of the Israelis that we should retire from this struggle.

There is another battlefield here in America where the Jewish people are being tested, and I pray that they win. That is the battle with assimilation, the struggle for continuity of Jewish life. History very clearly tells us that Jews can survive any persecution, but show a great tendency to assimilate and disappear where conditions are favorable. This seductive kiss of death is very hard to fight and I don't have all the answers. One thing is clear: where there is a strong intensity of religious upbringing, complete with Jewish day schools, the process of assimilation can be slowed. My prayer for the Jewish people would be a rapid growth in attendance in Jewish day schools. Also, the Jewish population will have to shift to a more traditional form of Judaism. In two or three generations more than 80% of Reform Jews will have disappeared. The main survivors will be Orthodox Jewry and the Lubavitch Movement.

In 1967, during a visit to Israel immediately following the Six Day War, I prayed at the Wall for the first time. I had expected the stones to be rough and weathered after all that time, but they were smooth from 2,000 years of touching and kissing. The gentle caresses of Jews over the ages had worn soft finger grooves in the hard rock. As I placed my hands on this magnificent relic of our forefathers, I felt a surge of light and energy the likes of which I had never known. In what had to have been but the flash of a second, I felt at one with Jews from all periods of history.

In an instant I saw the continuity of Jewish history and its unbreakable connection with Eretz Yisrael (Land of Israel). I understood how modern Israel is the beginning of the Third Temple Period and the spiritual heir to Joshua, Saul, David, Solomon, the Maccabees and Bar Kokhba. I frequently write about the security reasons for incorporating Judea, Samaria, and Gaza into the body of Israel. There is another side to this issue and that is the spiritual-religious side. The truth, which many find inconvenient, is that the Land of Israel was promised by G-d to Abraham and his seed in perpetuity. The Land of Israel is not speculative real estate to be bartered away for seductive promises of peace. The hills and valleys of Judea and Samaria contain the collective memory of the Jewish people. It was here that the Israelites first entered the Holy Land. And it was here they fought the battles, built the towns, elected their kings and were preached to by their prophets and judges. And it was on this soil that they wrote the Holy Scriptures we call our Bible.

In my blinding flash of insight at the Wall, I also understood that Israel on its own soil was more powerful than the sum of its weapons and men.

Jews who had wandered the Earth powerless for two millenniums attained great power when reunited with the soil of Israel.

One thing is clear to me: the Lord has blessed Israel by reuniting Jerusalem and bringing Judea, Samaria, and Gaza back under its control. It would be a horrendous sin against G-d and common sense for Israel to renounce this inheritance to which it is entitled. Israel holds these lands as a sacred trust for the Jewish people in perpetuity. It would not only be sinful, but also criminal, to abuse that trust by denying future generations of Jews their Holy Land—the Land of their Fathers—the one tiny spot on planet Earth given to them by G-d.

BEWARE THE RISEN PEOPLE

I have a vision and a dream that I must reveal as we approach these **Days of Awe**: In the name of G-d, the **Unforgetting** and the **Almighty**, I say to my people's enemies: Beware of the thing that is coming that will take what you would not give. That will free the people of Israel from your atrocities. I say to Israeli Prime Minister Benjamin Netanyahu: Be aware of the **Risen People** who will sweep the Arab scourge into the dustbin of history. Know that the Jewish soul will be set free. The spectacular victories of the Israeli army and the return to Zion demonstrated that power. But it wasn't a miracle. It was just the soul of the Jew coming to its own. It was just the Jewish soul freed at last to be itself.

And I see it coming: the Jewish soul released to be itself. I see a new proud Jewish government coming to power in Israel. A government that reclaims the Jewish **Holy Places** and restores Jewish sovereignty in all of *Eretz Yisrael*. I see Moslem control and Islamic sites removed from the **Temple Mount** to make it ready for **Moshiach**. I see the enemies of Israel, who raise up their hands to murder or injure Jews, driven from our **Holy Land**. I see the secular Jews of Israel and the world becoming more observant and returning to the **Torah**. I see religious Jews becoming more tolerant of diversity in Jewish practice.

I see a new Israeli foreign policy that grovels before no nation, no matter how powerful. I see Israel's Foreign Minister informing every nation that their embassies must be in Jerusalem. If they don't respect Israel's capital, then maybe they can have a consulate in Tel Aviv. I see the government demanding that the Vatican return all the property it has stolen from the Jewish people during the last 2,000 years. Maybe they will refuse and we could always hold their property in Israel as a down payment. The Vatican has been used to dealing with obsequious groveling Jews, but now they would see proud fearless Jews. I see an Israeli government that would change its relationship with America from one of subservience to one of equal alliance.

Yes, I have a dream that Jews will no longer debate the obvious: *like whether to hold onto what is theirs or trade it away; whether to struggle for survival or to give up from fatigue.* I have a dream that the Jews of the Kibbutz and the Jews of **YESHA** will be reborn as brothers and patriots. From the Galilee to Eilat, all the people of Israel will share the same dream of a powerful independent Zionist nation. I have a dream that this strong, proud independent Israel will win the respect of all the nations of the world, including the Arabs. Instead of the contempt it has earned in recent years, Israel will again be a light unto the nations. And finally, I have a dream that this new Israel will find the peace it so dearly deserves: a peace with strength and self-respect. As I look back at 4,000 years of Jewish history, I have but one urgent hope and prayer: We must make this dream a reality. **There is no alternative.**

May the Lord bless the leaders of Israel with the courage to pursue peace, and the wisdom to know when it is not attainable. May the Lord bless the Jews of the former Soviet Union and make their new lives rich with jobs and new friends to ease their transition into Israeli life. May the Lord bless the war-weary Israeli people with the stamina to bear up under the strain, if peace is not just around the corner. May they understand that their fate may be that of endless struggle to survive in a hostile world and may they have the strength to understand that there is still no alternative (ein brera). May the people of Israel prosper, and go from success to success never forgetting that their destiny lies in their might, their righteousness and their faith in HaShem. SHANA TOVA!

Four Editorials by Bernard J. Shapiro

OSLO: THE REALITY

(March 1998)

The true nature of Israel's "peace" partner ('Palestinian' Arabs) is revealed in their speeches and in their media. Their passionate demonstrations in favor Iraq and their pleas to Saddam to destroy Israel also reveal the truth. It is important to remember that when the Arabs refer to Palestine their definition is: *all the land between the River (Jordan) and the Sea (Mediterranean) with Jerusalem as its undivided capital.* They also usually mention that those who don't like this *"can drink the (salt) waters of Gaza"*. This definition can be gleaned from the intensive study of over 1000 speeches and articles by Palestinian Authority leaders, including Yasser Arafat. The research was done by Dr. Aaron Lerner (**Independent Media Review and Analysis**) David Bedein (**Institute for Peace Education**) and the Israel Government Press Office (**Prime Minister's Office**).

It is my conclusion, that Oslo is a process of appeasement and not peace. I believe that there is **NO** way to **"make it work in Israel's interest."** Those who believe that Oslo will lead to peace must certainly fall into the following categories:

1. Good people without adequate information to understand the facts.

2. Good people with a cognitive disorder that prevents them from understanding the facts.

3. Idiots and fools [this category does not exclude seemingly intelligent people with doctorates and great expertise in specialized fields. Yossi Beilin, for example, is quite learned but a fool nevertheless.]

4. Members of the Labor and Meretz Parties [see #3]

Bernard J. Shapiro

It should also be mentioned that there are several categories of people who believe in Oslo precisely because it will lead to the destruction of Israel. They are:

1. Anti-Semites

2. Anti-Zionists (same as #1)

3. The US State Department (see #1)

4. The Arab States (see #1)

5. The 'palestinian' Arabs (see #1)

6. The United Nations (see #1)

7. Most European Nations (see #1)

8. Michael Lerner, Thomas Friedman, Mike Wallace, Anthony Lewis, Woody Allen, Peace Now and other self-hating Jews

WHAT SHOULD BE DONE?

1. Announce that Arafat has terminated Oslo by his words and actions. Israel no longer views it as a valid document.

2. Pursue a vigorous Zionist agenda by building and settling all parts of **Eretz Yisrael**.

3. Adopt a Jewish constitution for Israel along the lines that Dr. Paul Eidelberg suggests.

4. Vastly improve the education of Israelis (both children and adults) in Jewish history, religion and Zionism. Education should be designed to inculcate patriotism, nationalism and love of **HaEretz** (Land of Israel) and **Am Yisrael** (the Jewish people)

5. Vastly increase the capability of the IDF and intelligence branches to ensure Israel's ability to preemptively crush any evil forces that threaten her.

6. Re-establish the rule of law by expelling all Arabs engaged in violent or political activities designed to damage the security of Israel and the safety of its citizens.

7. Terminate all interference and manipulation in Israeli policy by other nations, including friendly ones.

8. Strive to achieve economic and military independence from American foreign aid. Only by cutting the umbilical cord of US aid will Israel be truly free to pursue its unique destiny.

It is very late in the day for Israel. **It is time to call a "spade a spade."** Niceties aside there is tremendous damage being done daily to Israel by the Oslo process.

Please, if anyone has evidence that Oslo will bring peace and security to the people of Israel, I would like to hear it. In the five and half years since Oslo, I have seen mountains of evidence to the contrary. Among supporters of Oslo, I have seen only Chelm-like hopes for peace, totally without any basis in reality.

Auschwitz was **NOT** a Labor Camp. Oslo is **NOT** a peace process. Establishing a state of Palestine is **NOT** Zionism. Arafat is **NOT** a peacemaker. *Let us call things by their correct names.*

I have said these things before, and I plan to say them repeatedly until the necessary actions are taken to ensure their implementation. Only then will Israel's future be secure.

Bernard J. Shapiro

SIMPLE TRUTHS ABOUT COMPLICATED ISSUES

(April 1998)

1. Israel must be prepared for a massive disproportionate retaliation against Iraq if attacked. Better than retaliation for new missile attacks, Israel should try to pre-empt Saddam's ability to endanger her ever again. Israel's failure to defend itself during the 1991 Persian Gulf War left a damaging psychological scar on the Israeli psyche. The experience of sitting helpless in sealed rooms created the climate for the Oslo appeasement. Israelis felt weak and impotent. After the war, when asked why they supported Oslo, they said they were *"fatigued"* after four decades of war. They wanted to stop fighting their war of survival. So they accepted the false notion of Oslo with its plan of trading land for *"peace."*

2. There is no such thing as *"territories for peace."* It never existed in history and doesn't exist today. Albright's permutation of this concept, the **'phased redeployment plan'** (*a little territory for a little security*), is also a fraud and should be rejected. It has been four and half years since Oslo and Israel has given a lot and received nothing. Now the US wants to let the PA pocket their gains and then sell the **security rug** to the Israelis for the third or fourth time. If Albright's plan of a little security for a little withdrawal made sense, then total withdrawal (into the sea) would mean total security. They must think that Israelis are idiots. They may be right.

3. (There is a) continuity of Jewish history and its unbreakable connection with ***Eretz Yisrael*** (Land of Israel). Modern Israel is the beginning of the Third Temple Period and the spiritual heir to Joshua, Saul, David, Solomon, the Maccabees and Bar Kokhba. I frequently write about the security reasons for incorporating Judea, Samaria, and Gaza into the body of Israel. There is another side to this issue and that is the spiritual-religious side. The truth, which many find inconvenient, is that the ***Eretz Yisrael*** was promised by G-d to Abraham and his seed in perpetuity. The **Land of Israel** is not speculative real estate to be bartered away for some high sounding false promise of peace. The hills and valleys of Judea and Samaria contain the collective memory of the Jewish people. It was here that the Israelites first entered their **Holy Land**. And it was here they fought the battles, built the towns, elected their kings and were preached to by their prophets and judges. And it was on this soil that they wrote the **Holy Scriptures** we call our Bible. (**Jews, G-d & Israel**, 1992)

4. Israel on its own soil is more powerful than the sum of its weapons and men. Jews who had wandered the earth powerless for two millenniums attained great power when re-united with the soil of Israel. Anyone who has followed the Arab-Israeli conflict must be aware of the rising cost paid for Jewish blood. Before Israel was established, nations of the world took Jewish lives with impunity. Arabs learned that the iron fist of **Zahal** (Israel Defense Forces) exacts a high price for even one Jewish life. (**Jews, G & I**, 1992) [Then came Oslo and Jewish lives were cheap again.]

5. One thing is clear to me: the L-rd has blessed Israel by re-uniting Jerusalem and bringing Judea, Samaria, and Gaza back under its control. It would be a horrendous sin against G-d and common sense for Israel to renounce this inheritance to which it is entitled. Israel holds these lands as a sacred trust for the Jewish people for all time.

It would not only be sinful, but also criminal, to abuse that trust by denying future generations of Jews their Holy Land—Land of their Fathers; the one tiny spot on planet earth given to them by G—d.

(**Jews, G & I**, 1992)

6. My response to the Oslo Accords:

"The rush of events in the Middle East has been dizzying. The media hype, the talking heads, the worldwide expectations of peace in the Middle East are all quite staggering. Radio, TV, newspapers herald the coming of a new era of reconciliation between Israelis and Palestinians. The positive images are so abundant that any moment one might expect to see Isaiah on Nightline showing Ted Koppel video clips of lions lying down with lambs. Though studying the same history as many of those cheering recent developments, I see nothing to be happy about . . . . Despite the media hype surrounding these developments, let me make something very clear: A leopard does not change its spots. And you can say a ***berachaha***

(Hebrew blessing) over a ham sandwich, but that doesn't make it kosher. **And a deal with the PLO is like a dance on quicksand—before you realize it, you have sunk into the muck and slime."** (Press release, *Jewish Herald-Voice* September 3, 1993)

OBSERVATIONS & CONDEMNATIONS

(April 1998)

GENERAL OBSERVATIONS

The Freeman Center and all its members wish Israel a hearty Mazal Tov on the 50th anniversary of its independence. Unfortunately, our joy is diminished by our knowledge that the foolish pursuit of the Oslo Accords will ultimately cause Israel to disappear from the face of the earth. I have said it many times before, yet I must repeat the following statement on this special Yom Hatzmaut

A HARSH REALITY

We all want peace. We pray for peace in our Sabbath services every Friday night. After thousands of years, being victims of persecution, expulsion, extermination, and discrimination, it is natural that we yearn for peace with every ounce of our bodies and souls.

It is because our hunger for peace is so strong that we must be doubly cautious not to fall for a pseudo-peace that is really the wolf of war wrapped in sheep's clothing. Today none of us believe Chamberlain really negotiated "peace in our time" with Hitler. Why do some Jews believe that Peres and Rabin really negotiated PEACE with Arafat, one of today's Hitlers?

Israelis my age have fought in four wars and I understand their desire to be free of constant conflict. Unfortunately there is no magic cure. I wish I could write more optimistic words. Beyond the neighboring states that Israel is negotiating with now lies another ring of unmitigated hostility led by Islamic fundamentalists like those in Iran.

As Jews we are all involved in this historic struggle to survive. It is not our fate or that of the Israelis that we should retire from this struggle. The only peace the Arabs are prepared to give us is the peace of the grave.

In blood and fire was Israel born and on a hot anvil was she forged. The brave young soldiers of Israel must take a quick glance back to the crematoria of Auschwitz and then go forth to face the enemy knowing that there is still no alternative (ein breira).

LEBANON

Many Israelis, including both right and left, are under the illusion that they can leave Lebanon and be protected by Syria, Lebanon, the UN or the tooth fairy. Some believe the threat of massive Israeli retaliation will prevent violence on the northern border. No foreign group will ever protect Israel and no promises to Israel will ever be kept. Israel's ability to massively retaliate will be inhibited in the future, exactly as it is now.

On the other hand, it is not a hopeless situation where young Israeli soldiers go to become human targets of the Hizballah. We suggest the following: (1) Announce a massive retaliation policy against Syrian bases in Lebanon and Lebanese infrastructure including Beirut in the event of Hizballah attacks on IDF or SLA soldiers. (2) Then follow through without discussion with foreigners.

THE AMERICAN *'PEACE'* PLAN

After 50 years of independence it is past time for Israeli leaders to stop seeking advice or approval from the Americans. America is a wonderful country, but its foreign policy goals are not identical to Israel's. In fact during the last 50 years American diplomacy as tended to prevent the achievement of major Israeli goals. Israel's wars with the Arabs were never alloyed to become total victories. The Arabs were always resuscitated and allowed to re-group and re-arm for the next battle. Israel has been severely damaged by the major American effort at Camp David and Oslo. As for Europeans, they should be advised to discuss peace with Jews of Auschwitz.

ARAFAT AND THE PA

I am sick of Israeli leaders discussing what Arafat "has to do" before Oslo can proceed. Wake up, four years has passed and Arafat will not become a boy scout. Trust me. **"A leopard does not change its spots. And you can say a *berachaha* (Hebrew blessing) over a ham sandwich, but**

that doesn't make it kosher. And a deal with the PLO is like a dance on quicksand—before you realize it, you have sunk into the muck and slime." [Freeman Center press release, September 3, 1993] To all concerned with Israel's future: **Terminate Oslo now!**

NECESSARY CONDEMNATIONS

This has been a bad week for morality and integrity. We feel compelled by our sense of truth and justice to issue the following three condemnations:

1. We condemn British Foreign Secretary Robin Cook who came to Israel this week with a pro-Arab agenda. Cook intended to tour Har Homa with Feisal Husseini to dramatically push his belief that Jerusalem is "occupied Arab territory." He was dissuaded from this provocative act, though continued to babble Arab propaganda at every opportunity.

We have a long memory. We remember how the British gave 80% of the land reserved for the Jewish State by the League of Nations Mandate to set up a new Arab State for King Abdullah. We remember how the British slammed the doors of Palestine shut to Jews trying to escape the inferno of the Holocaust. We remember how they armed the Arabs to destroy the Yishuv. We remember how they turned over their fortresses (Taggart) to the Arabs before leaving in 1948. And we remember how they disarmed Jewish defenders of Israel. Yes, a lot of Jewish blood is on the hands of the British Foreign Ministry Officers. **We would advise Cook that we want neither his advice nor presence in** *Eretz Yisrael.*

2. We condemn the Vatican's new document on the Holocaust. Israel's Chief Rabbi Yisrael Meir Lau also rejected the Vatican statement as "too little too late." The Vatican, contrary to its promises to Jewish leaders, failed to apologize for the Church's role in making the Holocaust possible.

Again, we have a long memory. The crimes of the Catholic Church read like the definitive portrait of evil. Under Church direction Jews were pillaged, tortured, murdered, deported, forcibly converted, robbed and brutalized in ways so horrible that the mind cannot handle the horror. To this day the Vatican holds a vast storehouse of Jewish ceremonial objects and ancient Hebrew texts plundered from Jewish communities all over

Europe. During World War II, the Church became money launderer and protector of the Nazis. At the same time they condemned millions of Jews to extermination by not having the moral courage to say that mass murder was wrong. **We say to the Vatican: We don't want your self-serving documents.** *Return our property and then sink to your knees and beg forgiveness from the victims of your evil activities throughout nearly two thousand years.*

3. We condemn the Israeli Foreign Ministry for releasing a statement blaming the violence in Hebron on its Jewish community. This slanderous and totally false charge must be repudiated in the strongest terms by the Israeli leadership. After a week of Arab violence and attacks on Jews and Israeli soldiers, we are amazed and disappointed by this uncalled for statement. Shame on you. 4. And the report, LAW ENFORCEMENT IN HEBRON Discrimination and Perversion of Justice, made me mad as hell. See the accompanying story "LAW ENFORCEMENT IN HEBRON, Discrimination and Perversion of Justice" <http://www.freeman.org/m_online/apr98/hebron.htm>.

MY MESSAGE FOR ISRAEL'S

50th ANNIVERSARY

(May 1998)

History has many lessons for this generation. For Jews, the lessons are much harsher and much more clearly defined. The Holocaust looms as not only an overwhelming tragedy, but as a lesson in the failure of Jewish leadership. Too many people excuse that generation by claiming that the Nazi horror was beyond comprehension. This is foolishness. Every step that the Jews trod on that path of anti-Semitism from Hitler's rise to power in 1933 to the killings machines of Auschwitz was known to Jewish leaders within months. Their response was weak, timid and in many cases criminally negligent. The failure to confront President Roosevelt with a vigorous demand to save European Jewry will forever be a horrendous blot on our history.

The nations of the Western World committed the great sin of convincing Hitler that no one would allow the Jews refuge or even care about their survival. England, especially, preferred that the Jews be exterminated so that they would not immigrate to Palestine after the war. There is plenty of guilt to go around. The nations of the world have always been reckless with Jewish lives. The Jewish failure is much more shocking, as common decency would expect us to care about our own people.

I first began to study Jewish history in the early 1950's. To me the Holocaust was an enormous, overpowering evil that would seem to mock Jewish destiny. Then as I studied Zionism and the rise of Israel, I understood something significant. The Jews of Europe were ill prepared to defend themselves and were at the mercy of their gentile neighbors. In the geographical area encompassed by Hitler's armies, 90% of the Jewish population was exterminated. Jews often talk about the loss of a third of their people. This greatly underestimates the impact of the Holocaust. The Allies may have won World War II, but the Jews were, for the most part, dead and unable to celebrate the victory.

Bernard J. Shapiro

The Israeli war for survival during the years 1947-9 tells a remarkably different story. A Yishuv (Jewish community) numbering only 600,000 souls defeated at great cost five Arab armies and established the State of Israel. Some 6000 of their finest sons and daughters died in the conflict. That is 1% of the Jewish population compared to the 90% of European Jewry exterminated.

THIS WAS A REVOLUTION AND A LESSON IN THE EFFICACY OF JEWISH POWER.

No longer were the Jewish people a branch swept along by the currents of the non-Jewish river (world). Israel was a boat, powered by its own engine, that could navigate history as an independent nation. This was a quantum change and improvement in the Jewish condition of more than 2000 years.

As we celebrate the 50th Anniversary of Israel's birth, we must reflect on its long term viability. I fear that the seeds of Israel's destruction were planted in 1993 with the signing of the Oslo Accords. Just like Israel's birth changed forever the condition of the Jews, Oslo has given a great boost to the aspirations of 'palestinian' Arabs. Those aspirations include the destruction of Israel and its replacement with a State of Palestine. Oslo has given them the opportunity to utilize the **Phased Plan** (for the destruction of Israel) of 1974. As one watches the behavior of terrorist Yasir Arafat and his Palestinian Authority, it is clear that this plan is in operation.

The evidence is all there, for all to see: the failure to revise the PLO Covenant; the failure to fight terrorism and root out the infrastructure of Hamas and Islamic Jihad; the continued incitement of the their population against Jews and Israel; the use of Nazi themes in their propaganda; their falsification of history; their Nazi-like lies against the Israeli government; their attempts to seize territory outside their boundaries; their failure to extradite terrorist murderers; the blatant praise of terrorist murderers; their organization of attacks on Israeli civilians and soldiers; their participation in continued terrorism; their threats to resort to terrorism; their participation in treaties with Syria, Iran, and Iraq to attack Israel; and much more. All of the above are contrary to the Oslo Agreement signed in 1993 and all of this behavior continues today in 1998.

These violations by the PA are verifiable facts. The Israeli government of Prime Minister Benjamin Netanyahu knows all these things to be true. The reason I question Israel's long term viability is the failure of its leadership to **ACT** on these facts. Netanyahu is still negotiating with Arafat, despite his knowledge that every previous agreement with him has been violated immediately. This is what troubles me the most. The failure to *recognize reality* and then *make decisions* based on Israel's true interests. Believe me, creating and nurturing a renascent irridentist Palestine, is **NOT** in Israel's interests.

Israel's sovereignty and freedom of action seems to be increasingly restricted by the United States and Europe. Fifty years after Israel won its freedom to determine its own destiny, it is quite sad to see this growing dependence on the **"goodwill"** of the world's nations. Remember: *"Those who fail to learn from history, are condemned to repeat it."*

.... Bernard J. Shapiro, Editor

Bernard J. Shapiro

EDITOR'S NOTES FOR THE NEW YEAR

ELECTIONS

(January 1999)

As democracies are committed to do on a periodic basis, Israel will hold new elections on May 17th. Like all Israeli elections, the issues are being obscured and personalities have become paramount. It is way too early for me to give an intelligent analysis of platforms and prospects of the many parties and contenders for the office of Prime Minister. I hope that in the February issue of **THE MACCABEAN** I will be able to do so.

I would just like to give the reader a very general caution about judging candidates. The so-called centrist parties are apparently left-parties with a new public relations spin. Some so-called right-wing parties fail by most right-wing criteria. The Likud has become a center-left party, though many of its followers are in the Nationalist Camp.

Labor and Meretz have become surrogate Arab parties and this is proven daily by the support they get from Arab voters. By the way, Israel's Arab voters are not supporters of the 'Zionist entity' called Israel. They support 'Palestine.' Paul Eidelberg, one of Israel's most brilliant political/legal thinkers, has said of this phenomenon that democracy is not meant to be a suicide pact. I agree completely with him.

The important thing to remember at this critical time is the following: What you will be hearing from now until the elections will be primarily smoke and mirrors. The truth will be well hidden from view. Candidates will make promises they never intend to keep and party platforms will be a joke. American consultants like that rabid attack dog, James Carville, will try to spread muck and slime over the opposition candidates. I doubt that we will witness any dignity or intelligence in the campaign. There will be few if any discussions of the very serious issues facing Israel.

One could easily give in to despair . . . . but we won't! **THE MACCABEAN** will be there and will continue to discuss *REAL* issues that affect the survival and security of Israel.

IS PEACE GOING TO BREAK OUT?

The Harsh Reality

(June 1999)

The dangers facing Israel that we have written about are all still there. The election of Ehud Barak as Israel's new Prime Minister has not made even the slightest change in the Arab plans to eliminate the Jewish State from the Middle East. The anti-Semitism of Palestinian radio, television, newspapers and Islamic sermons is as Nazi like as ever. The goal of Arafat and his terrorist cohorts to create a new 'Palestine' from the river to the sea (replacing Israel on the map), has not changed. The use of PA territory as safe havens for terrorists and the terrorist infrastructure has not changed. The hostile diplomatic campaign against Israel, now using the 1947 Partition Resolution, has not ended. The illegal construction by Arabs on Israeli lands continues unabated. The murder and harassment of Jews by Arabs in Israel has also continued. The demand from the Arabs and the Israeli left to ethnically cleanse Jews from **YESHA** is growing louder.

One fact is clear: The election of Barak was supported by the Arab world, President Clinton, the U.S. State Department and with cheers from Israel's traditional enemies, including the extreme left.

With friends like these, Israel needs no enemies.

★

Reprinted from *IsraelWire* of May 26, 1999

To one and all of my critics:

Unfortunately there was **NO** rhetoric in my original note (**IS PEACE GOING TO BREAK OUT? The Harsh Reality**). Everything is easily verifiable. The continued anti-Semitism in the Arab World is a secret only to the Left. Those of you in Israel should turn on PA radio and TV or listen to the Islamic sermons on Friday night. Take a friend who knows Arabic to a PA school and look at the textbooks. And then notice that the murderers of Jews are sipping coffee in PA towns instead of being extradited for trial.

It is time that the Left took a look at the facts and stopped calling everything rhetoric and posturing. There is a **REALITY** out there that one must pay attention to.

Some Advice Prime Minister (Elect) Ehud Barak Didn't Ask For

AS THE NETANYAHU ERA ENDS, WHAT WE SUGGESTED IN 1996

(Editorial from June 1996 issue of THE MACCABEAN)

Some Suggested Do's & Don'ts For Netanyahu's New Government

Do restore **pride** and dignity to Israel's foreign policy.

Do restore **deterrence** to the Israel Defense Forces.

Do **crush** any resumption of the intifada.

Do **arrest** all members of the Palestine National Council guilty of crimes of violence.

Do **restore** Zionism and Jewish pride in Israel's school system.

Do **rid** the media of leftist jerks and create a vigorous information system with an aim to inform and not propagandize.

Do **demand** freedom for Jonathan Pollard.

Do **live up** to your campaign promise to free the economy, reduce taxes, and sell off all government industries not connected to security.

Do **put** Natan Sharansky in charge of immigration and absorption.

Do **take politics out of the Israel Defense Forces** and the Security Forces, even if this means removing leftist officers of high rank.

Do **respect the civil and human rights** of Israel's Arab inhabitants but . . . .

Don't **give them the political right to change Israel** from a Jewish State to a state with a lot of Jews.

Don't **go** to Egypt to talk to Mubarak. Let him come to you.

Do **support the** efforts of Dr. Paul Eidelberg in his quest to create an Israeli constitution that protects the Jewish character of Israel.

Don't **jump** every time the American State Department acts upset with your actions.

Do **annex** all of **YESHA** and re-affirm the Golan Annexation.

Do **pass** a law requiring a **two-thirds majority of the Knesset** and consent of the Prime Minister to alter above annexations.

Do **vigorously** settle Jews in Jerusalem and extend its municipal boundaries to Maale Adumim.

Do **carry out** the plan to add 500,000 Jews to YESHA.

Do as a **first step**, open all completed apartments for purchase and occupation.

And finally, do restore **Jewish rights to the Temple Mount** including the right to prayer.

[Editor's Note of June 29, 1999] I will grant that I was a bit arrogant telling an elected leader of Israel what he should or should not do. Please forgive my arrogance and ask yourself whether Bibi would still be in office had he followed this Zionist [not originally mine] advice? We all know he didn't, though he regretted this fact in the last months before the election. Wouldn't Barak be better off revitalizing the Zionism of his youth? **Believe me, in the next election his advisor might be from Gaza and not Texas.]**

Bernard J. Shapiro

EDITORIAL NOTES

In the 21st Century the Freeman Center will still be fighting

for Eretz Yisrael

(December 1999)

1. We will work to **PREVENT** the loss of the Golan and its 30% of Israel water plus strategic mountains

2. Israeli Prime Minister Ehud Barak has already agreed to recognize a Palestinian state. We will work to **MINIMIZE** the damage that will result.

3. We will actively **OPPOSE** the return of hostile Arabs west of the Jordan.

4. We will **SUPPORT** a unified Jerusalem as Israel's sole capital.

5. We will **DEMAND** the right of Jews to worship on the Temple Mount and support a policy that returns the whole area to Jewish control.

6. We will **EDUCATE** the Jewish and non-Jewish community on issues of importance for Israel's security.

WILL YOU BE WITH US? WE NEED YOUR HELP TO CARRY ON THIS IMPORTANT WORK. PLEASE HELP . . . .

Dear Readers:

After I read the story about Albright's visit to Syria and the plan for new Israeli-Syrian negotiations, I decided to put together a Freeman Center Peace Plan for Israel and Syria. It was very obvious that the US, the Syrians, the Europeans, and the UN had just about settled the issue and were in agreement on most parts of a proposed peace plan. It was also very obvious the Israeli leadership had NO PLAN whatsoever to protect Israeli security in the area. So here is my plan. Let me know what you think of it.

Bernard J. Shapiro

FREEMAN CENTER PEACE PLAN

FOR ISRAEL & SYRIA

(January 2000)

SYRIAN OBLIGATIONS

1. Syria must withdraw from the territory it occupied from Israel following the 1973 Yom Kipper War under the Kissenger Disengagement Agreement. This territory will give Israel an additional 10-15 kilometer buffer zone east of the present Golan Heights border. This will increase the chance for peace in the area by strengthening Israel strategically.

2. Syria will pay compensation to the families of Israel POW's murdered and tortured by the Syrian authorities.

3. Syria will pay reparations to Israeli farmers for constantly shelling them during the years 1949-67. Such compensation will include: damage to crops, farm machinery, loss of life and loss of income due to shelling.

4. Syria will completely democratize including: free democratic elections, human rights, women's rights and a free press.

5. Syria will agree that Jerusalem is Israel's capital and will place its embassy in Jerusalem.

6. Syria renounces all claims to the Golan Heights as well as its spurious claims to "Southern Syria."

7. Syria agrees never to go the war with Israel, even if every Arab country in the world decides to carry out a multinational jihad.

8. Syria agrees to destroy its missile and non-conventional war making ability including chemical, biological and nuclear.

9. Syria agrees to withdraw from Lebanon and cease aiding the Hizballah and other terrorist groups.

ISRAELI OBLIGATIONS

1. Israel agrees never to launch an aggressive war against Syria.

2. Israel agrees that Damascus is the Syrian capital and agrees to place its embassy in Damascus.

3. Israel agrees to open up free and fair trade with Syria.

4. Israel agrees not to interfere with the new Syrian democratic elections.

5. Israel will guarantee the new border with Syria and prevent terrorists from attacking Syria.

Well, this may not be complete. I probably could add a few move provisions, but I think it does the trick. I believe it is the best Israeli plan for relations with Syria ever proposed. If enacted, I fully believe that there would be PEACE (with Syria).

Your peace loving editor,

Bernard J. Shapiro

FREEMAN CENTER NOTE ON POLLS
(January 2000)

Most polls should be taken with a grain of salt. The answers are very dependent on how the question is asked. Pollsters usually manipulate the answers for political purposes. When I took statistics at Berkeley the first thing the professor told us was: "Statistics don't lie but statisticians do." The same can be said of pollsters. Words like peace, full peace, normal relations etc have no meaning in the real harsh world of the Middle East. Perhaps when *Moshiach* comes . . . .

Those words are used to confuse, deceive and manipulate. As a public service I am offering an honest question to be asked of Israelis relative to the Golan. I give my permission to Barak to use it for the referendum.

TO THE ISRAELI VOTER

[SUGGESTED POLL OR REFERENDUM QUESTION]

Do you agree to give the Israeli territory known as the Golan to the Nazi like anti-Semites (remember the recent blood libel accusations)?

Do you understand that this will increase the chance of war with Syria by increasing Israel's vulnerablity and eliminating the deterrent to Syria inherent in our position on the Golan?

Do you understand that 30% of Israel's water supply will be entrusted to the goodwill of the Syrians who murdered and tortured our POW's in violation of the international law and human decency?

Do you understand that the Americans will reward Syria for its great mitzvah of allowing Israel to surrender the Golan by rebuilding its army to the best high tech standards (like they did Egypt)?

Do you realize that a return to the June 4, 1967 boundaries rewards Syrian aggression and occupation of Israeli territory in violation of the 1949 Armistice Agreements?

Do you realize that this will become a precedent that will be used by Arafat to demand all of Judea, Samaria, Gaza, and Jerusalem?

With the full knowledge of the above which allows for informed consent, please indicate your choice of policy on the important question of the surrender of the Golan:

_____Defend the security and Survival of Israel and DO NOT surrender the Golan

_____Surrender the Golan and facilitate the further destruction of Israel and the mass murder of its citizens.

Bernard J. Shapiro

WHY NOT GIVE THE GOLAN HEIGHTS

TO THE FREEMAN CENTER

INSTEAD OF ASSAD?

(April 2000)

Over the last year I have noticed that a lot of Israelis and Americans believe that they have only one choice related to giving up the Golan Heights. And that choice is Syria's Assad. I am perhaps a little cautious when it comes to making strategic decisions that will affect Israel's future for all time. I am therefore proposing the Freeman Center as a better recipient of the Golan than Assad (Syria).

THE SCIENTIFIC AND HISTORICAL COMPARISON

1. Syria would expel all Jews from the Golan Heights and takeover their property
* The Freeman Center would lease the entire Golan Heights back to the residents for three bottles of Golan wine at Passover.

★

2. Assad is a terrorist, drug smuggler, Nazi loving anti-Semite and mass murderer who has killed tens of thousands of people.
* The Freeman Center has no ties with Nazis, terrorists, drugs and has never killed anyone.

★

3. Syria plans to attack Israel from its new improved strategic position on the Golan, overlooking Israel.
* The Freeman Center plans to set up a hang gliding tourist site with the Golan as the launching pad.

★

4. Assad never keeps his agreements
* The Freeman Center always lives up to its agreements.

★

5. Assad would divert 30 % of Israel's water supply.
* The Freeman Center would guarantee Golan water for Israel for all time.

★

6. Assad wants to shut down Israeli electronic surveillance site on Mount Hermon.
* The Freeman wants to improve the ski slopes on Mount Hermon and introduce fake snow for the off seasons.

★

7. Assad, upon receiving the Golan would then demand more concessions and more land from Israel.
* The Freeman Center, upon receiving the Golan, would request 4 additional bottles of Golan wine, realizing that they forgot to factor Purim into the negotiations.

It is obvious that the <u>Freeman Center would be a better recipient</u> for the Golan than the Syrians.
I would like ask you to take this short poll and then mail it to Clinton, Assad and Barak:
I believe that Israel should give the Golan to:
_____The Freeman Center
_____The drug smuggling, Nazi loving, anti-Semite, terrorist and mass murderer Assad
THANK YOU FOR PARTICIPATING IN THIS HISTORICALLY IMPORTANT POLL

FREEMAN CENTER NOTES

ON VIOLENCE IN ISRAEL

By Bernard J. Shapiro

The current violence in Israel related to the Temple Mount is, of course, totally unnecessary. It is a direct result of Israel's neglect of its sovereign rights there. The riots and the IDF response has been pitiful. Riots like we are seeing now should be crushed with the minimum of restraint. Barak brags that he uses maximum restraint, a policy perfect for Arab propaganda and media bias. One should bear in mind the old Jewish saying: "If you are merciful to the cruel, you will end up being cruel to the merciful."

We respectfully present our plan to sole this tragedy:

1. The Temple Mount is the holiest of all Jewish sites and should be visited daily by government officials and everyday citizens as befits a sovereign country.

2. The Islamic Waqf will not be happy with this arrangement and should therefore be thrown off the Mount. Full Israeli control should be instituted.

3. Jewish antiquities should be fully protected. and illegal construction stopped.

4. Jewish prayer on the Temple Mount should be stored.

Maximum military force to crush anyone who attacks Jews or IDF soldiers.

No more policy of moderation with Arafat. When he unlocks terrorism, a ton of sanctions should land on his head including rabid building YESHA.

Apparently Albright has summoned Barak and Arafat to Paris to try to stop the violence. Barak will under tremendous pressure to give up Jewish rights to the Mount. He should agree to NOTHING. The violence can be stopped with one word from Arafat and he should not be rewarded by this bloodletting. These riots indicate the direction of the Arabs in asserting their control of the Jewish Temple Mount. We should dedicate ourselves to prevent this and save our holiest site for Am Yisrael and Eretz Yisrael for all future time and every future generation.

Bernard J. Shapiro

TEN REASONS THE FREEMAN CENTER SHOULD DEAL WITH THE CURRENT CRISIS INSTEAD OF BARAK

(November 2000)

10. We would not allow Kofi Anan or any UN representative to come to Israel after their recent biased resolution condemning Israel.

9. We would not talk to Albright every five minutes and let her get involved in our foreign policy.

8. Same as #9 but for Clinton.

7. We would tell the Europeans and the Security Council to go to hell (in nice diplomatic language) for their bias towards the Arabs.

6. We would use our attack helicopters to knock out PA buildings including Orient House as well as all sources of live fire.

5. We would use our attack helicopters to knock out Arafat's three headquarters.

4. We would bring up tanks and shell Arab communities whose residents are attacking Jews and IDF soldiers.

3. In Lebanon we would destroy major infrastructures and then set the Syrian poppy fields in the Beka Valley on fire with napalm. No attempt should be made to protect Syrian soldiers.

2. Arab attackers should be rounded up and shipped to prison camps in the Negev.

And finally . . . .

1. We will not be wimps like Barak, we will keep deadlines, and we will use maximum force and minimum restraint to crush this Arab POGROM.

REFLECTION 2001

(January 2001)

As we enter a new year there are some thoughts I would like to share with you. The study of Jewish history in general and the Arab war of extermination against Israel in particular reveal a central persistent theme. The Jews are a gifted people, beneficial to the world community in vast disproportion to their numbers.

Despite the above, the world has plotted their destruction more times than can be counted. The next to last being the Nazi Holocaust and the present one being the Arab/Muslim war of extermination planned for Israel. All the great powers of the world who ignored the Jews cries for during the Holocaust are again turning their collective backs on Israel. And America seems to be a part of that group.

The hoax of a "peace process" is meant to cover the betrayal. Everyone knows that Israel will not be safe in shrunken non strategic borders. It is but a stage in Arafat's plan of "stages" to dismember the Jewish State.

Where are the leaders needed to face this apocalyptic threat?

Bernard J. Shapiro

REFLECTIONS AND REACTIONS

TO SHARON'S VICTORY

(March 2001)

Ariel Sharon's landslide victory and emergence as Israel's Prime Minister has elicited a multitude of reactions around the world and in the Middle East. The very size of the victory at over 25 percentage points tempts one to interpret the meaning of this shift in the Israeli electorate. Prime Minister Ehud Barak had been elected 19 months earlier by a large majority. What had happened? Below are reflections and reactions to Sharon's victory:

PM EHUD BARAK *Why He Lost*

Barak was driven by a post-Zionist ideology that insisted that peace was possible with the Palestinians. Before the election, disappointed and angry, he told an interviewer:

"I learned a few things in the past nine months. Because we had these great experts on the Palestinians who knew for sure where you could cut a deal. But it turned out that they didn't know. They were wrong. Because the Palestinians really do have intransigent national attitudes. They have been in the struggle for 50 years and they are ready for another 20." PM Ehud Barak in a pre-election interview (*Ha'aretz* 2/2)

Because of his failure to provide personal security to Israelis by crushing the Palestinian violence, he was rejected massively at the polls. Barak also embarrassed Israelis by being a "door mat" for Arafat, negotiating while violence continued. His frequent threats to cut off negotiations proved phony and the Arabs laughed at him. His concessions to the Palestinians went way beyond the national consensus and still Arafat snubbed him and demanded more.

PRIME MINISTER ELECT ARIEL SHARON *What His Election Means*

Some observers have noted that this election was against Barak but not against the "peace process" or for Sharon. This is nonsense. The Israeli electorate came out massively to support Sharon and his policies of security and Zionism. It is true that many leftist and Arabs chose to boycott the election or use blank ballots but this does not diminish the victory of Sharon. In fact Sharon received nearly 70% of the Jewish vote which is unprecedented in Israel's 53 year old history.

Sharon staked out policies that were preferred by the Israeli electorate, like: unity of Jerusalem as Israel's capital, sovereignty over the Temple Mount and other Jewish Holy sites, control Israel's strategic territory including the Jordan Valley, and of course support for the Jews of YESHA. All this was understood by the electorate and they supported it instead of Barak's constant never ending concessions.

MEDIA REACTION

The media, both Israeli and international) looked at Sharon's landslide and launched into many varieties of faulty analysis:

1. First they told us that 69% of Israel's population still supports peace. The implication was that Sharon would be forced to continue the Oslo negotiations. This is totally false. As an abstract, nearly everyone will say that they support "peace." It gets messy when you discuss the details. The brutal violence (pogrom) of the Palestinians and their anti-Semitic incitement against Jews (in their schools, TV, newspapers and sermons) has convinced a huge majority of Israelis that they are not a "partner for peace."

2. We are told that Sharon cannot form a narrow right wing/religious coalition and must seek a unity government with Labor. We are also told that if he does form a narrow coalition it will be short lived due to internal contradictions. At the Freeman Center, we prefer a Zionist/religious coalition in order to maintain the goals of Sharon's election campaign. Diluting the government with the likes of Shimon Peres or Haim Ramon will defeat that purpose. In fact, in post election interviews, Labor leaders had the *chutzpah* to say their decision to join a Sharon government depended on his adopting *their* positions on the "peace process."

Israel faces very serious security challenges at home and diplomatic challenges abroad. It would be my fervent prayer that the Zionist/religious parties will give Sharon the opportunity to work without constant governmental crises.

3. We are told by the media that Sharon is dangerous, bloodthirsty and will provoke a war in the Middle East. We have also been told that he provoked the current violence in Israel. Poppycock. The truth is that the existence on one Jew in Israel or on the Temple Mount is considered a provocation by anti-Semitic Arabs. In our sovereign Jewish state, we do not need to ask anyone permission to live and breathe. Sharon has been a proud defender of Israel throughout his whole life. The media likes to point to the Sabra/Shatila massacre as a black mark against his name. But none of it is true: See below:

That's not what the Kohan Commission found: "We have no doubt that no conspiracy or plot was entered into between anyone from the Israeli political echelon or from the military echelon in the I.D.F. and the Phalangists with the aim of perpetrating atrocities in the camps . . . We assert that in having the Phalangists enter the camps, no intention existed on the part of anyone who acted on behalf of Israel to harm the non-combatant population, and that the events that followed did not have the concurrence or assent of anyone from the political or civilian echelon who was active regarding the Phalangists' entry into the camps . . . . the direct responsibility for the perpetration of the acts of slaughter rests on the Phalangist forces "Source: The Beirut Massacre—The Complete Kahan Commission Report (authorized translation} Karz-Cohl Publishing, Inc.1983 {pp.54-55)

ARAB REACTION

The Arabs, especially, the Palestinians seem oblivious to how much they contributed to Sharon's stunning victory. In interview after interview they say that violence will continue until Israel surrenders to all of their demands. These demands would result in the destruction Israel and its replacement with Palestine. They don't seem to understand that Israelis were willing to try peace talks but reject suicide. They threaten to increase the violence with Sharon as Prime Minister but they are acting out violence every single day. There seems to be a serious disconnect in their policies.

They repeatedly tell reporters that they will only start negotiations where Barak left off at Taba. They seem not to understand that Barak had neither parliamentary nor public support for the concessions he made at Camp David II and Taba. The Palestinian leadership is fooling itself if it thinks it can revert to previous offers *they themselves rejected*. As Abba Eban once said: "The Arabs never miss an opportunity to miss an opportunity."

The Arab world is full of threats against Israel, but Sharon has never been afraid of threats. He will go about strengthening Israel's military and preparing it for any eventuality. You can also expect him to restore internal security and crush terrorism in Israel.

UNITED STATES REACTION

Both President George Bush and Secretary of State Colin Powell have warmly indicated that they will work with Sharon on regional Middle East issues. I believe that there will be much less pressure on the Palestinian-Israel negotiations and more on issues dealing with Iraq, Iran and oil supplies. My gut feeling is that President Bush will not put pressure on Israel to comply with specific policy guidelines. I foresee cooperation on a multitude of strategic issues and a much greater flow weapons technology to Israel.

The one thing I worry about is the attempt to cast problems with the Palestinians as morally equivalent. Powell recently called for restraint to avoid an escalation of violence in the region. The violence is all of Arab origin so what is he saying? Israel should "turn the other cheek," not protect its soldiers and civilians, and not stop terrorism. This, by the way, is an international problem dating back 53 years. The United Nations regularly condemns Israel for acting in self defense. The immoral bias of the UN would cause me to reject every one of its resolution out of hand.

EUROPEAN REACTION

European leaders who grovel before the terrorist Arafat are urging Sharon to renew the peace negotiations despite the backdrop of continuing Arab violence. I suggest that he politely tell them to mind their own business.

Bernard J. Shapiro

THE BOTTOM LINE

The ascent of Sharon to Prime Minister is more than a reward for a lifetime in the service of his country. It is an opportunity for Israel to restore Zionism and Jewish pride. It is an opportunity to restore Israeli military deterrence in the Middle East. Without such deterrence war would be more imminent. Sharon will prove that a tough stance on security issues, without appeasement, will win respect in the region and lead to a relaxation of tensions.

Where Barak wasted his time on the "peace process", I expect Sharon to devote time to solving Israel's socio-economic problems. He will try to bring together different parts of Israeli society, secular and religious, rich and poor, urban and rural, Ashkanzi and Sephardic.

The Freeman Center wishes Sharon success in his efforts for Israel. May he move from strength to strength.

11 THINGS I AM SICK AND TIRED OF

(September 2001)

There are a few things that make my blood boil. Here is a list and the explanations:

1. I am sick and tired of the slowly escalating actions of the IDF to fight terrorism.

The slow escalation allows PA terrorism to become immune to Israel's strategy. It allows them to smuggle more guns, mortars, anti-aircraft missiles into PA territory. Lately a 60mm heavy machine gun was able to strike Gilo from Bethleham. So much for the cease fire from Beit Jalla. This is much the same as bacterial infections. If the anti-biotic is not strong enough to eliminate it, then the disease will return in a much more virulent form.

2. I am sick and tired of the Israeli government's fear of collateral damage to the enemy.

The Arabs have no such qualms. In fact they target civilians in bestial suicide bombs. PA weapons factories, weapons storage depots and bomb making facilities should be blasted off the face of earth even if it causes civilian casualties. Remember that "he who is merciful to the cruel, will end up being cruel to the merciful."

3. I am sick and tired of Israeli PM Sharon's policy of restraint.

The adjustment to accepting the killing of Jews has become is an abomination. A Jew here or there murdered daily, pretty soon adds up to a lot. I remember when the Al Aska terror on Israel began last September, The IDF general staff re-opened a file called "Operation Thorns" which could re-take the PA areas. They estimated Israeli dead at 300.

Since then there have been almost 165 Jews killed which is more than half of estimated combat deaths with no apparent consequence to Arafat's ability to inflict casualties on Israel. There is one extremely important variable. The PA has used the last year to build bunkers, firing positions, smuggle in heavy weapons and organize an army of 80,000. The defeat of PA now would certainly be more costly. And it will grow with time. There is a very short window of time to defeat the PA terrorists with minimal losses. Many political analysts and military experts agree that Israel must take decisive action now.

4. I am sick and tired of the US State Department urging Israel to show "restraint."

Despite the fact that the CIA knows exactly WHO (PA) is attacking WHOM (Israel) the State Department continues call for a stop to the "cycle of violence." Whenever Israel is attacked viciously, there is rush to tell Israel "to turn the other cheek".

5. I am sick and tired of Shimon Peres trying to arrange another meeting with Arafat.

He claims to be seeking a cease fire and a return to negotiations. Let me be honest with you. I don't want negotiations with Arafat, I want to crush him and his terrorist gang. Arafat has violated all the provisions of Oslo (which I opposed strongly as a Pandora's Box). He broke 69 cease fire agreements since 1993 and before that broke hundreds of agreements with Jordan, the UN, the Arab nations and Lebanon. Arafat broke every provision of the Oslo agreement including anti-Semitic incitement against Israel. I wrote in a press release published 11 days before Oslo was I signed on the White House lawn:

Jewish Herald-Voice (Houston) September 2, 1993

Freeman Center says rush to embrace PLO is foolish and ultimately dangerous

'... *nothing more than an elaborate trap for Israel*'

Asserting that the rush to embrace the Palestinian Liberation Organization (PLO) is both foolish and ultimately dangerous, the Freeman Center For

Strategic Studies has declared: "The pro-Israel community should react with extreme caution to the moves in Jerusalem to recognize the PLO."

According to the Freeman Center, the PLO instituted a reign of terror, rape and murder locally as well as attacks on Israel in the two Arab countries where it gained a kind of 'self rule.'"

Shapiro continued: "Despite the media hype surrounding these developments, let me make something very clear: A leopard does not change his spots. You can say a *berachah* (blessing) over a ham sandwich, but that doesn't make it kosher. And a deal with the PLO is like a dance on quicksand—before you realize it, you have sunk into the muck and slime."

6. I am sick and tired of the continued UN presence within the borders of Israel.

It's time to remove them and assert Israel's sovereignty. Israel should work to have the world withdraw its recognition of Arab refugee camps and refugees. It should condemn the hypocritical treatment of the Arab countries for exploiting these people for political purposes. Israel should declare in a strong voice that there are NO refugees. That status is not permanent and obviously should not apply to people living in the same place for 53 years.

7. I am sick and tired of the international boycott of Jerusalem as Israel's capital.

Israel should unilaterally announce to the nations of the world that all embassies MUST be in Jerusalem. Consulates may be in Tel Aviv or any place they want. Israel no longer permits its eternal capital to be disrespected.

8. I am sick and tired that under both Labor and Likud governments, Arutz Sheva, Israel National Radio has not been fully legalized.

Whatever happened to freedom of speech found Arutz 7 should not only be allowed establish facilities on land but also a television channel. I am also sick and tired of government television being controlled by the extreme left that doesn't represent the Israeli public. A lot of the time they represent the Arabs and not Israel's.

9. I am sick and tired of Israel's trying to be Mister Nice Guy to a hypocritical world.

Europeans are increasingly comparing Israel to the Nazis. Over half of all the resolutions of the UN since its founding have directed against Israel. At the recent conference on how to condemn Israel in Durban, South Africa, UN head Kofi Anan condemned Israel for existing. The Arab world openly plots the destruction of Israel.

10. I am sick and tired of Israel tolerating Moslem restrictions and desecrations on the Temple Mount

The excuse that it would cause violence to exercise our rights there is absurd. Israel has the capability to enforce security. Virtually everything Israel wants do in the Land of Israel displeases the Arabs, who want us to leave. Jews should be allowed to pray on the Temple Mount and the destruction of Jewish antiquities by the Moslem waqf needs to be stopped immediately.

11. I am sick and tired of PA demonstrations of the fierceness of their terrorists and how they will destroy Israel.

I believe that we will defeat our current adversaries. We will succeed and survive from three sources of our strength: Love of *Tanach* (Torah), Love of *Eretz Israel* (Land of Israel, and Love of *Am Yisrael* (People of Israel) . . . . In blood and fire was Israel born, and on a hot anvil was she forged. Her youth understood that life in the new Jewish homeland would require sacrifice. With stories of the stench of burning flesh from the ovens of Auschwitz embedded deep in their psyches, the young Israeli soldiers fight with the firm conviction that there is still no alternative "*ein brera.*"

To that I would like to add something the American soldiers used to say during the heaviest fighting in Viet Nam. This is dedicated (slightly revised) to the brave IDF soldiers who face the enemy every day: Yeah though I walk through the Valley of Death, I will fear no evil because the Almighty fights with me for the Restoration of Zion and for love of HIS people, Israel.

Bernard J. Shapiro

STRAIGHT ANSWERS FOR TOUGH QUESTIONS

(May 2003)

Q. Will the new "Road Map" lead to peace in the Middle East?

A. On the contrary, if implemented, it will lead to greatly increased terrorism against Israel.

Q. Is Mahmoud Abbas really a moderate, peace-loving Arab, opposed to terrorism?

A. **NO!!** In fact he has a 23 year history as a vicious terrorist who financed and helped plan the Munich massacre of Israeli athletes. His opposition to terror is purely tactical and also a lie since he will certainly do **NOTHING** to eliminate it despite his words. He is also a Holocaust denier and neo-Nazi.

Q. Does Abbas have control over the PA?

A. Arafat still has complete control.

Q. Then why does the international media, world leaders (including Bush), and even Israeli PM Sharon act like this is an opening to begin negotiations that could lead to "peace?"

A. There is a distinction between international supporters of the Road Map and Israeli supporters. The world generally doesn't care about Israel's survival due to latent and open anti-Semitism and a desire to appease the Arabs.

Israelis (mostly leftists like Labor, Meretz and Peace Now) for some psychopathological reasons hate their Jewish heritage and will only be happy with self-destruction. In many ways they honestly supported Oslo as a way to absolve their "sin" of creating a Jewish State. Like obsessive compulsive psychotics they continue to expect Oslo to work if only Israel worked harder for its success, even though it was the Arabs who made it unworkable. They hit their heads against the brick wall of Oslo and then get a bloody headache. Being obsessive compulsive they keeping hitting their heads over and over again, each time expecting a different result. It will never happen and the Road Map is just Oslo revisited and much worse.

Q. Can't the IDF with its immense power be able to control it like it is doing now?

A. The Road Map leads to a Palestinian State which would be recognized by the entire world. Israel would find it much more difficult to cross a national border to fight terrorism. It would not be able to maintain its extensive intelligence network which has prevented 90% of attacks before they can be perpetrated.

Q. Wouldn't a Palestinian State be demilitarized with Israel controlling its borders and air space?

A. With reference to the writings of Louis Rene Beres (an international legal expert and strategic analyst from Purdue University), once a nation's sovereignty is recognized it is under no legal obligation to adhere to the conditions it agreed to before it became a State.

Q. Does this mean that planes flying into Israel's Ben Gurion International Airport would be vulnerable to Palestinian anti-aircraft missiles?

A. Yes! And even if there is an international treaty obligation not to fire on civilian aircraft, I would not expect the Palestinians to honor **ANY** agreement.

Q. Would a Palestinian State lead to the "End of the Conflict with the Arabs?"

A. No!! The Palestinian would still want to continue terrorism to drive the Jews into the sea. Their maps do not even show Israel existing in the Middle East. The same with the other Arab countries including Egypt. They are just biding their time while Israel is being weakened by the Palestinian State (the end result of the Road Map). Then they will launch a surprise attack to destroy what is left of Israel, bringing about a Second Holocaust.

Q. Why are all negotiations in the Middle East aimed at helping the terrorist Arabs, and none is to benefit Israel?

A. A better question is: Why do the Israelis participate in these one-sided talks?

Q. If America is truly Israel's best friend, why do they pursue the Road Map which could lead to Israel's destruction?

A. It is necessary to make clear distinctions when referring to the United States. Most important there are many supporters of Israel. For example: The US Congress, the American people (especially Evangelical Christians), the US Defense department (which works with Israel developing many high-tech weapon systems) plus a high proportion of the US Jewish population.

And then there is the US State Department which has a long history of trying to undermine Israel's security. Before WWII they restricted visas to Jews trying to escape the Nazis. They opposed the Partition Resolution of the United Nations in 1947 that led to Israel's re-birth as a nation. Even though Truman forced the US Ambassador to the UN to vote YES on the resolution, the State Department enacted an arms embargo on the new Jewish State. At the same time England and France were feverishly arming the Arabs. The Arabs announced publically that this would be a **War of Extermination** that would be remembered like the great **Mongolian massacres**.

Q. Is there any hope for Israel's survival in this hostile Arab/Muslim world? In fact, the whole world seems anxious to rid the planet Earth of Jews.

A. We must struggle to survive. Those who think that we are at the **End of Time** and can relax are grossly mistaken. The struggle of Israel and *Am Yisrael* (the Jewish People) continues. Peace will come with Moshiach and not any Road Map (really a much worse Oslo).

THE BOTTOM LINE

As Jews we are all involved in this historic struggle to survive. It is not our fate or that of the Israelis that we should retire from this struggle. The only peace the Arabs are prepared to give us is the **peace of the grave.**

Bernard J. Shapiro

NOTES ON ISRAELI POLICIES

(February 10, 2004)

On Israel Policy and Government

1. The Israeli prime minister should not be elected to be "dictator" and should be forced to govern with the consent of the electorate and the Knesset.

2. The Freeman Center believes, as David Ben-Gurion said at the Zionist Congress in Basel, Switzerland, in 1937, more than 65 years ago:

"No Jew has the right to yield the rights of the Jewish People in Israel. No Jew has the authority to do so. No Jewish body has the authority to do so. Not even the entire Jewish People alive today has the right to yield any part of Israel.

"It is the right of the Jewish People over the generations, a right that under no conditions can be cancelled. Even if Jews during a specific period proclaim they are relinquishing this right, they have neither the power nor the authority to deny it to future generations. No concession of this type is binding or obligates the Jewish People.

"Our right to the country—the entire country—exists as an eternal right, and we shall not yield this historic right until its full and complete redemption is realized."

3. Democracy requires that Israel's media (which uses national airwaves) should be removed from the hands of the extreme leftists and placed in responsible pro-Israel hands.

4. Israeli newspapers that incite against any Jewish segment of the population should be prosecuted.

5. Israel's Justice Department, Police, Prosecutors and Supreme Court must be stripped of their political bias in favor of extreme anti-Israel elements and become truly non-political.

6. Israeli industries must take responsibility for the pollution of the soil, air and water and take dramatic action to clean their operations.

7. Israel's Foreign Ministry must cease its failed policy of trying to explain its actions and trying to be nice to the Arabs. It should launch a broad campaign of psychological warfare against the Arabs and an aggressive campaign to win over public opinion. This means showing the world the horror and brutality of the Arabs, their lack of human rights, abuse of women (including genital mutilation), continued slavery, corruption and support (both financial and functional) of international terrorism.

In 1978, Chaim Herzog wrote a book in response to the United Nation's resolution that stated that Zionism is racism. The book was *Who Stands Accused: Israel Faces Its Critics* (Random House, 1978, 278 pages). Herzog brilliantly defended Israel and portrayed its critics in the harshest terms. Unfortunately, since the Oslo Appeasement of 1993, the Israeli Foreign Ministry has too often found itself in the position of putting a good face on its terrorist collaborators in the Palestine Authority. The result has been disastrous, not just on the ground in Israel in terms of dead and maimed Jews, but also in world public opinion.

By not telling the *truth* about the Arabs, the Arabs were able to repeat lies about Israel without an effective counter-attack. And lies they told, every hour, every day with constant repetition. Joseph Goebbels' Nazis taught them about how the bigger the lie the more it is believed and the utility of repetition of lies. Today, 59% of Europeans believe that Israel is the greatest danger to world peace. We must not throw up our hands and attribute everything to anti-Semitism (though that is certainly a factor) and must act forcefully and intelligently to present Israel's case to the world.

On Arabs and Terrorism

1. If Arabs do not like living in the same areas a Jews, we should remove the Arabs—*not* the Jews. This includes Judea, Samaria, Gaza and Jerusalem.

2. Arabs who are disloyal to the State of Israel should lose their voting rights in national elections. They could still vote in municipal or local elections.

3. Arabs who commit acts of violence against Jews should be either expelled or executed, depending on the degree of the violence.

4. The following will sound harsh, but remember that "he who is merciful to the cruel, will end up being cruel to the merciful." How to properly mete out justice in the case of hostile acts:

A. Throwing stones at Jews (in cars or walking)—Expulsion from Israel.

B. Throwing Molotov cocktails at Jews (in cars or walking)—Death sentence.

C. Collaboration in terrorist plot to kill Jews—Execution with bullets dipped in pork products (this prevents the terrorists from going to "paradise" in Islamic theology and acts a psychological deterrent to terrorism), after interrogation to gain maximum intelligence.

D. Participation in terrorist attack on Jews—Execution with bullets dipped in pork products, after interrogation to gain maximum intelligence.

E. Terrorists found guilty of killing, mutilating, kidnapping, or raping Jews—Execution with bullets dipped in pork products, after interrogation to gain maximum intelligence.

5. No terrorists should be kept alive to prevent future absurd prisoner exchanges.

6. Should an Israeli be captured by an enemy, the IDF should launch massive continuous attacks causing such pain and damage to the enemy as to force the return of the prisoner.

7. Military action should be aimed at "draining the swamp" instead of swatting mosquitoes (targeting just leaders).

8. Military action should be based on one massive campaign with *no* let up to allow the terrorists to re-group and re-arm. Once must think of fighting terrorism much the way a doctor treats an infection or cancer. If he doesn't

root it out completely, the disease will metastasize or grow back with the passage of a short time.

Should the above measures be taken, I believe Israel will put an end to the scourge of terrorism.

Bernard J. Shapiro

STRAIGHT ANSWERS FOR TOUGH QUESTIONS

(June 2004)

Q. Will Israeli PM Ariel Sharon's Gaza retreat plan lead to peace between Israel and the Arabs?

A. On the contrary, if implemented, it will lead to greatly increased terrorism against Israel.

Q. Will Egypt be able to prevent the smuggling of weapons into Gaza and control terrorism from there as Sharon says.

A. Of course not. Egypt is a major part of the problem—not the solution. Egypt has been one of the most anti-Semitic nations in the Arab world. They have done everything possible to sabotage any agreement between Israel and other Arabs. They have used their relationship with America to build a huge modern army that today threatens Israel. Egypt has done nothing to stop the smuggling of weapons into Gaza from its territory. At present there are huge stockpiles of anti-tank and anti-aircraft weapons in Sinai. There are also Kaytusha and other missiles that can hit targets deep into Israel. There is **ABSOLUTELY** no chance that Egyptian behavior will change after an Israeli retreat. *Only a fool would believe so.*

Q. Then why does the international media, world leaders (including Bush), and even Israeli PM Sharon act like this is an opening to begin negotiations that could lead to "peace?"

A. There is a distinction between international supporters of the Gaza surrender and Israeli supporters. The world generally doesn't care about Israel's survival due to latent and open anti-Semitism and a desire to appease the Arabs.

Israelis (mostly leftists like Labor, Meretz and Peace Now) for some psychopathological reasons hate their Jewish heritage and will only be happy with self-destruction. In many ways they honestly supported Oslo as a way to absolve their "sin" of creating a Jewish State. Like obsessive compulsive psychotics they continue to expect Oslo to work if only Israel worked harder for its success, even though it was the Arabs who made it unworkable. They hit their heads against the brick wall of Oslo and then get a bloody headache. Being obsessive compulsive they keeping hitting their heads over and over again, each time expecting a different result. It will never happen and the Gaza retreat is just a revival of the failed Oslo blunder.

Q. Will Israeli-American relations suffer if the Gaza retreat is rejected?

A. No, Israeli relations with America are based on many common political and strategic interests and can survive any temporary disagreement on policy. America will respect a strong Israel defending its security interests and fighting terrorism. A weak Israel will only earn contempt. Israel military industries are developing many weapon systems used by the US military. Some are jointly produced with American companies. Israeli intelligence services have been extremely important in America's war against international terrorism. And finally, President Bush's political base is with the Evangelical Christians, whose support for Israel is unshakeable.

Q. Can't the IDF with its immense power be able to control terrorism after a retreat from Gaza, like it is doing now?

A. Unilateral retreat from Gaza will inevitably lead to a terrorist Palestinian State which would be recognized by the entire world. Israel would find it much more difficult to cross a national border to fight terrorism. It would not be able to maintain its extensive intelligence network which has prevented 90% of attacks before they can be perpetrated.

Q. Wouldn't a Palestinian State be demilitarized with Israel controlling its borders and air space?

A. With reference to the writings of Louis Rene Beres (an international legal expert and strategic analyst from Purdue University), once a nation's sovereignty is recognized it is under no legal obligation to adhere to the conditions it agreed to before it became a State.

Q. Does this mean that planes flying into Israel's Ben Gurion International Airport would be vulnerable to Palestinian anti-aircraft missiles?

A. Yes! And even if there is an international treaty obligation not to fire on civilian aircraft, I would not expect the Palestinians to honor **ANY** agreement.

Q. Would a Palestinian State lead to the "End of the Conflict with the Arabs?"

A. No!! The Palestinian would still want to continue terrorism to drive the Jews into the sea. Their maps do not even show Israel existing in the Middle East. The same with the other Arab countries including Egypt. They are just biding their time while Israel is being weakened by the Palestinian State (the end result of Oslo, the Road Map, Geneva, and now the Gaza retreat). Then they will launch a surprise attack to destroy what is left of Israel, bringing about a Second Holocaust.

Q. Why are all negotiations in the Middle East aimed at helping the terrorist Arabs, and none is to benefit Israel?

A. A better question is: **Why do the Israelis participate in these one-sided talks?**

Q. If America is truly Israel's best friend, why do they pursue the Road Map and back Sharon's surrender to terrorism in Gaza, which could lead to Israel's destruction?

A. It is necessary to make clear distinctions when referring to the United States. Most important there are many supporters of Israel. For example: The US Congress, the American people (especially Evangelical Christians), the US Defense department (which works with Israel developing many high-tech weapon systems) plus a high proportion of the US Jewish population.

And then there is the US State Department which has a long history of trying to undermine Israel's security. Before WWII they restricted visas to Jews trying to escape the Nazis. They opposed the Partition Resolution of the United Nations in 1947 that led to Israel's re-birth as a nation. Even though Truman forced the US Ambassador to the UN to vote YES on the resolution, the State Department enacted an arms embargo on the new Jewish State. At the same time England and France were feverishly arming the Arabs. The Arabs announced publically that this would be a **War of Extermination** that would be remembered like the great **Mongolian massacres**.

Q. Is there any hope for Israel's survival in this hostile Arab/Muslim world? In fact, the whole world seems anxious to rid the planet Earth of Jews.

A. We must struggle to survive. Those who think that we are at the **End of Time** and can relax are grossly mistaken. The struggle of Israel and *Am Yisrael* (the Jewish People) continues. Peace will come with Moshiach and not any retreat from Gaza, Oslo or Road Map.

Q. Why is Israel like Charlie Brown?

A. As a kid, one of my favorite cartoons was Charlie Brown and his gang of offbeat characters. It is a little embarrassing to admit that my fondness for Charlie Brown extended way into my adulthood. There was something about him that seemed to correspond to my life. He was always trying to do good but forces beyond his control kept intervening.

One of those forces was a nasty little girl named Lucy. She would promise Charlie to hold a football so he could kick it. Simple enough, except she never followed through on her promises. She would pull the football away and Charlie always landed on his back, stunned at the betrayal.

It may sound over simplified to equate Israel with Charlie Brown, but I am going to do it. Israel repeatedly has tried to make peace, negotiate with the Palestinian Authority and Yasser Arafat and others. Of course they always end up on their back with more suicide bombings, shootings, and sniper attacks.

Charlie Brown never learned his lesson and neither has Sharon. Although he recently launched a wide ranging offensive to destroy the terrorist infrastructure in Gaza, he is still ready to retreat and let terrorism revive itself there once Israel has left.

Bernard J. Shapiro

THE BOTTOM LINE

As Jews we are all involved in this historic struggle to survive. *It is not our fate or that of the Israelis that we should retire from this struggle. The only peace the Arabs are prepared to give us is the* **peace of the grave.**

TO ISRAELI CONSULAR OFFICIALS

(March 2005)

I feel at the present time that I cannot visit you at the consulates and embassies of Israel. This because I feel in my heart and soul that the Government of Israel no longer represents either the Jewish or Israeli people. I do however have a recurrent dream about Israel's future (taken a bit from Martin Luther King). I have written about it in several articles—usually as a Rosh Hashana prayer.

This dream keeps me faithful to *Eretz Yisrael* despite the current crisis. I want to share it with you. See below.

Your friend and **Lover of Zion**,

Bernard

MY DREAM

As I survey the fragile planet we call home, my mind makes note of the chaos, blood, and tears. The cries of a million lost souls shatter the night in a million corners of the earth. The sensitive, compassionate among them try to feed the hungry, heal the sick, and clothe the naked. One by one their energies dissipate. They try to hold back the tide with a teaspoon and then see the impossibility of the task. The Jewish people are but a cosmic speck in this universe. To many Jews who feel deeply about their own people, that speck becomes the whole world. Other Jews are irrevocably tied to non-Jewish pursuits.

May we as a people open our eyes and begin to see the world as it really is. Without becoming depressed and morose, we must realize that there are powerful forces in the world that wish us ill. May we mobilize our strength to fight our enemies until they are defeated. May we not succumb to false prophets of peace. We all want peace. We pray for peace in our Sabbath services every Friday night. After thousands of years, being victims of persecution, expulsion, extermination, and discrimination, it is natural that we yearn for peace with every ounce of our bodies and souls. It is because our hunger for peace is so strong that we must be doubly cautious not to fall for a pseudo-peace. Today none of us believe Chamberlain really negotiated *"peace in our time"* with Hitler. Why do some Jews believe that Peres and Rabin really negotiated *"peace"* with Arafat, one of today's Hitlers? The Jewish people must learn the value of unity in the face of so many enemies who wish them ill.

I pray that Israelis who have fought in countless wars will understand that there is no magic cure, though they crave to be free of constant conflict. As Jews we are all involved in this historic struggle to survive. It is not our fate or that of the Israelis that we should retire from this struggle.

Immediately following the Six Day War, I prayed at the Wall for the first time. I had expected the stones to be rough and weathered after all this time, but they were smooth from 2000 years of touching and kissing. The gentle caresses of Jews over the ages had worn soft finger grooves in the hard rock. As I placed my hands on this magnificent relic of our forefathers, I felt a surge of light and energy the likes of which I had never known. In what had to have been but the flash of a second, I felt at one with Jews from all periods of history.

In an instant I saw the continuity of Jewish history and its unbreakable connection with **Eretz Yisrael** (Land of Israel). I understood how modern Israel is the beginning of the Third Temple Period and the spiritual heir to Joshua, Saul, David, Solomon, the Maccabees and Bar Kokhba. I frequently write about the security reasons for incorporating Judea, Samaria, and Gaza into the body of Israel. There is another side to this issue and that is the spiritual-religious side. The truth, which many find inconvenient, is that the Land of Israel was promised by **G-d** to Abraham and his seed in perpetuity. **The Land of Israel is not speculative real estate to be bartered away for seductive promises of peace. The hills and valleys of Judea and Samaria contain the collective memory of the Jewish people. It was here that the Israelites first entered the Holy Land. And it was here they fought the battles, built the towns, elected their kings and were preached to by their prophets and judges. And it was on this soil that they wrote the Holy Scriptures we call our Bible.**

In my blinding flash of insight at the Wall, I also understood that Israel on its own soil was more powerful than the sum of its weapons and men. Jews who had wandered the earth powerless for two millenniums attained great power when re-united with the soil of Israel.

One thing is clear to me: the Lord has blessed Israel by re-uniting Jerusalem and bringing Judea, Samaria, and Gaza back under its control. It would be a horrendous sin against G-d and common sense for Israel to renounce this inheritance to which it is entitled. Israel holds these lands as a sacred trust for the Jewish people in perpetuity. It would not only be sinful, but also criminal, to abuse that trust by denying future generations of Jews their Holy Land—the Land of their Fathers—the one tiny spot on planet earth given to them by G-d.

I say to the suffering people of Israel. We are an ancient people with a glorious history. Though we suffer from weak leadership, we are greater than our leaders. Our souls are greater than the terrorists and their allies in the Palestinian Authority. We will never be defeated by their bullets and bombs. We have never submitted. We have never renounced our claim to *Eretz Yisrael*. We are a **Holy People**, despite our pain. We have vision where our leaders sometime are blind. Our courage is greater than the mean and cruel world which has oppressed us.

BEWARE THE RISEN PEOPLE

I have a vision and a dream that I must reveal as we approach these **Days of Awe**: In the name of G-d, the **Almighty, Defender of His People, Israel**, I say to my people's enemies: Beware of the thing that is coming, that will take what you would not give. That will free the people of Israel from your atrocities. I say to Israeli Prime Minister Ariel Sharon: Be aware of the **Risen People** who will sweep the Arab scourge into the dustbin of history. Know that the Jewish soul will be set free. The spectacular victories of the Israeli army and the return to Zion demonstrated that power. But it wasn't a miracle. It was just the soul of the Jew coming to its own. It was just the Jewish soul freed at last to be itself.

And I see it coming, the Jewish soul released to be itself. I see a new proud Jewish government coming to power in Israel. A government that reclaims the Jewish **Holy Places** and restores Jewish sovereignty in all of *Eretz Yisrael*. I see Moslem control and Islamic sites removed from the **Temple Mount** to make it ready for **Moshiach**. I see the enemies of Israel, who raise up their hands to murder or injure Jews, driven from our **Holy Land**. I see the secular Jews of Israel and the world becoming more observant and returning to the **Torah**. I see religious Jews becoming more tolerant of diversity in Jewish practice.

I see a new Israeli foreign policy that grovels before no nation, no matter how powerful. I see Israel's Foreign Minister informing every nation that their embassies must be in Jerusalem. If they don't respect Israel's capital, then may have a consulate in Tel Aviv. I see the government demanding that the Vatican return all the property it has stolen from the Jewish people during the last 2000 years. Maybe they will refuse and we could always hold their property in Israel as a down payment. The Vatican has been used to dealing with obsequious groveling Jews, but now they would see proud fearless Jews. I see an Israeli government that would change its relationship with America from one of subservience to one of equal alliance.

Yes, I have a dream (apologies to MLK) that Jews will no longer debate the obvious: *like whether to hold onto what is theirs or trade it away; whether to struggle for survival or to give up from fatigue.* I have a dream that the Jews of the kibbutz and the Jews of **YESHA** will be reborn as brothers and patriots. From the Galilee to Eilat, all the people of Israel will share the same dream of a powerful independent Zionist nation. I have a dream that this strong, proud independent Israel will win the respect of all the nations of the world, including the Arabs. Instead of the contempt it has earned in recent years, Israel will again be a light unto the nations. And finally, I have a dream that this new Israel will find the peace it so dearly deserves. A peace with strength and self-respect. As I look back at 4000 years of Jewish history, I have but one urgent hope and prayer: We must make this dream a reality. **There is no alternative.**

May the Lord, bless the leaders of Israel with the courage to pursue peace, and the wisdom to know when it is not attainable. May the

Lord bless the Jews who return to Zion and give them jobs and new friends to ease their transition into Israeli life. May the Lord bless the war-weary Israeli people with the stamina to bear up under the strain, if peace not just around the corner. May they understand that their fate may be that of endless struggle to survive in a hostile world and may they have the strength to understand that there is still no alternative (ein brera). May the people of Israel prosper and go from success to success never forgetting that their destiny lies in their might, their righteousness and their faith in HaShem.

Bernard J. Shapiro

THE FREEMAN CENTER URGES CAUTION

ON THE ISRAEL PROJECT

(October-November 2005)

[Author's Note: This article will be seen as very controversial by many. I have avoided giving the personal names of many of the people involved to protect myself and the Freeman Center from legal action (But they know who they are, and they know how accurate this report is.) The extreme anti-democratic left has a history of trying to suppress free speech through lawsuits and judicial prosecution. This has happened to a great degree in Israel and a lesser degree in America. As a Jew, a Texan, an America and a Zionist, I do not fear their money or their lawyers. I will always speak out on issues of Israel's national security and survival.

This is a long and complicated article and one must read some of my supporting articles to understand the HARSH REALITIES. There is no shortcut to full understanding of these important issues.]

★

During the last year a new, seemingly pro-Israel organization, THE ISRAEL PROJECT, has emerged on the American scene. It is well financed and has produced some wonderful brochures and solicitation letters urging American Jews to support its mission of improving Israel's image in America and around the world. Of course, none of us disagrees with that mission. In fact, that has been my goal for over 46 years.

The problem with THE ISRAEL PROJECT is not its goal and mission statement, but with its extreme leftist PEACE NOW orientation. Its founders and financial supporters have the best of intentions, and far be it for me to doubt their love of Israel. The HARSH REALITY is that they are sadly mistaken as to the best policies for insuring Israel's security and survival. Unfortunately, as someone, who has studied the military, strategic, political and foreign policy aspects of the Arab War of Extermination against Jewish Israel, I must speak the TRUTH to my readers. This war has gone on for more than a 100 years and it is not going to end any time soon. (#3)

What has changed is the remarkable destruction wrought on Zionist ideology and Israeli security by PEACE NOW and its various "front" organizations. From an obscure leftist group, far from the Jewish mainstream, PEACE NOW, now controls the centers of power among American Jewry. It controls ideologically most Jewish Federations, most Jewish newspapers, Jewish news services, the Reform Jewish Movement, and the major Jewish Organizations and their associations.

In Israel it has moved from the leftist fringes of the Israeli political scene. Shalom Akshav (PEACE NOW) has taken control of several political parties, including the LABOR PARTY. Ariel Sharon's Likud/Left alliance which heads the Israeli government, the security services, the Israel Foreign, Defense and Justice ministries are all under the control of PEACE NOW IDEOLOGY now. The Israeli Supreme Court and the Judiciary as well as most Israeli newspapers and electronic media operate under PEACE NOW ideology.

One might ask, if this ideology has spread so fast and so far, why is it so bad for Israel. It will require the reader to do some study to understand the full seriousness of this threat to Israel. A quick-study guide is presented by me below in note#1 (PEACE NOW EXPOSED) printed below. Then read note #2 (MAKING PEACE WITH WOLVES).

[The danger to Israel's security and survival has been documented in several of my articles: See Notes: 5, 6, 7, 10 &11]

THE ISRAEL PROJECT presents itself to the public as a new organization dedicated to improving Israel's image through sophisticated hasbara, education and a network of students, Jewish leaders and others with the similar goal of improved public relations for Israel. What they don't tell you is that their organization is a "front" for the extreme leftist government of Sharon, Peres, Meretz, PEACE NOW (with the godfather of Israeli appeasement and post-Zionism, Yossi Beilin, in the background).

My personal experience with this group of leftists dates back several years. Circa 2003, I got information that a group was being formed to improve Israel's public relations (hasbara). I contacted the players in New York and offered my services free of charge. I never received a response. I sent them several of my articles dealing with Arab propaganda and how to defeat it as well as articles on improving hasbara in general. See Notes #4, 8, 9 & 10 to verify my expertise for over 40 years on this subject. I never received a response. After repeated inquiries, I was finally told that this project was controlled by the Israel Foreign Ministry (under Shimon Peres) and that I didn't have a security clearance for this job. The absurdity of refusing my offer of expert help for no fee baffled me for a while.

A little more than a year ago, I was contacted by a group of very wealthy Los Angeles Jews, who had at one time been supporters of the Freeman Center. They wanted to know what I would do to improve Israel's public relations, should I be given adequate funding. As most know, the Freeman Center, operates on a "hand to mouth" budget with extremely little funding. Of course, the pro-Israel \'bang for the buck\' is quite dramatic. In a given year, we produce and distribute about 100 times more (very serious, not peace fantasy) pro-Israel material than the entire Israel Foreign Ministry on 0.1% of their budget.

Naturally I was very excited about the prospect. Their cover story was that they were allowing several organizations to participate in the funding. I sent them a lot of material including financial statements from the Freeman Center. It was all a hoax. They promised to let me know the results in about six months. I never heard from them. My contact person with that organization was transferred and could not be reached

Being disappointed, I began to analyze the applications I had filled out for them. All of a sudden, I noticed one key question. It was: "Is your organization ideologically closer to PEACE NOW or the ZIONIST ORGANIZATION OF AMERICA. Had there been any chance of me getting funding, this answer of mine seemed to disqualify me.

When their solicitations, brochures and plans began to surface, it was easy for me to see that my ideas had been used. Unfortunately, they had been turned around (reverse engineering) to support the policy of appeasement and PEACE NOW. Israeli PM Sharon and Israeli FM Peres had been quite upset at the emergence of large groups that opposed the surrender of the Land of Israel to its terrorist enemies. While most American Jews remained passive, some 40 million Evangelical Christians refused to accept that

Sharon and Peres acted in name of G-d and Zionism. Some Zionist groups such as Americans For a Safe Israel, Zionist Organization of America, and the Freeman Center kept up a ceaseless information campaign on the dangers of expelling Jews from parts of Eretz Yisrael. This was done from both a religious and a security perspective.

The appeasers of terrorism had no legitimate arguments or grounds for their actions, so they were forced to act in a heavy handed and un-democratic manner in order to suppress free discussion on the serious issues of Israeli security and survival. The left, as I mentioned above, had pretty much taken control of American Jewry. Cracks, however, are beginning to appear in this tight control as the mountain of dead Jews grows higher in Israel and Jewish blood becomes cheap again. How long will Americans remain silent as rivers of blood begin to flow through Jerusalem, Hadera, Tel Aviv, Ashdod, Haifa, Netania. Jews will die on both sides of the security fence and soon the first commercial airliner will be shot down at Ben Gurion Airport.

Will the Israelis fight or die? The choice is as simple as that. The Peace Now activists prefer that Jews die rather than Arabs be inconvenienced. Zionism has been outlawed by the Israeli Left and its Supreme Court. The government of Israel has devoted itself to building a "Palestinian State" instead of building up Israel. Is this what you want?

It is not too late to rescue Israel from the apocalypse coming, should the current government continue the deconstruction of the State of Israel.

A step that American can do easily is to choose carefully the pro-Israel organizations you wish to support and to make sure they reflect your views. The Freeman Center recommends the following organizations (not a complete list): Americans For A Safe Israel, Zionist Organization of America, Freeman Center For Strategic Studies & Women in Green, David Horowitz's Center For Popular Culture and Accuracy in Media. The Freeman Center cautions about giving to the following non or anti-Zionist organizations (list not complete): THE ISRAEL PROJECT, American-Israel Public Affairs Committee, Anti-Defamation League, American Jewish Congress, New Israel Fund (for Israel's enemies), American Jewish Committee, Seeds of Peace & Tikkun.

Bernard J. Shapiro

The article below, US ATTITUDES ON ISRAEL IMPROVES by Nathan Burstein (THE JERUSALEM POST—Oct. 31, 2005) shows how THE ISRAEL PROJECT plans to manipulate public opinion to support appeasement of terrorism. By the way all polls are subject to political agendas. It is about how the questions are written or asked. For example the \'opinion elites\' in this poll all read the same biased news and listen to the same pro-appeasement propaganda of the Israel Foreign Ministry. Had they read THE MACCABEAN ONLINE or subscribed to the Freemanlist, their opinions would be quite different.

If you are in favor of PEACE NOW and prefer the deconstruction of Israel and the creation of a new terrorist State of Palestine, then THE ISRAEL PROJECT is perfect for you. If you are a true Zionist with a strong and passionate feeling for the unalienable right of the Jewish People for the Land of Israel, then please join and support the Freeman Center.

Shimon Peres once said that one need not study history since it is the future that counts. I am sorry to tell you, Shimon, that "those who do not learn from history are forced to repeat it" (George Santayana circa 1870). Jewish history has been filled with too much tragedy—I DON'T WANT TO REPEAT IT!

Need I say more?

REFLECTIONS OF A FRUSTRATED ZIONIST—YEAR END (2007)

(January 2008)

Much has happened in the last year. It has not been a good year for Zionism and the Jewish People. One could be optimistic and try to find the bright side of what has been happening. I am forced by nature to tell the truth in a realistic way. I am condemned to discuss harsh realities.

Some of my reflections:

1. The growth of religious Zionism would save Israel, IF there were TIME for it to take power. I fear that time is running out.

When will the Nationalist Camp realize that we are "at war already" with a PLO supported government that rules Israel? At what point will Israelis realize that the **CIVIL WAR** they fear, **IS ALREADY TAKING PLACE AND THEY ARE LOSING?** Why don't members of the Nationalist Camp understand that FORCE is being used by only ONE side which is the extremist pro-Arab anti-Semitic government. The monopoly on power must be broken or there is **NO** hope.

2. Appeals for aliyah to Israel are a joke. Sounds harsh and non-Zionist. I understand that. Let me make something "perfectly clear" as US President Richard Nixon used to say. As long as Israel is ruled by anti-Semites, who are more interested in protecting the Arab "right" to kill Jews, don't expect huge waves of aliyah. As long as the police, courts, Shin Bet, media continue to defame and persecute **TRUE ZIONISTS**, don't expect huge waves of immigration. As long as Land in Israel is controlled by the government (and the pro-Arab JNF) to the neglect of Jewish couples wanting to build affordable housing, don't expect a huge wave of immigration. As long as the IDF is used as a political tool to suppress freedom of speech and the G-d given right of the Jewish People to settle Eretz Yisrael, don't expect a huge wave of aliyah. As long as the bureaucracy in the Israel government ministries discourages individual enterprise, there will be no massive wave of immigration.

3. Israel's military/strategic policy has been on a sharp decline since the days of Former Israeli Pm Ben Gurion and Menachem Begin. When Israel agreed to allow the PLO to escape Beirut after the First Lebanon War in 1982, the decline began in earnest. The Freeman Center strategy would have been to agree to let them leave on ships that would have an "accident" en route killing all aboard.

Israel has, without a doubt, the best military in world. The Israel Defense Forces are quite capable of achieving any objective the Israeli government puts before it. The soldiers of the IDF are brave, patriotic and exceptionally well trained and equipped. Unfortunately Israel's political leadership is confused, inept and lacking in Zionist motivation.

Israel has been unable to stop the War of Extermination against it, because it lacks the political will to do what is necessary. The current campaign to secure the release of Cpl. Gilad Shalit, the captured IDF soldier, illustrates this fact. The Israeli government has given the military very limited objectives, primarily the release of the soldier. Proper strategic planning would use the sad situation of Shalit's capture to achieve a number of far reaching and important objectives.

Already Olmert has done several things that prevent the accomplishment of these aims. He has stopped the offensive in Gaza to allow time for negotiations to release Shalit. He has allowed Israel's enemy, Egypt, to intervene, and given the terrorists time to re-group and make demands.

The Israeli objectives should be:

1. The release of the soldier.

2. Elimination of the terrorist leadership in the PA.

3. Item #2 means successfully destroying the newly elected Hamas government.

4. Immediate annexation of all territory in Judea and Samaria that has strategic and religious value (which means all).

5. Withdraw citizenship and voting rights from Israeli Arabs who support terrorism against the State of Israel (which means most).

6. Create municipal councils but not sovereignty for Arab cities in the newly annexed areas.

7. Encourage Arab emigration by strict enforcement of taxes, building permits, national service requirements, and by providing funds to aid in emigration.

8. Dramatically increase Jewish immigration to Israel by reducing taxes and regulations on business. Immigration will soar once the lands of Judea and Samaria are opened up for massive Jewish settlement.

9. The Zionist/Jewish character of Israel must be affirmed and the cost of Jewish blood must rise dramatically as the government develops a zero tolerance for terrorism.

All of the above objectives are achievable. It is my hope that the Olmert government will be replaced soon with a new Zionist government committed to the objectives I have listed above.

10. The policy of restraint may have been practical during the pre-state days and even during the! early years of Israeli independence. These periods were characterized by weakness and relative dependence on foreign goodwill. Following the Six Day War in 1967, the need for restraint (havlagah) decreased and the damage it caused began to become more evident. Israel became the preeminent power in the Middle East, yet failed to grasp the strategic opportunities that came with such dominance. Here are some of the historical highlights of the failed policy of restraint:

1. Following the Six Day War (1967) and the capture of Jerusalem, Moshe Dayan turned over control of Judaism's most sacred place, the Temple Mount, to Moslem authorities. He did it to appease their sensibilities to the Israeli capture of the city. Jewish rights were ignored to please the defeated Arabs, who had plotted our destruction. Dayan also prevented a mass exodus of Arabs from YESHA, which ultimately led to the problems we face today.

2. During the War of Attrition with Egypt (1969-70), the Israeli forces adopted primarily a defensive posture. They built a system of bunkers (The Bar Lev Line) along the Suez Canal. Israeli soldiers were heavily pounded daily by Egyptian artillery. Finally they began to use aircraft to strike targets deep into Egypt. The policy of restraint kept them from striking anything but military and minor economic targets. Israeli soldiers died because the government was inhibited from causing Egypt \'real\' pain.

3. The Yom Kippur War of 1973 is a classic example of restraint run amok. Israeli military intelligence did not fail to recognize the approaching danger as has been the common account. In fact, Israel's leaders made the political decision not to utilize the great power of the IDF to crush the Egyptian and Syrian armies that they KNEW were planning to attack. Thousands of Israeli soldiers died needlessly.

4. The Camp David Accord with Egypt was another example of the failure to exert Israeli power. The oil fields of Sinai would have given Israel economic independence from America. The cost of redeployment from Sinai placed Israel in almost permanent debt to American diplomacy (increasingly pro-Arab). Did Israel achieve anything worthwhile at Camp David? I think not and I believe history will bear me out. Egypt has become one of the most ant-Semitic and hostile Arab countries in the world. As a result of Camp David, the Egyptian army now threatens Israel, having been equipped with the most modern American weapons.

5. During the War in Lebanon (1982), the IDF reached Beirut and then failed to complete the destruction of the PLO. Our enemies were allowed to escape and prepare to fight another day. Why didn't the Israeli Navy sink the ships loaded with PLO troops (including Arafat) as they fled Beirut? **RESTRAINT!**

6. In 1987 the intifada began and the Israeli forces showed great restraint and thus were incapable of crushing it. Of course, Israel received no credit in the Western media for such restraint. The failure to defeat this uprising began a process of demoralization among the Israeli population.

7. The Persian Gulf War (1991) and the SCUD attacks on Israel led to further demoralization. The failure to adequately respond to Iraq's

aggression and the humiliating sealed rooms, led to a rapid decline in Israeli morale and desire to defend itself. More and more Israelis began to feel impotent, weak and fatigued with the continuous battle for survival. The Oslo Accords were the logical outcome of this depression and feeling that they could not sustain the struggle.

8. The Oslo Accords (1993) were the ultimate failure of the policy of restraint. Israel like America actually was very powerful. The IDF was unequaled in the Middle East while the US was the most powerful nation in the world. Yet despite this power, Israel's leaders, were ready to grant equal status to a band of murderers and ultimately create a state of "Palestine" which would challenge its right to the Land and its capital of Jerusalem.

9. Israeli forces in Lebanon should have been given a free hand to \'punish\' all those who facilitate attacks on them including Syria, Lebanon, and Iran. There should be no more agreements that tie Israeli hands.

The damage caused by havlagah (restraint) has been immense and it far past time to reverse that policy. Americans have been viciously attacked in Africa, Yemen, and Saudi Arabia. The attempt to try to criminalize terrorism has been a dreadful mistake. Terrorism is sponsored by states who allow their territory and funds to help the organization of terrorist. The Oslo agreement allowed Arafat to set up terrorist headquarters in Israel's heartland. From there he sent terrorists to attack Israel. With plausible deniability he claims "he is not responsible."

12 THINGS I AM SICK AND TIRED OF:

1. I am sick and tired of the slowly escalating actions of the IDF to fight terrorism.

The slow escalation allows PA terrorism to become immune to Israel's strategy. It allows them to smuggle more guns, missiles, mortars and anti-aircraft missiles into PA territory. This is much the same as with bacterial infections. If the antibiotic is not strong enough to eliminate it, then the disease will return in a much more virulent form. I would suggest that the IDF launch a massive offensive against the terrorists until victory.

2. I am sick and tired of the Israeli government's fear of collateral damage to the enemy.

The Arabs have no such qualms. In fact they target civilians in bestial suicide and rocket attacks. PA weapons factories, weapons storage depots and bomb making facilities should be blasted off the face of earth even if it causes civilian casualties. Remember that "he who is merciful to the cruel, will end up being cruel to the merciful."

Also remember that the US Civil War, WWI and WWII were won by the massive inflection of casualties on the enemies' civilian populations.

3. I am sick and tired of Israeli PM Olmert's policy of restraint.

The adjustment to accepting the killing of Jews is an abomination. A Jew here or there murdered daily, pretty soon adds up to a lot of dead and maimed Jews. I remember when the Al Aksa terror on Israel began in September 2000, the IDF general staff opened a file called "Operation Thorns", a plan for the retaking of the PA areas. They estimated Israeli dead at 300. Since then there have been almost 1500 Jews killed, which is five times the estimated combat deaths (plus 10,000 wounded, many maimed for life), with no apparent consequences to the terrorists' ability to inflict casualties on Israel.

There is one extremely important variable. The PA (especially in Gaza) has used the last six years to build bunkers, firing positions, smuggle in heavy weapons and missiles, create an underground arms industry and organize an army of 100,000. The defeat of PA now would certainly be more costly. And it will grow with time. There is a very short window of time to defeat the PA terrorists with minimal losses. Many political analysts and military experts agree that Israel must take decisive action NOW.

4. I am sick and tired of the US State Department urging Israel to show "restraint."

Despite the fact that the CIA knows exactly WHO (PA) is attacking WHOM (Israel) the State Department continues call for a stop to the "cycle of violence." Whenever Israel is attacked viciously, there is rush to tell Israel "to turn the other cheek". Are we Christians or Jews? Does American follow the Christian policy expected of Israel?

5. I am sick and tired of Shimon Peres trying to arrange another appeasement for the PA.

He claims to be seeking a cease fire and a return to negotiations. Let me be honest with you. I don't want negotiations with either Hamas, Abbas or Assad. I want to crush them and their terrorist gangs.

6. I am sick and tired of the continued UN presence within the borders of Israel.

It's time to remove them and assert Israel's sovereignty. Israel should work to have the world withdraw its recognition of Arab refugee camps and refugees. It should condemn the hypocritical treatment of the Arab countries in exploiting these people for political purposes. Israel should declare in a strong voice that there are NO refugees. That status is not permanent and obviously should not apply to people living in the same place for 58 years.

7. I am sick and tired of the international boycott of Jerusalem as Israel's capital.

Israel should unilaterally announce to the nations of the world that all embassies MUST be in Jerusalem. (Consulates may be in Tel Aviv or any other place they want). Israel will no longer permit its eternal capital to be disrespected.

8. I am sick and tired that under both Labor and Likud governments, Arutz Sheva, Israel National Radio, has not been fully legalized.

Whatever happened to freedom of speech? Arutz Sheva should not only be allowed to establish facilities on land but also a television channel. I am also sick and tired of government television being controlled and dominated by the extreme left that does not represent the Israeli public. A lot of the time they represent the Arabs and not Israelis.

9. I am sick and tired of Israel's trying to be \'Mister Nice Guy\' to a hypocritical world.

Europeans are increasingly comparing Israel to the Nazis. Over half of all the resolutions of the UN since its founding have been directed against Israel. At the conference on how to condemn Israel in Durban, South Africa, UN head Kofi Anan condemned Israel for existing. In fact, at a recent meeting at the UN, there was a map of "Palestine", which included all of Israel. The Arab world openly plots the destruction of Israel. I am sick and tired of the vilification of "settlers".

10. I am sick and tired of Israel tolerating Moslem restrictions and desecrations on the Temple Mount.

The excuse that it would cause violence to exercise our rights there is absurd. Israel has the capability to enforce security. Virtually everything Israel wants do in the Land of Israel displeases the Arabs, who want us to leave. Jews should be allowed to pray on the Temple Mount and the destruction of Jewish antiquities by the Moslem waqf needs to be stopped immediately.

11. I am sick and tired of PA demonstrations of the fierceness of their terrorists and how they will destroy Israel.

Why not knock off a bunch of them during their demonstrations? Maybe they would be more circumspect.

12. And most important, the IDF and police should never be used for political purposes. Their purpose is to protect Israelis and not to expel them from their homes or persecute them.

✶

I **DO** believe that we will defeat our current adversaries. We will succeed and survive from three sources of our strength: **Love of Tanach (Torah), Love of Eretz Israel (Land of Israel, and Love of Am Yisrael (People of Israel).**

. . . . In blood and fire was Israel born, and on a hot anvil was she forged. Her youth understood that life in the new Jewish homeland would require sacrifice. With stories of the stench of burning flesh from the ovens of Auschwitz embedded deep in their psyches, the young Israeli soldiers fight with the firm conviction that there is still no alternative, "ein breira." (From personal diary 1992).

To that I would like add something the American soldiers used to say during the heaviest fighting in Viet Nam. This is dedicated (slightly revised) to the brave IDF soldiers who face the enemy every day: Yea, though I walk through the Valley of Death, I will fear no evil because the Almighty fights with me for the Restoration of Zion and for love of HIS people, Israel.

. . . . And for the Jews of YESHA, I believe that **He** will **NOT** allow Olmert to expel them from the heartland of ***ERETZ YISRAEL***. But remember, the Lor-d helps those who help themselves. Do not wait for a miracle—**BE THE MIRACLE!**

Bernard J. Shapiro

THE FREEMAN CENTER EXPOSED—THE GOOD AND THE BAD (?)

(January 2008)

Please read this message carefully.

The Freeman Center has been around for so long (since 1992) most people take it for granted. Readers depend on the Freemanlist daily news and commentary. We have always had a unique philosophy of being generous to other Zionist organizations and new authors. While most Jewish websites distribute only their own material, we send you a mixture of excellent material from many sources. Sort of a one stop shop for serious Zionists.

At the time we launched our website, there were less than 10 strong Zionist sites on the Internet. Today there are 10,000 Jewish sites, many of them Zionist. The new ones came up following our lead and copying our model. They had much more money and jazzier graphics. We have always concentrated on being primarily a text site for people wanting in depth reports and commentary on the news. In the USA, academics, the military, the government and many politicians read our reports. I don't claim to have convinced anybody of anything. We provided the information for sound judgments. Some understood it and some didn't.

Many love my no punches barred pro-Israel commentary on Israel and World events. Some object to how harsh my criticism is to the "democratically" elected government of Israel or the organized mainstream Jewish community in America. For my critics, I say, thank you. Why? If I pleased you and were popular, then I would not be worth "bucket of warm spit" (Harry Truman). Groucho Marx said it a little different: "I don't want to be a member of any organization that would have me."

Many important writers and political/military analysts got their start broadcasting on the web through the Freemanlist and in the Maccabean, including: Dan Nimrod, Lou Rene Beres, Yosef Bodansky, Boris Shusteff, Mark Langfan, Major Swawn M. Pine, Gerardo Joffe, Elyakim Haeztzni, David Wilder, Yoram Ettinger, Gary Cooperberg, Paul Eidelberg, Emanuel

Winston, David Basch, Ariel Natan Pasko, Steven Shamrak and many more.

At the time we stared the Freeman Center, including The Maccabean and the Freemanlist, the self-destructive process know as Oslo, was rearing its ugly head. The Freeman Center (along with Arutz Sheva, Paul Eidelberg, Herbert Zweibon-AFSI, Women in Green (Ruth and Nadia Matar) and Moshe Feiglin) immediately began to protest and explain the truth to a nation deluded into thinking that "peace" was around the corner.

Some of my critics tell me that I have two major flaws: I don't live in Israel and I am not 100% Orthodox by their definition. The first criticism can be answered with three names: Shimon Peres, Ehud Olmert and Yossi Beilin. The 30% of Israelis who continue to support Kadima, Labor, Meretz and Peace Now demonstrate clearly that living in Israel is no guarantee of either intelligence or Zionism. I can assure you that Jabotinzky's historical instincts were far sharper than David Ben Gurion. Jabotinzky died in 1940 and never lived in Israel.

The argument about religion is more difficult to answer for me as a devoted Jew and Zionist. I should be fully Orthodox. Yet I am flawed and not able to be 100%. I was raised in a Reform Congregation that had bylaws that required members to sign an oath NOT to support a Jewish State. (It was repealed in 1967) I think I have come a long way. Many Orthodox Jews, both in America and Israel are not even Zionist and allow the destruction of Eretz Yisrael, through their indifference and lack of political action. Many Christians in this country are very pro-Israel and stand with the Jews 100%. In fact, they are more Zionist than most Jews. Should there be a religious test for them also? Paul Eidelberg recently wrote: **"Bernard Shapiro is an outstanding and devoted Zionist. Would that Israel 's religious parties harbored his devotion to Eretz Yisrael ".**

You are my friends for many years, and I must tell you about my biggest flaw. I never took the steps necessary to become a big well financed organization. I always wanted to have the final say on Zionist ideology. This kept me from becoming dependent on big foundations and individuals that could make me moderate my positions on Israel. Fortunately there are some wonderful people that have kept me going all these years. Those

Bernard J. Shapiro

people have the heart and soul of true Zionists. While executives in major Jewish organizations in this country earn $250-500,000 a year, it was my choice to work for very little and now nothing.

Politicians in Israel are so corrupt that it nauseates me. In my case, you could offer me a $1 million dollars to change my views and broadcasts to accept surrender of our Holy Land. I would not take it.

This brings me to an important subject. Every year costs go up. Time is taking a toll of my older supporters who remember the Holocaust, Israel's Independence and the dreadful days before the Six Days War. The number of readers of the Freemanlist keeps growing and many of you send it to your friends (one reader up to 150 people on his list). I am very happy about that. The message of Jewish and Israeli survival and security in an apocalyptic era is of extreme importance to me.

But I need to be practical and pay our growing bills like: telecommunication, rent, webmaster, utilities, cyberspace, band width, security (which I have had to triple recently), computer repairs and much more. About 1% of our readers make a tax deductible contribution to the Freeman Center. I am appealing to you to do the mitzvah of supporting our important educational work. And, of course, if you do it in 2007 it can be used as a tax deduction on your 2007 income tax.

With Love of Israel and Faith in Hashem,

Bernard

PASSOVER AND JEWISH LIBERATION

(April 2008)

On this Passover (2008) I have many thoughts and reflections. Some might be of interest to you. There are three special **Holy Days** in Judaism that deal with the salvation and liberation of the Jewish People. We just celebrated Purim and read how Esther was able to save our people from the evil Hamen. Rabbis for thousands of years have foretold that Hamens will arise in every generation to destroy us. Unfortunately they have been correct.

At Passover we re-live the most decisive moment in Jewish history. We were not only liberated from bondage in Egypt, saw G-d's miracles, received the Ten Commandments, but were given **Eretz Yisrael** as our sacred inheritance. Like many gifts from HaShem, we had to earn it by hard work and many battles against our enemies.

There are three more Israeli National Holidays we celebrate at this time of year, **Yom ha-Sho\'ah** (Holocaust Remembrance Memorial), **Yom ha-Zikkaron** (Remembrance Day for fallen soldiers and terrorist victims) and finally **Yom ha-Azma\'ut** (Israel Independence Day). They are all related. The Holocaust, though it came half a century after the beginning of modern Zionism, forced the Jewish People to act to fulfill its mission. Unfortunately the Jewish people then went to sleep and are not preparing to prevent the Second Holocaust that is being planned for us by 1.5 billion Muslims. So much for all the Holocaust Museums and the slogan **NEVER AGAIN**

The intense anguish and knowledge that without a sovereign Jewish State protected by a Jewish Army, we had **NO** future in this World. The Hamens like Hitler would rise against us in every country until we were gone. Perhaps some future society would keep a few Jews in a protected **ZOO** so that the world could study this ancient people and their lost civilization.

Yom ha-Zikkaron is a day we remember the brave IDF soldiers who defended our beloved Israel. And on Israel Independence day we rejoice on the miracle of the Jewish people's re-birth in its Holy Land. I am not sure it is fair to ask young Israelis to fight terrorism and capture our enemies only to have them released by successive Israeli governments.

Sadly, it is getting increasingly harder for me to rejoice on **Yom ha-Azma\'ut** with each passing year. Since 1992, successive Israeli governments have been slowly destroying the foundation of Israeli Independence. The so called "peace process," which we all know is a surrender process to terrorism, is tearing the heart out of Zionism.

I have been criticized for calling Israeli leaders traitors for selling out Israel to its enemies. I not only stand by my statements, but have taken the opportunity to look the definition of treason in the Merriam Webster's Collegiate Dictionary. Here it is: ***"Betrayal of a trust."***

Ehud Olmert and Israel's previous governments (since 1992) have factually betrayed the Jewish Peoples trust by denying their covenant with G-d. HaShem gave them ***Eretz Yisrael*** in perpetuity. He did not give it to Olmert or any coalition of Israeli politicians to dispose of as if it were their own real estate.

DAVID BEN GURION, founding father and first Prime Minister of Israel, had this to say about territorial concessions at the Zionist conference in Basel (Switzerland) in 1939:

"I say from the point of view of realizing Zionism it is better to have immediately a Jewish state, even if it would only be in a part of the western Land of Israel. I prefer this to a continuation of the British Mandate . . . in the whole of the western Land of Israel. But before clarifying my reasoning, I have to make a remark about principle. If we were offered a Jewish state in the western Land of Israel in return for our relinquishing our historical right over the whole Land of Israel, then I would postpone the state. **No Jew has the right to relinquish the right of the Jewish people over the whole Land of Israel. No Jewish body has such authority, not even the whole Jewish people have the authority to waive the right (to the Land of Israel) for future generations for all time."**

And now the Olmert and his left wing elites are actively giving away Jerusalem. Is there no end to this treason (no apologies for telling the truth). Friends I have always tried to call things by their correct names. The Freemanlist does not call war—peace, black—white, tyranny—democracy, and certainly not our enemies by the false name of "peace partner."

The bottom line, I will celebrate all the Holy and Holidays, but some with a heavy heart and trepidation about the future.

Bernard J. Shapiro

THE FREEMAN CENTER VERSUS AIPAC

The Truth and the Consequences

(June 2008)

We recently were witness to the large AIPAC Conference in Washington, D.C. All the presidential candidates plus many Israeli and American political leaders spoke to the group. These included: Barack Obama, Hillary Clinton, Ehud Olmert, John McCain and Condoleezza Rice Ehud Olmert, Benjamin Netanyahu and other major political leaders.

There are many Americans (especially in the State Department, CIA, academic, Muslim and left-wing communities) who believe that AIPAC is an evil force that distorts US Middle East policy to our detriment. On the other hand, there are many pro-Israel Jews and Christians, who believe that it is indispensable in the defense of Israeli interests in Washington. Tens of millions of dollars are raised annually to support this organization.

The **Truth** is not found in these two views of AIPAC described above. Up until 1992, one could say that the second positive view of AIPAC was correct. For many years Tom Dine headed that organization and led a never ending battle supporting Israel and Zionism. The in the Israeli election of 1992, Labor leaders Yitzhak Rabin and Shimon Peres took over Israel. Rabin became Prime Minister and Peres a Foreign Minister.

Peres with his associate, extreme anti-Zionist Yossi Beilin, began negotiating with the outlawed terrorist PLO. It became necessary to emasculate AIPAC to prevent American Jewish criticism of the planed Oslo Agreements. Dine was ousted after many years of great service in a very nasty coup. AIPAC was now in the hands of pliable leaders who would follow every lead of the Israeli government, **NO MATTER HOW SELF DESTRUCTIVE.**

And those self destructive plans came one after another in rapid succession: Oslo, Hebron, Wye, Road Map, Expulsion of Jews from Gaza, restriction on building in Judea and Samaria, persecution of religious Jews and violation of their civil and human rights and finally the elimination of the Jewish right to self defense. Education in Israel ceased being patriotic or Zionist and building a Palestinian pseudo state became the goal of the Israeli Government. AIPAC said nothing and cheered the government's mad dash to dismantle the long sought for Jewish State.

THE BOTTOM LINE

There are still some TRUE Zionist organizations in America. The ones that have fought the longest and the hardest for Israel are American's For A Safe Israel, Freeman Center For Strategic Studies, Zionist Organization of America and Pastor John Hagee's Christians United For Israel. These are the organizations deserving of your support.

OUR PRO ISRAEL PHILOSOPHY COMPARED TO AIPAC

1. TRUE ZIONISTS: All of *Eretz Yisrael* belongs in perpetuity to the Jewish People

AIPAC: We will negotiate away any part of *Eretz Israel* the government believes will bring "peace"

2. ZIONISTS: Israel's right of self defense should be aggressive and not dependent of America or world opinion

AIPAC: Israel's defense should be based on what America allow and world public opinion find acceptable

3. ZIONISTS: It is moral and just to expel or transfer a hostile terrorists loving population from Israel. No racial implication, only behavioral characteristics. For example: Those who want to kill us should not be our neighbors.

AIPAC: It is immoral to transfer Arabs but it is Moral to transfer and expel Jews, as in Gush Katif and Yesha.

4. ZIONISTS: Gaza should be re-conquered, put under total siege, and starved until the Hamas terrorists surrender. That means no food, water,

medical supplies, electricity or fuel (which they use to fire rockets into Israel).

AIPAC: Humanitarian aid should flow to Gaza and a cease-fire that, leaves Hamas in place to continue the war, should be worked out

5. ZIONISTS: In order to save IDF lives, no consideration should be made for civilian "human shield" of Hamas. Standoff artillery and aircraft bombs should soften targets before ground invasion. Civilian casualties should be NO more considered than the Allies did during WWI in Dresden and Hiroshima.

AIPAC: The IDF military must act with great restraint, even if this means many more Israeli soldier's deaths.

6. ZIONISTS: No negotiations on the Golan, except demanding the Syrians return to the lines following the Israeli victory of 1973.

AIPAC: Whatever the Israeli government wants to do.

7. ZIONISTS: Protect all of Israel's water resources, including the Golan, the Judean-Samarian mountain aquifer, as well as prevent the pollution of water resources by sewage spill off Gaza coast and from Arab villages.

AIPAC: Support the Israeli governments plans to giveaway most of Israel's water resources to hostile enemies. And then they would want to replace this water through costly desalination schemes.

8. ZIONISTS: Would make Israel militarily independent of America and turn the relationship into a true alliance. Now it is an asymmetrical relationship, despite the fact Israel supplies the US approximately 5 times the military aid as America supplies Israel.

AIPAC: Loves to boast about its getting weapons from America, but never reveals the hidden cost. Every deal adds to the diplomatic pressure on Israel foreign policy. Every deal ends up in massive sales to Arab enemy countries like Egypt and Saudi Arabia. Every deal has some detrimental effect on Israel's local military industries.

9. ZIONISTS: Never discuss or give away any part of Jerusalem and also take over the Temple Mount from Islamic control. And of course allow regular Jewish prayer on the Mount.

AIPAC: Israel should not offend Muslims by asserting Jewish rights in Jerusalem and the Temple mount.

I could list many more differences between true American Zionist organizations and the pseudo Zionists at AIPAC. The above is enough for you to make a decision on who to support.

Bernard J. Shapiro

LET FREEMAN CENTER TAKE OVER ISRAEL FOREIGN MINISTRY—War crimes charges grow—

JERUSALEM SILENT

(February 2009)

FOR THE SAKE OF ISRAEL WE MUST DRAFT THE FREEMAN CENTER TO HANDLE PUBLIC RELATION FOR THE JEWISH STATE. THE FOREIGN MINISTRY HAS CAUSED GREAT DAMAGE TO THE GOOD NAME OF ISRAEL. I WOULD AGREE TO LET THE OFFICE WORKERS THERE CONTINUE TO TAKE CARE OF VISAS AND TOURISM (LIVNI LOVED TO SHOW ISRAEL, NOT AS LAND OF THE BIBLE, BUT AS SEXY BIKINI CLAD ISRAELI GIRLS).

THE FREEMAN CENTER CAN DO THE FOLLOWING:

1. Put up a vigorous Zionist defense of Israel at one tenth of one percent (0.01) the cost of the entire Israeli Foreign Ministry.

2. And they can do it with NO guilt feelings

3. They can do this with NO apologies to the World, USA, EU, Arabs, Muslims, UN for breathing the oxygen of Planet Earth. And, of course, being the only indigenous people living in its natural HOME, with the deed signed by the Almighty as a perpetual trust.

4. How do I know the Freeman Center can do all of above??? It is simple; we have been doing it since 1992. The RECORD is there. Go to www.freeman.org and see over 70,000 pages of the best news and commentary on Israel in THE MACCABEAN ONLINE www.freeman.org/online.htm

During this same period, the Israel Foreign Ministry devoted all of its resources to: a. Promoting the "tooth fairy" of Peace with Barbarians who want to destroy us. b. Undermining organization like the Freeman Center and myself personally who defended Israel's undiminished right to self-defense, security and survival in the dangerous world we find ourselves. c. Helping to tie the hands of the IDF and endangering the lives of our most precious commodity (our sons and daughters) to save the lives of Arabs, who wish us dead. They have accepted and defended the concept of restraint (havlagah) or "purity of arms." There is nothing pure or sacred about sacrificing Jewish blood on the ALTER of Left-wing pseudo-morality. Our enemies worship death—so help them achieve it. We believe in life—so let us save our own.

Please see articles below

Still a frustrated Zionist, after all these years-

Who still loves Israel and prays to HaShem that REALITY begin to be a guiding principle of Israeli policy.

Bernard

War crimes charges grow, Jerusalem silent

Feb. 27, 2009

Herb Keinon, THE JERUSALEM POST

As various individuals and organizations file petitions abroad against Israel for alleged war crimes, including at the International Criminal Court in The Hague, there is growing criticism in Jerusalem that Israel is taking too laid-back an approach to the matter, and not going on the offensive.

"[Attorney-General Menahem] Mazuz is involved, and a committee has been set up to deal with any lawsuits filed, but these are all defensive measures," one government source said. "We are not taking the offensive."

The best example of this, the official said, was Jerusalem's silence when the Palestinian Authority urged the ICC to investigate Israel's alleged war crimes during Operation Cast Lead in the Gaza Strip.

Some 210 groups, including the PA, have urged the ICC to deal with the matter and the ICC's prosecutor has said a "preliminary analysis" is underway.

Israel could have come out and said this was not the way the country's peace partner should act, but instead remained quiet, the government source said.

Another example of the low key approach was Israel's complete silence when an Arab League delegation entered Gaza this week to investigate alleged war crimes and report back to the League's secretary-general, Amr Moussa.

One Israeli Foreign Ministry official said that it would have been possible to sharply reply to the PA's actions, but because of Israel's pre-election, and now post-election, transition period, there was "no one to take the initiative."

The official further said that neither Prime Minister Ehud Olmert, who spent much of his tenure developing a relationship with the PA, nor Foreign Ministry Tzipi Livni, who led negotiations with it, had a political interest in publicly attacking it.

The official said that the policy was also dictated by other considerations, foremost that Israel did not want to give these petitions any more momentum, and a widespread feeling that the best way to "ride out" the current storm was to avoid giving the petitions more publicity.

"There is a consideration that the more you fight it, the more you raise the issue in the public consciousness, and that it's better to deal with it on a back burner," the official said.

The official pointed out that despite all the petitions and reports of imminent lawsuits, nothing concrete had emerged, and that when it seemed that something was about to, the Foreign Ministry responded.

For instance, the government responded swiftly and harshly, at least in a declarative manner, to a decision by a Spanish judge in January to open a probe of seven former top security officials for alleged war crimes in the 2002 bombing in Gaza that killed top Hamas terrorist Salah Shehadeh and 14 other people.

The investigation has been ordered against National Infrastructures Minister Binyamin Ben-Eliezer, who was defense minister at the time; Likud MK Moshe Ya'alon, who was chief of General Staff; Dan Halutz, then commander of the air force; Doron Almog, who was OC Southern Command; then-National Security Council head Giora Eiland; the defense minister's military secretary, Mike Herzog; and Public Security Minister Avi Dichter, who was head of the Shin Bet (Israel Security Agency).

Defense Minister Ehud Barak blasted the Spanish judge's decision, saying, "Someone who calls the assassination of a terrorist a crime against humanity lives in an upside-down world."

And Foreign Minister Livni, who immediately spoke with Spanish Foreign Minister Miguel Moratinos about the matter, directed the ministry's legal department to work quickly to annul the proceedings. She said that Israel "viewed gravely" the decision to open the probe. It was completely unacceptable, and Israel would give full legal backing to the seven officials, Livni said.

The cabinet has also addressed the issue, to a certain extent, both on the declarative and operative planes.

Last month, Prime Minister Olmert publicly said at a weekly cabinet meeting that Hamas was "using the international legal arena as one of the main arenas in which they are trying to hurt Israel and strike at its soldiers and commanders. With the typical moral acrobatics, these organizations and their supporters are trying to turn the attacker into the attacked and vice-versa."

At that meeting, Olmert appointed Justice Minister Daniel Friedmann to chair an interministerial team to coordinate the state's efforts to provide a legal defense for those who took part in the military operation. That committee has met and is mapping out where the potential problems are and how to deal with them.

But not everyone is pleased with the speed, or the results. Almog, who was advised by the security establishment not to go to Spain, was quoted this week as saying, "Unfortunately, this matter doesn't appear to be hurting the country too much, and so people are dealing with it with a grin. We need to develop an overall strategy and program to deal with this; otherwise the phenomenon will become more widespread and seriously hurt the country."

In 2005 Almog was advised not to disembark from an El Al jet when he landed in London because a warrant for his arrest had been issued for allegedly violating the Geneva Conventions in his capacity as head of the Southern Command.

NOTES TO BIBI AFTER HIS FIRST ELECTION—STILL IMPORTANT

(February 2009)

An Editorial from THE MACCABEAN June 1997
A CALL TO ACTION
We Must Return To Zionism

In 1897 in Basle, Switzerland, Theodore Herzl founded the World Zionist Organization. There were great accomplishments in the last 100 years. Much has happened to the Jewish people who found themselves on a roller coaster with many traumatic ups and downs. The Holocaust was the lowest point and the establishment of Israel was a high point. There was the great victory of 1967 and the trauma of 1973. Zionism flourished, Israel prospered, Judea, Samaria and Gaza were settled. The Ethiopian return to Zion brought tears to our eyes with pride. The great Russian migration to Israel literally changed the country for ever.

And then a cataclysmic and horrific event took place. A small clique of charlatans, with anti-Zionist delusions, took over the Israeli government in 1992. They deceived the Israeli voters by placing ("Mr. Security") Yitzhak Rabin at the head of their ticket. They promised security and then proceeded to dismantle the Jewish State. 100 years of Zionism are being undone in a few years. The new Likud government of Prime Minister Benjamin Netanyahu does not seem to have the political will to undo the damage of Oslo.

In the past few years, it seems that the main effort of Israeli governments was the creation of a Palestinian state. The word peace was perverted and distorted, coming to mean surrender and appeasement.

It is time for real Zionists to take charge of Israel's future. Zionists who will populate the lands of YESHA. And do it without apology or timidity. The leaders of Israel must pursue security policies without regard to the opinions of those who did nothing to help us during the Holocaust. The People of Israel must understand that they have caused a revolution in Jewish history. We have moved from weakness to the power of self-determination.

WE MUST NOT GO BACK TO THE OLD VULNERABLE DAYS. SURVIVAL INTO THE 21ST CENTURY REQUIRES SELF-SUFFICIENT POWER AND ACTIONS.

SOME THOUGHTS ON THE FAILURE TO IMPLEMENT REAL ZIONISM

It is obvious that the Palestinians will continue to violate their Oslo commitments. Their behavior is in keeping with their character. It is normal for them to kill Jews, break agreements, lie to the media and even abuse their own people. Like the wolf and the sheep, it is just nature that one will devour the other. The Palestinians are working very seriously to create a state from the river to the sea, with Jerusalem as their capital. We are not surprised.

What bothers us greatly, is the impotence (indeed in actions) of the Israeli government in protecting the vital interests of the Israeli people. Instead of lists of PLO violations, DO SOMETHING! DEMAND COMPLIANCE. In the old days, terrorists were destroyed in Gaza and Beirut by the long arm of ZAHAL (Israel Defense Forces). How is it that they can now find refuge in Nablus and Jericho?

We say to Netanyahu," Arafat and Mubarak are laughing at you. At the Freeman Center we are crying. We had worked for a stronger leadership. A leadership that would mobilize Israel to face the ominous challenges of the 21st Century."

TALKING ABOUT HAR HOMA

The Freeman Center urges the Israeli government NOT to talk about Har Homa. Instead talk about the PA endorsement of terrorism and their lack of compliance with existing agreements. Bibi should talk to Mubarak only in Jerusalem and only after Azam is released from Egyptian imprisonment. And then Mubarak could be asked to help rid Egypt's newspapers of anti-Semitic articles and cartoons and to allow its citizens to visit and trade with Israel. Har Homa is nobody's business but the Israeli people and any Arab, American, or European that brings it up should be shown the door

OSLO HAS CAUSED STRATEGIC DAMAGE TO ISRAEL'S SECURITY

The problem is the ability of the Palestinians to disrupt the IDF's mobilization schedule. Of course, the IDF can crush them in a head to head battle. But some 50,000 well armed terrorists (with anti-tank and anti-air missiles, Katyusha's etc) could slow Israel down while missile barrages from Syria, Iraq, and Iran containing VX nerve gas would contribute to general breakdown of Israel's ability to fight. Israel would still win, but at great cost. Do you remember the SCUD attacks and how much it disrupted life in Israel? Syria alone has 1000 missiles loaded with VX nerve gas and anthrax bacteria. We are talking chaos. Of course Israel can nuke these countries, but there is a great imbalance in this psychological deterrence factor. America and Russia operated on the principle of MAD (Mutually Assured Destruction) for 50 years. This will not work for Israel because its Arabs enemies see victory in DESTROYING Israel in a JIHAD. Arabs killed would go to paradise while the Jews would be sent straight to hell.

It is this imbalance in attitudes toward human life that makes the situation so unstable. The Freeman Center believes firmly in the principles of "preemption, preemption and preemption." No nation hostile to Israel should be allowed to possess non-conventional weapons. Regardless of public opinion they need to be taken out.

ISRAEL'S SOVEREIGNTY IN YESHA

Sovereignty is quite often a unilateral act. America's sovereignty in Texas and California was never recognized by Mexico and certainly was a unilateral act of based on superior military power. Israel's sovereignty in Eretz Yisrael has considerably more international sanction (League of Nations Mandate etc) than America ever had. That the international climate has shifted (to anti-Semitism) doesn't alter the issue. Of course with the granting of Eretz Yisrael to the Jews by HaShem there are certainly moral rights.

In the final analysis, Zionism was the Jewish people's act of unilateral sovereignty over what was morally and rightfully theirs BUT denied by mankind.

ISRAELI POWER

I wouldn't quibble over details, I would exercise our right and utilize our power for the good of the Jewish people. A lot of people misjudge the power of a united Jewish people in pursuit of justice for Israel. (Pray that we would unite!) We are not that weak, only intimidated by the big powers and the Arabs. Israeli strength has always been greater than the sum of arms and men. The Maccabees defeated numbers much greater than theirs. Bar Kochba held off the Roman Empire for many years before succumbing to the force of ONE HALF of Rome's Legions. I know they lost in the end, but many historians say that the huge losses of Rome in this battle with Bar Kochba and his men so weakened them that it led to Rome's decline. It is important to note that the Romans are NO MORE and we Jews control Israel and Jerusalem.

THE DOUBLE STANDARD

Some well meaning Jews believe that Israel should behave at a higher standard of morality than its Arab neighbors. They urge Jews to refrain from retaliating for Arab attacks.

While I have never supported murder for murder sake, killing the enemies that come to slay us is fully in keeping with Jewish law. Was it wrong for the fighters of the Warsaw Ghetto to kill Nazis? For the IDF to raid terrorist bases? For Netanyahu to travel to Beirut to kill PLO terrorists? To kill the enemies of Israel, before they commit murder, is certainly a mitzvah. And I am not talking about unjustified murder. I am talking about real enemies including those who throw Molotov cocktails and other lethal objects. The double standard is really a form of anti-Semitism.

A complete discussion of this subject can be found in chapter 10 (Why Jews Must Behave Better Than Everybody Else) of Professor Ed Alexander's new book, THE JEWISH WARS (no relation to the book by Josephus about Masada).

An Editorial from the May 1997 issue of THE MACCABEAN.
NETANYAHU, OUR PRODIGAL SON
What Should The RIGHT Do About Bibi's Plight
By Bernard J. Shapiro

Israeli Prime Minister Benjamin (Bibi) Netanyahu is in trouble. While he will not be charged with a crime, there is no question that his political standing has fallen. How he came to be embroiled in the most damaging scandal of his political career is also well know. I would like to discuss the proper response of the National Camp to unfolding events.

Bibi has been like the prodigal son who takes the family inheritance and squanders it foolishly. He was elected on a Zionist platform by one of the largest Jewish majorities in Israeli history (over 11%). His election was a clear signal from the voters of concern about the direction of the Oslo Process. Yet like the prodigal son, he took the political power, given him by the electorate, and began to use it to complete the self-destructive process begun by the previous Labor/Meretz/PLO government.

Bibi's current troubles stem from his desire to secure a majority in the Knesset for the abandonment of Hebron. He desperately needed the votes of Shas, an ultra-Orthodox political party with a long history of fraud and scandal. While I am not a religious scholar, it has occurred to me, that Bibi may be feeling the Wrath of HaShem for his share in undermining the Jewish claim to Hebron, burial place of the Patriarchs. We know from the TANACH that HaShem loved and cared deeply for Abraham, Isaac and Jacob. Perhaps He is showing His displeasure at Bibi's actions.

With all that said, I must confess the following: Bibi is OUR prodigal son. We must guide him back to the Right path. Now there is no substitute. The Left has unsheathed their long knives and has begun to lust for blood. The viciousness of the Israeli media and the politically corrupted police and judiciary must be stopped. They seek to overturn the voter's democratic choice by innuendo, slander and damaging leaks. The charges against Bibi are at their very worse a form of political "backroom" bargaining. Such behavior has been common to every Israel government since 1948. In fact it was David Ben Gurion, Israel's first premier, who initiated the policy of "paying off" the ultra Orthodox to join his coalition.

Do we value the concept of "equal protection under the law" and judicial impartiality? The Left is guilty of far greater crimes against the State than Bibi. How many of you remember Alex Goldfarb who was given a new Mitsubishi to bolt the Tsomet Party and give Peres and Rabin a majority for the Oslo Accord? Was the late Yitzhak Rabin ever charged with the cold-blooded murder of 17 Jewish teenagers in 1948 during the Altalena incident. The Israeli police never investigated whether Shimon Peres, Yossi Beilin and others violated Israel law by:

(1) collaborating with the enemy

(2) damaging Israeli security by aiding known terrorists

(3) perpetrating the self-destructive hoax of Oslo against the will of the Israeli people

(4) plotting with enemies of Israel to turn over strategic territory to them which would facilitate their destruction of the Jewish State.

The Left is also guilty of compromising the quality of the IDF by promoting fellow leftist officers instead of the most qualified. The leftist police have pursued an agenda of punishing Jews who defend themselves against Arab attack. And then the government releases Arab murderers to kill more Jews. The Israeli television channels are so biased that it is easier for Yasser Arafat to get an interview than the Prime Minister. Leftist educators have recently launched a campaign to strip everything Jewish or Zionist from Israel's schools. Speakers who have unconventional views are prevented from speaking on college campuses. Freedom of speech is only for the Left. I could go on. The Leftist rot in Israel runs very deep.

The bottom line is this: Israeli society has many problems. Bibi is certainly not the worst problem. We must support him during this current crisis. It could work to our favor. With the National Unity government removed from the table, Bibi is more dependent than ever on his Nationalist coalition. The Left is literally salivating for his fall. Bibi and his traditional allies must re-unite and proceed with the management of Israeli affairs in a more activist Zionist fashion. That means ACTUAL building permits in YESHA (in a simplified process) instead of mere TALK ABOUT PERMITS.

The new revitalized coalition must consider doing the following:

1. ACTUALLY DEMANDING RECIPROCITY from Arafat instead of just TALKING about it.

2. Demanding that all provisions of Oslo be complied with. This includes everything from the PLO Covenant, extradition of terrorists, disarming and destruction of Hamas and Islamic Jihad infrastructure, reducing the size of the PLO army to stated terms, turning in of all prohibited weapons (anti-tank, anti-air, grenades, bombs etc), and an end to incitement against Israel and Jews, etc.

3. All of above to be done within 60 days or Oslo is terminated. PERIOD.

4. The Leftists must be weeded out of government media, the police, Consular Corp and the judiciary

5. Moledet should be brought into the government even if this means that the Third Way (no bargain for the Nationalists) decides to leave.

This is only a beginning. First we need to salvage this government and then make it RIGHT.

Bibi, Jonathan Is Worried

An Editorial in the November 1996 issue of THE MACCABEAN

Long before I had ever heard of Benjamin Netanyahu (Bibi), I had read about his older brother Jonathan, Hero of Entebbe. In 1980, I read a book of Jonathan's letters entitled: SELF-PORTRAIT OF A HERO, The Letters Of Jonathan Netanyahu [1963-1976]. A lot of reviewers at the time spoke about the beautiful prose, the passion and the great potential of this hero cut down in his youth. While I saw all those things, it was Jonathan's deep love of Israel and his fervent patriotism that attracted me most. There was something else that one could sense on every page. That was his deep understanding of Jewish history and the role of Israel in it. One of my favorite passages, which I have quoted often, could have been written today in the context of the Oslo Accords. Here is that excerpt:

"I see with sorrow and great anger how a part of the people still clings to hopes of reaching a peaceful settlement with the Arabs. Common sense tells them, too, that the Arabs haven't abandoned their basic aim of destroying the State; but the self-delusion and self-deception that have always plagued the Jews are at work again. It's our great misfortune. They want to believe, so they believe. They want not to see, so they shut their eyes. They want not to learn from thousands of years of history, so they distort it. They want to bring about a sacrifice, and they do indeed. It would be comic, if it wasn't so tragic. What a saddening and irritating lot this Jewish people are!"

I am sure that Bibi, growing up in the shadow of his fallen brother, must have felt an overpowering need to succeed. There must have been a need to learn more, achieve more, to rise to the top of his chosen field. The struggle was partly to "make his brother proud," and partly to prove to himself that he was made of the 'right stuff." That is, the stuff with which HEROES are made.

And Bibi did it all: military excellence, diplomacy at the highest level, and finally political success in his brilliant campaign for prime minister. He has proven his worth to everyone, including himself. Now, poised at center stage during the most critical time of Israel's history, Bibi seems to have lost his inner direction. Often he speaks with a voice that would make Jonathan cheer, and then his actions leave much to be desired. For example, on October 24, 1996, the Prime Minister's office sent me a list of the ten most egregious PLO violations (printed in this issue) of the Oslo Accords. It was quite devastating: this account demonstrating the PLO's total disregard for its peace obligations.

This impressive list could be used as a part of a major Israeli public relations (hasbara) campaign to justify terminating its obligations to implement Oslo, including the abandonment of Hebron. Unfortunately, Bibi will NOT do this. He should have given the list to PLO terrorist chief, Yasser Arafat, with the admonition that all implementation of Oslo would cease until complete compliance. He didn't. Bibi has spoken often of the need for reciprocity, while continuing to negotiate without it.

The Battle for Eretz Yisrael

I want to tell a little story to explain what I believe is happening to Bibi. My grandfather, Harry W. Freeman, settled in Texas at the turn of the century. He was already fighting injustice to women and Afro-Americans by 1912, liquidating white slavery in Galveston by 1930 and speaking about the dangers of Hitler and Nazism in 1933. Growing up in Texas I used to love the rodeo which came to Houston once a year. One of my favorite contests was the wild bronco bull ride. Cowboys would mount these ferocious creatures and hold on tight until they were thrown. It all lasted little more than 12 seconds. It was much later that I learned that a leather strap was tied tight behind the bull's testicles to make him buck more ferociously. Even the biggest, strongest and most experienced Texans were able to ride the bull for only a few seconds.

This brings me back to Bibi, who is trying to ride the "Oslo bull." The Palestinian Arabs are filled with rage and hatred of Jews with all the ferocity of the bull angered by the leather strap. Much of their rage comes straight from Nazi anti-Semitism, brought to the Middle East by their former mufti, Haj Amin el-Husseini. The Palestinian Arabs, filled with both Nazi and Islamic hatred of Jews, make the Oslo bull impossible to ride. Their aspirations for a state that REPLACES Israel is evident to anyone who takes the time to listen to what they are saying. As much as Bibi would like to master the Oslo process and protect Israeli interests, it is impossible. It is a bull he can never ride. This is a harsh reality. There is a history lesson that Jonathan understood well: Enemies must be defeated and destroyed. The idea that one makes peace with your enemies is just a hoax of the Left.

The Americans did not make peace with the Native Americans, they destroyed them. The same is the case with Hitler's Germany and the Emperor's Japan. Midge Dector had this to say about says this about peace:

"For there is no such thing as making peace. Nations who are friendly do not need to do so, and nations or people who are hostile cannot do so. To cry peace, peace when there is no peace, the prophet Jeremiah taught us long ago, is not the expression of hope, not even superstition, but a reckless toying with the minds and hearts of people whose very future

Bernard J. Shapiro

depends on their capacity to rise every day to the harsh morning light of the truth."

Bibi must recognize the essential truth that both his brother and Dector have expressed so eloquently. He must read his own list of PLO violations. And then he must get off the Oslo bull and lead his people, Israel, to victory. Jews the world over are praying that he will fulfill his great destiny as a leader of Israel. They pray that he will pursue with all his vigor the Zionist goals of settling the Land, protecting the Holy Places, and ingathering the Jewish exiles. They pray that he will strengthen the military and infuse it with the high morale of days past. In my heart I know that Jonathan is watching over Bibi with love and affection. And Bibi, in my heart I fear that he is as worried as me.

THE ISRAEL QUILT

(April 2009)

Those few of you who are native Houstonians will remember the Shapiro cousins, Armand, Bernard and Doug. We were a close-knit group and hung around with a whole generation of young Jews growing up, during the 1940s and '50s, in the Riverside area (Highway 288 goes over my original house now). Of course, we grew up and went our separate ways.

Armand became a successful businessman and financier, making millions of dollars. I had a multifaceted career as bookseller, pro-Israel activist, editor and writer. I was sort of the Don Quixote of the group. My impossible dream was that the Jewish People would wake up and prevent a Second Holocaust. They haven't yet.

Doug was the scientific genius of the group. We all first became aware of this when he was expelled from Bellaire High School for a science experiment gone terribly wrong. His brilliance took him to Harvard, where he earned a medical degree. After practicing in Washington for three years, he became bored and went to London and got a Ph.D. in animal behavior. Doug traveled the world doing research on coral reef fish. He stayed on a small facility (its main inhabitants were large iguanas) off the coast of Puerto Rico for about a decade, where he discovered a sex-changing coral reef fish.

Wanting to see civilization again, he took a job as head of the biology department at Eastern Michigan University and then became a drug researcher at Pfizer and Johnson & Johnson. Houstonians have benefited greatly from his work.

Now, a new creative genius has entered the Shapiro family. Charlynn and Doug were married about a decade ago. Charlynn has developed over many years a remarkable ability to design and create quilts of phenomenal beauty. In her words, she described the Israel quilt she made for me:

"One day in the early summer, my husband, Doug, was talking on the phone to his cousin, Bernard. Bernard asked him something about my quilts. Doug mentioned it to me, and before I knew it, I was lying awake at night, trying to figure out how I might make a quilt for Bernard. I knew from Doug how passionately he loved the Jewish people and Israel, the Jewish homeland. I decided to start sewing."

"Although I had no plan or pattern, I knew immediately what some of the blocks would be: the dove with an olive branch (we all hope for peace, don't we?), a rainbow, the Exodus, Pesach, Chanukah, Shabbat, the two blocks that refers to 'the land of milk and honey.'

"The quilt also needed to have blocks signifying some of the customs, festivals and celebrations unique to the Jewish people.

"Included are blocks of chuppah, Sukkot, a Bat Mitzvah and a Bar Mitzvah. Fruits, wheat, the Israeli flag and the Hebrew aleph bet symbolize the Land of Israel (Eretz Yisrael). The 12 colored stones represent Jacob's sons: the 12 Tribes of Israel. The front of the quilt is full of vibrant color. (Whoever saw a white fig?) All of the blocks were completed before I decided how to put them together. The back of the quilt shows a small view of the Western Wall in Jerusalem.

"It took seven months to complete, including research time. On a trip to New York, I found a Judaica store, where I bought a set of Hebrew flash cards. Unfortunately, one of the cards was missing. Doug's son Aidan, who is studying Hebrew in college, helped me identify which letters should be included (consonants only).

"Another trip to New York, and I found the bees for the beehive. After the quilt top was completed, I learned from a website that, in ancient times, honey was made from dates, not honeybees. I decided to leave it as it was (artistic license).

"I named the quilt 'Lâ'chaim'—to life. It was the most original and fun quilt that I have made so far. Now, I am really inspired to do more quilts with a Jewish theme."

I have encouraged Charlynn to make a similar quilt to give to a Jewish or Israel museum, so that the general public can enjoy her work. From the photo, you will note that the quilt is a traditional American style. In Israel and at quilt fairs nationwide, there are many quilters using the quilt to paint a picture, much like artists using oil or watercolors. There are many abstract designs. I find the structure, discipline and concentration on one theme a major plus for Charlynn's quilt. To me it outshines all of the modern innovations and is true to the original spirit of the quilt.

Bernard J. Shapiro

MY PRAYER FOR ROSH HASHONAH—5770

Author Note: Each year for the past many years, I have re-issued this prayer. Unfortunately my prayers don't seem to be answered. I know they are the prayers of many of my readers also. What to do?

My rage and anger at the situation we face has grown this last year, especially with the election of an anti-Israel American President. This prayer is hopeful. It also demonstrates my mixed state of rage and hope.

I think that all Lovers of Zion have similar feelings . . . . Please read and **MAKE IT HAPPEN THIS YEAR, 5770** . . . . Bernard]

MY PRAYER FOR ROSH HASHONAH—5770

(September 11, 2009)

As I survey the fragile planet we call home, my mind makes note of the chaos, blood, and tears. The cries of a million lost souls shatter the night in a million corners of the earth. The sensitive, compassionate among them try to feed the hungry, heal the sick, and clothe the naked. One by one their energies dissipate. They try to hold back the tide with a teaspoon and then see the impossibility of the task. The Jewish people are but a cosmic speck in this universe. To many Jews who feel deeply about their own people, that speck becomes the whole world. Other Jews are irrevocably tied to non-Jewish pursuits.

May we as a people open our eyes and begin to see the world as it really is. Without becoming depressed and morose, we must realize that there are powerful forces in the world that wish us ill. May we mobilize our strength to fight our enemies until they are defeated. May we not succumb to false prophets of peace. We all want peace. We pray for peace in our Sabbath services every Friday night. After thousands of years, being victims of persecution, expulsion, extermination, and discrimination, it is natural that we yearn for peace with every ounce of our bodies and souls. It is because our hunger for peace is so strong that we must be doubly cautious not to fall for a pseudo-peace. Today none of us believe Chamberlain really negotiated "peace in our time" with Hitler. Why did some Jews believe that Peres and Rabin really negotiated "peace" with Arafat, one of today's Hitlers?

Why do many still believe that it is possible to make peace with the barbarians who surround Israel and wish only to destroy it. (Santayana said and it is true today: "Those who do not learn from history are forced to repeat it.") The Jewish people must learn from history and learn the value of unity in the face of so many enemies who wish them ill.

I pray that Israelis who have fought in countless wars will understand that there is no magic cure, though they crave to be free of constant conflict. As Jews we are all involved in this historic struggle to survive. It is not our fate or that of the Israelis that we should retire from this struggle.

I have a vision and a dream that I must reveal. In the name of G-d, the Almighty, Defender of His People, Israel, I say to my people's enemies: Beware of the thing that is coming, that will take what you would not give. That will free the people of Israel from your atrocities. I say to Israeli Prime Minister 'Bibi' Netanyahu and his Defense Minister Ehud Barak: Be aware of the Risen People who will sweep the Arab scourge into the dustbin of history. Know that the Jewish soul will be set free. The spectacular victories of the Israeli army and the return to Zion demonstrated that power. But it wasn't a miracle. It was just the soul of the Jew coming to its own. It was just the Jewish soul freed at last to be itself.

And I see it coming, the Jewish soul released to be itself. I see a new proud Jewish government coming to power in Israel. (May Bibi be the one I prayed for or is he another weak leader??) A government that reclaims the Jewish Holy Places and restores Jewish sovereignty in all of Eretz Yisrael.

I see Moslem control and Islamic sites removed from the Temple Mount to make it ready for Moshiach. I see the enemies of Israel, who raise up their hands to murder or injure Jews, driven from our Holy Land. I see the secular Jews of Israel and the world becoming more observant and returning to the Torah. I see religious Jews becoming more tolerant of diversity in Jewish practice.

I see a new Israeli foreign policy that grovels before no nation, no matter how powerful. I see Israel's Foreign Minister informing every nation that their embassies must be in Jerusalem. If they don't respect Israel's capital, then they will be given permission to have a consulate in Tel Aviv. I see the government demanding that the Vatican return all the property it has stolen from the Jewish people during the last 2000 years. Maybe they will refuse and we could always hold their property in Israel as a down payment. The Vatican has been used to dealing with obsequious groveling Jews, but now they would see proud fearless Jews. I see an Israeli government that would change its relationship with America from one of subservience to one of equal alliance.

Yes, I have a dream (apologies to MLK) that Jews will no longer debate the obvious: like whether to hold onto what is theirs or trade it away; whether to struggle for survival or to give up from fatigue. I have a dream that the Jews of the kibbutz and the Jews of YESHA will be reborn as brothers and patriots. From the Galilee to Eilat, all the people of Israel will share the same dream of a powerful independent Zionist nation. I have a dream that this strong, proud independent Israel will win the respect of all the nations of the world, including the Arabs. Instead of the contempt it has earned in recent years, Israel will again be a light unto the nations. And finally, I have a dream that this new Israel will find the peace it so dearly deserves. A peace with strength and self-respect. As I look back at 4000 years of Jewish history, I have but one urgent hope and prayer: We must make this dream a reality. There is no alternative.

May the L-rd, bless the leaders of Israel with the courage to pursue peace, and the wisdom to know when it is not attainable. May the L-rd bless the Jews who return to Zion and give them jobs and new friends to ease their transition into Israeli life. May the Lord bless the war-weary Israeli people with the stamina to bear up under the strain, as peace is not just around the corner.

May they understand that their fate may be that of endless struggle to survive in a hostile world and may they have the strength to understand that there is still no alternative (*ein brera*). May the people of Israel prosper and go from success to success never forgetting that their destiny lies in their might, their righteousness and their faith in HaShem.

"For Zion's sake I shall not hold my peace, And for Jerusalem's sake I shall not rest."

LECTURE ON ISRAEL FUTURE SECURITY AND SURVIVAL
by Bernard J. Shapiro
Chairman of the Freeman Center For Strategic Studies
Labor Day - September 7, 2009

Thank you Dr. Frank and Alice Lanza for giving me the financial and moral support to make this evening possible.

A special warm thanks to my old friends Rabbi Jack Segal and Dr. Richard H. Rolnick. Both of you mean more to me than words can explain. I have learned and grown over the years by being close to you. Through good and bad times your words of wisdom have motivated me to keep working for Israel.

INTRODUCTION

In 1934, Harry W. Freeman, my grandfather, was already lecturing about the dangers of Hitler and Nazism. Nobody listened. The Holocaust was not prevented. Today, in 2009 there are 1.9 billion Arab & Moslem people who plan a second Holocaust against the Jews of Israel and the world. The governments and people of Europe not only acquiesce but actively aid in this genocidal plan through diplomatic and material support. The American State Department encourages the Arabs by actively striving to weaken Israel's strategic and military superiority. Their first stage is to use the so called 'peace process' to weaken Israel and strip it of its strategic territories. They are being aided by the same hypocrites and accomplices in the West who failed to aid the Jews of Europe in their darkest hour. Unfortunately, even left-wing Israelis have fallen victims to the seductive lure of peace and have begun a policy of appeasement similar to that tried with Hitler. The results will be no different.

The Arab propaganda full of slanders and libels; the media bias against Israel replete with double standards and the rewriting of history are all working to the same end: the de-legitimating of Israel. Israel is the only country considered by many to be GUILTY OF ORIGINAL SIN by virtue of its very existence. This process of de-legitimating has as its goal creating a world climate in which the DESTRUCTION of Israel is acceptable. Many in the Jewish community are either apathetic or fail to recognize this threat. Fortunately the Jews have new allies in the Evangelical Christian Community and in the Hindu community that has suffered Moslem depredations for about1400 years.

I founded the FREEMAN CENTER FOR STRATEGIC STUDIES in order to create a powerful voice to arouse the Jewish community to the action necessary to frustrate the evil designs of the enemies of Israel and the Jewish People. I need your help to accomplish this mission.

The following are functioning parts off the Freeman Center:

THE MACCABEAN ONLINE
Monthly Internet Magazine archived
THE FREEMANLIST
Daily Email broadcasts of news and commentary
THE FREEMAN BLOG
THE FREEMAN WEBSITE
Multiple good sources of information
EXCELLENT GRAPHIC PRESENTATIONS
Important issues covered

WORK CONTINUES DAILY DESPITE MANY DIFFICULTIES SINCE 1992

SOME THINGS YOU MAY KNOW AND SOME YOU MAY NOT

Harvard University's Judaica Division and Purdue University are archiving articles from THE MACCABEAN ONLINE (back to 1996)

EBSCO, The largest database in the United States is archiving THE MACCABEAN ONLINE. It will be available to ALL Universities, Schools (K-12), Libraries, Military and Government Institutions.

★

As I survey the fragile planet we call home, my mind makes note of the chaos, blood, and tears. The cries of a million lost souls shatter the night in a million corners of the earth. The sensitive, compassionate among them try to feed the hungry, heal the sick, clothe the naked. One by one their energies dissipate. They try to hold back the tide with a teaspoon and then see the impossibility of the task. The Jewish people are but a cosmic speck in this universe. To many Jews who feel deeply about their own people, that speck becomes the whole world. Other Jews are irrevocably tied to non-Jewish pursuits. Many Christians believe that their fate and that of their loved ones is also tied to the fate of the Jewish People.

We are all, Jews, Christians, and Hindus living in one World threatened by a global Jihad that would consume us all.

Bernard J. Shapiro

MIRACLES IN THE HOLY LAND - THERE ARE MANY - MOST OF YOU KNOW OF SOME - BUT THIS IS WORTH REPEATING

AFTER THE ROMANS DESTROYED JERUSALEM AND DROVE THE JEWS OUT

A Roman legionnaire stands on a hill overlooking Jerusalem. He watches the city burn and proclaims proudly, "Judea capta est" Judea is destroyed. It will never rise again. Rome's rulers even decreed a change of name for Judea. Henceforth it would be named after the Philistines (or Palestine) and the Jewish connection would be obliterated forever.

Yet, like the legendary Phoenix, rising from the ashes of its own destruction, the new nation of Israel burst onto the international scene in 1948, with the lusty cry of a newborn infant, yearning to breathe free. Five Arab armies rushed to invade Israel and crush the life from the new Jewish State. With unbelievable bravery and heroism the new state survived. Six thousand of its young defenders gave their lives that Israel might live.

In blood and fire was Israel born, and on a hot anvil was she forged. Her youth understood that life in the new Jewish homeland would require sacrifice. With stories of burning flesh from the ovens of Auschwitz embedded deep in their psyches, the young Israeli soldiers fought with the firm conviction that there was "no alternative" (ein brera).

[Originally written and published in 1992 as a founding statement of the Freeman Center For Strategic Studies.]

Mark Twain wrote ABOUT JEWS and first published in HARPER'S magazine, September 1887.

If the statistics are right, the Jews constitute but one quarter of one percent of the human race. It suggests a nebulous dim puff of stardust lost in the blaze of the Milky Way. Properly, the Jew ought hardly to be heard of; but he is heard of, has always been heard of. He is as prominent on the planet as any other people, and his importance is extravagantly out of proportion to the smallness of his bulk.

His contributions to the world's list of great names in literature, science, art, music, finance, medicine and abstruse learning are very out of proportion to the weakness of his numbers. He has made a marvelous fight in this world in all ages; and has done it with his hands tied behind him. He could be vain of himself and be excused for it. The Egyptians, the Babylonians and the Persians rose, filled the planet with sound and splendor; then faded to dream-stuff and passed away: the Greeks and the Romans followed and made a vast noise, and they are gone; other peoples have sprung up and held their torch high for a time but it burned out, and they sit in twilight now, or have vanished.

The Jew saw them all, survived them all, and is now what he always was, exhibiting no decadence, no infirmities of age, no weakening of his parts, no slowing of his energies, no dulling of his alert and aggressive mind. All things are mortal but the Jew; all other forces pass, but he remains. What is the secret of his immortality?

As Mark Twain implied, their secret is that the Almighty loves his children, Israel.

*

Let Me Tell You About
A HARSH REALITY
Facing Jews and others.

We all want peace. We pray for peace in our Sabbath services every Friday night. After thousands of years, being victims of persecution, expulsion, extermination, and discrimination, it is natural that we yearn for peace with every ounce of our bodies and souls.

It is because our hunger for peace is so strong that we must be doubly cautious not to fall for a pseudo-peace. Today none of us believe Chamberlain really negotiated "peace in our time" with Hitler.

Israelis my age have fought in 7 wars and a 120 year war against terror.

Bernard J. Shapiro

I understand their desire to be free of constant conflict. Unfortunately there is no magic cure. I wish I could speak more optimistic words. Beyond the neighboring states that Israel is negotiating with now lies another ring of unmitigated hostility led by Islamic fundamentalists like those in Iran, Syria and Saudi Arabia. Even the so called Peace Agreements with Egypt and Jordan have not real substance. Those countries will turn on Israel the moment it is opportune for them.

As Jews, Christians and Hindus we are all involved in this historic struggle to survive. It is not our fate or that of all non-Moslems, that we should retire from this struggle. The only peace the Arabs are prepared to give us is the peace of the grave.

NATURE OF PEACE

Great issues of war and peace as related to Israel are being debated by Jews and Christians across America. Israelis are debating the same issues among themselves. There are strong opinions on both sides of the Atlantic as well as both sides of the major issues. What seems to be lacking in all these discussions is the proper historical context. Professor Paul Eidelberg formerly of Bar-Ilan University reviews the historical facts.

Between 1945 and 1978 the longest time without a war going on someplace was a mere 26 days. On an average day there are 12 wars being fought somewhere on earth. The consensus of scholars has been that the norm of international relations is not peace but war. As Eidelberg reports, "Indeed, the occurrence of 1,000 wars during the last 2,500 years indicates that "peace" is little more than a preparation for war. Which means that peace treaties are WORTHLESS, to say the least."

Eidelberg then quotes from a book by Lawrence Beilenson, entitled THE TREATY TRAP, saying, "After studying every peace treaty going back to early Roman times, Beilenson concludes that treaties are made to be broken. In fact, he shows that treaties for guaranteeing the territorial integrity of a nation are useless to the guaranteed nation, and worse than useless insofar as they engender a false sense of security. Such treaties can only benefit nations governed by rulers intending to violate them whenever expedient."

Midge Dector says this about "peace" and I must explain: As a political scientist, she was not talking about peace with G-d, with our friends and loved ones.

Her statement below was intended to mean peace between nations at war.

She says: What I want to say is something that virtually the whole history of the 20th and 21st century teaches us and yet something we refuse to learn. And that is, when applied to the affairs of nations, peace is an evil word. Yes I said evil. And the idea of peace as we know it is an evil idea. From the peace of Versailles to "peace in our time" at Munich...each declaration of peace or expressions of longing for peace ended in slaughter. Not necessarily immediately and not necessarily directly, but slaughter all the same...

For there is no such thing as making peace. Nations who are friendly do not need to do so, and nations or people who are hostile cannot do so.

To cry peace, peace when there is no peace, the prophet Jeremiah taught us long ago, is not the expression of hope, not even superstition but a reckless toying with the minds and hearts of people whose very future depends on their capacity to rise every day to the harsh morning light of the truth.

On September 3, 1993, I wrote the following on Oslo and it was published in a Press Release in the Jewish Herald-Voice (Houston):

"The rush of events in the Middle East has been dizzying. The media hype, the talking heads, the worldwide expectations of peace in the Middle East are all quite staggering. Radio, TV, newspapers herald the coming of a new era of reconciliation between Israelis and Palestinians. The positive images are so abundant that any moment one might expect to see Isaiah on Nightline showing Ted Koppel video clips of lions lying down with lambs. Despite the media hype surrounding these developments, let me make something very clear: A leopard does not change its spots. And you can say a berachaha (Hebrew blessing) over a ham sandwich, but that doesn't make it kosher. And a deal with the PLO is like a dance on quicksand --before you realize it, you have sunk into the muck and slime."

IS PEACE POSSIBLE BETWEEN ISRAEL AND THE ARAB WORLD?

It is possible only when the Arab/Moslem world creates secular democratic states not subservient to the rule of Islam. The problem for Israel is the very hostile attitude that Islam has not only toward Jews, but also Christians and Hindus. Islam is all encompassing and guides behavior, law and religion. It perceives the world as two separate parts:

1. The first is Dar el-Islam or the World of Islam

2. All the rest is Dar el-Harb or the world of war -- that is non-Muslim nations that have yet to be conquered.

JIHAD or Holy War is the instrument to conquer the non-Moslem world. Another concept in the Koran essential to understand when relating to Moslems is the law of HUDAIBIYA which dates back to Muhammad. It states clearly that "Muslims are permitted to lie and break agreements with non-Muslims." This applies to business, personal life and politics. Would a peace treaty be worth much if the other party is Moslem?

Islam divides the world between Believers and Infidels. Do you really think it is possible to make peace or negotiate a people with this religious background.

HITLER AND THE ARABS

"Hitler, Goebbels and Goering were pathological and pragmatic liars. Arafat also lied at Oslo as he fully intended to carry out his staged plan of 1974. Under this plan he would accept any part of Palestine until he could conquer the remainder. The Nazis lied so convincingly and so hugely that most statesmen from other countries could not believe that what they were hearing was a lie. One of Hitler's biggest lies was constantly to assure the world of peaceful intentions while obviously planning war. Arafat has done the same.

The only reason that the Arabs have not yet done to the Israeli Jews what Hitler did to their forefathers in Europe is that they have thus far lacked the military means and weapons of mass destruction which were at Hitler's disposal, to do so.

That the Arabs have not done so to date has not been due to any reluctance on their part, but because, this time, there has been this difference:

The Jews in Europe had no army to defend them. Thank G-d, the Jews in Israel have not only the Israel Defense Forces but the Mighty Hand of the Almighty to defend them!

May Israel be wiser in relation to this death wish of her neighbors, than the Jews in Europe were. They belittled the writings and speeches of Hitler and the Nazis and were massacred as a result. May it not happen again with Abbas and his Fatah, Hamas, Islamic Jihad, Iran, Syria and the new Hitlers of the 21st century!

THE LEFT

This is where the left went wrong. And of course this includes our new radical Leftist President here in America. They believed that you could make peace with your enemies by being nice, making concessions, and in every way appeasing their demands. Yet they immediately forgot that these people were just that: the enemy.

Islam is the enemy. In the Middle East they have armies, anti-aircraft and anti-tank missiles, armored cars, mortar launchers, snipers etc. Rather than negotiate peacefully they have launched several wars, both regular and terrorist against Israel and its Jewish citizens. I might remind the audience that they have also attacked us here in America and at American facilities overseas. And the recent terrorist assaults on India at Mumbai, remind us that this is a worldwide struggle. But tonight I focus on Israel security and survival.

Bernard J. Shapiro

ANTI-SEMITISM AND JEWISH SELF-DELUSION

Unfortunately, Jews throughout history have deluded themselves about their position in society. They pursue utopian solutions to complex political problems and disputes. Jews rejoiced as the enlightenment spread across Europe in the 18th and 19th centuries. Many were eager to give up their Jewishness and become German, French, Italian, and English. In the final analysis those societies viewed them as Jews. Self-delusion came into collision with reality and left us with the stench of burning flesh from the ovens of Auschwitz. Many Russian Jews eagerly supported the communist idea of a worker's utopia with no nationalities and no religion. Reality taught them that their neighbors still considered them Jews.

The left-wing in Israel believes in a common humanity of shared values with the Arabs. In the face of all empirical evidence to the contrary they believe peace is possible. In the book Self Portrait Of A Hero: The Letters of Jonathan Netanyahu (1963-1976), Jonathan Netanyahu, the fallen hero of Entebbe and brother of Benjamin, said it best:

"I see with sorrow and great anger how a part of the people still clings to hopes of reaching a peaceful settlement with the Arabs. Common sense tells them, too, that the Arabs haven't abandoned their basic aim of destroying the State; but the self-delusion and self-deception that have always plagued the Jews are at work again. It's our great misfortune. They want to believe, so they believe. They want not to see, so they shut their eyes. They want not to learn from thousands of years of history, so they distort it. They want to bring about a sacrifice, and they do indeed. It would be comic, it wasn't so tragic. What a saddening and irritating lot this Jewish people are!" Need I say more?

THE BLINDING FLASH OF INSIGHT

In 1967, only days after the war ended, I found myself rushing to Jerusalem to touch the Holy Wall near the Temple Mount, on the previously Arab side of a spit Jerusalem.

As I touched and said my prayers I felt a huge surge of energy go through my body.

I suddenly understand how modern Israel is the beginning of the Third Temple Period and the spiritual heir to Joshua, Saul, David, Solomon, the Maccabees and Bar Kokhba. I frequently write about the security reasons for incorporating Judea, Samaria, and Golan into the body of Israel. There is another side to this issue and that is the spiritual-religious side. The truth, which many find inconvenient, is that the Land of Israel was promised by G-d to Abraham and his seed in perpetuity. The Land of Israel is not speculative real estate to be bartered away for some high sounding (but false) promises of peace. The hills and valleys of Judea and Samaria contain the collective memory of the Jewish people. It was here that the Israelites first entered the Holy Land. And it was here they fought the battles, built the towns, elected their kings and were preached to by their prophets and judges. And it was on this soil that they wrote the Holy Scriptures we call our Bible.

THE OSLO ACCORDS: A FAILURE - IS PEACE IMPOSSIBLE NOW

1. Giving world recognition to a terrorist organization as a representative of a legitimate national entity

2. Terrorism - over 1500 killed 20 thousand maimed and injured

3. Armed Palestinian force in the heart of Judea, Samaria, and Gaza

4. Incitement against Jews, Nazi like Anti-Semitism on PA TV, sermons, newspapers and in schools

5. Abbas (and Hamas) support massive violence and terrorism against Jews and turns his back on promise of negotiations for peace

6. Potential loss of strategic territory: Judean-Samarian mountain ridge

7. Loss of 30% of its water resources

8. Greatly divided Israel when unity was necessary to face the Arab threat

9. And finally, the Arab/Muslim world rejects a Jewish state in their midst for deeply held cultural, religious and anti-Semitic reasons. These are non-negotiable.

9. A victory for post-Zionism and a decline in Israeli patriotism

10 The recent acceptance of a Palestinian state by Bush, Blair, Obama and Israeli leaders will lead to the destruction of Israel.

THINGS AMERICANS MUST LEARN QUICKLY - BEFORE IT IS TOO LATE

1. The current American government is doing many things that impact negatively on our security

2. Negotiating with evil is morally wrong. Like all deals with the devil, YOU LOSE YOUR SOUL. Evil in today's world includes: Iran, Hamas, Syria, Hizbollah, Fatah, Islamic Jihad, Sudan and many other - all Moslem

3. The relationship with Israel helps protect America - Many think America supports Israel but it goes both ways. In fact the contribution of Israel to America in Intelligence, High Tech Military products, medicine, telecommunications, agriculture, irrigation, pharmaceuticals and many others outweighs American contributions to Israel by a factor of 5-1.

4. The moral factor. Israel is the canary in the coal mine. To the Jihadists, Little Satan and America is the Great Satan. After Europe falls soon and Israel is destroyed then America will be target number one. Jihadists have already infiltrated this country to a degree few Americans understand.

They control Middle East Studies at most universities, force text books to distort history, have hundreds of underground cells waiting to be activated.

5. Our government has decided to ignore the threat and treat terrorism as criminal problem and not a real WAR.

6. The Obama/Clinton/Rahm Emanuel Foreign policy supports terrorists and condemns Israel to destruction.

7. Remember what the Bible says. Those that curse Israel will be cursed. Those that Bless Israel will be blessed.

A FUTURE MIRACLE

Israel is playing a waiting game. She knows that Iran driven by historical memory, overweening pride, and Allah"s cult of hatred, will strike; but Israel will have the warning time required to strike first and the Jews, victims of the Holocaust, will indeed strike first. This will be the beginning of a new Middle East that hardly anyone dreams of. Even before Iran is devastated, the Israel Defense Forces will deliver crippling blows to Hizbollah, Hamas, Fatah, and Syria. Israel will eliminate the entire terrorist network west of the Jordan River. Countless Arabs will flee from Judea and Samaria as well as from Gaza. The peace charade will be over. The mendacity and puerilities of Lilliputian politicians will be silenced. The Lion of Judah will have triumphed.

Israel must be truly sovereign.

Its power is greater than the sum of its arms and men. Fighting on its own soil, with the L-rd on its side it can never be defeated.

The Bible says that Sons of Darkness will come from the North (Iran, The Arabs and Russia) and Battle the Sons of Light. This Battle will take place in Israel at Armageddon. I have stood on top that spot, called by its original Hebrew name, Meggido. You can see the Tiberious, the Sea of Galilee, the Jordan River on the East and the Mediterranean on the West.

This small and sacred land holds the future of mankind. I pray that America stands with Israel in this final battle. Public opinion polls show overwhelming support for Israel but the new Democrat government has other ideas. I fear that we here will suffer the wrath of G-d if His people are abandoned.

Bernard J. Shapiro

On a final Note:

THE BOTTOM LINE

I know much more about the capabilities of the Israeli military than is commonly understood. Certain places in our government are purposely down grading the offensive capacity of Iran and other countries of evil. The result will be WAR with horrible consequences for all.

If you are interested we can go into that during the Q & A.

Freeman Center Disgusted at Bibi Groveling

Before Anti-Semites of Europe

by Bernard J. Shapiro (2011)

When I founded the Freeman Center back in 1992, I gave a copy of Bibi's book, A PLACE AMONG THE NATIONS, to everyone joining. I was very impressed at the clear understanding of history and the Jewish place in it. I especially appreciated the chapter on Czechoslovakia and how it related to the current Arab-Israeli issues.

Now, we see the pitiful image of Israel's PM running after the princes of Europe hat in hand. Does he have no pride? Does he not know how powerful Israel is really? Has he not read the articles of Paul Eidelberg and Yoram Ettinger broadcast here for the world to see?

Despite protestations of Israel's Supreme Court of the Arab People (and not Jews), there is NO SUCH THING AS INTERNATIONAL LAW!!! The only thing that has ever mattered in world history is POWER. Machiavelli knew it. So did Lao Tsu, Muhammed, Pol Pot, Genghis Khan, Julius Caesar, Napoleon, Mao, Churchill, Roosevelt and Stalin.

Power can be used for good or evil. The defense of Israel and the Jewish People is the most righteous use of power in the course of human history.

The world that Bibi so earnestly seeks to befriend has spent the last 2000 years killing, raping, forcibly trying to convert us. They have stolen our treasure and reaped the benefit of our culture, our science, and our religion. And finally they exterminated us like vermin.

The Jews have always been the most productive, creative people on this planet. While making up less than 1% of the world's population, they made up over 33% of Nobel Prize winners in all fields from medicine to economics.

The Muslims have brought to the world NOT life, but death. Instead of a polio vaccine they invented car bombs, homicide bombers and human shields.

We must ask ourselves: Why has the world embraced this death cult over Israel and the Jewish People?

My response is simple. I don't give a damn. Let them do as they wish, Israel is strong and can take any action it needs to defend its interests.

What Israel lacks is strong leadership. I would second the motion of Paul Eidelbeg that Caroline Glick would make a good PM.

And then create a strong Zionist coalition without the pro-Arab parties of Labor and Meretz. The Arab Parties should be immediately expelled from the Knesset as traitors.

I will continue on the future of Israel under strong leadership in further articles. The article below is what got me ranting. FYI, in a war between NATO and Israel, Israel would win quickly. The West has no stomach for real combat. Picking on Libyia, Serbia is one thing, Israel is another.

CHAPTER THIRTEEN: CORRESPONDENCE WITH SHIMON PERES

OCTOBER 3, 1974
THE JEWISH HERALD-VOICE

ISRAEL'S NEW DEFENSE MINISTER ... A Personal Perspective

EXCLUSIVE REPORT
BY
BERNARD SHAPIRO

SHIMON PERES

Shimon Peres, Israel's new Minister of Defense is an enigma to most Americans. His predecessor, Moshe Dayan, was well known for his military career. While Peres has worked most of his public life to strengthen Israel's security, a lot of what he has done has been of necessity secret. In this brief article I will try to give a rough outline of his accomplishments and project how he will respond to Israel's security needs in the future.

Shimon Peres was born in 1923 and became active in defense work in his early teens. By the time he was 26 Ben Gurion, who was impressed by his talents, placed him in charge of the fledgling Navy Department of the Defense Ministry. Three years later he became Director General of the Defense Ministry and by 1959 was named Deputy Minister of Defense. He remained in office until 1965 when a split in the labor party sent him into the opposition along with Ben Gurion and Dayan. While Ben Gurion was the nominal head of the Rafi party formed in 1965 when the labor party split, it was Peres who really organized and led the party. In 1967 in the crisis before the Six Day War it was Peres who mobilized public opinion to force Prime Minister Eshkol to form a national coalition government with Dayan as Defense Minister. Since 1967 Peres served in a variety of positions including Minister responsible for the Administered Territories, Minister for Immigrant Absorption, Minister for Transport and Communications, and finally Minister of Information.

During his early years with the Defense Ministry, Peres is credited with forging the alliance with France that brought Israel the weapons with which to win the wars of 1956 and 1967. He frequently travelled on secret missions to Germany and other countries, including the U.S. in search of weapons Israel desperately needed. He was instrumental in building up the arms industry in Israel including the important aviation industry now producing fighter planes and missiles. Peres is also credited with encouraging Israel's advanced nuclear research. He is the author of two books: *The Next Phase* published in 1965 which predicted many of the changes taking place in Israel today and *David's Sling* published in 1970 which described the history of the arming of Israel.

As a politically motivated youth living in Israel in 1965, I had the opportunity to hear all of Israel's leaders during the election campaign of that year. No one impressed me more than Shimon Peres. His straight forward manner of talking and his ability to answer questions directly to the point convinced me that he could be trusted as a leader of Israel. Peres was one of Ben Gurion's favorite proteges and he learned a lot from his teacher. Peres is a pragmatist, able to focus on achievable ends without losing sight of the ideal. Israel finds itself in a very difficult security situation where the hope of peace sometimes obscures the unrelenting Arab hostility. With a man like Peres in the government we can be assured that Israel's security will not be traded for some momentary relaxation of tension.

We can expect Israel's new Defense Minister to work even harder to make Israel independent of imported arms and the concomitant political pressure. Peres has already set new standards of efficiency and hard work at both the Defense Ministry and the military industries. His legendary ability to work 18 hours a day is an impressive example for all of Israel's workers. He is a technocrat in its purist sense as one who gets things done quickly and efficiently. Peres also has Ben Gurion's great sense of history and Israel's place in it. He is a man of clear vision and unshakeable courage who will stand fast and not waver when questions of principle are at stake.

Shimon Peres rose to his present position by a politically daring challenge of the Labor Party executive. By choosing to run against the party favorite, Itzhak Rabin, and winning almost half of the votes of the Labor Party Central Committee, he has assured himself of a position of leadership in the party for the foreseeable future. It would not surprise me to see Peres become prime minister of Israel in the future.

PATRONIZE OUR ADVERTISERS

BERNARD SHAPIRO
5730 CHEENA DR.   723-2588
HOUSTON, TEXAS 77035

Date 12/10 19 73

Pay to the order of __Zahal__ $1000.00

__One Thousand and 00/100__ Dollars

Bank of Houston
HOUSTON, TEXAS

For _____   Bernard Shapiro

PAY TO THE ORDER OF
BANK OF ISRAEL
ACCT.
MINISTRY OF DEFENCE
FINANCE DPT.

Pay to the order of any bank, Banker or Trust Company
Prior endorsements guaranteed
BANK OF ISRAEL — JERUSALEM

PAY ANY BANK REC
F.R.B. HOUSTON
THE PHILADELPHIA
NATIONAL BANK
PHILADELPHIA, PA.
34

ADVERTISEMENT

כא רשימת פועלי ישראל (רפ״י) כא

ANOTHER OPEN LETTER FROM THE ISRAEL LABOR LIST-RAFI

Dear Reader,

In another few weeks Israel will hold its sixth general election to the Knesset. You have been witness to a political campaign maybe second to none in its concentration on personal vilification. It has been characterized by an almost complete avoidance of the important issues facing the nation. Well, the main issue really is the strengthening of Israel's democracy, but the major threat to its survival comes not from the man who has led Israel and the Jewish people for the last 50 years but from a new political entity known as the "Alignment".

The threat is very subtle, but also very real and is contained in a single clause of the Mapai-Achdut Avoda alignment agreement. It consists of an undertaking by Mapai not to actively support electoral reform for the next four years of the Sixth Knesset term. This in itself would not be so bad if Israel's present electoral system were reasonably good, but it isn't. Israel's proportional representation system has all the evils of its European counterparts plus certain evils peculiar to Israel which cause it to grow increasingly undemocratic.

Under Israel's proportional representation system (PR) there is no direct contact between the voter and the candidate for office. The party oligarchy decides who will enter the Knesset and not the voters who are allowed only to choose between the various parties. The result is that the members of the Knesset have a direct obligation to their party machine and only an indirect (and often indifferent) obligation to the voters and the nation as a whole. As destructive to democracy as PR is in normal cases it is even more so in the case of Israel.

This is so because while the majority of Israel's population arrived after the establishment of independence, almost all of the leadership positions in the major parties are held by veterans who came to the country before the state. Upward mobility is almost impossible here as elected officials apparently must die in order to be replaced. Young persons joining political parties grow old before positions open for them.

The result of this process in Israel is that today the persons "elected democratically" are truly representative of less than a fourth of the electorate. Whole sections of the population are not fairly represented in the Knesset and in the central committees of all the major parties. Sabras, who make up a third of the population, hold few positions of importance in the parties or the government. New immigrants, who make up half of Israel's population, have little or no representation in the political institutions that govern their lives. Outside of Tel Aviv, Haifa, and the coastal plain lie great stretches of Israeli territory whose citizens, in the developing areas of Dimona, Lachhish, Ashdod, Beersheba, and Kiryat Shmona, cry out for representation. Will their voice be heard?

The present system encourages the splintering of Israel's electorate into many parties, thus depriving the voter of any hope that his party will get a clear mandate. Every government must be a coalition of several parties and this gives the small party the power to extort from the majority agreements to enact legislation *against* the will of the majority of Israel's citizens. Under the present system governments can rise or fall because of intrigues between the coalition partners or demands of a smaller party (as in the Shalom dispute) *without any* crisis in the confidence of the electorate. Thus we have a situation in Israel today where the Knesset is not only unrepresentative of the people and may pass legislation against the will of the people, but also is prevented from improving in the future because of barriers to the democratic process built into the present electoral system. What can be done?

The Israel Labor List (Rafi) is the only political party that is demanding electoral reform and it will refuse to join any coalition that will not leave it due to work to improve the democratic process in Israel. Electoral reform for Israel means the end to nation wide PR and the introduction of single member constituency elections, or at least regional PR. With one or two persons elected from a specific district, the voter will know who is his representative and will have a voice in electing him or her. And of course the candidates elected will be answerable directly to the voters and not to the party officials. Thus freed of party control the Knesset member will be able to ignore party dogma when it conflicts with his conscience or with the wishes of his constituents.

Talented young persons and the independent voter will be free to contest in the elections without the approval of party bureaucracies. The mayors of cities should also be elected in a personal campaign instead of the PR system used now with the horse trading it involves and its many other defects.

Those of you who come from England and America will easily recognize the advantages of electoral reform. It is the hope of the Israel Labor List (Rafi) that you will understand the necessity and the urgency of this issue. Israel's democracy is really at stake. We hope that you will join the masses of young people, new immigrants, and others concerned with Israel's future in voting for Rafi.

By Bernard Shapiro
1965

THE MINISTER OF DEFENCE

Tel-Aviv, May 31, 1977

Mr. Bernard Shapiro,
The House of Books, Inc.,
9215 Stella Link Road,
Houston, Texas 77025,
USA

Dear Bernard,

    Please accept my warmest thanks for your moving letter. We have in the meantime suffered a severe blow in the elections and shall have to start everything all over again.

    But Vespasian has already said, according to Flavius Josephus: "As it is not fitting the person of merit to take pride without limit in good times, so it is not fitting a man of valour to despair in time of trouble, as good and bad alternate rapidly. The exemplary man is the one who did not boast in time of happiness, so that he may also bear his troubles with ease of mind".

    I thank you very much for the two books. They seem, at first glance, to be very interesting, and I shall rely on your good taste in the future too.

    With my friendly wishes,

Yours sincerely,

Shimon Peres
Minister of Defence

MINISTER SHIMON PERES

December 27, 1973

Mr. Bernard Shapiro
House of Books Inc.
9215 Stella Link Road
Houston, Texas 77025
U.S.A.

Dear Mr. Shapiro: [handwritten: Bernard]

Thank you very much for your letter of December 10, 1973 and for the $1,000 check made out to Zahal enclosed with it.

I quite agree with you that research into and development of new means of combat is a matter of great priority for the State of Israel and therefore your wish that your donation should be allocated for this purpose is most commendable; but, practically speaking, very little research and development work of this nature can be accomplished for $1,000.

Accordingly, I would like to suggest that we return to your first inclination - to allocate your donation for the benefit of wounded veterans.

I am holding your check until I hear from you your confirmation that we may use your donation for the benefit of wounded veterans.

With best regards,

Sincerely,

Shimon Peres

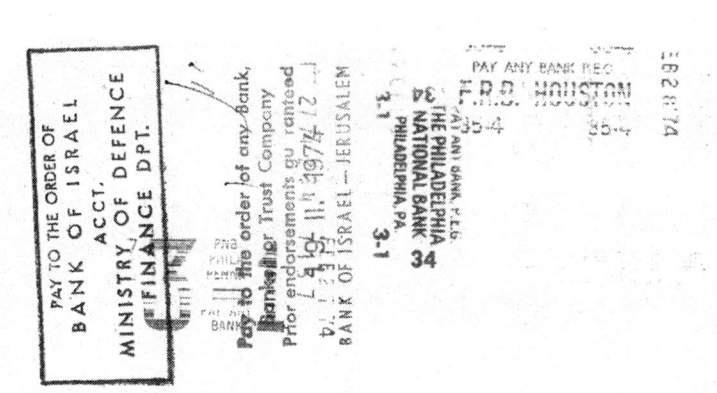

Bernard Shapiro
5730 CHEENA DR.   723-4688
HOUSTON, TEXAS 77035

No. 593

DATE 12/10 19 73

PAY TO THE ORDER OF __Zahal__ $1000.00

__One thousand__ _____ DOLLARS

Bank of Houston
HOUSTON, TEXAS

FOR _____

Bernard Shapiro

⑈1130⑈0096⑈   30⑈1516⑈51⑈   ⑈0000100000⑈

PAY TO THE ORDER OF
BANK OF ISRAEL
ACCT.
MINISTRY OF DEFENCE
FINANCE DPT.

Pay to the order of any Bank,
Bankalier Trust Company
Prior endorsements guaranteed
BANK OF ISRAEL — JERUSALEM

PAY ANY BANK P.E.O.
F.R.B. HOUSTON
THE PHILADELPHIA
NATIONAL BANK
PHILADELPHIA, PA.
34
3-1

ראש הממשלה
THE PRIME MINISTER

Jerusalem   May 25, 1986
              Ref.: 1-DSR-559-1

Mr. Bernard Shapiro
House of Books, Inc.
9215 Stella Link Road
Houston, Texas 77025
U S A

Dear Bernard,

    Thank you very much for your letter to me of March 11, 1986. Unfortunately the books you mention in the letter reached me only today.

    I have taken due note of your remarks. You have always been a wise counsellor.

    The national unity government, after 20 months in office, can today credit itself with impressive achievements, in important areas of life. The withdrawal of the IDF from Lebanon -- served to consolidate our national security, while safeguarding the lives of our soldier-sons. We succeeded in halting the inflationary spiral -- which threatened to sweep the national economy into the abyss. We are now on the threshold of a new economic momentum -- which will comprise the encouragement of exports, the replacement of imports, and a structural reorganization of the economy.

    On the political level, we have broadened the gateway between Israel and Egypt -- and, despite attempts to intimidate and to terrorize us, both countries remain resolved to deepen the ties between us as a prelude to a comprehensive peace in the region. The Hashemite King has also come a long way to meet us on the road to the negotiating table, while the PLO continues to prove that it is an obstacle to peace, as we have postulated.

    The present government of Israel can also pride itself on the fact that, in its time, internal tensions in the country have been greatly reduced: between Ashkenazim and Sephardim, between the different political parties, between religious and secular elements, between Jews and Arabs. Israel's image in the world has also improved. Leaders and governments are attentive to our views; they appreciate our firm stand against terrorism; and they understand that our continuing struggle, here in Israel, is based not only on power, but also on justice.

    Please continue to convey to me your thoughts and comments.

In friendship,
Shimon Peres

VICE PREMIER
AND MINISTER OF FOREIGN AFFAIRS

ממלא מקום ראש הממשלה
ושר החוץ

Jerusalem, March 15, 1987

Mr. Bernard Shapiro
House of Books, Inc.
9215 Stella Link Road
Houston, Texas 77025
U.S.A.

Dear Bernard,

Thank you very much for your very detailed letter.

Thank you also for the books you sent me, which were much appreciated. The choice, as always, was excellent. One thing, at least, is certain: reading books about stopping smoking is less dangerous than smoking.

In response to your various comments:

The conditions you pose for the convening of an international conference have indeed been included in all my talks and statements on the subject, and we will continue to insist upon their fulfillment.

Regarding demonstrations on behalf of Soviet Jewry — this is apparently the difference between American democracy and the Russian regime, but I am convinced that we will, in the end, open the gates of the Soviet Union to Jewish emigration. With regard to Soviet Jewish emigration to America, our efforts in this area are directed only to those Jews who request visas to Israel, and whom Israel is ready and willing to absorb.

Finally, on the West Bank: Regardless of what merit your ideas may or may not have, we must recognize that the problem is essentially demographic, and not geographic.

On a lighter note, I am delighted to hear that you will be visiting Israel with your wife and son this June, and will be pleased to meet with you then.

Sincerely,

Shimon Peres

VICE PREMIER
AND MINISTER OF FOREIGN AFFAIRS

ממלא מקום ראש הממשלה
ושר החוץ

Jerusalem, April 15, 1987

Mr. Bernard Shapiro
House of Books, Inc.
9215 Stella Link Road
Houston, Texas 77025
U.S.A.

Dear Bernard,

Thank you very much for your good wishes for Boston, and for, as always, seeing to it that I do not lack for reading material. You will no doubt be pleased to learn that I have taken at least one of your recent suggestions to heart, and have stopped smoking -- though I don't promise always to be quite so compliant.

Once again, I look forward to seeing you and your family in Israel this June.

Sincerely,

Shimon Peres

VICE PREMIER
AND MINISTER OF FOREIGN AFFAIRS

ממלא מקום ראש הממשלה
ושר החוץ

Jerusalem, September 14, 1987

Mr. Bernard Shapiro
House of Books, Inc.
9215 Stella Link Road
Houston, Texas 77025

Dear Bernard,

Thank you very much for your letter and good wishes, and your comments on the Lavi.

The future of the Lavi project was for me one of the most decisive issues facing the government. In seeking a solution to this difficult question -- a search which kept me awake nights -- it was clear to me that the decision would be crucial to Israel's national security, both militarily and economically.

I considered it vital to guarantee the following:

1. Israel's research and development capabilities.

2. The Israeli defense industry's continued ability to produce advanced aircraft.

3. Maximum continued employment for the research and production workers in the Israel Aircraft Industries.

4. The maintenance of the budget and taxation framework and the prevention of renewed inflation.

5. Maximum possible coordination with the United States, which in effect finances the project.

In examining the options before us, it seemed to me that the two polar positions -- cancellation of the Lavi project or its continuation -- were unacceptable, each for its own reasons. I felt it my responsibility to try and find a middle course between these options -- a course which may perhaps not be easy, but which is imperative to protect vital national interests.

It is in the spirit of these thoughts that, in coordination with the Defense and Finance Ministers, I formulated a proposal designed to guarantee the five goals listed above. This proposal, to our satisfaction, was adopted as a government resolution on August 30, 1987.

With best wishes to you and your family for the New Year,

Sincerely,

[signature]

VICE PREMIER
AND MINISTER OF FOREIGN AFFAIRS

ממלא מקום ראש הממשלה
ושר החוץ

Jerusalem, February 21, 1988

Mr. Bernard Shapiro
9215 Stella Link
Houston, Texas 77025
U.S.A.

Dear Bernard,

Thank you for your letter of January 30, 1988, which I read with great interest as usual.

With regard to the current situation, as you know we made a major effort to create a peace momentum which unfortunately has stalled, due to Arab timidity and the recalcitrance of the Likud. Now the U.S. is exploring a new initiative that is to lead to direct negotiations after an international opening. These negotiations will be aimed at achieving an interim solution, to be followed by a final settlement. I believe that today, given the enormous burden of the cost of war, both on us and on the Arab countries, we have an historic opportunity to achieve peace, and we must seize it. Should we fail to do so, the consequences for future generations will be grave.

As to Israel's image, our problem is that, in modern times, television can be an effective weapon. There is little we can do to prevent negative coverage, since in a scene of soldiers fighting rock-throwing youths, sympathy will always be with the youth. What we can and will do, as you suggest, is to launch a major effort to obtain balanced coverage of the realities. I understand that the recent CBS 48-hour broadcast was a step in this direction. I am convinced that the more the American media will concentrate on the sources of the conflict, the better our image will be.

With best wishes,

Sincerely,

Shimon Peres

CHAPTER FOURTEEN: CORRESPONDENCE WITH OTHER LEADERS

November 28, 1970

P R E S S   R E L E A S E

HOUSTONIAN TELLS RUSSIANS "Let my people go"

Bernard Shapiro, a third generation Houstonian, sent a telegram yesterday to the Russian Ambassador in Washington saying simply "Let my people go."

Mr. Shapiro explained to reporters that his grandfather, Harry W. Freeman, settled in Houston from Russia at the turn of the century. He was an escapee from Czarist persecution of the Jews. Here in Houston he founded his family and practiced law. You might recall that it was Mr. Freeman who fought white slavery in the area as well as working with Judge Dannenbaum to give Negroes the right to vote in Texas.

There are millions of Jews in Russia today who want freedom from communist domination and who would love to be allowed to come America or Israel, where they can live in freedom. They have a tremendous contribution to give to the free world and we must not forget them.

Mr. Shapiro, who is currently the President of the House of Books, Inc., says he is not afraid of Russian retaliation for his telegram. The Russians are very sensitive to Public Opinion in the West and only a public outcry against the treatment of Jews in the Soviet Union will help liberate them.

822, Sindh Colony,
Prof. G. C. ASNANI.
Aundh, Pune 411007.
M.Sc., Ph.D.
Tel. : 91- 020 - 588 0347
United Nations Service (Retd.)
E-mail: asnani@giaspn01.vsnl.net.in
URL :
http://www.balasai.net/asnani

Date: 1st Jully 1999.

To : Dr. Yossef Bodansky
C/o. Freeman Centre for Strategic Studies.
P. O. Box No. 35661
Houston, Tx77235-5661, USA
E-mail: Bsaphir@aol.com

Dear Dr. Bodansky,
                    I thank you very much for sending me your book " Islamic Anti-Semitism as a Political Instrument " through Freeman Centre for Strategic Studies, Houston.

      The facts and figures presented in the book clearly show that you have understood Islam in its true colours. Islam is a big challenge to the very existence of the whole human race, not only Jews. Either we have to become blind followers of " Prophet " Mohammed or get tortured till death by his other blind followers. If the Christians, especially of USA, do not understand this plain fact, USA will not be a safe place for Democracy or Human Rights; USA will be swallowed up by the fanaticism of Islam along with its Democracy and Human Rights.

      Thanking you once again for writing a book with such a profound scholarliness for the benefit of the whole human race and with best regards,

Yours sincerely,

(G. C. Asnani)

THE WHITE HOUSE
WASHINGTON

October 21, 1970

Dear Mr. Shapiro:

Your comments about my new initiative for peace in southeast Asia were especially gratifying to me. I greatly appreciated your very thoughtful message and I hope that our efforts to reach an honorable and enduring end to the war will merit your confidence and support.

With best wishes,

Sincerely,

Richard Nixon

Mr. Bernard Shapiro
9215 Stella Link Road
Houston, Texas 77024

THE WHITE HOUSE
WASHINGTON

April 26, 1993

Mr. Bernard J. Shapiro
Director
Freeman Center For Strtegic Studies
Post Office Box 35709
Houston, Texas 77235-5709

Dear Bernard:

    I appreciate your taking the time to write.

    It's important to me to hear the thoughts and experiences of people who care about the future of America and the world. We face many challenges ahead, and in order for us to come together and build consensus, we must all share our ideas and concerns.

    Your letter is valuable to me. Thank you.

Sincerely,

Bill Clinton

4114 Gairloch Lane
Houston, Texas 77025

May 17, 1968

The Hon. Levi Eshkol
Prime Minister
State of Israel
Jerusalem, Israel

Dear Mr. Eshkol:

Shalom!

Many friends of mine all over this country are anxious to settle in Israel. However, we see no practical way of doing this outside the framework of the Multi-Purpose Settlement as originated by Uri Goldschmidt of Tel Aviv.

Many of us have studied Hebrew at ulpanim and attempted aliya before but failed to get integrated into Israeli life for lack of a secure base from which to operate. All of us are well educated and could easily (with time) become the leaders of our local Jewish communities. We have decided, however, that we would rather be "little Israelis" than big Zionists in America.

Some of us will bring with them the technical know how to set up light industries at the settlement to provide employment to others.

The local Jewish press is beginning to run ads and articles about the MPS and I expect to be able with in the next week to form a local (Houston) group of a dozen or more.

In the best interest of Israel's future destiny I appeal to you to help cut out the red-tape and bureaucratic complications that Uri Goldschmidt and his followers must go through in order to settle in Israel in a community of their own.

Thanking you in advance for your aid, I remain

Sincerely yours,

Bernard Shapiro

Jerusalem, May 5h, 1973

Dear Mr. Shapiro,

I was glad to hear that your plans are progressing well.

Needless to say that I shall be glad to meet you when you come to Israel. We have recently moved to live close to Mount Scopus. We do not yet have a telephone and it seems it will take sometime till this neighbourhood will connected. Anyhow you can find me through my address as specified on the other side of this letter or the Hebrew University.

Sincerely yours

Y. Yadin

MINISTER OF COMMERCE AND INDUSTRY
JERUSALEM, ISRAEL

29/3/72

Dear Bernard,

Thank you for your nice letter and congratulations.

As you see, I have finally "landed" in a field where I can make some use for my "Business School" training. Very interesting and a lot of problems.

I am all for your "aliya", and I am at your service for this purpose. Regards to your family – Shalom
Haïm

CHIEF OF THE GENERAL STAFF BRANCH
ISRAEL DEFENCE FORCES

Tel-Aviv, February 8, 1970

Mr. Bernard Shapiro,
8951 Braesmont Ave., 207,
Houston, Texas 77035,
U.S.A.

Dear Mr. Shapiro,

Thank you very much for your letter, your contribution and your moving thought.

A gesture such as yours is a symbol for every Jew, and, as long as there are people like you in the world, the Jewish nation will remain united.

I wish you all the best and sincerely hope that you will be able to carry out your plans and to immigrate to Israel with your wife.

With warmest regards,

Yours sincerely,

Haim Bar-Lev — Lt.-General
Chief of the General Staff

February 9, 1989

9215 Stella Link
Houston, Texas 77025
U.S.A.

Itzhak Shamir, Prime Minister
Prime Minister's Office
Jerusalem, Israel

Dear Mr. Shamir:

I would like to make a small contribution to the pool of ideas that you have before you to solve present crisis in Judaea and Samaria and Gaza.

   Stage One: Israel must overcome the psychological barriers to unilateral action. I know you are committed to the Camp David framework But Nobody else seems to be. No Arab much less Palestinian will go back to it. The MAXIMUM Israel can offer in negotiations is less than the MINIMUM the Arabs would accept.
   You must make the crucial decision to act alone, carving out a solution in Israel's best interest.

   Stage Two: You've made your decision to act alone, now you must give your actions the best face (public relations wise) possible, minimizing damage to U.S.-Israeli relations. You hold an election in every settlement and village in the territories to determine the status of each village. The ballot has three choices: residents may decide either
   A. Continue status quo
   B. Merge with Israel
   C. Become part of a fully autonomous Palestine with all rights of a state except military and the right to harm Israel.

   A boycott of the election will be considered a vote for the status quo and will be announced as such beforehand. The Jewish settlements will certainly vote to join Israel and this can be accomplished before the whole world as democratic due process. The Arabs may boycott the election but with good public relations Israel will come out smelling like a rose.

   Stage Three: The Arabs boycott the election, the intifadia continue what to do next:
   A. Gradually pull troops out of Arab areas and redeploy them along the roads linking Jewish settlements.
   B. Treat any interference with road travel the same as terrorism and crush the perpetrators.
   C. Arabs attacking settlers and being killed will not play in the media the same negative way Arabs stoning troops in their own vilages has done.

Stage Four: Gaza A. There is nothing in Gaza but problems. My best advice is to evacuate it and then:
B. Surround it with a security fence and patrol the perimeter for terrorists.
C. Move Jewish settlers to Judaea or Samaria at government expense.
D. Allow Gaza Arabs to work in Israel with proper I.D. and good behavior.

Stage Five: Declare Arabs in Judaea and Samaria autonomous, whether they like it or not. Then:
A. Withdraw Israeli civil administration
B. Allow Arabs to work in Israel with proper I.D. and behavior.
C. Maintain vigilant control of roads linking Jewish settlements with Israel and each other. Respond with maximum force to any attempt to cut roads or harass drivers.
D. Publicly announce that Israel's adminstration of Arab areas is over and that they are free to do as they please (call themselves Palestine if they wish) AS LONG AS THEY DO NOT DEVELOP A MILITAI OR DO ANY HARM TO ISRAEL.

This policy is relatively easy to sell abroad and can certainly be defend in the U.S. with little or no loss to American-Israeli relations. Speaking of public relations, I find that Israel has done the worst possi job. I for one am sick and tired of having the good name of Israel vilified and smeared every day on radio, T.V., newspapers and magazines. Some suggestions: 1.The Arabs killed should never be described as 'demonstrators' but as rioters, terrorists, or Arabs who were attacking soldiers or police. Agressive use of comparative history should be used to show how truly humane the Israeli soldiers are(e.g. in the Watts riot in Los Angeles dozens of blacks were killed in a matter of days).
2. Video spots should appear on American television showing manequins dressed in Israeli army uniforms being attacked by rock trowing Arabs. The camera zooms in on the manequins as they are broken to piece by the rocks. A voice overlay says in a calm voice:Israeli soldiers are not dummies----THEY SHOOT BACK.

I hope this letter gives you some ideas. Nothing would please me more than to help you in your quest for peace and security for Israel.

Hoping to hear from you soon,
Sincerely yours,

Bernard Shapiro
Bernard Shapiro, President
House of Books, Inc.

HOUSTON CHAPTER
PRESIDENT
Bernard Shapiro
VICE - PRESIDENT
Michael Abramowitz
SECRETARY - TREASURER
Barbara Gordin
COMMUNITY COORDINATOR
Janabeth Lakenmacher

AMERICANS FOR A SAFE ISRAEL
P.O. Box 35709
Houston, Texas 77235-5709

June 9, 1990

Mr. Yitzhak Shamir
Prime Minister
Government of Israel
Jerusalem, Israel

Dear Mr. Shamir:

On behalf of myself and my organization, I would like to offer you a hearty congratulations on your success in forming a new government. We look forward to your leadership in overcoming Israel's formidable problems.

As an organization we feel that the following things should be given top priority:
1. Rescue and settlement (including jobs and homes) of Soviet Jewry.
2. The parallel realization of the incorporation of Judaea and Samaria in the State of Israel and the granting (unilaterally) of limited self-rule to the Arab inhabitants there of.
3. The rapid development of high-tech industries to provide jobs and maintain superiority over the Arabs.
4. Electoral Reform (which we believe will greatly add to your parliamentary majority).
5. Continue to pursue "Peace for Peace" with all Arab countries (not the nonsense of "Peace for Territories" which we believe will led to war).
6. Liberate the Israeli economy from bureaucratic controls and let Jewish capital transform the country.

Our group is devoting a lot of energy trying to improve Israel's image and would appreciate some help on your part. What I am trying to say delicately, please be careful of the way you announce things. A careful turn of phrase, a friendly word and statement of peaceful intent can mask even harsh actions.

Best wishes for great success.

Sincerely yours,

Bernard Shapiro,

לשכת ראש הממשלה
PRIME MINISTER'S BUREAU

Jerusalem, February 26, 1989
111-4

Mr. Bernard Shapiro
House of Books, Inc.
9215 Stella Link Road
Houston, Texas 77025

Dear Mr. Shapiro,

I am writing on behalf of the Prime Minister, Mr. Yitzhak Shamir, to thank you for your recent letter, which was brought to his attention.

We have noted your opinions and proposals, which are under consideration.

The Prime Minister appreciates your interest in and concern for our country and sends you best wishes from Jerusalem.

Yours sincerely,

Z.H. Hurwitz
Adviser to the Prime Minister

NEWS, VIEWS & REVIEWS
BERNARD J. SHAPIRO

Political Analysis and Commentary on Israeli and Jewish Affairs

December 1, 1992

Haim Bar-Lev,
Ambassador to Russia
c\o Ministry of Foreign Affairs
Jerusalem, Israel

Dear Ambassador Bar-Lev:

I hope you are well and fine. Congratulations on your new position as Ambassador to Russia.

You haven't hear from me in a long time. I used to send you checks for the IDF when you were facing the Egyptians during the War of Attrition.

Your appointment to Moscow caused me to search through my old papers to find a piece of memorabilia for you. I succeeded and I am sending it to you in a round about way to avoid offending the Russians.

This newspaper headline was printed at an amusement park in New Orleans back in 1970. I was angry and frustrated that everything you did to force the Egyptians to stop the fighting, was counteracted by the Soviets. They kept upping the ante until they were even involved in air combat themselves. I fantasized that somehow you would defeat the Russians and enter Moscow in triumph.

Twenty-two years later, Russia (the Soviet Union) is no more and you in fact entered Moscow in triumph.

And Israelis are always saying that the age of prophecy is over!

My bookstore is closed (after 23 years) and I have become a pro-Israel journalist (something of a rarity). Enclosed a couple of my columns. Don't be mad at me as I have drifted to the right (as defined in Israeli politics) and think Rabin is losing touch with reality as far as the Arabs are concerned.

I have saved all your letters from the 70's and view you as a hero of Israel. Best wishes in Moscow. Dress warm!

Sincerely,

Bernard J. Shapiro

P.O. Box 35709 ✡ Houston, Texas 77235-5709
Telephone & Fax: (713) 723-6016

FREEMAN CENTER FOR STRATEGIC STUDIES

BERNARD J. SHAPIRO
DIRECTOR

June 30, 1993

The Honorable Yitzhak Rabin
Prime Minister of Israel
Jerusalem
Israel

Dear Prime Minister Rabin:

Your election was based primarily on economic issues and the internal disarray in the opposition Likud Party.

Your election did not give you a broad mandate to effect territorial changes in the Peace Process. In America, for example, a two thirds vote of the states is necessary to change the constitution. Your paper thin electoral margin does not give you the authority to make the major changes you propose.

There are only two ways to achieve this mandate:

1. New elections
2. A referendum on any peace agreement or territorial change

The first method (elections) could cause a change in government. The second method (referendum) has the advantage of allowing you to remain in power with a well-defined mandate. This strengthens your hand in the negotiations with the Arabs by establishing "red lines" beyond which you are prevented from going.

Significantly, it also allows you to hear and understand the will of the majority of Israeli voters (e.g., democracy).

Failure to take either of these two steps will ultimately lead to disaster. For example:

P.O. Box 35709 ✩ Houston, Texas 77235-5709
Telephone & Fax: (713) 723-6016

FREEMAN CENTER FOR STRATEGIC STUDIES

BERNARD J. SHAPIRO
DIRECTOR

June 6, 1994

General Ariel Sharon, MK
Likud Party Office
The Knesset
Jerusalem, ISRAEL

Dear General Sharon:

I recently returned from a month of research and study in Israel. My primary goal was to develop a method to rally the Nationalist forces in such a way as to achieve victory over the Left-wing parties currently ruling the country.

I have now put my thoughts on paper and wish to share them with you. While I believe that my specific plan will work, it is important to remember that the crucial part in winning with any plan is the enthusiasm and whole hearted support it is given. It has certain glitzy and show business characteristics. These are necessary to create the excitement needed to revive the Right.

Although this plan is also being sent to other leaders of the Nationalist camp, I have been an admirer of yours for many years. Did you get the photo from your trip to Houston of you, with the Hindu-Jewish Friendship Forum, that I sent you while I was in Israel.

Enclosed: (1) Victory Plan For Israel (2) the May-June issue of **THE MACCABEAN**, the monthly publication of the Freeman Center For Strategic Studies.

Respectfully,

Bernard J. Shapiro

P.O. Box 35709 ✿ Houston, Texas 77235-5709
Telephone & Fax: (713) 723-6016

FREEMAN CENTER FOR STRATEGIC STUDIES
P.O. Box 35709
Houston, Texas 77235-5709
Phone or Fax (713) 723-06016

March 25, 1994

Prime Minister Yitzhak Rabin
Israeli Government
Jerusalem, Israel

Dear Prime Minister Rabin:

I am against removing the Jews of Hebron. It will destroy the unity of the Jewish people and **could lead to civil war**. Hebron is holiest city to Jews following Jerusalem. Jews should have the right to live wherever they wish.

It is long past time for you to reconsider your choice of allies. You have alienated half of the Jewish people in order to curry favor with terrorists. The former may never forgive you and later are laughing at you each time they extract another concession. In the end they will tear up the agreement you tried so hard to preserve.

Sincerely,

Bernard J. Shapiro, Director

> **JEWS CONCERNED FOR THE FUTURE OF ISRAEL**
> 3040 Post Oak Blvd., Suite 1515
> Houston, TX 77056-6512
> Telephone: (713) 961-3255, Fax: (713) 961-1205

June 9, 1994
The Honorable Yitzhak Rabin,
Prime Minister of Israel
Prime Minister's Office
Jerusalem, ISRAEL
Dear Prime Minister Rabin:

We are a group of American Jews with strong feelings for Israel and great concerns about its security and well-being. There is a great diversity of opinions among us, but one thing is abundantly clear: We feel that the present policy of the Labor/Meretz government related to the Israel/PLO agreement (DOP) could be improved in many areas.

Although we have several areas of concern, this letter contains only the most important. We believe this agreement fails to protect the legitimate interests of the Jewish communities in Judea, Samaria and Golan. Not only is their security potentially threatened, but also there is no provision for land and water to allow for their future growth. We believe that full disclosure of written commitments regarding future Israeli concessions to the Palestinians is essential for both the Israeli public and Jewish communities abroad. Such full disclosure would allow free and open discussion of all important issues.

Israel's present negotiating strategy appears to us to be one of appeasement of every Palestinian request and demand. The truth is that there will be no end to the demands as the Palestinians keep changing the nature of what will satisfy them.

The failure to insist on compliance on the part of the PLO with its solemn commitments is quite unsettling. We would like to see Israel publicize the PLO non-compliance to influence world opinion regarding which party is responsible for holding back the peace process.

Finally, we believe that Israel shares America's democratic tradition of free speech, and urge you not to try to stifle voices of dissent in this country. Please remember that we are lifelong friends and supporters of Israel. When we voice our concerns with Israeli policy, it is the concern of a relative for a loved one.

Respectfully,

Phillip Aronoff
Uzi Halevy
Isaac Kleinman
Louis Lechenger
Sheldon Miller

Gary Polland
Ben Ronn
David Ronn
Bernard J. Shapiro

FREEMAN CENTER FOR STRATEGIC STUDIES

BERNARD J. SHAPIRO
DIRECTOR

Consul General Meir Romem
Consulate General of Israel

January 2, 1995

Dear Meir:

Once again your government has proven its abiltiy to appease those very same Arabs that wish them dead.

I condemn in the strongest terms Israel's failure to defend the right of the Jewish People to its Holy Land.

The consequences will be devastating and not to the liking any member of the current government.

Regretfully,

Bernard J. Shapiro

Prime Minister's Bureau   לשכת ראש הממשלה

יועץ ראש הממשלה ומנהל הלשכה
Head of the Prime Minister's Bureau

July 2, 1995
ד' בתמוז התשנ"ה

Mr. Bernard J. Shapiro, Director
Freeman Center for
Stategic Studies
P.O. Box 35709
Houston, Texas 77235-5709
U.S.A.

Dear Mr. Shapiro,

On behalf of the Prime Minister, Mr. Yitzhak Rabin, I acknowledge receipt of your postcard regarding Jerusalem.

Jerusalem has been the focus of our yearning and the embodiment of our dreams for thousands of years. Loyal to our heritage and our values, we will always allow free access and freedom of religious worship to people of all creeds. Jerusalem, however, has always been, and will always be the heart of the Jewish people, and will continue to be the capital of the State of Israel. It is the policy of this Government to preserve Jerusalem united, under Israeli sovereignty.

We appreciate your sharing your views and concerns with us.

Sincerely yours,

Eitan Haber

3 Kaplan St. Hakirya, Jerusalem 91007, Israel. Tel: 972-2-705512

FREEMAN CENTER FOR STRATEGIC STUDIES
P.O. Box 35709-395 Houston, TX 77235-5709
Telephone or Fax: (713) 723-6016 E-mail: BSAPHIR@AOL.COM
Internet: gopher://gopher.jer1.co.il/11/Politics/research/free

FAXED 8-25-95

EXECUTIVE DIRECTOR
Bernard J. Shapiro

BOARD OF DIRECTORS
Richard B. Rolnick, MD
  Chairman
Bruce Goldfaden
Rael Jean Isaac
Louis Lechenger
Dan Nimrod
Gary M. Polland
Herbert Zweibon

ADVISORY COMMITTEE
Michael Abramowitz
Christopher Barder
David Basch
Eugene Blum
Yossef Bodansky
Arvind Ghosh
Monica Goldfaden
Zvi Kalisky, MD
Alexander King
Helene Klein
Bob Lang
Zvi Lando
Mark E. Langfan
Yechiel M. Leiter
Yehuda Poch
Monroe Spen
Janice Starkie
Johnny Weintraub
Nathan Wolkovitz
Herbert Wisenberg
Robert K. Zurawin, MD

RESEARCH ASSOCIATES
David Basch --
  Philosopher / Political Analyst
Yossef Bodansky --
  World Terrorism Analyst
Arvind Ghosh --
  Hindu Historian & Publisher
Mark E. Langfan --
  Military/Strategic Analyst
Dan Nimrod --
  Jewish / Israeli Historian
Yehuda Poch --
  Zionist / Israeli Research
Bernard J. Shapiro --
  Political Analyst

RABBINICAL ASSOCIATES
Rabbi Moshe Cahana
Rabbi Stuart Federow
Rabbi Joseph Radinsky
Rabbi Jack Segal

August 24, 1995

President Ezer Weizmann
Office of the President
State House
Jerusalem, Israel
Via Fax: 011-972-2-660445

Dear President Weizmann:

On behalf of our worldwide membership and myself, I would like to express my condolences to you over the recent terrorist bombing in Jerusalem. The loss of even one Jew is too much. The bereavement of one Israeli family is shared by Jews around the world.

President Weizmann, I must be honest with you at this grave time. The Oslo Process will lead to the demoralization and eventual destruction of Israel. The Labor/Meretz government of Prime Minister Yistzhak Rabin and Foreign Minister Shimon Peres can not solve the problem of terrorism. In fact, they are in bed with the terrorists. Their whole "peace" process represents a collaboration with the world's most infamous terrorist, Yassir Arafat. Recent video tapes demonstrate to even the most trusting Israeli that the Palestinian *Jihad* against Israel and the Jewish people has not ended. Indeed, it has been **accelerated** by the Israeli government's willingness to provide safe havens for terrorists.

This government has collaborated with the enemy; given away our **Sacred Land** and **Holy Places**; divided the **People of Israel**; beaten women and children; suppressed our freedom of speech; endangered our water supply; released terrorist murders into our midst; surrendered our strategic mountains; created a Palestinian State; broken **G-D's Covenant with Abraham**; defamed religious Jews and their **TORAH** and even jeopardized Jewish rule in **Jerusalem** and our right to the **Temple Mount**.

DAYENU! ENOUGH OF THEIR TYRANNY!

By their actions they have forfeited and any claim to legitimacy. Only new elections can restore democratic Zionist rule to ISRAEL. We urge you, President Weizman to have the courage to issue a call for new elections.

FREEMAN CENTER FOR STRATEGIC STUDIES
P.O. Box 35661 ✧ Houston, Texas 77235-5661
Phone or Fax: 713-723-6016 ✧ E-Mail: BSaphir@aol.com
Web Site (URL): http://freeman.io.com

EXECUTIVE DIRECTOR
Bernard J. Shapiro

THE MACCABEAN
Bernard J. Shapiro, *Editor*

BOARD OF DIRECTORS
Richard H. Rolnick, MD (Houston)
  Chairman
Rael Jean Isaac (NY)
Ira Kahn (Chicago)
Louis Lechenger (Houston)
Dan Nimrod (Quebec, Canada)
Gary M. Polland (Houston)
Herbert Zweibon (New York)

ADVISORY COMMITTEE
Michael Abramowitz (Houston)
Yedidya Atlas (Jerusalem)
Christopher Barder (England)
David Basch (West Hartford)
Eugene Blum (Baltimore)
Yossef Bodansky (MD)
Rabbi Moshe Cahana (Houston)
Rabbi Stuart Federow (Houston)
Arvind Ghosh (Houston)
Zvi Kalisky, MD (Houston)
Helene Klein (San Francisco)
Bob Lang (Israel)
Mark E. Langfan (New York)
Yechiel M. Leiter (Israel)
CPT Shawn M. Pine (San Antonio)
Yehuda Poch (Israel)
Rabbi Joseph Radinsky (Houston)
Boris Shusteff (NY)
Janice Sturkie (Houston)
Johnny Weintraub (Houston)
Nathan Wolkovits (Houston)
Gail & Emanuel Winston (Chicago)
Herbert Wisenberg (Houston)
Robert K. Zurawin, MD (Houston)

RESEARCH ASSOCIATES
David Basch --
  Philosopher / Political Analyst
Yossef Bodansky --
  World Terrorism Analyst
Arvind Ghosh --
  Hindu Historian & Publisher
Mark E. Langfan --
  Military/Strategic Analyst
Dan Nimrod --
  Zionist / Israeli Research
CPT Shawn M. Pine --
  Military/Strategic Analyst
Boris Shusteff --
  Zionist / Israeli Research
Bernard J. Shapiro --
  Political Analyst
Emanuel A. Winston --
  Middle East Analyst

April 8, 1998

COPY

The Honorable Benjamin Netanyahu
Prime Minister of Israel
Prime Minister's Office
Jerusalem, ISRAEL

Dear Prime Minister Netanyahu:

First I would like to wish you and your family a *Happy and Healthy Passover*.

Enclosed is the skeleton of a plan to counter the increasingly effective Arab propaganda campaign in the United States. It occurs to me that part of it, especially the historical parts, could also be used in Israel to educate a population excessively exposed to post-Zionist disinformation.

Also enclosed is an article, **ARAB PROPAGANDISTS JOIN FORCES WITH ANT-SEMITES**. While written in 1965, it remains extremely accurate in its analysis and was certainly prescient for its time.

The only real question is whether your government is **serious** about fighting the hasbara battle. For example, your Consul General in Houston (Tzion Evrony) though a nice enough guy does almost no Hasbara of significance. It is left to me at the Freeman Center to duplicate and distribute your Government Press Office press releases and documents. Michael Freund supplies me with the material and I distribute it broadly to Jewish activists and members of the Senate and Congress.

[As a side note, I am apparently still on a blacklist from the Rabin-Peres days. This excludes me from Consular functions for the Jewish leadership. Do you want this to continue?]

While I don't always agree with your policies, I am committed 100% to battling the Arab propaganda that now pervades our media and college campuses. I am here to help.

Best Wishes. *With Love of Israel,*

Bernard J. Shapiro, Executive Director
Freeman Center For Strategic Studies

AUTHOR BIOGRAPHY

Bernard J. Shapiro

Executive Director and Political Analyst

Bernard J. Shapiro was born in Houston, Texas and received his higher education at the University of California at Berkeley, where he received degrees in both Political Science and in Communication and Public Policy. Shapiro lived in Israel for several years following graduation and has traveled there dozens of times to remain abreast of current developments. He has been an advocate for Israel for more than 50 years.

Shapiro is the founder and executive director of the **Freeman Center For Strategic Studies** and editor of its monthly magazine, **The Maccabean Online** (political analysis and commentary on Israeli and Jewish affairs). From 1993-1999 he also was editor of the Maccabean, an expanded, print version of the Maccabean Online that was distributed to Freeman Center members, Jewish leaders and educational institutions around the world. He is also the editor of the Freeman Center's email list, the FREEMANLIST.

The Freeman Center was named after Shapiro's grandfather Harry W. Freeman.

For many years (1990-1995), Shapiro was the political analyst on Israeli and Jewish affairs for the Jewish Herald-Voice, writing his weekly column: News, Views, & Reviews. He has served the Jewish community in several capacities including founder and president of the Student Zionist Organization at the University of California at Berkeley, associate director of the Jewish National Fund in Houston, consultant to the Anti-Defamation League of B'nai B'rith in Miami, and founder and president of the Houston chapter of Americans For A Safe Israel (AFSI).

Shapiro's primary objective during all these years has been to improve Israel's image in this country as well as counteract Arab propaganda in the community and on college campuses. In pursuit of this goal, he intends to maximize solidarity with Israel among the Jewish community and combat media bias. To carry our his stated objective, he has been active in other Jewish organizations including: the Community Relations Committee of the Jewish Federation of Greater Houston (1991-1994); the Houston Advisory Board for the American Israel Public Affairs Committee (AIPAC 1991-1996); and Zionist Organization of America (ZOA) (since 1960); and Americans For a Safe Israel (AFSI) as member and executive committee 1990 to present.

Prior to founding the Freeman Center, Shapiro was proprietor, manager, and buyer for the House of Books, Inc. (1969-92), Houston's main source for Jewish books as well manager and buyer for Houston Paperback Distributors.

SUGGESTIONS FOR FURTHER READING

HISTORY OF ISRAEL

Oslo's Gift of "Peace": The Destruction of Israel's Security . . . . Christopher Barder. $12.95

Front Page Israel, The Jerusalem Post 1932-2010; $50

Peace Now: Blueprint for National Suicide . . . . Dan Nimrod, 1984, Dawn Publishers; $10.00

A HISTORY OF ISRAEL From the Rise of Zionism to Our Time

Howard M. Sachar. Knopf. 1976, 883 pages.

A HISTORY OF ISRAEL Volume II From the Aftermath of the Yom

Kippur War. Howard M. Sachar. Oxford. 1987. 319 pages.

FROM TIME IMMEMORIAL The Origins of the Arab-Jewish Conflict Over Palestine. By Joan Peters. Harper & Row.1984. 601 pages.

A HISTORY OF ZIONISM Walter Laqueur. Holt Rinehart Winston. 1972.

A PLACE AMONG NATIONS Israel And The World, Benjamin Netanyahu. Bantam. 467 pages. 1993.

THE IDEA OF THE JEWISH STATE Ben Halpern. Harvard University Press. 1969.

MY PEOPLE Abba Eban, Random House. 1984.

THE PRIME MINISTERS An Intimate Narrative of Israeli Leadership Yehuda Avner Toby Press 2010

THE ROAD TO NOWHERE A Layman's Guide to the Middle East Conflict Balfour Yitzhak ben-Gad, Books 2004

THE FIGHT FOR JERUSALEM Radical Islam, The West, and the future of the Holy City Dore Gold REGNERY PUBLISHING 2004

ISRAEL IN THE WORLD Changing Lives Through Innovation Helen & Douglas Davis Weidenfield & Nicolson 2005

THE OSLO SYNDROME Delusions of a People Under Seige Kenneth Levin Smith & Kraus 2005

THE HIGH COST OF PEACE How Washington's Middle East Policy Left America Vulnerable to Terrorism Yosef Bodansky FORUM 2002

RABIN OF ISRAEL Robert Slater. St. Martin's. 1993.

BATTLEGROUND: Fact & Fantasy in Palestine Samuel Katz. Shapolsky.1985. 322 pages.

ISRAEL A Personal History David Ben-Gurion. Funk & Wagnalls. 1971. 862 pages,

The Jewish Revolution *Jewish Statehood* Israel Eldad

Dr. Israel Eldad advocates a form of Zionism that is unpopular in conventional society . . .

The Secret War Against the Jews: *How Western Espionage Betrayed The Jewish People*, John Loftus St. Martins Press 1994

Israel's Secret Wars: A History of Israel's Intelligence Services [Paperback] Ian Black Grove Press (1992) ISBN-10: 9780802132864

Start-up Nation: *The Story of Israel's Economic Miracle* [Hardcover] Dan Senor Paperback: Twelve

ELECTORAL REFORM

Demophrenia, Israel and the Malaise of Democracy . . . . Paul Eidelberg; $14.95

Jewish Leadership: Lest Israel Fall . . . . Paul Eidelberg; $14.95

WARS OF ISRAEL & ISRAEL DEFENSE FORCES

ATLAS OF THE ARAB-ISRAELI CONFLICT Martin Gilbert. Macmillan Editions in 1974, 1976, 1979, 1992

THE REVOLT Story of the Irgun Menachem Begin. Steimatzky. 1951.

MOSHE DAYAN: The Story of My Life Moshe Dayan. William Morrow. 1976.

WARRIOR: The Autobiography of Ariel Sharon Ariel Sharon. Simon and Shuster. 1989.

Shackled Warrior *Israel and the Global Jihad,* **Caroline Glick, GEFEN PUBLISHING, 2008**

Dangers of a Palestinian State Prof. Raphael Israeli, 1994

Jerusalem Diaries In tense times ISRAEL BOOKS **Judy Lash-Balint**

State of Siege User's Manual ISRAEL BOOKS **Doron Goldenberg**

How does it feel to fear that at any time a next bomb could explode alongside you? What is it like to go to school on a bus . . .

Yoni's Last Battle Iddo Netanyahu

The Rescue at Entebbe, 1976

A gripping account of the famous operation in Entebbe, Uganda in July 4, 1976.

The Letters of Jonathan Netanyahu Jonathan Netanyahu

The Commander of the Entebbe Rescue Force

" . . . if I should have to sacrifice my life to attain its goal, I'll do so willingly"

(from the book)

The Jews' Secret Fleet Murray S. Greenfield

The Untold Story of North American Volunteers who Smashed the British blockade

Mossad Exodus Gad Shimron

The Daring Undercover Rescue of the Lost Jewish Tribe

The First Tithe Israel Eldad

An inside look at the secret workings of the pre-State Lehi underground was revealed as the Jabotinsky Institute

THE ARAB-ISRAELI WARS War and Peace in the Middle East From the War of Independence through Lebanon Chaim Herzog. Random House. 1982. 392 pages.

GENESIS 1948: The First Arab-Israeli War Dan Kurzman. NAL. 1972.

A HISTORY OF THE ISRAELI ARMY (1870-1974) Zeev Schiff. Straight Arrow. 1974.

THE LESSONS OF MODERN WAR Vol I: The Arab-Israeli Conflict 1973-1989 Anthony H. Cordesman and Abraham R. Wagner. Westview Press. 1990.

BROKEN COVENANT *American Foreign Policy and the Crisis Between the US and Israel,* Moshe Arens 1995

EVERY SPY A PRINCE The Complete History of Israel's Intelligence Community. Dan Raviv and Yossi Melman. Houghton Mifflin. 1990. 466 pages.

THE MOSSAD Israel's Secret Intelligence Service INSIDE STORIES. Dennis Eisenberg, Uri Dan and Eli Landau. Paddington Press. 1978. 272 pages.

DAVID'S SLING The Arming of Israel Shimon Peres. Weidenfeld & Nicolson. 1970. 322 pages.

CHARIOTS OF THE DESERT The Story of the Israeli Armoured Corp David Eshel. Brassey's. 1989.

NO MARGIN FOR ERROR The Making of the Israel Air Force

Ehud Yonay. Pantheon. 1993.

THE YOM KIPPUR WAR The Insight Team. London Sunday Times. 1974.

DUEL FOR THE GOLAN The 100-Hour Battle That Saved Israel Jerry Asher. Morrow. 1987.

The Quest for Justice in the Middle East The Arab Israeli Conflict in Greater Perspective. Gerald A. Honigman CREATION HOUSE 2009

ISRAEL NUCLEAR DETERRENCE A Strategy for the 1980's Shai Feldman. Columbia University Press. 1982.

SHIELD OF ZION The Israel Defense Forces N. Lorch. Howell. 1992.

ARAB PROPAGANDA AND MEDIA BIAS

THE CASE FOR ISRAEL Alan Dershowitz John Wiley & Sons, Inc. 2003

MYTHS AND FACTS A Concise Record of the Arab-Israeli Conflict Mitchell G. Bard and Joel Himelfarb. Near East Report. 1992.

ARAB ATTITUDES TO ISRAEL Dr. Yehoshafat Harkabi. 1972, Israel Universities Press. 527 pages

.POLITICS, LIES, AND VIDEOTAPE 3000 Questions & Answers on the Mideast Crisis. Yitschak Ben Gad. Shapolsky. 1991479 pages.

THE NEW ANTI-SEMITISM Phyllis Chesler Jossey Bass 2003

THE MEDIA'S WAR AGAINST ISRAEL Edited by Stephen Karetzky. Shapolsky. 1986.

DOUBLE VISION: How the Press Distorts America's View of the Middle East Zeev Chafets. William Morrow. 1985.

EYE ON THE MEDIA David Bar-Ilan The Jerusalem Post 1993

The Jewish Revolution

Jewish Statehood **Israel Eldad**

Dr. Israel Eldad advocates a form of Zionism that is unpopular in conventional society . . .

FREEMAN CENTER BOOKS

ARAB-ISRAELI CONFLICT A Resource Book Edited by Bernard J. Shapiro Freeman Center For Strategic Studies Second Edition * 1993 * 210 pages 8.5 by 11 flexibound * $17.50

A very pro-Israel collection of articles, commentary, historic maps& outlines, political cartoons, and much more. Three sections: History of Israel, Arab Propaganda and Media Bias, and Current Issues

Facing Israel. The best and toughest pro-Israel journalism you will ever read.

JEWS, GOD, & ISRAEL Straight Talk On Tough Issues

By Bernard J. Shapiro Freeman Center For Strategic Studies

1993 * 229 pages 8.5 by 11 flexibound * $17.50

This is a souvenir collection of over 110 of Bernard J. Shapiro's best hard-hitting columns in the *Jewish Herald-Voice* (Houston). They are arranged by subject and there is a new introduction to each section. Includes several articles that never appeared locally.

Jews, G-d & Israel, The Battle for Eretz Yisrael (Original edition, 1996, 250 pages) By Bernard J. Shapiro (This new edition is updated to 2011. Current edition is out of print.)

ON ISLAM

Islamic Anti-Semitism as a Political Instrument .... Yossef Bodansky Freeman Center For Strategic Studies

The Koran and the Kafir (Islam and the Infidel) .... A. Ghosh $7.95

Islam, the Arab National Movement .... Anwar Shaikh, The Principality Pub. $9.95

The Wrath of Allah .... Robert E. Burns $12.95

Peace: The Arabian Caricature A Study of Anti-Semitic Imagery **Arieh Stav** Analyzes the anti-Jewish caricatures found in Arab publications . . .

THE LEGACY OF JIHAD *Islamic Holy War and the Fate of Non-Moslems*

PEACE: *The Arabian Caricature A Study of Anti-Semitic Imagery* Arieh Stav NATIF PUBLISHING, Analyzes the anti-Jewish caricatures found in Arab publications . . . by Andrew G. Bostom, MD Prometheus Books, 2005

INTERNATIONAL TERRORISM *Challenge and Response* edited by Benjamin Netanyahu THE JONATHAN INSTITUTE 1989

THE GREAT ARAB CONQUESTS Hugh Kennedy Da Capo Press 2007

HATRED'S KINGDOM How Saudi Arabia Supports the New Global Terrorism, Dore Gold REGNERY PUBLISHING 2003

NEVER AGAIN Rabbi Meir Kahane Z"L

THEY MUST GO Rabbi Meir Kahane Z"L

LISTEN WORLD LISTEN JEW Rabbi Meir Kahane Z"L

FREEMAN CENTER FOR STRATEGIC STUDIES

Into the 21st Century

Defending Eretz Yisrael For All Future Generations

We know from our history that the battle for *Eretz Yisrael* will continue far into the future. There are two ways you can ensure that the Freeman Center will be there, spreading the truth and defending the Jewish right to Israel:

You are urged to make a tax deductible gift to the Freeman Center.

And you should also consider making a bequest to the Freeman Center in your will.The Freeman Center receives no public funds and exists solely on private contributions.

★

WE NEED YOUR FINANCIAL SUPPORT TO CONTINUE OUR

MANY VALUABLE EDUCATIONAL SERVICES.

Contributions the Freeman Center are fully tax deductible under Internal Revenue Code 501(c)(3).

Our Employer Identification Number is 76-0387722. We are incorporated as a non-profit corporation in the State of Texas, Charter Number 01257855. Contributions should be sent to:

The Freeman Center

P.O. Box 35661

Houston, TX 77235-5661.

Thank you for supporting our battle for *Eretz Yisrael*.

★

CPSIA information can be obtained at www.ICGtesting.com
Printed in the USA
LVOW092107261111

256579LV00002B/79/P